T0309493

Advancing the Service Sector with Evolving Technologies:

Techniques and Principles

John Wang
Montclair State University, USA

Managing Director:	Lindsay Johnston
Senior Editorial Director:	Heather Probst
Book Production Manager:	Sean Woznicki
Development Manager:	Joel Gamon
Development Editor:	Michael Killian
Acquisitions Editor:	Erika Gallagher
Typesetter:	Deanna Jo Zombro
Print Coordinator:	Jamie Snavely
Cover Design:	Nick Newcomer, Greg Snader

Published in the United States of America by
Business Science Reference (an imprint of IGI Global)
701 E. Chocolate Avenue
Hershey PA 17033
Tel: 717-533-8845
Fax: 717-533-8661
E-mail: cust@igi-global.com
Web site: http://www.igi-global.com

Copyright © 2012 by IGI Global. All rights reserved. No part of this publication may be reproduced, stored or distributed in any form or by any means, electronic or mechanical, including photocopying, without written permission from the publisher. Product or company names used in this set are for identification purposes only. Inclusion of the names of the products or companies does not indicate a claim of ownership by IGI Global of the trademark or registered trademark.

Library of Congress Cataloging-in-Publication Data

Advancing the service sector with evolving technologies : techniques and
principles / John Wang, editor.
     p. cm.
 Includes bibliographical references and index.
   ISBN 978-1-4666-0044-7 (hbk.) -- ISBN 978-1-4666-0045-4 (ebook) -- ISBN
978-1-4666-0046-1 (print & perpetual access) 1. Service industries--
Information technology. 2. Customer services--Information technology. 3.
Service-oriented architecture (Computer science) 4. Web services. I. Wang,
John, 1955-
 HD9980.5.A384 2012
 658'.05--dc23
                              2011041823

British Cataloguing in Publication Data
A Cataloguing in Publication record for this book is available from the British Library.

All work contributed to this book is new, previously-unpublished material. The views expressed in this book are those of the authors, but not necessarily of the publisher.

Table of Contents

Preface..xiv

Chapter 1
Predicting Ambulance Diverson 1
    Abey Kuruvilla, University of Wisconsin Parkside, USA
    Suraj M. Alexander, University of Louisville, USA

Chapter 2
Hybrid Value Creation in the Sports Industry: The Case of a Mobile Sports Companion as IT-
Supported Product-Service-Bundle 11
    Jan Marco Leimeister, Kassel University, Germany
    Uta Knebel, Technische Universitaet Muenchen, Germany
    Helmut Krcmar, Technische Universitaet Muenchen, Germany

Chapter 3
Connect Time Limits and Performance Measures in a Dial-Up Modem Pool System 25
    Paul F. Schikora, Indiana State University, USA
    Michael R. Godfrey, University of Wisconsin Oshkosh, USA
    Brian D. Neureuther, State University of New York, College at Plattsburgh, USA

Chapter 4
ICT Usage by Greek Accountants 46
    Efstratios C. Emmanouilidis, University of Macedonia, Greece
    Anastasios A. Economides, University of Macedonia, Greece

Chapter 5
Exploring the Adoption of Technology Driven Services in the Healthcare Industry 66
    Umit Topacan, Bogazici University, Turkey
    A. Nuri Basoglu, Bogazici University, Turkey
    Tugrul U. Daim, Portland State University, USA

Chapter 6
Temporal Aspects of Information Technology Use: Increasing Shift Work Effectiveness................... 87
    Roslin V. Hauck, Illinois State University, USA
    Sherry M. B. Thatcher, University of Louisville, USA
    Suzanne P. Weisband, University of Arizona, USA

Chapter 7
Implementation Success Model in Government Agencies: A Case of a Centralized Identification
System at NASA 105
    Yair Levy, Nova Southeastern University, USA
    Theon L. Danet, NASA Langley Research Center, USA

Chapter 8
SERREA: A Semantic Management System for Retail Real Estate Agencies 120
    Ángel García-Crespo, Universidad Carlos III de Madrid, Spain
    Ricardo Colomo-Palacios, Universidad Carlos III de Madrid, Spain
    Juan Miguel Gómez-Berbís, Universidad Carlos III de Madrid, Spain
    Fernando Paniagua Martín, Universidad Carlos III de Madrid, Spain

Chapter 9
Mass Customisation Models for Travel and Tourism Information e-Services: Interrelationships
Between Systems Design and Customer Value 135
    Marianna Sigala, Democritus University, Greece

Chapter 10
Technology Fears: A Study of e-Commerce Loyalty Perception by Jordanian Customers 158
    Ahmad Khasawneh, Hashemite University, Jordan
    Mohammad Bsoul, Hashemite University, Jordan
    Ibrahim Obeidat, Hashemite University, Jordan
    Iyad Al Azzam, Yarmouk University, Jordan

Chapter 11
Predictive Models in Cybercrime Investigation: An Application of Data Mining Techniques 166
    A. S. N. Murthy, Indian Police Service, Karnataka, India
    Vishnuprasad Nagadevara, Indian Institute of Management Bangalore, India
    Rahul De', Indian Institute of Management Bangalore, India

Chapter 12
Deploying New Perspectives of Network Organizations for Chronic Diseases' Integrated
Management 178
    Isabella Bonacci, Federico II University, Italy
    Oscar Tamburis, ICAR – CNR, Italy

Chapter 13
Marketing and Reputation in the Services Sector: Higher Education in South Africa
and Singapore 193
    Johan De Jager, Tshwane University of Technology, South Africa
    Werner Soontiens, Curtin University of Technology, Australia

Chapter 14
Data Mining in Nonprofit Organizations, Government Agencies, and Other Institutions.................. 208
> *Zhongxian Wang, Montclair State University, USA*
> *Ruiliang Yan, Indiana University Northwest, USA*
> *Qiyang Chen, Montclair State University, USA*
> *Ruben Xing, Montclair State University, USA*

Chapter 15
Understanding Expectations, Perceptions and Satisfaction Levels of Customers of Military
Engineer Services in India 219
> *Anand Parkash Bansal, Indian Institute of Management Bangalore, India*
> *Vishnuprasad Nagadevara, Indian Institute of Management Bangalore, India*

Chapter 16
Service Registry Design: An Information Service Approach 239
> *Luís Ferreira Pires, University of Twente, The Netherlands*
> *Arjen van Oostrum, University of Twente, The Netherlands*
> *Fons Wijnhoven, University of Twente, The Netherlands & Wilhelms University of Muenster,*
>   *Germany*

Chapter 17
Operational Performance Analysis of a Public Hospital Laboratory 260
> *Kamrul Ahsan, Auckland University of Technology, New Zealand*
> *Abdullahil Azeem, Bangladesh University of Engineering and Technology, Bangladesh*

Chapter 18
A Mashup Application to Support Complex Decision Making for Retail Consumers 277
> *Steven Walczak, University of Colorado at Denver, USA*
> *Deborah L. Kellogg, University of Colorado at Denver, USA*
> *Dawn G. Gregg, University of Colorado at Denver, USA*

Chapter 19
Using the Critical Incident Technique to Identify Factors of Service Quality in Online Higher
Education 295
> *María J. Martínez-Argüelles, Open University of Catalonia, Spain*
> *José M. Castán, University of Barcelona, Spain*
> *Angel A. Juan, Open University of Catalonia, Spain*

Compilation of References 312

About the Contributors 349

Index 359

Detailed Table of Contents

Preface xiv

Chapter 1
Predicting Ambulance Diverson 1
Abey Kuruvilla, University of Wisconsin Parkside, USA
Suraj M. Alexander, University of Louisville, USA

The high utilization level of emergency departments in hospitals across the United States has resulted in the serious and persistent problem of ambulance diversion. This problem is magnified by the cascading effect it has on neighboring hospitals, delays in emergency care, and the potential for patients' clinical deterioration. We provide a predictive tool that would give advance warning to hospitals of the impending likelihood of diversion. We hope that with a predictive instrument, such as the one described in this paper, hospitals can take preventive or mitigating actions. The proposed model, which uses logistic and multinomial regression, is evaluated using real data from the Emergency Management System (EM Systems) and 911 call data from Firstwatch® for the Metropolitan Ambulance Services Trust (MAST) of Kansas City, Missouri. The information in these systems that was significant in predicting diversion includes recent 911 calls, season, day of the week, and time of day. The model illustrates the feasibility of predicting the probability of impending diversion using available information. We strongly recommend that other locations, nationwide and abroad, develop and use similar models for predicting diversion.

Chapter 2
Hybrid Value Creation in the Sports Industry: The Case of a Mobile Sports Companion as IT-Supported Product-Service-Bundle 11
Jan Marco Leimeister, Kassel University, Germany
Uta Knebel, Technische Universitaet Muenchen, Germany
Helmut Krcmar, Technische Universitaet Muenchen, Germany

Integrated product-service packages (hybrid products) can open new markets and target groups to companies. However, existing approaches to service or product development do not sufficiently address simultaneous development and domain-specific issues. A very promising new field for such bundles is the health and fitness industry. In this research, we designed and built an IT-supported training system for running, the Mobile Sports Companion (MSC), which closely interlocks a product and corresponding services using an iterative development process. We tested the pilot system with 14 recreational athletes. The results of the field test show that the MSC proved to be a promising tool to offer athletes an effective individual, flexible, and mobile training. However, the system, as it is, did not sufficiently represent the human trainer behind it, thus lowering its acceptance and the credibility of its recommendations. Our next step is to integrate features that could strengthen the athlete-trainer relationship. The MSC could turn out to be a promising field for future e-business applications in the sports service industry.

Chapter 3
Connect Time Limits and Performance Measures in a Dial-Up Modem Pool System 25
Paul F. Schikora, Indiana State University, USA
Michael R. Godfrey, University of Wisconsin Oshkosh, USA
Brian D. Neureuther, State University of New York, College at Plattsburgh, USA

Managing customer service is critical for both nonprofit and for-profit dial-up modem Internet service providers. When system operators face excess demand, they can either add capacity or adapt their management techniques to deal with their limited resources—this article considers the latter. We examine system configuration options and the resultant effects on customer service levels in a simulated dial-up modem pool operation. Specifically, we look at a single pool operation and examine the effects of imposing time limits in a seriously overloaded system. We analyze the results on several key customer service measures. The results show that imposing these limits will have a distinct, nonlinear impact on these measures. Customer productivity and actual system load are shown to have major impacts on the performance measures. Interactions between several system and environmental parameters are also discussed.

Chapter 4
ICT Usage by Greek Accountants.. 46
Efstratios C. Emmanouilidis, University of Macedonia, Greece
Anastasios A. Economides, University of Macedonia, Greece

This study investigates Greek accounting offices use of Information and Communication Technologies (ICT). Initially, a comprehensive questionnaire was developed. It contains 35 questions with multiple answers and 2 open questions tailored to the accountants. One hundred accountants' offices in a Greek county answered the questionnaire. The findings present their current ICT infrastructure and their use of ICT and accounting e-services. Greek accounting offices have made improvements in adopting new technology in their everyday work. All use email, antivirus software, and the Web. Most submit VAT (Value Aided Tax), Taxation Statements, and APS (Analytical Periodic Statement) via Internet. However, most are not cautious about backing up their data daily; they do not create electronic files for all their documents; they do not update their software via Internet; and they do not use advanced software applications. Finally, they expect the government and the Accountants' Chamber to finance their ICT infrastructure.

Chapter 5
Exploring the Adoption of Technology Driven Services in the Healthcare Industry 66
Umit Topacan, Bogazici University, Turkey
A. Nuri Basoglu, Bogazici University, Turkey
Tugrul U. Daim, Portland State University, USA

Recent developments in information and communication technologies have helped to accelerate the diffusion of electronic services in the medical industry. Health information services house, retrieve, and make use of medical information to improve service quality and reduce cost. Users—including medical staff, administrative staff, and patients—of these systems cannot fully benefit from them unless they can use them comfortably. User behavior is affected by various factors relating to technology characteristics, user characteristics, social environment, and organizational environment. Our research evaluated the determinants of health information service adoption and analyzed the relationship between these determinants and the behavior of the user. Health information service adoption was found to be influenced by service characteristics, user characteristics, intermediary variables, facilitating conditions, and social factors.

Chapter 6

Temporal Aspects of Information Technology Use: Increasing Shift Work Effectiveness.................. 87
Roslin V. Hauck, Illinois State University, USA
Sherry M. B. Thatcher, University of Louisville, USA
Suzanne P. Weisband, University of Arizona, USA

The dynamic nature of organizations and technologies require a comprehensive understanding of how organizational forms and information technology interact. While previous research and theories of information technology have investigated aspects such as organizational structure, individual and group behavior, and inter-organizational relationships, shift work, an important temporal aspect often found in service organizations, is surprisingly absent in the literature. The purpose of this paper is to examine the effect that shift work has on employee use and satisfaction with information technology. The results of a field study of a police organization indicate that information technology systems are valued differently by workers on different shifts. The authors discuss how this research helps advance theories of technology use and effectiveness (such as task-technology fit and technology acceptance model) and present important practical implications of this study for strategic alignment of technology in the areas of systems design, implementation, addressing the needs of peripheral workers, and resource management.

Chapter 7

Implementation Success Model in Government Agencies: A Case of a Centralized Identification
System at NASA 105
Yair Levy, Nova Southeastern University, USA
Theon L. Danet, NASA Langley Research Center, USA

A recent presidential directive mandated that all U.S. government agencies establish a centralized identification system. This study investigated the impact of users' involvement, resistance, and computer self-efficacy on the implementation success of a centralized identification system. Information System (IS) usage was the construct employed to measure IS implementation success. A survey instrument was developed based on existing measures from key IS literature. The results of this study indicated a strong reliability for the measures of all constructs (user involvement, computer self-efficacy, user's resistance, and IS usage). Factor analysis was conducted using Principal Component Analysis (PCA) with Varimax rotation. Results of the PCA indicate that items of the constructs measured had high validity, while Cronbach's Alpha for each factor demonstrates high reliability for all constructs measured. Additionally, results of a structural equations modeling analysis using Partial Least Square (PLS) indicate that computer self-efficacy and user involvement had positive significant impact on the implementation success. However, the results also demonstrated that user's resistance had no significant impact on IS usage, while end user involvement had a strong negative impact on user's resistance.

Chapter 8

SERREA: A Semantic Management System for Retail Real Estate Agencies 120
Ángel García-Crespo, Universidad Carlos III de Madrid, Spain
Ricardo Colomo-Palacios, Universidad Carlos III de Madrid, Spain
Juan Miguel Gómez-Berbís, Universidad Carlos III de Madrid, Spain
Fernando Paniagua Martín, Universidad Carlos III de Madrid, Spain

In the scenario of market competition in the Retail Real Estate Agencies (RREA) business, having exact information regarding properties in supply and their associated demand is a differentiating factor for organizations. The Semantic Web represents an opportunity to create extensible services that hold precise information concerning these types of markets. The objective of the current initiative is to use this market data as a competitive advantage for organizations. In this article, the authors propose SERREA, a management system for RREA based on semantics and constructed using Web Services, which has been implemented successfully in one of the leading agencies in Spain. The goal of this paper is to show how RREA benefits from using Semantic Technologies in the context of their business operations.

Chapter 9

Mass Customisation Models for Travel and Tourism Information e-Services: Interrelationships
Between Systems Design and Customer Value 135
Marianna Sigala, Democritus University, Greece

Online travel firms exploit current ICT advances for developing mass customization (MC) capabilities and addressing the needs of the sophisticated travellers. However, studies investigating MC in services and specifically in tourism are limited. By adopting a customer-focused approach, this paper addresses this gap by analysing the following issues: a) the ICT and product dimensions that online firms can customise for developing and implementing different MC models; and b) the customer value and benefits provided by the different MC models. After reviewing and illustrating the interrelationships of studies coming from the fields of customer value, MC and IS design, the author proposes a customer value based framework for developing MC models. The applicability and practical implications of this framework are demonstrated by analysing the MC practices of three online travel cyberintermediaries. Finally, the paper summarises the formulation of research propositions investigating the influence of users' characteristics on the customer value and benefits sought by MC practices and on the design of the IS platforms supporting MC services.

Chapter 10

Technology Fears: A Study of e-Commerce Loyalty Perception by Jordanian Customers 158
Ahmad Khasawneh, Hashemite University, Jordan
Mohammad Bsoul, Hashemite University, Jordan
Ibrahim Obeidat, Hashemite University, Jordan
Iyad Al Azzam, Yarmouk University, Jordan

The Internet and all other types of networks have changed life in general and doing business in particular, and as a result, many companies are now conducting and transferring their businesses online. In this paper, the authors evaluate whether loyalty issues are the major obstacles to the growth of e-commerce in Jordan. A survey conducted for the study reveals that technology fears are major barriers to loyalty in Internet banking and e-commerce activities among consumers. The results suggest that unless the technology fears of adopters are acknowledged, some of them are not successful.

Chapter 11
Predictive Models in Cybercrime Investigation: An Application of Data Mining Techniques 166
A. S. N. Murthy, Indian Police Service, Karnataka, India
Vishnuprasad Nagadevara, Indian Institute of Management Bangalore, India
Rahul De', Indian Institute of Management Bangalore, India

With increased access to computers across the world, cybercrime is becoming a major challenge to law enforcement agencies. Cybercrime investigation in India is in its infancy and there has been limited success in prosecuting the offenders; therefore, a need to understand and strengthen the existing investigation methods and systems for controlling cybercrimes is greatly needed. This study identifies important factors that will enable law enforcement agencies to reach the first step in effective prosecution, namely charge-sheeting of the cybercrime cases. Data on 300 cybercrime cases covering a number of demographic, technical and other variables related to cybercrime was analyzed using data mining techniques to identify and prioritize various factors leading to filing of the charge-sheet. These factors and the respective priority rankings are used to suggest various policy measures for improving the success rate of prosecution of cybercrimes.

Chapter 12
Deploying New Perspectives of Network Organizations for Chronic Diseases' Integrated
Management.. 178
Isabella Bonacci, Federico II University, Italy
Oscar Tamburis, ICAR – CNR, Italy

The social frame of healthcare organizations in Europe (and in particular in the Italian Public Sector), as a combination of relational, formal and informal aspects, is one of their most relevant sources of complexity, which leads to different approaches about decisional, clinical and organizational processes (Cicchetti, 2004). These issues have been enlightened as well by the increasing social incidence of chronic-degenerative pathologies, such as Diabetes Mellitus type 2. In this regard, the Italian national e-government strategy has first pointed out the need for paths of integration and interoperability among information systems to ensure a safe exchange of information (CNIPA, 2008). The activity of "integrated design" of information flows between doctors and patients allows the creation and development of reticular organizational forms in which many non contiguous actors work at the same time on the diagnosis and care process. This paper shows how the adoption of the Social Network Analysis (SNA), as theoretical and methodological perspective that emphasizes the social reality as reticular framework (Moreno, 1987), can provide an innovative approach for the study of the "pathology networks" and the "integrated management" of Diabetes Mellitus type 2, where ICT solutions are (or are about to be) currently involved.

Chapter 13

Marketing and Reputation in the Services Sector: Higher Education in South Africa
and Singapore.. 193

Johan De Jager, Tshwane University of Technology, South Africa
Werner Soontiens, Curtin University of Technology, Australia

Over the past few decades the tertiary sector has developed from a predominantly inward focussed industry serving public interest to an internationalised and commercially competitive industry. Resulting from this fundamental change is a drive to better understand the most prominent dimensions that impact on internationalisation, more particularly, the expectations and experiences of students. Although some of these can be argued to be country specific, and thus differentiate between markets, others are universal and impact on the overall industry. One of the latter is a pressure to consider and treat students as clients introducing all the dynamics of service delivery and management. The primary objective of this paper is to identify the most important variables related to marketing and reputation issues when selecting a university in South-Africa and compare the same for Singapore students. This study revealed that the most important consideration for the South African sample, regarding marketing and reputation related variables when choosing an institution of higher education, is the academic reputation of the institution, while the marketing activities were regarded as priority by the Singaporean sample.

Chapter 14

Data Mining in Nonprofit Organizations, Government Agencies, and Other Institutions.................. 208

Zhongxian Wang, Montclair State University, USA
Ruiliang Yan, Indiana University Northwest, USA
Qiyang Chen, Montclair State University, USA
Ruben Xing, Montclair State University, USA

Data mining involves searching through databases for potentially useful information, such as knowledge rules, patterns, regularities, and other trends hidden in the data. Today, data mining is more widely used than ever before, not only by businesses who seek profits but also by nonprofit organizations, government agencies, private groups and other institutions in the public sector. In this paper, the authors summarize and classify the applications of data mining in the public sector into the following possible categories: improving service or performance; helping customer relations management; analyzing scientific and research information; managing human resources; improving emergency management; detecting fraud, waste, and abuse; detecting criminal activities; and detecting terrorist activities.

Chapter 15

Understanding Expectations, Perceptions and Satisfaction Levels of Customers of Military
Engineer Services in India 219

Anand Parkash Bansal, Indian Institute of Management Bangalore, India
Vishnuprasad Nagadevara, Indian Institute of Management Bangalore, India

Customer satisfaction and client orientation concepts are needed in all service providing organisations, including those engaged in construction and infrastructure provision within the public sector where the public perception about their services is at its lowest. This study measures the expectations and perceptions of various service elements among clients of Military Engineer Services (MES) in India. Customers' survey mode was used to measure the expectations, perception, importance and satisfaction. The perceived quality of services provided by this department was measured with SERVQUAL instrument on selected attributes using the Gap approach for identifying priorities. Additionally, this study also examines the influence of demographic characteristics of clients on expectations and perceptions of the clients. The results can be used by similar organisations for cultural and structural change to increase accountability and performance, in which the results indicate that the three most important dimensions in the order of importance among the clients of MES are tangibles, responsiveness and reliability.

Chapter 16
Service Registry Design: An Information Service Approach 239
    Luís Ferreira Pires, University of Twente, The Netherlands
    Arjen van Oostrum, University of Twente, The Netherlands
    Fons Wijnhoven, University of Twente, The Netherlands & Wilhelms University of Muenster,
        Germany

A service registry is a Service-Oriented Architecture (SOA) component that keeps a 'catalogue' of available services. It stores service specifications so that these specifications can be found by potential users. Discussions on the design of service registries currently focus on technical issues, while service registries should take into consideration information needs of business domain users. In this regard, the authors consider service registries as information services and develop a comprehensive framework for designing service registries. This framework introduces aspects that determine a design space for service registries. In this design space, the authors identify views, requirements, processes, and means in the design of a service registry that supports the lifecycle information of a service. A vital part of these requirements is further implemented and demonstrated in a prototype built as a 'proof-of-concept' for the framework. This paper also discusses a case study used to evaluate the prototype. In this case study, a registry prototype has been populated with realistic services of a large insurance company, and 21 experienced IT and business professionals from a consultancy organization evaluated the prototype for its user satisfaction.

Chapter 17
Operational Performance Analysis of a Public Hospital Laboratory 260
    Kamrul Ahsan, Auckland University of Technology, New Zealand
    Abdullahil Azeem, Bangladesh University of Engineering and Technology, Bangladesh

Efficient utilization of scarce resources is an issue for any healthcare system. In developing countries, proper tools, techniques, and resources must be widely used in healthcare operational planning. Considering the necessity of effective resource planning, this study focuses on the rural healthcare system of Bangladesh and concentrates on the sub-district government hospital laboratory. The authors' determine possible ways to improve operations of laboratory facilities. To analyze existing system efficiency, sample laboratory data is fed into a simulation model. This paper identifies several possible ways for future expansion and suggests using simulation for better planning and analysis.

Chapter 18

A Mashup Application to Support Complex Decision Making for Retail Consumers 277

    Steven Walczak, University of Colorado at Denver, USA

    Deborah L. Kellogg, University of Colorado at Denver, USA

    Dawn G. Gregg, University of Colorado at Denver, USA

Purchase processes often require complex decision making and consumers frequently use Web information sources to support these decisions. However, increasing amounts of information can make finding appropriate information problematic. This information overload, coupled with decision complexity, can increase time required to make a decision and reduce decision quality. This creates a need for tools that support these decision-making processes. Online tools that bring together data and partial solutions are one option to improve decision making in complex, multi-criteria environments. An experiment using a prototype mashup application indicates that these types of applications may significantly decrease time spent and improve overall quality of complex retail decisions.

Chapter 19

Using the Critical Incident Technique to Identify Factors of Service Quality in Online Higher Education 295

    María J. Martínez-Argüelles, Open University of Catalonia, Spain

    José M. Castán, University of Barcelona, Spain

    Angel A. Juan, Open University of Catalonia, Spain

Information technologies are changing the way in which higher education is delivered. In this regard, there is a necessity for developing information systems that help university managers measure the quality of online services offered to their students. This paper discusses the importance of considering students' perception of service quality. The authors then identify key factors of service quality, as perceived by students, in online higher education. To this end, the Critical Incident Technique (CIT) is proposed as an effective qualitative methodology. Some benefits of this methodology are highlighted and an exploratory research is carried out in a real environment to illustrate this approach. Results from this research explain which quality dimensions are considered the most valuable to online students. Information provided by this methodology can significantly improve strategic decision-making processes in online universities worldwide.

Compilation of References 312

About the Contributors 349

Index 359

Preface

THE CURRENT STATE, OBJECTIVE, AND FUTURE TRENDS OF GREEN IT FOR SERVICES

Introduction

Environmental issues have become an important topic of concern over the past decade, and Information Technology (IT) services have not been left out of this trend, and for good reason. With the vast and rapid pace of technology, there is no reason why IT cannot be "green" and environmentally friendly, especially given the large influence of IS/IT on the current global business environment. There are some key components of Green IT, and the direction that it will be taking in the future will be discussed here.

Green IT, also referred to as Green Computing, is the focus on environmental sustainability for the IT sector. A definition of this is, "the study and practice of designing, manufacturing, using, and disposing of computers, servers, and associated subsystems—such as monitors, printers, storage devices, and networking and communications systems—efficiently and effectively, with minimal or no impact on the environment" (Murugesan, 2009, p.25). This is a global concern, as it aims at minimizing hazardous materials usage while at the same time increasing energy efficiency and recyclability, in the context of IT hardware, software, and services.

A well-designed Green IT system can be very sophisticated, and may include different networks, hardware, and people with varying skills and backgrounds. The realm of Green IT encompasses Green Outsourcing, Green Consulting, Green Network Services and lastly, Green Package Software. A Forrester report foresees an increasing demand for Green IT services, estimated to grow by 60 percent each year (Samson, 2008).

The notion of Green information technology services refers to a somewhat large set of services available to businesses, both large and small, to help them reduce their carbon footprint in the world, while also making attempts to save money. According to Wilson (2009), 97% of senior level information technology executives have been discussing implementing green technologies into their businesses, and 45% have already started using some of these strategies. This can be considered a great improvement, as most companies in the past have only tossed around and debated these ideas, but did not take concrete steps to implement them. Another trend in this survey is that of an individual company's increased awareness of their impacts on the environment. While the impetus of this in the past was on cost savings, a recent and critical finding from this survey points to the fact that these companies are now genuinely becoming interested in their ability to do less harm and to make a positive impact on the environment. The Greening of IT has definitely become a driving force in the business world, but it still has a long way to go (Beitollahi & Deconinck, 2011).

One of the main focus areas of Green IT is to reduce IT emissions and the impacts of the broad spectrum of IT use, while subsequently increasing the sustainability of these technologies and their impacts. But many wonder who is or should be responsible for this initiative in a firm, besides the most obvious, the CIO. While the "greening" of IT has become a very specialized industry that is changing very rapidly, as more companies become interested in sustainability, these "green" efforts are taking off, and people are being recruited from many different industries to help manage the myriad of techniques that can be employed. Not only are there workers with expertise in the area of energy conservation, but also needed are those skilled in electrical systems, energy auditing, chip design, and more efficient battery, system, and server design (Sanchitanand, 2009; Marsan & Meo, 2011).

Many companies want to "go green" overnight, but the task can be more complex and involved than it appears at first glance. Hedman and Henningsson (2011) suggest three ways in order to change a business, from "appearing to be green" to a radical 360 degree transformation. One model of change is the "storefront". A storefront business promotes themselves as one that is green "without changing any of its business activities; in effect, the 'storefront' company investigates existing activities to see if it can label any of them as green IT..." (p.55). This strategy does not, in reality, include any internal changes in their processes or business operations, but makes an attempt to parallel their current ideas with those that are "green." While more along the lines of "window dressing" and being "for show", few new "green" strategies are being implemented. Hedman & Henningsson's second approach involves improving a given company's current operations, including any viable "green IT" changes and strategies. This strategy is great for companies that are really interested in being green, but don't have the time, the ability or the funds to drastically alter their company. The last category the authors describe what they call "the redesign." In this model, the company takes the a firm and solid initiative to implement Green IT into every area of their business, and this may require the hiring of someone experienced to head this project. Because of the scale and complexity of this initiative, it is typically only done in cases where there is a significant upside to a drastic change, and also sufficient recognition and resources to manage the risk in the case of failure or results that are unexpected. In short, it should be recognized that while the payoff of Green IT can be substantial, the risks can also be considerable. While Green IT is such a hot topic due to broad current interest of a "Green Revolution," there is not enough research being done in this area. Jenkin, Webster and McShane (2010) have developed a framework as to what direction this research should be going proceeding. Currently, most of the research is done on Green IS, which is (S) systems-focused as opposed to (T) technology-focused, and concentrate on how to improve these kinds of systems in terms of greater efficiency, less emissions, and reduced costs. Example of these could include more efficient super computers and data centers, for example. The author's framework suggests moving the general direction of research into a new direction, especially taking account of the four components that they find to be vital, these being motivating forces, environmental initiatives, environmental orientations and environmental impacts.

It should be understood that the transition to a sustainable, low-carbon footprint economy represents an enormous challenge. It is concerned with allocating sufficient resources so as to transform our economy in a relatively prompt manner, but also keeping in mind the critical need to maintain environmental and "green" considerations, while at the same time not undermining the prospects for prosperity in the future. Specifically, investments in Green IT, technologies, and technologies will need to focus on resource productivity, renewable energy, clean technology, green business, climate adaptation and ecosystem protection, to name a few. These may bring about tangible effects that can be measured and quantified. However, investments in eco-system enhancement and climate adaptation might not be able to demonstrate conventional financial returns at all, even though they are protecting vital ecosystem services for the future, may have effects which are important to the environment, and can also help reduce unemployment (Jackson & Victor, 2011).

In addition, environmentally modified national accounts offer a quantifiable sustainability concept for produced and natural capital maintenance. For practical reasons, sustainability economics should therefore have their primary focus on sustainable economic performance and growth. In the case of efforts to coordinate these with other social goals, this is probably better left to the political realm (Bartelmus, 2010).

Current Research in Green IT

Ecosystem Services

The concept of ecosystem services is an approach widely discussed and employed to clarify and to assess the dependence of human society on ecosystems and landscapes. Landscapes may be thought of as merely for aesthetic effect, but may have impacts upon the environment and ecosystems, that must be recognized. In order to better understand and evaluate the potential performance of ecosystems and landscapes and the quality needed or demanded by society, Bastian, Haase, and Grunewald (2011) suggest returning to a landscape potential concept originally developed by landscape ecologists in the 1970s. Employing both the original concepts and new approaches proposed by the authors, the result is a proposed EPPS framework – ecosystem (or landscape) properties, potentials and services – which is presented as a better way to link both potentials and services to help undertake planning, management practice, and governance endeavors. The empirical part of their paper shows the potential applications and effects of the EPPS framework in an urbanized region.

Green Cloud Computing Model

Another interesting and viable research area concerns the problem of data centers hosting cloud applications, which due to their high processing and input/output needs consumes huge amounts of electrical energy, contributing to high operational costs and adding additional burdens to the carbon footprints of the environment. The focus and goal of "Green" Cloud computing is not only to minimize operational costs, but also to reduce the environmental impact of data centers. Beloglazov, Abawajy, & Buyya (2011) define an architectural framework, and also principles for, more energy-efficient Cloud computing. Based on this architecture, they presented their vision, including research opportunities, resource provisioning, and allocation algorithms for more energy-efficient management of Cloud computing environments, and other methods and techniques. The proposed energy-aware allocation heuristics distribute data center resources to client applications in such a way that energy efficiency of the data center is improved, while also maintaining a high level of Quality of Service (QoS).

The VALUE Model (Combining Cost–Benefit and Multiplier Analyses)

Increased urbanization has put a great deal of pressure on the availability of land, and its value in being used for "Green" purposes. One problem lies in the fact that investments in green infrastructure are difficult to assess in terms of a quantified value. However, it is also a fact that the creation and designation of green spaces has had a proven positive effect on people living and working, in a given neighborhood. In order to convince the public and other stakeholders of the usefulness of investments in green spaces, it is necessary to give a correct, understandable and easily repeatable method to value these kinds of investments. Vandermeulen, Verspecht, Vermeire, Van Huylenbroeck, and Gellynck (2011) present a model that can be used to express the value of green infrastructure investments in economic terms. The goals of evaluating a project at both the site and regional scales will give a complete overview of all direct, indirect and use values of the investment. In addition, by using cost–benefit as well as multiplier analyses, it is possible to come up with concrete, estimated monetary values. This article shows that the employment of this model can help to justify the support for, and investment in, green spaces.

Layered Green Performance Indicators

Kipp, Jiang, Fugini, and Salomie (2011) present a layered Green Performance Indicators (GPI) approach, allowing for a clearly defined classification of the "greenness" of an IT service centre at different hierarchical levels. In particular, the correlation and linkages between the GPIs at different levels were presented, and IT service centres are continuously monitored through a suitable energy sensing and monitoring infrastructure. Then, energy related data will be collected and the corresponding GPI values will be computed. In order to better evaluate the correlation between GPIs at various levels, data mining algorithms and statistical methods are used to analyze the collected data, with the goal of providing some indication of the predictive relationship between the GPIs, with a particular emphasis on the relationship between high level (application, business processing, QoS - Quality of Service) GPIs and low-level, hardware-related GPIs.

Integrating LCA and Dynamic Simulation

With sustainability increasingly becoming an important factor in business decisions and planning, companies are now looking for methods and tools to help gain a fuller picture of the environmental impacts caused by their manufacturing and supply chain activities. In line with Nwe, Adhitya, Halim, and Srinivasan (2010), life cycle assessment (LCA) is a widely-used technique for measuring the environmental costs associated with a specific product or service. However, one drawback is that LCA takes a high-level view and assumes that there is a fixed supply chain structure and operation. Moreover, it does not explicitly consider the effect of any supply chain design and practices that can make a positive environmental impact. The authors presented an approach integrating LCA indicators and dynamic simulation techniques to address "green" supply chain design and operations. The environmental impact indicators are incorporated into a dynamic model of the supply chain, along with the needs of maintaining desired levels of profit and customer satisfaction, so that the sustainability of various design and operational decisions can be assessed in a comprehensive manner.

Optimization Models

Overall, energy consumption from wireless networks is increasing rapidly, and in some countries amounts to more than 55% of the entire communication sectors' usage. As such, energy forms a non-negligible, and in some cases, substantial part of the operational costs of mobile operators. With the advent of new wireless technologies, exhibiting a growth rate factor of roughly 10 fold every 5 years, and also the dramatic increase in the number of users, results in a projected doubling of the power consumption of cellular networks infrastructures every 4–5 years. Lorincz, Capone & Begušić (2011) present an approach to create possible mobile network energy savings through optimized management of on/off states, and the transmission of access station power based on traffic estimates associated with different hours (or days) of the week. They propose an optimization approach based on ILP models that minimizes energy consumption while desired area coverage and sufficient capacity for guaranteeing quality of service. The proposed model can capture system characteristics, including considering different management constraints that can be considered, based on varying traffic requirements and application scenarios. Obtained results show that the potential exists for substantial energy savings, up to more than 50%, by employing the proposed management strategies.

Simulation Models

By exploring the concept of productivity in post-growth economies and using a simulation model of the UK economy, Jackson and Victor (2011) showed how a two-fold strategy – comprised both of work-time reduction, and a sectorial shift to 'green services' – could contribute to achieving more desirable carbon footprint targets in the UK. The proposed model demonstrated how such a strategy might help to maintain full employment, even while there may be a slowdown in the economy as a whole. The employment of the dual methods could contribute to achieving 'deep' carbon emission reduction targets while at the same time helping to sustain an increased level of employment. This paper has the contribution of impacts of these strategies on labour (and labour productivity) in the transition to a more sustainable economy.

Matsumoto (2010) presented a simulation model for reuse business markets. The model includes the models of decision making of major actors and players in reuse markets, and it formally describes the relationship between both the factors associated with these reuse businesses, and also the different patterns associated with reuse markets. On the basis of the model formulated in this paper, future research has been directed towards refining the model so that it can support the decision making strategies of both companies and governments. The model can be refined, first, by dividing a single parameter into several sub-parameters. In addition, the model proposed in this paper provided a basis to help make these refinements possible.

As a result of Payments for Ecosystem Services (PES), conservation investments are increasingly being implemented for the protection and restoration of ecosystem services around the world. Chen, Lupi, An, Sheely, Viña and Liu (2011) present an agent-based simulation model to demonstrate the evolution and impacts of social norms on the enrollment of agricultural land in a PES program. They applied the model to land plots that have been enrolled in China's Grain-to-Green Program (GTGP), with the purpose of examining re-enrollment in an alternative payment program when the current payments ceased. In the study, conducted at the Wolong Nature Reserve (Sichuan province, China) where several thousand plant and animal species, including giant pandas, may benefit from the reenrollment program. The authors found that a larger portion (over 15%) of GTGP land can be reenrolled at the same payment if social norms were leveraged. The form of leveraging was accomplished by allowing more than 10 rounds of interactions among landholders regarding their reenrollment decisions.

Two-Stage Game Theoretic Model

Environmental concern is increasingly gaining strength and attention in a large majority of industries throughout the world. One of the areas that cause substantial environmental burdens from the business sector is in transportation and logistics activities. In particular, a major factor in managing and evaluating transportation and delivery environmental implications, are the characteristics of organizational transportation fleets. As a result of heightened environmental concerns, many organizations in a wide variety of industries have recognized that effective planning and management of their transportation fleets requires recognition of the fleets' environmental burden and impact.

For a more meaningful understanding of this interaction and the resulting equilibrium behavior of firms, Bae, Sarkis, and Yoo (2011) analyzed the situation with the help of a quality-price two stage game theoretic model, originally developed and used in the economics literature. By applying a widely respected solution concept of the model, they derived numerous insightful results, such as the fact that government R&D subsidies are more effective for overall industry performance, and that the employment of tighter regulatory standards can be more effective towards the adoption of a "green fleet." Overall, using their current model the qualitative results and insights from the simulation show the capabilities of the game theoretic model here to provide some very robust analyses and implications.

Green IT Research Using Surveys and Interviews

Sadly, many ecosystem services are currently in decline. As a result, local ecological knowledge and associated practices are essential to sustaining and enhancing ecosystem services such as those for gardens and other kinds of "green spaces." Barthel, Folke, and Colding (2010) focused on the "social–ecological memory" of such gardens and had demonstrated its significance in terms of managing ecosystem services. The authors examined and investigated where and how ecological practices and knowledge are retained and transmitted by the garden communities; and their associated reification processes that results in artifacts, rules-in-use and the structures of the gardens themselves. The research method involved performing surveys and interviews over a four-year period, with a sample of several hundreds of gardeners. The authors found some interesting results, namely that allotment gardens function as a kind of community-of-practice, where participation and reification interact, and social–ecological memory is a shared source of resilience of the community. The function of these can be described as being both emergent and persistent, as they highlighted the critical role of urban gardens in maintaining and supporting ecosystem services in times of crisis and change. In particular, the stewards of urban green areas and the social memory that they carry may help to effectively counteract and stem the further decline of critical ecosystem services.

It is an established fact that the value chain of many business enterprises is increasingly required to demonstrate the profitability of a firm's primary activities, starting from inbound logistics to operations, outbound logistics, marketing sales, and finally to services. In the research conducted by Lai and Wong (2012), the adoption of Green Logistics Management (GLM) presents an opportunity for Chinese manufacturing exporters to competently respond and address the escalating expectations of the international community in terms of meeting increased levels of resource conservation, while at the same time exhibiting both environmental concern, and profitability. Based on a survey of Chinese manufacturing exporters, they found that the commonly held view that economic motivation is related to the adoption of GLM is not supported. However, it was found that GLM positively affects both environmental and operational performance, and the existence of regulatory pressure enhances the GLM-performance relationship.

Young (2010) found that municipal forestry departments are giving greater attention to the management of municipal green space to enhance ecosystem services. This is being perceived as an increasingly important consideration for the goals and actions of their departments. Through a survey, this area was investigated in greater detail. The results of the survey brought forth a number of interesting results: first, the majority perceived traditional services such as tree planting and maintenance, and social aspects such as beautification and enhancing public health and well-being to be high departmental priorities. In addition, respondents rated managing municipal green space to produce ecosystem services, such as efforts to bring about better energy and climate management; improved water quality, habitat and biodiversity; as more important to their department than traditional objectives such as the maintenance of property values or the protection of power lines, for example.

Björklund (2011) used a mail survey to investigate the nature and character of different factors that can influence the environmental aspects of purchasing transportation services. Factor analysis suggests that the factors can, to a large extent, be grouped according to the actors involved. The most significant factors related to the internal management, firm image, resources of the firm, customer demands, carriers, and means of governmental control. In additions, the majority of the factors function as drivers. Differences have been identified when comparing the surrounding environment of the environmental aspects of purchasing transportation services with the surrounding environment commonly described in the more general purchasing and environmental management literature.

A Combination of Different Models

Urban growth boundaries (UGBs) have been are used throughout the world by planners to plan, design, and control urbanization by demarcating urban and rural boundaries. Currently, few UGB models exist to assist in the development of future urban growth boundaries. Tayyebi, Pijanowski, and Tayyebi (2011) present an urban growth boundary model (UGB) which utilizes artificial neural networks (ANN), geospatial information systems (GIS) and remote sensing (RS) to simulate the complex geometry of urban boundaries, using the unique feature of integrated raster and vector formats. A variety of goodness of fit land change model statistics are presented, many of which can be applied to purely raster-based land change models. They summarize the use of UGBs in urbanization planning around the world, and describe how this model can be used to assist planners in developing and better using future urban growth boundaries. This is critical because an understanding can provide greater insights into how to better understand, evaluate, and manage urban expansion.

Trappey, Trappey, and Wu (2010) developed a hybrid qualitative and quantitative approach, using fuzzy cognitive maps and genetic algorithms, to model and evaluate the performance of RFID-enabled reverse logistic operations. The use of fuzzy cognitive maps provides the advantage to linguistically express the causal relationships between the various reverse logistic parameters. The other evaluation, inference analysis using genetic algorithms, helps to enable performance forecasting and decision support for improving reverse logistic efficiency. In addition, Weber and Allen (2010) used an integrated, multi-scale approach to evaluate aspects of environmental mitigation and stewardship as they relate to transportation projects.

Climate Impacts of Planning Policies

Regulating a local climate through the use of urban green areas is an important urban ecosystem service, as it reduces the extent of the urban heat island and other effects, and as a result can enhance quality of life in an urban area. Through local and regional planning policies, land use changes can be effected in an urban area, which can then have an impact on the regulation of local climates. Schwarz, Bauer, & Haase (2011) describe a method for estimating the impacts of current land use as well as local and regional planning policies on local climate regulation, using a study of evapotranspiration and land surface emissivity as the main indicators. This method can be implemented by practitioners as a way of evaluating the effectiveness of these policies. For example, a case study on the application of this method was discussed, and involved work done in Leipzig, Germany. The results gathered from six selected planning policies in Leipzig indicated their distinct impacts on climate regulation and especially the role its spatial extent. The proposed method was found to easily produce a meaningful qualitative assessment of the impacts of planning policies on climate regulation.

Exploring Transportation Planning Issues

As host to a World Expo in 2012, Korea has been exploring the need to construct new inter-regional transportation facilities so as to improve the physical, economic and social structure of the host city. Kim (2011) examined the transportation planning tasks that should be done during the course of preparing for the Expo and to define tasks, measures, and goals to effectively address this objective. The paper conducted a review of four different aspects, the orientation of the government's low carbon green growth initiative, the governance system, the transportation facilities and traffic operational systems, and the participation of the local community. These were selected as some of the critical factors affecting the needs, and also the potential success of the Expo's transportation needs. These factors are key considerations in the preparations for the Expo, especially because Korea needs to prepare for the Expo by associating and joining the low carbon green growth policy implemented by the central government with the Expo's theme "The Living Ocean and Coast."

Future Trends of Green IT

The notion, goal, and implementation of Green IT services is a category of technology planning, design, and innovation that has become a necessity for our future not only for its environmental benefits, but also for its savings in terms of energy, costs, and other resources. Lamb (2009) described Green IT as "the study and practice of using computing resources efficiently." It is focused on reducing the environmental impact of industrial processes and innovative technologies, and their usage, in part caused by the Earth's growing population. Since we have no doubt seen many signs of the worldwide climactic changes that have caused many potentially disastrous events, and while some may not immediately see the direct connection between IT use and climactic change, anything that can severely affect the environment can be a contributor to undesired global change. In order to help move toward a "greener" future for IT in general, it would be useful to start at the source. Thomas Friedman made a valid point, that in order to achieve a greener product the materials itself must be environmental safer. "You can't make a product greener whether it's a car, a refrigerator, or a traffic system, without making it smarter - smarter materials, smarter software or smarter design" (Lamb, 2009, p.215).

Green IT Strategy

Green IT strategy is not only about buying more carefully and efficiently, but is also an approach in terms of how we go about thinking about the resources, energy and products that we use. One goal is to stay focused on saving energy for the organization, the individual and also the government, which is a worthy and practical perspective, but not the only one. The employment of alternative approaches and technologies, including emerging infrastructure technologies, for example, virtualization and distributed computing, can help to offer a higher level of flexibility and environmental sustainability.

Virtualization allows companies to obtain feedback, or to gather a more detailed view on the services that they are providing. It is the most critical emerging technology because it can be more efficient in terms of resource utilization, facility space savings, reduced power and cooling costs, while at the same time reducing the server footprint and energy usage. Reduced energy usage is made possible by using smaller servers and storages that have a larger capacity and more efficient processing. Also, it can help to reduce carbon emissions and protect the environment by using cleaner and more efficient technologies. With server virtualization, IT departments can change virtual server configurations, without the time-consuming labor required to maintain physical servers.

Distributed computing is made up of multiple independent computers, which communicate through a network and interact with each other through communications links, in order to achieve a goal. Each computer has a program that is installed in it and represents a direct link to the server. This setup can also bring about a more environmentally-friendly approach to computing.

Environmental Impact of IT

Green IT can help to benefit the goals of global environmental sustainability. Few can argue against the fact that environment conservation is essential, and that "green" IT can be used to help alleviate many of the problems normally associated with pollution, urban sprawl, and emissions from manufacturing facilities. "Although we all want to stop destroying our environment, Green IT is as much about doing the right thing as corporate citizens as it is about making the best business decisions from a cost and growth prospective" (Velte, Velte & Elsenpeter, 2008, p.24). The future of a Green IT environment will depend on everyone; however, people are often unaware as to the ways in which to contribute to environmental conservation or to the linkages between the environment and seemingly unrelated business decisions. For example, according to Murugesan (2008), many people are unaware that the "simple" disposal of electronic devices such as batteries, obsolete computers, and hardware devices can negatively impact our environment. Simply stated, Green IT benefits the environment in many ways including improving energy efficiency, lowering greenhouse gas emissions, using less harmful materials, and encouraging reuse and recycling.

Green IT's Growing Future

One of the most important elements of the future for green IT is that we must have better control over energy use at the data centers supporting a corporation. Some of the organizations or companies that have started using Green IT are Google and Microsoft. Through proper planning and development, they have built green data centers in the Pacific Northwest, and are expecting their future utility expenses to greatly decrease because of the efficiency and energy savings of their data centers.

In addition, the creation of green PC's by using nontoxic materials that would consume less power, be easier to assemble and have an extended useful lifetime are all benefits that are appreciated and welcome.

Low Carbon Finance

There have been excellent results demonstrated by commercial banks in China, active in the implementation of green credit policy. While some local governments actively promote the green credit policy, there have been many problems encountered in the implementation of low carbon finance in China. In the future, China is actively developing a strategic plan for low-carbon finance development, improve the legal framework for financial supervision, regulate the development of carbon finance, and foster low-carbon financial innovation mechanism. In addition, there have been expressed the goal to innovate and develop a variety of low-carbon financial instruments, improve low carbon financial intermediation services, and actively promote an international carbon trading process, using the denominated RenMinBi.

Rebound Effect and Backfire

Households are expected to play a pivotal role in reducing greenhouse gas (GHG) emissions in the UK, and the government is encouraging households to take specific steps to help meet desired targets. However, as Druckman, Chitnis, Sorrell & Jackson (2011) discovered, only a portion of the GHG emission reductions estimated by simple engineering calculations are generally achieved in practice due to a "rebound" effect resulting from the prescribed actions. Furthermore, emissions may increase in some instances, a phenomenon known as "backfire". Their study instead focuses on the benefits and importance of shifting consumption to lower GHG intensive categories and also investing making investments in low carbon technologies

A Holistic Strategic Analysis Framework

Zhang, Liu and Li (2011) suggest a holistic strategic analysis framework including considerations for the environment and "green" IT. In the past, IT system design was driven mainly by two essential factors: technical merits and cost considerations. Environmental aspects have only begun to emerge under the separate and distinct "green" IT perspective. Since the evaluation of any environmental and climate impacts may be complicated and involve a great many parameters, some of which are indirect and hidden, it is often difficult to come up with a rational analysis without the use of a more holistic framework. As such, the authors propose to extend the goal-oriented requirements modeling language, GRL, to model the rationality behind IT system design, with particular attention to how the environment related considerations come into play in such design and decision making. The framework is sufficiently flexible to facilitate decision making using different environmental settings.

Conclusion

The world is changing at a blistering pace and technology seems to be leading the way, but the technology that is available isn't always implemented or used in the most efficient way. While there are many proposals and suggestions for Green IT, many of them have not been widely understood, studied, or implemented. This is where a lot of research into Green IT services should be heading, as while inventing new strategies is essential, finding ways and means to have them widely implemented and applied has yet to fully accomplished. We have presented strategies and tools that can be used in order to help ease companies into Green IT and the programs and processes associated with it, but only time will tell if Green IT will take off. The recent interest in the environment and protecting it is very positive and will further boost awareness. The advances made in Green IT outsourcing and consulting have shown much promise, and hopefully these services and processes will become accepted in the business community, globally.

Financial concerns, constraints, global competition, and conflicting demands from within and organization complicate the many issues and directions that this area of research can take. As a result, in some ways research progress in this area has not been as dynamic and substantial as many think it should be. While Green IT is becoming a force to be reckoned with financially, more research is needed, and hopefully the future will bring a greater interest in this area. With increasing external pressure from government and consumers, this may be the time when a positive radical change will take place. Experts predict that this area of research will develop dramatically in the future, and as a result would benefit all.

The future of Green IT is still very hopeful and almost limitless, and, as technologies and attitudes change, the ways to efficiently maximize its power will change as well. That will be the ever evolving and dynamic future of Green IT and the services it provides.

John Wang
Montclair State University, USA

Jeffrey Hsu
Farleigh Dickinson University, USA

REFERENCES

Bae, S. H., Sarkis, J., & Yoo, C. S. (2011). Greening transportation fleets: Insights from a two-stage game theoretic model. *Transportation Research Part E, Logistics and Transportation Review, 47*(6), 793–807. doi:10.1016/j.tre.2011.05.015

Bartelmus, P. (2010). Use and usefulness of sustainability economics. *Ecological Economics, 69*(11), 2053–2055. doi:10.1016/j.ecolecon.2010.06.019

Barthel, S., Folke, C., & Colding, J. (2010). Social–ecological memory in urban gardens—retaining the capacity for management of ecosystem services. *Global Environmental Change, 20*(2), 255–265. doi:10.1016/j.gloenvcha.2010.01.001

Bastian, O., Haase, D., & Grunewald, K. (2011). Ecosystem properties, potentials and services – The EPPS conceptual framework and an urban application example. *Ecological Indicators*, In Press, Corrected Proof, Available online Sept. 29, 2011.

Beitollahi, H., & Deconinck, G. (2011). A dependable architecture to mitigate distributed denial of service attacks in network-based control systems. *International Journal of Critical Infrastructure Protection*, In Press, Corrected Proof, Available online Sept. 29, 2011.

Beloglazov, A., Abawajy, J., & Buyya, R. (2011). Energy-aware resource allocation heuristics for efficient management of data centers for Cloud computing. *Future Generation Computer Systems*, In Press, Corrected Proof, Available online 4 May 2011.

Björklund, M. (2011). Influence from the business environment on environmental purchasing — Drivers and hinders of purchasing green transportation services. *Journal of Purchasing and Supply Management, 17*(1), 11–22. doi:10.1016/j.pursup.2010.04.002

Brown, D., & Wilson, S. (2009). *The black book of outsourcing: 2009 green outsourcing survey*. John Wiley & Sons Inc.

Chen, X.D, Lupi, F., An, L., Sheely, R., Viña, A., & Liu, J. (2011). Agent-based modeling of the effects of social norms on enrollment in payments for ecosystem services. *Ecological Modelling*, In Press, Corrected Proof, Available online Sept. 29, 2011.

Druckman, A., Chitnis, M., Sorrell, S., & Jackson, T. (2011). Missing carbon reductions? Exploring rebound and backfire effects in UK households. *Energy Policy, 39*(6), 3572–3581. doi:10.1016/j.enpol.2011.03.058

Hedman, J., & Henningsson, S. (2011). Three strategies for green IT. *IT Professional Magazine, 13*(1), 54–57. doi:10.1109/MITP.2010.141

Jackson, T., & Victor, P. (2011). Productivity and work in the 'green economy': Some theoretical reflections and empirical tests. *Environmental Innovation and Societal Transitions, 1*(1), 101–108. doi:10.1016/j.eist.2011.04.005

Jenkin, T., Webster, J., & McShane, L. (2010, Sep). An agenda for "green" information technology systems research. *Information and Organization, 21*(1), 17–40. doi:10.1016/j.infoandorg.2010.09.003

Kim, K. S. (2011). Exploring transportation planning issues during the preparations for EXPO 2012 Yeosu Korea. *Habitat International, 35*(2), 286–294. doi:10.1016/j.habitatint.2010.10.002

Kipp, A., Jiang, T., Fugini, M., & Salomie, I. (2011). Layered Green Performance Indicators. *Future Generation Computer Systems*, In Press, Corrected Proof, Available online Sept. 29, 2011.

Lai, K.-H., & Wong, C. W. Y. (2012). Green logistics management and performance: Some empirical evidence from Chinese manufacturing exporters. *Omega, 40*(3), 267–282. doi:10.1016/j.omega.2011.07.002

Lamb, J. (2009). *The greening of IT: How companies can make a difference for the Environment*. Pearson. IBM Press.

Liu, J. G., & Shen, Z. Q. (2011). Low carbon finance: Present situation and future development in China. *Energy Procedia, 5*, 214–218. doi:10.1016/j.egypro.2011.03.038

Lohr, S. (2009, April 29). Bringing efficiency to the infrastructure. *The New York Times, Energy & Environment*, p. F1.

Lohr, S. (2011, August 23). Why flash is the future of storage in Data centers. *The New York Times, Technology* p.1.

Lorincz, J., Capone, A., & Begušić, D. (2011). Optimized network management for energy savings of wireless access networks. *Computer Networks*, *55*(3), 514–540. doi:10.1016/j.comnet.2010.09.013

Marsan, M. A., & Meo, M. (2011). Energy efficient wireless Internet access with cooperative cellular networks. *Computer Networks*, *55*(2), 386–398. doi:10.1016/j.comnet.2010.10.017

Matsumoto, M. (2010). Development of a simulation model for reuse businesses and case studies in Japan. *Journal of Cleaner Production*, *18*(13), 1284–1299. doi:10.1016/j.jclepro.2010.04.008

Murugesan, S. (2008). Harnessing green IT: Principles and practices. *IEEE IT Professional*, *10*(1), 24–25. doi:10.1109/MITP.2008.10

Nwe, E. S., Adhitya, A., Halim, I., & Srinivasan, R. (2010). Green supply chain design and operation by integrating LCA and Dynamic Simulation. *Computer Aided Chemical Engineering*, *28*, 109–114. doi:10.1016/S1570-7946(10)28019-7

Schwarz, N., Bauer, A., & Haase, D. (2011). Assessing climate impacts of planning policies—An estimation for the urban region of Leipzig (Germany*). Environmental Impact Assessment Review*, *31*(2), 97–111. doi:10.1016/j.eiar.2010.02.002

Tayyebi, A., Pijanowski, B. C., & Tayyebi, A. H. (2011). An urban growth boundary model using neural networks, GIS and radial parameterization: An application to Tehran, *Iran. Landscape and Urban Planning*, *100*(1-2), 35–44. doi:10.1016/j.landurbplan.2010.10.007

Tebbutt, D., Atherton, M., & Lock, T. (2008). *Green IT for Dummies*. John Wiley & Sons.

The use of economic valuation to create public support for green infrastructure investments in urban areas. *Landscape and Urban Planning*, In Press, Corrected Proof, Available online 20 August 2011.

Trappey, A. J. C., Trappey, C. V., & Wu, C.-R. (2010). Genetic algorithm dynamic performance evaluation for RFID reverse logistic management. *Expert Systems with Applications*, *37*(11), 7329–7335. doi:10.1016/j.eswa.2010.04.026

Vandermeulen, V., Verspecht, A., Vermeire, B., Van Huylenbroeck, G., & Gellynck, X. (2011).

Velte, T., Velte, A., & Elsenpeter, R. (2008). *Green IT:Reduce your information system's environmental impact while adding to the bottom line*. McGraw-Hill.

Weber, T. C., & Allen, W. L. (2010). Beyond on-site mitigation: An integrated, multi-scale approach to environmental mitigation and stewardship for transportation projects. *Landscape and Urban Planning, Volume*, *96*(4), 240–256. doi:10.1016/j.landurbplan.2010.04.003

Wilson, C. (2009). Putting the green in green. *Telephony*, *250*(5), 36–37.

Wilson, M. (2009). Survey: Green IT now essential. *Chain Store Age*, *85*(7), 52–52.

Young, R. F. (2010). Managing municipal green space for ecosystem services. *Urban Forestry & Urban Greening*, *9*(4), 313–321. doi:10.1016/j.ufug.2010.06.007

Zhang, H., Liu, L., & Li, T. (2011). Designing IT systems according to environmental settings: A strategic analysis framework. *The Journal of Strategic Information Systems*, *20*(1), 80–95. doi:10.1016/j.jsis.2011.01.001

Chapter 1
Predicting Ambulance Diverson

Abey Kuruvilla
University of Wisconsin Parkside, USA

Suraj M. Alexander
University of Louisville, USA

ABSTRACT

The high utilization level of emergency departments in hospitals across the United States has resulted in the serious and persistent problem of ambulance diversion. This problem is magnified by the cascading effect it has on neighboring hospitals, delays in emergency care, and the potential for patients' clinical deterioration. We provide a predictive tool that would give advance warning to hospitals of the impending likelihood of diversion. We hope that with a predictive instrument, such as the one described in this paper, hospitals can take preventive or mitigating actions. The proposed model, which uses logistic and multinomial regression, is evaluated using real data from the Emergency Management System (EM Systems) and 911 call data from Firstwatch® for the Metropolitan Ambulance Services Trust (MAST) of Kansas City, Missouri. The information in these systems that was significant in predicting diversion includes recent 911 calls, season, day of the week, and time of day. The model illustrates the feasibility of predicting the probability of impending diversion using available information. We strongly recommend that other locations, nationwide and abroad, develop and use similar models for predicting diversion.

BACKGROUND

A majority of Emergency Departments (EDs) across the United States perceive they are at or over capacity (Lewin Group, 2002). As ED visits have been on the rise, the number of hospital EDs and beds available at hospitals has decreased (Nawar, Niska, & Xu, 2007; U.S. General Accounting Of-

fice [GAO], 2003) In literature, several authors discuss factors contributing to ED saturation, ranging from high patient acuity and bed shortages (Derlet, Richards, & Kravitz, 2001) to lab delays and nursing shortages (Richards, Navarro, & Derlet, 2000).

When EDs reach their capacity, ED staff is unable to promptly care for new arrivals, and services within the hospitals are unable to ac-

DOI: 10.4018/978-1-4666-0044-7.ch001

Copyright © 2012, IGI Global. Copying or distributing in print or electronic forms without written permission of IGI Global is prohibited.

commodate the specific needs of new ambulance arrivals; hence ambulances must be diverted to other facilities that can provide critical care. This situation, referred to as "Ambulance Diversion," not only results in delays in emergency care (Redelmeier, Blair, & Collins, 1994), but could also contribute to patients' clinical deterioration (Glushak, Delbridge, & Garrison, 1997). We attempt to develop a mathematical model whereby hospitals/EMS agencies in a region can use 911 calls and diversion status of hospitals to predict the likelihood of the occurrence of diversion.

LITERATURE REVIEW

A study of the literature shows that the rising trend in ambulance diversions started causing concern during the late 1980s (Richardson, Asplin, & Lowe, 2002), resulting in reports, position papers and task forces studying this problem from the early 1990s (Frank, 2001; Vilke, Simmons, Brown, Skogland, & Guss, 2001; Pham, Patel, Millin, Kirsch, & Chanmugam, 2006). However, owing to the elevated utilization level of EDs, ambulance diversion continues to be an issue today and is a common and increasing event that delays emergency medical care (Redelmeier et al., 1994).

A wide range of literature exists, discussing the problem and various solutions have been suggested. A U.S. General Accounting Office survey (2003) found that while about two of every three EDs reported going on diversion at some point in fiscal year 2001, a much smaller portion—nearly 1 of every 10 hospitals—was on diversion more than 20 percent of the time. A cohort of twenty-two master's degree candidates from the University of Virginia (2001) did a detailed study on diversion at Richmond hospitals, and outlined problems and solutions, analyzed via a simulation model. A government study (U.S. House of Representatives, 2001), quoting instances of diversion from the local press in all states, reported that ambulance

diversions have impeded access to emergency services in the metropolitan areas of 22 states. Vilke et al., (2001) tested the hypothesis that, if one hospital could avoid ED diversion status, need for bypass could be averted in the neighboring facility. They concluded that reciprocating effects can be decreased with one institution's commitment to avoid diversion, thus decreasing the need for diversion at a neighboring facility. Neely, Norton, and Young (1994) found that ambulance diversions increase transport times and distances. One community served by four hospitals reduced ambulance diversion during a year, by 34% (Lagoe, Kohlbrenner, Hall, Roizen, Nadle, & Hunt, 2003). This was accomplished by sending daily diversion statistics to hospital chief executive officers and ED directors and managers, along with each hospital individually implementing its own measures to reduce diversion hours. Schull, Mamdani, and Fang (2004) found that there was an increase of diversion hours during the months of November and December and correlated it to the effect of flu on diversion. Only two papers in medical literature referred to 911 calls being used in a transport decision. Anderson, Manoguerra, and Haynes (1998) explored the effect of diverting poison calls to a poison center and Neely et al. (1994) found that diversion of 911 patients correlated strongly with unavailability of specific categories of beds.

Several communities have also produced policies to honor patient requests regardless of diversion status and to limit the total time of diversion for each hospital. Some large metropolitan areas have established oversight task forces to study and track the diversion issue in their communities (GAO, 2003). Some communities have addressed this issue with political mandates by non-medical personnel banning the use of diversion (Anderson, 2003). One city's solution (Lagoe & Jastremski, 1990) was the installation of an ambulance diversion system, whereby ambulances carrying patients with relatively minor injuries were diverted, when necessary, from the city's busy emergency departments to less crowded ones in neighboring counties.

A model that is able to predict the likelihood of a hospital or a combination of hospitals going on ambulance diversion would give advance warning to hospitals and allow them to take proactive steps to prevent it. The region itself would be better served by, for example, rerouting ambulances to alternate medical establishments. This would reduce transportation time and free up ambulances quicker for the next emergency. A survey of the literature yielded only one model for predicting an impending diversion. This model used the "work score" of an ED to predict ambulance diversion (Epstein & Tian, 2006). However, the model was developed for individual hospitals and does not consider the diversion status of other hospitals in the region; also, the workscore is not an easily available independent variable.

The model presented in this paper defines the joint probability of the diversion status of a collection of hospitals, based on readily available data, such as 911 calls and current status of hospitals. The objective of this paper is to propose a methodology and evaluate its feasibility for predicting the likelihood of ambulance diversion using readily available data, such as 911 calls and the diversion status of hospitals. Its purpose is to encourage metropolitan areas to develop similar models to predict ambulance diversion.

SELECTION AND EVALUATION OF METHODOLOGY

Since the purpose of this paper is to encourage metropolitan areas to develop similar models to predict the likelihood of ED diversion, we used multinomial logistic regression, a widely accepted statistical methodology that relates independent variables to the likelihood of a dependent event. The model developed uses data such as 911 calls and the diversion status of hospitals in the region,

which is readily available from health/EMS agencies. 911 calls have been used for transport decisions (Anderson et al., 1998), and there is a strong association between the number of ambulance patients and diversion (Schull, Lazier, Vermeulan, Mauhenney, & Morrison, 2003). Since the first call made by, or for, a potential ED patient is to "911," the number of calls for transport to hospitals in the region is an obvious leading indicator of the patient load at an ED. Other variables that could affect the number of patients at an ED include the time of year or season (such as flu season), the day of week, and time of day; hence, these variables are also used as independent variables in the model.

The proposed methodology was evaluated through a retrospective examination of real ambulance diversion and emergency 911 call data for the Kansas City metropolitan area. 911 call data was obtained for the Kansas City metropolitan area for the year 2003 and first 6 months of 2004. Twenty-nine of the 36 hospitals in the region were on diversion at some point during that period. The emergency 911 call data for the Kansas City metropolitan area was obtained from the Metropolitan Ambulance Services Trust (MAST), the ambulance service authority for the area. The data included the time a call was received, the type of emergency, and the hospital to which the patient was initially transported. The diversion data was obtained from "EMSystems," a program that tracks diversion status of hospitals. The system helps emergency departments report their status and thus coordinate and communicate with the other hospitals/EMS agencies in the region. EMSystems includes the time at which a hospital went on diversion, the reasons for going on diversion, and how long it stays on diversion.

Three hospitals with the most instances of diversion from the region were selected for analysis. The number of variables used in the model increases exponentially as the number of hospitals increases. Also, preliminary experiments indicated that a logistic model was useful in determining the probability of diversion at each of the hospitals based on the 911 calls, particularly for hospitals where diversion was most frequent. For these reasons, this study focuses on the three hospitals with the highest incidence of diversion. The preliminary logistic model was modified to account for the correlations among the diversion statuses of hospitals within a region, because the state of any one hospital affects the impending state of other hospitals. For instance, consider a region with two hospitals A and B, and Hospital A is similar to Hospital B with respect to any specialized types of patients it accepts, such as trauma patients. The current state of Hospital A clearly affects the future state of Hospital B because Hospital B has responsibility for a larger patient population when Hospital A is on diversion and vice-versa (Vilke et al., 2001).

In order to simultaneously consider the current ED state at each of the hospitals to predict the probability of diversion at any one of the hospitals, a multivariate multinomial model was constructed. While the individual logistic models provided valuable information on their own, the collective valid are coded as 0, 1,..., K - 1; the vector x denotes the p covariates. The logit functions are represented as:

$$g_k(x) = \ln\left(\frac{P(Y = k \mid x)}{P(Y = 0 \mid x)}\right) = x'\beta, k = 1..., K - 1.$$

where β is a vector of unknown coefficients

Thus, the conditional probability that a hospital is in a specific state, that is on diversion or not, is given by the following equations:

$$P(Y = 0 \mid x) = \frac{1}{1 + \sum_{i=1}^{K-1} e^{g_i(x)}}$$

$$P(Y = k \mid x) = \frac{e^{g_k(x)}}{1 + \sum_{i=1}^{K-1} e^{g_i(x)}}, k = 1,..., K - 1.$$

One of the key assumptions of the multinomial model is that the observations are independent. Thus for each of the models, only one out of every d observed values of the response variable is used, so that no variable representing 911 calls in a period is used twice. If all the observations of the response variable were used, nearly all observed 911 data would be used d times ($t-d+1$ to period t), in establishing the model, which would make the assumption of independence less plausible. This approach also significantly decreased the computation time and improved the overall fit of the models. The data processing and statistical analysis were accomplished using Microsoft Excel and the statistical packages R and SAS.

The data on ambulance diversion and 911 calls is partitioned into bins of length 1 hour. For each bin, the response variable gives the conditional probability of the future state of the three hospitals. There are eight possible outcomes that could occur in the next period which can be denoted by O, A, B, C, AB, AC, BC, and ABC. These are coded as $k = 0, 1, ..., 7$, respectively. The letters denote which hospitals are on diversion. For example, AC represents the state where hospitals A and C are on diversion, but hospital B is not. The state O represents the situation where none of the hospitals are on diversion.

There are several explanatory variables that are represented in the vector x. This includes the state of diversion during the current hour, which is a categorical variable with the same eight possible states as the response variable. Also, included is another categorical variable representing the period of the day, which is defined by partitioning the day into early morning (midnight–6 a.m.), morning (6 a.m.–noon), afternoon (noon–6 p.m.), and evening (6 p.m.–midnight). Additionally, indicator variables enable distinguishing between different years, weekdays and weekends, and seasons, such as flu season (which we have specified as being the months of November and December). In addition, three variables c_t, c_{t-1}, and c_{t-2} that represent the number of 911 calls during the current hour, the previous hour, and the hour before the previous hour, are included. The explanatory variables included in the model are shown in Table 1.

The multinomial logistic regression model is defined using the explanatory variables and the

historical data on the state of the hospital EDs. The statistical significance of the variables is shown in the analysis of effects table, Table 2.

As indicated in the table, only the variable for weekend is not statistically significant at a 5% level; however, it is a natural variable to include in the model.

Table 1. Codes for the data set

Variable Name	Description	Codes
Current	The current state of diversion.	O = no hospitals on diversion A = only A is on diversion B = only B is on diversion C = only C is on diversion AB = A and B are on diversion AC = A and C are on diversion BC = B and C are on diversion ABC = all hospitals are on diversion
Period	The period of the day.	0 = early morning (midnight–6am) 1 = morning (6am–noon) 2 = afternoon (noon–6pm) 3 = evening (6pm–midnight)
Weekend	An indicator variable for the weekend.	0 = weekday 1 = weekend
Year	An indicator variable for the year 2003.	0 = year 2004 1 = year 2003
Flu	An indicator variable for the flu season.	0=not flu season 1=flu season
	The number of 911 calls during the current hour.	Non-negative integer
	The number of 911 calls during the previous hour.	Non-negative integer
	The number of 911 calls during the hour before the previous hour.	Non-negative integer

Table 2. Effect table for factors considered

Effect	df	Chi-Square	P-Value
CURRENT	49	13590.9257	<.0001
PERIOD	21	154.9376	<.0001
WEEKEND	7	12.5411	.0841
YEAR	7	46.2325	<.0001
FLU	7	35.9705	<.0001
	7	110.5531	<.0001
	7	31.6680	<.0001
	7	17.9957	.0120

The Deviance and Pearson goodness-of-fit statistics also give no evidence against the model. The odds ratios are shown in Tables 3, 4, and 5.

DISCUSSION

The results indicate that the most recent 3 hours of the overall number of 911 calls are significant in predicting whether hospitals will go on diversion. Beyond that, the calls do not seem to be significant in predicting diversion. Also, other factors like the current state of diversion, indicator variables for flu, and quarter of day and the year were highly significant. The logistic model that has been developed illustrates the feasibility of predicting the probability of diversion. Since a number of EMS agencies are currently using online technologies with the data necessary for prediction readily available, this type of analysis might be timely. An early warning of impending diversion provided by this model could enable hospitals and EMS agencies to take appropriate actions to prevent and mitigate the effects of diversion. Such actions would include reallocation of resources and directing the transport of patients by EMS. The multinomial model presented in this paper is shown to be able to effectively predict the condi-

Table 3. Odds ratios for weekend, year, and flu effects

Odds Ratio Estimates			
		Point	95% Wald
Effect	Future	Estimate	Confidence Limits
weekend 0 vs 1	ABC	1.091 0.725 1.642	
weekend 0 vs 1	ABO	0.700 0.494 0.990	
weekend 0 vs 1	AOC	0.898 0.677 1.190	
weekend 0 vs 1	AOO	0.835 0.662 1.052	
weekend 0 vs 1	OBC	1.042 0.750 1.448	
weekend 0 vs 1	OBO	0.788 0.617 1.007	
weekend 0 vs 1	OOC	1.087 0.906 1.304	
yr 0 vs 1	ABC	1.949 1.268 2.993	
yr 0 vs 1	ABO	1.249 0.873 1.786	
yr 0 vs 1	AOC	1.618 1.219 2.147	
yr 0 vs 1	AOO	1.129 0.905 1.409	
yr 0 vs 1	OBC	1.640 1.188 2.264	
yr 0 vs 1	OBO	1.036 0.817 1.313	
yr 0 vs 1	OOC	1.617 1.373 1.906	
flu 1 vs 0	ABC	1.621 0.964 2.725	
flu 1 vs 0	ABO	0.575 0.338 0.977	
flu 1 vs 0	AOC	1.218 0.841 1.764	
flu 1 vs 0	AOO	0.820 0.600 1.122	
flu 1 vs 0	OBC	1.561 1.082 2.254	
flu 1 vs 0	OBO	1.329 0.993 1.779	
flu 1 vs 0	OOC	1.520 1.241 1.860	

Table 4. Odds ratios for different periods

Odds Ratio Estimates			
		Point	95% Wald
Effect	Future	Estimate	Confidence Limits
period 1 vs 0	ABC	4.359 1.899 10.005	
period 1 vs 0	ABO	1.752 1.053 2.915	
period 1 vs 0	AOC	4.662 2.794 7.778	
period 1 vs 0	AOO	2.020 1.458 2.799	
period 1 vs 0	OBC	1.604 0.926 2.776	
period 1 vs 0	OBO	0.795 0.574 1.100	
period 1 vs 0	OOC	1.305 0.997 1.707	
period 2 vs 0	ABC	6.403 2.967 13.819	
period 2 vs 0	ABO	1.654 0.861 3.175	
period 2 vs 0	AOC	5.153 3.053 8.697	
period 2 vs 0	AOO	1.188 0.794 1.776	
period 2 vs 0	OBC	1.500 0.827 2.719	
period 2 vs 0	OBO	0.751 0.485 1.162	
period 2 vs 0	OOC	1.215 0.905 1.631	
period 3 vs 0	ABC	1.017 0.516 2.002	
period 3 vs 0	ABO	0.599 0.348 1.032	
period 3 vs 0	AOC	1.019 0.641 1.621	
period 3 vs 0	AOO	0.527 0.372 0.749	
period 3 vs 0	OBC	1.381 0.859 2.220	
period 3 vs 0	OBO	1.028 0.723 1.462	
period 3 vs 0	OOC	1.045 0.815 1.339	

tional probability of diversion at hospitals that are frequently on diversion. The model illustrates that the number of 911 calls and other factors are more closely linked with the occurrence of diversion, than with the duration of diversion. Hospitals have internal factors they take into consideration when they decide to go on diversion, such as average waiting time, number of patients in the waiting room, or number of ambulances waiting. These policies and decisions are currently hospital specific and need to be integrated to derive maximum benefits from models, such as those presented in this paper, that signal impending diversion. The model presented in this paper could probably be improved by including additional causal factors like downstream inpatient bed availability to predict diversion. Also, the model is specifically developed using Kansas City EM system and 911 call data. The authors encourage the development of similar models for other regions in the United States. Similar models could also be developed in metropolitan areas of Canada or UK or where similar systems exist for collecting data on ambulance arrivals as well as emergency call data and where diversion is a public health issue.

Table 5. Odds ratios for calls during different times

Odds Ratio Estimates			
		Point	95% Wald
Effect	Future	Estimate	Confidence Limits
Calls during time t			
Xt1	ABC		1.120 1.058 1.186
Xt1	ABO		1.072 1.015 1.131
Xt1	AOC		1.073 1.031 1.116
Xt1	AOO		1.029 0.994 1.065
Xt1	OBC		1.139 1.086 1.195
Xt1	OBO		1.089 1.049 1.131
Xt1	OOC		1.130 1.102 1.159
Calls during time t-1			
Xt2	ABC		1.065 1.004 1.129
Xt2	ABO		1.029 0.973 1.088
Xt2	AOC		1.088 1.044 1.133
Xt2	AOO		1.067 1.029 1.105
Xt2	OBC		1.056 1.007 1.108
Xt2	OBO		1.000 0.962 1.040
Xt2	OOC		1.058 1.031 1.086
Calls during time t-2			
Xt3	ABC		1.012 0.956 1.072
Xt3	ABO		0.961 0.909 1.017
Xt3	AOC		1.004 0.966 1.044
Xt3	AOO		0.967 0.934 1.002
Xt3	OBC		1.058 1.009 1.110
Xt3	OBO		1.011 0.972 1.051
Xt3	OOC		1.026 1.000 1.053

ACKNOWLEDGMENT

The authors wish to thank Todd Stout, President, First Watch Solutions; Jonathan D. Washko, President, Washko & Associates; Gil Glass, Director of Operations and the Metropolitan Ambulance Services Trust at Kansas City, Missouri, for providing the impetus and data for this study; Ryan Gill, Assistant Professor, University of Louisville, for assisting with data analysis; the Editor-in-Chief of the journal, Professor John Wang; and reviewers for their invaluable input in developing this paper.

REFERENCES

Anderson, B. (2003, February 25). Fresno County bans diversion of ambulances. *Sacramento Bee*. p. A1.

Anderson, B. D., Manoguerra, A. S., & Haynes, B. E. (1998). Diversion of 911 calls to a poison center. *Prehospital Emergency Care, 2*(3), 176–179. doi:10.1080/10903129808958867

Cohort. (2002). *Metropolitan Richmond hospital diversions: A system analysis and change proposal*. Project report, Systems and Information Engineering Executive Master's Program. Charlottesville, VA: University of Virginia.

Derlet, R. W., Richards, J. R., & Kravitz, R. L. (2001). Frequent overcrowding in U.S. emergency departments. *Academic Emergency Medicine, 8*(2), 151–155. doi:10.1111/j.1553-2712.2001.tb01280.x

Epstein, S. K., & Tian, L. (2006). Development of an emergency department work score to predict ambulance diversion. *Academic Emergency Medicine, 13*(4), 421–426. doi:10.1111/j.1553-2712.2006.tb00320.x

Frank, I. C. (2001). ED crowding and diversion: Strategies and concerns from across the United States. *Journal of Emergency Nursing: JEN, 27*(6), 559–565. doi:10.1067/men.2001.120244

Glushak, C., Delbridge, T. R., & Garrison, H. G. (1997). Ambulance diversion. Standards and Clinical Practices Committee, National Association of EMS Physicians. *Prehospital Emergency Care, 1*(2), 100–103. doi:10.1080/10903129708958797

Hosmer, D., & Lemeshow, S. (2000). *Applied Logistic Regression* (2nd ed.). New York: John Wiley & Sons.

Lagoe, R. J., & Jastremski, M. S. (1990). Relieving overcrowded emergency departments through ambulance diversion. *Hospital Topics, 68*(3), 23–27.

Lagoe, R. J., Kohlbrenner, J. C., Hall, L. D., Roizen, M., Nadle, P. A., & Hunt, R. C. (2003). Reducing ambulance diversion: A multihospital approach. *Prehospital Emergency Care, 7*, 99–108. doi:10.1080/10903120390937184

Lewin Group. (2002). *Emergency department overload: A growing crisis*. Chicago: American Hospital Association.

Nawar, E. W., Niska, R. W., & Xu, J. (2007). *National hospital ambulatory medical care survey: 2005 Emergency department summary* (Advance data from vital and health statistics No. 386). Hyattsville, MD: National Center for Health Statistics. Retrieved March 30, 2009, from http://www.cdc.gov/nchs/data/ad/ad386.pdf

Neely, K. W., Norton, R. L., & Young, G. P. (1994). The effect of hospital resource unavailability and ambulance diversions on the EMS system. *Prehospital and Disaster Medicine, 9*(3), 172–177.

Pham, J. C., Patel, R., Millin, M. G., Kirsch, T. D., & Chanmugam, A. (2006). The effects of ambulance diversion: A comprehensive review. *Academic Emergency Medicine, 13*(11), 1220–1227. doi:10.1111/j.1553-2712.2006.tb01652.x

Redelmeier, D. A., Blair, P. J., & Collins, W. E. (1994). No place to unload: A preliminary analysis of the prevalence, risk factors, and consequences of ambulance diversion. *Annals of Emergency Medicine, 23*(1), 43–47. doi:10.1016/S0196-0644(94)70006-0

Richards, J. R., Navarro, M. L., & Derlet, R. W. (2000). Survey of directors of emergency departments in California on overcrowding. *The Western Journal of Medicine, 172*(6), 385–388. doi:10.1136/ewjm.172.6.385

Richardson, L. D., Asplin, B. R., & Lowe, R. A. (2002). Emergency department crowding as a health policy issue: Past development, future directions. *Annals of Emergency Medicine, 40*(4), 388–393. doi:10.1067/mem.2002.128012

Schull, M. J., Lazier, K., Vermeulan, N., Mauhenney, S., & Morrison, L. J. (2003). Emergency department contributors to ambulance diversion: A quantitative analysis. *Annals of Emergency Medicine, 41*(4), 467–476. doi:10.1067/mem.2003.23

Schull, M. J., Mamdani, M. M., & Fang, J. (2004). Community influenza outbreaks and emergency department ambulance diversion. *Annals of Emergency Medicine, 44*(1), 61–67. doi:10.1016/j.annemergmed.2003.12.008

U.S. General Accounting Office. (2003). *Hospital emergency departments: Crowded conditions vary among hospitals and communities* (GAO-03–460). Washington, DC: Author. Retrieved March 30, 2009, from http://www.gao.gov/new.items/d03460.pdf

U.S. House of Representatives. (2001). *National Preparedness: Ambulance Diversions Impede Access to Emergency Rooms*. Washington, DC: Special Investigative Division, Minority Staff for Representative Henry A. Waxman, Committee on Government Reform, U.S. House of Representatives.

Vilke, G. M., Simmons, C., Brown, L., Skogland, P., & Guss, D. A. (2001). Approach to decreasing emergency department ambulance diversion hours. *Academic Emergency Medicine, 8*(5), 526.

This work was previously published in International Journal of Information Systems in the Service Sector, Volume 2, Issue 1, edited by John Wang, pp. 1-10, copyright 2010 by IGI Publishing (an imprint of IGI Global).

Chapter 2
Hybrid Value Creation in the Sports Industry:
The Case of a Mobile Sports Companion as IT-Supported Product-Service-Bundle[1]

Jan Marco Leimeister
Kassel University, Germany

Uta Knebel
Technische Universitaet Muenchen, Germany

Helmut Krcmar
Technische Universitaet Muenchen, Germany

ABSTRACT

Integrated product-service packages (hybrid products) can open new markets and target groups to companies. However, existing approaches to service or product development do not sufficiently address simultaneous development and domain-specific issues. A very promising new field for such bundles is the health and fitness industry. In this research, we designed and built an IT-supported training system for running, the Mobile Sports Companion (MSC), which closely interlocks a product and corresponding services using an iterative development process. We tested the pilot system with 14 recreational athletes. The results of the field test show that the MSC proved to be a promising tool to offer athletes an effective individual, flexible, and mobile training. However, the system, as it is, did not sufficiently represent the human trainer behind it, thus lowering its acceptance and the credibility of its recommendations. Our next step is to integrate features that could strengthen the athlete-trainer relationship. The MSC could turn out to be a promising field for future e-business applications in the sports service industry.

DOI: 10.4018/978-1-4666-0044-7.ch002

Copyright © 2012, IGI Global. Copying or distributing in print or electronic forms without written permission of IGI Global is prohibited.

INTRODUCTION

Services account for a large part of the value added in manufactured goods in developed countries (Sheehan, 2006). Severe competition and cost pressures limit the growth of many companies across various industries, and, especially in the case of small and medium enterprises, threaten their existence. This has contributed to the expansion of the service economy over the last several decades. Integrated product-service packages (hybrid products) can enable innovative offerings and open new markets and target groups to companies (Organisation for Economic Cooperation and Development, 2006). However, companies mostly design services and products in separate processes, services being a mere add-on component to the product (Ernst, 2005). This separation can also be observed in the research literature. Many widespread process models focus on product construction, such as systems engineering (Daenzer, 1977), various Verein Deutscher Ingenieure (VDI) guidelines (e.g., VDI 2223) (Verein Deutscher Ingenieure, 2004), the Three-Tier-Model (Giapoulis, 1996), or software engineering, such as the Unified Software Development Process (Jacobson, Booch, & Rumbaugh, 1999) or eXtreme Programming (Beck, 2000). Alongside this extensive literature about product development, there is also a distinct literature describing new approaches to service development (see Bullinger & Scheer, 2003; Hermann, Krcmar, & Kleinbeck, 2005; Scheer & Spath, 2004), but they do not sufficiently address integrated, parallel development. Recent publications recognize this gap and present suggestions for integrated models (Spath & Demuß, 2006). However, the concept remains rather abstract and general. In addition, it does not consider domain-specific issues. In this research, we try to fill part of this gap while focusing on an example product development in the health and fitness market in Germany, a newly emerging and very promising field for innovative solutions like Computer Supported Collaborative Sports (Wulf, Moritz, Henneke, Al-Zubaidi, & Stevens, 2004).

Personal health and well-being gain more and more attention in today's industrial societies. In Germany, the sports, fitness, and recreation market has a market volume of more than 50 billion Euros. With an annual growth rate of 6% (Deloitte & Touche, 2005), it is one of the booming markets in the health sector. The reasons for the rising attention are mainly twofold: For one thing, health awareness has increased throughout large parts of the population, being considered an important part of a modern lifestyle. Moreover, consequences of unhealthy personal lifestyles on the economy become more and more evident. Ailments as a consequence or complication of being overweight and/or a lack of physical activity, such as cardiovascular diseases, back problems, and diabetes, account for approximately one fifth of the present health costs of German health insurance companies (Scriba & Schwartz, 2004), heavily burdening health insurance companies and employers. Schwarzer (2004) summarizes the results of various studies showing the correlation between certain diseases and lack of exercise. They amount to economic costs of about 530 million Euros per year in Germany (von Lengerke & John, 2005).

In spite of these developments, the market for fitness and health service providers, such as gyms or equipment manufacturers, in Germany has been steadily declining over the past 5 years (for a detailed market analysis see Kamberovic, Meyer, & Orth, 2005). Cost pressure and competition threaten small providers especially; many are put out of the market by emerging large franchise chains. To regain competitive advantage, especially above low cost operators, they need to offer innovative products and services going beyond the mere provision of sports equipment and occasional supervision that are common today.

Personal training, that is individual supervision and support of each athlete by a trainer, could be a way of addressing both of the above-mentioned problems. On the one hand, personal training is known to produce successful and effective results in competitive sports as well as in companies' management health coaching, and thus is also very likely to show effects in the mass market as well. On the other hand, personal training as a service could be a means of differentiation for small fitness providers. The major obstacle for translating the service of personal training into recreational sports and health management is cost. Health service providers cannot multiply their support services without an immense increase in personnel cost, whereas the clients, be it consumers or institutions on behalf of consumers, will not be willing and able to spend a considerably higher amount on health services. As in many other industries, the solution to this dilemma could be (partial) process automation.

The idea of automating sports training and health services is not new. Many vendors have already tried to integrate IT-based training support into a variety of devices, such as heart rate monitors or mobile phones. The most important vendor in the German market is Polar, whose major products are running and cycling computers. Apart from Polar, there are many small and very small vendors with different offerings (e.g., PCS-port.de, Technogym Wellness Wizard, iWorkout, PumpOne, etc.). However, virtually all existing systems fall short of solving the above-mentioned issues of integrating service into design. Most vendors try to achieve a full automation of the sports training, concentrating their efforts on hard- and software development, while totally neglecting the design of a corresponding service. Therefore, most systems on the market neglect necessary use scenarios for efficient training. Most systems are designed bottom-up based on and limited to the characteristics of an existing device or software. To make the design fit for use, it should be derived top-down from use scenarios, as well as users' goals and requirements.

Focus on single parameters. Existing systems base their training plans almost exclusively on heart rates. This is an appropriate method, when

determined correctly, but many systems operate on rules of thumb, neglecting important influencing factors, such as physical well-being, stress, daily form, and sometimes even age, sex, and sport discipline. Other effective methods for determining training intensities (for an overview see Neumann & Hottenrott, 2002) are not applied.

Require previous knowledge. Many systems offer possibilities for data analysis but no guidance on how to interpret this data. Users who have little knowledge of training methods might not be in the position of adjusting the training to their needs. Especially in case of illness, professional advice is necessary.

Depend on the users' discipline. Most existing systems are fully automated; no relationship between trainer and athlete is established. But especially inactive risk groups are not likely to motivate themselves for their training. To have a continued effect, the training must become part of the user's lifestyle and be supervised and supported by either a trainer or an institution

The objective of this research was to design, build, and evaluate an IT-supported training system for running (MSC) that closely interlocks a product components and corresponding services. The development of both components was simultaneous; the result was an integrated product-service bundle, which was then evaluated in a field test.

DEVELOPING THE MOBILE SPORTS COMPANION

Research Framework

This research is designed as an explorative study. As a research object, "mobile information systems for fitness sport" is very new and not well-investigated, and general theories about the research object do not yet exist. Stating and validating hypotheses purely deduced from theory, as is common in empirical-analytical research designs, are difficult to apply here. According to

Ulrich (1981), explorative research starts "... in practice, is focused on analyzing the context of use and ends in practice."

The intention of this research is to design an innovative system to improve real-world situations, following the tradition of the Action Research Method, which can be briefly described by its three main characteristics (Rapoport, 1970), (Lau, 1997):

1. The researcher actively intervenes in a social organization to advance both the organization's well-being and scientific knowledge.
2. The project consists of phases of interventions and of reflection for research purposes.
3. The researcher has to live up to the ethical challenges of the intervention.

Therefore, the effects of the mobile sports companion are tested in a pilot study (field test). Such field tests can, on the one hand, test the feasibility and effects of an innovation in a natural environment, and on the other, hand allow the identification of new demands that need to be addressed in further development. They have the advantage of high external reliability (Witte, 1997). For the design of social innovations, such explorative methods are most fruitful (Szyperski, 1971; Schwabe & Krcmar, 2000b), as recent examples in healthcare (Leimeister, Ebner, & Krcmar, 2005) and government (Schwabe & Krcmar, 2000a) have shown.

Research Design and Development Process

Since system requirements were neither completely nor exactly defined, a linear model did not seem to fit the uncertainty that arose from the field. An iterative model seemed to be more appropriate for several reasons. It allows to build the system step by step, and to evaluate the outcome of each interval of the iterative development periodically. Moreover, the type of development can be shaped according to the demands of the situation. To achieve this, we used Arnold, Leimeister, and Krcmar's (2003) Community Platform Engineering Process "CoPEP."

The heart of this process model is an iterative process, adapted from the generic spiral process model (Boehm, 1988; Wigand, Picot, & Reichwald, 1998). It is combined with a prototyping approach. Each consists of four phases: planning, analysis, engineering, and evaluation. Different than in the original spiral model, a much stronger focus is put on the building of prototypes and the involvement of users in evaluations. The goal of the engineering phase of each iteration is the generation of a prototype (hardware, software, and services) in order to get a tangible version of parts or the whole product (for a promising conceptualization of service systems see Mora, Raisinghani, O'Connor, & Gelman, 2009) very early in the development process (for a similar, but rather heavyweight approach to service design see Moller, Chaudhry, & Jorgensen, 2008). Each prototype undergoes an evaluation at the end of its development cycle in cooperation with experts. After each evaluation phase, the next iteration starts over with planning again, but uses information that was learned from the previous iteration in the design.

We adapted CoPEP's iterations to our research topic, and decided to involve target users in the evaluations in addition to experts as their representatives. Figure 1 shows the adapted process model that was used for the development of the mobile sports companion. The method used for evaluation was a mixture of interviews and group discussions. We presented the results of each cycle to a group of experts (iteration 1 and 2) and to a group of users (iteration 3 and 4) during the development phase. User and expert feedback was integrated into the planning of the next iteration. Finally, the finished prototype was tested in a field study.

Through an early involvement of various stakeholders in the development cycle and the visualization of parts of the end product through

Figure 1. Development process (adapted from Arnold et al., 2003)

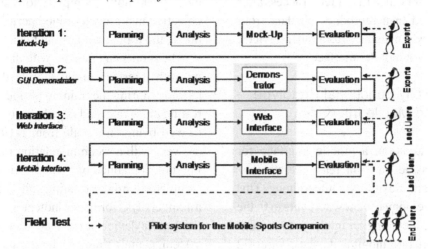

prototyping, the described process counteracts the danger of dragging wrong requirements fixed in the beginning along to the end product. General requirements get more detailed as the development process goes on and mistakes created in the beginning of the process can be repaired.

Results of the Iterations

Iterations 1-3: Mock-Up to Web Interface

In the first iteration, we conducted in-depth interviews with a group of four experts. The experts represented four different scientific disciplines, including training theory, sports psychology, sports medicine, and runners training. The basic idea was to define a service level for training supervision and support in between the high service level offered to professional athletes and the virtually non-existent service level offered in recreational sports; detailed enough to ensure an effective training, but as simple as possible. Through brainstorming and discussions, the experts specified the relevant measurement categories, interdependencies, and interplays between them and developed a relatively simple model for training supervision and control. We then determined which data must

be collected by professional trainers, which data should be collected and documented by the runners themselves, and which calculations the system was to make automatically. Limits and tolerance regions were determined. This model required the service to be made up of two components: first, a face-to-face support where trainer and athlete meet in person, and second, computer-mediated or fully automated support, where users interact with the system only. Based on this input, we developed a mock-up (i.e., a paper and pencil-prototype) of the mobile sports companion, which was approved by the experts.

In the second iteration, we implemented the runner's perspective in a first clickable prototype. The previously described experts checked if all relevant data was collected correctly, and tested the usability of the prototype. Their feedback was documented and implemented in the next iteration.

The third iteration produced a functional prototype, including a Web interface for the runners and trainers and a server backend. Apart from the experts, four lead users tested and evaluated the system by means of a structured questionnaire. The lead users generally felt that the quality of their training was improved but complained about the missing flexibility and the long time needed for documentation, as they had to memorize their training parameters, then find Internet access after the training, and then reproduce all data from memory or copy it manually from other devices. They wished for a mobile interface.

Iteration 4: Fully Functional Prototype with Web and Mobile Interfaces

In the fourth iteration, a mobile interface for the runners was added to increase the athletes' independence and flexibility while training. This implied the development of new software to fit the mobile device, including an interface to receive data from heart rate monitor devices. Figure 2 shows the data flows in the system.

At the beginning of a training period, trainer and runner meet personally. The trainer gathers basic information on the runner, such as height, weight, resting pulse rate, sport history, and conducts a standardized fitness test. Together, trainer and runner define the runner's training objectives. Using the trainer web interface, the trainer creates a personal electronic file for the runner. Based on the training objectives and considering the runner's physical condition, the system suggests value ranges for the number, length, frequency and intensity of training units

the runner should complete to reach his or her objective in a predetermined period. Within this range, the trainer adjusts the plan.

The runner can interact with the system either by Web interface or by mobile device. Every morning during the training period, he enters his resting pulse rate, and rates his subjective feeling of well-being on a scale from 1-10. The system answers with a recommendation to do the training unit as planned or to modify it. After having completed the day's training unit, the runner feeds a number of performance indicators—either using the mobile device or the Web interface—into the system, namely time and duration of the training, perceived well-being, and average heart rate. Heart rates can be transmitted directly from the heart rate monitor to the mobile device. Once uploaded, the system analyzes the data, compares planned and actual values, and assigns the result to the stages of a traffic light (green = ok; yellow = contact trainer; red = stop training, contact trainer urgently).

The trainer can access all data uploaded to the system by his runners, and monitor and supervise their progress. The traffic light system allows him to screen the state of all runners quickly, and to focus on the more problematic cases (i.e., red light)

Figure 2. Data flows

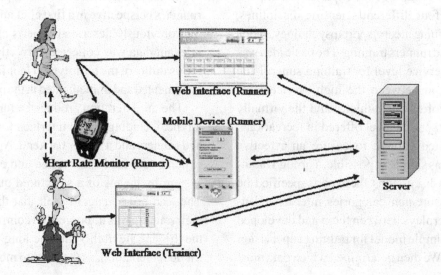

first. This cycle repeats until the training objectives are realized or until the next control meeting. Independent from the system's recommendations, if necessary, the athletes can contact their trainer at any time via a "contact trainer" button.

As in the previous iteration, four lead users evaluated the system. The mobile client was highly appreciated, as it enhanced the user's flexibility in documenting their training units. They also found the daily recommendations for their training very useful. Overall they felt that the quality of their training had improved. On the other hand, they felt a strong dependence from their trainer. As a consequence of these results, some more functions were added to the system in close cooperation with the before-mentioned experts.

To better supervise the runners' progress and by this increase the quality of the training, we increased the service level and introduced periodical test runs and corresponding analyzing tools. In addition, a tool for weekly comparison of the planned and actual training units was implemented. The trainer was given more possibilities to adjust the system-generated training plans according to his own recommendations. With these alterations, the system was ready to be tested by a larger number of users.

Field Test

Purpose

The purpose of the field test was to examine:

1. If the mobile sports companion could support users in reaching their training goals (perceived usefulness)
2. How users felt to train with an automated training system (use, perceived ease of use, perceived well-being)
3. If the mix of face-to-face, computer-mediated, and fully automated service components gave the impression of continuous individual support (perceived service level)

4. How the system could be further adapted to the user's needs

It is important to state that the MSC was evaluated as a whole; it is not adequate for an integrated product-service bundle to try and evaluate the single components separately.

Setting

The field test was conducted with 14 employees of a telecommunication company, 9 male and 5 female, all between 25 and 40 years old. The participants represented the whole range from sports novices to experienced runners. Figure 3 shows their training habits and weight classification.

For the field test, the training period and goal was standardized for all participants: being able to run a half marathon (21 km) after 12 weeks of training, following an individual training plan managed through the mobile sports companion. The training period began with a thorough analysis of the participants' anthropometric data, such as height, weight, sports experience, past and present diseases, and medications. It also included a lactate threshold test—an individual performance test to assess the physiological condition of each of the runners, lactate being a key indicator for determining training intensity and evaluating training results in endurance sports. In addition, the participants assessed their perceived exertion on a Borg scale[2]. Based on the diagnostic data, the individual training plans were created.

We provided all participants with a mobile device (PDA) and a heart rate monitor. They were asked to document their resting pulse rate and perceived well-being everyday, first thing in the morning. In reaction, the system recommended them to train as planned, do not train and recreate, or to contact the trainer. The training units were divided into three categories with different training intensities (for details on the intensity

Figure 3. Characteristics of the participants of the field test

	Training Units / Week			
	0–1	2–3	4–5	Total
male	4	3	2	9
female	3	2	0	5
Total	7	5	2	14

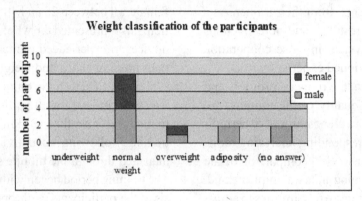

levels see Neumann & Hottenrott, 2002), setting a time and pulse rate.

After 4, 8, and 12 weeks, all runners made a test run at given constant speed over a given distance. The heart rate served as an indicator for endurance improvement. The participants repeated the Borg rating. At the end of the 12 weeks training period, the lactate threshold test was repeated.

To evaluate the subjective training success, perceived well-being and motivation, we used a structured questionnaire both at the beginning and at the end of the training period. Figure 4 illustrates the procedure.

Figure 4. Field test procedure

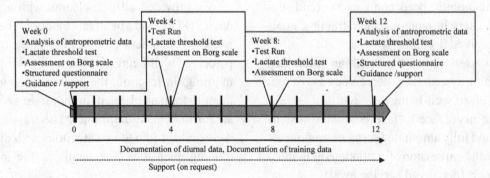

Technology

The server was implemented as a J2EE web application based on the Struts framework. A MySQL database in the backend worked as a persistent data memory. A Web service interface at the server using the Apache Axis framework enabled the communication between the mobile devices (the clients) and the server. The client software was written in C# and based on the .NET 2.0 Compact Framework. It runs on PDAs with Microsoft Windows Mobile 2003 or newer versions.

In the field test, the participants used mobile devices (PDAs) of the type O2 XDA II, XDA III, and XDA mini S respectively. The interface for the communication with the heart rate monitor was optimized for Polar S625X, as it is one of the most widespread heart rate monitors in the German market. Integrating the Polar device into the system was most challenging, as the communication protocol was not laid open.

A role concept defined the right to access and manipulate data; it comprised the three roles of trainer, runner, and administrator.

Empirical Results

The first questionnaire was administered at the beginning of the field test. It was completed by all 14 participants. The second questionnaire was administered at the end of the testing period. It was only completed by 10 participants. Two of the participants had already left and another two participants were not able to keep the appointed date of the survey.

Empirical Results

Use and Perceived Ease of Use

On average, the users tended to agree that by use of the MSC, they trained more regularly than before. However, they did not document their training data and even less their diurnal data very accurately. Most of them felt especially the measuring of the resting pulse rate in the mornings as too time-consuming and annoying. Another reason could be the usability of the Web and mobile interfaces. Though their usability is rated slightly positively, the users do not judge it well (Table 1). Some users reported repeated difficulties in loading up their data from the mobile device to the server.

Perceived Usefulness

In respect to perceived usefulness, the respondents tended to assess the quality of their training and training supervision. Moreover, they clearly agree that using the MSC has advantages for them and consider technical devices in general as helpful for training (Table 2).

Table 1. Usage and usability of the MSC

	mean	std. dev.
By use of the MSC, I trained more regularly than before.	0.4	1.9
I have documented my diurnal data regularly.	-0.7	1.7
I have documented my training data regularly.	-0.2	1.6
The web interface was easy to use.	0.5	0.8
The mobile interface was easy to use.	0.7	0.8
*Annotation: 5-point scale from "totally agree"=+2 to "do not agree at all"=-2		

Table 2. Perceived ease of use

	mean	std. dev.
With the MSC I feel better supervised and supported*	0.7	1.2
By use of the MSC, the quality of my training was increased.*	0.4	1.6
Using the MSC has advantages for me.*	1.2	1.2
Technical devices during training are...**	0.8	0.9
*Annotation: 5-point scale from "totally agree"=+2 to "do not agree at all"=-2 ; **+2=very helpful to -2=not helpful at all		

The physiological data confirmed these perceptions. In the lactate threshold tests, the heart frequency measuring, as well as the self-assessment according to the Borg scale, the participant's performance had continuously increased.

Perceived Well-Being

After 12 weeks of training, the participants had the impression that their fitness level had increased, though still being far from ideal. They also felt more energetic and satisfied with their bodies (Figure 5).

Perceived Service Level

It was the idea of the field test that the trainers stayed in the background as much as possible, leaving the sportive guidance to the MSC. Personal interference should only happen if an athletes training data was so unexpected that the trainer's traffic light turned "red." This however was not accepted well by the participants. Most of them repeatedly tried to contact the trainers instead of relying on them to communicate their recommendations via the MSC, if necessary at all. When the trainers gave no or very little additional information, some participants were extremely dissatisfied, and the research team had once again to explain the reasons for their approach. Nevertheless, in the final discussion, the majority of the group wished for more personal advice.

We think that the greater part of this reaction was due to an organizational misunderstanding in the beginning. The participants of the field study were recruited with the assistance of the corporate health service provider, not personally by the research team. As the task of contacting potential participants was passed on from one person to the other within the service provider, they might have communicated a wrong picture of the MSC. Some of the participants were told they would receive personal feedback to all actions performed in the program (not only in case of problems and via the MSC channel). Naturally, these (wrong) expectations were not satisfied. In future studies, we will address this issue with standardized information material and training for the recruiters as well as for the participants starting the program.

Nevertheless, offering a feedback channel within the MSC, such as an "E-Mail to trainer" button will be considered in future studies to enable the participants to give proactive information (e.g. did not exercise because of illness) and for urgent questions. The principal exercise guidance however will still be communicated via the MSC.

SUMMARY AND OUTLOOK

We developed a concept and iteratively implemented a prototype of a semi-automatic training system. The starting point in each iteration was the

Figure 5. Perceived well-being

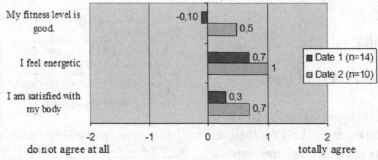

athlete's requirements and the necessary service elements deduced from them. We field-tested the prototype with 14 volunteers with different sports experience. In general, the MSC proved to be a promising tool to offer athletes an individual, flexible, and mobile training. In contrast to most automated training systems on the market, the MSC concept integrates personal services like the initial health checkup or face-to-face meetings with a trainer. However, the system, as it is, did not do a good job of representing the human trainer behind it, thus lowering its acceptance and the credibility of its recommendations. As a consequence, the service component seemed insufficient to the test users.

Based on the experience gained in these studies, we have two major action points for further developing the MSC. First, we must adapt the computer-mediated and automated service components to better resemble an individual support, and second, we must reduce cost and effort of the face-to-face service components. The next steps for our research are:

1. Develop motivational features: The voluntary participation of the field-test participants attests to a certain degree of intrinsic motivation for being physically active. However, training progress is a long-term process. Many people will not discipline themselves to follow the plan without strong extrinsic incentives. A combination of motivational features implemented in the software, for example, game elements (Lin, Mamykina, Lindtner, Delajoux, & Strub, 2006) and virtual group experience (Mueller & Agamanolis, 2005) would contribute to the perseverance in following the training plan. Incentives, for instance set by a company for their employees, could enforce this trend.

2. Set individual goals: Running a half marathon in 12 weeks proved to be too high a goal for the greater part of the participants. Especially in the field of recreational or preventive sports, more general goals such as "loose weight" or "stay fit" should be addressed (Stevens, Wulf, Rohde, & Zimmermann, 2006).

3. Extend and diversify methods of performance measuring and training plan design: The training plan design and control based on the lactate threshold proved to be very time-consuming and tiring for both athletes and trainers. Based on personal goals and proficiency level, other ways of testing and planning might be appropriate. Training documentation could be enhanced by further data, such as GPS data, weather, amount of sleep etc.

4. Establish trainer-athlete relationship: Seeing the trainer for control sessions and in case of unexpected events was not enough to give athletes the impression of a good supervision, even if they knew he would check their training data on the server. We need to examine if this perceived deficiency can be reduced by altering the look and feel of the software, and at what time the trainer has to interfere personally. Based on the frequency of this interference and on the variations of data collection and performance tests mentioned above, a large variety of service levels could be developed. Business models and pricing are further questions in this area.

5. Further field tests including control groups: A large-scale field test including control groups who train without the support of the MSC would allow a comparison of cost and effect.

We developed the MSC along an iterative process model, turning learning from earlier stages into requirements for later stages. Service components were considered from the beginning. Experts and users were integrated in all phases of development. The process seemed appropriate to collect and react to user suggestions and requirements in all phases of the development. However, in the pilot test the MSC did not fully satisfy all participants. Therefore, we have to further explore and evaluate our method.

In this research, our pilot study was carried out in a German telecommunications company with a quite homogenous group concerning education and cultural background. For future work, we plan to explore the MSC in multi-cultural environments in Germany (e.g., with the staff of a manufacturing company) and in international contexts. The creation of business models and the design of value networks that could offer the MSC also hold great potential for further research.

LIMITATIONS OF THE STUDY

This research has certain limitations. First, the test group was rather small, the statistic calculations showed a considerable variance. Second, as the members of the test group participated voluntarily and out of interest in the study, their motivation and positive attitude towards the MSC is not necessarily representative. Third, there was no control group to compare the effect of the MSC-supported training to a conventional training. Finally, self-report measures as we applied among others, can always be biased by the participants' intended or unintended false answers.

We believe that the major advantage of MSC is that it allows supervision of and situational reactions to user behavior, but at the same time, the computer-mediated delivery and supervisor support functions allow a fast and efficient supervision and administration. Therefore, practice will find the MSC and similar designs eligible and useful for large-scale corporate or public health programs, providing an alternative to conventional interventions requiring personal presence.

REFERENCES

Arnold, Y., Leimeister, J. M., & Krcmar, H. (2003). *COPEP: A development process model for a community platform for cancer patients.* Paper presented at the XIth European Conference on Information Systems (ECIS), Naples, Italy.

Beck, K. (2000). *Extreme programming explained.* Upper Saddle River, NJ: Addison-Wesley.

Boehm, B. W. (1988). A spiral model of software development and enhancement. *Computer, 21*(5), 61–72. doi:10.1109/2.59

Borg, G. (1998). *Borg's perceived exertion and pain scales.* Champaign, IL: Human Kinetics.

Bullinger, H.-J., & Scheer, A.-W. (2003). *Service engineering: Entwicklung und gestaltung innovativer dienstleistungen.* Berlin, Germany: Springer.

Daenzer, W. F. (1977). *Systems engineering: Leitfaden zur methodischen durchführung umfangreicher planungsvorhaben.* Köln, Zürich: Peter Hanstein.

Deloitte & Touche. (2005). *Der deutsche pitness- und wellnessmarkt.* Munich, Germany: Deloitte & Touche GmbH.

Ernst, G. (2005). Integration von produkt und dienstleistung—hybride wertschöpfung.

Giapoulis, A. (1996). *Modelle für effektive konstruktionsprozesse.* Aachen, Germany: Shaker.

Hermann, T., Krcmar, H., & Kleinbeck, U. (Eds.). (2005). *Konzepte für das service engineering—modularisierung, prozessgestaltung und produktivitätsmanagement.* Heidelberg, Germany: Physica.

Jacobson, I., Booch, G., & Rumbaugh, J. (1999). *The unified software development process.* Glenview, IL: Addison-Wesley Longman.

Kamberovic, R., Meyer, M., & Orth, S. (2005). Eckdaten der deutschen fitnesswirtschaft. 67.

Lau, F. (1997). A review on the use of action research in information systems studies. In A. S. Lee, J. Liebenau & J. I. DeGross (Eds.), *Information Systems and Qualitative Research: Proceedings of the IFIP TC8 WG 8.2 International Conference on Information Systems and Qualitative Research*, Philadelphia (pp. 31-68). London: Chapman & Hall.

Leimeister, J. M., Ebner, W., & Krcmar, H. (2005). Design, implementation and evaluation of trust-supporting components in virtual communities for patients. *Journal of Management Information Systems, 21*(4), 101–131.

Lin, J., Mamykina, L., Lindtner, S., Delajoux, G., & Strub, H. (2006). Fish'n'Steps: Encouraging physical activity with an interactive computer game. In P. Dourish & A. Friday (Eds.), *Proceedings of the International Conference on Ubiquitous Computing*, Orange County, USA (pp. 261-278). Berlin, Germany: Springer.

Löllgen, H. (2004). Standard der sportmedizin: Das anstrengungsempfinden (RPE, Borg Skala). *Deutsche Zeitschrift fur Sportmedizin, 55*(11), 299–300.

Moller, C., Chaudhry, S. S., & Jorgensen, B. (2008). Complex service design: A virtual enterprise architecture for logistics service. *Information Systems Frontiers, 10*(5), 503–518. doi:10.1007/s10796-008-9106-3

Mora, M., Raisinghani, M., O'Connor, R., & Gelman, O. (2009). Toward an integrated conceptualization of the service and service system concepts: A systems approach. *International Journal of Information Systems in the Service Sector, 1*(2), 36–57.

Mueller, F., & Agamanolis, S. (2005). Sports over a distance. *ACM Computers in Entertainment, 3*(3), 4. doi:10.1145/1077246.1077261

Neumann, G., & Hottenrott, K. (2002). *Das große buch vom laufen*. Aachen, Germany: Meyer & Meyer.

Organisation for Economic Co-operation and Development. (2006). *Innovation and knowledge-intensive activities*. Paris: Author.

Rapoport, R. N. (1970). Three dilemmas in action research. *Human Relations, 23*(4), 499–513. doi:10.1177/001872677002300601

Scheer, A.-W., & Spath, D. (2004). *Computer aided service engineering*. Berlin, Germany: Springer.

Schwabe, G., & Krcmar, H. (2000a). *Digital material in a political work context—The case of Cuparla*. Paper presented at the 8th European Conference on Information Systems (ECIS 2000), Vienna, Austria.

Schwabe, G., & Krcmar, H. (2000b). *Piloting a socio-technical innovation*. Paper presented at the 8th European Conference on Information Systems (ECIS 2000), Vienna, Austria.

Schwarzer, R. (2004). *Psychologie des gesundheitsverhaltens. Einführung in die gesundheitspsychologie* (3rd ed.). Göttingen, Germany: Hogrefe.

Scriba, P. C., & Schwartz, F. W. (2004). Bewegung. Prävention und gesundheitsförderung—wege zur innovation im gesundheitswesen? *Internist, 45*(2), 157–165. doi:10.1007/s00108-003-1131-1

Sheehan, J. (2006). Understanding service sector and innovation. *Communications of the ACM, 49*(7), 43–48. doi:10.1145/1139922.1139946

Spath, D., & Demuß, L. (Eds.). (2006). *Entwicklung hybrider produkte—gestaltung materieller und immaterieller leistungsbündel* (2nd ed.). Berlin, Germany: Springer.

Stevens, G., Wulf, V., Rohde, M., & Zimmermann, A. (2006). *Ubiquitous fitness support starts in everyday's context*. Paper presented at the 6th World Conference on the Engineering of Sport, Munich, Germany.

Szyperski, N. (1971). Zur wissensprogrammatischen und forschungsstrategischen orientierung der betriebswirtschaft. *Zeitschrift für Betriebswirtschaft, 23*, 261–282.

Ulrich, H. (1981). Die betriebswirtschaftslehre als anwendungsorientierte sozialwissenschaft. In M. N. Geist & R. Köhler (Eds.), *Die führung des betriebes. Festschrift für curt sandig* (pp. 1-26). Stuttgart, Germany: Poeschel Verlag.

Verein Deutscher Ingenieure. (2004). *VDI richtlinie 2223—methodisches entwerfen technischer produkte*. Berlin, Germany: Beuth.

von Lengerke, T., & John, J. (2005). Gesundheitsökonomische aspekte der adipositas—bisherige ergebnisse der kooperativen gesundheitsforschung (KORA). *Cardio News, 8*(3), 46.

Wigand, R., Picot, A., & Reichwald, R. (1998). Information, organization and management: Expanding corporate boundaries. Chichester, UK: Wiley.

Witte, E. (1997). Feldexperimente als innovationstest—die pilotprojekte zu neuen vedien. *Zeitschrift für betriebswirtschaftliche* [zfbf]. *Forschung, 49*(5), 419–436.

Wulf, V., Moritz, E., Henneke, C., Al-Zubaidi, K., & Stevens, G. (2004). Computer supported collaborative sports: Creating social spaces filled with sports activities. In *Proceedings of the Third International Conference on Entertainment Computing (ICEC 2004)* (pp. 80-89). Springer.

ENDNOTES

1. An earlier version of this article appeared in the *Proceedings of the Fifteenth European Conference on Information Systems*. H. Österle, J. Schelp, R. Winter (Eds.) (pp. 81-92), St. Gallen, Switzerland: University of St. Gallen.

2. The Borg Rating of Perceived Exertion or Borg Scale is a method of determining the intensity of physical activity. Perceived intensity is rated on a scale from 6 (no exertion at all) to 20 (maximal exertion). A person who wants to engage in moderate-intensity activity would aim for a Borg Scale level of "somewhat hard" (12-14) (Borg, 1998). The Borg Scale is widely used in clinical studies and in professional sports, and it is considered an appropriate method for controlling physical activity intensity (Löllgen, 2004).

This work was previously published in International Journal of Information Systems in the Service Sector, Volume 2, Issue 1, edited by John Wang, pp. 11-25, copyright 2010 by IGI Publishing (an imprint of IGI Global).

Chapter 3
Connect Time Limits and Performance Measures in a Dial–Up Modem Pool System

Paul F. Schikora
Indiana State University, USA

Michael R. Godfrey
University of Wisconsin Oshkosh, USA

Brian D. Neureuther
State University of New York, College at Plattsburgh, USA

ABSTRACT

Managing customer service is critical for both nonprofit and for-profit dial-up modem Internet service providers. When system operators face excess demand, they can either add capacity or adapt their management techniques to deal with their limited resources—this article considers the latter. We examine system configuration options and the resultant effects on customer service levels in a simulated dial-up modem pool operation. Specifically, we look at a single pool operation and examine the effects of imposing time limits in a seriously overloaded system. We analyze the results on several key customer service measures. The results show that imposing these limits will have a distinct, nonlinear impact on these measures. Customer productivity and actual system load are shown to have major impacts on the performance measures. Interactions between several system and environmental parameters are also discussed.

INTRODUCTION

Schikora and Godfrey (2006) examined connect time limits in a dial-up modem pool (DMP). In that study, they examined the impact on the performance measures of the percent of lost

DOI: 10.4018/978-1-4666-0044-7.ch003

customers and the percent of customers disconnected when connect time limit restrictions were placed on the system. They found that imposing DMP time limits affected these key customer service measures. The study presented here is an extension of that previous work, providing more detailed results and examining the interaction of key experimental factors.

Copyright © 2012, IGI Global. Copying or distributing in print or electronic forms without written permission of IGI Global is prohibited.

Universities, corporations, and Internet service providers have long provided external access to computer networks using a DMP. Modems allow data to be transmitted over standard analog telephone connections, providing long-distance access to a central computer from any place that has a telephone connection and a modem-equipped computer. Though the data transfer rates through a modem-to-modem connection are much slower than the transfer rates of a direct network connection, modems are essential for providing flexible external access to a central network for most users.

With the rapid growth in the use of home computers and the increasing popularity of the Internet over the past decade, DMP operators experienced a corresponding increase in demand for their service (Naldi, 1999). Advances in broadband availability have since reduced demand for DMP service. However, narrowband users still account for 32% of active Internet users in the United States (Website Optimization LLC, 2006), 30% of Internet users in Australia (Daniel, 2006), and 70% of Internet users in New Zealand (Auckland, 2006). Even on the African continent, government leaders are urging broadband Internet providers to lower prices because broadband remains high priced and is leading to slowed down growth in Internet usage in South Africa (Miniwatts Marketing Group, 2004). Despite the promise of high-speed connectivity, dial-up access remains a viable, low-priced means by which a significant percentage of users still access the Internet. Walczak and Parthasarathy (2006) have argued that customer discontinuance and switching remain major issues for Internet service providers. In addition, Titus (2007) outlines advantages of dial-up modems and the convenience they offer in the electronics industry in the United States. He offers an outlook for the incorporation of dial-up modems by engineers to other modems. Further, an article in *The Economist* ("The Slow Death of Dial-up," 2007) states that even though there is a decrease in the use of dial-up to access the internet, several segments of society are expected to continue to use

dial-up as their primary means for accessing the Internet. In fact, the article states, "The rumour of dial-up's death has been greatly exaggerated." Therefore, our research analyzes how to improve service to dial-up customers of Internet service providers. Specifically, we examine the situation where demand for service exceeds the capacity of an existing DMP system.

The easiest way to remedy excess demand for DMP service is simply to increase capacity by enlarging the size of the DMP—often a viable option for a for-profit operator given that increased demand leads to increased revenues. However, this approach is expensive, so increasing capacity should not be done without regard for operating efficiencies. In the case of smaller or nonprofit operators (e.g. universities), additional capacity often is not a viable option due to budget constraints. In the case of system downsizing in markets with reduced demand, very high system utilization may result and persist for some time immediately after system resizing. Regardless of the provider's demand forecast, or whether the provider is for-profit or non-profit, system operators should be concerned with the efficiencies of their system and should focus more on using available resources efficiently. Krueger (2003) suggests using COM Port Redirector software to replace Desktop modems. This allows modem users to share a dial-out modem pool on a centralized server on their corporate network.

This article examines DMP system configuration and management issues when user demand meets or exceeds the capacity of a DMP system. In such a situation, users wanting to access the system often will receive a busy signal (in standard queuing terminology, they are *blocked*). They then have the option of continuing to try to access the system by redialing (retrials), or giving up and leaving the system, possibly returning later. Those customers who give up and leave the system without being served are considered *lost*. [Care should be taken to note the meaning of a *lost customer* here. Customers are lost only in the sense of the current service encounter. They are assumed to return at some later point to try for service again. Therefore, customers are lost in the sense that they leave the current service provider for another.] While the blocking probability is an important performance measure in typical queuing systems, a more important performance measure in DMP systems is the percentage of customers that are lost. The widespread implementation of auto-redialing in personal computer systems minimizes the negative impact of blocking on any one connection attempt, from a customer service standpoint. Instead, the major negative impact on customer service occurs when a customer gets frustrated enough after repeated redials to give up and go away without receiving service.

With a fixed system configuration and stable demand over a foreseeable horizon, the system administrator has few choices to improve this customer service measure. We examined the practice of imposing per-call connect-time limits on users to distribute capacity more equitably among the user base. Various levels of time limits were studied, and we report on the resultant effect on two key customer service measures: the percentage of lost customers and the percent of callers disconnected before their primary work tasks are complete. The next section of this article discusses the general problem structure as a type of *retrial queue*. The problem statement is then presented, followed by a review of the existing research and a description of the experiment methodology. Results of the experiment are then presented and discussed. Finally, a summary and suggestions for future research are discussed.

General Problem Structure

DMPs can be used in various system structures, based on the type of service provider, and the number of pools available to a local customer set (those that can access the pool with a local telephone call). The service provider can be local, providing service to a defined set of customers in

a local—perhaps city or county-wide—area. An example of this type of provider is a university or community bulletin board service. A service provider also can be regional, providing service to customers in many different areas through local access numbers, all of which link up to a single central computer system. An example is a regional Internet service provider that serves a wide area within a state or several states. Finally, a service provider can be national, with local access numbers throughout the nation. A national provider could have all local numbers link up to a central system, similar to a regional provider, or it could group local service areas into different regions, with each region having its own central computer system that is linked to every other regional system, or perhaps linked to a single central computing system. Regional and national providers also could allow access from outside the local service areas through long-distance (possibly toll-free) connections. The communications links of a national provider resemble the hub-and-spoke systems in many transportation networks.

Regardless of the type of system, DMP systems fit a general queuing model known as a *retrial queue*. A retrial queue operates in the following manner: a customer arrives at the system and if all servers are busy, the blocked customer leaves the service area but may return after some random time (Falin, 1990). In a DMP system, a customer leaves the service area by hanging up after receiving a busy signal. Previously blocked customers waiting to return (retry) for service are said to be *in orbit* (or in the *orbit queue* or *retrial queue*). The orbit queue is comprised of customers who have received a busy signal but are redialing, or plan to redial very soon. The retrial queue is not a physical queue in the traditional sense—the orbit is an artificial construct to account for the blocked customers who will be returning for service. As such, there is no queuing discipline in orbit, and determination of the next customer to be served once a server becomes free is a random process. Customers in orbit are, in a sense, competing with other orbiting customers and new arrivals for the next available server. Retrial systems also can contain an explicit queue, as in a customer service call center, where blocked customers can wait in a first come, first served (FCFS) queue. DMP systems generally have no explicit queue, so blocked customers either leave or enter the orbit queue.

In addition to the physical structure of the system, DMPs can be defined further by their *availability*. The number of separate modem pools available defines what is called the availability of the system. When there is a single pool (by definition accessed through a single telephone number), any free server (modem) in the system can be accessed by any customer. This type of system is called a *full-available* system. Alternatively, with a non-full available system, the modems serving a local area are broken into m different pools, with each pool i ($i = 1, 2,... m$) accessed by a different phone number. Any caller into a pool i can access only the modems in that pool (Yang and Templeton 1987).

A DMP pool with retrial queuing (Figure 1) can be thought of as a two-station queuing network (Greenberg & Wolff, 1987). The modem pool is the first station; and customers in orbit waiting to redial comprise the second station, an infinite capacity queue. There is no waiting space in the system other than in the orbit queue.

Callers arrive at some rate, λ, by dialing in from a remote telephone. If a modem is free when the customer arrives, then the customer is assigned immediately to that modem for service, which is completed at some rate, μ. When service is complete, the customer leaves the system. If all of the modems are busy when the customer arrives, then with some probability, r_1, the customer enters orbit with the intent of redialing at some time in the future, and with probability $1 - r_1$, the customer leaves the system. Customers in orbit retry for service at some rate, ν. If an orbiting customer finds an idle modem upon retrying, the customer is assigned immediately to that modem for service. If the customer finds the system full, then the customer either re-enters orbit with some probability, r_2, or with probability $1 - r_2$, leaves the system (Wolff, 1989). The probabilities r_1 and r_2 may be considered constants (non-loss or geometric loss), or more generally, some function of the number of retrials the customer already has made (wait-based loss).

Problem Statement

What sets DMP retrial queues apart from most other commonly-studied queuing systems is that in the DMP system, the customer often determines the length of the session. Regardless of the speed of an individual server—in this case a modem—the

Figure 1. Typical modem pool retrial queue system

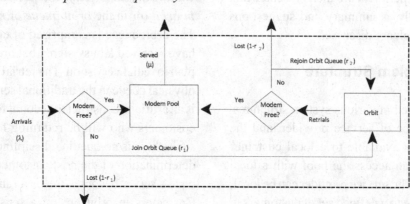

customer determines when to terminate the service encounter by hanging up. We assume that a customer arrives at the system with a predetermined amount of work to be done, requiring a certain amount of time and system resources to process. However, a user frequently will stay connected, and thus occupy a server, for some time longer than necessary to process the work. The excess time the user stays connected can be thought of as nonproductive time. In many instances, the nonproductive time for a customer will be quite significant, often exceeding the productive portion of the service time. We collected data from peak usage times at a DMP at a large Midwestern university. This pool, comprised of 192 modems, had been managed under a policy of unlimited connect time, and was overloaded very heavily for much of each day. An analysis of the connect-time data revealed a striking fact: a very small percentage of the customers—approximately 6%—accounted for *half* of the carried load. In most queuing systems, where service times are assumed to be distributed exponentially, some skewing of the service time is expected, but in this system, that characteristic was grossly exaggerated. Figure 2 shows a histogram of the length of 15,000 calls randomly sampled from this data. Several points can be noted from this graph. First, most calls are

fairly short in length—in fact, over half of the calls sampled were 15 minutes or less. Also standing out in this plot is how very skewed to the right the distribution is. To make a reasonably sized graph, all of the calls over 10,000 seconds (2.78 hours) in length are grouped together as "More." The call lengths in this category vary widely, with a maximum connect time of 654,001 seconds (181.67 hours, or 7.57 *days*). It is reasonable to assume that in these extended-length calls, a great deal of the capacity used is being wasted on nonproductive connect time. Therefore, the purpose of this study was to determine the effectiveness of reducing non-productive time through the use of connect-time limits and on the resultant impact on customer service measures.

Connect-time limits restrict the amount of time any user could be connected to the pool during a single call. Once the limit has expired for a particular service encounter, the call would be disconnected and the user would have to redial if he/she needed more time. Connect-time limits are attractive in that the capability to implement them is inherent in most existing systems. Connect-time limits have the added benefit of being difficult, if not impossible, to circumvent. Additionally, these limits have a certain appearance of fairness because all users are subject to the same time

Figure 2. Histogram of service length

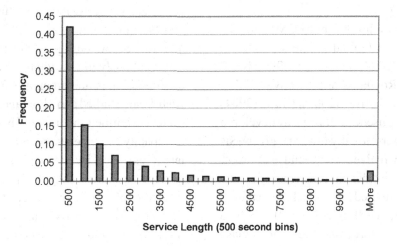

Service Length (500 second bins)

constraints and compete for available resources on equal footing. Of course, a negative impact of these limits is that some customers will be disconnected before their work is done. Compounding that problem for some users may be the fact that there is no notice prior to disconnection. If the call is disconnected in the midst of a file transfer, the entire transfer must be reinitiated on the next call, unless the caller is using software that allows recovery from an incomplete file transfer due to a system disconnect.

LITERATURE REVIEW

Retrial queues are encountered commonly in computer and telecommunication networks, and can be thought of as a type of network with re-servicing after blocking. They are not encountered commonly in manufacturing or service operations, where blocked customers are either queued or considered lost, so research on retrial queues generally is limited to pure queuing, telecommunication, or statistical journals. The research on retrial queues is fairly extensive and extremely rigorous in mathematical analysis. A complete literature review of the field is beyond the scope of this study, and would, to a great extent, duplicate the work in previous surveys (see Amador & Artalejo, 2009; Artalejo & Gómez-Corral, 2008; Falin, 1990; Kernane, 2008; and Yang & Templeton, 1987).

Published research relevant to DMPs in particular has been very limited to date, with the exception of Chiou (2004); Goodman (1999); Naldi (1999); Novak, Rowland, and DaSilva (2003); and Schikora and Godfrey (2003). Chiou (2004) surveyed Internet users in Taiwan to develop a model of consumers' loyalty toward a given ISP. He found that perceived value and trust were significant factors influencing customers' loyalty. Goodman (1999) studied modem delay as it relates to Voice over Internet Protocol (VoIP). He cited industry's lack of effort toward reducing delays

in modem transmission. Then he recommended methods for optimizing existing modems and designing lower delay modems. Naldi (1999) measured the frequency and duration of calls placed to Internet service providers (ISPs) on a single telephone switch. He concluded that the Poisson distribution could be used to characterize the arrival of calls (using 15 minute intervals). Further, he found that the mean duration of calls during peak times ranged from 25 to 40 minutes. Being focused on a particular system implementation, the specific results are of limited use in a general study. Schikora and Godfrey (2003) analyzed the use of linear regression, neural networks, and data mining software for building predictive models of DMP system performance. They found varying levels of performance among the studied methods when predicting output statistics for the university DMP studied. This study was tangential to the work presented here.

With respect to modem queues in general, Lambert, Van Houdt, and Blondia (2008) determined the optimal fraction of the uplink channel capacity that should be dedicated to the contention channel in a Data Over Cable Service Interface Specification (DOCSIS) cable network to minimize its mean response time. They ran several simulations to confirm the accuracy of their decomposition technique, and they further explored the impact of a variety of systems parameters (such as the number of cable modems, the initial backoff window size, the correlation structure of the arrival process, and the mean packet sizes) on the optimal fraction. As multiple cable modems connect simultaneously to a single trunk line, the system configuration is fundamentally different than the DMP being studied here. Fontanella and Morabito (2002) examined the tradeoff between investing in capacity (service channels) and satisfying the target user service level of Brazilian Internet Service Providers. They analyzed and illustrated this trade-off utilizing a three step approach: (i) determining user arrival and service processes in chosen periods, (ii) selecting an appropriate queuing model using some simplifying assumptions, and (iii) generating trade-off curves between system performance measures. Their approach to the constrained capacity problem focused on adding capacity, making it essentially different from our approach of imposing time limits on the existing DMP structure.

There are just two published works that specifically addressed the issue of connect-time limits and their effects on DMP performance. Novak et al. (2003) used a network-specific simulation model to study the effect of session limits on a single measure of service—blocking probability—for a single pool, university DMP. They found that connect-time limits did not reduce blocking probability significantly unless limits were set very short (less than or equal to 1 hour). On the other hand, their results showed a significant decrease in blocking probability from adding capacity to the single modem pool (although later in the article they noted that reductions in blocking probability from adding capacity often have been short-lived). In their study, the authors did not model customer retrials explicitly. Instead, retrials were considered implicitly as part of the modeled inter-arrival rate. Schikora and Godfrey (2006) used a general simulation model to study a similar full-available university DMP. They modeled arriving customers with a random amount of work to be completed and explicitly modeled retrials. The article summarized two key performance measures: percent of lost customers (those who leave the system after repeated blocking without being served), and percent disconnected customers (those disconnected before their work was complete).

RESEARCH DESIGN AND METHODOLOGY

This research examines the impact of per-call connect-time limits on the performance of overloaded DMPs. The research is based on the assumption that the service provider desires to distribute limited resources more evenly among the full customer base, especially during periods of system overload. Specifically, we study how system performance measures change when connect-time limits are imposed on a full-available (single pool) system. DMP operators often experience cycles of excess demand (peak periods) followed by excess capacity (lull periods). We are, of course, interested in those periods where demand exceeds capacity and new customers are likely blocked. Due to the nature of these systems, excess capacity from lull periods cannot be *stored* for use during periods of excess demand, so we can study the system under peak period demand conditions without concern for the impact of the lull periods.

The question to be answered in this research is straightforward: What is the relationship between time limits, other variable system parameters, and system performance? We are not simply interested in whether the proposed changes have a significant effect on the system—it is rather obvious that imposing timeout limits on an overloaded system with a highly skewed service time distribution will significantly impact the performance measures of interest. Rather, we are interested in how the system performance changes as the operating rules change, and whether we can predict system performance for a given set of operating parameters. A simulation model was developed to study this type of system. Standard graphical analysis was used to provide descriptive results presented later in this article.

System Performance Measures

Several important customer service and managerial performance measures were analyzed in this study. The objective of connect-time limits is to distribute system capacity over a wider customer base by reducing wasted capacity. If the limits succeed, one would expect to see more customers served with a corresponding reduction in wait time in the orbit queue. Relevant service-related measures of performance for this type of system include:

- **Percent of Lost Customers:** Percent of new arrivals who leave the system without receiving service.
- **Average Time in Queue:** How long customers have to wait in the orbit queue before receiving service or leaving the system. This can be measured in number of retries or in time units.
- **Blocking Probability:** Percent of customers who receive a busy signal on their initial arrival to the system.
- **Nonproductive Use:** Percent of system use accounted for by nonproductive time (this is a measure of wasted capacity).
- **Percent Disconnected:** Percent of customers who are disconnected *before their work is complete*. These customers are differentiated from customers who are disconnected during purely nonproductive time.

From a customer service standpoint, the first four measures were expected to improve with time limits, and the last was expected to worsen. Additionally, the simulation study examined the managerial performance measure of server utilization, defined as overall modem-time-units used divided by total modem-time-units available. Due to the high demand situations studied, time limits were expected to have minimal impact on this performance measure.

It can be argued that two performance measures are of primary interest here: percent lost customers and percent disconnected customers. Taken together, they measure the key positive and negative impacts of time limits. While time in queue and blocking probabilities are very important measures in many queuing systems, their negative effects are minimized here by the automated redialing capability of most users' computers. Multiple redials after blocking are common and handled by the computer automatically. During the resultant

time in queue waiting for the connection to be made, customers can occupy their time with other productive or entertaining endeavors. Therefore, these two performance measures are not as critical in this type of queuing system.

Simulation Design

A simulation study was performed to examine the effect of per-call time limits on the listed performance measures. The simulation model was coded in the C programming language, using a version of the SIMLIB library of functions (Schikora & Godfrey, 2003) with slight modifications. The use of a general purpose programming language and the SIMLIB functions allowed us to model all of the details of the DMP pool operation explicitly, including the orbit queue and customer retrials/reconnects.

Data for building the simulation model were collected from the actual DMP operations at a large public Midwestern university, and used to determine realistic modeling parameters and experimental factors for the simulation study. These data then were incorporated into the simulation model, which included both fixed parameters and experimental factors. Descriptions of the parameters and factors follow.

Four fixed parameters were modeled in the simulation: number of modems, service time distribution, inter-retrial time distribution, and reconnect persistence. A discussion of each follows.

1. Number of Modems - The total number of modems available remained fixed, so results could be compared across identical resources. Because the DMP data were used also to help determine service rates, it was reasonable to choose a system size based on the real-world example. There were 192 modems available in the actual DMP, and our simulation used a fixed resource size of 200 modems. We assumed that there were

no modem failures, although this assumption could easily be relaxed in future research.

2. Service Time Distribution - The *BestFit* software package from Palisade Corporation was used to fit a distribution to the available service time data. Analysis indicated that either a Weibull or a Pearson VI distribution—both commonly used to model task completion times—would fit the empirical data best. We assume readers generally are more familiar with the Weibull distribution, so it was used to model the customer service times in the simulation. This distribution had a shape parameter α of 0.651262 and a scale parameter β of 1524.1, with a mean of 2022 seconds, or 34.6 minutes.

3. Inter-retrial Time Distribution - The retrial rate defines how quickly customers in orbit try again for service, and usually is expressed as the distribution of inter-retrial times (IRT). In this study, IRT is defined as the time between when a customer's computer hangs up after receiving a busy signal, and when the computer next contacts the service center, the call either is connected to the service center or is given another busy signal. Because most retrial queue literature models the IRTs with an exponential distribution, it might seem appropriate to do the same here. However, it is important to note that prior research has focused on the *human* customer having to initiate the retrial attempt. In this study, it is reasonable to assume that most of the retrial attempts are made by the *machine* part of the customer—the computer. Usually computers are set up to redial automatically and *immediately* upon receiving a busy signal. As such, IRTs for an individual customer will be distributed so tightly as to be nearly constant. Therefore, we treated individual retrial times in a service encounter as a constant drawn from a tightly distributed uniform distribution. The IRT for any single customer was modeled as a constant, drawn from a Uniform

(5, 10) distribution (measured in seconds). The range of the distribution was based on personal experience with auto-redial capabilities of most computers.

4. Reconnect Persistence - This defines the probability that a customer who is disconnected from the DMP will try to redial. We assumed that this probability equals 1 if a customer is disconnected before all productive work is completed and 0 if a customer is disconnected after all productive work is completed. The work time for the reconnecting customer was set to the work time unsatisfied in the initial call, with an additional non-productive time element randomly generated to fit the current factor in the simulation runs. After the initial reconnect attempt, the retrial process for reconnecting customers is modeled the same as for new arrivals.

Four experimental factors were varied across simulations: the length of connect-time limits, the percent nonproductive time, mean system utilization, and retrial persistence. A description of these factors follows:

1. Length of Connect-Time Limits - Four levels of time limits were simulated: 30 minutes, 60 minutes, 120 minutes, and no time limit.

2. Percent Nonproductive Time - We modeled the assumption that each call contains some nonproductive time by generating a random variable, with a range of [0, 1], that represents the percentage of the overall service time in a call that, without limits, would be purely nonproductive time. There were no empirical data with which to model this assumed ratio. Therefore, we followed a recommendation of Law and Kelton (2000) and assumed that the ratio had a beta distribution, with shape parameters α_1 and α_2. By varying the shape parameters as an experimental factor, we varied the mean productivity of arriving

customers. Values for the levels of this factor are listed in Table 1, and the resultant distribution plots are shown in Figure 3.

3. Mean System Utilization - The mean arrival rate of customers was varied to adjust the mean system utilization ρ across simulations. Because we were interested in analyzing the overloaded system, arrival rates were set to achieve various levels of congestion in the system. Based on empirical data and a chi-square goodness-of-fit test, this arrival process was modeled with a Poisson process defined by a mean arrival rate of λ. With mean system utilization ρ defined as $\lambda/c\mu$ ($c = 200$ in this case), the mean arrival rate λ was then set at different levels to achieve the desired ρ. This factor was set to three different levels: 1.0, 1.25, and 1.5. These levels might seem extreme at first, but note that the mean service time includes both nonproductive and work time. The system load accounted by work time is less than the level of ρ in each simulation, sometimes significantly so, and this is expected to be important when time limits are imposed. In addition, the high levels of ρ allow us to model the realistic situation where more customers are trying to access the system than can be accommodated without time limits.

Retrial Persistence (R) - Actual customer retrial behavior was unknown. It seemed reasonable, however, that customers very likely would attempt a retrial after a busy signal on an initial arrival, but their likeliness to redial would decrease with the number of unsuccessful prior attempts. To model that behavior, we assumed that all new arrivals would join the orbit queue if they received a busy signal. We then defined R as the probability that customers in orbit would rejoin the orbit after receiving a busy signal upon their first retrial attempt. The probability that a customer in orbit

would redial after the nth failed redial attempt was defined by r_n, which we assumed to be of the form:

$$r_n = R^n \tag{1}$$

The probability a customer would leave the system upon the nth failed redial attempt is simply $1 - r_n$. Next, we defined N as the number of redials a customer would make before leaving the system. Given (1), we can determine the probability density function (p.d.f.) – the probability that N will equal any particular number:

$$P(N = n) = \left(\prod_{i=0}^{n-1} R^i\right)\left(1 - R^n\right) \ n = 1, 2, 3, \dots . \tag{2}$$

The expected number of redials a customer would make before leaving the system is given by:

$$E(N) = \sum_{n=1}^{\infty} \left[\left(\prod_{i=0}^{n-1} R^i\right)\left(1 - R^n\right) n\right] \tag{3}$$

Due to the exponential product nature of Equation (3), R must be very high to achieve any reasonably sized $E(N)$ for this particular application. This gives the function the desired quality of highly likely initial retrials. It is this very same nature that causes the p.d.f. to reach a point where it rapidly decreases, properly reflecting the customer's increased frustration at repeated busy signals. Four levels of R were considered. Values

Table 1. Beta distribution parameters for percent nonproductive time

Level	Beta Distribution Parameters		
	α_1	α_2	Mean
Very Low	1.5	5	0.231
Low	2.5	4	0.385
High	4	2.5	0.615
Very High	5	1.5	0.769

Figure 3. Beta distribution plots for nonproductive to work time ratios

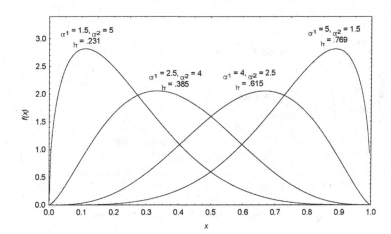

for the levels of this factor are listed in Table 2. Representative retrial probability density plots are shown in Figure 4.

Experimental Design

Table 2 summarizes the parameters and factor levels used in this simulation study. The combination of the different factors resulted in 4 x 4 x 3 x 4 = 192 cells in the simulation design. For each cell, a simulation study was performed with multiple

Table 2. Summary of simulation design elements

Parameter	Fixed/ Varied	Level(s)
Number of Modems	Fixed	200
Service Pattern	Fixed	Weibull (.651262, 1524.1)
Inter-retrial Times (seconds)	Fixed	Uniform (5,10)
Reconnect Persistence	Fixed	0 or 1
Length of Time Limits in minutes (*limit*)	Varied	30, 60, 120, no limit
Mean Percent Nonproductive Time (*ratio*)	Varied	.231,.385,.615,.769
Mean System Load (ρ)	Varied	1.0, 1.25, 1.5
Retrial Persistence *R* (mean retrial attempts)	Varied	.995,.9993,.9997,.99985 (18, 47, 72, 102)

replications. In each replication, the simulation began with the system empty. Therefore, a suitable warm-up period had to be determined to eliminate the effects of transient states in the system and to ensure that data collected represented steady-state operations (Schikora & Godfrey, 2006). Following standard graphical analysis of various test simulations, this warm-up period was set at 10 hours. Each simulation was then run for a simulated 96 hours, resulting in 86 hours of simulated data collected per simulation run. Each simulation was replicated 20 times to reduce the effect of random variations on the simulated results. The total number of simulation runs was therefore 192 x 20 = 3840. Results for each cell in the design (20 per cell) were collected, and the mean performance measures for each cell were computed and used in the results analysis.

RESULTS

Analysis for this research was based primarily on visual inspection of plots of performance measures against the different simulation factors. In describing the results, we looked at both the primary effects of the simulation factors on the performance measures and all relevant two-way interactions. This was accomplished by plotting

Figure 4. Representative retrial p.d.f. for various R

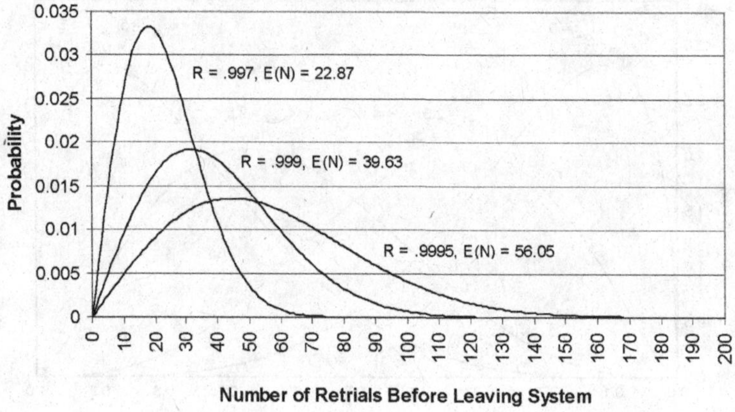

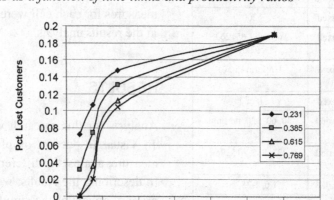

performance measures against each pair of factors that affected the performance measure. To aid in gaining insight into the interactions, each interaction was plotted in two separate graphs, alternating factors on the x-axis in each graph. The data plotted are averages across the factors not plotted in each particular graph. For example, Figure 5 plots Percent Lost Customers as a function of time limits and customer productivity ratios. For each of the 16 points plotted, the value plotted is the average output of all simulation cells that match that limit and ratio. For some performance measures, one or more factors had no effect on the

results. In these instances, interactions involving those factors were not examined.

In graphing the interactions, some accommodation had to be made for plotting data associated with the no-time-limit level. A common method of graphing such data is to choose a numerical value that is substantially larger than the other observed values to substitute for the infinite level. This allows the researcher to show the data associated with the infinite value, but plot them far enough away from the other observed values to not greatly affect the underlying general shape of the curve. In this research, the largest time limit for a single pool is 2 hours, or 7,200 seconds.

Figure 5. Plot of PM1 as a function of time limits and productivity ratios

For the sake of graphing the data, the infinite time limit was assigned a value four times the largest limit—28,000 seconds.

There were 52 different data plots originally examined in the research project. For the sake of brevity, and to focus on the key performance measures, we limit our discussion here to the following two key customer service performance measures:

- PM1: Percent of lost customers (percent of new arrivals that leave the system without receiving service) and PM2: Percent disconnected (percent of customers who are disconnected *before their work is complete*). These are differentiated from customers who are disconnected during purely nonproductive time. Data plots relevant to these two performance measures are shown in Figures 5 through 12. Complete result data sets and remaining data plots are available from the authors on request.

PM1: Percent of Lost Customers

Plots relevant to this section include Figures 5 through 10. Time limits have a definite and nonlinear impact on the percent of lost customers. Generally, as the limit is decreased, there is a reduction in this performance measure, as would be expected (Figures 5–7). The reduction in lost customers is fairly steep within the range of limits considered in this study. An exception occurs when plotting the effect of limits under different levels of ρ (Figure 6). When the system load is 1.0, the effect of time limits on lost customers appears minimal and linear. This is due most likely to the relatively low incidence of lost customers with no time limits and $\rho = 1.0$—as such, there is little room for improvement. It is interesting to note the significant reduction in lost customers due to just the highest of limits. The longest time limit results in about a one-third reduction in the percent of lost customers on average, from 19.0% to 13.4% —a net gain of 5.6% of all customers who enter service. This compares to an increase in PM2 (percent disconnected) from 0 to 2.2%. It is expected that for most service providers, this would be a worthwhile tradeoff. The magnitude of the reduction is smaller with lower inefficiency ratios (more productive customers, Figure 5), and lower levels of ρ (Figure 6), indicating an interaction between time limits and these two factors.

The system load ρ and customer inefficiency ratio also have an impact on the percent of lost customers. As ρ increases, there is an increase in the incidence of lost customers, as would be expected when more customers are arriving per time

Figure 6. Plot of PM1 as a function of time limits and system load

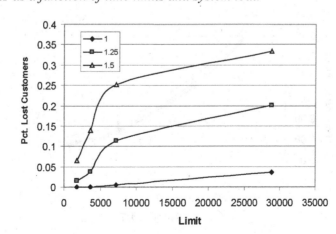

Figure 7. Plot of PM1 as a function of time limits and R

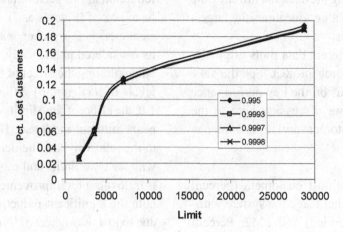

Figure 8. Plot of PM1 as a function of productivity ratios and system load

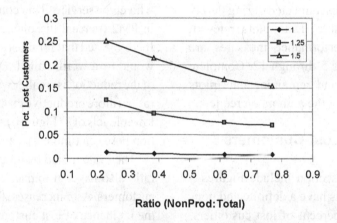

Figure 9. Plot of PM1 as a function of productivity ratios and R

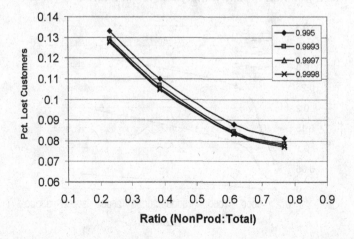

Figure 10. Plot of PM1 as a function of system load and R

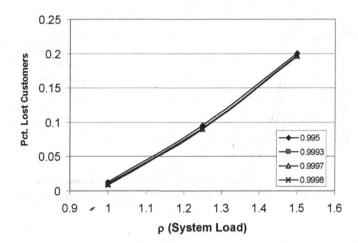

unit and competing for the same limited resources (Figures 6, 8, 10). Similarly, as customers become less productive with their online time, fewer customers are lost, as the number of disconnected customers making reconnect attempts drops (Figures 5, 8, 9). Surprisingly, customer persistence has a minimal effect on the number of lost customers. A slight negative trend in lost customers is evident as R increases, but it may, for all practical purposes, be considered negligible over the range of R considered in this study (Figures 7, 9, 10).

There appear to be interactions between all the factors except R. The shorter the time limit, the greater the effect of customer productivity on PM1 (Figure 5). Conversely, the longer the time limit, the greater the effect of ρ on lost customers (Figure 6). The effect of customer productivity on percent of lost customers also is increased, as the system becomes more overloaded (Figure 8). Note that with $\rho = 1.0$, customer productivity has virtually no effect on this performance measure, while with $\rho = 1.5$, variation in customer productivity accounts for a swing of about 40% in the value of this measure. This implies that operators of very heavily overloaded systems should be much more concerned about their customers' online productivity than operators of systems who

that are merely at the saturation point. Measuring the actual system load in a fully saturated system is difficult, however, as lost customers are not seen by the system.

PM2: Percent disconnected

Plots relevant to this section include Figures 11 and 12. This performance measure shows the percent of customers disconnected before their productive work time is completed. This is the main negative impact of imposing time limits; the results here must be weighed against the benefits of time limits to help practitioners better understand the overall impact of time limits. This performance measure is affected by only two factors in the experiment: time limits and customer productivity. As time limits decrease, more customers will be disconnected before their work is done. In addition, as customers become less productive with their use of online time, it is less likely that a customer still will be working productively when the time limit is reached. Figure 11 shows that the effect of time limits is very nonlinear, and as time limits are shortened, PM2 increases at an increasing rate. As time limits approach 0, PM2 approaches its upper limit of 100%.

Figure 11. Plot of PM2 as a function of time limits and productivity ratios

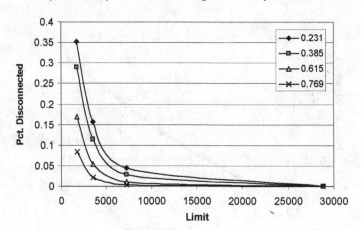

Figure 12: Plot of PM2 as a function of productivity ratios and time limits

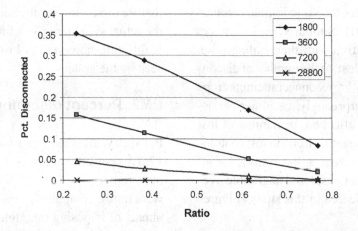

Customer productivity also has a definite effect on PM2, but unlike time limits, the effect of customer productivity appears to be quite linear (Figure 12). As customers become more unproductive online, it is less likely that a customer who is disconnected by a time limit still is doing productive work when cut off. There is also an apparent interaction between customer productivity and time limits. With no time limits, customer productivity has no effect, because customers are never disconnected. As time limits decrease, the effect of customer productivity becomes more significant. If customers tend to be extremely productive with their online time, then decreasing time limits will, at some point, increase this performance measure, very rapidly, which is undesirable. However, if customers tend to waste a lot of their online connect time, then decreasing time limits will result in a much more moderate increase in this measure. In any case, the effect of limits on this performance measure has to be weighed against the benefits of limits on other performance measures. As such, it is fortunate that this sole negative performance measure is dependent on only one other factor in the system. If a system operator could determine the general productivity of customers, the system operator could better estimate the general effect of time limits on this measure.

SUMMARY AND FUTURE RESEARCH

As expected, the implementation of time limits has a significant and nonlinear effect on every performance measure studied, including those not presented here. Generally, implementation of time limits has an increasingly greater effect as the time limits decrease. An examination of the call length distribution helps explain this nonlinearity, as decreasing the time limits has an increasingly greater impact on the number of customers affected by the limits. This implies that in the lower range of possible time limits, the choice of the exact time limit has a large impact on the number of customers directly impacted by the limits, and therefore greatly impacts the various performance measures. It also implies that imposing a call limit that is too long will have minimal effect on performance measures. In this study, the greatest effects of time limits are seen generally in the range below approximately three times the average service call length of 2078 seconds (34.6 minutes). Above 6000 seconds (100 minutes), the effect of limits tends to flatten out, as the limits impact fewer customers. This does not imply that longer time limits are not worth considering, however. As pointed out earlier, the longest time limit significantly reduces the number of lost customers in moderately and heavily overloaded systems.

For most performance measures, there is a strong interaction between time limits and customer productivity. Time limits are more effective at improving the "good" performance measures when customers are less productive in their use of online time. This is not surprising--as fewer productive customers waste more time, wasted time can be reduced by time limits. Less productive customers also are less likely to attempt to reconnect after being disconnected, thus reducing general congestion in the system. However, very productive customers will limit the benefits to be gained from imposing time limits. Considering the "bad" performance measure PM2, the relationship between time limits and customer productivity is reversed. Time limits have a greater impact on this measure as customers become *more* productive. This again makes sense because more productive customers are more likely to be in the midst of their work when disconnected by a time limit.

These two points taken together make it clear that the expected overall results from imposing a time limit, and thus the decisions to impose a limit and to determine its length, are highly dependent on the general productivity of customers in the system. Systems with nonproductive customers who generally waste resources can expect significant benefits from time limits, with minimum negative effects. Systems with conscientious, productive customers can expect limited overall benefits from time limits, but suffer greatly with respect to PM2.

In deciding about time limits then, the system operator should have a measure of customer productivity to get a clearer picture of what to expect from time limits. It also would help to develop a cost-benefit model that prices out the cost of time limits—increased PM2—and the value of the benefits gained in PM1 and other measures previously discussed. To simplify such a model, an argument can be made that the most important of these measures from a customer service standpoint are those discussed here: PM1, the percent of lost customers, and PM2, customers disconnected before their work is completed. Each measure directly impacts the customers' ability to obtain the service to which they are entitled, and thus is crucial to any measure of customer service. In most queuing systems, the wait in queue is also a critical measure. However, in a DMP system, with the computer doing all of the redialing, a customer can do other things while waiting to connect, and it is reasonable to assume that the wait becomes a lesser issue for the customer. Because the wait in queue is less important to a customer, the initial blocking probability also becomes less important. With the computer performing the wait in queue, so to speak, the customers are less concerned with getting connected on the first try, as long as they can get into the system on one of the redials. Therefore, a meaningful cost-benefit model could be developed by examining the tradeoff between PM1 and PM2. By putting a value on each percentage reduction in lost customers, and a cost on each percentage increase in customers disconnected while still working, the net result of different time limits could be evaluated with a meaningful single cost-benefit measure.

The general nature of this tradeoff can be shown with a simple comparison of PM1 and PM2. If we assume that a one percent change in either measure has the same unit value to the system, we can plot the net benefit/cost of imposing a certain time limit compared to no time limit at all. First we define $PM1_{a,b}$ as the measure of PM1 at time limit level a and customer productivity level b. $PM2_{a,b}$ is similarly defined. For the models with no time limit, $a = \infty$. We then define the following:

$$\Delta PM1_{a,b} = P1_{\infty,b} - PM1_{a,b} \qquad (4)$$

$$\Delta PM2_{a,b} = P2_{\infty,b} - PM2_{a,b} \qquad (5)$$

$$\beta_{a,b} = (\Delta PM1_{a,b} + P2_{\infty,b}) \times 100 \qquad (6)$$

Equation 6 defines the net unit benefit by imposing time limit a on a customer base with productivity level b. Positive values of $\beta_{a,b}$ equate to a net benefit from imposing that limit on that customer base; negative values equate to a net loss/ cost. Figure 13 plots the values of $\beta_{a,b}$ and shows that the nature of the tradeoff is highly dependent on the productivity ratio of the customer base. When customers tend to waste time online, the values of $\beta_{a,b}$ are all positive and there appears to be an optimum time limit level, somewhere in the middle of the levels tested, that maximizes $\beta_{a,b}$. As the customer base gets more productive, the net benefit of imposing time limits is restricted to the longest time limits. These results assume an equal value placed on both PM1 and PM2. An argument could be made that PM1 should have a higher value than PM2 – it is better to have been served and disconnected than never to have been served at all. As PM1 takes on higher values relative to PM2, the net benefit increases and remains positive across a wider range of a and b. To demonstrate, we compute and plot the following in Figure 14, showing the cost-benefit tradeoff with PM1 twice as valuable as PM2.

$$\beta 2_{a,b} = (2 \times \Delta PM1_{a,b} + P2_{\infty,b}) \times 100. \qquad (7)$$

Figure 13. Plot of $\beta_{a,b}$ net performance measure tradeoff

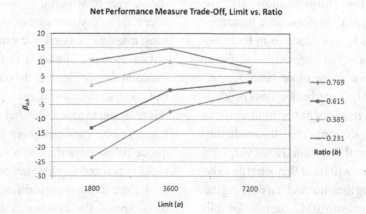

Figure 14. Plot of β2$_{a,b}$, net performance measure tradeoff, double weight for PM1

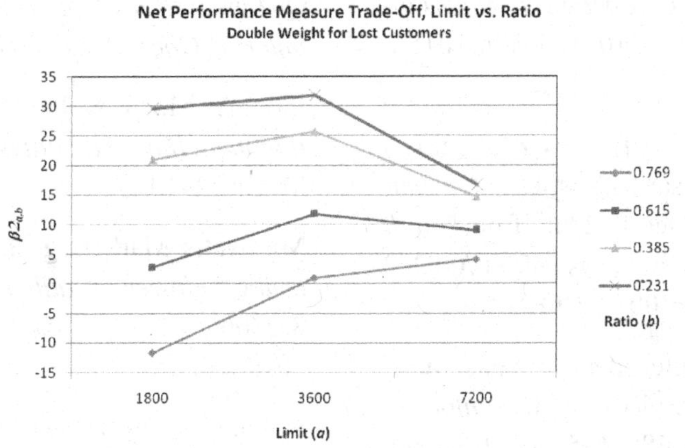

Net Performance Measure Trade-Off, Limit vs. Ratio
Double Weight for Lost Customers

Keys to a valid analysis of this type are estimates of actual customer productivity and the true system load. Customer productivity could be estimated by data throughput logs for actual calls in the system. True system load is more difficult to measure, as customers lost during peak periods of system overload are not seen by the system. The system operator can easily see *when* the system is overloaded, but not by *how much* it is overloaded. A good estimate of this measure requires access to telephone system logs.

While imposing time limits is an obvious method to improve customer service levels in overloaded DMP systems, other options are available. DMP operators can choose to segment their customers and resources by shifting to a non-full-available system structure, splitting modems into different pools with different access numbers. Different time limits would be applied to the different pools, thereby allowing customers with greater needs to try to access the longer limit pools. Similarly, customers with minimal needs could try to access the shorter time limit pools, with a greater expectation of being served due to the shorter time limits. Results of a study examining such an approach are forthcoming.

Further research may possibly extend this work to the field of broadband Internet connections that are gaining in market penetrations. While the DMP system is constrained by a finite number of physical connections, broadband systems can manage significantly larger numbers of users, but are constrained by a fixed volume of bandwidth in a given physical configuration. Time constraints would not be as relevant in such a system, but rather the concept of *bandwidth throttling* could be used to manage user demand in a capacity-constrained system. A study of proper management techniques in such a scenario would require a completely different methodology from this article.

Finally, it would be interesting to explore the relationship between this study and customer service issues in a customer call center. The service system structure bears many similarities to the DMP system explored here. There are a finite number of servers that customers dial into, and often customers cannot immediately enter service. The main differences are that the call centers typically have electronic queues, and the service times are a factor of both the customers and service agents.

REFERENCES

Amador, J., & Artalejo, J. R. (2009). The M/G/1 retrial queue: New descriptors of the customer's behavior. *Journal of Computational and Applied Mathematics, 223*(1), 15–26. doi:10.1016/j. cam.2007.12.016

Artalejo, J. R., & Gómez-Corral, A. (2008). Advances in retrial queues. *European Journal of Operational Research, 189*(3), 1041. doi:10.1016/j.ejor.2007.05.035

Auckland, J. S. (2006, April). New Zealand is a nation of dial-up users says statistics NZ. *Computerworld*. Retrieved Oct. 8, 2006, from http://www.computerworld.co.nz/news.nsf/NL/00D725EF22F3F254CC25714200179B6F

Chiou, J. (2004). The antecedents of consumers' loyalty toward internet service providers. *Information & Management, 41*, 685–695. doi:10.1016/j.im.2003.08.006

Daniel, A. (2006, August). Internet usage in Australia. *Kinesis Interactive Design*. Retrieved Oct. 8, 2006, from http://www.kinesis.com.au/article_stats.asp

Falin, G. A. (1990). Survey of retrial queues. *Queueing Systems, 7*(2), 127–168. doi:10.1007/BF01158472

Fontanella, G. C., & Morabito, R. (2002). Analyzing the trade-off between investing in service channels and satisfying the targeted user service for Brazilian internet service providers. *International Transactions in Operational Research, 9*(3), 247–259. doi:10.1111/1475-3995.00354

Goodman, B. (1999). Internet telephony and modem delay. *IEEE Network, 13*(3), 8–16. doi:10.1109/65.767132

Greenberg, B. S., & Wolff, R. W. (1987). An upper bound on the performance of queues with returning customers. *Journal of Applied Probability, 24*, 466–475. doi:10.2307/3214270

Kernane, T. (2008). Conditions for stability and instability of retrial queuing systems with general retrial times. *Statistics & Probability Letters, 78*(18), 3244–3248. doi:10.1016/j.spl.2008.06.019

Krueger, M. (2003). Dial-out modem pools. *Buildings, 97*(11), 16.

Lambert, J., Van Houdt, B., & Blondia, C. (2008). Queues in DOCSIS cable modem networks. *Computers & Operations Research, 35*(8), 2482–2496.

Law, A. M., & Kelton, W. D. (2000). *Simulation modeling and analysis* (3rd ed.). New York: McGraw-Hill.

Miniwatts Marketing Group. (2004). *ISOC-ZA trying to lower broadband costs*. Retrieved Oct. 8, 2006, from http://www.internetworldstats.com/af/za.htm

Naldi, M. (1999). Measurement-based modeling of internet dial-up access connections. *Computer Networks, 31*, 2381–2390. doi:10.1016/S1389-1286(99)00091-2

Novak, D. C., Rowland, D., & DaSilva, L. (2003). Modeling dialup internet access: An examination of user-to-modem ratios, blocking probability, and capacity planning in a modem pool. *Computers & Operations Research, 30*, 1959–1976. doi:10.1016/S0305-0548(02)00119-3

Schikora, P. F., & Godfrey, M. R. (2003). Efficacy of end-user neural network and data mining software for predicting complex system performance. *International Journal of Production Economics, 84*, 231–253.

Schikora, P. F., & Godfrey, M. R. (2006). Connect time limits and customer service levels in dial-up modem pools. *Journal of Network and Systems Management, 14*(2), 181–188. doi:10.1007/s10922-006-9031-z

The slow death of dial-up. (2007). *The Economist, 382*(8519), 13-14.

Titus, J. (2007). Dial-up modems still ring a bell. *Electronic Component News, 51*(12), 21.

Walczak, S. & Parthasarathy, M. (2006). Modeling online service discontinuation with nonparametric agents. *Information Systems and e-business Management, 4*(1), 49-70.

Website Optimization, L. L. C. (2006). *Home connectivity in the US*. Retrieved Oct. 8, 2006, from http://www.websiteoptimization.com/bw/0603/

Wolff, R. W. (1989). *Stochastic modeling and the theory of queues*. Englewood Cliffs, NJ: Prentice Hall.

Yang, T., & Templeton, J. G. C. (1987). A survey of retrial queues. *Queueing Systems*, *2*(3), 201–233. doi:10.1007/BF01158899

This work was previously published in International Journal of Information Systems in the Service Sector, Volume 2, Issue 1, edited by John Wang, pp. 26-48, copyright 2010 by IGI Publishing (an imprint of IGI Global).

Chapter 4
ICT Usage by Greek Accountants

Efstratios C. Emmanouilidis
University of Macedonia, Greece

Anastasios A. Economides
University of Macedonia, Greece

ABSTRACT

This study investigates Greek accounting offices use of Information and Communication Technologies (ICT). Initially, a comprehensive questionnaire was developed. It contains 35 questions with multiple answers and 2 open questions tailored to the accountants. One hundred accountants' offices in a Greek county answered the questionnaire. The findings present their current ICT infrastructure and their use of ICT and accounting e-services. Greek accounting offices have made improvements in adopting new technology in their everyday work. All use email, antivirus software, and the Web. Most submit VAT (Value Aided Tax), Taxation Statements, and APS (Analytical Periodic Statement) via Internet. However, most are not cautious about backing up their data daily; they do not create electronic files for all their documents; they do not update their software via Internet; and they do not use advanced software applications. Finally, they expect the government and the Accountants' Chamber to finance their ICT infrastructure.

INTRODUCTION

The profession of accountancy has experienced unprecedented change during the past 20 years. It has moved from paper-based to PC-based, and the Internet has become prevailing tendency. Similar to other professions in the service sector (Levy,

DOI: 10.4018/978-1-4666-0044-7.ch004

Murphy, & Zanakis, 2009; Lexhagen, 2009), the recent technological developments have given accountants the opportunity to incorporate information systems in their profession. They use the PC, to a large extent, for customers' book keeping and liquidation of income tax statements. They spend a large amount of time processing and producing many documents (Bhansali, 2006a). Also, they use the Internet extensively for submitting tax

Copyright © 2012, IGI Global. Copying or distributing in print or electronic forms without written permission of IGI Global is prohibited.

statements to the government (Anderson, Fox, & Schwartz, 2005; Garen, 2006). The recent advances in e-government (Chatzopoulos & Economides, 2009; Economides & Terzis, 2008; Terpsiadou & Economides, 2009) have pushed accountants to follow. Furthermore, more than 2,000 accounting firms have Web sites registered with "The List of CPA Firms Directory" (Roxas, Peek, Peek, & Hagemann, 2000).

Many software packages are available to help accountants with book keeping. However, many of these software packages become quite complicated and present problems of interoperability and usability, among others. Human-computer interface issues are extremely important for online service applications (Pinhanez, 2009). In parallel, many accountants lack the time or the patience to learn the skills needed to take full advantage of these advances. Even worse, the technology continues to move forward, getting more complicated and thus widening the gap between potential and actual use (Zarowin, 2004).

While technology's impact on the accountants' profession has been considerable, there are many more developments to come. Thus, accountants must be technologically proactive (Johnston, 2005). During the next few years, the profession of accountancy will face unexpected new challenges (Bhansali, 2006b).

This study investigates the level of ICT use by accounting offices in a Greek county. In the next section, previous studies on these issues are presented. Then the methodology is described. The presentation of the results follows. Finally, conclusions are drawn and future research is suggested.

PREVIOUS RESEARCH

Not many previous studies exist on the use of ICT by accounting offices. Some detailed studies were conducted by the American Institute of Certified Public Accountants (AICPA).

Gallun, Heagy, and Lindsey (1993) distinguished between small and large public CPAs (Certified Public Accountants) and accountants in large enterprises (industry accountants) in the United States. They found that large accounting offices used more LANs (Local Area Networks) than small ones. Also, most accountants did not appear to worry very much about viruses and other security issues. Most used laser printers along with the essential dot matrix, and the most popular brand was Hewlett-Packard. Finally, a small percentage used portable printers.

Khani and Zarowin (1994) showed that 23% of enterprises in the United States supplemented all forms electronically (e.g., liquidation of income tax statements), and 15% planned to do it in the future. Regarding security, 31% faced virus problems. Also, 37% used an antivirus program, 68% of which used Norton. Regarding backup, 83% backed up their data, 80% of which did this daily and 16% weekly. E-mail was used by 39% of the offices.

Prawitt, Romney, and Zarowin (1997) classified U.S. accountants in the following categories: 1) in big accounting offices (Big 6—national), 2) in intermediate (regional) offices, 3) in small offices (local and individual offices), 4) in organisations (business and nonprofit), 5) in schools (academic), and 6) in governmental organisations. The most popular operating system was Microsoft Windows. All accountants in the first two categories used networks. The most popular application office suite was Microsoft Office (Word, Excel, Access, and PowerPoint). All accountants used applications for managing their contacts and timetables, and the most popular application was ACT! by Sage. (The small use of Microsoft Outlook was interesting.)

Bush (2000) found that 96% of U.S. accountants had access to the Internet. More than half reported that they "surf" every day. Also, 65% of men and 47% of women reported that the Internet created more opportunities for them. Finally, 47%

expected an increase in using the Internet for accounting research.

Anders and Fischer (2004) found that the New York accountants were absolutely satisfied with the programs of accountancy that they used for third consecutive year. Also, an increase was observed in the creation of Web pages by accountants aiming at the satisfaction of their customers.

Zarowin (2006) found that many accounting offices of all sizes transformed their offices to electronic ones. In 2003, only 38% prepared invoices electronically. In 2005, the percentage increased to 46%. In 2003, 64% used internal local networks (Intranets) for the storage and processing of customers' data. In 2005, the percentage increased to 72%. Finally, the number of accounting offices that stored their customers' documents only in the computer without printing them (electronic paperless office) showed an enormous increase of 103% from 2003 to 2005.

The use and development of Web pages for advertising by companies in the European Union during 2000–2003 increased, by 19% (Voiculescu, 2003). Advertising was the main reason for using and developing web pages (59%). It is remarkable that income acquisition was in third place (11%), behind customer service (26%).

Gullkvist and Ylinen (2005) found that the most important reasons for the development of e-accounting systems by Finnish accounting agencies were the following: more efficient use of time resources, higher internal performance, availability of accounting information, and perceived requirements from authorities. Lack of time can clearly been seen as one of the key obstacles delaying the adoption of the e-accounting systems among small and medium-sized enterprises.

The accountancy profession is feeling the strain of increased responsibility, away from the traditional roles for which accountants were trained (Mintel International Group Ltd., 2005). Although the triggering factors for stress and increasing staff turnover are high, little is currently being done to improve the situation. A resounding 84% of U.S.

companies said their accounting department was leading the compliance initiatives in the company. The same 84% stated that increasing compliance requirements have put them under greater pressure due to the increase in scope and volume of their work, and yet 88% were still manually re-keying data into spreadsheets for reporting and analysis (Mintel International Group Ltd., 2005).

Although many Inland Revenue Service offices support electronic tax filing (Economides & Terzis, 2008), many accountants continue not to use these new electronic services. Each of the previous studies investigated only a specific area of accountants' ICT use. For example, one study examined the types of networking technologies adopted; another examined the types of software used; and another examined the accountants' Web sites. Therefore, a comprehensive survey needed to be developed to capture the complete view of accountants' ICT use. Furthermore, most studies investigated accountants in the United States. Thus, a need also existed to investigate accountants' ICT use in other countries.

METHODOLOGY

Based on the OECD (Organization for Economic Co-operation and Development) (2002) model, our experience in surveying other services' areas, opinions of accountants after extensive discussions with them, and the previous studies presented above, we developed a comprehensive questionnaire to find out the utilization of ICT by accountants. Specially, fruitful discussions with members and officials of a local Accountants' Club helped us finalize the questionnaire.

We wanted to discover the ICT infrastructure that accounting offices in a Greek province owned and used. Also, we investigated what kind of accountant-specific software and e-government services the accountants used. We also wanted to identify the problems they faced in their daily accounting work regarding ICT. Suggestions to the Greek government and the Greek Accountants' Chamber could then be made.

The questionnaire contains 30 closed-type questions with multiple choice answers and 2 open-type questions. We classified the questions into four categories:

1. General information about the accounting enterprises (5 questions),
2. ICT infrastructure of the enterprise (18 questions),
3. Internet use and Web presence (4 questions), and
4. Accounting software applications and services (8 closed + 2 open questions).

One hundred twenty accounting offices are in the survey's region. The research was carried out at 100 accounting offices (private as well as belonging to enterprises) in this Greek county, using interviews at each office. The remaining 20 offices did not participate due to their lack of available time. We faced several obstacles in trying to interview the accountants due to their limited time.

We selected the specific survey's region because we have personal relationships with many accountants in this region, and expected that they would take the time to answer our questionnaire. During 2006–2007, we visited 75 offices and personally interviewed the staff. Twenty-five offices were interviewed by phone.

RESULTS

General Information about the Accounting Enterprises

Most accounting offices (53) employed four to nine people, followed by offices (37) with less than three people. There were also 10 offices employing more than nine people.

Almost all offices (98) were autonomous private offices, while 2 were large enterprises. This was expected since most Greek accountants work mainly as free professionals, having their own private offices.

Most offices (63) were active in the profession for more than 15 years. Most (31) were active for 23 years. Only 13 offices were relatively new in the profession (less than 6 years).

ICT Infrastructure

As expected, all offices used Internet and e-mail, since they need to use the e-government services of Inland Revenue Service. Wide Area Networks (WAN) were only used by two offices, the large enterprises (Figure 1).

It is important to note that 63 offices set up LAN networks for better internal office operation. Considering the offices that have LANs, 21% employed 1–3 people, 62% employed 4–9 people, and 17% employed 10 or more people. This shows that the use of networks in small and medium-sized enterprises is becoming a necessity.

The number of PCs was proportional to the number of personnel. In particular, 58 offices owned 4–10 PCs, and 42 offices owned 1–3 PCs. However, no office owned more than 10 PCs although 11 offices employed more than 10 people. Not all personnel were concurrently working on PCs; some were occupied at exterior works (e.g.,

Figure 1. ICT usage

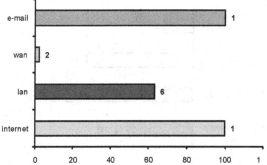

visiting the Inland Revenue Service, the Social Security Organization, and banks).

Out of the 63 offices that set up LAN networks, 21 used Client-Server technology and 42 used Peer-to-Peer (P2P) technology (Figure 2). This was expected for such small LANs since the P2P networks cost less and do not require specialised personnel for maintenance. It is also noteworthy that among the 37 offices that did not set up any network infrastructure, 29 planned to set up one in the near future, while 8 did not.

Furthermore, 26 offices used a separate file server for central storage of all their files (in both Client-Server and P2P networks), 4 used Print Server (only in Client-Server networks), 12 used Backup Server (only in Client-Server networks), and none used Mail Server. Since most offices employed few employees, they usually met each other in person at the office. The 26 offices that used a file server realised that they were able to protect important files by placing them centrally and would not waste time updating the same data on separate PCs.

It is also interesting to note that among the offices that used Client-Server, 10% owned 1–3 PCs (Figure 3). Also, among the offices that used P2P, 62% owned 4–10 PCs. Accountants may not have been fully aware of the different benefits offered by each one of these networking technologies. Usually, an office imitates others and decides to invest in something others suggest. Cost is also a very important factor in this choice. Instead of

Figure 2. LAN types and plans to use LANs

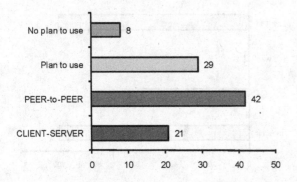

buying a new server, many small offices transformed an old PC into a File Server.

The offices that did not plan to set up a LAN were small offices, usually with one PC and sometimes two or three. Roughly half of the offices that planned to set up a LAN owned 1–10 PCs (Figure 4).

Only 34 offices owned laptops apart from PCs. Some accountants worked from homes using laptops at these offices.

As expected, 92 offices owned Dot Matrix printers since printing is essential for their daily work, for example printing customers' books (Figure 5). It is interesting to note that 30 offices had black and white Laser printers and 16 offices owned colour Laser printers. These offices were mainly large offices with many customers, as well as the two big enterprises. More than half of the offices owned new multi-machines (fax, Inkjet printer, scanner together), which is economically sound for small offices. Forty-two offices owned old fax machines. The new offices preferred to buy multi-machines. Sixty-six owned inkjet printers, which are the most economical for printing a few pages. Seven offices owned separate scanners. Only 16 offices owned photocopy machines (mainly big offices with many customers).

All offices used antivirus programs, while hardly any of the 76 offices used separate firewall programs apart from that included in Windows XP Operating System (Figure 6). Also, 12 offices used full data backup systems. These were mainly big offices and the two large enterprises, which had explicit backup policies. Due to the high cost of such technologies, the remaining offices did not use such technology. Instead, they used more economical ways of backing up their data. The offices that did not use a firewall program were mainly small offices with few PCs; they did not wish to purchase separate programs, since the firewall included in Windows XP worked well.

Regarding security problems faced by the offices during the previous year, 18 faced virus or spy-ware problems, 11 faced unauthorized access

Figure 3. Relationship between "LAN type" and "Number of PCs"

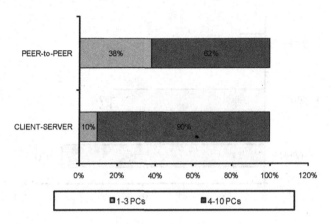

Figure 4. Relationship between the "Plans for LANs" and "Number of PCs"

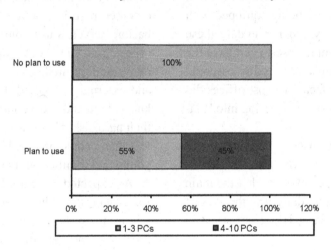

Figure 5. Printers usage

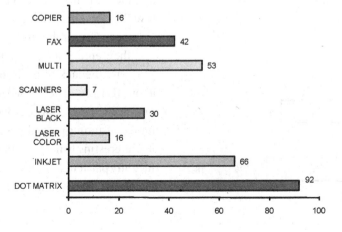

Figure 6. Security protection mechanisms

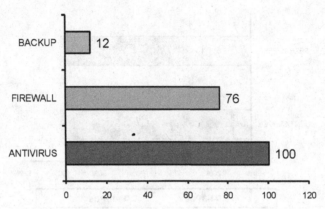

into their PCs, and 1 faced a program exploitation problem (Figure 7). The main reason for these problems was that despite being equipped with antivirus programs, they did not update these programs daily or, in some cases, even have the programs activated. The unauthorized access could be associated with the fact that most offices did not use password and user name to log into Windows.

Seventy-nine offices backed up their critical data daily, 11 did this weekly, and 10 did this monthly (Figure 8). They claimed that the main reason for not backing up daily was the lack of time and their belief that it is not important to back up daily.

Figure 7. Security problems

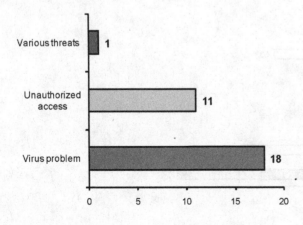

Regarding the media used for back up (Figure 9), most offices (86) backed up on the local disk (another partition or another file), 16 used a backup server, 8 used the old zip-drive, and 29 offices used CD-DVD. Twenty-one offices used more modern methods such as USB flash disk and external USB hard disk. Only two offices knew about and had a complete image backup of their hard disk. These two offices were small with less than people people, but these workers were young and familiar with new technology.

As expected, they used Microsoft's software for general use. They used Windows XP as the operating system, and the Microsoft Office 2000–2003 as their office suite. Most companies did not know about open source software.

Sixty-eight offices used password and user name to log in to the Windows system. The remainder 32 offices were mainly small offices with few PCs, and they did not consider it essential.

Regarding problems due to introducing ICT into their enterprises, 18 offices considered, as a problem, the lack of information and knowledge about ICT; 16 offices had problems with the terminology; and 13 offices were burned up by the time-consuming procedures (Figure 10). However, it is interesting to note that most offices (58) did not face any particular problem, and 5 offices were not interested in any of these problems. (Most offices

Figure 8. Backup frequency

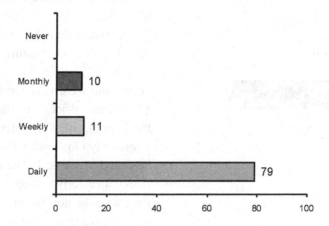

Figure 9. Data media backup

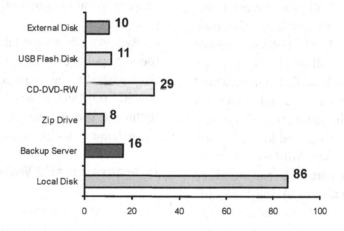

Figure 10. ICT problems

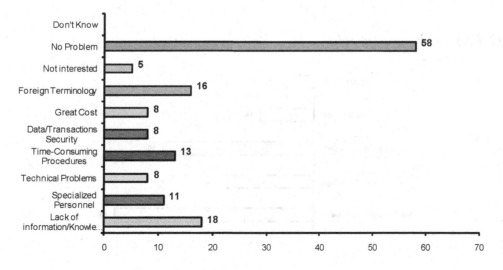

Figure 11. VoIP usage

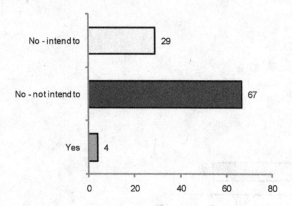

declared that they were not interested in this new technology.

Regarding their degree of familiarization with ICT and their continuing training policy, most offices (58) maintained a continuous training policy and were very familiar with ICT (Figure 13). In these offices, most accountants recognized the benefits of ICT. Internet explosion helped immensely. On the other hand, a few offices (eight) hesitated to use ICT. These were mainly old offices with elderly accountants, who could not keep pace with the new technologies and simply used only the essential items for their daily work. Sixty-four offices were very familiar with ICT, but they did not have any training policy, which happens mainly in small offices with one or two people.

Regarding their expectations of their Chamber (oe-e.gr, pol.org.gr) or the government, 71 offices wished to be financed to purchase or use new ICT products (Figure 14). Accountants were willing to use the new technologies, but they needed money to proceed.

were staffed by young accountants who eagerly follow any new technological innovations.)

Regarding the use of VoIP (Voice over Internet Protocol) technology, only four offices had used Skype (Figures 11 & 12). Most offices declared that this technology is still unreliable, and they will wait until it becomes perfect to use it again. Sixty-seven offices said they had not used it but intended to do so in the future, while 23 offices declared that they did not intend to use it at all. Their reasons for not using VoIP were that this technology is still new, unreliable, and there is no sufficient information about it. At that time, only two Greek telecommunications companies provided VoIP in parallel with other services, and they did not advertise it enough. Sixteen offices

Internet Use and Web Presence

In this section, we present the results of our research on accountants' Internet use. It is important to note that a Greek accounting office should have an Internet connection to connect to the Inland

Figure 12. Reasons for not using VoIP

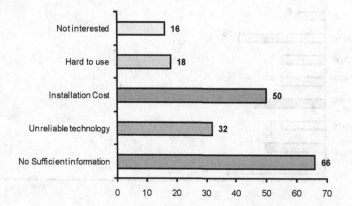

Figure 13. ICT familiarity and training policy

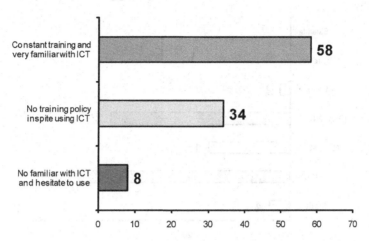

Figure 14. What accountants want from government and chamber

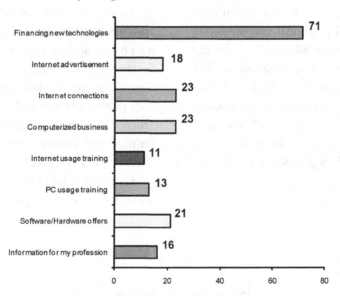

Revenue Service (TAXIS NET: www.taxisnet.gr). Forty-three offices used ISDN (Integrated Services Digital Network), while 53 offices adopted the new ADSL (Asymmetric Digital Subscriber Line) technology (Figure 15). However, four still used simple PSTN (Public Switched Telephone Network) connections via modems; these offices are small and staffed by elderly accountants who did not wish to upgrade their infrastructure. No office used wireless or satellite connections.

More than half of the offices used an ADSL connection due to the aggressive policy of the main Greek telecommunication company (OTE). Recently, OTE lowered the price of ADSL, making it affordable for any office. Correlating these results with their upgrading plans, we see that most of the 53 offices that planned to upgrade their Internet connection used ISDN. Accountants also embraced ADSL technology because it was economically and technically accessible.

Figure 15. Internet connection type

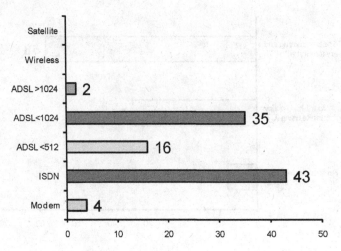

Only three offices had Web sites, which were developed by external personnel and hosted by an ISP server. Most accounting offices did not exclusively employ ICT specialists or an ICT service company, because they believed they needed a Web site only for advertising purposes. However, they did not consider this function essential. This conclusion is also supported by the fact that only five offices planned to create Web pages in the near future.

As we have mentioned, an accounting office must have an Internet connection for transactions with public services, such as the Inland Revenue Service. Consequently, all offices said the main reason they used the Internet was to communicate with public services and ministries (Figure 16). Thirty-four offices also cited e-banking as a reason for their Internet use. Fifty-eight offices used the Web to find information.

They rated the problems that affect their Internet use equally (Figure 17). These problems

Figure 16. Internet usage reasons

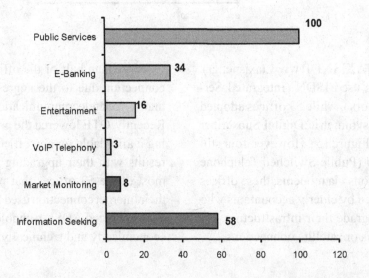

Figure 17. Internet problems evaluation

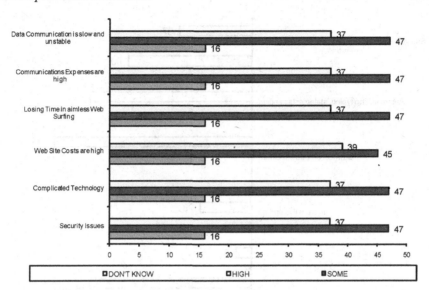

were related to security, complicated technology, Web site cost, loosing time in surfing, communication costs, and slow and unstable data communications. Most offices (47) considered these problems serious, 37 considered them fair, and 13 did not care. Therefore, most accountants were hesitant about the Internet.

Accounting Software Applications and Services

In this section, we report on the accountants' use of accounting software and related services.

The usual work of a Greek accountant is the book keeping of A and B categories. In the Greek market, there are software packages operating in a network environment that are useful for this purpose. These software packages can be used simultaneously by several people, depending on the licence. In 63 offices, such software packages were used by two or more people in a network environment. In the remaining 37 offices, a single person used them. This occurred mainly in small offices.

In Greece, all enterprises are obliged to send a VAT (Value Added Tax) statement periodi-

cally (every quarter for A & B categories) to the Inland Revenue Service. According to existing legislation, accountants do not have to send these statements electronically via TAXIS NET even if such possibility is provided. Most offices (82) periodically sent the VAT statement electronically, exploiting the electronic services offered by the state. Few offices (18) submitted their statement in person to the Inland Revenue Service.

While almost all of these software packages support data exchange with MS Office, no office used this feature. The accountants may not have known about this possibility or did not need it.

Although these software packages could be upgraded via the Internet, in real time (live update), most offices (61) did not download the new versions. They may have not been familiar with this process, or they did not know it existed. On the other hand, 26 offices checked for new versions once per month, and 13 offices did so daily.

When we examined the types of printers used to print out reports from these software packages, we found that 92 offices used all varieties. Eighty-nine did this daily and three did weekly. The remaining eight offices, which are small offices, owned and used only one printer (Figure 18).

Figure 18. A' & B' books category services usage

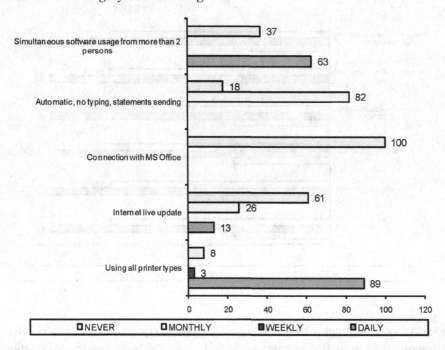

Next, we investigated the book keeping of C category. Large enterprises, with high turnover, must keep C category books. Thus, the book keeping of C category is mainly done by large offices with much experience. Regarding the simultaneous use of software packages by two or more people, we have the same results as the book keeping of A and B categories, that is, accountants used networking technology. Sixty-three offices used this technology daily and 37 never. In these 37 offices, offices were included that did not serve customers of the C category.

None of the offices used the software's ability to connect to MS Office. For C category book keeping, accountants must frequently update their software packages. In terms of upgrading via the Internet in real time, 53 offices never updated in this manner, 13 monthly, 5 weekly, and 29 daily. Regarding printing work related to C category book keeping, 66 offices, with many of these customers, printed daily. However, 28 offices did not have such customers and therefore did not need to print this work, 3 offices printed

a few times per month because they had one or two such customers, and 3 offices printed a few times per week (Figure 19).

Only eight offices used CRM (Customer Relationship Management) systems daily, and the remaining 92 offices did not know about CRM. These eight offices were mainly large offices with many customers. Similarly, only the two large enterprises used ERP (Enterprise Resource Planning) systems daily (Figure 20). Only large companies with a specialized accountants' section used ERP.

On the matter of payroll services in Greece, all enterprises that pay personnel are obliged to send the APS (Analytic Periodical Statement) to the Organisation of Social Security (IKA) every month. IKA offers accountants multiple ways to submit this statement. Currently, the two most popular methods are: 1) creating a compatible file using the payroll program and sending it to IKA, and 2) typing the elements into suitable forms on the Web site of IKA (www.ika.gr) and completing the sending of APS (Analytic Periodical State-

Figure 19. C' books category services usage

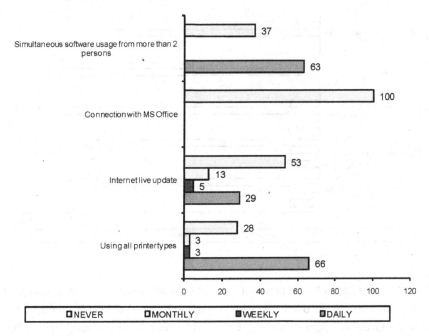

ment). The first method is used by 92 offices monthly (Figure 21). The second method is used by 71 offices monthly. Eight offices did not use any payroll software.

Three offices upgraded their payroll software online daily, 87 monthly, and 10 never.

Concerning electronic communication with banks or other institutions of social insurance (as well as the exchange of electronic data), 79 (respectively 82) offices never had such interactions, 10 (respectively 8) monthly, and 11 (respectively 10) daily (Figure 21).

Figure 20. ERP, taxation software and CRM Services usage

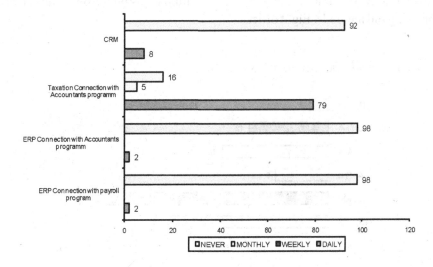

Figure 21. Payroll services usage

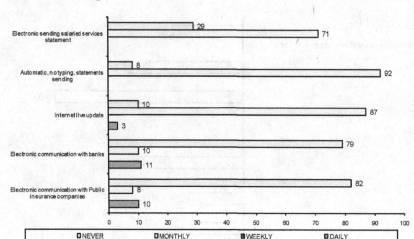

Ninety offices used Windows-based accounting software whereas only three used the old DOS-based software. Greek accounting software companies helped by adapting their products to new technological innovations.

Figure 22 shows the specific accounting software programs offices used. UNION is used by 37 offices, while SINGULAR is used by 24. EPSILON-net is a powerful program, but it is more expensive; therefore, it is used by only 12 big companies.

However, accounting offices did not utilize the new ways of upgrading their software. Seventy-nine upgraded via post (CD) (Figure 23). Although new technology is available, many offices insisted on using old methods. Eight offices upgraded their software directly via the Internet (live update) over a broadband Internet connection, and 34 offices upgraded after downloading and installing the update file.

The accountants kept themselves informed about new developments in their profession via multiple means. Ninety-two offices read periodicals, 53 offices read TaxHeaven (www.gus.gr), 37 offices read e-Forologia (www.e-forologia.gr), 26 offices read the online e-magazine EPSILON7 (http://www.epsilonnetwork.gr/epsilon7), and 29 offices were informed by discussions in various forums (Figure 24). Thus, many accountants were informed not only through traditional written press but also via the Internet.

Figure 22. Program's brands that accountants use

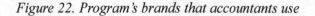

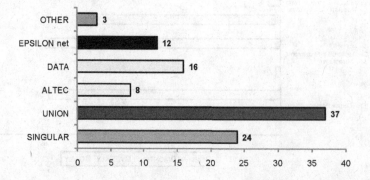

Figure 23. Program's update

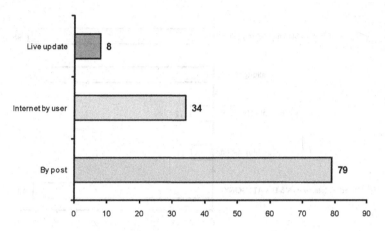

Figure 24. Frequent profession's informing

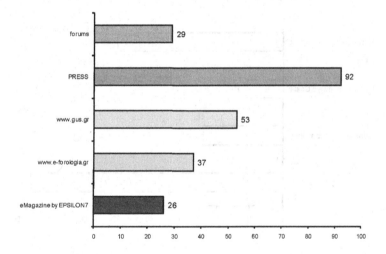

As we have reported, many accountants used the new e-services provided by TAXIS NET. Although sending VAT statements regarding the A and B book keeping categories electronically is not mandatory, 92 offices did in this manner. Also, 95 offices sent their customers' final Taxation Statements to TAXIS NET. The accounting offices realized the benefits of using the new online services that the government provided (Figure 25).

Finally, Greek accountants were not familiar with the "paperless office" that prevails in the United States. Only two offices created an electronic file for each customer by scanning the forms and storing them in e-files. Also, no office could send invoices to their customers in electronic form. Instead, they preferred to key the invoices' data into the corresponding software. They did not use these technologies because 76 offices did not consider them to be important, and 50 did not have much time for such work (Figure 26).

Finally, almost all offices considered the following factors very important for their software packages: convenience of learning, ease of use, reputation of the software's company, live update ability, specifications and functions, customer support, user friendliness, and online service (Figure 27).

Figure 25. Greek government services (TAXIS NET) usage

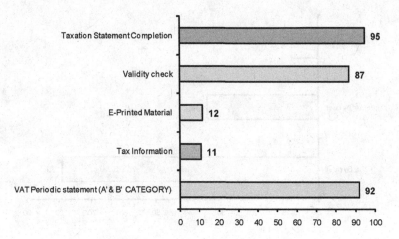

Figure 26. Reasons of not using "paperless Office"

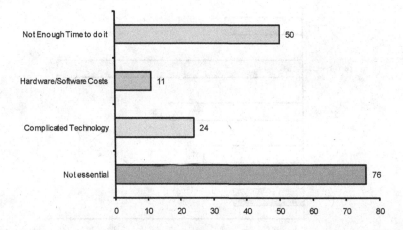

Figure 27. Software evaluation criteria

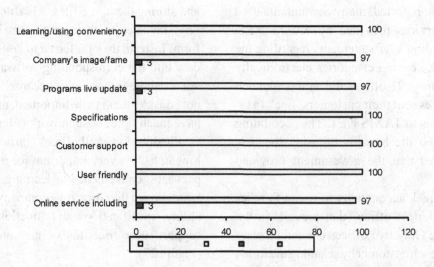

CONCLUSION

The purpose of this study was to provide insights into the level of ICT use by the accounting offices in a Greek county.

The Greek state provided various e-government services to accountants, which urged the accounting offices to use and develop an ICT infrastructure. Various Greek public organizations provide e-services. For example, the Ministry of Finance has the Web site for TAXIS NET (www.taxisnet.gr) and the Ministry of Employment provides the Web site for IKA (www.ika.gr). These e-government services help accounting offices to save time and better serve their customers.

The findings from this survey show that the accounting offices in a Greek county kept pace with ICT technological innovations. For example, Internet was widely used by them. However, elderly accountants seemed to be more resistant to adopt the new technologies.

Briefly, the positive points were the following:

- Many (63) offices set up a LAN, and 29 of the remaining offices planned to do so in the future. The accountants recognized the benefits of having a LAN in their enterprise. Software companies helped with this implementation by allowing their programs to be used in a network environment without extra cost.
- All the offices had antivirus programs for their PCs.
- Few (18) offices faced viruses' problems during the past year.
- Many (58) offices did not face any problems using ICT.
- Many (82) offices used the electronic submission of VAT (in A and B category book keeping) via TAXIS NET, which is not mandatory.

The negative points were the following:

- Few (26) offices used separate file servers to store their data.
- Few (12) offices used complete backup systems for their data.
- Only 79 offices backed up their data daily.
- Very few (2) offices had a complete image backup of their hard disk.
- Very few (4) offices used VoIP for small time duration. They said this service was unreliable, and they did not have much information regarding how to use it.
- Many (43) offices still used the old ISDN Internet connection, although the prices of ADSL had fallen enough to be economically comparable with ISDN.
- Very few (3) offices developed their own Web site.
- Very few (8) offices used CRM programs for daily operations.
- Still, 3 offices used DOS-based professional applications.
- Many (79) offices upgraded their software packages via post (receiving the upgrades in a CD), although almost all software packages had live update ability.
- Very few (2) offices created electronic files of their customers' documents (paperless office).

Although there were two open questions, many accountants did not make any suggestions but the following suggestions were made:

- Enable direct and complete interconnection between their software programs and the public e-services of the Inland Revenue Service (TAXIS NET) and the Organisation of Social Security (IKA) without having to type the same data into forms on the these Web sites. Currently, this ability is provided for some services.
- Provide the possibility of sending a customer's first VAT statement electronically. Currently, a new customer should record

his first statement in person with the Inland Revenue Service. Afterward, he can send the statements electronically.

- Provide the possibility of sending the liquidation VAT statement electronically via the Internet. Currently, a pilot project offers this ability.
- Training on accounting software should be offered by the software companies not only in Athens (the capital of Greece) but also in the province.

Limitations of this study include the specific province and country sample of the accounting offices. A future study could cover all Greek regions, as well as other countries. Also, a cross-sector comparison with enterprises in other service professions could be made. Nevertheless, we hope that the results of this study provide an insight into the use ICT and electronic services by Greek accountants. These results could be a starting point for further research in this area.

REFERENCES

Anders, S. B., & Fischer, C. M. (2004). A hard look at tax software: 2004 survey of New York State practitioners. *The CPA Journal.* Retrieved October 14, 2006, from http://www.nysscpa.org/cpajournal/2004/704/infocus/p18.htm

Anderson, T., Fox, M., & Schwartz, B. N. (2005). History and trends in e-filing: A survey of CPA practitioners. *The CPA Journal.* Retrieved October 14, 2006, from http://www.nysscpa.org/cpajournal/2005/1005/essentials/p66.htm

Bhansali, C. (2006a). The question every practicing accountant must ask. *Accounting Technology*, June. Retrieved March 22, 2007, from http://www.webcpa.com/

Bhansali, C. (2006b). A partial solution to a Daunting problem. *Accounting Technology*, September. Retrieved March 22, 2007, from http://www.webcpa.com/

Bush, C. T. (2000). Accountants are thriving on the Web, says survey. *Journal of Accountancy*, *190*(5), 20.

Chatzopoulos, K. C., & Economides, A. A. (2009). A holistic evaluation of Greek municipalities' websites. *Electronic Government, an International Journal (EG), 6*(2), 193-212.

Czech Statistical Office. (2002). *Technology used by enterprises.* Retrieved October 11, 2006, from http://www.czso.cz/eng/edicniplan.nsf/o/9602-04-2003-1__technology_used_by_enterprises

Economides, A. A., & Terzis, V. (2008). Evaluating tax sites: An evaluation framework and its application. *Electronic Government, an International Journal (EG), 5*(3), 321-344.

Gallun, R. A., Heagy, C. D., & Lindsey, H. C. (1993). How CPAs use computers. *Journal of Accountancy, 175*(1), 38–41.

Garen, K. (2006). Driving the firm of the future. *Accounting Technology,* June. Retrieved February 9, 2007, from http://www.webcpa.com/

Gullkvist, B., & Ylinen, M. (2005). E-accounting systems use in Finnish accounting agencies. In M. Seppä, M. Hannula, A-M. Järvelin, J. Kujala, M. Ruohonen, & T. Tiainen (Eds.) *Frontiers of e-Business Research. Proceedings of the e-Business Research Forum 2005* (pp. 109-117). Tampere, Finland: e-Business Resilience Centre.

Johnston, R. P. (2005). A tour of tomorrow's technology. [from http://www.aicpa.org/PUBS/JOFA/joaiss.htm]. *Journal of Accountancy, 200*(4), 95–97. Retrieved November 23, 2006.

Khani, P. E., & Zarowin, S. (1994). The technology used by high-tech CPAs. *Journal of Accountancy, 177*(2), 54–58.

Levy, Y., Murphy, K. E., & Zanakis, S. H. (2009). A value-satisfaction taxonomy of IS effectiveness (VSTISE): A case study of user satisfaction with IS and user-perceived value of IS. *International Journal of Information Systems in the Service Sector, 1*(1), 93–118.

Lexhagen, M. (2009). Customer perceived value of travel and tourism web sites. *International Journal of Information Systems in the Service Sector, 1*(1), 35–53.

Mintel International Group Ltd. (2005). Retrieved October 14, 2006, from http://www.mintel.com

Organization for Economic Co-operation and Development. (2002). *The OECD model survey of ICT usage in the business sector.* Retrieved September 8, 2006, from http://www.oecd.org

Pinhanez, C. (2009). A service science perspective on human-computer interface issues of online service applications. *International Journal of Information Systems in the Service Sector, 1*(2), 17–35.

Prawitt, D., Romney, M., & Zarowin, S. (1997). A journal survey: The software CPAs use. *Journal of Accountancy, 183*(2), 52–66.

Roxas, M. L., Peek, L., Peek, G., & Hagemann, T. (2000). A preliminary evaluation of professional accounting services: Direct marketing on the Internet. *Journal of Services Marketing, 14*(7), 595–605. doi:10.1108/08876040010352763

Terpsiadou, M. H., & Economides, A. A. (2009). (in press). The use of information systems in the Greek public financial services: The case of TAXIS. *Government Information Quarterly.*

Voiculescu, A. (2000). *Strategic implications of electronic commerce for UK businesses.* Retrieved October 14, 2006, from http://www.aurelvoi-culescu.com/

Zarowin, S. (2003). Hot stuff: What you need and what you don't your technology setup may be sufficient for your needs. *Journal of Accountancy, 195*(4), 28.

Zarowin, S. (2004). Top tools for CPAs: Technology products that make your work go faster and smoother. *Journal of Accountancy, 194*(5), 26.

Zarowin, S. (2006). Rate yourself in the paperless race: Have you overcome your resistance to the new technology? *Journal of Accountancy, 201*(5), 50–54.

This work was previously published in International Journal of Information Systems in the Service Sector, Volume 2, Issue 1, edited by John Wang, pp. 49-70, copyright 2010 by IGI Publishing (an imprint of IGI Global).

Chapter 5
Exploring the Adoption of Technology Driven Services in the Healthcare Industry

Umit Topacan
Bogazici University, Turkey

A. Nuri Basoglu
Bogazici University, Turkey

Tugrul U. Daim
Portland State University, USA

ABSTRACT

Recent developments in information and communication technologies have helped to accelerate the diffusion of electronic services in the medical industry. Health information services house, retrieve, and make use of medical information to improve service quality and reduce cost. Users—including medical staff, administrative staff, and patients—of these systems cannot fully benefit from them unless they can use them comfortably. User behavior is affected by various factors relating to technology characteristics, user characteristics, social environment, and organizational environment. Our research evaluated the determinants of health information service adoption and analyzed the relationship between these determinants and the behavior of the user. Health information service adoption was found to be influenced by service characteristics, user characteristics, intermediary variables, facilitating conditions, and social factors.

INTRODUCTION

The healthcare industry has grown rapidly over the past three decades and projected growth is likely to continue or even expand in the coming decades. As a result it is facing significant challenges on

a number of fronts: healthcare reimbursement is decreasing, demand for larger volumes of healthcare services, and increased pressure to publicly report quality data are a few of the factors driving change. While the healthcare industry has been slow to adopt technology, it will be forced to do so in the coming decade to meet not only the

DOI: 10.4018/978-1-4666-0044-7.ch005

Copyright © 2012, IGI Global. Copying or distributing in print or electronic forms without written permission of IGI Global is prohibited.

known challenges identified above but also other challenges that have not yet been identified in this rapidly changing marketplace.

Health expenditures per capita, as a percent of gross domestic product (GDP), doubled between 1970 and 2001 in the United States for a total expenditure of $14.1 trillion in 2001 (Levit, Smith, Cowan, Lazeby, Sensening, & Catlin, 2003). This growth is driven by a number of factors, the primary drivers being increased demand for healthcare services and increasing cost of services. The number of Americans over the age of 65 is projected to increase by a factor of 2.5 by 2040 (Lee & Tuljapurkar, 1994). As a result of improved economic and technical environments, these "baby boomers" will not only increase the total volume of healthcare services provided (Reinhardt, 2000) but also drive the type of healthcare services required. Baby boomers also have more disposable income than previous generations and as a result elect to have more elective procedures than any generation before them (Knickman, Hunt, Snell, Marie, Aleczih, & Kennell, 2003).

In the healthcare sector, electronic information and communication technologies are intensively used to provide and support healthcare operations (Hsieh, Hjélm, Lee, & Aldis, 2001). However, compared to other industries diffusion of such technologies have been slow in the healthcare sector. This article focuses on this problem and identifies factors that may influence the adoption of such services. Telemedicine, and specifically remote monitoring, was picked as the case to analyze in this paper. Telemedicine systems were deployed in many medical fields. Remote monitoring systems were developed to capture disease specific measurements electronically. For example, data from insulin-dependent diabetes (Biermann, Dietrich, Rihl, & Standl, 2002) and asthma patients (Glykas & Chytas, 2004) are being captured remotely. Also, some systems are used for consultation purposes (Berghout, Eminovic, Keizer, & Birnie, 2007).

Therefore, this research will have the following objectives

1. To search and find major determinants of health information service adoption among users (medical staff, administrative staff and patients)
2. To find individual, social, service and technological components of adoption
3. To assess desirability of a service electronic interface prototype
4. To establish a more general framework that can be tested statistically in future studies

In this study, we developed an electronic health service prototype for patients suffering from diabetes and obesity where its foundation had been set in preliminary work (Topacan, Basoglu, & Daim, 2008). Patient data is collected through various devices, such as a mobile phone, stethoscope, and glucose meter. Collected data is then stored on a medical server. Healthcare providers can monitor the patients through this system and make suggestions as necessary. As a result, we found that health information service adoption decisions of users were influenced by service characteristics, user characteristics, intermediary variables, facilitating conditions, and social factors.

LITERATURE REVIEW

Adoption Theories

Service adoption is influenced by various factors including user characteristics and requirements, service characteristics, and social factors. During the past decades, many theoretical models were developed by researchers to explain the human behaviors in the adoption process. Theory of Reasoned Action (TRA) (Fishbein & Ajzen, 1975) is one of the well known models. Fishbein and Ajzen (1975) used two main constructs, namely attitude toward behavior and subjective norm, to predict the behaviors. Following the TRA model, many researchers attempted to expand it by adding new constructs or by applying it in different contexts. Theory of Planned Behavior (TPB) (Ajzen, 1991) was developed by adding perceived behavioral control to the TRA (Figure 1). Technology Acceptance Model (TAM) (Davis, 1989) was applied in the IS context to predict technology acceptance. TPB and TAM (Figure 2) are just two of such models expanding TRA. According to Davis (1989), two fundamental determinants of system use are perceived ease of use and perceived usefulness. The relative strength of usefulness-utilization relation is stronger than that of the relationship between ease of use and utilization (Davis, 1989). These findings are validated in many different studies (Venkatesh & Davis, 2000; Chau & Hu, 2002).

Healthcare Systems

Healthcare providers use various technologies to decrease cost, increase access to healthcare and improve quality in the medical services (Gagnon et al., 2003). Telemedicine is one of these technologies that enable "remote medical procedures and examinations between patients and medical providers via telecommunication technologies such as the Internet, or telephone" (Al-Qirim, 2007). Chau and Hu (2002) studied healthcare professionals' decisions regarding acceptance of telemedicine. They compared TRA and TAM and found that TAM is a more suitable model than TRA in predicting the technology acceptance in the medical sector (Chau & Hu, 2002). Others found factors that influence acceptance of both medical providers and patients. How the service is perceived and used by the users significantly affects adoption process.

With the rapid development of telecommunication systems, intelligent monitoring and control systems have become the major application areas of telemedicine. Such applications include 'Smart

homes' for telecare by means of movement detectors, oxymeters, tansiometers, and various other devices (Rialle, Lamy, Noury, & Bajolle, 2003), such as a ring-sensor that monitors patient's blood oxygen saturation (Yang & Rhee, 2000) and a Web-based electrocardiogram monitoring application facilitating collection, analysis and storage of patient data (Magrabi, Lovell, & Celle, 1999). Many different devices and techniques are used to collect more accurate patient information. A spoken dialogue system was designed by Giorgino et al. (2005) to test the reliability of a speech recognition system. Finally, compared to traditional patient care, telemedicine systems provide many benefits to the physicians and patients. Brink, Moorman, Boer, Pruyn, Verwoerd, and Bemmel (2005) found electronic health information and monitoring systems help physicians in early detection of occurring head and neck cancer

Figure 1. Theory of planned behavior (Ajzen, 1991)

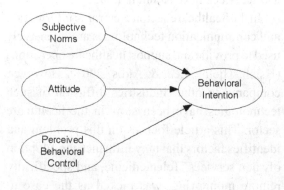

Figure 2. Technology acceptance model (Davis, 1989)

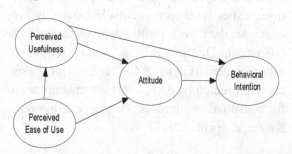

problems. Telemedicine systems are reported to reduce number of clinic visits significantly (Chae, Lee, Ho, Kim, Jun, & Won, 2001).

Factors Influencing Adoption

Effort expectancy, defined as "the degree of ease associated with the use of the system," (Venkatesh, Morris, Davis, & Davis, 2003) is one of the factors related to service characteristics. The more users think that the service is complex to use, the slower their adoption. Also, compatibility, which is defined as "the degree to which an innovation is perceived as being consistent with the existing practices, values, needs and experiences of the healthcare professional," influences acceptance of information and communication technologies in the case of occupational therapists (Schaper & Pervan, 2003). Besides, availability, quality, and value of the information provided by the service are other important characteristics (Aubert & Hamel, 2001). In addition, some of the adoption factors are related to individual characteristics. Chen, Yang, Tang, Huang, and Yu (2008) studied user specific characteristics such as age, educational level, and

job experience to explore the intention of nurses towards Web-based learning. Also, user satisfaction which is defined as "the overall evaluation of a user's experience in using the system and the potential impact of the system," significantly influences the adoption process (Yusof, Kuljis, & Papazafeiropoulou, 2008). Moreover, users' intrinsic motivation about adoption and perceptions about ease of use are influenced by the satisfaction of the user with the medical care (Wilson & Lankton, 2004). Apart from service and users, adoption is influenced by the organizational, environmental, or external characteristics as well. Rewarding and financial incentives were found to accelerate adoption of computerized physician order entry with clinical decision support systems (Simon, Rundall, & Shortell, 2007). Gagnon et al. found that social norms are one of the significant predictors of physicians' intention toward using medical technology (Gagnon et al., 2003). Table 1 summarizes the factors cited in the literature.

Table 1. Factors influencing adoption

Class	Literature
User Characteristics	Aubert & Hamel, 2001; Bruner & Kumar, 2005; Chang, Hwang, Hung, Lin, & Yen, 2007; Chau & Hu, 2002; Chen et al., 2008; Dishaw & Strong, 1999; Gagnon et al., 2003; Schaper & Pervan, 2003; Thompson et al., 1991; Venkatesh & Davis, 2000; Venkatesh et al., 2003; Wilson & Lankton, 2004; Yusof et al., 2007
Service Characteristics	Aubert & Hamel, 2001; Bruner & Kumar, 2005; Chang et al., 2007; Dishaw & Strong, 1999; Karahanna, Straub, & Chervany, 1999; Liu & Ma, 2005; Schaper & Pervan, 2003; Thompson et al., 1991; Tung et al., 2008; Venkatesh & Davis, 2000; Yusof et al., 2008
Ease of Use	Aubert & Hamel, 2001; Bruner & Kumar, 2005; Chang et al., 2007; Dishaw & Strong, 1999; Chen et al., 2008; Chau & Hu, 2002; Karahanna et al., 1999; Liu & Ma, 2005; Schaper & Pervan, 2003; Taylor & Todd, 1995; Thompson et al., 1991; Tung et al., 2008; Venkatesh & Davis, 2000; Venkatesh et al., 2003; Wilson & Lankton, 2004
Social Factors	Aubert & Hamel, 2001; Chau & Hu, 2002; Karahanna et al., 1999; Schaper & Pervan, 2003; Taylor & Todd, 1995; Thompson, et al., 1991; Venkatesh & Davis, 2000; Venkatesh et al., 2003
Usefulness	Aubert & Hamel, 2001; Bruner & Kumar, 2005; Chau & Hu, 2002; Chen et al., 2008; Dishaw & Strong, 1999; Karahanna et al., 1999; Liu & Ma, 2005; Schaper & Pervan, 2003; Taylor & Todd, 1995; Tung et al., 2008; Venkatesh & Davis, 2000; Venkatesh et al., 2003; Wilson & Lankton, 2004; Yusof et al., 2008
Facilitating Conditions	Aubert & Hamel, 2001; Chang et al., 2007; Gagnon et al., 2003; Karahanna et al., 1999; Schaper & Pervan, 2003; Thompson, et al., 1991; Venkatesh et al., 2003;

METHODOLOGY

Research Method

Prior to the study, a health information service prototype was developed for patients and their healthcare providers. The service was designed to

- Collect patient data via various devices like stethoscope, treadmill, bascule, mobile phone
- Support collecting patient information and transmitting to the healthcare providers
- Facilitate the early detection of health problems by means of monitoring patient data

Qualitative research method was applied in the study to analyze the topic and to take advantage of interviewees' creative ideas and experiences. Semi-structured open-ended questions were asked to the potential users, physicians, and nurses. The interviewee list was prepared such that distributions of gender, age, and work experience were balanced. At the beginning of the interview, interviewees were informed about the service with a presentation that takes approximately 5 minutes. After presentations, physicians used the prototype developed for physicians and potential users the one developed for them. Finally, the interview was conducted by asking 14 questions (see Appendix A for questions).

In the analysis phase, the following steps have been realized

- Interviews' audio-records were deciphered and written in a file sentence by sentence.
- The sentences were examined so that we can extract casual relationships where an outcome is attributed by one or more factors and consequently dependent and independent variables were set. A sort of modified attribution coding has been realized

(Silver, 2004). The variables list also grew out of this conception.

- A second expert also repeated the same relationship coding. In case of any discrepancy, a discussion has occurred to resolve the conflict.
- All produced casual relationships that were weighted based on how critical they were perceived by the interviewees. The weight was accepted as 1 by default. If the participant mentioned the same factor more than once or gave special emphasis, the relationship was assigned a score of 1.5.
- After content analysis and coding, the relationship scores were summed and divided by total weights, and depicted in Table 5 for further analysis.

Proposed Service

A home based telemonitoring service was designed for obesity and diabetic patients. The service (Figure 3) mainly consisted of

- Hypothetical devices that were capable of sending data via Bluetooth technology
  - Treadmill for cardio information
  - Bascule for weight information
  - Stethoscope for blood pressure
  - Glucose meter for blood glucose level
- Prototype of the patients' application developed for mobile devices to collect information about patient
- Prototype of the physicians' application developed for mobile devices to get patient information
- Prototype of the PC application installed in the desktop computer of physicians to monitor patient status
- A medical server to store and manage patient data collected from various sources

Both the patients' and physicians' prototypes work as follows:

Figure 3. Proposed service

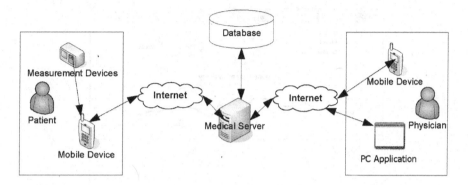

The mobile device reads the menu to patient/physician. The patient/physician selects operation by pronouncing the operation name and saying the keyword "OK." The service listens the voice of patient/physician and syntheses it. After the service hears "OK," it goes onto the next step based on the selected operation. Thus, a dialogue occurs between patient/physician and the service. In Appendix B, many typical dialogue examples have been given. Table 2 shows the functions of the electronic service.

The proposed system also has reminder services for both patients and physicians. If the patient takes medicine at regular times, the service warns him or her when this time comes. Also, if the patient does not enter any information at a specific time, the service prompts him or her to enter. Moreover, physicians can define reminders based on specific patient data. As an example, they can define so that the service can warn them when the patient's blood glucose level decreases to below "3 mmol/l" (dialogue and sample warning texts are in the Appendix B). Developed PC application prototype enables physician to monitor all of the patient's data, such as what the patient eats, how much calorie he or she gets, and what exercises he or she does. Figure 4 shows a sample screen of the prototype. In this screen, physicians can generate calorie, fat, protein, blood sugar, and weight graphs of the patient for a specific period.

RESULTS

Profile of Interviewees

Twenty-five people participated in this study. Educational level, age group, gender, computer literacy, and mobile phone experience variables were taken into consideration in the selection process. Age of the interviewees ranged between 22 and 50. Fifteen were female and 10 were male. Educational level of the sample consisted of high school graduates, university graduates, and graduate students. Table 3 contains details about the profile of interviewees.

Table 2. Menu of the services

Patients Menu	Physicians Menu
- Enter Meal	- Calorie Information
- Enter Information	- Blood Glucose Information
---- Enter movement or exercise	- Blood Pressure Information
---- Enter Trauma	- Exit
---- Enter pain	
---- Enter drug	
---- Return main menu	
- Meal Suggestion	
- Get Calorie Information	
- Exit.	

Figure 4. PC application screen

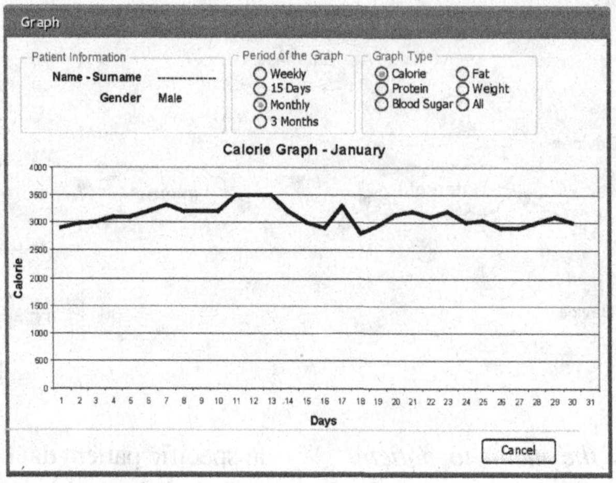

Findings

Service Characteristics

Service characteristics should match the user needs and requirements for better performance and effortless adoption (Goodhue, 1995).

Content: Potential users attempt to use services that meet their needs and requirements. Thus, required information content differs based on doctors' area of specialization and patients' disease types in the case of health information services. As an example, general surgery doctors need cardio information and diabetic patients show concern for blood glucose level. One of the comments was:

...As a general surgeon, I do not care what patient eats or drinks. I just care about his/her blood pressure, electrocardiogram ... if I were

an internal specialist; I probably would use the service because information content fits with an internal specialist's or a dietician's data requirements (Male, Doctor, 32).

An anesthesia expert said the following about the content;

... I do not care about the weight, the calories, or the blood pressure. Pruritus, headache, and nausea information are more useful in my profession (Female, Doctor, 32).

Users think that appropriate, comprehensive, and quality content improve the usefulness of the service. The relationship between content quality and usefulness is also supported in the literature (Ozen & Basoglu, 2006).

Table 3. Interviewees' profile

	Number	Average Age (in years)	Computer Experience (in years)	Mobile Phone Experience (in years)
Doctor	6	40	18	10
Nurse	2	32	8	7
Potential User	17	27	10	9
Total	25	31	12	9

Cost: One of the major predictors of behavior intention to use an IS system is the perceived cost (Mathieson, Peacock, & Chin, 2001). Tung, Chang, and Chou (2008) defined cost as the monetary expense for using the electronic information system. It negatively affects the adoption of the service. One of the participants said the following:

... my usage preference of the service depends on the cost of it. If it costs much, I do not prefer to use it (Male, Potential User, 25).

Another comment is given below:

If the cost of using the service exceeds the cost of visiting a doctor, I prefer face-to-face communication with a doctor (Female, Potential User, 23).

Based on the participants' comments, the more costly the service, the less people prefer to use it. Thus, the findings about the cost were parallel with the literature (Tung et al., 2008).

Sound quality: The voice used in the mobile device to communicate with the patient/physician was that of a mechanical male. Most of the participants disliked the voice and proposed a more human one.

The voice of the service is mechanical and hoarse. Sometimes, it is very difficult to understand what it says (Female, Potential User, 30).

Also, another comment from a participant:

It should be a female voice (Male, Potential User, 30).

Participants are more comfortable with a non-mechanical female voice in the conversation with mobile device.

Security: Security affects the adoption of IT services (Cheng, Lam, & Yeung, 2006). Security is the condition of protecting user specific data against others.

Security is very important for me. I do not prefer to share the data that shows my health status with others (Male, Potential User, 47).

Mobility: Users can benefit from a mobile service anywhere at any time. According to Kleinrock (1996), two of the well-known dimensions of mobility are time and place independence. What participants said about the mobility also supports these findings. Especially, doctors pay more attention to the mobility characteristics of the service in the adoption process because they could reach patient data even if they were outside of the hospital. One of the doctors commented about mobility:

I may refer this service to my colleagues because doctors can monitor their patients on the weekends and holidays. You are not confined to office hours to access the patient information (Female, Doctor, 32).

Mobility affects usefulness of the service in a positive way. Another comment about mobility indicated:

... there are similar services on the Internet. You enter what you eat to the application and it calculated how many calories it has. The most significant advantage of the proposed service is that it can be used in a mobile device. You can get advice whenever you need" (Female, Doctor, 37).

Thus, mobile applications were found more useful by the potential users because they could use these applications whenever the need arose.

Time factor: Time factor is a person's belief about the time spent interacting with the service and the response time of the service concerning patient status. If entering data to the service takes too long, users prefer seeing the doctor. Biermann et al. (2002) also found that 30% of the patients prefer entering extra data into a system if it is not time-consuming.

... the time I spend during data entrance affects my usage decision. If I spend a lot of time while entering information about me, I would not prefer using it. I visit the doctor instead of using it (Female, Potential User, 23).

Participants emphasized that time is a significant factor that affects adoption. Thus, designers should develop services that do not require much time. Users do not prefer to spend much time using the service.

User Characteristics

Health status: With some health conditions, like chronic illness, patients need more healthcare than normal conditions. Although Wilson and Lankton (2004) did not find a strong relationship between patients' healthcare need and intention to use provider-delivered e-health, participants in the study would use an e-health service if they had a disease.

I do not need to use the service because my health status is good. However, I wish to use it on account of ill health (Male, Potential User, 47).

Age: Behavior of the user toward computer use is also influenced by the user's age (Liu, Pothiban, Lu, & Khamphonsiri, 2000). Chen et al. (2008) studied age as a determinant of intention of nurses toward Web-based learning. Others examined age as a moderator variable in the technology adoption context (Chau & Hu, 2002; Venkatesh et al., 2003). The following is one of the participants' comments about age:

I do not need the help of others while using the service. I think all of the doctors can use it except aged ones (Male, Doctor, 50).

In the study, it was found that both potential users and doctors considered age as a factor that affects effortless use of the service. It is a general belief that older people would have difficulties adopting or using a technological device.

Users' time constraint: Participants think that people who do not have enough time to visit a doctor may prefer to use the service.

Hard-working people who do not spare time to visit a doctor, but they want to be under control of the doctor may prefer to use (Male, Potential User, 47).

Subsequently, in addition to service-related time factors like quick data entry and rapid response, users' time limitations also affect the attitude of users toward using health services.

Intermediary Characteristics

Usefulness: Usefulness is the key determinant of attitude in the technology acceptance research field. Davis (1989) defined usefulness as "the degree to which a person believes that using a particular system would enhance his or her job performance," and found that usefulness is the strongest predictor of behavioral intention. Many researchers support Davis' findings about usefulness (Taylor & Todd, 1995; Venkatesh et al., 2003). Venkatesh et al. (2003) called usefulness as performance expectancy and defined it as "the degree to which an individual believes that using the system will help him or her to attain gains in job performance." One of the comments of the participants about usefulness is:

I ask people who use the service for its functionalities and try to understand how I can benefit from it in my job. Then, I make a decision whether or not to use the service (Female, Nurse, 25).

Another comment:

If I think that information given from the service is useful for me, I start using the service (Male, Potential User, 25).

Many comments were about the usefulness of the service. Therefore, it can be said that health information service users pay great attention to how the service would improve their job performance. These findings are in parallel with previous research findings (Davis, 1989; Taylor & Todd, 1995; Venkatesh et al., 2003).

Ease of use: Perceived ease of use (EoU) defined as "the degree to which a person believes that using a particular system would be free of effort" is one of the core constructs in TAM (Davis, 1989). Significant effect of EoU on behavior intention was also confirmed by many other researchers (Taylor & Todd, 1995; Venkatesh & Davis, 2000). Moreover, comments of potential users about the EoU supported these findings. Two of these comments are given below:

There are some questions in my mind. One of them is about ease-of-use. Effortless use of the service affects my intention about service usage (Male, Potential User, 25).

... the more the service is simple and easy to use, the more people will intend to use it (Male, Doctor, 50).

Social Influence

Social influence contains three main constructs: subjective norms defined as "The person's perception that most people who are important to him think he should or should not perform the behavior in question" (Ajzen, 1991), social factors, which is "The individual's internalization of the reference group's subjective culture, and specific interpersonal agreements that the individual has made with others, in specific social situations" (Thompson, Higgins, & Howell, 1991), and image defined as "The degree to which use of an innovation is perceived to enhance one's image or status in one's social system" (Moore & Benbasat, 1991; Venkatesh et al., 2003). In the study, eight of the interviewees answered the question that

stated "Do you attempt to use the service if you notice someone who uses it?" as follows:

I try the service if I see someone who uses it (Male, Doctor, 50).

In the study, participants referred to the subjective norms and image constructs of social influence. People are influenced by others' opinions and behaviors. People may use a service if he or she believes that becoming one of the service users will improve his or her social status.

Facilitating Conditions

User guidance: In the previous studies, facilitating conditions were found significant when they were examined with intermediary variables like age or experience. For example, it was found that they only matter for older users (Venkatesh et al., 2003). However, in the research, participants did not mention age or other variables when talking about the facilitating conditions. They indicated that all of the users need some help to use the service:

Users may need a user's guide that explains how to use the service (Female, Potential User, 22).

DISCUSSION

As a result of the data gathered through these interviews, we propose a health service adoption taxonomy, which is shown in Figure 5 and the weights of variables in Table 4. It has been produced with the constructs that were found significant by the participants and researchers cited in this article.

According to the taxonomy, health service adoption has five main aspects: service characteristics, user characteristics, intermediary variables, social factors, and facilitating conditions. Three of these aspects contain some subcategories.

Figure 5. Proposed health service adoption taxonomy

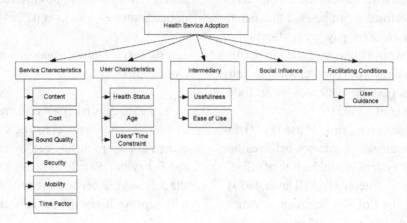

Table 4. Weights of health service adoption taxonomy

Class	Study
Service Characteristics	55%
User Characteristics	26%
Intermediary	8%
Social Factors	6%
Facilitating Conditions	5%

While cost, content, sound quality, security, mobility, and time factor constitute subcategories of the service characteristics, health status, age, and time constraint compose users' sub categories. Usefulness and EoU are two of the intermediary variables.

Finally, a theoretical framework is developed (Figure 6). This framework draws upon both prior research, such as TAM and TRA, and the findings of this study. A larger scale data would help us to test the relationship proposed in this framework.

We found that service characteristics have more impact on usefulness when compared with other variables. Rich and accurate content were indicated to be more useful by the interviewees. Also, two of the participants said that the service

Figure 6. Propositions for future research

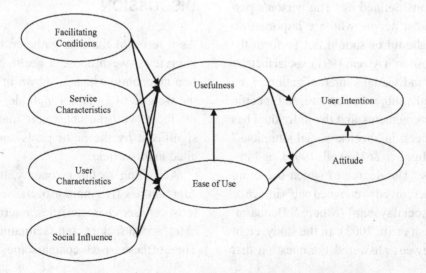

capabilities, such as reminders for medicine time, make the service more useful. Mobility offers advantages to the service by enhancing job performance of the doctors as well. Variables in Table 5 are collected from 17 different technology acceptance and adoption papers (see Table 1 for details), and grouped according to relevant classes. Then, occurrence number of these classes has been determined to calculate the percentage values in the *literature* column in Table 5. Values in the *study* column in Table 5 are computed by dividing sum of weights of each class studied in this paper to the grand total weight of these classes. According to Table 5, classes are examined equally in the literature. However, most of the comments in this study were about the service characteristics, indicating a major need to research service characteristics.

When we examined the data acquired from the interviews (see Appendix C), we observed further implications of our findings. These implications can be interpreted as future propositions as listed in Table 6.

These propositions will need to be tested with further data collection.

Table 5. Literature and study comparison

Class	Literature	Study
User Characteristics	24%	26%
Service Characteristics	21%	55%
Ease of Use	16%	3%
Social Factors	15%	6%
Usefulness	15%	5%
Facilitating Conditions	9%	5%

CONCLUSION

This article contends that health information service adoption decisions of users are influenced by service characteristics like cost, content, sound quality, security, mobility, and time factor; user characteristics like health status, age, and users' time constraint; social factors; and facilitating conditions like user guidance. In line with previous technology adoption studies, usefulness and ease of use are found two significant determinants of user behavior.

Based on the findings, electronic health service designers and developers may focus on financial cost of the developed service. The cost of the service should be less than the cost of visiting a doctor. Moreover, content of the service should be related to the doctors' profession and users' requirements. Users attach importance to reach accurate, relevant, and quality information in a minimum response time. Another implication is that security and time factors should be taken into consideration when designing such services. Users do not prefer using services that are insecure and require a lot of time. Also, similar to prior research (Tung et al., 2008; Venkatesh & Davis, 2000), people intend to use systems that are effortless and improve job performance of the user.

For future study, a comprehensive quantitative research with large sample size can be conducted to test validity of the results. Proposed prototype can be expanded by adding new functionalities and capabilities to examine their affect on the health service adoption process.

Table 6. Propositions developed for future study

Ease of Use is influenced by the following attributes of the health services: user guidance, sound quality, age, and language.
Usefulness is influenced by the following attributes of the health services: content, service capability, mobility, and job fit.
Attitude of the potential users is influenced by the following attributes of the health services: cost, health status, social influence, usefulness, content, users' time constraint, and security. *Content quality is influenced by the following attribute of the health services: communication standards.* *Service quality is influenced by the following attribute of the health services: sound quality, communication standards, and language.*

REFERENCES

Ajzen, I. (1991). The theory of planned behavior. *Organizational Behavior and Human Decision Processes, 50*(2), 179–211. doi:10.1016/0749-5978(91)90020-T

Al-Qirim, N. (2007). Championing telemedicine adoption and utilization in healthcare organizations in New Zealand. *International Journal of Medical Informatics, 76,* 42–54. doi:10.1016/j.ijmedinf.2006.02.001

Aubert, B. A., & Hamel, G. (2001). Adoption of smart cards in the medical sector: The Canadian experience. *Social Science & Medicine, 53,* 879–894. doi:10.1016/S0277-9536(00)00388-9

Berghout, B. M., Eminovic, N., Keizer, N. F., & Birnie, E. (2007). Evaluation of general practitioner's time investment during a store-and-forward teledermatology consultation. *International Journal of Medical Informatics, 76,* 384–391. doi:10.1016/j.ijmedinf.2007.04.004

Biermann, E., Dietrich, W., Rihl, J., & Standl, E. (2002). Are there time and cost savings by using telemanagement for patients on intensified insulin therapy? A randomised, controlled trial. *Computer Methods and Programs in Biomedicine, 69,* 137–146. doi:10.1016/S0169-2607(02)00037-8

Brink, J. L., Moorman, P. W., Boer, M. F., Pruyn, J. F. A., Verwoerd, C. D. A., & Bemmel, J. H. (2005). Involving the patient: A prospective study on use, appreciation and effectiveness of an information system in head and neck cancer care. *International Journal of Medical Informatics, 74,* 839–849. doi:10.1016/j.ijmedinf.2005.03.021

Bruner, G. C., & Kumar, A. (2005). Explaining consumer acceptance of handheld Internet devices. *Journal of Business Research, 58,* 553–558. doi:10.1016/j.jbusres.2003.08.002

Chae, Y. M., Lee, J. H., Ho, S. H., Kim, H. J., Jun, K. H., & Won, J. U. (2001). Patient satisfaction with telemedicine in home health services for the elderly. *International Journal of Medical Informatics, 61,* 167–173. doi:10.1016/S1386-5056(01)00139-3

Chang, I. J., Hwang, H. G., Hung, M. C., Lin, M. H., & Yen, D. C. (2007). Factors affecting the adoption of electronic signature: Executives' perspective of hospital information department. *Decision Support Systems, 44,* 350–359. doi:10.1016/j.dss.2007.04.006

Chau, P. Y. K., & Hu, P. J. H. (2002). Investigating healthcare professionals' decisions to accept telemedicine technology: An empirical test of competing theories. *Information & Management, 39,* 297–311. doi:10.1016/S0378-7206(01)00098-2

Chen, I. J., Yang, K. F., Tang, F. I., Huang, C. H., & Yu, S. (2008). Applying the technology acceptance model to explore public health nurses' intentions towards web-based learning: A cross-sectional questionnaire survey. *International Journal of Nursing Studies, 45*(6), 869–878. doi:10.1016/j.ijnurstu.2006.11.011

Cheng, T. C. E., Lam, D. Y. C., & Yeung, A. C. L. (2006). Adoption of internet banking: An empirical study in Hong Kong. *Decision Support Systems, 42,* 1558–1572. doi:10.1016/j.dss.2006.01.002

Davis, F. D. (1989). Perceived usefulness, perceived ease of use, and user acceptance of information technology. *MIS Quarterly, 13*(3), 319–339. doi:10.2307/249008

Dishaw, M. T., & Strong, D. M. (1999). Extending the technology acceptance model with task-technology fit constructs. *Information & Management, 36,* 9–21. doi:10.1016/S0378-7206(98)00101-3

Fishbein, M., & Ajzen, I. (1975). *Belief, attitude, intention and behavior: An introduction to theory and research.* Reading, UK: Addison-Wesley.

Gagnon, M. P., Godin, G., Gagné, C., Fortin, J. P., Lamothe, L., & Reinharz, D. (2003). An adaptation of the theory of interpersonal behavior to the study of telemedicine adoption by physicians. *International Journal of Medical Informatics, 71*, 103–115. doi:10.1016/S1386-5056(03)00094-7

Giorgino, T., Azzini, I., Rognonia, C., Quaglinia, S., Stefanelli, M., & Gretter, R. (2005). Automated spoken dialogue system for hypertensive patient home management. *International Journal of Medical Informatics, 74*, 159–167. doi:10.1016/j.ijmedinf.2004.04.026

Glykas, M., & Chytas, P. (2004). Technological innovations in asthma patient monitoring and care. *Expert Systems with Applications, 27*, 121–131. doi:10.1016/j.eswa.2003.12.007

Goodhue, D. L. (1995). Understanding user evaluations of information systems. *Management Science, 41*, 1827–1844. doi:10.1287/mnsc.41.12.1827

Hsieh, R. K. C., Hjelm, N. M., Lee, J. C. K., & Aldis, J. W. (2001). Telemedicine in China. *International Journal of Medical Informatics, 61*, 139–146. doi:10.1016/S1386-5056(01)00136-8

Karahanna, E., Straub, D. W., & Chervany, N. L. (1999). Information technology adoption across time: A cross-sectional comparison of pre-adoption and post-adoption beliefs. *MIS Quarterly, 23*(2), 183–213. doi:10.2307/249751

Kleinrock, L. (1996). Nomadicity: Anytime, anywhere in a disconnected world. *Mobile Networks and Applications, 1*(4), 351–357.

Knickman, J. R., Hunt, K. A., Snell, E. K., Marie, L., Alecxih, B., & Kennell, D. L. (2003). Wealth patterns among elderly Americans: Implications for healthcare affordability. *Health Affairs, 22*, 168–174. doi:10.1377/hlthaff.22.3.168

Lee, R. D., & Tuljapurkar, S. (1994). Stochastic population forecasts for the United States: Beyond high, medium and low. *Journal of the American Statistical Association, 89*, 175–189. doi:10.2307/2290980

Levit, K., Smith, C., Cowan, C., Lazeby, H., Sensenig, A., & Catlin, A. (2003). Trends in U.S. healthcare spending 2001. *Health Affairs, 22*, 154–164. doi:10.1377/hlthaff.22.1.154

Liu, J. E., Pothiban, L., Lu, Z., & Khamphonsiri, T. (2000). Computer knowledge, attitudes, and skills of nurses in People's Hospital of Beijing Medical University. *Computers in Nursing, 18*(4), 197–206.

Liu, L., & Ma, Q. (2005). The impact of service level on the acceptance of application service oriented medical records. *Information & Management, 42*, 1121–1135. doi:10.1016/j.im.2004.12.004

Magrabi, F., Lovell, N. H., & Celle, B. G. (1999). A web-based approach for electrocardiogram monitoring in the home. *International Journal of Medical Informatics, 54*, 145–153. doi:10.1016/S1386-5056(98)00177-4

Mathieson, K., Peacock, E., & Chin, W. W. (2001). Extending the technology acceptance model: The influence of perceived user resources. *The Data Base for Advances in Information Systems, 32*(3), 86–112.

Moore, G. C., & Benbasat, I. (1991). Development of an instrument to measure the perceptions of adopting an information technology innovation. *Information Systems Research, 2*(3), 192–222. doi:10.1287/isre.2.3.192

Ozen, Ç., & Basoglu, N. (2006, July 9-13). Impact of man-machine interaction factors on enterprise resource planning (ERP) software design. In *Technology Management for the Global Future, 2006 (PICMET 2006)* (Vol. 5, pp. 2335-2341). IEEE.

Reinhardt, U. E. (2000). Healthcare for the aging baby boom: Lessons from abroad. *The Journal of Economic Perspectives, 14*, 71–83.

Rialle, V., Lamy, J. B., Noury, N., & Bajolle, L. (2003). Telemonitoring of patients at home: A software agent approach. *Computer Methods and Programs in Biomedicine, 72*, 257–268. doi:10.1016/S0169-2607(02)00161-X

Schaper, L. K., & Pervan, G. P. (2003). ICT and OTs: A model of information and communication technology acceptance and utilization by occupational therapists. *International Journal of Medical Informatics, 71*, 103–115. doi:10.1016/S1386-5056(03)00094-7

Silver, J. (2004). *Attributional coding in essential guide to qualitative methods in organizational research.* Thousand Oaks, CA: SAGE Publications.

Simon, J. S., Rundall, T. G., & Shortell, S. M. (2007). Adoption of order entry with decision support for chronic care by physician organizations. *Journal of the American Medical Informatics Association, 14*, 432–439. doi:10.1197/jamia.M2271

Taylor, S., & Todd, P. (1995). Assessing IT usage: The role of prior experience. *MIS Quarterly, 19*(4), 561–570. doi:10.2307/249633

Thompson, R. L., Higgins, C. A., & Howell, J. M. (1991). Personal computing: Toward a conceptual model of utilization. *MIS Quarterly, 15*(1), 124–143. doi:10.2307/249443

Topacan, U., Basoglu, A. N., & Daim, T. U. (2008, July 27-31). Exploring the success factors of health information service adoption. In *Portland International Conference on Management of Engineering & Technology, 2008 (PICMET 2008)* (pp. 2453-2461). IEEE.

Tung, F. C., Chang, S. C., & Chou, C. M. (2008). An extension of trust and TAM model with IDT in the adoption of the electronic logistics information system in HIS in the medical industry. *International Journal of Medical Informatics, 77*, 324–335. doi:10.1016/j.ijmedinf.2007.06.006

Venkatesh, V., & Davis, F. D. (2000). A theoretical extension of the technology acceptance model: Four longitudinal field studies. *Management Science, 45*(2), 186–204. doi:10.1287/mnsc.46.2.186.11926

Venkatesh, V., Morris, M. G., Davis, G. B., & Davis, F. D. (2003). User acceptance of information technology: Toward a unified view. *MIS Quarterly, 27*(3), 425–478.

Wilson, E. V., & Lankton, N. K. (2004). Modeling patients' acceptance of provider-delivered e-health. *Journal of the American Medical Informatics Association, 11*(4), 241–248. doi:10.1197/jamia.M1475

Yang, B. H., & Rhee, S. (2000). Development of the ring sensor for healthcare automation. *Robotics and Autonomous Systems, 30*, 273–281. doi:10.1016/S0921-8890(99)00092-5

Yusof, M. M., Kuljis, J., Papazafeiropoulou, A., & Stergioulas, L. K. (2008). An evaluation framework for health information systems: Human, organization and technology-fit factors (HOT-fit). *International Journal of Medical Informatics, 77*, 386–398. doi:10.1016/j.ijmedinf.2007.08.011

APPENDIX A: INTERVIEW QUESTIONS

1. Have you ever used a mobile service?
   a. If you have used, which mobile service(s) did you use?
   b. Are you interested in new technologies?
2. Would you want to use the proposed service?
   a. According to you, which functionality/properties of the service are beneficial?
   b. In your opinion, which functionality/properties of the service are inadequate?
3. Do you advise the service to your colleagues and friends?
   a. According to you, which functionality/properties of the service do you advice?
   b. According to you, which functionality/properties of the service do not you advice?
4. If you encounter someone who uses the service, do you attempt to use it?
5. What do you think about the one that uses the service?
6. Did you need help while using the service?
   a. If you need, in which part of the service do you need help?
7. Do you think the service is ease of use? What type of difficulties did you encounter while you were using the service?
8. Is the information given by the service useful? Which information is the most useful for you?
9. Do you suggest any extra information for the service?
10. How much money would you want pay for using the service?
11. Do you mind privacy and security of your data stored in the service?
12. Do you think that people intend to use this service? In your opinion, who are the people that need this service at most?
13. What do you think about the interface's sound used in the service?
14. Do you have any additional comment for the proposed service?

APPENDIX B: DIALOGUE BETWEEN PATIENT/PHYSICIAN AND THE SERVICE

Patient Dialogue

Service: Hello. What is your username?
Patient: Tiger *(okay)*
Service: Enter your password.
Patient: Enter 1224 *(okay)*
Service: Select your operation. Enter Meal, Enter Information, Meal Suggestion, Get Caloric Information, Exit.
Patient: Enter Meal *(okay)*
Service: What did you eat or drink?
Patient: I eat hamburger *(okay)*
Service: How much you eat or drink
Patient: One *(okay)*
Service: Do you eat or drink anything else?

Patient: Yes *(okay)*

Service: What did you eat or drink?

Patient: I drink coke *(okay)*

Service: How much you eat or drink?

Patient: I drink one bottle *(okay)*

Service: Do you eat or drink anything else?

Patient: No *(okay)*

Service: Select your operation. Enter Meal, Enter Information, Meal Suggestion, Get Calorie Information, Exit.

Patient: Meal Suggestion *(okay)*

Service: You can eat 1 Cups of Spaghetti, 3/4 Cup Tossed Salad, 1 Cup Apple Juice. Do I repeat or return main menu.

Patient: Repeat *(okay)*

Service: You can eat 1 Cups of Spaghetti, 3/4 Cup Tossed Salad, 1 Cup Apple Juice. Do I repeat or return main menu.

Patient: Return main menu *(okay)*

Service: Select your operation. Enter Meal, Enter Information, Meal Suggestion, Get Calorie Information, Exit.

Patient: Enter Information *(okay)*

Service: Select your operation. Enter movement or exercise, Enter Trauma, Enter pain, Enter drug, Return main menu

Patient: Enter Pain *(okay)*

Service: What is your pain?

Patient: I have headache and chest pain *(okay)*

Service: Select your operation. Enter movement or exercise, Enter Trauma, Enter pain, Enter drug, Return main menu

Patient: Enter movement or exercise *(okay)*

Service: What type of movement or exercise you did?

Patient: Today, I run 3000 meters and ride a bicycle 6000 meters.

Service: Select your operation. Enter movement or exercise, Enter Trauma, Enter pain, Enter drug, Return main menu

Patient: Enter drug *(okay)*

Service: Enter drug information.

Patient: I get one sulfonylurea.*(okay)*

Service: Select your operation. Enter movement or exercise, Enter Trauma, Enter pain, Enter drug, Return main menu

Patient: Return Main Menu *(okay)*

Service: Select your operation. Enter Meal, Enter Information, Meal Suggestion, Get Calorie Information, Exit.

Patient: Get Calorie Information *(okay)*

Service: Today you got 4200 cal and you can got 1000 more in today. Do I repeat or return main menu.

Patient: Return main menu *(okay)*

Service: Select your operation. Enter Meal, Enter Information, Meal Suggestion, Get Calorie Information, Exit.

Patient: Exit

Service: Bye bye

Warning to Take Medicine

Service: Hello Mrs. James. This is a reminder service of the Medical Record Server. It is time to take sulfonylurea. Bye Bye.

Warning to Enter Information

Service: Hello Mrs. James. This is a reminder service of the Medical Record Server. You do not enter any information to the system last 8 hours. Thank you. Bye Bye.

Physician Dialogue

Service: Hello. What is your username?

Physician: Tiger *(okay)*

Service: Enter your password.

Physician: Enter 1224 *(okay)*

Service: Select your operation. Calorie Information, Blood Glucose Information, Blood Pressure Information, Exit

Physician: Calorie Information *(okay)*

Service: What is your patient name?

Physician: Peter Brown *(okay)*

Service: Peter Brown got 3000 calories in today. He can take 1230 more calories. Do I repeat or return main menu.

Physician: Return main menu *(okay)*

Service: Select your operation. Calorie Information, Blood Glucose Information, Blood Pressure Information, Exit

Physician: Blood Glucose Information *(okay)*

Service: What is your patient name?

Physician: Mary Brown *(okay)*

Service: There are two Mary Brown. What is the birth date of Mary Brown?

Physician: 4th of April *(okay)*

Service: Blood glucose of Mary Brown is 6 mmol/l and recorded at 10:00 am in today. Do I repeat or return main menu.

Physician: Repeat

Service: Blood glucose of Mary Brown is 6 mmol/l and recorded at 10:00 am in today. Do I repeat or return main menu.

Physician: Return main menu *(okay)*

Service: Select your operation. Calorie Information, Blood Glucose Information, Blood Pressure Information, Exit

Physician: Exit

Service: Bye Bye

Warning to Physician

Service: Hello Mr. James. This is an alert service of the Medical Record Server. Blood Glucose level of patient Mary Brown decreases under 3 mmol/l. Bye Bye.

APPENDIX C: DATA EXTRACTED FROM THE INTERVIEWS (TABLE 7)

Table 7.

Class	Independent	Content Quality		Service Quality		Ease of Use		Usefulness		Attitude		Grand Total	
		No.	%	No.	Percent	No.	Percent	No.	Percent	No.	Percent	No.	Percent
Service Characteristics	Communication standards	2	0.71%	2	0.71%							4	1.42%
Service Characteristics	Sound Quality			5	1.77%	8	2.84%					13	4.61%
Service Characteristics	Language			2	0.71%	5	1.77%					7	2.48%
Service Characteristics	Accurate Input			1	0.35%			2	0.71%	3	1.06%	6	2.13%
Service Characteristics	Output Quality			1	0.35%			2	0.71%	2	0.71%	5	1.77%
User Characteristics	User Involvement			1	0.35%			2	0.71%	2	0.71%	5	1.77%
Service Characteristics	Customizable			1	0.35%			1	0.35%			2	0.71%
Facilitating Conditions	User Guidance					10	3.55%					10	3.55%
User Characteristics	Age					7	2.48%			8	2.84%	15	5.32%
Service Characteristics	Input Type					4	1.42%			3	1.06%	7	2.48%
User Characteristics	Experience					4	1.42%			3	1.06%	7	2.48%
Service Characteristics	Input Quantity					3	1.06%			1	0.35%	4	1.42%
Service Characteristics	Sound					3	1.06%			1	0.35%	4	1.42%

continues on following page

Table 7. Continued

Class	Independent	Content Quality		Service Quality		Ease of Use		Usefulness		Attitude		Grand Total	
		No.	%	No.	Percent	No.	Percent	No.	Percent	No.	Percent	No.	Percent
Service Characteristics	Length of Menu Items					3	1.06%				0.35%	3	1.06%
User Characteristics	Tech-savvy					2	0.71%			5	1.77%	7	2.48%
Facilitating Conditions	Help Button					2	0.71%			2	0.71%	4	1.42%
Service Characteristics	Device Type					2	0.71%					2	0.71%
Service Characteristics	Service Complexity					1	0.35%			1	0.35%	2	0.71%
Service Characteristics	Input Quality					1	0.35%					1	0.35%
Service Characteristics	Content							16	5.67%	12	4.26%	28	9.93%
Service Characteristics	Service Capabilities							5	1.77%	2	0.71%	7	2.48%
Service Characteristics	Mobility							3	1.06%	6	2.13%	9	3.19%
Service Characteristics	Job Fit							3	1.06%	4	1.42%	7	2.48%
Service Characteristics	Rapid Response							1	0.35%	1	0.35%	2	0.71%
Service Characteristics	Service Accuracy							1	0.35%	1	0.35%	2	0.71%
Service Characteristics	Cost									16	5.67%	16	5.67%
User Characteristics	Health Status									16	5.67%	16	5.67%
Social Influence	Social Influence									15	5.32%	15	5.32%
Intermediary	Usefulness									14	4.96%	14	4.96%
User Characteristics	Users' Time Constraint									9	3.19%	9	3,19%
Service Characteristics	Security			1	0.35%					9	3.19%	10	3,55%

continues on following page

Table 7. Continued

Class	Independent	Content Quality		Service Quality		Ease of Use		Usefulness		Attitude		Grand Total	
		No.	%	No.	Percent	No.	Percent	No.	Percent	No.	Percent	No.	Percent
Service Characteristics	Time Factor									8	2.84%	8	2.84%
Service Characteristics	Face-to-face Communication									6	2.13%	6	2.13%
Intermediary	Ease of Use			1	0.35%			1	0.35%	6	2.13%	8	2.84%
User Characteristics	Income									4	1.42%	4	1.42%
User Characteristics	Educational Level									3	1.06%	3	1.06%
User Characteristics	Gender									3	1.06%	3	1.06%
User Characteristics	Requirement									3	1.06%	3	1.06%
Social Influence	Image									2	0.71%	2	0.71%
Service Characteristics	Service Quality									1	0.35%	1	0.35%
User Characteristics	Trust									1	0.35%	1	0.35%
Grand Total		2	0.71%	15	5.32%	55	19.50%	37	13.12%	173	61.35%	282	100.00%

This work was previously published in International Journal of Information Systems in the Service Sector, Volume 2, Issue 1, edited by John Wang, pp. 71-93, copyright 2010 by IGI Publishing (an imprint of IGI Global).

Chapter 6
Temporal Aspects of Information Technology Use:
Increasing Shift Work Effectiveness

Roslin V. Hauck
Illinois State University, USA

Sherry M. B. Thatcher
University of Louisville, USA

Suzanne P. Weisband
University of Arizona, USA

ABSTRACT

The dynamic nature of organizations and technologies require a comprehensive understanding of how organizational forms and information technology interact. While previous research and theories of information technology have investigated aspects such as organizational structure, individual and group behavior, and inter-organizational relationships, shift work, an important temporal aspect often found in service organizations, is surprisingly absent in the literature. The purpose of this paper is to examine the effect that shift work has on employee use and satisfaction with information technology. The results of a field study of a police organization indicate that information technology systems are valued differently by workers on different shifts. The authors discuss how this research helps advance theories of technology use and effectiveness (such as task-technology fit and technology acceptance model) and present important practical implications of this study for strategic alignment of technology in the areas of systems design, implementation, addressing the needs of peripheral workers, and resource management.

DOI: 10.4018/978-1-4666-0044-7.ch006

Copyright © 2012, IGI Global. Copying or distributing in print or electronic forms without written permission of IGI Global is prohibited.

INTRODUCTION

The dynamic nature of organizations and technologies necessitate that we develop a comprehensive understanding of how organizational forms and information technology interact to affect work. While previous research and theories of information technology have investigated aspects such as organizational structure, individual and group behavior, and inter-organizational relationships, an important temporal aspect of service organizations, shift work, is surprisingly absent in the literature.

Although studies have investigated many aspects of shift work, the majority of these studies have not considered relatively recent organizational changes. Perhaps one of the biggest changes that we have seen in organizations is in the use of information and communication technology to enable new ways of working. For example, prior to the introduction of email, the Internet, and knowledge management systems, night shift workers were limited with regard to the people and resources that they were able to access, most of which operated on a 9-to-5 schedule. Now, night shift workers are able to utilize different technologies to access resources that were not previously available to them. Thus, this research examines how information technology unleashes the potential to leverage shift work in a way that has not yet been studied.

In May 2004, more than 17.7% of wage and salary workers, or approximately 21 million employees in the United States worked alternative shifts that at least partially fell outside of the standard working hours (i.e., hours other than 9am-5pm) (McMenamin, 2007). Shift work in general refers to a schedule of work that falls outside the standard daytime working hours (Spurgeon & Cooper, 2000). Shift work is most prevalent in organizations providing 24-hour services. For example, it is estimated that 55% of protective service employees, 42% of employees in food services, 37% of employees in transportation services, and 36% of health service employees are shift workers (Beers, 2000). With the increased need for organizations to work effectively across time zones in the international arena (Holsapple, Luo, & Morton, 2000) and given the advent of technologies that support work without temporal boundaries, shift work has become a more prevalent means of work in all types of organizations (Fandray, 2000). Thus, it is imperative to understand the relationship between shift work and information technology use.

There is considerable literature on the effects of shift work on a number of different types of physiological, organizational, and social variables (Furnham & Hughes, 1999). Research on the relationship between shift work and physiological outcomes has shown that night shift workers are more likely to suffer from sleep problems, body function problems, and gastrointestinal disorders than day shift workers (e.g., Bøgglid, Burr, Tüchsen, & Jeppesen, 2001; Morshead, 2002; Oexman, Knotts, & Koch, 2002). Studies looking at shift work and organizational variables have shown that working the night shift is related to job dissatisfaction (Barton, 1994; Furnham & Hughes, 1999) and job stress (Barton & Folkard, 1991; Kandonlin, 1993). Night shift workers also suffer more familial and home conflicts (e.g., Dunham, 1977; Demerouti, Geurts, Bakker, & Euwema, 2004) as community and life activities are often built around a traditional 9-5 day. While the effects of shift work on physiological, organizational, and social variables have been studied, there is little in the literature examining the relationship between shift work and information technology use. Thus, we are interested in exploring the effects that a shift system has on information technology use and productivity.

To frame our examination of shift and technology, we focus on the work context of professional service providers who must provide job coverage 24 hours a day, 7 days a week. Emergency medical technicians, patrol officers, nurses, fire fighters, and television news crews are examples of these service providers. These types of jobs require trained individuals who must often make immediate decisions based on the information and resources currently available to them (Geisler, 2009; Tucker, Edmondson, & Spear, 2002).

In this paper, we present the results of a field study at a police organization to explore the effects that shift work has on information technology use, effectiveness, and satisfaction with technology. To explain these expected effects we build off of and extend existing theories in the areas of task-technology fit and technology acceptance models. The results of this study will help organizations that use a shift system better understand how information technology use can differ between employees working different shifts.

LITERATURE REVIEW

Although there are different types of shift work that have been studied in the literature (see e.g., Kogi, 1985), the type of shift work that is of interest to our study is fixed shift-work. Fixed shift-work refers to the type of permanent, non-rotating shift work where specific activities are done during specific day or night shifts (Blau & Lunz, 1999; Sagie & Krausz, 2003). Because fixed shift employees continuously work the same shift, we can be more certain that the work patterns and behaviors that are of interest of this study are truly established.

An underlying issue of our study is that in many organizations employing a shift system, the type of work required during the night shift can be inherently different from work required during the day shift. In other words, the context of work (i.e., the night shift) affects the content of the work, (i.e, work characteristics) (Bøgglid et al., 2001). Before discussing the effects of shift on technology use, we must first review the underlying mechanisms that differentiate work performed during the night from work performed during the day. There are three aspects of work that may be different depending on the shift one

works: level of routinization, workload differences, and resource need and availability.

Routinization refers to the degree to which the content of the job (i.e., tasks) are standard with little variability (Baba & Jamal, 1992). Studies indicate that routinization levels are inherent to the work context found during different shifts. Blau and Lunz (1999) in their study of medical technologists found that day shift technologists had a lower level of routinization (i.e., more task variety) than night shift technologists. While Blau and Lunz's 1999 study found that the night shift was related to higher job content routinization, the sample used in the study were medical technicians responsible for conducting various laboratory tests. However, the opposite may also be true in different work contexts; for example, work during the night shift for protective services such as the police may result in lower routinization of tasks.

Another way in which shift can affect work is by affecting workload, the amount of work conducted by a worker in a specified time period. Different industries will use different measures of workload. For example, in a police organization, workload can be measured by the number of cases that an officer or detective handles (see e.g., Punkett & Lundman, 2003), while in the medical field context, workload can be measured by number of activities performed on patients (see e.g., Cass, Smith, Unthank, Starling, & Collins, 2003). Previous research has found a relationship between workload and shift work. For example, researchers observed a drop in work activities and workload for nurses on the night shift (Grant, 1979). In contrast, Sagie and Krausz (2003) looked at the relationship between shift work and psychological correlates for nurses working in different shifts and in different departments. Nurses who worked the night shift perceived a higher workload than nurses who worked other shifts (Sagie & Krausz, 2003).

A third aspect of shift work is the need for, and availability of, resources. Resources come in many forms such as knowledge from other individuals, paper documents, technological support, supervisors, and social support derived from coworkers. The ability and level of effort needed for employees to access resources are important factors in problem solving (Tucker et al., 2002). Without the ability to access key resources, an employee will be less likely to engage in problem-solving activities (Geisler, 2009). During the day shift, workers have a greater window of opportunity to access more resources and more types of resources since more individuals tend to work during day shifts (Dunham, 1977; Zedeck, Jackson, & Marca, 1983). Night shift workers have limited access to resources and are often faced with the challenge of finding and accessing required resources. For example, during the day shift, nurses have access to many other nurses and physicians while nurses working the night shift are more limited in their access to these resources (Maloney, 1982).

Given that these aspects of shift (i.e., routinization, workload, and resource availability) affect employee effectiveness, it is reasonable to assess the extent to which technology supports tasks when done in different shifts. Using the theory of task-technology fit to develop our hypotheses, we examine the impact of shift on technology use, technology satisfaction, and employee effectiveness.

HYPOTHESIS DEVELOPMENT

The task-technology fit (TTF) model has been used in numerous contexts to explain the usage of different information technologies (see e.g., Dennis, Wixom, & Venderberg, 2001; Dishaw & Strong, 1998). TTF research indicates that the utilization of information technology and its positive impact on individual performance is a result of the fit between the technology and the tasks it supports (Goodhue & Thompson, 1995). The better the fit between what the technology is able to do and the needs defined by the job task, the higher the individual's performance. Task

technology fit is an ideal framework for studying shift work because tasks take on different characteristics when conducted in different shifts.

As we have discussed previously, the level of available resources and the need for resources can be influenced by the shift worked. For example, nurses may not need a wide variety of resources in a non-intensive care unit during the night shift as the population of patients is stable and the tasks are relatively routine. On the other hand, during the day shift, a nurse in the same non-intensive care unit may need more and different resources since existing patients may leave, new patients arrive, and doctors are prescribing new forms of care for various patients (Maloney, 1982). In police work the type of task required of police officers is affected by the shift as many criminals operate under the cover of night. Thus, the type and amount of resources needed for patrol officers working the night shift vary substantially from that required during the day shift (Stephens & Long, 2000). Given the tasks and needs of night shift workers, there is a better "fit" between what information technology can offer for night shift workers than for day shift workers.

Access to certain resources and expertise may only be available during the day (Dunham, 1977). For example, police officers who work the day shift can easily contact detectives, who work typical day shift hours, for information on a particular suspect or case (Stephens & Long, 2000). Because detectives typically do not work at night unless they are processing a specific crime, officers in the night shift do not have access to detectives as a resource and are forced to find alternative resources. Buren and Stenzel (1984) found that over half of the police departments using permanent shift assignments felt that the lack of communication between personnel working different shifts was a concern. Nurses must contend with the fact that during the night shift there are fewer physicians and staff available for consultation (Grant, 1979). Therefore, in a society where the majority of people work from 9-to-5, the potential for access to human-related sources of knowledge decreases for night-shift workers (Dunham, 1977). Use of information technology can improve resource access for employees working the night shift.

We know from earlier studies that employees who are peripheral to an organization or isolated in some fashion can benefit from technology. Scientists who are not in research intensive institutions (e.g., have fewer resources for conducting research) benefit more from the use of technologies than their mainstream counterparts (Hesse, Sproull, Kiesler, & Walsh, 1993; Luo & Olson, 2006). Similarly, we expect that night-shift employees who have task variability may benefit from information technology as they may be able to access some of the information they desire.

While task-technology fit suggests that specific technologies should be used for specific tasks, individuals do not always act as recommended. The theory of reasoned action (TRA; Fishbein & Ajzen, 1975) and its extension, the theory of planned behavior (TPB; Azjen & Madden, 1986) posits that behaviors (e.g., to use a particular technology) stems from user intention to engage in the behavior. The antecedents of user intention are an individual's attitude, the subjective norm towards the behavior, and perceived behavioral control (Agrawal, 2000; Ajzen & Madden, 1986). Thus, it is not only important to consider the extent to which a technology is right for the task but it is also important to understand employees' attitudes and intentions about using a particular technology.

The Technology Acceptance Model (TAM) developed by Davis (1989) draws from both TRA and TPB to refer specifically to the adoption of information technology and includes perceived usefulness and ease of use into the model. TAM argues that technology will be accepted and used when a user believes that the technology is useful to her/him. TAM has been tested extensively with various types of technologies such as groupware (Lou, Luo, & Strong, 2000), CASE tools (Dishaw & Strong, 1999), spreadsheets (Venkatesh & Da-

vis, 1996) and e-learning (Liao & Huang, 2009). The TAM model has been modified by a number of researchers to include antecedents to perceived usefulness and perceived ease of use. For example, in TAM2 Venkatesh and Davis (2000) include the constructs of individual differences, system characteristics, social influence, and facilitating conditions as being determinants of perceived usefulness and ease of use.

In our current study, we expand the theories of technology adoption to include the specific organizational arrangement of shift-work. The shift that an employee works is one factor that may influence the perceived usefulness of a technology. Day-shift employees have relatively more access to social networks and other resources available at a low cost (in terms of time and effort), and will view the technology to be less useful and thus, be less likely to use available technologies. On the other hand, we expect that night-shift employees will perceive technology to be highly useful and be more likely to accept and use technology as it is a resource existing in a resource-constrained environment relative to day-shift employees.

H1a: Professional service employees who work during the night shift will report a higher level of general computer use than employees who work during the day shift.

H1b: Professional service employees who work during the night shift will report a higher level of work-related information systems use than employees who work during the day shift.

Few studies have investigated the extent to which shift work affects effectiveness. On the one hand, working during non-traditional shifts has been found to increase health problems, decrease satisfaction, increase family conflicts, and increase sleep deprivation (Barton, 1994; Furnham & Hughes, 1999; Morshead, 2002; Demerouti et al., 2004). All of these may lead to decreases in performance as measured by an increase in errors and accidents (Monk & Folkard, 1985).

On the other hand, employees working day shifts (e.g., 9-5) may be constantly interrupted by supervisors or coworkers (Bohle & Tilley, 1998) reducing the amount of time they can spend on a task (Grant, 1979). In environments where there is a lot of uncertainty and task variability (e.g., police depts., hospitals, fire stations) individual decision-making may be influenced by politics and relationships rather than by data or unbiased information (Choo, 1998). Thus, when individuals are acting alone and without the influence of others, they will rely on the information to which they have access. In addition, Dalton and Mesch (1990) found positive effects (e.g., decreased absenteeism and turnover) of shift workers because of the increased autonomy and responsibility afforded shift workers. Thus, controlling for any differences due to workload, we expect that effectiveness will be higher for employees working the night shift than employees working the day shift.

H2: Professional service employees who work during the night shift will have higher levels of effectiveness than service employees who work during the day shifts.

We have argued that shift affects both technology use and effectiveness. In fact, we expect that technology use may be one of the reasons why night shift workers have higher rather than lower levels of effectiveness than day shift workers. Thus, employees who make decisions based on information provided to them by the information technology system may experience higher levels of effectiveness than those who do not use the technology (Dawes, 1996; Hesse et al., 1993; Nunn, 2001). Previous studies have shown that information from computer systems may contain fewer organizational and political barriers than information from human sources (Andersen, 2005; Sproull & Kiesler, 1986). In addition, employees who use work-related information

technology systems may receive quick feedback enabling them to be more efficient and make good decisions (Northrop, Kraemer, & King, 1995). The efficiency and decision-making effects are likely only for those who use work-related information technology systems. This relationship is also supported by the Task-Technology Fit model (Goodhue & Thompson, 1995). Night shift workers who need access to information to complete their tasks will turn to technology for their information due to the lack of other available resources. Thus, there will be a "fit" between the task and the technology for night shift workers. Given this, we predict a mediating role of work-related information systems.

H3: Work-related information systems use will mediate the relationship between type of shift worked and effectiveness.

Although IT may provide accurate and timely information to night shift workers, night shift employees are less likely to be satisfied with the information technology and their access to information than day shift workers. Previous studies have found that night workers were more dissatisfied with the physical conditions of their work (Furnham & Hughes, 1999). Since night shift workers have fewer options than day shift workers in their ability to accumulate information from different sources, night shift workers are very dependent upon the resources to which they have access (Manning, 1996). When the system does not give them the information they need or when they have problems with the technology, they have fewer options than day shift workers to get answers to their questions.

In addition, a number of studies have shown that co-worker and supervisor support provide positive attitudinal benefits for employees (Colvin & Goh, 2005; Kirmeyer & Lin, 1987). During night shifts, which tend to be more isolating than day shifts, there is less personal support (Bøgglid et al., 2001; Furnham & Hughes, 1999; Hurrel,

1987). For example, Bosch and Lange (1987) found that social isolation was a key problem for nurses working weekend and night shifts in the Netherlands. Stephens and Long (2000) found that police officers who talked about work events were better able to alleviate stress than officers who did not talk about work events. The use of technology can change the nature of the relationships between individuals. For example, Schultze and Orlikowski (2004) found that the use of information technology reduced the frequency of interaction between sales reps and customers as well as altered the nature and quality of information that was shared. Thus, we expect that despite the effectiveness improvements seen by night shift workers who use technology, night shift workers will feel less satisfied about the technology and their ability to access information.

H4a: Professional service employees who work during the night shift will report less satisfaction with work-related information systems than service employees who work during the day shift.

H4b: Professional service employees who work during the night shift will report less satisfaction with access to information than service employees who work during the day shift.

METHODS

Research Setting and Sample

The present study was conducted among police officers in two patrol divisions working in the primary law enforcement organization for a metropolitan area with approximately 500,000 people. For a period of six-months, data was collected in the form of archival records and rosters. In addition to having a fixed night shift system, officers in law enforcement, particularly patrol officers, are primarily car-based and incident-driven (Maltz, Gordon, & Friedman, 2000). As in many

police organizations across the United States, officers work their shifts alone in one-person cars. Measures drawn from the archival records included amount of work (workload) and work effectiveness (number of arrests). Division rosters designated the shift that officers were scheduled to work for the year.

In addition to the archival data, surveys were also collected. Of the approximately 240 officers from the two divisions, 166 officers completed the questionnaire, yielding a response rate of 69 percent. To ensure that there were no differences between respondents and non-respondents we compared the demographic characteristics of officers who participated in the study to the general population of officers in the entire organization. Overall, officers in the general population were on average about thirty-five years old, had an average tenure of six years, and were 85% male. The average age of the officer who participated in the study was thirty-three and the average tenure was sixty-four months or 5.3 years. The gender breakdown for officers included in our sample was 88% male and 12% female. We also tested for non-response bias for workload level and effectiveness by conducting t-tests and found no significant difference between officers who completed the survey and those who did not.

Measures

Shift. The dataset was divided into two shift categories: DAYS and NIGHTS. Patrol officers who worked in the DAYS group worked the majority of their hours during daylight hours (from 7:00am to 5:00pm). Officers who were in NIGHTS worked during primarily night hours (5:00pm to 7:00am). Of the 166 subjects participating in the study, 85 worked DAYS and 81 worked NIGHTS. The mean workload levels of officers during the night and day shifts were not significantly different ($F(1, 164) = .135, p = .713$). Task variety levels between day shift officers and night shift officers were also pretty similar. To examine task variety we conducted interviews and ride-alongs with a sampling of police officers from each squad all of whom participated in the survey. Day shift officers conducted an average of ten different activities and night shift officers conducted an average of nine different activities. However, there were differences between the types of tasks conducted during the day shift and the night shift. Patrol officers working both day and night shifts commonly conducted routine traffic stops, apprehended stolen vehicles, responded to domestic violence reports, and interacted with drivers thought to be driving under the influence of alcohol. Activities more common to day-shift officers included bank robberies, checking on the welfare of neighbors or employees who have not been seen or heard from, responding to house burglar alarms, responding to calls from businesses (for example, to investigate a disturbance or loitering/solicitations), investigating reports of shoplifting, and dealing with problems associated with transients. Night-shift officers, on the other hand, were more likely to encounter crimes in progress, crimes related to drugs/narcotics, shootings, prostitution, and calls regarding disturbances of the peace (based on ride-alongs and interviews with 24 patrol officers). Work activities described by the officers are consistent with those reported in a number of studies describing police work (Cordner, 1979; Famega, 2005; Liederbach, 2005). Thus, while workloads and routinization levels (e.g., task variety) were similar, the actual tasks themselves varied considerably (Famega, 2005). In addition, as a night shift officer reported during one of our interviews, resources in the forms of other police personnel were severely diminished in night shifts.

Effectiveness. Effectiveness refers to the number of criminal arrests made by each study participant. Arrests are made based on evidence that a criminal violation has occurred and that there is sufficient evidence for prosecution. Arrests can be made based on a call in progress as well as a result of an issued warrant. Number of arrests is an important statistic used by the police agency for determining organizational effectiveness and all officers have an equal opportunity to make arrests over a period of time (Schroeder, personal communication, March 9, 2006). Therefore, number of arrests by officer was used in this study as a measure of individual effectiveness. The number of arrests was captured from the police organization's management database over a period of six months. The number of arrests that each officer made over this time period was matched to the survey data.

General Computer Use. All police officers have access to computer terminals in the police substation as well as to the terminals in their vehicles. To assess the level of computer use, subjects were first asked to report their level of use on five items: computers in general, the Internet, a word processing application (e.g., MS Word), a spreadsheet application (e.g., MS Excel), and a browser (e.g., Internet Explorer). Subjects were asked to rate each of the five items using a five-point Likert scale anchored from "never" to "many times every day." The Cronbach alpha for this item is .80.

Work-Related Information System Use. In addition to the general measure of computer use, we included the use of a number of specific information systems for police work, located on the substation terminals. Subjects were asked to rate their level of use on a five-point scale for each of the three systems: the criminal records management system, a multimedia criminal database, and a photo database. For each system, subjects rated their level of use: from "never" to "many times every day." Because we are interested in the level of usage across the three different police information systems this measure was created by summing the scores for the three items.

User Satisfaction with Work-Related Information Systems. To measure end user satisfaction with the work-related information systems for police work, a variation of Rocheleau's (1993) end user satisfaction scale was used. The measure, which included twelve items, asked officers to rate the extent to which the system allowed them to access the precise information they need, whether the system is accurate, whether the information returned by the system is timely, if the content of the system meets their needs, whether the information returned by the system is clear, whether they are able to get sufficient information from the system and whether the system's information is up-to-date. Responses were based on a 5-point Likert scale ranging from "almost never" to "almost always," and had a Cronbach alpha of .93.

Satisfaction with Information Access. In addition to asking about satisfaction with specific police information systems, we also asked officers to rate their satisfaction with the level of information that they could access. We modified Rocheleau's (1993) measure of satisfaction by removing four measures that referred to specific system characteristics and to address information access more generally. The 8-item measure for satisfaction with information access has a Cronbach alpha of .91.

Control variables. Given that newer and younger police officers may be the officers more likely to work the night shift, *age* was used as a control variable in this study. By controlling for age, we can better focus on the effect that shift has on our outcome variables. We also control for

workload as patrol officers who have more cases may be more likely to make arrests. Finally, we control for *computer self-efficacy* as previous studies have found that self-efficacy is a significant factor in determining technology use (Compeau & Higgins, 1995).

RESULTS

Means, standard deviations, and correlation matrix of all the variables in the study are presented in Table 1. As the table shows, our control variables are related to the variables we suspected. Age is strongly correlated with shift ($r = -.26$, $p<.001$) suggesting that younger officers were more likely to work at night. Computer self-efficacy is significantly correlated with both general computer use ($r =.45$, $p<.001$) and work-related IT systems use ($r=.20$, $p<.05$). Workload is significantly related to number of arrests ($r=.22$, $p<.01$). Officers working the night shift had more arrests ($r =.26$, $p<.001$), used computers more often ($r =.20$, $p<.01$), and used work-related IT systems more often ($r =.17$, $p<.001$) than did officers working the day shift. Officers who worked the night shift rated their satisfaction with the work-related IT systems lower than day officers ($r = -.17$, $p<.05$). There was also a significant positive correlation between

Table 1. Means, standard deviations, and correlations

	Variable	Mean	(s.d.)	1	2	3	4	5	6	7	8
1	Age	32.98	(7.53)								
2	Workload	208	(85)	-.23**							
3	Computer self-efficacy	5.62	(2.02)	-.26***	.10						
4	Shift[a]			-.26***	.03	12					
5	General computer use	8.46	(4.18)	-.11	.03	.45***	.20**				
6	Work-related IS use	4.25	(2.41)	-.03	-.12	.20*	.17*	.30***			
7	Effectiveness/Arrests	26.56	(18.36)	-.05	.22**	.19*	.26***	.17*	.21**		
8	Sat. with info access	3.45	(.64)	.08	-.04	.01	-.09	-.06	-.07	-.06	
9	Sat. with work-related IS	3.62	(.57)	.10	.02	-.02	-.17*	-.09	-.12	-.00	74***

***$p <.001$, **$p <.01$, *$p <.05$

[a]Shift: day shift is coded as 0 and night shift is coded as 1

Table 2. The effects of shift on information technology use, effectiveness, and satisfaction

Independent Variable	General Computer Use		Work-related IS use		Effectiveness		Satisfaction with work-related IT		Satisfaction with Info Access	
	Step 1	Step 2	Step 1	Step 2	Step 1	Step 2	Step 1	Step 2	Step 1	Step 2
Age	.00	.04	-.01	.04	.04	.11	.07	.02	09	.07
Workload	-.01	-.01	-.12+	-.14+	.21**	.22**	-.002	-.004	-.02	-.03
Self-efficacy	.45***	.44***	.21**	.20*	.18*	.17*	-.05	-.04	.03	.04
Shift		.16*		.17*		.26***		-.18*		-.07
F	13.48***	11.51***	3.37*	3.68**	4.66**	6.73***	.44	1.50	.47	.55
Adj R²	.186	.204	.041	.075	.063	.123	-.011	.012	-.01	-.01
Δ Adj R²	.201	.023	.059	.025	.08	.064	.008	.029	.009	.005

***$p < .001$, **$p < .01$, *$p < .05$, +$p < .10$

both general computer use and work-related IT systems use with the number of arrests made ($r = .17$, $p < .05$ and $r = .21$, $p < .01$, respectively).

The results of the hierarchical multiple regression analyses are presented in Tables 2 and 3. In Step 1, the control variables, age, workload, and self-efficacy were entered. The main effect of shift was entered in Step 2. We predicted in Hypothesis 1a that night shift officers will use computers in general more often than day officers. We found support for this hypothesis; officers who worked the night shift reported a higher level of computer use than day officers ($\beta = 0.16$, $p < .05$). Because Hypothesis 1a examines general computer use, we also looked specifically at the use of police information systems. We found a significant main effect for shift on the use of these work-related information systems (Hypothesis 1b). Officers who worked the night shift reported using these technologies more often than day officers did ($\beta = 0.17$, $p < .05$). We found support for Hypothesis 2 which stated that officers working the night shift would have higher levels of effectiveness as measured by number of arrests ($\beta = 0.26$, $p < .001$).

In support of Hypothesis 3, the level of work-related IT use partially mediates the relationship between shift and effectiveness as described in

Hypothesis 2. Using the method described in Baron and Kenny (1986), we tested for mediation by regressing both shift and work-related information systems use on productivity (see Table 3). In the full model, the beta for shift was .23 ($p < .01$) and the beta for work-related IS use was .19 ($p < .05$), indicating that work-related information system use partially mediates the relationship between shift and effectiveness.

Table 3. The mediating role of information technology use on the shift-effectiveness relationship

Independent Variable	Effectiveness	
	Step 1	Step 2
Age	.04	.10
Workload	.21**	.25***
Self-efficacy	.18*	.13+
Shift	.26***	.23**
Work-Related IS use		.19*
F	4.66**	6.79***
Adj R²	.063	.150
Δ Adj R²	.08	.096

***$p < .001$, **$p < .01$, *$p < .05$, +$p < .10$

To further test the relationship between effectiveness and work-related IT use within the night shift, we ran an additional model testing only the night shift officers. As seen in Table 4, we found a main effect of work-related IT use on effectiveness ($\beta = 0.25$, $p < .05$). This finding provides stronger support for the idea that during the night shift, the most effective officers are those who use work-related IT. We also tested relationship between effectiveness and work-related IT on the sample of day shift officers. As we predicted, we did not find a main effect for work-related IT use ($\beta = 0.11$, $p =$ ns). Therefore, work-related IT is particularly important to night shift officers as it has a direct impact on their effectiveness; an impact that is not replicated for day shift officers.

We expected that night officers would report a lower level of satisfaction with work-related information systems (Hypothesis 4a) as well as a lower level of satisfaction with the information that they access (Hypothesis 4b). Hypothesis 4a was supported as patrol officers who worked in the night shift reported less satisfaction with the work-related information system than those working in the day shift ($\beta = -.18$, $p < .05$; Table 2). Support for Hypothesis 4b was not found.

DISCUSSION AND IMPLICATIONS

The aim of this study was to investigate the effects that shift work can have on effectiveness and how information technology is viewed and used. The results of this study suggest that information technology systems have different value for workers on different shifts even if the task goals are the same. Therefore, the inclusion of shift work in future studies will lead to a better understanding of how the context of work (i.e., shift) affects the use of technology by affecting the content of work (i.e., availability and need for resources).

An important finding in this study is that night shift patrol officers had higher levels of effectiveness partially as a result of using work-related information technology systems. We also found that night shift officers not only use specific work-related information systems more often than their day shift counterparts, they also used computers in general more often. Furthermore, we found that the use of work-related IT mattered more to night shift officers than to the day shift officers in terms of increasing effectiveness (i.e., making arrests). Compared to their day shift counterparts, night shift officers must use technology-related tools for information access as they have fewer

Table 4. The effects of work-related IT use on effectiveness (within each shift)

Independent Variable	Effectiveness: Night Shift		Effectiveness: Day Shift	
	Step 1	Step 2	Step 1	Step 2
Age	.27*	.24*	-.12	-.11
Workload	.34**	.40***	-.02	-.12
Self-efficacy	.11	.06	.29*	.27*
Work-related IT use		.25*		.11
F	5.16**	5.47***	3.39*	2.78*
Adj R²	.135	.183	.079	.079
Δ Adj R²	.167	.056	.113	.011

***$p < .001$, **$p < .01$, *$p < .05$

resources with which to complete their tasks. This empirical finding supports a conceptual argument made by Luen and Al-Hawamdeh (2001) that police officers who are able to assess, assimilate and use knowledge effectively will be able to perform effectively. Although day shift officers have the same ability to access these new technologies, they were less likely to access them than were night shift officers.

In addition to using more work-related IT, there may be other differences in the work environment that lead night shift officers to have higher levels of task effectiveness than day shift officers. For example, as described earlier, the nature of cases during the night and day shifts differs. Night shift officers often deal with crimes-in-progress (e.g., burglaries) and there is more opportunity to make immediate arrests. Furthermore, criminals may be more easily found during the night at their places of residence so more arrests may take place. We are not suggesting that the sole reason that night shift officers are more effective is that they use more work-related IT systems; our results confirm this as the use of work-related IT systems is a *partial* mediator of the relationship between shift and effectiveness. Our results however do suggest that when officers make use of the IT systems provided to them by the organization that there are beneficial outcomes for the organization.

Finally, the model testing system satisfaction suggests that increased reliance on a technology also causes increased expectations (Levy, Murphy, & Zanakis, 2009). When those expectations are not met, satisfaction may decrease. Thus, police officers working the night shift were less satisfied with their technology than were officers in the day shift. Brown and Brudney (2003) provide an alternative explanation for why there is a *positive* relationship between shift and information systems use and a *negative* relationship between shift and satisfaction with information systems. Brown and Brudney, in a study of police officers, found that while all officers agree information technology was important, only officers that preferred a structured approach to problem solving were satisfied with the technology tools available to them. Although we did not measure problem-solving preferences, it is not inconceivable that officers working the night shift prefer non-structured approaches to problem-solving.

By investigating the role of work shift in affecting individuals' technology use, we are essentially looking at temporal rhythms of work. Temporal rhythms or patterns of work refer to the "broad temporal pattern of the work iterated over time" (Reddy & Dourish, 2002, p. 348). The temporal work rhythm of shift breaks down work into different types and intensities of activities that are useful in determining the needs of the different shift workers. Although the two-fixed shift system that was used in this study is a broad pattern or a large-scale rhythm dictated by the organization itself, we were able to find key differences in effectiveness as well as the use of technology. Therefore, understanding different temporal rhythms of work can be an important aspect in the study of individual outcomes and technology use.

Our study on the effects that shift work can have on information technology use and perceptions has strong implications for affecting organizational effectiveness. Organizational leaders should carefully schedule shift work along with information technology needs, access, and training; thus providing an important organizational resource to night shift workers that can greatly enhance productivity and effectiveness. By better meeting the informational needs of the night shift population, organizations can strategically utilize information technology to compensate for the lack of other informational resources that are readily available to day shift workers.

Our focus on technology use among employees working in different shifts has some important theoretical implications. First, one of the most influential frameworks of technology use, the Technology Acceptance Model (TAM; Davis, 1989), should be extended to consider the ways that context influences the characteristics of work.

Figure 1. Potential TAM extension including the organizational influences of shift work (adapted from Venkatesh & Bala, 2008)

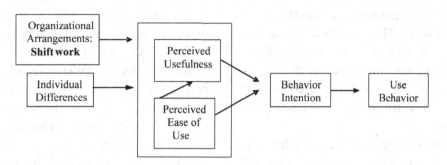

While our results clearly show the benefits of technology use in the police context, the TAM model might consider organizational arrangements that influence personal motivations for technology use. We have included Figure 1 to show how the basic TAM model can be extended to include organizational arrangements, such as shift work. In this case, working different shifts affects the perceived usefulness and perceived ease of use of the information technology.

Other aspects of shift (differences in levels of routinization and task variety) may also influence the extent to which individuals see value in adopting and using technologies. Choo (1998) has suggested that information technology systems are not helpful in environments with high task uncertainty and task variability as individuals in these conditions prefer to rely on political decision-makings. Our study suggests that when resources are limited, officers use information technology systems more often; and when they use these systems more often, there are positive outcomes. We believe that in cases where individuals work autonomously, it is important to manage their attitudes about technology; however, this may be especially difficult when employees work in shifts.

As we have discussed, another framework for understanding the extent to which technology is used and accepted is that of Task-Technology Fit (Goodhue & Thompson, 1995). This model explains how employees with a particular set of tasks

need to find the right technologies to help them complete their tasks. The problems arise when the set of tasks assigned to an employee is so large and varying that the technology may only help in some subset of tasks. If there are other ways that an employee can access the resources or information needed to complete a task, technology may be deemed unnecessary or redundant. Thus, the same task in different contexts may not require the same technology. This study shows that although the goal of the task is the same (e.g., reducing crime), the time during which the task takes place (i.e., night versus day) can affect the degree to which the technology is useful. Thus, the boundaries of task-technology models should be extended and empirically tested to include dynamic factors such as shift work to better address the fit between the user's needs and the technology.

Future studies should investigate the role of shift work and information technology in other types of organizations, such as call centers, hospitals, and manufacturing operations. The effects of night and day shift work are likely to be vastly different among these different organizational forms. Hospitals and police departments are similar in that night shift workers are often as busy as day shift workers and face emergencies relatively frequently. Night shift workers in call centers and manufacturing operations may have more routine tasks and they may be less busy than those on the day shift. Although the value of technology may be equally important (due to the lack of other information resources) the degree to which the technology is used, updated, and valued may be extremely different. Thus, in investigating the relationship between shift work and technology in other contexts, one must consider the degree to which tasks are varied and routinized, as well as the extent to which there are differences in workload levels.

In this study, we discuss the need for different information resources across different temporal work groups. To better understand patterns of work and resource needs, future research should look at specific types and levels of resources accessed by the different temporal groups. In addition, examining the different characteristics and values associated with different types of resources (e.g., social network-based resource versus repository-based resource) can provide additional insights on the relationship between shift work and technology use.

An extremely important and practical implication of this research is in the area of systems design. This research indicates the importance of addressing the needs of peripheral workers, such as night shift workers, in the design of information systems. Although the voices of these workers are likely to be underrepresented in the requirement determination process, the resulting technology may serve a more crucial need for this group of workers as compared to the "mainstream" day shift workers. In addition, this process may determine that night shift workers and day shift workers do fundamentally different tasks.

This research can also guide managers in better resource allocation for different types of workers within an organization. By focusing on the specific needs of peripheral workers, like night shift employees, human resource departments can have a better understanding of the relationship that exists between shift work and technology use. The result is a strategy of technology deployment that will not only lead to better resource utilization for the organization, but also better address the needs of their employees.

As shift work continues to be an alternative mode of work for many organizations, especially in the service sector (McMenamin, 2007), how information technology is viewed and utilized becomes pivotal. In order for organizations to fully address the needs of all employees, including shift workers, they need to closely examine how information technology resources are used in the absence of other "traditional" resources. To the best of our knowledge, this is one of the first studies to look at shift work and its effect on technology needs and use. We believe that this study indicates the importance of looking at temporal aspects of work as part of an organization's structure when examining technology use from both from a practitioner's and researcher's point of view. Not only does this research affect organizations that utilize a shift system, it also impacts our current theories and models of organizational forms and technology use.

ACKNOWLEDGMENT

The authors wish to acknowledge IJISSS Editor-in-Chief Professor John Wang and the anonymous reviewers for their valuable input on a previous version of this paper. This work was supported in part by the National Science Foundation under award number 0218304. Any opinions, findings and conclusions or recommendations expressed in this material are those of the authors and do not necessarily reflect those of the National Science Foundation

REFERENCES

Agrawal, R. (2000). Individual acceptance of information technologies. In Zmud, R. W. (Ed.), *In framing the domains of IT management: Projecting future… through the past* (pp. 85–104). Cincinnati, OH: Pinnaflex Education Resources.

Ajzen, I., & Madden, T. J. (1986). Prediction of goal directed behavior: Attitudes, intentions, and perceived behavioral control. *Journal of Experimental Social Psychology*, *22*(5), 453–474. doi:10.1016/0022-1031(86)90045-4

Andersen, T. J. (2005). The performance effect of computer-mediated communication and decentralized decision making. *Journal of Business Research*, *58*(8), 1059–1067. doi:10.1016/j.jbusres.2004.02.004

Baba, V. V., & Jamal, M. (1992). Routinization of job context and job content as related to employees' quality of working life: A study of Canadian nurses. *Journal of Organizational Behavior*, *12*(5), 379–386. doi:10.1002/job.4030120503

Baron, R. B., & Kenny, D. A. (1986). The moderation-mediator variable distinction in social psychological research: Conceptual, strategic, and statistical considerations. *Journal of Personality and Social Psychology*, *51*(6), 1173–1182. doi:10.1037/0022-3514.51.6.1173

Barton, J. (1994). Choosing to work at night: A moderating influence on individual tolerance to shift work. *The Journal of Applied Psychology*, *79*(3), 449–454. doi:10.1037/0021-9010.79.3.449

Barton, J., & Folkard, S. (1991). The response of day and night nurses to their work schedules. *Journal of Occupational Psychology*, *64*(3), 207–218.

Beers, T. M. (2000). Flexible schedules and shift work: Replacing the '9-to-5' workday? *Monthly Labor Review*, *123*(6), 33–40.

Blau, G., & Lunz, M. (1999). Testing the impact of shift schedules on organizational variables. *Journal of Organizational Behavior*, *20*(6), 933–942. doi:10.1002/(SICI)1099-1379(199911)20:6<933::AID-JOB940>3.0.CO;2-V

Bøgglid, H., Burr, H., Tüchsen, F., & Jeppesen, J. (2001). Work environment of Danish shift and day workers. *Scandinavian Journal of Work, Environment & Health*, *27*(2), 97–105.

Bohle, P., & Tilley, A. J. (1998). Early experience of shiftwork: Influences on attitude. *Journal of Occupational and Organizational Psychology*, *71*(1), 61–79.

Bosch, L. H. M., & Lange, W. A. M. (1987). Shift work in health care. *Ergonomics*, *30*(5), 773–791. doi:10.1080/00140138708969767

Brown, M. M., & Brudney, J. L. (2003). Learning organizations in the public sector? A study of police agencies employing information and technology to advance knowledge. *Public Administration Review*, *63*(1), 30–43. doi:10.1111/1540-6210.00262

Buren, R. M., & Stenzel, W. W. (1984). The impact of police work scheduling on patrol productivity. *Public Productivity Review*, *8*(3), 236–252. doi:10.2307/3380465

Cass, H. D., Smith, I., Unthank, C., Starling, C., & Collins, J. E. (2003). Improving compliance with requirements on junior doctors' hours. *British Medical Journal*, *327*(2), 270–273. doi:10.1136/bmj.327.7409.270

Choo, C. W. (1998). *The knowing organization*. New York: Oxford University Press.

Colvin, C. A., & Goh, A. (2005). Validation of the technology acceptance model for police. *Journal of Criminal Justice*, *33*(1), 89–95. doi:10.1016/j.jcrimjus.2004.10.009

Compeau, D. R., & Higgins, C. A. (1995). Computer self-efficacy: Development of a measure and initial test. *Management Information Systems Quarterly*, *19*(2), 189–211. doi:10.2307/249688

Cordner, G. W. (1979). Police patrol work load studies: A review and critique. *Police Studies Intnl Review of Police Development*, *2*(2), 50–60.

Dalton, D. R., & Mesch, D. J. (1990). The impact of flexible scheduling on employee attendance and turnover. *Administrative Science Quarterly, 35*(2), 370–387. doi:10.2307/2393395

Davis, F. D. (1989). Perceived usefulness, perceived ease of use, and user acceptance of information technology. *Management Information Systems Quarterly, 13*(3), 319–340. doi:10.2307/249008

Dawes, S. S. (1996). Interagency information sharing: Expected benefits, manageable risks. *Journal of Policy Analysis and Management, 15*(3), 377–394. doi:10.1002/(SICI)1520-6688(199622)15:3<377::AID-PAM3>3.0.CO;2-F

Demerouti, E., Geurts, S. A. E., Bakker, A. B., & Euwema, M. (2004). The impact of shiftwork on work-home conflict, job attitudes and health. *Ergonomics, 47*(9), 987–1002. doi:10.1080/00140130410001670408

Dennis, A. R., Wixom, B. H., & Vandenberg, R. J. (2001). Understanding fit and appropriation effects in group support systems via meta-analysis. *Management Information Systems Quarterly, 25*(2), 167–193. doi:10.2307/3250928

Dishaw, M. T., & Strong, D. M. (1998). Supporting software maintenance with software engineering tools: A computed task-technology analysis. *Journal of Systems and Software, 44*(2), 107–120. doi:10.1016/S0164-1212(98)10048-1

Dishaw, M. T., & Strong, D. M. (1999). Extending the technology acceptance model with task technology fit constructs. *Information & Management, 36*(1), 9–21. doi:10.1016/S0378-7206(98)00101-3

Dunham, R. (1977). Shift work: A review and theoretical analysis. *Academy of Management Review, 2*(4), 624–634. doi:10.2307/257514

Famega, C. N. (2005). Variation in officer downtime: A review of the research. *Policing: An International Journal of Police Strategies and Management, 28*(3), 388–414. doi:10.1108/13639510510614528

Fandray, D. (2000). Eight days a week: Meeting the challenge of the 24/7 economy. *Workforce, 79*(9), 35-42.

Fishbein, M., & Ajzen, I. (1975). *Belief, attitude, intention and behavior: An introduction to theory and research*. Reading, MA: Addison-Wesley.

Furnham, A., & Hughes, K. (1999). Individual difference correlates of nightwork and shiftwork rotation. *Personality and Individual Differences, 26*(5), 941–959. doi:10.1016/S0191-8869(98)00199-8

Geisler, E. (2009). Tacit and explicit knowledge: Empirical investigation in an emergency regime. *International Journal of Technology Management, 47*(4), 273–285. doi:10.1504/IJTM.2009.024430

Goodhue, D. L., & Thompson, R. L. (1995). Task-technology fit and individual performance. *Management Information Systems Quarterly, 19*(2), 213–236. doi:10.2307/249689

Grant, N. (1979). *Time to care*. London: Royal College of Nursing.

Hesse, B. W., Sproull, L. S., Kiesler, S. B., & Walsh, J. P. (1993). Returns to science: Computer networks in oceanography. *Communications of the ACM, 36*(8), 90–101. doi:10.1145/163381.163409

Holsapple, C. W., Luo, W., & Morton, R. S. (2000). Computer support of shift work: An experiment in a GSS environment. *Journal of Computer Information Systems, 41*(1), 1–6.

Hurrell, J. J. (1987). An overview of organizational stress and health. In L. R. Murphy & T. F. Schoenberg (Eds.), *Stress management in work settings*. Washington, DC: National Institute of Occupational Safety and Health (U.S. Government Printing Office).

Kandolin, I. (1993). Burnout of female and male nurses in shift work. *Ergonomics*, *36*(1-3), 141–147. doi:10.1080/00140139308967865

Kirmeyer, S. L., & Lin, T.-R. (1987). Social support: Its relationship to observed communication with peers and superiors. *Academy of Management Journal*, *30*(1), 138–151. doi:10.2307/255900

Kogi, K. (1985). Introduction to the problems of shift work. In Folkard, S., & Monk, T. (Eds.), *Hours of work* (pp. 165–182). Chichester, UK: Wiley.

Levy, Y., Murphy, K. E., & Zanakis, S. H. (2009). A value-satisfaction taxonomy of IS effectiveness (VSTISE): A case study of user satisfaction with IS and user-perceived value of IS. *International Journal of Information Systems in the Service Sector*, *1*(1), 93–118.

Liao, C., & Huang, W. (2009). Community adaptability, computer and internet self-efficacy, and intention of blended e-learning. *International Journal of Society Systems Science*, *1*(3), 209–226. doi:10.1504/IJSSS.2009.022816

Liederbach, J. (2005). Addressing the "elephant in the living room:" An observational study of the work of suburban police. *Policing: An International Journal of Police Strategies and Management*, *28*(3), 415–434. doi:10.1108/13639510510614537

Lou, H., Luo, W., & Strong, D. (2000). Perceived critical mass effect on groupware acceptance. *European Journal of Information Systems*, *9*(2), 91–103.

Luen, T. W., & Al-Hawamdeh, S. (2001). Knowledge management in the public sector: Principles and practices in police work. *Journal of Information Science*, *27*(5), 311–318. doi:10.1177/016555150102700502

Luo, A., & Olson, J. S. (2006). Informal Communication in Colaboratories. In *Proceedings of the conference on computer-human interaction*. New York: Association for Computing Machinery.

Maloney, J. P. (1982). Job stress and the consequences on a group intensive case and non-intensive care nurses. *ANS. Advances in Nursing Science*, *4*(2), 31–42.

Maltz, M. D., Gordon, A. C., & Friedman, W. (2000). *Mapping crime in its community setting: Event geography analysis*. New York: Springer Verlag.

Manning, P. K. (1996). Information technology in the police context: The "sailor" phone. *Information Systems Research*, *7*(1), 52–62. doi:10.1287/isre.7.1.52

McMenamin, T. M. (2007). A time to work: Recent trends in shift work and flexible schedules. *Monthly Labor Review*, *139*(12), 3–15.

Monk, T., & Folkard, S. (1985). Shift work and performance. In Folkard, S., & Monk, T. (Eds.), *Hours of work* (pp. 239–252). Chichester, UK: Wiley.

Morshead, D. M. (2002). Stress and shiftwork. *Occupational Health & Safety (Waco, Tex.)*, *71*(4), 36–38.

Northrop, A., Kraemer, K. L., & King, J. L. (1995). Police use of computers. *Journal of Criminal Justice*, *23*(3), 259–275. doi:10.1016/0047-2352(95)00019-M

Nunn, S. (2001). Police information technology: Assessing the effects of computerization on urban police functions. *Public Administration Review*, *61*(2), 221–234. doi:10.1111/0033-3352.00024

Oexman, R. D., Knotts, T. L., & Koch, J. (2002). Working while the world sleeps: A consideration of sleep and shift work design. *Employee Responsibilities and Rights Journal*, *14*(4), 145–157. doi:10.1023/A:1021189305076

Punkett, J. L., & Lundman, R. J. (2003). Factors affecting homicide clearances: Multivariate analysis of a more complete conceptual framework. *Journal of Research in Crime and Delinquency*, *40*(2), 171–193. doi:10.1177/0022427803251125

Reddy, M., & Dourish, P. (2002). A finger on the pulse: Temporal rhythms and information seeking in medical work. In *Proceedings of the conference on computer supported collaborative work.* New York: Association for Computing Machinery.

Rocheleau, B. (1993). Evaluating public sector information systems. *Evaluation and Program Planning, 16,* 119–129. doi:10.1016/0149-7189(93)90023-2

Sagie, A., & Krausz, M. (2003). What aspects of the job have most effect on nurses? *Human Resource Management Journal, 13*(1), 46–62. doi:10.1111/j.1748-8583.2003.tb00083.x

Schultze, U., & Orlikowski, W. J. (2004). A practice perspective on technology-mediated network relations: The use of internet-based self-serve technologies. *Information Systems Research, 15*(1), 87–106. doi:10.1287/isre.1030.0016

Sproull, L., & Kiesler, S. (1986). Reducing social context cues: electronic mail in organizational communication. *Management Science, 32*(11), 1492–1512. doi:10.1287/mnsc.32.11.1492

Sprugeon, A., & Cooper, C. L. (2000). Working time, health, and performance. In Cooper, C. L., & Robertson, I. T. (Eds.), *International review of industrial and organizational psychology* (Vol. 15). Chichester, UK: Wiley.

Stephens, C., & Long, N. (2000). Communication with police supervisors and peers as a buffer of work-related traumatic stress. *Journal of Organizational Behavior, 21,* 407–424. doi:10.1002/(SICI)1099-1379(200006)21:4<407::AID-JOB17>3.0.CO;2-N

Tucker, A. L., Edmondson, A. C., & Spears, S. (2002). When problem solving prevents organizational learning. *Journal of Organizational Change Management, 15*(2), 122–137. doi:10.1108/09534810210423008

Venkatesh, V., & Bala, H. (2008). Technology acceptance model 3 and a research agenda on Interventions. *Decision Sciences, 39*(2), 273–315. doi:10.1111/j.1540-5915.2008.00192.x

Venkatesh, V., & Davis, F. D. (1996). A model of the antecedents of perceived ease of use: Development and test. *Decision Sciences, 27*(3), 451–481. doi:10.1111/j.1540-5915.1996.tb01822.x

Venkatesh, V., & Davis, F. D. (2000). A theoretical extension of the technology acceptance model: Four longitudinal field studies. *Management Science, 46*(2), 186–204. doi:10.1287/mnsc.46.2.186.11926

Zedeck, S., Jackson, S. E., & Marca, E. S. (1983). Shift work schedules and their relationship to health, adaptation, satisfaction, and turnover intention. *Academy of Management Journal, 26*(2), 297–310. doi:10.2307/255977

This work was previously published in International Journal of Information Systems in the Service Sector, Volume 2, Issue 2, edited by John Wang, pp. 1-18, copyright 2010 by IGI Publishing (an imprint of IGI Global).

Chapter 7

Implementation Success Model in Government Agencies:
A Case of a Centralized Identification System at NASA

Yair Levy
Nova Southeastern University, USA

Theon L. Danet
NASA Langley Research Center, USA

ABSTRACT

A recent presidential directive mandated that all U.S. government agencies establish a centralized identification system. This study investigated the impact of users' involvement, resistance, and computer self-efficacy on the implementation success of a centralized identification system. Information System (IS) usage was the construct employed to measure IS implementation success. A survey instrument was developed based on existing measures from key IS literature. The results of this study indicated a strong reliability for the measures of all constructs (user involvement, computer self-efficacy, user's resistance, and IS usage). Factor analysis was conducted using Principal Component Analysis (PCA) with Varimax rotation. Results of the PCA indicate that items of the constructs measured had high validity, while Cronbach's Alpha for each factor demonstrates high reliability for all constructs measured. Additionally, results of a structural equations modeling analysis using Partial Least Square (PLS) indicate that computer self-efficacy and user involvement had positive significant impact on the implementation success. However, the results also demonstrated that user's resistance had no significant impact on IS usage, while end user involvement had a strong negative impact on user's resistance.

DOI: 10.4018/978-1-4666-0044-7.ch007

Copyright © 2012, IGI Global. Copying or distributing in print or electronic forms without written permission of IGI Global is prohibited.

INTRODUCTION

In 2004 Presidential Directive (PD) 12 mandated that all United States (US) government agencies enhance security, increase government efficiency, reduce identity fraud, and protect personal privacy (The White House, 2004). All US government agencies should establish a mandatory, government-wide standard for secure and reliable forms of identification issued by the Federal Government to its employees and contractors (The White House, 2004). The PD 12 provided justification for central identification and account administration infrastructure. However, the complexity arises in the implementation of a centralized identification system (CIS). As a result, it was the central aim of this study to look at several constructs that may impact the success (or failure) of a CIS implementation as mandated by the PD 12. Evaluation of information systems (IS) success is a complex and perplexed issue (DeLone & McLean, 1992, 2003). Several factors are believed to impinge upon the success experienced by organizations regarding their deployment of IS (Hunton & Beeler, 1997; Jiang, Waleed, Muhanna, & Klein, 2000; Lane, Palko, & Cronan, 1994). Those factors generating the largest amount of research activity have involved the influence of individual differences upon IS design, implementation, and usage (DeLone & McLean, 1992, 2003). However, very little attention has been given in literature to IS implementation success in the context of government and federal agencies. The assumption taken by this work is that in the context of IS implementation, government and federal agencies can be viewed as a unique sub-set of the general service sector as they provide services to the government and/or other entities. Additionally, if government and federal agencies are being viewed as non-for-profit service providers, the implementation success of functional systems, such as CIS, may be warranted a separate investigation (Ebbers & van Dijk, 2007). Therefore, this study was aimed at assessing the impact of key user perceptions on the success (or failure) of a CIS in the context of a federal agency.

THEORETICAL BACKGROUND

Introduction

Prior research has been conducted on various models of implementation success (DeLone & McLean, 1992, 2003). However, such models have been repeatedly validating a somewhat fixed set of constructs such as user satisfaction, system quality, information quality, and IS service quality. Although such construct are valid, the aim of this study was to go beyond such strongly validated constructs and investigate other individual constructs that appear promising as predictors of IS implementation success. Specifically, the implementation success as described under this investigation concentrated only on the constructs of user involvement, user resistance, computer self-efficacy, and IS success. Thus, a brief review of the literature for each of these key constructs is provided and serves as the theoretical foundation for this study.

User Involvement

The construct of involvement, defined as a psychological construct, needs to be differentiated from other psychological construct and user perceptions, particularly attitude (Barki & Hartwick, 1994). While many different definitions of attitude have been proposed over the years, the classical work by Fishbein and Ajzen (1975) defined attitude as a general conceptualized construct that is referred to an affective judgment of a person towards another person, object, or an event. User involvement is conceptually different than attitude as it focuses on the feelings one has about his/her own feelings of belonging to a larger group of individuals, rather than his/her own affective judgment of external entities. User involvement refers to participation in the system development process by representatives of the target user group (Ives & Olson, 1984). Baronas and Louis (1988) suggested that when employees are given the opportunity to enhance their control during a system implementation, they will adapt to the resultant changes and more readily accept the system. With increased user involvement, users will have an increased desire to participate in development (Barki & Hartwick, 1994). Hunton and Beeler (1997) concluded that the key IS success factor is to provide users with a sense of overall responsibility and system ownership. They indicated that having users involved early in the implementation stage will increase their sense of overall ownership, which results in successful implementation (Hunton & Beeler, 1997).

Adams, Berner, and Wyatt (2004) investigated the role of user involvement and user resistance in the context of IS implementation in healthcare. Based on a case study, they also suggested that user resistance and user involvement are two key constructs in the success or failure of IS implementation within healthcare organizations. Barki and Hartwick (1994) suggested that predevelopment states of user involvement toward a proposed IS are positively related to a user's desire to participate in upcoming development activities. They also indicated that additional research is needed to understand the role of user involvement in any IS related endeavor.

User Resistance

Research on IS implementation problems indicated that user resistance to change appears to be a key factor in the success of such endeavors (Jiang et al., 2000). Jiang et al. (2000)'s study attempted to make it explicit, based on system type, key reasons for user resistance and the remedies designed to promote implementation success. Using a sample of 66 managers, they developed taxonomy to identify reasons for user resistance. They concluding by indicating that although user

resistance is a key construct contributing to IS implementation success, "there are significant differences in the reasons users resist [different types of ISs]" (Jiang et al., 2000, p. 32). Ebbers and van Dijk (2007) indicated that the construct of user resistance should be investigated in the context of IS implementation success in government agencies as prior models may not properly represent issues related to such organizations. Myers and Avison (2002) indicated that implementations of new systems that alter the balance of power by users in organizations are resisted by those who lose power and accepted by those who gain it. Fjermestad and Romano (2003) indicated that reducing user resistance is a key construct for the success of system implementation and maybe effected by user involvement during earlier stages of the system development. However, they noted that additional research is needed to explore such relationships in other contexts. Jiang et al. (2000) also found that user resistance is critical for the success of IS implementations. They also indicated that additional research is needed to investigate the role of user resistance in the success of IS implementations.

Computer Self-Efficacy

Self-efficacy (The White House, 2004), the belief that one has the capability to perform a particular behavior, is an important construct in social psychology (Compeau & Higgins, 1995). Lucas, Walton, and Ginzberg (1988) provided some of the earliest evidence of the individual behavioral factors that influence IT adoption. Compeau and Higgins (1995) built upon Bandura's (1977, 1982, 1986) research on self-efficacy theory to propose and develop the construct of computer self-efficacy (CSE). They indicated that CSE is a more focused construct than SE, in that it relates to an individual's beliefs about their abilities to competently use computers to perform an activity. Compeau and Higgins (1995) stated that understanding the factors that influence an individual's use of IS has always been a key goal of IS research. Their model was developed to test the influence of CSE, outcome expectations, affect, and anxiety on IS usage. Significant relationships were found between CSE and outcome expectations, as well as between CSE, affect, anxiety, and IS usage (Compeau & Higgins, 1995). Compeau and Higgins (1999) indicated that additional research is needed to fully understand the role of CSE in adoption of IS as well as its impact on implementation success and the generalizability of CSE to other contexts.

Information Systems Success

The classical work of DeLone and McLean (1992) developed a model to organize the diverse research attempting to identify factors that contribute to IS success. DeLone and McLean (1992) built upon the work of Ives and Olson (1984)'s and Zmud (1979)'s extensive reviews on the measurement of IS success. Ives and Olson (1984) adopted two classes of IS outcome variables: system quality and system acceptance. They indicated that user involvement leads to improved system quality as well as increased user acceptance, which in turn increase IS usage. Baroudi, Olson, and Ives (1986) developed a measure of IS usage by incorporating a list of activities developed by the organization's system project managers. They indicated that user involvement increase IS usage, while IS usage serves as a surrogate measure of IS success (Baroudi et al., 1986). Additionally, Jones and Young (2006) noted that IS usage is the most critical issue that top IS executives are faced with when implementing new IS in their organization.

Doll and Torkzadeh (1998) developed a multidimensional IS usage measure. They indicated that IS usage is a critical construct in the system-to-value chain that links upstream research on the causes of IS success with downstream research on the organizational impacts of IS (Doll & Torkzadeh, 1998). The goal of their research was to make a preliminary effort to rethink the IS usage construct and develop appropriate instrumentation. According to Doll and Torkzadeh (1998), several factors have impeded the development of new multidimensional IS usage measures: (1) a primarily upstream IS research agenda, where a unidimensional IS usage construct is an adequate indicator of implementation success; (2) the lack of a theory base in the IS literature that provides a taxonomy of usage behaviors; and (3) the realization that, where use is mandatory, measures of IS usage may indicate only compliance, not IS success. They indicated that the potential of the IS usage construct depends on how it is conceptualized and operationalized (Doll & Torkzadeh, 1998). Doll and Tokzadeh's (1998) empirical results provided evidence of the instrument's reliability, validity, and general applicability. DeLone and McLean (2003) recommended that researchers consider adopting and applying this more comprehensive systems usage instrument.

DeLone and Mclean (2003) revisited their original work on the IS Success Model (DeLone & McLean, 1992). Their follow up work indicated that over 285 studies used their original model (DeLone & McLean, 2003). They discussed the important IS success research contributions of the prior decade, focusing especially on research efforts that apply, validate, challenge, and propose enhancements to their original model. They indicated that IS usage is an appropriate measure of IS success. However, some scholars noted that additional research on the implementation of new and unique technologies is still warranted (Jones & Kochtanek, 2004).

METHODOLOGY

This study was based on a quantitative assessment of four constructs. The four constructs assessed were: user resistance (URES), user involvement (UI), computer self-efficacy (CSE), and IS usage (ISU). IS usage was assumed to be a surrogate measure of CIS implementation success. This study used a survey instrument to collect quantitative data on the three independent variables (URES, UI, CSE) and the dependent variable (ISU) based on prior measures validated in IS research. Figure 1 shows the conceptual model that was used for this study.

This study posed four hypotheses:

Hypothesis 1: *User's computer self-efficacy* has a positive impact on *information systems usage.*

Hypothesis 2: *User's internal resistance* has a negative impact on *information systems usage.*

Hypothesis 3: *User involvement* has a positive impact on *information systems usage.*

Hypothesis 4: *User involvement* has a negative impact on *user's internal resistance.*

Instrument

An attempt was made in this study to use the original non-revised/non-reduced measures as much as possible. Thus, as a result of the literature review, Web-based survey was designed based on existing validated measures found in literature that identified the source or one of the original measures for all measured constructs. This study utilized the measure proposed by

Barki and Hartwick (1994) to assess the construct of UI. The validated measure of user resistance by Jiang et al. (2000) was used to assess URES. Additionally, the classical validated and reliable measure of CSE by Compeau and Higgins (1995) was used to assess the construct of CSE. Finally, Doll and Torkzadeh's (1998) validated and reliable measure of IS usage was slightly revised and used in this study to measure the dependent variable, IS usage. Appendix A depicts the specific items used in the study.

User Involvement Measure

Barki and Hartwick (1994) presented a theoretically–grounded perspective to account for effects of involving users during implementation, and provided an initial test of their model. They developed and validated a measure using a 7-point, bipolar scale to measure frequencies from (1) 'insignificant involvement' to (7) 'highly involved'. This study used Barki and Hartwick's (1994) measure of UI.

Computer Self-Efficacy Measure

Compeau and Higgins (1995) stated that understanding CSE is important to the successful implementation of systems in organizations.

Figure 1. Implementation success model of centralized identification system

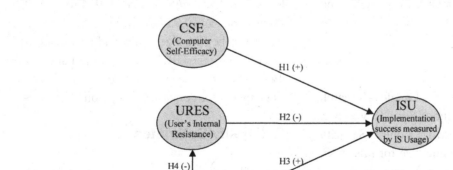

This study used their validated, reliable measure of user's CSE and its impact on implementation success of the centralized identification system at NASA. Compeau and Higgins (1995) developed and validated a 10-item CSE measure on a scale of (1) 'lowest level of confidence' to (10) 'highest level of confidence'. This study used the original Compeau and Higgins' (1995) CSE instrument to measure the CSE construct.

User Resistance Level Measure

Jiang at al. (2000) stated that user resistance can create a negative impact on the success of IS implementation. They developed a measure to assess URES. This study used their 7-item URES measure on a 7-point scale, where (1) represented 'lowest negative impact' and (7) represent 'highest positive impact'.

Information Systems Usage Measure

This study measured implementation success by using Delone and McLean's (2003) IS usage (ISU) variable derived from their success model. This study used the instrument proposed by Doll and Torkzadeh (1998) to measure end users' reported IS usage as part of the evaluation of IS. Following Doll and Torkzadeh (1998), this study used a 9-item measure to assess ISU. A 5-point Likert-type scale was used where (1) 'not at all', (2) 'a little', (3) 'moderately', (4) 'much', and (5) 'a great deal'.

Data Collection

This study took place at NASA Langley Research Center (LaRC). The rollout of this CIS was part of an initiative put by Network Control Security Branch (NCSB). The sample size for this study was approximately 700 participants. Each participant received an email from the IT Security Manager stating the purpose of the survey and the importance of participating in it. The Web-enabled survey was emailed to system users. Over 230 responses were submitted representing a response rate of over 33%. Following Mahalanobis distance multivariate analysis, four cases were removed for demonstration of outliers. Moreover, according to Levy (2006), response-set is when respondents mark the same score on all items in the survey. Response-set represent a minor threat to data analysis and should be considered for removal prior to fill analyses (Levy, 2006). Thus, nine more cases were removed due to response-set.

Data Analyses and Results

An exploratory factor analysis was done using Principal Component Analysis (PCA) method to verify the construct validity of the measures. This procedure is used to study the correlations among a large number of interrelated quantitative variables by grouping the variables into a few factors; after grouping, the variables within each factor are more highly correlated with variables in that factor than with variables in other factors (Mertler & Vannatta, 2001).

The PCA analysis was based on Varimax rotation and forced to four factors because there were four constructs measured. The overall cumulative variance was 70.5% based on the four factors. The partial correlation between the item and the rotated factor helped to formulate an interpretation of the factors or components. All partial correlations were between 0.784 and 0.914 for the CSE items, 0.627 and 0.937 for the UI items, 0.527 and 0.871 for the IS usage items, and between 0.613 and 0.770 for the URES items. Table 1 shows the block structure of each construct and demonstrating support for construct validation.

Reliability Estimates

Reliability estimates were calculated for each construct's responses using Cronbach's Alpha. Research indicates that reliability estimates exceeding 0.70 are desirable (Mertler & Vannatta,

Table 1. Varimax rotated component matrix (N=218)

Item	Component			
	1	**2**	**3**	**4**
CSE7	**0.914**	0.003	0.111	0.025
CSE10	**0.906**	-0.035	0.059	0.036
CSE5	**0.904**	-0.030	0.055	0.010
CSE9	**0.888**	-0.052	0.058	0.027
CSE6	**0.886**	-0.014	0.046	-0.046
CSE4	**0.884**	-0.004	0.090	-0.116
CSE8	**0.861**	0.005	0.152	-0.052
CSE3	**0.842**	0.067	0.113	-0.109
CSE1	**0.837**	0.079	0.135	-0.061
CSE2	**0.784**	0.139	0.166	-0.131
UI3	0.052	**0.937**	0.068	0.046
UI4	0.081	**0.935**	0.091	0.127
UI5	0.057	**0.915**	0.084	0.133
UI1	0.108	**0.908**	0.029	-0.004
UI7	0.003	**0.905**	0.127	0.193
UI8	0.116	**0.761**	0.144	0.158
UI2	-0.099	**0.657**	0.048	0.104
UI6	-0.045	**0.627**	-0.010	0.242
ISU2	0.069	0.151	**0.871**	0.062
ISU1	0.040	0.201	**0.835**	0.057
ISU3	0.096	0.147	**0.833**	0.018
ISU7	0.221	0.136	**0.800**	0.020
ISU8	0.143	0.038	**0.782**	0.054
ISU4	0.049	-0.033	**0.689**	0.040
ISU9	-0.008	-0.093	**0.641**	-0.050
ISU6	0.110	-0.076	**0.619**	0.073
ISU5	0.111	0.076	**0.527**	-0.111
URES2	-0.063	0.030	0.088	**0.770**
URES6	-0.062	0.184	-0.031	**0.742**
URES4	0.025	0.060	-0.062	**0.736**
URES5	-0.068	0.093	0.047	**0.695**
URES3	0.043	0.254	-0.007	**0.651**
URES7	-0.048	0.321	0.115	**0.638**
URES1	-0.079	0.062	0.014	**0.613**

2001). The Cronbach's Alpha were 0.911 for UI, 0.831 for URES, 0.965 for CSE, and 0.901 for ISU demonstrating high reliability for all construct measures. Table 2 shows the summary of each construct's Cronbach's Alpha.

Partial Least Square (PLS)

Data was analyzed using Partial Least Square (PLS) (Chin, 1998; Chin, Marcolin, & Newsted, 2003) with SmartPLS 2.0 (beta) (Ringle, Wende, & Will, 2005). As a sub-type method of structured equation modeling (SEM), PLS is widely used in IS research (Gefen & Straub, 2005). With the demonstration of the good reliability results indicated above and nice block-structure results of the PCA analysis, the constructs under investigation appears to provide adequate convergent and discriminant validity. Results of the standardized PLS path coefficients model for the proposed theoretical model are presented in Figure 2. The numbers noted above the arrows in the model represent the path coefficient, where results indicated that all path coefficients were significant at least at the .05 level. Results of the R-squared (R^2) values are indicated in the upper right corner above the given constructs where R^2 is applicable. Wetzels, Odekerken-Schröder, and Van-Oppen (2009) suggested a global fit measure (GoF) for PLS path modeling as a geometric mean of the average communality and average R^2. They also indicated three cut-off points for GoF GoF_{small}=0.1, GoF_{medium}=0.25, and GoF_{large}=0.36. Following such global fit measure, the calculated GoF for this model (Figure 2) is 0.6325 that well exceeds the .36 cut-off point value of the large, indicating that the overall proposed theoretical model (Figure 1) is sound.

Results of the PLS analysis demonstrated that CSE had a significant positive impact on ISU ($\beta_{CSE \rightarrow ISU}$= 0.407, p <.001), UI had a significant positive impact on ISU ($\beta_{UI \rightarrow ISU}$= 0.230, p <.05), UI had a significant negative impact on URES ($\beta_{UI \rightarrow URES}$= -0.676, p <.001), and URES demon-

Table 2. Reliability analysis-Cronbach Alpha (N=218)

	User Involvement (UI)	User Resistance (URES)	Computer Self-Efficacy (CSE)	IS Usage (ISU)
Reliability Coefficients (Cronbach's Alpha)	0.911	0.831	0.965	0.901
No. of Items	8	7	10	9

Figure 2. Results of the PLS analysis (N=218)

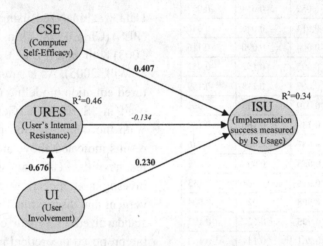

strated a non-significant negative impact on ISU. Such results indicated that hypotheses 1, 3, and 4 are supported, while hypothesis 2 is not supported.

Ordinal Logistic Regression

According to Marcoulides, Chin, and Saunders (2009), PLS has a key limitation with its linearity. They noted that "the latent variables in PLS are estimated as exact linear combinations of their indicators (or manifest block variables)" (p. 173). Additionally, Marcoulides, and Saunders (2006)

Table 3. Summary of hypotheses results

Hypothesis	Relations:	Sig. Positive Impact
H1:	CSE → ISU	Yes
H2:	USER → ISU	No
H3:	UI → ISU	Yes
H4:	UI → USER	Yes

criticized PLS for its assumption of linearity. In order to add for the robustness of the findings provided by the PLS analysis, an ordinal logistic regression (OLR) was also performed. According to Mertler and Vannatta (2001), "logistic regression requires that no assumptions about the distribution of the predictor variables (IVs) need to be made by the researcher... the predictors do not have to be normally distributed, linearly related, or have equal variances within each group" (p. 314). Moreover, they noted that "Logistic regression is able to produce nonlinear models, which again adds to its overall flexibility" (p. 314). Thus, reporting here the results of OLR appears warranted to augment those found by the PLS analysis.

Unlike nominal scales, values on an ordinal scale can be 'ordered' to reflect differing degrees or amount of the characteristic under study (Mertler & Vannatta, 2001). As this study utilized survey items that are ordinal, OLR analysis was also conducted to test hypotheses H1, H2, and H3.

The OLR model developed a predictive model using the three independent variables (UI, URES, and CSE) as predictors of the dependent variable (ISU). Results of the OLR model provided weights for each of the independent variables in order to predict the probability of the dependent variable. OLR results indicated that two of the three independent variables were significant (p<.01, marked with *, p<.001 marked with **, in Table 4). The results indicated that the OLR model is reliable: -2 Log Likelihood=209, χ^2(df=3)=26.1, p <.001. Results of OLR analysis are presented in Table 4.

Results of the OLR analysis are consistent with those of the PLS results, aside from the H4 testing, which this OLR model didn't account for. As such, the OLR results also confirmed that URES provided no significant contribution to the prediction of the probability of ISU. Results also demonstrated that CSE was significant (p<.0001) in predicting the probability of ISU. While results also demonstrated that UI was significant (p=.006) in predicting the probability of the dependent variable, ISU.

DISCUSSION AND CONCLUSION

Summary of Results

The central problem that this study investigated was the challenge that occurred with NASA's implementation of a CIS. As a result, it was the central aim of this study to look at key constructs that may impact the success (or failure) of CIS implementation. More specifically, this study investigated the impact of user involvement, computer self-efficacy, and user resistance on the CIS implementation success at a NASA center. This study was built on prior validated instruments that analyze and measures assessed. This study hypothesized that if organizations incorporate the concept of user involvement, recognize the impact of resistance levels, and identify the importance of computer self-efficacy before the implementation process; it will increase the chance of a successful implementation. Based on an empirical data collected at a NASA center, results showed that computer self-efficacy and user involvement are significant predictors of IS usage. Additionally, results showed that user resistance appears to have little or no effect on IS usage, at least in the context of this federal agency. Moreover, results of this study showed that user involvement is significantly impacting user resistance, however, this did not translate into a significant effect on IS usage. Although such results may appear counter intuitive, it may very well be that user resistance is somewhat overshadowed by other stronger constructs. Also, prior research such as Fjermestad and Romano (2003) as well as Myers and Avison (2002) indicated that user resistance is a viable construct in the pursuit of IS implementation success. However, such research was done based on utility type systems (i.e., customer relations management system, Web-based services, etc), while this study concentrates on operational and functional type systems, specifically an identification system. Additionally, the development and implementation of functional type systems, such as identification systems, is somewhat different

Table 4. Results of the OLR analysis in predicting IS usage (N=218)

	Estimate	Std. Err.	Wald	df	Sig.		95% Confidence Interval	
User Involvement (UI)	0.596	0.217	7.585	1	*0.006*	*	0.172	1.021
User Resistance (URES)	-0.027	0.258	0.011	1	0.916		-0.478	0.533
Computer Self-Efficacy (CSE)	0.268	0.067	15.919	1	*0.000*	**	0.136	0.399

* p<.01 ** p<.001

than utility type systems in the fact that functional type systems are used by all members of the organization. This notion is supported by Jiang et al. (2000) who indicated that the specific type of an IS may have a significant mediating effect on the effect of user resistance on the IS implementation success. As such, resistance for a system that may perceive by the users to be required functional system in the future may deem to be insignificant. However, the role of user resistance in functional systems such as identification system may warrant additional investigation.

Implications of the Study

This study has several implications for researchers and practitioners. According to Levy and Green (Forthcoming), considerable amount of IS research has been done over the years to develop and validate models using students as the main source of study participants. Thus, researchers in the field of IS implementation success may value the results of this study due to its unique data in US federal agency (i.e., NASA), rather than the use of students. Additionally, the results of this research may aid other researchers when attempting to investigate the impact of government issued policies, such as the US's PD in this study. This study also has significant implications for practitioners in the service sector as well as for those from government agencies. The first implication for practice is the recognition of computer self-efficacy as the key success construct in the implementation of IS within government organizations. Government decision makers who are in charge of IS development and implementation should provide the nurturing environment for their users to enhance their computer self-efficacy by providing them with field workshops and other avenues that might increase their computer self-efficacy. The second implication for practice is the recognition of user involvement in the development stage of a system as a key factor that may impact the success of the IS implementation.

Government decision makers who are in charge of IS development and implementation should pay close attention ensuring the involvement of system users in all the stages of the development to increase the likelihood of the system success.

Limitations of the Study

There is one key limitation to this study. It relates to the fact that this study measured data from a single NASA center. Although there appears to be little variation in government agencies like NASA between centers on the issues measured in this study, some considerations should be made when attempting to generalize the results found here to the service sector. Moreover, in the US there is a considerable amount of service organizations that are either spin-offs of previous government organization's projects or service organizations founded by prior government individuals, the results found here maybe valid for such service organizations.

Future Research

Future research may include several avenues. First, future studies may attempt to validate such findings of this work in other government agencies that provide services and also in government agencies of other countries. For example, additional work can look at the impact of user involvement, computer self-efficacy, and user resistance on the IS implementation success in agencies of the European Union, China, etc. Moreover, additional work can look at the impact of such constructs related to e-government services. Second, another set of studies may attempt to investigate the predecessor causes for the two constructs that were found significant in this work. For example, more work should look at the way organizations can increase computer self-efficacy of its employees. Additionally, more work should investigate techniques to increase user involvement in the system development and implementation phases of IS within government agencies. Third, as a CIS could have an impact on the daily work in organizations it might be important to add the social impact of such implementation to the model. Additional work may attempt to combine other social aspect and test it in the context of service oriented organizations.

ACKNOWLEDGMENT

The authors would like to thank all the anonymous NASA employees that participated in this study. The authors would like to thank the editor-in-chief Professor John Wang, as well as the anonymous referees, for their careful review and valuable suggestions. Additionally, the authors wish to acknowledge the input of participants at the Decision Science Institute (DSI) 2008 conference in Baltimore, MD, Nov 2008, where an earlier version of part of this article was presented.

REFERENCES

Adams, B., Berner, E. S., & Wyatt, J. R. (2004). Applying strategies to overcome user resistance in a group of clinical managers to a business software application: A case study. *Journal of Organizational and End User Computing, 16*(4), 55–65.

Bandura, A. (1977). Self-efficacy: Toward a unifying theory of behavioral change. *Psychological Review, 84*(2), 191–215. doi:10.1037/0033-295X.84.2.191

Bandura, A. (1982). Self-efficacy mechanism in human agency. *The American Psychologist, 37*(2), 122–147. doi:10.1037/0003-066X.37.2.122

Bandura, A. (1986). *Social foundations of thought and action.* Englewood Cliffs, NJ: Prentice-Hall.

Barki, H., & Hartwick, J. (1994). Measuring user participation, user involvement, and user attitude. *Management Information Systems Quarterly, 18*(1), 59–82. doi:10.2307/249610

Baronas, A., & Louis, M. (1988). Restoring a sense of control during implementation: How user involvement leads to system acceptance. *Management Information Systems Quarterly, 12*(1), 111–123. doi:10.2307/248811

Baroudi, J., Olson, M., & Ives, B. (1986). An empirical study of the impact of user involvement on system usage and information satisfaction. *Management of Computing, 29*(3), 232–238.

Chin, W. W. (1998). Issues and opinions on structural equation modeling. *Management Information Systems Quarterly, 22*(1), 7–16.

Chin, W. W., Marcolin, B. L., & Newsted, P. R. (2003). A partial least squares latent variable modeling approach for measuring interaction effects: Results from a monte carlo simulation study and an electronic mail adoption study. *Information Systems Research, 14*(2), 189–217. doi:10.1287/isre.14.2.189.16018

Compeau, D., & Higgins, C. (1995). Computer self-efficacy: Development of a measure and initial test. *Management Information Systems Quarterly, 19*(2), 189–211. doi:10.2307/249688

Compeau, D., & Higgins, C. (1999). Social cognitive theory and individual reactions to computing technology: A longitudinal study. *Management Information Systems Quarterly, 23*(2), 145–159. doi:10.2307/249749

DeLone, W., & McLean, E. (1992). Information systems success: The quest for the dependent variable. *Information Systems Research, 3*(1), 60–95. doi:10.1287/isre.3.1.60

DeLone, W., & McLean, E. (2003). The DeLone and McLean model of information systems success: A ten-year update. *Journal of Management Information Systems, 19*(4), 9–30.

Doll, W., & Torkzadeh, G. (1998). Developing a multidimensional measure of system-use in an organizational context. *Information & Management, 33*(4), 171–185. doi:10.1016/S0378-7206(98)00028-7

Ebbers, W. E., & van Dijk, J. A. G. M. (2007). Resistance and support to electronic government, building a model of innovation. *Government Information Quarterly, 24*(3), 554–575. doi:10.1016/j.giq.2006.09.008

Fishbein, M., & Ajzen, I. (1975). *Belief, attitude, intention and behavior: An introduction to theory and research*. Reading, MA: Addison-Wesley.

Fjermestad, J., & Romano, N. (2003). An integrative implementation framework for electronic customer relationship management: Revisiting the general principles of usability and resistance. In *Proceeding of the Proceedings of the 36th Hawaii International Conference on System Sciences,* Big Island, HI.

Gefen, D., & Straub, D. (2005). A practical guide to factorial validity using PLS-graph: Tutorial and annotated example. *Communications of the Association for Information Systems, 16*(5), 91–109.

Hunton, J., & Beeler, J. (1997). Effects of user participation on systems development: A longitudinal field experiment. *Management Information Systems Quarterly, 21*(4), 359–388. doi:10.2307/249719

Ives, B., & Olson, H. (1984). User involvement and MIS success: A review of research. *Management Science, 30*(5), 586–603. doi:10.1287/mnsc.30.5.586

Jiang, J., Waleed, J., Muhanna, A., & Klein, G. (2000). User resistance and strategies for promoting acceptance across system types. *Information & Management, 37*(1), 25–36. doi:10.1016/S0378-7206(99)00032-4

Jones, M. C., & Young, R. (2006). ERP usage in practice: An empirical investigation. *Information Resources Management Journal, 19*(1), 23–42.

Jones, N. B., & Kochtanek, T. R. (2004). Success factors in the implementation of a collaborative technology and resulting productivity improvements in a small business: An exploratory study. *Journal of Organizational and End User Computing, 16*(1), 1–20.

Lane, P. L., Palko, J., & Cronan, T. P. (1994). Key issues in the MIS implementation process: An update using end user computing satisfaction. *Journal of End User Computing, 6*(4), 3–14.

Levy, Y. (2006). *Assessing the value of e-learning systems*. Hershey, PA: Information Science Publishing.

Levy, Y., & Green, B. D. (In Press). An empirical study of computer self-efficacy and the technology acceptance model in the military: A case of a U.S. Navy combat information system. *Journal of Organizational and End User Computing,* 1-23.

Lucas, H., Walton, E., & Ginzberg, M. (1988). Implementing packaged software. *Management Information Systems Quarterly, 12*(4), 537–549. doi:10.2307/249129

Marcoulides, G. A., Chin, W. W., & Saunders, C. (2009). A critical look at partial least squares modeling. *Management Information Systems Quarterly, 33*(1), 171–175.

Marcoulides, G. A., & Saunders, C. (2006). PLS: A silver bullet? *Management Information Systems Quarterly, 30*(2), iii–ix.

Mertler, C. A., & Vannatta, R. A. (2001). *Advanced and multivariate statistical methods: Practical application and interpretation*. Los Angeles, CA: Pyrczak Publishing.

Myers, M., & Avison, D. (2002). *Qualitative research in information systems*. Thousand Oaks, CA: Sage Publications.

Ringle, C. M., Wende, S., & Will, A. (2005). *SmartPLS 2.0 (beta)*. Retrieved March 11, 2009 from http://www.smartpls.de/

The White House. (2004). *Policy for a common identification standard for federal employees and contractors*. Retrieved March 16, 2008 from http://www.whitehouse.gov/news/releases/2004/08/20040827-8.html

Wetzels, M., Odekerken-Schröder, G., & Van-Oppen, C. (2009). Using PLS path modeling for assessing hierarchical construct models: Guidelines and empirical illustration. *Management Information Systems Quarterly, 33*(1), 177–195.

Zmud, R. (1979). Individual differences and MIS success: A review of the empirical literature. *Management Science, 25*(10), 966–979. doi:10.1287/mnsc.25.10.966

APPENDIX: SURVEY INSTRUMENT

User Involvement (UI) items:

I was able to make changes to the formalized agreement of work to be done during implementation

The Information Systems staff kept me informed concerning progress and/or problems during implementation

I formally reviewed work done by Information Systems staff during implementation

I developed test data specifications for this system

I reviewed the results of system tests done by the Information Systems staff

The Information Systems staff held a "special event" to introduce the system to me

I participated in designing the user training program for this system

I participated in developing the user procedures manual for this system

User Resistance (URES) items:

I feel this system implementation will create a loss of status in my current job

I feel this system implementation will affect my salary or potential increase in salary

I feel this system implementation will alter interpersonal relationships

I feel this system implementation will change my job duties

I feel this system implementation will change my decision making approach

I feel this system implementation will create a loss of power for me in my current position

I feel this system implementation will create a personal level of uncertainty on the purpose of the implementation

Computer Self-Efficacy (CSE) items:

I could complete the identification using this system if there was no one around to tell me what to do as I go

I could complete the identification using this system if I had never used a system like it before

I could complete the identification using this system if I had only the software manuals for reference

I could complete the identification using this system if I had seen someone else using it before trying it myself

I could complete the identification using this system if I could call someone for help if I got stuck

I could complete the identification using this system if someone else had helped me get started

I could complete the identification using this system if I had a lot of time to complete the job for which the software was provided

I could complete the identification using this system if I had just the built-in help facility for assistance

I could complete the identification using this system if someone showed me how to do it first

I could complete the identification using this system if I had used similar systems before this one to do the same job

Information System Usage (ISU) items:

I use this system to assist me in the identification process
I use this system to help explain my identification issues
I use this system to analyze if problems occur with my identification
I use this system to control my identification process
I use this system to help me manage my identification accesses
I use this system to monitor my own performance
I use this system to plan my identification accesses
I use this system to keep my supervisor informed
I use this system to document to others my identification accesses

This work was previously published in International Journal of Information Systems in the Service Sector, Volume 2, Issue 2, edited by John Wang, pp. 19-32, copyright 2010 by IGI Publishing (an imprint of IGI Global).

Chapter 8
SERREA:
A Semantic Management System for Retail Real Estate Agencies

Ángel García-Crespo
Universidad Carlos III de Madrid, Spain

Ricardo Colomo-Palacios
Universidad Carlos III de Madrid, Spain

Juan Miguel Gómez-Berbís
Universidad Carlos III de Madrid, Spain

Fernando Paniagua Martín
Universidad Carlos III de Madrid, Spain

ABSTRACT

In the scenario of market competition in the Retail Real Estate Agencies (RREA) business, having exact information regarding properties in supply and their associated demand is a differentiating factor for organizations. The Semantic Web represents an opportunity to create extensible services that hold precise information concerning these types of markets. The objective of the current initiative is to use this market data as a competitive advantage for organizations. In this article, the authors propose SERREA, a management system for RREA based on semantics and constructed using Web Services, which has been implemented successfully in one of the leading agencies in Spain. The goal of this paper is to show how RREA benefits from using Semantic Technologies in the context of their business operations.

INTRODUCTION

The importance of Information Systems (IS) in different domains in today's society is without doubt. Moreover, according to Targowski (2009) Web technology is key solution for the provision of e-Service systems. In the domain of Real Estate, the importance of technology has been emphasized by numerous authors since the 1990s (e.g., Weber, 1990; Fung et al., 1995; Rodriguez et al., 1995; Bible & Hsieh, 1996; Pace & Gilley, 1997), a trend which continued during the 21st century (Crowston et al., 2001; Fryrear et al., 2001; Zeng & Zhou,

DOI: 10.4018/978-1-4666-0044-7.ch008

Copyright © 2012, IGI Global. Copying or distributing in print or electronic forms without written permission of IGI Global is prohibited.

2001; Kummerow & Lun, 2005; Pagourtzi et al., 2006; Krol et al., 2008).

Turban et al. (2003) present several advantages for the use of Information Technology (IT) in Real Estate, such as saving time for the client and the broker, and improving the organization of properties according to criteria, facilitating the search process. According to Crowston et al. (2001), Real Estate is an information-intensive business. Agents, who are pure market-intermediaries, connect buyers to sellers and do so through control and dissemination of information, being particularly vulnerable to changes in the availability of such information.

In a general sense, according to Kummerow and Lun (2005), a Real Estate Agency entails brokerage - bringing together buyers and sellers (sales and leasing). Thus, retail real estate may be referred to as the activity responsible for successfully performing the management of retail stores, in the context of sales and leasing. Examining the work of Q4 in 2008 by Cushman and Wakefield (2008), the demand for retail, particularly in prime locations, continues to be active in various countries (Austria, Greece, France, Germany), while in others (Italy, Portugal, Spain) investment is in a period of "wait and see", given that the profitability of prime shopping centers is about 6%.

In this scenario, in spite of the global economic situation, which has decelerated growth, RRE continues to be an attractive area for investment and technological development, and also is presenting a dramatic increase in its interactions with new technological artifacts, known as highly specialized service systems (Spohrer & Kwan, 2009). This paper presents SERREA, a platform for RREA support designed using semantic technology for the definition of the characteristics of retail stores. The application, which has been developed to act as support to the service which a particular RREA offer, enables them to provide an improved service using the application of a set of leading technologies, including semantics. This application is different from other RREA solutions.

Many of the features of the application are similar (search, locate...), but semantics brings a well defined meaning, that in words of Berners-Lee, Hendler and Lassila (2001) can "enable computers and people to work in co-operation better". In other words, semantics and ontologies can bring new features to service sector: better integration of services and improved cooperation among organizations. The aim of this paper is twofold. On the one hand, to introduce SERREA as a novel and promising solution that supports RREA business process using semantic technologies and, on the other hand, by means of the application of a questionnaire, to show results of its implementation in a particular RREA.

The remainder of the paper is organized as follows. The next section defines the state of the art in semantics, semantic information systems and their use in the RREAs environment. This is followed by a description of SERREA, detailing its architecture and implementation. Subsequently, the paper provides a case study of this implementation in a Spanish RREA. Next section analyzes the results of the evaluation of the tool. Lastly, the paper presents the principal conclusions and future work of the study.

STATE OF THE ART

The platform presented in the current work integrates two types of technologies, or more specifically, two distinct IT philosophies. In the first place, it incorporates the vision of the Semantic Web for the annotation and efficient use of the information which characterize the different retail stores. In the second place, the platform benefits from the technology provided by Web Services to equip the system developed with extensible features.

The arrival of the Semantic Web represents a revolution for the form of access and storage of information. The term "Semantic Web" was coined by Berners-Lee, Hendler, and Lassila (2001), to describe the evolution from a document-based web towards a new paradigm that includes data and information for computers to manipulate. The Semantic Web enables automated information access based on machine-processable semantics of data. The Semantic Web was defined by these authors as "an extension of the current web in which information is given well defined meaning," and can "enable computers and people to work in co-operation better". The Semantic Web provides a complementary vision as a knowledge management environment (Warren, 2006) that, in many cases has expanded and replaced previous knowledge and information management archetypes (Davies, Lytras, & Sheth, 2007). Ontologies (Fensel, 2002) are the technological cornerstones of the Semantic Web, because they provide structured vocabularies that describe a formal specification of a shared conceptualization. Ontologies were developed in the field of Artificial Intelligence to facilitate knowledge sharing and reuse (Fensel et al., 2001). Ontologies provide a common vocabulary for a domain and define, with different levels of formality, the meaning of the terms and the relations between them. Knowledge in ontologies is mainly formalized using five kinds of components: classes, relations, functions, axioms and instances (Gruber, 1993). Classes in the ontology are usually organized into taxonomies. Sometimes, the definition of ontologies has been diluted, maybe because taxonomies are considered to be full ontologies (Studer, Benjamins, & Fensel, 1998). The formal semantics underlying ontology languages enables the automatic processing of the information in ontologies and allows the use of semantic reasoners to infer new knowledge. The shift enabled by the use of machine understandable ontologies can outperform the current endeavors that require finding data spread out across the Web or dynamically drawing inferences, which are continually hampered by their reliance on ad-hoc, task specific frameworks.

The fundamental aim of the Semantic Web is to answer the ever-growing requirement for data integration on the Web. The benefit of adding semantics consists of bridging nomenclature and terminological inconsistencies to include underlying meanings in a unified manner. Given that a universally shared data format is not likely to arise and diffuse, the Semantic Web provides an alternative solution to represent the comprehensive meaning of integrated information and promises to lead to efficient data management by establishing a common understanding (Shadbolt, Hall, & Berners-Lee, 2006). In this new scenario, the challenge for the next generation of the Social and Semantic Webs is to find the right match between what is put online and methods for doing useful reasoning with the data (Gruber, 2008).

Regarding semantic web methodologies, there are methodologies for building ontologies from scratch (Staab, Studer, Schnurr, & Sure, 2001) and methodologies for the collaborative and cooperative construction of ontologies (Noy & Musen, 2003). Moreover, there are several methods to develop semantic web applications and semantic web services. See Wahl and Sindre (2009) for a detailed review.

In recent years, Semantic Web research has resulted in significant outcomes and the adoption of this technology from the market and the industry is becoming closer (Lytras & García, 2008). With regard to the application of the Semantic Web in real systems, there have been numerous applications of the Semantic Web in service environments. Applications have been seen in the field of the hiring of human resources, such as Prolink (Gómez-Berbís et al., 2008), in the collaborative development of software, for example, platforms such as Global Software Repository (Colomo-Palacios et al., 2008), logistics (Corcho, Losada, & Benjamins, 2008), or tourism (García-Crespo et al., 2009a).

Especially, for the real estate sector, searching and comparing offers on the internet is extremely time-consuming and not very efficient (Langegger & Wöß, 2007). Taking into account the importance of the functional environment of Real Estate, a multitude of efforts have developed and implemented initiatives in this application environment which benefit from the Semantic Web (e.g., Stubkjær, 2000; Michalowski et al., 2004; Pretorius, 2005; Zhang et al., 2005; Hess & de Vries, 2006; Langegger & Wöß, 2007). Many of the initiatives focus on the adoption of semantic technology to improve searches for property and facilitate integration between different systems. However, these solutions do not consider the specific characteristics of RREAs in the definitions of the technologies used.

Lastly, in relation to Web Services, the standard definition is that stated by the W3C (2004): A Web service is a software system designed to support interoperable machine-to-machine interaction over a network. Other systems interact with the Web service in a manner prescribed by its description using SOAP messages, typically conveyed using HTTP with an XML serialization in conjunction with other Web-related standards. The benefits of Web services include the decoupling of service interfaces from implementations and platform considerations, the enablement of dynamic service binding, and an increase in cross-language, cross-platform interoperability (Ferris & Farrell, 2003). The subsequent section describes the tool developed which combines the two technologies in a novel solution specifically customized for RREAs. Firstly, an overview of the tool is provided, followed by a detailed description of the architecture.

Semantic Management System for Real Estate Agents (SERREA): Overview Architecture

The SERREA architecture presents a set of significant decisions about the organization of the software system, by selecting a number of structural elements and their interfaces. Components might be related to the behavior as specified in the collaboration among those elements, turning those structural and behavioral elements into pro-

gressively larger subsystems and the architectural style that guides this organization.

This section introduces a loose-coupled view of the architecture. The explanation of this view is aided by describing the architecture in a layered design. The advantage of layering is the conceptual distinction and functionality between layers, given that each layer has a particular and precise functionality. Layers exhibit a bottom-up dependency relationship, indicating that the upper layers rely on some functionality of the lower layers. Layered architectures are used in different domains, and particularly in communication systems where each layer implements a different aspect of the information exchange. The layer view is shown in Figure 1.

The architecture is comprised of three operating layers. Firstly, the User Layer is composed by a number of devices / Graphical User Interfaces (GUI, for short) through which users can interact with the SERREA architecture. Secondly, the Business Logic Layer encompasses the Reasoning, Inference and Business Logic Management functionalities. It is connected to the User Layer through the Web Services Interface, a Service Oriented Architecture based on the Service Bus concept, where a number of loosely-decoupled software components or interfaces can communicate through Web Services Interfaces. Finally, the Persistence and Storage Layer is composed by Semantic Repositories, storing both the Domain Ontologies and Semantic Annotations. In the following, we will detail several of the core components in each layer:

The User Interface Layer has two core software GUIs, namely the Intranet GUI and the Internet GUI:

- Intranet GUI: Provides the functionalities which realize the interaction with the user who works in the intranet for the management of business activities. Additionally, it offers a semantic annotation retrieval functionality for the user, based on both the

Figure 1. SERREA architecture

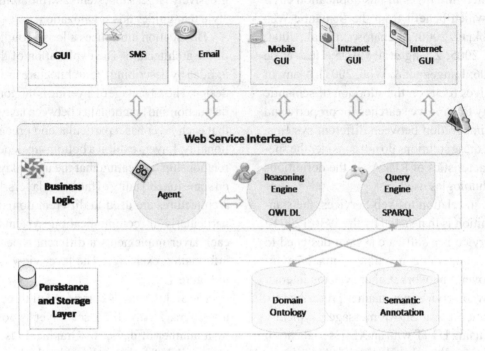

Reasoning Engine and the Query Engine use encapsulated by Web Service. In the former, retrieval is envisaged as location of a subset of concepts by means of Description Logics subsumption. In the latter, the retrieval is provided by SPARQL (Prud'hommeaux & Seaborne, 2008) definitions to find, manage and query Resource Description Framework (RDF) triples following particular criteria. Agreeing with Pinhanez (2009) that software tools and online service applications are intrinsically different, proposed GUI has been designed been aware of service science in order to take full advantage of the service science perspective.

- Internet GUI: The Internet GUI provides a subset of the functionalities of the Intranet GUI, designed to display properties to registered users on the Web.
- Web Service Interface: The element responsible for defining the functionality of the platform, with the objective that it

can be used by different GUIs. This interface can transmit its messages via an HTTP Post (like any other SOAP-based service) but also using HTTP Get request. Traditionally a HTTP Get request should be used when the request will not cause any changes to the serve where at a HTTP Post request could cause some change on the server. Since in SERREA every service is annotated with the type of request it should be used, client applications can benefit of using either HTTP Post or HTTP Get to adapt the invocation to their interest and preferred way of communication.

The Business Logic Layer provides cutting-edge functionalities through the following components:

Agent: The agent component collects, manages, and processes the information regarding what is available on the market and what is demanded, and brings together demanders and suppliers. It is responsible for systematically checking the existence of elements which fulfill the characteristics demanded by clients. At the moment that a match is encountered, the client is notified by email or SMS. The preferences of the users are stored in such a form that they can be utilized by the search algorithm based on the application of the Ordered Weighted Averaging (OWA) operator (Yager, 1988) and the Multi Attribute Utility Theory (MAUT)-based feature comparison. In MAUT, given a request (a retail real estate product) r with the attribute values a_i = [0, 1] and relative weights w_i = [0, 1]:

$$r = ((a_1, a_2, .., a_m), (w_1, w_2, ..., w_m))$$

and a real estate product p with the attribute values b_i = [0, 1]:

$$p = (b_1, b_2, .., b_n)$$

the score is calculated according to this function:

$$score(r, p) = \sum_{i=1}^{m} w_i * util(a_i, b_i)$$

While the scoring function calculates the overall score of an offer in respect to the user's preferences, an utility function $util(a_i, b_i) \rightarrow [0,1]$ calculates the utility of each single attribute accounting for the overall score. When scores for all existing results have been calculated, the results can be used to rank product offers and select the best matching candidates. On the other hand, OWA is a vector of weights which is used to weigh multiple ordered attributes. The implementation of the agent component is based in Java as a standalone application, where most of the check procedures are hardcoded. It uses standard Java communication libraries for email and SMS notification and also provides a rough implementation of the OWA algorithm. A combination of weighted scoring and OWA operators was presented by Langegger and Wöß (2007).

- Reasoning Engine: This component derives facts from a knowledge base, reasoning about the information with the final purpose of formulating new conclusions. In the SERREA framework, we use OWL Description Logics as the OWL flavor which will be used to reason. Hence we are based on the Description Logics knowledge representation mechanism. For the implementation of the Reasoning Engine, we use Pellet, a Java-based Description Logics reasoned which also provides SPARQL querying and RDF management through the Jena framework. From the development perspective, we simply use the subsumption-based DL reasoning to find sets and subsets of annotations based on logical constraints.

- Query Engine: The Query Engine component uses the SPARQL RDF query language to make queries into the storage systems of the back end layer. The semantics of the query are defined not by a precise rendering of a formal syntax, but by an interpretation of the most suitable results of the query. This is because SERREA stores mostly RDF triples or OWL DL ontologies which also present an RDF syntax.

In the knowledge representation research field, there are technologies that not only ease knowledge representation, but also enable the sharing and reuse of knowledge components. One of these technologies is ontologies, which allow static knowledge representation. Ontologies enable knowledge sharing and reuse, thus reducing the effort needed to implement expert systems. Ontologies were conceived in the scope of Artificial Intelligence as a means to facilitate sharing and reuse. Since the 1990s, ontologies have been a latent research topic and different research communities have been involved in their evolution such as knowledge engineering, natural language processing, and knowledge representation. One of the reasons of the increasing popularity of the study of ontologies is what they promise: a shared and common understanding of a particular domain which can be communicated between people and software applications. In summary, the use of ontologies provides a chance to increase the likelihood of successfully enacting any task related to knowledge and information management. Both the Domain Ontology and the Semantic Annotations are implemented with the Web Ontology Language (OWL) in its OWL-DL flavor, what allows the reasoning based on Description Logics explained previously. The ontologies were implemented using Protégé, the most extended world-wide framework for the creation and management of ontologies. Protégé is a free, open source ontology editor and a knowledge acquisition system. Protégé is written in Java and relies on Swing to create its user interface.

Finally, the Persistence and Storage Layer consists of a semantic data store system that enables ontology persistence, querying performed by the Business Logic layer components, and offers a higher abstraction layer. This enables fast storage and retrieval of large amounts of OWL DL ontologies together with their RDF syntax while keeping a small footprint and a lightweight architecture approach. Examples of these systems could be the OpenRDF Sesame RDF Storage system, or the Yet Another RDF Storage System (YARS), which deal with data and legacy integration. In our case, for the implementation, we used the Jena Framework as the backbone technology, for two main reasons. Firstly, Jena relies on a MySQL database. The semantic information (ontologies and annotations) stored in Jena are provided with RDF and OWL support and has been used for storing the Semantic Information. Jena is a framework for Java that provides an API for writing and extracting data from OWL descriptions.

IMPLEMENTATION

The implementation of the architecture as a whole has been based on Sun Microsystems J2EE (Java to Enterprise Edition) technology. J2EE is a widely used platform for server programming in the Java programming language, adding libraries which provide functionality to deploy fault-tolerant, distributed, multi-tier Java software, based largely on modular components running on an application server. Fundamentally, parts of the architecture such as the agents, reasoning engine and user profiles have been developed using existing Java applications. Particularly in the reasoning engine case we use self-contained loosely coupled software components providing such functionality. Current reasoning approaches on the Semantic Web are grounded on classical logic, with its notions of deduction, semantics, model-theory, soundness and completeness.

For the liaison between the business logical and the presentation layer, it is based on the Model-View-Controller design pattern, where the GUI layer corresponds with the view, the business logic layer corresponds with the controller, and the persistence layer corresponds with the model. For the GUI a web interface enhanced with AJAX technology has been chosen. With the objective of enabling the geo-location of properties, the Google Map interface has been used for interaction with the platform. The communication of the different software components is hence based on the standard J2EE communication mechanisms, despite it could also be based on more decoupled frameworks such as Web Services.

Regarding the Domain Ontology, semantic annotation and communication between these different parts they are all based on the Web Ontology Language (OWL), a family of knowledge representation languages for authoring ontologies, and is endorsed by the World Wide Web Consortium. This family of languages is based on two (largely, but not entirely, compatible) semantics: OWL DL and OWL Lite semantics are based on

Description Logics which have attractive and well-understood computational properties, while OWL Full uses a novel semantic model intended to provide compatibility with RDF Schema.

Furthermore, the Semantic Annotation and Query functionalities provide retrieval and selection of propositions contained in large-scale semantic repositories. Retrieval and selection are needed to support ceiling-free reasoning since they need to be able to dynamically reduce or expand the data set we are working with depending on factors such as cost of processing or confidence in result. For any particular task the choice of selection method depends most crucially upon three factors:

- Cost/Benefit. The affordability of different scales of reasoning process and the expected cost-per-statement of the process. In other words, both the size and nature of the propositional content under consideration and the intended nature of the reasoning process must be taken into account when choosing a selection method.
- Provenance. The source of a proposition is evidence of its relevance to a particular reasoning task. For example, propositions that have been derived from or linked to a document collection can be selected by using clustering and search methods from information retrieval.
- Context. The context of the reasoning process can be used as a filter on the relevance of propositional content. For example, a degree of similarity to content on the user's desktop or in their browser history is an indication of relevance in certain conceptual search scenarios.
- Determination of the optimal mapping between these three factors and the selection methods that the project will adapt and develop requires quantification of the performance of each method when operating according to parameters derived

from a representative sample of task environments. In other words, we must apply empirical measures to gather data for our theory of selection and of selection method choice.

Finally, the main software architecture principles followed by the SERREA architecture are defining structural issues in the SERREA software system that include global control structure, protocols for communication, synchronization and data access, assignment of functionality to design elements, physical distribution, composition of design elements, scaling and performance and selection among design alternatives based on the J2EE technology framework which provides full support for them from an implementation viewpoint.

CASE STUDY

The company NEREAL (fictitious name) was established in Madrid, Spain in 2005. NEREAL aims to exploit the experience held by one of its two partners, here named ILA, a textile firm of Spanish origin which has achieved the largest number of business expansions of the decade since the year 2000. ILA's business model was conceived as a RREA in prime locations, which correspond to the main commercial streets of large cities. ILA's business model includes both buying operations as well as the renting of business premises in these zones, principally for international companies in the textile industry. The operating strategy of NEREAL is overall, highly personalized, given that both negotiations with clients as well as with owners is done by ILA.

Subsequent to two years of performance, the success achieved by the company in the operations undertaken by ILA leads them to consider changing their organizational strategy, which changes the size of the company, and in parallel, the business model. The company considers the creation of a network of agents for the location of business premises in various Spanish cities. However, this move evokes the requirement that the management of the offer and the request should be supported by automated techniques which aid ILA in making the offer to companies in expansion. These agents should be empowered to make notifications regarding the discovery of premises which fulfill existing requests or demands. The number of clients of the company is moderate, and therefore its requests are highly varied and depend on the circumstance and intuition of the decision makers in the client organizations. Thus, NEREAL decides to implement SERREA for the management of its relations with clients and providers.

In addition to the diverse capacities related to the operations of the company, the use of SERREA focuses on two fundamental aspects. In the first place, the company adapts SERREA so that the agents input the commercial premises which characterize the subsequent offer, or which simply represent leads (without communication with the owner of the property).

In the second place, SERREA is utilized to store customer preferences. At the moment at which a lead or a property is added, ILA is informed, as well as the corresponding account agents, using email and SMS to inform them of the new availability. ILA continues to be responsible for communication with important clients, even though it delegates other agents to negotiate with the owners of commercial premises and carry out the administrative affairs of negotiation with clients. The information is completed with the references of the system to national property/site values, as well as spatial information regarding the property. Lastly, the property is always geolocated using XY coordinates, storing these coordinates in a persistent repository.

In the first year of use of the tool, a total of 700 leads were codified in SERREA, of which 37 resulted in a successful deal, 86% of which were renting operations and 14% sales deals. The preferences of the clients were codified by an ILA agent based on his notes, and analyzing the agent's data, the matching realized by SERREA was considered crucial for the closing of operations (specially for operations in Madrid, the location of the headquarters of the company). In this year, NEREAL presented an increase of 26% in its commissions, 28% its operations and 21% its EBITDA. Today, NEREAL continues operations using SERREA as a management system and a communication tool with its agents.

EVALUATION

Research Design

Evaluation of the proposal was required in order to determine the level of acceptance of SERREA among NEREAL workers. With the objective of calculating the level of adjustment of the proposal, a study was designed which was aimed towards NEREAL workers. This evaluation was carried out by means of the application of a questionnaire. The questionnaire was applied after the subjects had used the SERREA tool for a period of time not less than nine months.

The questionnaire was composed of three sections. In the first place, the subject was required to provide identification data: age and gender. Secondly, the users were asked about the different perceptions they had about the use of SERREA. Users were asked to answer three questions regarding SERREA: Overall evaluation, User experience and Performance. The responses to these questions were coded using a Likert scale ranging from 1 to 4 points, with the following values. 1: Limited, 2: Regular, 3: Good, 4: Very Good. Thirdly, the subject was asked about the capacities of SERREA compared with other Real Estate applications used by them in their previous jobs. To do so, users explain with their own words their experience in tools devoted to Real Estate. After that, users compare SERREA with their previous experience in Real Estate tools using Likert scale ranging from 1 to 5 points (1: SERREA is clearly worse than other tools, 2: SERREA is slightly worse than other tools, 3: More or less the same, 4: SERREA is slightly better than other tools, 5: SERREA is clearly better than other tools). After that, users were asked to identify the differencing features in SERREA (Faceted Search, Annotation…) and rank them.

Questionnaires were sent to targeted individuals via email and filled out by them with the online supervision (via chat) of one member of the research team.

Sample

The sample was composed of NEREAL workers and ex-workers. These workers use SERREA as a tool to support their work in NEREAL. The sample was composed of 2 women (14%) and 12 men (86%), with an average age of 34.7. Among respondents, four of them are not currently working in NEREAL, but they have left the company recently (less than 6 months). All respondents had previous experience in top RREAs either in Spain or abroad.

Results

The results of the surveys, which were filled in using electronic documents, were subsequently coded in the statistical analysis tool Statistical Package for the Social Sciences (SPSS). In Table 1, the average and standard deviation of the responses offered by the subjects are shown in relation to overall evaluation, user experience and performance.

Taking into account the results provided, those related to "User experience" are more than promising. This value presents an average of 3.79 points over 4, with a highly adjusted standard deviation of 0.43, which indicates that, apart from the scoring being high, the agreement between the subjects is more than acceptable. Thus, the attempts to

develop the Graphical User Interface of SERREA so that it would be attractive to users have been judged positively by test users. Apart from this, and taking into account results displayed in Table 1 and Figure 2, all factors are above 3 points and present moderate standard deviation figures (high concentration of values and low disparity).

On the other hand, users reported a total of four tools used by them in their previous jobs: Salesforce (6 users), SAP (4 users), Sage (3 users) and in-house developments (6 users). None of these tools implement semantic technologies yet. Figure 3 shows the results of the comparisons made by users among these tools and SERREA (1: SERREA is clearly worse than other tools, 2: SERREA is slightly worse than other tools, 3: More or less the same, 4: SERREA is slightly better than other tools, 5: SERREA is clearly better than other tools).

The comparison among SERREA and other Real Estate (or general purpose tools customized to operate in a Real Estate scenario) tools is also very promising. SERREA can be seen as a useful tool compared to In-house developments (SERREA is clearly better in 5 of 6 opinions) and also compared with Sage, and, in a lower but important level, with solutions like SAP or Salesforce.

Finally, users identified a total of 6 characteristics of SERREA as differencing features. Table 2 displays characteristics, occurrences and average rank.

Table 1. Overall evaluation, user experience and performance: average and standard deviation

	Average	Std. Deviation
Overall evaluation	3.21	0.58
User experience	3.79	0.43
Performance	3.29	0.61

The frequency of the scores in the scale defined for the different factors may be viewed in Figure 2 (Values: 1: Limited, 2: Regular, 3: Good, 4: Very Good):

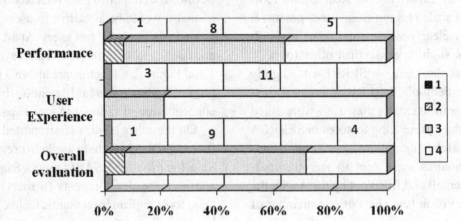

Figure 2. Overall evaluation, user experience and performance: score frequencies

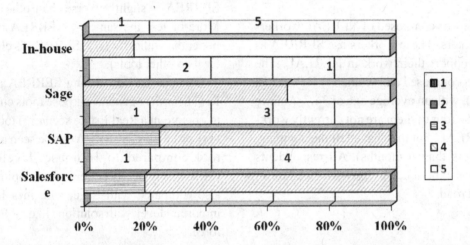

Figure 3. Overall evaluation, user experience and performance: score frequencies

Taking into account the results provided in Table 2, SERREA top 3 features are pure semantic features. In particular, "Faceted Search" is perceived as the leading feature. In "Faceted

Table 2. SERREA top features

	Occurrences	Avg. Rank
Faceted search	14	1
Semantic annotation tool	14	2
Keyword Search	14	3
Finder agent	8	4
SMS	8	5
Email integration	7	6

Search", based on previous works (García Crespo et al., 2009b; García Crespo et al., 2009c) a number of RDF based faceted navigation mechanisms were developed that help the user to navigate through the results. With faceted metadata, the information space is partitioned using orthogonal conceptual dimensions of the data. These dimensions are called facets, and represent the characteristics of the information elements. These facets are used then to select or filter the relevant elements in a certain information space, leading users to the exact information needed. These facets are the properties defined in the domain ontologies.

Secondly, the "Semantic annotation tool" provides the functionality of linking a particular object with a given concept, populating ontologies in an easy and effective way. Finally, "Keyword Search" also presents good values, but, due to the popularity of this feature in both semantic and non-semantic tools, this feature has been judged as less relevant by subjects.

Taking into account the test, and from the perspective of the results, the implementation of SERREA may be considered a success: pure semantic features are perceived as the main features of SERREA and SERREA as a whole is perceived as a useful tool in RREA domain.

CONCLUSION AND FUTURE WORK

In the environment of market competition in Retail Real Estate, dynamism and exactness of information represent two of the characteristics of successful organizations. Taking into account that Retail Real Estate is an information-intensive business and that the agents are pure market intermediaries, control in the dissemination of information also represents a feature which is highly valued by agencies that today information systems cannot afford in a full way. SERREA contributes these capacities to the management of information in an environment defined as Retail Real Estate. On the one hand, as a result of the application of agents based on semantics, it enables the instantaneous delivery of information to interested parties. Additionally, the use of semantic technology facilitates the precision of the information, which constitutes the novel solution in SERREA. Here, the benefit of adding semantics consists of bridging nomenclature and terminological inconsistencies to include underlying meanings in a unified manner. Lastly, control of the dissemination of information is achieved due to the use of profiles for access to the information.

Regarding its implementation, SERREA has been tested in a Spanish top RREA domain with good results. On the one hand, this agency has improved its results and on the other hand, users opinions and evaluations of SERREA can be considered more than promising. In this scenario, the aim of testing if semantic technologies, and more in particular, SERREA can be useful to RREAs is passed with good marks.

The development of SERREA represents the beginning of a prolific applied research domain. Therefore, as future research efforts three differentiated lines are proposed. In the first place, with the objective of integrating semantic multimedia capacities into the platform, the researchers propose to incorporate semantic annotation capacities to multimedia video formats. This characteristic would contribute a value added feature, providing a service to the client by enabling him/her to view with precision the elements of the property which fulfill his/her requirements through multimedia video formats. The semantic annotation of multimedia formats on the Internet represents a common future line of work for Semantic Web researchers. Using this feature, a given user could locate a movie in which a given building appears. More precisely, this user could point the exact minute and second in which a certain part of a given building appears in the movie.

In the second place, the aim is to test the introduction of a new component into the architecture used to match supply and demand to exploit the advantages provided by such matching. Lastly, it is aimed to integrate Web 2.0 capacities with semantic web features into the system for the addition of information concerning the property, that is, analyze, classify and store automatically the opinions of users about the property or the commercial site for advanced decision making support using Natural Language Processing (NLP) techniques and opinion mining procedures.

REFERENCES

W3C. (2004). *Web services architecture*. Retrieved August 30, 2009 from http://www.w3.org/TR/2004/NOTE-ws-arch-20040211

Berners-Lee, T., Hendler, J., & Lassila, O. (2001). The semantic web. *Scientific American, 284*(5), 34–43. doi:10.1038/scientificamerican0501-34

Bible, D. S., & Hsieh, C. H. (1996). Applications of geographic information systems for the analysis of apartment rents. *Journal of Real Estate Research, 12*(1), 79–88.

Colomo-Palacios, R., Gómez-Berbís, J. M., García-Crespo, A., & Puebla-Sánchez, I. (2008). Social global repository: Using semantics and social web in software projects. *International Journal of Knowledge and Learning, 4*(5), 452–464. doi:10.1504/IJKL.2008.022063

Corcho, O., Losada, S., & Benjamins, R. (2008). Semantic web-enabled protocol mediation of logistics domain. In García, R. (Ed.), *Semantic web for business: Cases and applications*. Hershey, PA: IGI Global.

Crowston, K., Sawyer, S., & Wigand, R. (2001). Investigating the interplay between structure and information and communications technology in the real estate industry. *Information Technology & People, 14*(2), 163–183. doi:10.1108/09593840110695749

Cushman & Wakefield. (2008). *Marketbeat Q4 2008*. Retrieved August 30, 2009 from http://www.mapic.com/App/homepage.cfm?appname=100543&moduleid=279&campaignid=13036&iUserCampaignID=46044210

Davies, J., Lytras, M. D., & Sheth, A. P. (2007). Semantic-web-based knowledge management. *IEEE Internet Computing, 11*(5), 14–16. doi:10.1109/MIC.2007.109

Fensel, D. (2002). *Ontologies: A silver bullet for knowledge management and electronic commerce*. Berlin: Springer.

Fensel, D., van Harmelen, F., Horrocks, I., McGuinness, D. L., & Patel-Schneider, P. F. (2001). OIL: An ontology infrastructure for the semantic web. *IEEE Intelligent Systems, 16*(2), 38–45. doi:10.1109/5254.920598

Ferris, C., & Farrell, J. (2003). What are web services? *Communications of the ACM, 46*(6), 31. doi:10.1145/777313.777335

Fryrear, R., Prill, E., & Worzala, E. M. (2001). The use of geographic information systems by corporate real estate executives. *Journal of Real Estate Research, 22*(1-2), 153–164.

Fung, D., Kung, H., & Barber, C. (1995). The application of GIS to mapping real estate values. *The Appraisal Journal, 16*(11), 446–449.

García Crespo, A., Chamizo, J., Rivera, I., Mencke, M., Colomo Palacios, R., & Gómez Berbís, J. M. (2009a). SPETA: Social pervasive e-tourism advisor. *Telematics and Informatics, 26*(3), 306–315. doi:10.1016/j.tele.2008.11.008

García Crespo, A., Colomo Palacios, R., Gómez Berbís, J. M., & García Sánchez, F. (2009b). *SOLAR: Social link advanced recommendation system*. Future Generation Computer Systems.

García Crespo, A., Gómez Berbís, J. M., Colomo Palacios, R., & García Sánchez, F. (2009c). Digital libraries and web 3.0: The CallimachusDL approach. *Computers in human behaviour.*

Gómez-Berbís, J. M., Colomo-Palacios, R., García-Crespo, A., & Ruiz-Mezcua, B. (2008). ProLink: A semantics-based social network for software project. *International Journal of Information Technology and Management, 7*(4), 392–404. doi:10.1504/IJITM.2008.018656

Gruber, T. R. (1993). A translation approach to portable ontology specifications. *Knowledge Acquisition, 5*(2), 199–220. doi:10.1006/knac.1993.1008

Gruber, T. R. (2008). Collective knowledge systems: Where the social web meets the semantic web. *Web Semantics: Science. Services and Agents on the World Wide Web, 6*(1), 4–13.

Hess, C., & de Vries, M. (2006). From models to data: A prototype query translator for the cadastral domain. *Computers, Environment and Urban Systems, 30*(5), 529–542. doi:10.1016/j.compenvurbsys.2005.08.008

Krol, D., Trawinski, B., & Zawila, W. (2008). Integration of cadastral and financial-accounting systems. *International Journal of Intelligent Information and Database Systems, 2*(3), 370–381. doi:10.1504/IJIIDS.2008.020448

Kummerow, M., & Lun, J. C. (2005). Information and communication technology in the real estate industry: Productivity, industry structure and market efficiency. *Telecommunications Policy, 29*(2-3), 173–190. doi:10.1016/j.telpol.2004.12.003

Langegger, A., & Wöß, W. (2007). Product finding on the semantic web: A search agent supporting products with limited availability. *International Journal of Web Information Systems, 3*(1-2), 61–88. doi:10.1108/17440080710829225

Lytras, M. D., & García, R. (2008). Semantic web applications: A framework for industry and business exploitation - what is needed for the adoption of the semantic web from the market and industry. *International Journal of Knowledge and Learning, 4*(1), 93–108. doi:10.1504/IJKL.2008.019739

Michalowski, M., Ambite, J. L., Thakkar, S., Tuchinda, R., Knoblock, C. A., & Minton, S. (2004). Retrieving and semantically integrating heterogeneous data from the web. *IEEE Intelligent Systems, 19*(3), 72–79. doi:10.1109/MIS.2004.16

Noy, N. F., & Musen, M. A. (2003). The PROMPT suite: Interactive tools for ontology merging and mapping. *International Journal of Human-Computer Studies, 59*(6), 983–1024. doi:10.1016/j.ijhcs.2003.08.002

Pace, R. K., & Gilley, O. W. (1997). Using the spatial configuration of the data to improve estimation. *The Journal of Real Estate Finance and Economics, 14*(3), 333–340. doi:10.1023/A:1007762613901

Pagourtzi, E., Nikolopoulos, K., & Assimakopoulos, V. (2006). Architecture for a real estate analysis information system using GIS techniques integrated with fuzzy theory. *Journal of Property Investment and Finance, 24*(1), 68–78. doi:10.1108/14635780610642971

Pinhanez, C. (2009). A service science perspective on human-computer interface issues of online service applications. *International Journal of Information Systems in the Service Sector, 1*(2), 17–35.

Pretorius, A. J. (2005). Visual analysis for ontology engineering. *Journal of Visual Languages and Computing, 16*(4), 359–381. doi:10.1016/j.jvlc.2004.11.006

Prud'hommeaux, E., & Seaborne, A. (2008). *SPARQL query language for RDF.* Retrieved August 30, 2009 from http://www.w3.org/TR/rdf-sparql-query

Rodriguez, M., Sirmans, C. F., & Marks, A. P. (1995). Using geographic information systems to improve real estate analysis. *Journal of Real Estate Research, 10*(2), 163–174.

Shadbolt, N., Hall, W., & Berners-Lee, T. (2006). The semantic web revisited. *IEEE Intelligent Systems, 21*(3), 96–101. doi:10.1109/MIS.2006.62

Spohrer, J., & Kwan, S. K. (2009). Service science, management, engineering, and design (SSMED): An emerging discipline - outline & references. *International Journal of Information Systems in the Service Sector, 1*(3), 1–31.

Staab, S., Studer, R., Schnurr, H. P., & Sure, Y. (2001). Knowledge processes and ontologies. *IEEE Intelligent Systems, 16*(1), 26–34. doi:10.1109/5254.912382

Stubkjær, E. (2000, August 13-29). Information communities - A case study in the ontology of real estate. In B. Brogaard (Ed.), Rationality and Irrationality, *Proceedigns of the 23rd International Wittgenstein Symposium*, Kirchberg am Wechsel, Austria (Vol. 8, No. 2, pp. 159-166).

Studer, R., Benjamins, V. R., & Fensel, D. (1998). Knowledge engineering: Principles and methods. *Data & Knowledge Engineering, 25*(1-2), 161–197. doi:10.1016/S0169-023X(97)00056-6

Targowski, A. (2009). The architecture of service systems as the framework for the definition of service science scope. *International Journal of Information Systems in the Service Sector, 1*(1), 54–77.

Turban, E., Lee, J. K., King, D., & Chung, H. M. (2003). *Electronic commerce - a managerial perspective*. Upper Saddle River, NJ: Prentice Hall.

Wahl, T., & Sindre, G. (2009). A survey of development methods for semantic web service systems. *International Journal of Information Systems in the Service Sector, 1*(2), 1–16.

Warren, P. (2006). Knowledge management and the semantic web: From scenario to technology. *IEEE Intelligent Systems, 21*(1), 53–59. doi:10.1109/MIS.2006.12

Weber, B. R. (1990). Application of geographic information systems to real estate market analysis and appraisal. *The Appraisal Journal, 58*(1), 127–132.

Yager, R. R. (1988). On ordered weighted averaging aggregation operators in multicriteria decisionmaking. *IEEE Transactions on Systems, Man, and Cybernetics, 18*(1), 183–190. doi:10.1109/21.87068

Zeng, T. Q., & Zhou, Z. (2001). Optimal spatial decision making using GIS: A prototype of a real estate geographical information system. *International Journal of Geographical Information Science, 15*(4), 307–321. doi:10.1080/136588101300304034

Zhang, D., Chen, M., & Zhou, L. (2005). Dynamic and personalized web services composition in e-business. *Information Systems Management, 22*(3), 50–65. doi:10.1201/1078/45317.22.3.20 050601/88745.7

This work was previously published in International Journal of Information Systems in the Service Sector, Volume 2, Issue 2, edited by John Wang, pp. 33-47, copyright 2010 by IGI Publishing (an imprint of IGI Global).

Chapter 9

Mass Customisation Models for Travel and Tourism Information e-Services:
Interrelationships Between Systems Design and Customer Value

Marianna Sigala
Democritus University, Greece

ABSTRACT

Online travel firms exploit current ICT advances for developing mass customization (MC) capabilities and addressing the needs of the sophisticated travellers. However, studies investigating MC in services and specifically in tourism are limited. By adopting a customer-focused approach, this paper addresses this gap by analysing the following issues: a) the ICT and product dimensions that online firms can customise for developing and implementing different MC models; and b) the customer value and benefits provided by the different MC models. After reviewing and illustrating the interrelationships of studies coming from the fields of customer value, MC and IS design, the author proposes a customer value based framework for developing MC models. The applicability and practical implications of this framework are demonstrated by analysing the MC practices of three online travel cyberintermediaries. Finally, the paper summarises the formulation of research propositions investigating the influence of users' characteristics on the customer value and benefits sought by MC practices and on the design of the IS platforms supporting MC services.

DOI: 10.4018/978-1-4666-0044-7.ch009

Copyright © 2012, IGI Global. Copying or distributing in print or electronic forms without written permission of IGI Global is prohibited.

INTRODUCTION

During the 19th century the industrial revolution took place and mass production was the common manufacturing term used; i.e., products were produced in large quantities at low and afford-able prices. The success of mass production was undeniable as products were manufactured on massive levels, in direct response to consumer demands. In the 21st century, however, consum-ers became more sophisticated and demanding regarding issues pertaining to the design, quality and functionality of their products and services (Clemons, Gao, & Hitt, 2006; Clemons, Gù, & Spitler, 2003). The tourism industry does not constitute an exception from such developments. In particular, the following factors have increased tourists' demand for affordable and reliable ser-vices that correspond exactly to their specific individual needs (Sigala, 2005): increased online price and product transparency; the use of customer recommendation and information personalisation systems by online firms that allow customers to participate in and customise processes such as product development, design and production (e.g., Dell, Travelocity.com dynamic package possibili-ties). Moreover, as the disposable income, the time and flexibility of travellers' increases, demand for pre-packaged and static packaged tours decreases. Moreover, an increasing number of travellers are nowadays willing: to afford little more money for buying personalised tourism services; to spend some time to plan and organise their own vaca-tions by assembling and selecting their own tour package components; and to create their own flexible trip itineraries.

For addressing individuals' requests, travel information service companies have traditionally followed a niche marketing strategy by focusing on specific travellers and offering them differentiating travel products-services at premium prices (e.g., specialised travel agents). However, current com-petition prevents firms from charging for product customisation, while ICT advances and tools (e.g.,

collaborative filtering) enable firms to adopt flex-ible operating procedures that reduce the cost of product customisation at mass production output levels, i.e., mass customisation operating models (MC). Indeed, recent research provides evidence of a positive relationship between increased ICT investments and a firms' capability to produce a large product variety (Gao & Hitt, 2004).

In e-tourism, MC practices are mainly reflected on the wide adoption and development of per-sonalised travel services and dynamic packaging (Anite, 2002; Sigala & Christou, 2005). However, despite the business necessity of MC in tourism, research in MC in tourism, as well as in services in general, is scarce (Peters & Saidin, 2000). Indeed, most of the MC studies have primarily focused on investigating the operational and technologi-cal capabilities of mass customisers specifically within the manufacturing sector (Papathanas-siou, 2004). Thus, limited academic debate and evidence are currently provided identifying the MC models and analysing how the latter can be designed for delivering enhanced customer value. This is because previous studies on MC typologies have adopted a business value chain and process centric approach for categorising MC models (e.g., Spira, 1996), as MC implementation demands the integration and participation of customers in value chains. However, when MC implementation is centred around value chains rather than customer value, customer adoption of MC is not guaranteed (Piller et al., 2004). Previous MC typologies also implicitly assume that the success of MC increases as customer involvement in the value chain in-creases. Nevertheless, this assumption does not consider whether customers are also willing, have the competencies and/or perceive and get any value by participating in value chains and becoming co-producers of personalised services. Therefore, there is a need to adopt a customer value centric approach for identifying and analysing how to develop MC models that can deliver customer value and benefits.

This paper aims to develop an overall framework that can be used for identifying, developing and categorising different types of MC models from a customer value centric approach. By focusing on MC implementation in the context of online travel information service companies, the study does not only address the gaps of MC within the service sector, but it also investigates a major competitive necessity in e-tourism. To achieve this, the study first analyses the drivers, the concept and the application of MC in general and then, it focuses on MC in the context of online travel and tourism information services. As a result, the paper identified and reviewed the various types and dimensions of MC models and then, it proposed a customer value centric framework for analysing the MC models and customer values delivered by online travel firms. When MC is implemented over the Internet, its supporting information system (IS) platform needs to be appropriately designed in order to provide users with different MC functional, utilitarian and emotional values (Franke, & Piller, 2004; Oon & Khalid, 2001; Kamali & Loker, 2002; Liechty, Ramaswamy, & Cohen, 2001). Recently and Lexhagen (2009) has also demonstrated the need to design and assess travel websites by adopting a customer-value centred approach. To that end, the proposed framework also identifies the different IS design issues that need to be considered when designing the online MC IS platform so that the latter would address and fit the physical, cognitive and affective profile of its users. In this vein, the framework is developed by borrowing and synthesising concepts from the fields of human-technology interaction, IS design and customer value. The applicability of the dimensions and customer values of the proposed MC framework are illustrated by analysing the online MC services provided by three travel cyberintermediaries. Because all travellers do not give the same importance to functional and emotional MC customer values, while other contextual (e.g., type of task to be performed) and social community (e.g., peer groups) factors may also affect travellers' preferences and needs regarding the design, the functionality and the customer values provided by the IS platform supporting the MC services. Hence, the study concludes by developing several research propositions aiming to guide further research investigating the design of IS platforms supporting the development and provision of MC models and customer values.

MASS CUSTOMISATION: CONCEPT, DRIVERS AND IMPLEMENTATION

The term *mass customization* was coined by Stan Davis (1987) who predicted that the more a company was able to deliver customized goods on a mass basis relative to its competition, the greater would be its competitive advantage. This view is also supported by Pitt, Bertham, and Watson (1999) and Duray and Milligan (1999). Pine, Victor, and Boynton (1993) described the synergy of mass customization as a 'new' competitive strategy challenging 'old' strategies such as mass production. Hart and Taylor (1996) offered an operational definition of MC claiming that 'MC is the use of flexible processes and organizational structures to produce varied and often individually customised products/services at the price of standardised, mass produced alternatives'. MC means that firms can reach the same large customer numbers as in mass production, but they have the additional ability to address their customers individually as in customised markets (Parker, 1996). Flexibility, variety and responsiveness of processes as well as resource reconfiguration are all essential to MC, while companies need to understand what customers really want and then respond quickly with an offering which costs the customer relatively little more than standardised, mass produced alternatives (Duray & Milligan, 1999; Pine et al., 1995; Boynton et al., 1993).

The justification for the development of MC systems is based on three main ideas and developments (e.g., Pitt et al., 1999; Duray & Milligan,

1999; Pine et al., 1995; Duray, 2000): a) new flexible manufacturing systems and ICT enable production systems to deliver higher variety at lower cost; b) an increasing demand for product variety and one-to-one customization; and c) the shortening of product life cycles and the expanding industrial competition that have led to the breakdown of many mass industries and the need to adopt production strategies focused on individual customers. Pine's (1993) market turbulence map identified the following additional drivers to MC: the 'quality consciousness' of customers considered as 'meeting whatever the customer wants', and the competitive activity.

Considering e-tourism, the following trends have led to the urgency to adopt MC practices in the travel and tourism intermediary sector (Anite, 2002; Sigala & Christou, 2005): reduction of commissions provided to intermediaries by tourism suppliers; the need of travel intermediaries to find new revenue models by providing enhanced customer value and new customer services; the possibility of dynamic packaging to provide new revenue streams and customer loyalty; the rise of no-frills airlines that have increased the number and willingness of travellers to travel independently and to create their own itineraries and tour packages; and the increased online competition amongst cyberintermediaries and tourism suppliers both offering flexible and customisable travel information services and products. Overall, the ability to sell in the mass travel market by simultaneously addressing individual travellers' needs through personalisation tools is no longer considered as a differentiating factor, but rather as a competitive necessity. Indeed, the number of cyberintermediaries adopting personalisation practices has boomed (Anite, 2002).

Duray et al. (2000) and Duray (2002) identified two critical dimensions for implementing MC: the basic nature of customization; and the means for achieving customization at or near mass production cost. The first dimension concerns the stage and level of customer's involvement within the value chain process (e.g., at the design, production, assembly, delivery and/or usage stage) and it is used for determining the degree of customization. The second dimension is related to modularity. Modularity is used as the critical aspect for gaining scale volume or 'mass' in MC, since a modular approach: can reduce the variety of components while offering a greater range of end products; allows part of the product to be made in volume as standard modules; and creates product distinctiveness through combination or modification of the modules. Overall, modularity provides both economies of scale and economies of scope, as component modularity restricts the range of choice and so, it decreases the possible variety of components which in turn allows repetitive manufacturing.

Modularization in the travel product is easy to identify as travel services consist of different modules (e.g., accommodation, flights, leisure activities) for each one of which a traveller can select specific providers and services and then, assemble each module and option together for creating a personalised vacation (i.e., the creation of a dynamic package). Furthermore, each travel module can be further modularised into smaller components, e.g., on Virgin Express' website, a traveller can design and buy customised flight services by selecting the location and leg-room of his/her seat, pre-order and pre-pay for any special in-flight catering service etc. Travel websites also offer travellers the opportunity to personalise their services by engaging and participating at different stages of the travel value chain process. For example, at the product design stage, travellers can select different travel modules and components for designing customised vacations; at the travel consumption-production stage, travellers can co-produce as well as influence the selection and consumption of tourism experiences by reading, uploading, and distributing personal travel reviews and feedback in online travel communities and social networks (e.g., www.tripadvisor.com, www.expedia.com); at the purchase stage, travellers can choose the payment form (e.g., type of credit card etc) of their personalised travel experience as well as select the method for receiving the information and confirmation of their purchase, bookings and travel documents (e.g., by e-mail, SMS). Many travel cyberintermediaries allow travellers to personalise and customise the content and the functionality of the travel website even further. For example, travellers may upload their profile and personal travel data (such as dietary preferences, airport closed to their home, airline frequent flyer card numbers), so that the website's search engines and content are automatically configured to consider these personal parameters when filtering and suggesting travel information, availability and other travel options. This personalisation function of the website is usually referred to as *'my...'* (e.g., my yahoo, my travelocity, my expedia).

MASS CUSTOMISATION TYPOLOGIES: A CUSTOMER CENTRIC APPROACH

Previous Typologies of MC Strategies and Dimensions

Previous research in MC has been dispersed and so, many studies have attempted to summarise previous findings in order to categorise MC implementation models and strategies in appropriate types. This is because typologies that analyse and differentiate the implementation characteristics and impacts of different types of MC models could help in further building and testing a MC theory (Doty & Glick, 1994; Kotha & Vadlamani, 1995). Previous studies (e.g., Lampel & Mitzberg, 1996; Pine et al. 2005) classifying the types of MC implementation models have used the two previously discussed MC dimensions (i.e., modularisation and customer involvement in the value chain) for identifying different types of MC. Based on these MC typologies, customer involvement at the early stages of the value chain

reflects higher levels of MC implementation than customer involvement at later stages (which is regarded as cosmetic MC), because the former enables substantial changes to happen at the product design and fabrication stages. For example, MC can range from low customisation levels (i.e., involvement at the product delivery stage whereby customers simply "adapt" products' packaging), up to high customisation levels (i.e., when customers determine the customization of the sale, design, fabrication, and assembly of products). Table 1 summarises this literature by placing the types of MC implementation models proposed by different authors according to the level and stage of customer involvement within the value chain (i.e., the first dimension of MC as identified by Duray et al., 2000) that these models represent. The table also illustrates and explains how these types of MC implementation models are applied in the e-tourism field (Sigala & Christou, 2005).

As many authors (Piller & Moller, 2004; Piller, 2005; Franke & Piller, 2003; Sigala, 2006) have previously recognised, the above mentioned typologies of MC implementation have led firms to adopt an operations-centric approach to MC. This is because, the suggested MC typologies gave emphasis on the need to find ways to integrate and involve customers within value chains, which in turn led firms to focus mainly on how to design their processes for better integrating and engaging customers into their operations. However, as Berger, Moslein, Piller, and Reichwald (2005) advocated this operations-led approach to MC implementation provides limited insight into the value and the benefits that customers get from their involvement and contributions to MC implementation. In other words, although this approach provides useful guidelines on how to design business operations for integrating customers within value chains, it does not explain why customers should and would be willing to take an active role in business operations. Other authors (e.g., Sigala, 2006; Franke & Piller, 2003; Piller, Schubert, Koch, & Möslein, 2005; Huffman & Kahn, 1998)

Table 1. Generic levels of MC applied in the travel sector

MC generic levels	Pine et al. (1995)	Lampel & Mitzberg (1996)	Pine (1993)	Spira (1996)	MC in travel
8. Design	Collaborative, transparent	Pure customization			Collaborative design of travel products between supplier-customer and within travellers virtual communities
7. Fabrication		Tailored customization			Flexible Itineraries determined by the traveller
6. Assembly		Customized standardisation	Modular production	Assembling standard components into unique configurations	Traveller selection of travel modules and components from a supplier's predetermined choice list: dynamic packaging
5. Additional custom work			Point of delivery customization	Performing additional custom work	Customizing features / services of travel products, e.g. excess weight, destination tours, insurance
4. Additional services			Customized services, quick response	Providing additional services	Personalised services, e.g. SMS alerts for flights cancellations, delays
3. Packaged and distribution	Cosmetic	Segmented standardisation		Customizing packaging	Selection of distribution-delivery systems, e-mail, SMS delivery of an 3D e-ticket and e-boarding pass
2. Usage	Adaptive		Embedded customization		Adaptation of pre-defined packaged tour
1. Standardisation		Pure standardisation			Pre-defined packaged tour designed by the intermediary

have also claimed that this operations centric approach to MC does not answer questions related to the following customer related issues: does the higher degree and level of customer involvement in value chain lead to greater customer value and benefits? do customers always require to get more involved with product customisation? which are the dimensions of the services' modules-components whose customisation can provide enhanced customer value? what types of customer value are delivered by (different) MC models? do all types of customers require and demand to customise all these dimensions of services' modules – components? are there any customers' and/or contextual factors that demand the customisation of specific services' modules – components? Moreover, as the adoption of any technology based innovation depends on the users' perceptions regarding the technology's easy of use and usefulness [e.g., see Christou and Kassianidis (2003) and Kargin, Basoglu, and Daim (2009) for a review and analysis of the implications of the Technology Acceptance Model (TAM)], frameworks suggesting the development of successful types of MC models should be based on and identify the service dimensions and components that create and deliver enhanced MC driven customer value and benefits. To achieve that, the following section adopts a customer-oriented approach that emphasises the need of MC to deliver customer value (Piller et al., 2005; Franke & Piller, 2003) for proposing a framework for modelling the design and implementation of MC models. Specifically, the framework identifies and is built on the services' modules-components that can be mass customised in order to directly enhance the customer value that travellers get from online mass customised travel information services.

MC in Online Travel Information Services: A Customer Centric Framework

The previous discussion revealed that successful MC strategies should focus on and identify how customer engagement in business operations should provide and deliver customer values. In this vein, when examining the types of MC implementation, Piller et al. (2004) adopted a customer-centric approach for identifying the customer values that customers get when they customise the following product features (the discussion is also enhanced in order to provide examples of customer values provided by MC types found within the tourism sector):

Adaptation of form: Mass customisation can be used for adapting a product's form and design. Customers' motivations, value and benefits for adapting products'/services' aesthetic features include: better product-service fit with other products (e.g., customisation of the watch's colour to match the colours of one's cloths) and customer needs (e.g., customisation of the size and the colours of the fonts and the background colour of a website to match the user's eye abilities); expression of personal style, taste and personality (e.g., customisation of the website backgrounds, the mobile phone's colours, screens, ring-tones and the travel information and products in order to fit with the user's profile and personality).

Adaptation of fit: Another factor (less related to aesthetics) motivating customers to individualise products is the need to get customer value and benefits deriving from customised products/services that fit customers'

characteristics and needs. Practical reasons are most important: e.g., garment adaptation to individual's physical structure and body measure; in-flight catering customised to the religious and dietary customers' needs; leisure activities and sightseeing tours that match tourists' interests; button sizes of mobile phones according to one's finger sizes. For example, the destination portal of Switzerland allows travellers to find an appropriate conference centre based on their preferences and needs (e.g., distance from airports and city centres, capacity and layout designs, the provision of other business services), while users of the destination portal of Germany can search and find a spa centre and/or hotel that provide the appropriate wellness services and treatments that match their personal health circumstances and needs.

Adaptation of function: customers get also value and so, they are motivated to individualise products-services, because customised products deliver benefits of better functionality. Many customers are known to the dilemma of modern products, which in most cases have way too much functionality, but which, in a great measure, will never be used by a single customer. As products-services are getting more and more complex, the harder it becomes for the customer to handle and use such products-services. Sometimes customers may even expect different functionality (Dellaert & Stremersch, 2005). Thus, firms usually integrate services-products with the whole variety of expected functionalities in order to satisfy a lot of different customers and/or develop multi-functional devices, products and services, and then, firms ask customers to customise functionality based on their needs and preferences. As customers begin to long for products that have exactly those functionalities that they want them to have, customers' ability to customise product functionality is becoming very critical. Recognising this functionality confusion amongst users, Vodaphone has recently launched two devices (called Vodafone simply) equipped with three buttons that allow users to directly divert to the three most popular and highly needed functionalities of mobile phones, i.e. make a call, access voice mail and send an SMS. Additional practical examples of MC models adapting product functionality include: travelocity.com allows travellers to configure its lowest fare tracking system, so that the latter will automatically search the web for special offers and tours that match the user's profiles and requests (e.g., search for flights to specific destinations at specific dates and days of week) and then it will alert travellers about the search results on pre-specified interval periods and by using pre-specified mediums (e.g., SMS or e-mail alerts) previously determined by the traveller.

Adaptation of modalities: This dimension of MC identifies the values that customers get when they can determine the functionality and the forms of the production and delivery of products and services. For example, the customer may want to choose by herself/himself, which firm and personnel should perform a specific service and which production method should be used. The customer may also be enabled to influence the service delivery time and place. Many only travel firms allow travellers to create their own profile based on which information provision and search as well as website interface are customised; (for example the website system searches and provides information only about the airlines or hotels for which the user has previously provided a loyalty card on his profile; flights' availability will be provided only for flights departing from airports located nearby the traveller's home). Travellers can also customise the delivery

options for receiving products and services (e.g., travel alerts delivered by SMS or through e-mails; tickets delivered by post, SMS and/or e-mail). Finally, travellers can also choose and customise the payment forms by simply selecting the information and payment options that they have previously uploaded into their profile.

Overall, the possibility to interactively influence and adapt the features of a product/service according to one's personal needs and preferences (and so, to obtain value and benefits), is one of the most fundamental motivation persuading customers to invest time and efforts to participate in MC operations such as creating and updating online their personal profiles and customising recommender systems. In other words, in exchange of resources and time spent for providing personal information and for customising products, customers expect to obtain extra benefits and value (such as, fast and easy purchases of products-services customised to user' needs, time savings, enhanced product usefulness and functionality addressing personal needs and desires). As previously analysed, these types of customer value can be easily obtained when customers have the possibility to customise the form, the fit, the functionality and the modality of the product-service. The applicability of this customer centric framework for implementing MC was verified by Sigala (2006) who measured and provided evidence of the different types of customer value (functional, social, emotional, epistemic and conditional value) that users get when they customise the following features of their mobile phone services: form, code, substance, layer, visual aspects and interaction.

However, the product and services of online travel and tourism information providers are closely interlinked with and are inseparable from the ICT system that supports them. In this vein, in order to propose MC strategies in the online travel sector that are customer effective, one should also identify the features of the ICT system whose form, fit, functionality and modality has to be adapted for creating customer value (Franke & Piller, 2004; Oon & Khalid, 2001; Kamali & Loker, 2002; Liechty et al., 2001). To decompose the travel ICT systems into its design features, the following three major layers of digital communication systems were used (Benkler, 2000): physical, code and content layer.

The decomposition of the ICT system in its components is argued as a useful framework for identifying and modelling MC implementation models because:

- It is consistent with the concept of modularisation, which is one of the two MC dimensions facilitating MC implementation; so, ICT components represent modules whose features can be customised in terms of their form, fit, modality and functionality for enhancing customer value;

- Most travellers frequently do not know what they want as well as they do not have the knowledge and expertise to identify, select and customise the appropriate modules for addressing their individual needs. Thus, the identification and the analysis of various customisation options for each tourism module and component can help and educate travellers on how to easier identify and specify the modules' dimensions that can satisfy their needs;

- The components-modules of the ICT system can directly influence customer value. For example, recent research provided evidence of the different types of value that customers get, when they create MC mobile phone services by customising the ICT components (in terms of fit, form, functionality and modality) of their mobile phones services to their individual preferences and needs (Sigala, 2006). Earlier, Sigala (2002) has also demonstrated how to adapt the form and the functionality of e-learning systems and tools, so that the

learning platform can reflect and match the learners' cognitive styles, learning orientations and preferences.

The physical layer includes the physical technological device and the connection channel used to transmit communication signals. The *code or middle layer* consists of the protocols and software that make the physical layer run. By customising the code, the user can customise and control its interaction with the technology (i.e. determine the way and time of accessing and delivering information services, e.g. e-mail alerts etc). On top, there is a *content layer*, which consists of multimodal information. It includes both the substance and the form of multimedia content (Saari, 2002). Substance refers to the core message of the information. Form implies aesthetic and expressive ways of organising the substance, such as using different modalities and structures of information (Saari, 2002). In this vein, travellers can select the colour and mode of information (e.g., choose between text, 3D pictures, webcams etc) that better match their personality, preferences and style. Travellers can also request to solely see or search the information (substance) that is relevant to their profile; for example, if they travel always with their spouse or children, then search engines and information results about hotel availability are designed and filtered to consider their family needs; similarly if they travel always with airlines that are members of the "star alliance" group in order to accumulate air miles, then search results about flights' availability will include flight availability only by "star alliance" member airlines. In general, customisation of the information/content can be individual-centric when the content is personalised based on the user's profile, or it can be more community-centric when the content is customised based on other users' profiles and behaviours (i.e., collaborative filtering).

These ICT components are amenable for further numerous customisations. Content can be selected, grouped, and organised, form can be tailored to suit individual needs and preferences (e.g., My Excite allows users to select their preferred website fonts, themes, colours etc) and delivery methods can be tailored by selecting the communication-technology platform to receive information updates and alerts. The possibilities to change the content structure and the interrelations amongst the three layers of the ICT system provide additional numerous opportunities for designing mass customised travel information services that add customer value. For example, imagine the situation whereby a traveller creates an online profile and informs the content of his personal calendar by including the anniversaries and celebrations of all his/her friends. The company can create different interrelations amongst customised content giving the option to the user to further determine and customise how the personalised calendar content can be interrelated-connected with other travel related functions, e.g., the automatic delivery of e-mails to the persons who celebrate an anniversary, the automated and programmed purchase of user pre-selected services (e.g., a flight ticket to visit the friend on his/her celebration and the reservation of a meal at a favourite restaurant). In another occasion, content interrelation can help a business man whose flight is cancelled or changed; in this case, content interrelations in the online travel information services should be created, so that the businessman's hotel reservations are automatically changed and the respective hotel is also automatically informed, alternative flight arrangements are made for other travel itineraries etc. Overall, such personalised online travel services provide travellers with a wide variety of benefits-value, e.g., functional (e.g., time savings and convenience) as well as emotional (e.g., empathy and responsiveness). The aim of the following section is to analyse in depth the types of customer value that travellers gets from MC online travel services.

Types of Customer Value Fostered by MC Types

Current research on the customisation-personalisation of information systems (IS) places great emphasis on the utilitarian value of personalised information delivery (Abidi, 2003). Nevertheless, other dimensions of value provided by customised IS are nowadays being recognised that are also equally important to the users' experience. For example, users are often active in tailoring ICT systems to better reflect their own personality and identity (e.g., ring tones, backgrounds) (e.g., Guay, 2003), but these forms of user initiated personalisation have been overlooked in the literature (Saari & Turpeinen, 2003; Sigala, 2006). In reviewing the literature, Abidi (2003) identified different dimensions of personalisation such as, special attention and empathy, customization of products-services, pseudo-personalization of messages, depersonalization/re-personalization of the relationship by the ICT, etc. In her study investigating the customer value of MC mobile phone services, Sigala (2006) identified the following types of perceived customer value: functional-convenience value; social value; emotional value; conditional value; epistemic value; and control value – freedom of choice. By synthesising this literature, MC customer values are clustered into two major dimensions of personalization (Abidi, 2003; Sigala, 2006):

The utilitarian MC: Utilitarian mass customisation and personalisation also refers to service features that mainly aim to provide functional value and convenience in service provision rather than experiential value (emotional). For example, the creation of a traveller's profile will enable him/her to make online bookings faster, as he/she will not need to re-enter personal data. In general, this dimension of MC refers to the individualization, the made-to-order customization, the tailor of the offer or else the MC done with the customers in a routine bases. Examples of this dimension of MC may include the following: pseudo-, routine personalisation reflecting user recognition on the website by his name and – or user adaptation of website information and interface.

The emotional/symbolic MC: this type of MC refers to the customisation of service features aiming to provide customers with emotional and/ or symbolic value (e.g., social recognition). Although this MC dimension is above all established in interpersonal service-encounter, current studies also speak about emotional personalization in person-computer service encounter (like e-commerce). For example: Moon (2002) argued that there is social interaction even between the PC and the user; Hopkins and Raymond (2004) investigated the emotional user responses of telepresence; Gretzel et al. (2004) showed how destination recommendation systems can use personality user characteristics for customising content and for creating appropriate user emotional responses; Vrehopoulos et al. (2004) proved how the layout and the structure of an e-store can affect utilitarian, cognitive and emotional user values such as perceived usefulness, easy of use, time savings, entertainment; in investigating the dimensions of website interactivity, Chen and Yen (2004) provided evidence on the impact interactive website features on constructs related to customer values such as user control, playfulness, reciprocal communication, social presence, choice, information selection. Lexhagen (2009) provided evidence of travel website features that evoke and provide emotional customer values to travellers. Sigala (2006) measured the impact of MC features of mobile phone services [(such as customisation of ring tones with songs matching users' personality; mobile phone screens designed with photos taken by the user; personalised SMS alerts providing customised information

services (e.g., horoscopes)] on the emotional value, social recognition and esteem value perceived by mobile phone users. Overall, these studies provide evidence that it is possible to create MC models that deliver emotional/symbolic values in e-commerce platforms and that technology mediated servicescapes are also ideal for supporting customer interactions over the time and establishing a personal and more intimate relationship and social bonding between the e-retailer, the customer and customer communities.

In other words, utilitarian MC focuses on providing functional customer values, while emotional MC focuses on delivering emotional and social customer values. Saari (2002) summarised the features of the ICT components whose customisation can enhance emotional and utilitarian customer values as they are presented in Table 2. Saari's arguments are also expanded (in Table 2) in order to illustrate how these ICT layers can be customised for designing MC models within the context of online travel and tourism information services. The applicability of this framework is also demonstrated in Table 3, whereby the framework is used for analysing several examples of MC information services currently provided by three major travel cyberintemediaries.

Information Systems Design: Trends and Interrelations with IS Supporting MC Implementation and Customer Values

The adoption of MC services in an e-commerce environment heavily depends on the design of the IS platform that customers can use for customising products and services (Franke & Piller, 2004; Oon & Khalid, 2001; Kamali & Loker, 2002; Liechty, Ramaswamy, & Cohen, 2001). In general, it is also widely advocated that the user adoption and satisfaction from the use of an IS enhance when: a)

Table 2. ICT features for functional and emotional types of MC

Layer	Key factors	Online travel services
Physical	**Hardware** - large or small vs. human scale - mobile or immobile - close or far from body (intimate personal- social distance)	Travellers can select the ways and devices (e.g. by SMS, e-mail, transfer of information and synchronisation of PC with the PDA and iPhone) for: receiving travel information alerts, storing and accessing travel information, receiving travel bookings and itineraries, receiving electronic tickets etc
Code	**Interaction** - degree of user vs. system control, proactivity through user interface **Visual-functional aspects** - way of presenting controls in an interface visually and functionally	**Customisation of interaction** Travellers can request, control and customise the delivery (frequency and timing) of automated e-mail alerts that provide them with customised travel information services such as flight changes and delays, arrival of flights, traffic alerts, weather conditions etc **Customisation of functional aspects** Travellers can request, control and customise the services and functionality of website software: e.g. a tracker software can be configured so that it searches and alerts travellers (by e-mail SMS etc) about changes in prices and availability of pre-specified flights, hotels, etc
Content	**Substance** - the essence of the event described - type of substance (factual/imaginary; genre, other) - narrative techniques used by authors **Form** 1. Modalities: text, video, audio, graphics, animation, etc. 2. Visual layout - ways of presenting various shapes, colours, font types, groupings and other relationships or expressive properties of visual representations - ways of integrating modalities into the user interface 3. Structure - ways of presenting modalities, visual layout, other form elements and their relations - linear-non linear structure: sequential, parallel, narrative techniques, hyper-textuality	**Customisation of SUBSTANCE:** Travellers can upload and create their travel profile and preferences so that the website content is customised and filtered to their profile. Website content can be customised to any of the 4Ps (product, price, promotion, place) dimensions of the travel services, e.g. search for flights only when economy fare class tickets are available, search for and display hotel availability only for hotel chains for which the user holds a loyalty card, etc **Customisation of FORM:** Travellers can customise issues related to the information modality of the website: text, 3D pictures, web cams of destinations. For example, travellers may request to search and review hotels for bookings only when hotels provide online photographs of their rooms

Table 3. Examples of MC from online cyberintemediaries

	Orbitz.com	Expedia.com	Travelocity.com
Physical	**Orbitz** provides mobile access to its customised services so that users can also use their mobile phones to: o Retrieve their travel itinerary in My Trip o Check their flight status o See hotel deals & availability for same-day travel in selected markets o Contact customer service **Multichannel delivery of content:** Orbitz Insider provides Podcasts via RSS or iTunes. Thus, users can select the type and timing of information to be delivered to them as well as the delivery medium (e.g. iPod, RSS reader)	The user can request the receipt of **personalised deals via RSS** Expedia users can get personalized travel deals delivered right to them—when and where they want them. If users have a personalized homepage (like My Yahoo!, My AOL, or a Google Homepage), it only takes a few simple clicks to get the deals users want. Users just specify to Expedia which destinations they would like to watch, what type of trip they prefer, what type of package they prefer (luxury or standard), from where they want to travel, and Expedia sends them personalised travel information to their personalised portal.	The user can request and get personalised information (e.g. Flight reminders, status alerts, gate change notifications etc) through various media (e.g. mobile phone, fax, PDA, or pager). **RSS personalised Deals Feeder:** users can find out fast when fares to their favorite destinations drop by at least 20%. Users just choose the destinations they like Travelocity to watch, and the company keeps them informed through My Yahoo, My MSN, Pluck or another RSS news reader of the user's choice.
Code	Users can ask for automated customised e-mail alerts (user driven functionality) relating to travel news, special offers, and Fare Sales alerts for flights departing from any airport the user prefers - specifies. Users can also request e-mail alerts for local weather forecasts as well as they can specify the timing parameters for the delivery of this information Orbitz's TLC alerts for flight delays, cancellations, street closures, gates changes etc (users can specify the timing of the alerts, between 3-5 hours before departure, as well as the device for receiving alerts, e.g. mobile phone, pager, PDA, phone, e-mail etc) *The above mentioned MC services are provided to the user by the firm itself.* Orbitz also provides users the possibility to search, share and read personalised real-time information updates (e.g. about security wait times, traffic & parking, taxi lines) that are uploaded from fellow travelers in a mash-up application including google maps and a social network of travelers **(such MC information services are created by the travelers' community itself, i.e. MC enabled and supported by a community of travelers)** **The e-mail alerts that an Orbitz's user can configure and request to receive before his trip include:** o Hotel information including traveller confirmation number, hotel address and phone number o 3-day weather forecast for traveller destination o Confirmation information on activities traveller may have booked for his/her trip o Links to city guides so you can plan your activities before you go o Links to Insider Podcasts that will give you unique insights on select cities o Quick tips from previous Orbitz hotel guests on dining & more	Expedia allow the users to request and configure individualised e-mail alerts and marketing messages for travel deals Fare Alert software, created and provided by Expedia, allows users to personalise and automate the search of individualised travel deals. When users download Fare Alert, a small, unobtrusive icon is installed onto their desktop. Users can double-click the icon any time to see the current low fare, and when Expedia finds a fare that meets or beats your pre-set price limit, a small window will pop up briefly to notify users.	Travelocity FareWatcher(SM) is a free, personalized subscription service that tracks the best round trip fares published by airlines for up to five city pairs of users' choice. When users subscribe, they decide which cities to track, for how long (how many days and/or depending on price level changes) and whether they want to be notified of changes to those fares via email or in the personalised user FareWatcher webpage. The FareWatcher(SM) page is available 24 hours a day, tracking the fares that are most important to users (i.e. MC possibilities between the user and the firm) Travelocity's innovative ExperienceFinder(sm) planning tool: this is a toolkit supporting users to design their personalised travel experience based on their profile, preferences, wish lists and reviews, critics of a social network of travellers (i.e. co-creation of MC services amongst a community of travellers) Users can request the delivery of timely notifications about sales, special promotions, and Travelocity exclusives so that they can get the best deals on the right time and the right device while deals are still available

continues on following page

Table 3. Continued

	Orbitz.com	Expedia.com	Travelocity.com
Content	**Product customisation: Orbitz** gives the possibility to users to create their profile (that may include for example user's membership in hotel, rent a car, airlines frequent customer programmes, preferred departure city and aircraft seat, in flight meal requirements), so that information can be filtered and provided according to this user profile, as well as the user will not have to re-enter these personal data in every transaction and website search. Product customisation can also be configured for up to 25 friends accompanying the user in any trip, but friends profile has also to be uploaded online. Orbitz provides dynamic packaging possibilities whereby travellers can assembly their personalised travel packages **Price customisation:** users can request E-mail alerts for special offers and prices and newsletters delivery whose content can be individualised based on the specified interests (activities, lifestyle and destinations) of the user. Subscribed Orbitz users get a webpage with special prices and offers that are customised according to their profile, loyalty programmes and website usage. **Payment and Delivery customisation:** The user can also specify payment methods (type of credit cards) and shipping addresses for information- tickets delivery. *The following personalised services are also offered by Orbitz in order to support users in their efforts to create personalised travel packages:* Orbitz Insider Podcasts keep users up to speed on what's happening in the greatest cities - User can subscribe to get and use podcasts for: o Hearing unique insights from experienced travellers o Learn about different neighbourhoods & what makes them special o Get the inside scoop on events around the city each month o Discover local favourites off the beaten path, like restaurants, shops & more Orbitz's pre-trip e-mail alert provides users with **several links to different databases and services** of Orbitz (e.g. Podcasts, city guides etc). This interconnection of content and functionality creates further opportunities for developing infinitive MC possibilities	**Product customisation:** Expedia gives the possibility to users to create their profile (membership in hotel, rent a car, airlines frequent customer programmes, departure city, seat preferences, in flight meal requirement), so that information can be filtered and provided according to this profile, while the user does not have to re-enter the data at every transaction. Profile customisation also available to users' friends and co-travellers. Expedia also allows its members to book travel for their co-workers or friends by updating and accessing their profile (friends and colleagues should have first given permission to their friend to do so). Travel arrangements are made directly in a co-worker's or friend's account, so travel plans are accessible to them via Expedia.com whether they are on the road, at home, or in the office, 24 hours a day, 7 days a week. Users can customised website content and information search by: • Specifying home airport for flights checking. • Specifying preferred routes • Specifying preferred destinations Dynamic packaging possibilities whereby the user assembly its own personalised tour package **that is priced** on real time with a unique price that is different from the profile of other users **Price customisation:** From time to time, Expedia.com sends coupons to its customers, generally via postal mail or e-mail (users need to first request and customise these alerts), these alerts also provide users with individualised promotional coupons and prices - deals based on their profile. **Payment customisation:** Users that have pre-uploaded their preferred payment information on their profile are given the opportunity of express booking by simply confirming credit card details The Fare Alert of Expedia provides users with several other **links to complementary information** (hotel deals, car rentals etc) which in turn provide users with the possibility to link and **create infinitive number of MC products and e-services**	**Product customisation: Travelocity** gives the possibility to users to create their profile (membership in hotel, rent a car, airlines frequent customer programmes, departure city, seat preferences, in flight meal requirement), so that information can be filtered and provided according to this profile, while the user does not have to re-enter the data at every transaction. Profile customisation also available to users' friends and co-travellers. Provision of dynamic packaging possibilities whereby the travellers can assembly their personalised travel packages **Payment customisation: Pre**-specification of credit card details, and then users need to simply confirm payment methods at the purchase stage **Delivery options: users can select from and use 3 e-mail addresses for the personalised delivery of information:** 1) formal e-mail; 2) e-mail for real deals; 3) e-mail for special offers **My offers: a** webpage functionality that provides users with personalised special offers individualised to the users' travel details: e.g. a users that has bought a flight to New York can be offered a special price for renting a DVD movie or a New York destination guide in order to watch during the journey

IS design fits the human-computer interface, and b) IS services are customised to the user characteristics and to the technology task that he/she has to complete (Vessey & Galletta, 1991; Baecker et al., 1995; Goodhue & Thompson, 1995). The following analysis reviews the current trends related to these issues of IS design and then, it identifies their interrelations with the design of IS used for supporting MC implementation.

Concerning the concept of fit between the IS and its user, fit has been conceptualized so far as physical fit, cognitive fit and only recently as affective fit (Te'eni, 2005). Physical fit (e.g., ergonomic fit) allows for comfortable operation by minimizing physical effort in accomplishing a task and considering user's overall well-being (Buxton, 1986). Cognitive fit seeks to match the information representation displayed to the user's mental model of the task demands. Similarly, cognitive fit minimizes the cognitive effort for transforming representations and performing a task, reduces the propensity for error and reduces the effort and time required to complete the task (Vessey & Galletta, 1991). Incongruence between the cognitive style of the user (learning style) and the IS design may reduce student performance (Sigala, 2002). Affective fit is conceptualized as interface design considerations that promote user's positive affect, or in a more generalized form as fit with a user's desired affective state. Research in the role and importance of affective fit is currently being developed and is related to system design methodologies that are people oriented (Avital & Te'eni, 2006). In terms of performance, research studies have mainly focused on performance dimensions and measures that relate to task related criteria of efficiency, accuracy, or productivity (Zhang & Na, 2004; Avital & Te'eni, 2006).

On the other hand, interpreting performance solely in terms of productivity has been sufficient some years ago when technology was viewed as a tool whose major role was to increase operational efficiency and productivity. However, technology tools and IS' role have been advanced and

transformed. Nowadays, IS are interactive and communicative and they are expected to provide several opportunities for instilling and enhancing users' innovation, creativity, affective behaviour and well-being.

To address these gaps in IS design, Avital and Te'eni (2006) introduced the concept of *generativity* and developed two corresponding IS design considerations namely *generative capacity* and *generative fit*. In reviewing the concept generativity in several social sciences, Avital and Te'eni (2006) concluded that the generative capacity is the ability to rejuvenate, to produce new possibilities and configurations, to reframe the way we see and we understand the world, to think out-of-the-box and to challenge the normative status quo. In this vein, they (2006) argued that a systems' task-related performance has two unique components namely *operational efficiency and generative capacity*. Operational efficiency is the kind of task performance that is usually observed in the literature and it relates to tasks with low ambiguity, finite in nature, well-articulated and in which one is expected to be efficient, accurate and on time. Generative capacity, however, relates to one's ability to deal with a task with high ambiguity, open-ended in nature, unclear in a considerable part and in which one is expected to be innovative, expansive and to make a difference. In other words, *generative capacity* refers to one's creativity, ingenuity and mental dexterity. Hence, in applying generative capacity in IS design, Avital and Te'eni (2006) defined *generative fit* as the interface and IS design considerations that have a positive effect on the generative capacity of the system. In other words, generative fit refers to the extent to which a particular IT artifact, or part thereof, is conducive to evoking and enhancing that generative capacity. In their case study, Avital and Te'eni (2006) provided evidence that IS designed by adopting generative dimensions can help IS users to enhance their: creative work, unstructured syntheses, serendipitous discoveries, and any other form of computer-aided tasks that involve unexplored outcomes, or who expect fresh configurations, or aim at boundary spanning results. Unlike other types of fit, generative fit is inherently dynamic and enhances human processes, and Avital and Te'eni (2006) study illustrated that generative fit has a critical impact on user related affective-based performance criteria and particularly on the user's well-being. Recently, Levy, Murphy, and Zanakis (2009) have also provided evidence of the role and the impact of user-perceived cognitive value of IS on the effectiveness and user satisfaction from IS.

Avital and Te'eni (2006) identified the following IS design parameters and factors that can enhance and create generative fit:

- *Integration of systems and information databases:* Integrated platforms and databases that can provide real-time information and flexible interoperability between heterogeneous systems can promote system-wide boundary-crossing, across-the-board sharing, and cross-fertilization.
- *Communication:* Providing ubiquitous access and fast connectivity to knowledge based systems.
- *Intelligence:* adaptive systems that incorporate continuous learning and continuous improvement based on user feedback and other performance measures.
- *Visualization:* incorporating human-centred visualization tools that provide integrative views, scaling, zoom in and out, and easy movement in the task space.
- *Rejuvenation:* supporting iterative processes and generating an infinite number of configurations. Building an integrative path for innovation.

Based on the above mentioned developments in the area of IS design, the following conclusions are derived related to the interrelations between the current trends in IS design and the design of IS supporting the implementation of MC online services:

- Research in IS design increasingly recognise the need to design IS interfaces and capabilities that will not only improve the utilitarian – functional value that the system provides to the user. Equally, IS design should consider and include features that also enhance the affective-emotional value provided to the users as well as enhance users' cognitive capabilities for processing more information and creating new services. Such arguments are directly related to the features and the functionality (discussed in Tables 2 and 3) of the ICT systems supporting the MC of online services in order to provide both the functional – convenience (i.e., cognitive capabilities of users) as well as the emotional-symbolic customer values.

Avital and Te'eni (2006) identified the above mentioned five IS design parameters enabling generative fit, which also relate and refer to the ICT features identified in Table 2 that can be mass customised for providing both functional and emotional value to users. So, integration and rejuvenation relate to the capability to integrate different systems, platforms and databases; visualisation relates to the customisation of the physical layer, while communication relates to the customisation of the code layer.

- The concept of generative fit in IS design implies that users should be able to generate infinitive possibilities and configurations. In a similar vein, it was previously showed that the interrelations between the ICT components create numerous MC possibilities. Therefore, it can be argued that by creating integration capabilities amongst the ICT components, the generative ability of the IS increases, which in turn allows the IS and its users to continually identify and create infinitive types of mass customised information services based on the users' needs, context and circumstances.

Overall, it becomes evident that recent research in IS design follows similar people-oriented paths as the proposed framework for designing and implementing MC models that deliver customer value within the context of travel information e-services. By following people-oriented approaches emphasis is given on creating different types of customer value namely functional (task related operational efficiency), cognitive (rejuvenation of infinitive customised services) and emotional (affective and user well-being) value.

VARIABLES MODERATING THE USER IMPACT AND CUSTOMER VALUE OF MC INFORMATION SERVICE: IMPLICATIONS FOR FUTURE RESEARCH

When a user interprets information, a complex set of hierarchical variables may influence the users' psychological response to mass customised information e-services, such as presence and experience of the information, learning and emotion. These variables may be clustered as Mind (individual differences and social similarities of perceivers), Content (information substance and form embedded in technology with certain ways of interaction) and Context (social and physical context of reception) (Saari, 2002). For example, searching for travel information for buying a routine flight ticket and searching for travel information for creating personalised vacations in unknown destinations are two totally different tasks whose completion, even by the same user, would require different utilitarian and emotional values and functionalities from the IS supporting the MC online travel services. In the first case, the traveller will prefer and seek to use MC features that make his

online booking process faster and easier, in the second case, the traveller would prefer services and MC features that will help him/her to: select travel products and services that enhance his/her experiential and emotional value when creating his/her itinerary, evaluating and selecting travel components (e.g., features reducing the customer perceived risk and stress due to the information chaos by ensuring that the personalised travel package that was created is socially recognised and positively reviewed and evaluated by other travellers). Being able to systematically and reliably predict the appropriateness between the IS features to be mass customised and the travellers' preferences and/or values sought is the key for using mind-based ICT systems for creating MC information e-service and targeting them to particular market segments at the most appropriate times and contexts.

Based on previous studies, it can be hypothesised that the following travellers' characteristics may affect users' preferences on the types of the MC features and the value expected to be gained. The level of customer involvement with the product may also effectively moderate the type of MC benefits sought by travellers. For example, travellers may find some travel and tourism services of greater personal relevance and importance (e.g. a honey moon trip, a family vacation versus a business strip) (Christou, 2006). It appears that travellers with higher product involvement levels would attach greater importance to confidence, social and emotional benefits and value to be provided by MC features rather than utilitarian benefits (Christou & Kassianidis, 2003). Avital & Te'eni, (2006) also recognised that the extent of desired operational efficiency, the fit of an IS design (i.e., functional value) and the extent of generative capacity (cognitive and affective) may differ according to the characteristics of the computer related task. For some tasks operational efficiency is critical and generative capacity is counterproductive (e.g., tasks related to manufacturing control systems), for other tasks operational efficiency is not relevant and generative capacity is critical (e.g. tasks related to scenario planning). Two extreme circumstances may exist: a) a *convergent action* requiring users to be concrete, accurate, effective, and fast and with little or no deviation from standard operating procedures; and b) a *divergent action* requiring users to be imaginative, creative, innovative, and provocative and with little or no conformism. Overall, it is proposed that future studies can investigate the following proposition: *User involvement influences the type of MC features and value-benefits that travellers consider important. Under conditions of high involvement, travellers will value the psychological benefit of increased confidence derived from features of MC e-services (such as suggestions based on the opinions, reviews and experiences of other travellers) more than features of MC e-services that provide utilitarian benefits (such as faster online bookings).*

Travellers' participation in MC depends not only on their willingness to take part in the service production and personalised design process, but also on their capability to evaluate and select the most appropriate service components that match their profile and preferences (Pillar et al., 2004). However, whereas product involvement signals the interest or willingness of travellers to carry out complex and analytic processes for customising their services, expertise affects the extensiveness of this customization process and the users' ability to engage in such a process. Expertise makes the travellers' cognitive structures more complex, increases travellers' ability to differentiate across many competing alternatives and options, prompting finer discriminations with greater reliability. Not only are experts better equipped to understand the meaning of service customization, but they also need a lower amount of cognitive effort for any specific level of comprehension. Thus, expertise will affect the travellers' process for customizing travel and tourism services. In addition, expert travellers may engage in a more complex problem solving activity simply because they are aware

of a greater amount of relevant issues to be kept informed about or because they are more capable of formulating specific questions and requests about a larger amount of e-service attributes. Thus, it is proposed that future research should test the following proposition: *The higher the travellers' expertise the higher their expectations for the availability and the use of features of MC that enable them to customise travel and tourism information e-services.*

Travellers' expectations about the importance, availability and impact of MC features may also differ based on their *gender and cultural profile.* Women tend to be rated higher for empathy and communication than men, and so, they may emphasize the affective features of MC e-services more than males, because females show a relatively high tendency towards emotion, tender-mindedness and empathy. Males may show greater focus on features of MC e-services that concentrate on functionality and form, as they tend to be more autonomous and to show relatively tendency toward emotion. Furthermore, travellers from Asian cultures are usually risk averse, so they may not prefer to take control and participate in the customisation of travel and tourism e-services, as this may increase their perceived purchase risk, i.e. the possibility that the user-customised product may not be able to satisfy their need or be of good value. On the other hand, travellers from western cultures tend to be more innovators as well as adventure and risk seekers. Thus future research could test the following hypothesis: *Users' gender and cultural profile affect their preferences and use of features of MC e-services as well as their expectations of MC customer values sought.*

Moreover, research in the area of IS design enabling online MC has solely focused on IS features supporting company-to-customer interactions and ignoring the issue that communities of customers (and so, customer-to-customer online interactions) can also take part in online MC processes. IS design issues enabling and supporting customer-to-customer interactions for supporting online MC are currently becoming important and critical when considering the wide diffusion of Web 2.0 tools. For example, wikis and blogs allow multiple interaction and communication possibilities (e.g., many-to-many, one-to-many) as well as generate a huge social intelligence that in turn provides a useful information resource that users can use for customising services online. Piller et al. (2005) defined the types of MC that exploit communities of customers as communities for collaborative co-design and advocated that the latter are important for the success of MC because they reduce the mass confusion phenomenon, i.e., the complexity, effort, and perceived risk that customers feel when involved in co-design activities. Analytically, Piller et al. (2005) identified three customer community features that overcome the mass confusion phenomenon: 1) generation of customer knowledge for pre-configuration of customised services; 2) support of collaborative co-design fostering in forms of problem solving; and 3) building of trust and reduction of perceived risk for MC users. In this vein, future research on the design of IS supporting MC should also aim to identify the IS design characteristics and functionality that can support and enable the creation of the following three features of customers' communities: community knowledge, collaborative problem solving and trust building. Future research could also focus on demonstrating the different types of customer value (e.g. functional, social, cognitive, emotional) that web 2.0 tools can provide for supporting MC implementation.

However, Piller et al. (2005) identified and solely talked about the functional and technical assistance that communities of co-design provide to users, ignoring the emotional and social benefits that customers also expect to get from their engagement in MC processes. On the contrary, research on virtual communities and recent studies on social networking provide evidence that users' participation in collaborative activities is driven by the fulfillment of a variety of needs-motives such as the gain of self-esteem, self-actualisation,

cognitive needs, peer-pressure, belongingness etc. Therefore, future research should also focus on investigating and measuring the values of social support as well as the functional values that virtual communities and online social networks (such as facebook.com and blogs) may provide to customers when engaged in the implementation of online MC.

CONCLUSION

The website cost can increase by more than 3 million Euros when individualisation and MC capabilities are added. But, are all types and levels of individualisation and mass customisation worth it? Studies argue that customisation pays for itself as it greatly affects customer loyalty and online average spending. As nowadays most travel and tourism websites offer customisation options, online travellers are increasingly getting used to being treated as individuals and MC strategies are loosing their business differentiation competitive value. In this vein, this paper has assisted in answering such questions in the following ways.

First, the study helped in identifying and categorising different types of online MC implementation models by proposing a customer value oriented framework that specifies the types of customer value that users get by customising different features of the IS used to support the implementation of MC. This analysis has filled in a gap in the literature regarding MC implementation in services and particularly in the context of web-based travel and tourism information e-services. Since online travel and tourism information services are interlinked with the ICT system that delivers and supports them, the ICT layer framework was used for developing the customer value centred MC models' typology. In general, two main types of MC implementation strategies were found: the utilitarian MC and the symbolic/emotional MC. The implications and interrelations of this framework with the current trends related to IS design were also recognised and reviewed.

Second, the study has also identified the different customer values and benefits that customers can obtain from the different features and functionalities of MC e-services. However, studies in usability, affective computing and mind-based IT entail that emotional MC dimensions have different psychological user responses and behaviour than simply pseudo-utilitarian MC. For this reason, several research propositions were analysed and proposed in order to indicate how future studies can examine the importance and the impact of different MC types and features on travellers' preferences and usage patterns of MC models. In other words, the respective research propositions have helped in speculating the different user characteristics and contextual factors that may affect the types of features and MC models that different users may require at different contexts. However, as customisation preferences are complex and may differ across users and contexts, future studies would need to use large scale and cross-cultural samples of users and e-services in order to refine and validate these research propositions.

Finally, given the current diffusion of web 2.0 tools and their wide use for supporting MC implementation, future research should also aim to: a) identify the design features and functionality of web 2.0 tools that enable the creation and the generation of knowledge, trust and problem solving capabilities amongst customers taking part in MC implementation; and b) identify and measure both the functional and the emotional values that customers obtain from virtual communities engaged and supporting MC implementation and processes.

REFERENCES

Abidi, A. (2003). *Customer relationship personalisation on the Internet: a conceptual framework*. Paper presented at the Mass Customisation Conference, Munchen, Germany.

Anite. (2002). *Dynamic packaging: the consumer's choice*. London: Anite Travel Systems.

Avital, M., & Te'eni, D. (2006, June 12-14). From generative fit to generative capacity: Exploring an emerging dimension of information systems fit and task performance. In *Proceedings of the 14th European Conference on Information Systems (ECIS)*, Goteburg, Sweden.

Baecker, R. M., Grudin, J., Buxton, W. A. S., & Greenberg, S. (1995). Designing to fit human capabilities. In *Human-computer interaction: Towards the year 2000* (pp. 667–680). San Francisco: Morgan Kaufman.

Benkler, Y. (2000). From consumers to users: Shifting the deeper structures of regulation. *Federal Communications Law Journal, 52*, 561–563.

Berger, C., Moslein, K., Piller, F., & Reichwald, R. (2005). Co-designing the customer interface for customer-centric strategies: Learning from exploratory research. *European Management Review, 2*(3), 24–39.

Chen, K., & Yen, D. (2004). Improving the quality of online presence through interactivity. *Information & Management, 42*, 217–226.

Christou, E., & Kassianidis, P. (2003). Consumers perception and adoption of online buying for travel products. *Journal of Travel & Tourism Marketing, 12*(4), 56–68. doi:10.1300/J073v12n04_06

Clemons, E., Gao, G., & Hitt, L. (2006). When online reviews meet hyperdifferentiation: A study of craft beer industry. In *Proceedings of the 39th Hawaii International Conference on System Sciences*.

Clemons, E., Gu, B., & Spitler, R. (2003). Hyperdifferentiation strategies: Delivering value, retaining profits. In *Proceedings of the 36th Hawaii International Conference on System Sciences*.

Davis, S. M. (1987). *Future perfect*. Reading, MA: Addison-Wesley.

Doty, H., & Glick, W. (1994). Typologies as a unique form of theory building: Towards improvement understanding and modelling. *Academy of Management Review, 19*(2), 230–251. doi:10.2307/258704

Duray, R. (2000). Approaches to mass customization: Configurations and empirical validation. *Journal of Operations Management, 18*(6), 605–625. doi:10.1016/S0272-6963(00)00043-7

Duray, R. (2002). Mass customization origins: mass or custom manufacturing? *International Journal of Operations & Production Management, 22*(3), 314–330. doi:10.1108/01443570210417614

Duray, R., & Milligan, G. (1999). Improving customer satisfaction through MC. *Quality Progress, 32*(8), 23–41.

Duray, R., Ward, P. T., Milligan, G. W., & Berry, W. L. (2000). Approaches to MC: configurations & empirical validation. *Journal of Operations Management, 18*, 605–625. doi:10.1016/S0272-6963(00)00043-7

Franke, N., & Piller, F. (2003). Key research issues in user interaction with user toolkits in a mass customization system. *International Journal of Technology Management, 26*(5-6), 578–599. doi:10.1504/IJTM.2003.003424

Franke, N., & Piller, F. (2004). Toolkits for user innovation and design: An exploration of user interaction and value creation. *Journal of Product Innovation Management, 21*(6), 401–415. doi:10.1111/j.0737-6782.2004.00094.x

Gao, G., & Hitt, L. (2004). IT and product variety: Evidence from panel data. In *Proceedings of the 25th International Conference on Information Systems (ICIS)*, Washington, DC.

Goodhue, D. L., & Thompson, R. L. (1995). Task-Technology fit and individual performance. *Management Information Systems Quarterly, 19*(2), 213–237. doi:10.2307/249689

Gretzel, U., Mitsche, N., Hwang, Y., & Fesenmaier, D. (2004). Tell me who you are and I will tell you where to go: Travel personality testing for DRS. In A. Frew (Ed.), *Proceedings of the ICT in Tourism ENTER 2004*, Vienna, Austria (pp. 205-215). Berlin: Springer Verlag.

Guay, L. (2003). Create your identity, create your product. In *Proceedings of the 2003 World Congress on Mass Customization and Personalization (MCPC 2003)*, Munich, Germany.

Hart, C., & Taylor, J. R. (1996). *Value creation through MC: Achieving competitive advantage through mass customization*. Ann Arbor, MI: University of Michigan Business School seminar.

Hopkins, C., & Raymond, M. (2004). Consumer responses to perceived telepresence in online advertising: moderating role of involvement. *Marketing Theory, 4*(1-2), 137–162. doi:10.1177/1470593104044090

Huffman, C., & Kahn, B. (1998). Variety for sale: Mass customization or mass confusion. *Journal of Retailing, 74*(4), 491–513. doi:10.1016/S0022-4359(99)80105-5

Kamali, N., & Loker, S. (2002). Mass customization: On-line consumer involvement in product design. *Journal of Computer-Mediated Communication, 7*(4). Retrieved July 5, 2005 from http://jcmc.indiana.edu/vol7/issue4/loker.html

Kargin, B., Basoglu, N., & Daim, T. (2009). Adoption factors of mobile services. *International Journal of Information Systems in the Service Sector, 1*(1), 15–34.

Kotha, S., & Vadlamani, B. (1995). Assessing generic strategies: an empirical investigation of two competing typologies in discrete manufacturing industries. *Strategic Management Journal, 16*(1), 75–83. doi:10.1002/smj.4250160108

Lampel, J., & Mintzberg, H. (1996). Customizing MC. *Sloan Management Review, 38*, 21–30.

Levy, Y., Murphy, K. E., & Zanakis, S. H. (2009). A Value-satisfaction taxonomy of IS effectiveness (VSTISE): A case study of user satisfaction with IS and user-perceived value of IS. *International Journal of Information Systems in the Service Sector*, *1*(1), 93–118.

Lexhagen, M. (2009). Customer perceived value of travel and tourism websites. *International Journal of Information Systems in the Service Sector*, *1*(1), 35–53.

Liechty, J., Ramaswamy, V., & Cohen, S. H. (2001). Choice menus for mass customization: An experimental approach for analyzing customer demand with an application to a Web-based information service. *JMR, Journal of Marketing Research*, *39*(2), 183–196. doi:10.1509/jmkr.38.2.183.18849

Moon, Y. (2002). Personalization and personality: Some effects of customizing message style based on customer personalities. *Journal of Consumer Psychology*, *12*(4), 313–326. doi:10.1207/15327660260382351

Oon, Y. B., & Khalid, H. M. (2001). Usability of design by customer websites. In Tseng, M. M., & Piller, F. (Eds.), *The Customer Centric Enterprise* (pp. 283–301). New York: Springer.

Papathanassiou, E. (2004). MC: management approaches and internet opportunities in the UK financial sector. *International Journal of Information Management*, *24*, 387–399. doi:10.1016/j.ijinfomgt.2004.06.003

Parker, M. (1996). *Strategic transformation and information technology: Paradigms for performing while transforming*. Englewood Cliffs, NJ: Prentice-Hall.

Peters, L., & Saidin, H. (2000). IT and the mass customisation of services: The challenge of implementation. *International Journal of Information Management*, *20*(4), 103–119. doi:10.1016/S0268-4012(99)00059-6

Piller, F. (2005). *Innovation and Value Co-Creation: Integrating Customers in the Innovation Process*. Cambridge, MA.

Piller, F., Moeslein, K., & Stotko, C. (2004). Does mass customisation pay? An economic approach to evaluate customer integration. *Production & Planning*, *15*(4), 435–444. doi:10.1080/0953728042000238773

Piller, F., & Moller, M. (2004). A marketing approach for mass customization. *International Journal of Computer Integrated Manufacturing*, *17*(7), 583–593. doi:10.1080/0951192042000273140

Piller, F., Schubert, P., Koch, M., & Möslein, K. (2005). Overcoming mass confusion: Collaborative customer co-design in online communities. *Journal of Computer-Mediated Communication*, *10*(4). Retrieved from http://jcmc.indiana.edu/vol10/issue4/piller.html.

Pine, B. J. II. (1993). *Mass customization: The new frontier in business competition*. Boston: Harvard Business School Press.

Pine, B. J. II, Peppers, D., & Rogers, M. (1995). Do you want to keep your customers forever. *Harvard Business Review*, *73*(2), 103–114.

Pitt, L., Bertham, P., & Watson, R. (1999). Cyberserving: Taming service marketing problems with the world wide web. *Business Horizons*, *42*(1), 11. doi:10.1016/S0007-6813(99)80044-5

Saari, T. (2002). Designing mind-based media and communications technologies. In *Proceedings of Presence 2002 Conference*, Porto, Portugal.

Saari, T., & Turpeinen, M. (2003). *Psychological customisation of information: Basic concepts, system architecture and applications*. Paper presented at the Mass customisation Conference, Munchen, Germany.

Sigala, M. (2002). The evolution of Internet pedagogy: Benefits for tourism and hospitality education. *Journal of Hospitality, Leisure. Sports and Tourism Education, 1*(2), 29–45.

Sigala, M. (2005). Integrating customer relationship management in hotel operations: Managerial and operational implications. *International Journal of Hospitality Management, 24*(3), 391–413. doi:10.1016/j.ijhm.2004.08.008

Sigala, M. (2006). Mass customisation implementation models and customer value in mobile phones services: Preliminary findings from Greece. *Managing Service Quality, 16*(4), 395–420. doi:10.1108/09604520610675720

Sigala, M., & Christou, E. (2005, July 27-31). MC in the travel trade: Reality check in the Greek travel-tour operator sector. In *Proceedings of the Annual I-CHRIE Convention*, Las Vegas, NV.

Spira, J. (1996). Mass customization through training at Lutron Electronics. *Computers in Industry, 30*(3), 171–174.

Te'eni, D. (2005). Designs that fit: An overview of fit conceptualizations in Human Computer Interaction. In Zhang, P., & Galletta, D. (Eds.), *Human-Computer Interaction and Management Information Systems – Foundations. Advances in Management Information Systems, 4.* Armonk, NY: M. E. Sharpe.

Vessey, I., & Galletta, D. (1991). Cognitive fit: An empirical study of information acquisition. *Information Systems Research, 2*(1), 63–84. doi:10.1287/isre.2.1.63

Zhang, P., & Na, L. (2004). An assessment of human-computer interaction research in management information systems: Topics and methods. *Computers in Human Behavior, 20*(2), 125–147. doi:10.1016/j.chb.2003.10.011

This work was previously published in International Journal of Information Systems in the Service Sector, Volume 2, Issue 2, edited by John Wang, pp. 48-69, copyright 2010 by IGI Publishing (an imprint of IGI Global).

Chapter 10
Technology Fears:
A Study of e-Commerce Loyalty Perception by Jordanian Customers

Ahmad Khasawneh
Hashemite University, Jordan

Mohammad Bsoul
Hashemite University, Jordan

Ibrahim Obeidat
Hashemite University, Jordan

Iyad Al Azzam
Yarmouk University, Jordan

ABSTRACT

The Internet and all other types of networks have changed life in general and doing business in particular, and as a result, many companies are now conducting and transferring their businesses online. In this paper, the authors evaluate whether loyalty issues are the major obstacles to the growth of e-commerce in Jordan. A survey conducted for the study reveals that technology fears are major barriers to loyalty in Internet banking and e-commerce activities among consumers. The results suggest that unless the technology fears of adopters are acknowledged, some of them are not successful.

INTRODUCTION

The situation of the internet has changed globally since 1999 (Al-Jaghouob & Westrup, 2003). Internet plays a significant role in commerce and business in the whole world (Bagchi et al., 2007), which connects millions of people and millions of computers at the same time (Ali, 2004; Khasawneh, 2008). The number of Internet users are increasing day after day (Kulchitsky, 2004), and it is used in many sectors, especially in conducting business on the internet (Khasawneh & Stafford, 2008), because Internet achieves more work without any increase in cost, and improves the quality of services as well (Stafford et al., 2006). But, this does not mean every online business can be a success (Mistry, 2005), because Internet and the

DOI: 10.4018/978-1-4666-0044-7.ch010

Copyright © 2012, IGI Global. Copying or distributing in print or electronic forms without written permission of IGI Global is prohibited.

new information and communication technologies encourage and help hackers and online criminals to attack any kind of business and disrupt it; this makes loyalty a major issue to tackle, as hackers might access and steal customers' personal information and details. In addition, since the internet gives people the ability to access any web site everywhere, they can search for better products and services, and as a result this increases the competition among companies. Internet provides a long range of opportunities and advantages for both business holders and customers as well, such as, reducing cost, saving times and so on. On the other hand, Internet enables hackers and internet criminals who attempt to enter and assault computer systems to obtain information illegally.

LITERATURE REVIEW

Loyalty has been researched and proved by many researches that it is a critical and significant factor that leads any company to expand in its size, besides being popular and famous in the whole world. The cost of retaining customers to be loyal is less than acquiring new customers; as a result, this leads to increase profits (Lake & Hicky, 2002).

There are many definitions for loyalty and loyal customers. (Bowen & Chen, 2001) identify loyal customers as those who have good feelings of appreciation for the company's brand and commit to stay buying products or services and recommend them to other customers. Customer loyalty will last or remains as long as the customers will stay with specific company brand and trade mark (turban et al., 2004). Applix (quoted in Sterne, 2000, p. 295) defines loyalty as "a feeling that results from an organization's ability to deliver three things to their customers: knowledge, anticipation of future requirements and superior communication".

Nowadays companies are struggling to create and maintain online loyal customers because there are new factors appearing with Internet, (Vatariausombut et al., 2004) claim the following factors that affect online customers loyalty: saving cost in online searching, internet and network technologies provide many tools and software that help customers in finding their needs effectively and efficiently by providing them the related information at lower costs and time as well. Thus customers can use these tools in searching on the internet and then buying the cheapest thing, Internet enables new business entrants to enter with minimum costs, new companies can imitate some of the famous and reputable companies and then use the technologies in building their website more powerful than the existing. As a result this leads to new strong competitors, and reduces the uniqueness of companies as well (Fletcher, 1995).

LOYALTY BENEFITS

Loyalty generates many benefits and advantages for the companies which have loyal customers. (Humby et al., 2003) claim that loyalty Increases sales, when customers become loyal to any organization they commit themselves to come back to the same organization instead of competitors, and loyal customers are willing to buy products or services from different sales channels as well (Duffy, 2003). As a result this increases the company's sales, increases the customization of marketing communications and tracks customers' styles as well.

Loyalty helps companies in doing one to one marketing because the loyal customers keep doing their transactions just in a specific company. This generates much data about customers' preferences. The company can then use the data in customising products and services for its loyal customers; in addition it helps the company to know the way that their customers do shopping and what kinds of products and services they choose, in order to change its performance to another form to match customer needs. Further it reduces the cost of transactions, marketing, lost customer expenses (Turban et al., 2004).

MEASURING LOYALTY

Loyalty assists the company to promote trust; and loyal customers will start talking about their company to other people. This will cause other people to trust the company and try their products and services; and loyalty improves company's brand. Loyal customers when they have bad feelings about the products or services for the brand that they are loyal to it, they are only complaining instead of going to other brands because the real loyal customers feel that they own the brand and try to make it strong and famous Loyal customers are not the same in the degree of their loyalty into specific brand or vendor; there are levels and categories of loyalty. There are many ways to measure customer loyalty. Bowen and Chen (2001) claim that the loyalty can be measured by three different approaches; behavioural measurements, attitudinal measurements, and composite measurements. Behavioural measurements refer to customers who have repeated buying behaviour for the same brand of products or services, but the weakness of this approach is that it does not show the real customer's emotion about the brand. Attitudinal measurements deal with customers who have good feelings about the brand, but they do not try it or continue to buy it because of its price but they recommend it to other customers. The third one, Composite approach, combines the behaviour and attitudinal measures together to measure the customers' loyalty who have repeated buying behaviour while at the same time having good feelings about the brand.

Loyalty can be created through many ways, (Vatariausombut et al., 2004) recommend companies which are interested in creating and maintaining customer loyalty to have a powerful security system, excellent customer service, have good reputation, as well as excellence of quality of products and services and an awareness of their customer's concerns. (Sterne, 2000) suggests the following three steps in building loyalty:

1. Make customers satisfied with the information and knowledge that the company provides them. There are four different types of knowledge and information that customers expect from any company in order to convince them that the company is more familiar and knowledgeable than its competitors:
   - Information about the company such as its history, strength and positions in the market.
   - Information about the market, for instance, market behaviour, and performance.
   - Information about the products or services such as offers, packages and prices.
   - Information about customers, for example, the way that customers deal with the company.
2. Predication of customer's requirements: This process consists of three sub processes:
   - Predictions of new products or services that might be valuable to the customer's needs and requirements.
   - Developing new technical services that might mitigate or avoid problems that customers may face.
   - Prediction of products or improvement of services depending on customer's feedback.
   - Keep in touch brilliantly with the customers in order to let them know about what it's the current situation of the market in order to make them feel that they constitute the important key in the market.

CATEGORIES OF LOYALTY

Loyal customers are not the same in the degree of their loyalty into specific brand or vendor; there are levels and categories of loyalty. (Dick & Basu,

1994) characterize the loyalty into four different categories depending on the customer's feeling about products or services and his/her repeated patronage: Loyalty, Latent loyalty, spurious loyalty, and No loyalty, and the customers are classified according to these four types of loyalty as well:

- Loyal customers: the customers who have great feelings about the products or services but with high repeat patronage.
- Latent loyal customers: the customers who have great feelings about the products or services but with low repeat patronage.
- Spurious loyal customers: the customers who have ordinary and low fellings about products or services and with high repeat patronage.
- No loyal customers: the customers who have low feelings about products or services as well as repeat patronage.

Rowley (2005) proposes the following different types of loyalty: captive loyalty, convince-seeker loyalty, contented loyalty, and committed loyalty.

1. Captive loyalty where customers remain buying products or services because there is no choice for them to change to other products or services and their feeling about the brand is unbiased and neutral. However this type is under risk to change via many factors such as new competitors, developments, changes in customers' social life and culture and other situations that might make customers to be not captive.

2. Convince-seeker loyalty; where customers routinely buying products and services and they do transactions usually related to the brand. This kind of customers does not have any feeling or attitude to brand excluding some of them. The threats that might face this kind of loyalty are new offers from other competitors such as buy one get one free, half price offers and others.

3. Contented loyalty where customers have high good feelings about the brand and they keep buying depending on the brand but they do not have the willingness to expand their buying on products or services from the same company. The threats that might face this kind of loyalty are better customer services from competitors, bad product quality as well as customer services, and low interest in developing new products.

4. Committed loyalty where customers are committed to continue buying products or services from the same brand, and are willing to expand their buying from the same brand, and also advice other customers to try a specific brand and to be committed to it as well. The threats that might face this kind of loyalty are frequent product failures and bad customer service and new services or products from competitors that really provide obvious benefits.

LOYALTY AND TRUST

The relationship between trust and loyalty is obvious and it has been proved by many researchers who claim that there is a positive relationship between trust and loyalty (Auh, 2005; Ballester & Aleman, 2001). Trust is imperative to build and maintain long relationships between customers and companies as well as to encourage to purchase and interact with companies especially in electronic commerce (Bernstel, 2002). (Ha, 2004) has declared that the customers which trust specific companies are loyal to it more than other customers. Trusted customers towards companies have the confidence that these companies deal with them legally and morally, and accordingly those customers will stay dealing the company which they have trusted for a long time and to which they will be loyal.

METHOD AND PROCEDURE

A mail survey was developed based on literature; content validity was established by established through individual interviews with IT professionals in bank and financial organization experts. The survey then was developed and was pre-tested to review the survey instrument for clarity, completeness, and readability. A pilot test was conducted using a random sample of IT professionals.

Schools are the vector for Internet adoption in Jordan (Ein-Dor et al., 1999), and since major official universities are from the very beginning have provided the pivotal nodes of network evolution, the ideal sample for investigating privacy issues in e-commerce use pattern in emerging Middle Eastern Internet markets might well be college students.

Granted, students are convenient for such research, and are often considered highly desirable as a sample frame due to the beneficial effects of homogeneity of but in this case university students also represent the majority of the current consuming Internet public of study, and, as such, can support excellent levels of external validity for studies of the diffusion of ICT in Middle Eastern nations.

The full survey was sent to 500 internet users were randomly selected from various education institutions in Jordan. A survey questionnaire was used to measure privacy issues perception and attitude toward e-commerce and Internet banking. We designed questionnaire based on the research objectives discussed. From 500 questionnaire distributed only 270 were collected and usable for analysis. Available evidence suggests that despite the possible inaccuracy involved with self-reported data in an absolute sense, it is usually the best possible and most appropriate approach for investigating decisions among individuals.

RESULTS AND DISCUSSION

Frequency distributions were performed and found that 58% were female and 42% were male and respondent age were in range of 20-25 years (78%) followed by 25-35 years (18%) of the overall total and 68% of them use the Internet daily and 70% uses the Internet banking. Although most of the respondent believe that using the Internet banking and shopping will make their life easier and is more convenient. Half of them think that it is safe and secure.

It is obvious from the above table that people resist using online banking if their privacy (personal and financial information) is exposed to other parties; it explains that 70% of the respondents are extremely concerned and worried about their privacy and they will be more far away from online banking if they know or have doubt that their privacy will be exposed by the bank.

This table shows the role of reputation in online loyalty. It shows that approximately 70%

Table 1. My resistance to use online banking increases if my bank shares my personal information with other companies

Strongly agree	35%
Agree	35%
Neither	15%
Disagree	10%
Strongly Disagree	5%

Table 2. Loyalty and online loyalty cross tabulation

	Online Loyalty YES	NO
Loyalty YES	25	11
Loyalty NO	0	45
Total	25	56

Table 3. How do you act towards companies that you are loyal to?

Repeat buying	45%
Repeat buying and tell other people	45%
Tell other people without repeat buying	5%
No further action	5%

of people are loyal to specific company; they are also loyal to it if it goes to be an online company. Hence the reputation of company is very important for maintaining and building online loyalty.

Table 3 shows how customers reward the company that they are loyal to, 45% from respondent who are loyal to specific company reward the company through repeat buying and telling other people about it, whereas 45% reward the company through repeat buying only, and only 5% reward the company by telling other people about it without repeat buying.

Table 4 shows the relationships between trust and loyalty. It illustrates that trust and loyalty are not the same, 60% of respondents who trust a specific company are not loyal to it whereas 40% say that if they trust a specific company they are loyal to it. From this result the researcher observes that trust helps in building loyalty but it does not mean that if there is trust, there is loyalty.

DISCUSSION

Perceived product or service quality is defined as customers' decision about the advantage of a product or service and its form from the customers'

Table 4. If you trust a company does it mean that you will be loyal to it?

Yes	40%
No	60%

feelings and attitudes, resulting from evaluation of the performance (Dean, 2002; Wong & Sohal, 2003; Sivadas & Baker, 2002). Thus if customers find that the quality of products or service is the same or more than they expect, they will be loyal to them. A positive relationship between the quality of products or services and the customer loyalty has proved. In addition, because in electronic commerce there is no physical interaction meaning customers can not touch the products and check it physically before purchasing it they have doubts about online purchase. However if they receive their products with the high quality they will be loyal to the company and committed to them because they are not cheated by online companies where many of them are fakes.

We found some customers are loyal to specific company if they have found that the company has low prices for their products and services, while another one, Also respondents who is experienced in marketing claimed that the layout of the web site does not affect the customer loyalty, as customer satisfaction comes from customer services and quality of products or services that the customer receives. The brand name affects and creates reputation. Furthermore other claims that the customers' conveniently plays a significant part in building and maintaining customer loyalty. The way that they provide special offers is important also in retaining customer loyalty for a long time.

CONCLUSION AND IMPLICATIONS

There are a number of opportunities for future research. A longitudinal case study would provide more conclusive evidence as to process the analysis. This analysis in no way comprises the full set of possible variables that may explain adoption behavior. The discussion of loyalty, privacy and trust will continue to be the focus of future research; the prevalence of the Internet will drive more technology into the banking and finance industry. The findings also have important practical implications for IS adoption and for manager understanding of customer requirement. Such an understanding can assist system developers in the planning of intervention mechanisms. A better understanding of the technological safeguards will increase the level of trust and privacy in the technology and therefore loyalty. Furthermore, the system developers need to focus on building customer trust as the findings indicate active adopters have stronger beliefs about the reliability, competence and integrity.

ACKNOWLEDGMENT

The author acknowledges the Editor-in-Chief of the journal, Professor John Wang, and the anonymous reviewers for their indispensable input that improved the paper significantly.

REFERENCES

Al-Jaghouob, S., & Westrup, C. (2003). Jordan and ict-led development: towards a competition state? *Information Technology & People, 16*(1), 93–110. doi:10.1108/09593840310463032

Ali, J. M. H. (2004). Information technology in the Middle East. *Journal of Global Information Technology Management, 7*(1), 1–4.

Auh, S. (2005). The effects of soft and hard service attributes on loyalty: The mediating role of trust. *Journal of Services Marketing, 19*(2), 81–92. doi:10.1108/08876040510591394

Bagchi, K., Udo, G., & Kirs, P. (2007). Global diffusion of the internet xii: The internet growth in Africa: some empirical results. *Communications of AIS, 19*, 325–351.

Ballester, E., & Aleman, L. (2001). Brand trust in the context of consumer loyalty. *European Journal of Marketing, 35*(11-12), 1238–1258. doi:10.1108/EUM0000000006475

Bernstel, J. (2002). Why Canada wins in online banking. *Banking Marketing, 34*(4), 12–17.

Bowen, J., & Chen, S. (2001). The relationship between customer loyalty and customer satisfaction. *International Journal of Contemporary Hospitality Management, 13*(5), 213–217. doi:10.1108/09596110110395893

Dean, A. (2002). Service quality in call centres: Implications for customer loyalty. *Managing Service Quality, 12*(6), 414–423. doi:10.1108/09604520210451894

Dick, A., & Basu, K. (1994). Customer loyalty: towards an integrated framework. *Journal of the Academy of Marketing Science, 22*(2), 99–113. doi:10.1177/0092070394222001

Duffy, D. (2003). Commentary internal and external factors which affect customer loyalty. *Journal of Consumer Marketing, 20*(5), 480–485. doi:10.1108/07363760310489715

Fletcher, K. (1995). *Marketing management and information technology* (2nd ed.). Hertfordshire, UK: Prentice Hall.

Ha, H. (2004). Factors influencing consumer perceptions of brand trust online. *Journal of Product and Brand Management, 13*(5), 329–342. doi:10.1108/10610420410554412

Humby, C., Hunt, T., & Phillips, T. (2003). *Scoring points how tesco is wining customer loyalty.* London: Kogan Page.

Khasawneh, A. M. (2008). Information technology in transitional economies: The mobile internet in Jordan. *Journal of Global Information Technology Management, 11*(3), 4–23.

Khasawneh, A. M., & Stafford, T. F. (2008). Mobile computing in developing nations: the case of use and adoption in Jordan. In *Proceedings of the 2008 Global Information Technology Management Conference,* Atlanta, GA.

Kulchitsky, D. R. (2004). Computerization, knowledge, and information technology initiatives in Jordan. *Administration & Society, 36*(1), 3–37. doi:10.1177/0095399703257263

Lake, N., & Hickey, K. (2002). *The customer service workbook*. London: Kogan Page.

Mistry, J. J. (2005). A conceptual framework for the role of government in bridging the digital divide. *Journal of Global Information Technology Management, 8*(3), 28–46.

Rowley, J. (2005). The four cs of customer loyalty. *Marketing Intelligence & Planning, 23*(6), 574–581. doi:10.1108/02634500510624138

Sivadas, E., & Baker-Prewitt, J. (2002). An examination of the relationship between service quality, customer satisfaction, and store loyalty. *International Journal of Retail & Distribution Management, 28*(2), 73–82. doi:10.1108/09590550010315223

Stafford, T. F., Turan, A. H., & Khasawneh, A. M. (2006). Middle East.com: diffusion of the internet and online shopping in Jordan and Turkey. *Journal of Global Information Technology Management, 9*(3), 43–61.

Sterne, J. (2000). *Customer service on the internet: building relationships, increasing loyalty, and staying competitive* (2nd ed.). New York: Wiley.

Turban, E. (2004). *Electronic commerce 2004: a managerial perspective* (International ed.). Upper Saddle River, NJ: Prentice Hall.

Vatariasusombut, B. (2004). How to retain online customers. *Communications of the ACM, 47*(6), 65–69.

Wong, A., & Sohal, A. (2003). Service quality and customer loyalty perspectives on two levels of retail relationships. *Journal of Services Marketing, 17*(5), 495–513. doi:10.1108/08876040310486285

This work was previously published in International Journal of Information Systems in the Service Sector, Volume 2, Issue 2, edited by John Wang, pp. 70-77, copyright 2010 by IGI Publishing (an imprint of IGI Global).

Chapter 11
Predictive Models in Cybercrime Investigation:
An Application of Data Mining Techniques

A. S. N. Murthy
Indian Police Service, Karnataka, India

Vishnuprasad Nagadevara
Indian Institute of Management Bangalore, India

Rahul De'
Indian Institute of Management Bangalore, India

ABSTRACT

With increased access to computers across the world, cybercrime is becoming a major challenge to law enforcement agencies. Cybercrime investigation in India is in its infancy and there has been limited success in prosecuting the offenders; therefore, a need to understand and strengthen the existing investigation methods and systems for controlling cybercrimes is greatly needed. This study identifies important factors that will enable law enforcement agencies to reach the first step in effective prosecution, namely charge-sheeting of the cybercrime cases. Data on 300 cybercrime cases covering a number of demographic, technical and other variables related to cybercrime was analyzed using data mining techniques to identify and prioritize various factors leading to filing of the charge-sheet. These factors and the respective priority rankings are used to suggest various policy measures for improving the success rate of prosecution of cybercrimes.

INTRODUCTION

With the growing penetration of the Internet and Information and Communication Technologies (ICT) in countries around the world, and, in particular, in developing countries, it is expected that along with the benefits that accrue there will also be problems. These problems have to do with both the technology as well as the use of the technology. Criminal and mischievous elements around the world are intent on using or abusing the open facilities of the ICT technologies for their benefit or entertainment. The central problem of

DOI: 10.4018/978-1-4666-0044-7.ch011

Copyright © 2012, IGI Global. Copying or distributing in print or electronic forms without written permission of IGI Global is prohibited.

law enforcement and regulations is to establish the framework within which abuses with and through the use of ICT is checked.

A problem of law enforcement and regulations with regard to ICT spread is that the many features and facilities of the technologies are growing and evolving. Few still know all the possible ways in which the technologies will be used. It is clear that the Internet provides a lot of information that is beneficial, but it is not obvious as to what manner the information may be used. Law enforcement and regulatory agencies around the world are struggling to define what policies to adopt to both restrict abuse and to enhance use of ICT.

In a developing country like India, the penetration rates of the Internet and of ICT are low but growing. Table 1 shows some data on Internet and ICT penetration in India as compared to two developed countries – Sweden and USA. Though the numbers are low for India, for all the indicators, owing to the large population base, the problems of usage and enforcement are very high. For instance, the number of Internet subscribers in India is 10.36 million as on December 2007 and another 57.83 million have access to Internet through various other media (TRAI, 2008).

The concern for monitoring and controlling crimes committed using ICT is called Cybercrime. That this is of growing importance was reflected in a recent conference (in September 2007) organized by the Indian Central Bureau of Investigation (CBI) in association with the software industry. Participants from 37 countries attended the conference. The main thrust of the conference was to have effective international cooperation in dealing with cybercrimes which covers legal standardization, standardization of procedural obligations, capacity building, and partnership with other agencies. This conference underscored the fact that cybercrime has become a major issue for law enforcement agencies in recent years.

OBJECTIVES AND SCOPE

The broad goal of this study is to understand and strengthen existing investigation methods, systems and practices for controlling cybercrime. A specific objective of this study is to identify the enabling factors which will facilitate charge-sheeting of cybercrime cases in India. The scope of study is limited to analyzing cybercrimes reported to law enforcement agencies in five states of India, namely Karnataka, Tamil Nadu, Andhra Pradesh, Kerala and Delhi.

The rest of the paper begins with a section on the definition of cybercrime, which is followed by a review of cybercrime prevention efforts from around the world and also a review of academic literature on cybercrime. This is followed by a discussion of the methodology of data collection and analysis. In the next sections the results are presented along with an analysis of the findings.

Background: What is Cybercrime?

It is extremely difficult to determine when the first crime involving a computer actually occurred. In 1801 Joseph Jacquard, a textile manufacturer in France, designed the forerunner of the computer

Table 1. Internet and ICT penetration in India and two developed countries. Source: UN E-Government Survey, 2008.

Country	Per capita income (US $)*	Internet per 100 persons**	PCs per 100 persons**	Mobile users per 100 persons**	Landline users per 100 persons**
Sweden	46,060	76.97	83.49	105.92	59.52
USA	46,040	69.1	76.22	77.40	57.15
India	950	5.44	1.54	14.83	3.64

punched card. This device allowed repetition of a series of steps in the weaving of special fabrics. So concerned were Jacquard's employees with the threat to their traditional employment and livelihood that they resorted to sabotage in order to discourage Mr. Jacquard from further use of this technology. This could be considered as the first "computer" crime to have been committed (United Nations, 1994).

Cybercrime Definition

Even after many years, a global definition of computer crime has not been arrived at. The functional definitions have become the norm. Cybercrimes can be classified into 3 categories:

- Against Individuals: These are the crimes or acts committed against a person. These crimes include harassment through e-mails, cyber-stalking, dissemination of obscene material on the Internet or intranet, defamation, hacking/cracking etc. In addition, these include crimes against property of an individual, computer vandalism, transmitting virus, Internet intrusion and unauthorized control over computer system.
- Against Organizations: These are crimes committed against an organization including Government departments, private firms, companies, groups of individuals; possession of unauthorized information and cyber-terrorism against the government or any other organization. Distribution of pirated software could also be included in this category of cybercrimes.
- Against Society at large: These are crimes that impact the society at large. Pornography is a typical example of such crimes.
- Technical or non-technical: The threats to individuals from the Internet and Internet services can be grouped as "technical" and "non-technical." The technical threats are computer virus, worms or spyware. The non-technical include theft, fraud, impersonation, deception, extortion, abuse, defamation and invasion of privacy.

In India, the Information Technology Act was enacted in June 2000, to provide the legal frame work for defining cybercrime in the country. The two major objectives of the act are facilitation of e-commerce and e-governance through legal recognition of e-records and digital signatures. The act enables the CBI to be the nodal agency in India to coordinate with Interpol in regard to cooperation for investigation from other law enforcement agencies.

It is interesting to note that two of the most important cybercrimes are hacking and distributing obscenity that contribute to more than sixty percent of cybercrimes in India.

REVIEW OF CYBERCRIME AND PREVENTION

The incidence of cybercrime is a global phenomenon. One of the comprehensive surveys on cybercrime is the Global economic crime survey 2005, carried out by Price Waterhouse Coopers (2005). It covered 3634 respondents spread over 34 countries. One of the significant findings is that the actual cybercrime is much more than perceived. The biggest concerns for the future are asset misappropriation which is the most visible of economic crimes and cybercrimes. The survey found that a typical perpetrator of economic crime in India was a graduate male between 31-50 years. With respect to crime detection, about 7 percent could be attributed to investigation by law enforcement agencies, 15 percent to internal audit, 22 percent to whistle blowing and 7 percent to internal tip-off to a regulatory authority. According to the survey, economic crimes, worldwide, have a lasting impact on reputation, brand image, share price, staff morale and business relationship of the commercial entities involved.

The Computer Security Institute (CSI) survey on computer crime and security is an annual feature. The 2008 survey was based on the responses from 522 computer security practitioners in various corporations, government agencies, financial institutions, medical institutions and universities (Richardson, 2008). According to the survey, the most expensive computer security incidents were those involving financial fraud with an average reported cost of close to $500,000 (for those who experienced financial fraud). The second-most expensive, on average, was dealing with "bot" computers within the organization's network, reported to cost an average of nearly $350,000 per respondent. The overall average annual loss reported was just under $300,000.

A report by McAfee (2007) points to the serious issues regarding cybercrime, and, in particular, to the threats to national security. The report highlights the well-funded and well-organized nature of these crimes, which are committed not only for money, but also for political reasons. Espionage and social engineering techniques are used to spot weaknesses in network security and for phishing for accounts and passwords. It appears that even intelligence agencies of different countries are getting into the act of surveillance and probing for weaknesses of national networks. Experts believe that cybercrime represents the biggest security threat to nations in the future.

In Australia, research has shown that the level of computer crime is not accurately measured. According to the study by the Australian Centre for Policing Research (2000), a vast majority of cases that are detected are not reported to the police. Some of the future challenges identified by the study are decoding encryption, proving identity, improving the reporting of electronic crime, and enhancing the exchange of information and intelligence.

The investigations that directly followed the September 11, 2001 attacks also disclosed the use of the internet to obtain information that could be used to plan attacks or obtain materials needed to make or improvise chemical, biological or radiological weapons. The United Nations 11th National Congress on Cybercrime Trends asserted that the relationship between government crime control efforts and the role of private sector companies involved in the production of hardware/software and in the delivery of services continued to be a major issue. This continues to be a major issue at the policy and legislative level as well as investigation and law enforcement level in many countries.

Irish organizations are significantly affected by cybercrime. Irish cybercrime survey (ISSA/UCD, 2006) suggested that the basic training which is mainly awareness training is a must for every investigator without which it is very difficult to proceed with the investigation.

Review of Literature on Cybercrime

The research literature on cybercrime follows two broad streams. The first concerns the issues regarding an appropriate legal framework that can enable governments and policing and security agencies to define, investigate and prosecute cybercrime (Cangemi, 2004; Huey & Rosenberg, 2004; Pocar, 2004; Bassett et al., 2006; Lu et al., 2006; Passas & Vlassis, 2007). Researchers point to the need for international cooperation to define crimes (Pocar, 2004; Hossain & Shahidullah, 2008), determine jurisdictional issues (where the crime is committed and who has to investigate) (Pocar, 2004; Passas & Vlassis, 2007), and identify procedures to collect evidence that is admissible in court (Huey & Rosenberg, 2004; Bassett et al., 2006).

The second stream focuses on the analysis of cybercrime data to detect patterns and evolve strategies for prevention, and investigation and prosecution. Cybercrime data is obtained from crime investigations and reports, and is available in a wide range of formats. Much of it is available over periods of time. The quality of the data is varied, often with large pieces missing. This has given impetus to data mining techniques that can deal with time-series data, in different formats, and of varied quality. Researchers have thus examined issues related to the tools that can be used for different types of crime data (Chen et al., 2004) and the manner in which data can be aggregated for analysis (Ritschard et al., 2008).

Research also shows that a beneficial effect of cybercrime is that it forces technology to evolve, to tackle the emerging threats (Anonymous, 2006).

DATA

The cybercrime investigation process in India is as follows: the process is initiated with the filing of complaints by the victim. This is also referred to as filing of the "First Information Report (FIR)". Sometimes it is possible that the concerned police person may not register the complaint, but may initiate inquiry into the complaint. In such a case, the inquiry report is approved by the higher authorities and the complaint is treated as closed.

On the other hand, if the FIR is registered, it may result in different outcomes. The two most desirable outcomes are (1) the investigation is completed and the case results in a charge sheet and (2) the case is investigated and proves to be a mistake of fact. The other possible outcomes are that investigation continues, or goes undetected or not investigated at all. Figure 1 presents the process and the possible outcomes.

For the purpose of this study, cybercrime is taken as the crimes registered by cybercrime police stations and cyber cells in the cities of Bangalore, Hyderabad, Chennai, Thiruvananthapuram and Delhi. These include most of the cases registered under Information Technology Act 2000 and a few cases registered under Indian Penal code.

The data pertaining to 291 cybercrime cases mostly in the form of copies of First Information Reports (FIRs) and final reports pertaining to states of Karnataka, Tamil Nadu, Andhra Pradesh, Kerala, and Delhi is used. There were 157 FIRs from Karnataka where as the remaining 134 were

Figure 1. Process of cybercrime investigation in India

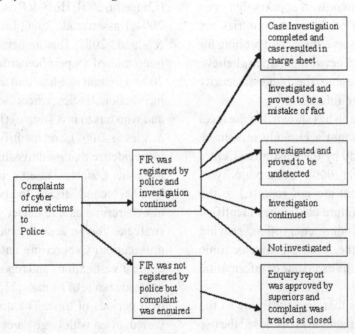

from the other four states. While the FIRs are generally hand written documents without any structured format, the nature of information that is to be recorded is well defined. All the information available in the FIRs is translated into 34 variables. The details of these 34 variables are given below in Table 2:

DATA ANALYSIS

The data is analyzed to identify the factors that will lead to filing the charge sheet. Two different techniques, namely, classification trees and artificial neural networks are used to analyze the data.

Classification trees work best with nominal or binned variables; hence, the data was prepared accordingly. In the case of C5.0 classification trees, the splitting of the records at each node is done based on the information gain. Entropy is used to measure the information gain at each node. This method can generate trees with variable number of branches at each node. For example, when a discrete variable is selected as an attribute for splitting, there would be one branch for each value of the attribute. C5.0 builds a tree by splitting the observations at each node based on a single attribute or variable. If no split that could significantly reduce the diversity of a given node can be found, the process of splitting is stopped and the node is labeled as a leaf node.

Table 2. Data variables

1. Crime number, section and cyber police station: This is to track back a case. It is a unique identifier of the record.
2. Age of Complainant: Binned into 4 categories
3. Gender of Complainant/VICTIM
4. Nature of Victim: either an Individual, or an Organization
5. Type of Organization: Four different types were defined
6. Marital status of the Complainant
7. Type of Damage to the Victim (Copy right, Data/software/source code, Reputation, Other
8. Type of Offence: Hacking, Obscenity, Copy Right violation, Others
9. Occupation of Complainant:
10. Investigation/Enquiry time for finalizing case: binned into 4 categories
11. Arrest period: binned into 4 categories
12. Arrest Status: Arrest is not mandatory but very important to obtain vital clues
13. Case Status (Case Finalization): This is very important for knowing whether police have successfully investigated a case-charge sheeted- or not (C). If there are no clues for detecting the crime, it is reported as undetected (U). If false complaints are given to settle civil disputes between parties, after investigation, it is reported to the court as false (F). It may take several months/years to know that the case is false or can not be detected. Even after several years, some cases may be still under investigation (I)
14. Motive of Accused
15. Tool for commission of offence
16. Gender of Accused
17. Age of Accused: binned into 4 categories
18. Tenure of Employee Involved: Binned into four categories
19. Damage amount (in lakhs): binned into 5 categories (10 lakhs=1million)
20. Time Lag in Noticing or Reporting: Binned into five categories
21. Identification of the Accused
22. Co-operation of Complainant
23. Occupation of accused
24. Dominant factor in offence: Behavior, Environment, Technology
25. Number of Offenders Single, Multiple, Not known
26. Details of IP Address
27. Server log details furnished
28. Co-operation of Service Provider
29. Co-operation of other agencies involved
30. Involvement of Cyber Cafe
31. Server Location: Foreign, Indian, Not Known
32. Type of Information: Data or Voice
33. Penal Act: Information Technology Act 2000 or Indian Penal Code (IPC)
34. Network Crime or Otherwise

When all the nodes become leaf nodes, the tree is fully grown. At the end of the construction of the tree, each and every observation has been assigned to a leaf node. Each leaf can now be assigned to a particular class and a corresponding error rate. The error rate at the leaf node is nothing but the percentage of misclassifications at the leaf node. The error rate for the entire tree is the weighted sum of the error rates of all the leaf nodes.

Artificial neural networks (ANN) are generally based on the concepts of the human (or biological) neural network consisting of neurons, which are interconnected by the processing elements. ANNs are composed of two main structures namely nodes and links. Nodes correspond to the neurons and links correspond to the links between neurons. ANN accepts the values of inputs into what are called input nodes. This set of nodes is also referred to as the input layer. These input values are then multiplied by a set of numbers (also called as weights) that are stored in the links. These values, after multiplication, are added together to become inputs to the set of nodes that are to the right of the input nodes. This layer of nodes is usually referred to as the hidden layer. Many ANNs contain multiple hidden layers, each feeding into the next layer. Finally, the values from last hidden layer are fed into an output node, where a special mapping or thresholding function is applied and the resulting number is mapped to the prediction. ANN is created by presenting the network with inputs from many records whose outcome is already known. For example, the data on age, gender and occupation of the complainant with respect to the first record are input into the input layer. These values are fed into the hidden layer and after processing (by combining these values using appropriate weights) the prediction is made at the output layer. If the prediction made by the ANN matches with the actual known status of the cybercrime (say either charge sheeted or undetected), then the prediction is good and the ANN proceeds to the next record. If the prediction is wrong, then the extent of error (expressed in numerical values) is apportioned back into the

links and the hidden nodes. In other words, the values of the weights at each link are modified based on the extent of error in prediction. This process is referred to as the backward propagation. Artificial neural networks are found to be effective in detecting unknown relationships. ANNs have been applied in many service industries (Wong et al., 1997), such as health to identify the length of stay and hospital expenses (Nagadevara, 2004), air lines (Faraway & Chatfield, 1998) and for predicting the categories of the members of loyalty programs (Nagadevara, 2008).

Profile of Data Sample

As mentioned earlier, the data for the study consisted of 291 cases dealing with cybercrime. About half of the complaints are made by individuals where as the remaining half or made on behalf of the complainant organization. More than 65 percent of the complainants were male. Most of the complaints deal with hacking accounting for about 49 percent. Obscenity was the second most common complaint accounting for about 26 percent. The most common nature of cases was with respect to theft of data or source code or loss of reputation because of the crime. The motive for the crime was predominantly monetary gain. Needless to say 87 percent of the crimes were committed using computers where as about 7 percent were committed using a mobile phone. In about 70 percent of the cases, the case was reported within one month. In most of the cases, the server logs were not available, nor were the IP numbers. Similarly, the details of the service provider involved in the crime were also not available.

RESULTS AND DISCUSSION

The entire database was divided into two subsets. The first subset contains the records of cybercrimes reported in the state of Karnataka. The second subset contains the cybercrimes reported in the rest of the country. The variable "Case Status" was used as the dependent variable for the purpose of building the classification trees and artificial neural networks for prediction. The data is analyzed for the entire database as well as for each subset separately. Classification trees for Karnataka and the rest of the country are presented in Figure 2

and Figure 3 respectively. There are four possible values of the dependent variable namely, "Filing Charge Sheet", "Investigation Continuing", "False Reporting" and "Undetected". The accuracy levels of the classification trees are fairly high with 80 percent accuracy for the State of Karnataka, 85 percent for the rest of the country and 82 percent for the entire database.

Figure 2. Classification tree for cybercrimes reported in Karnataka

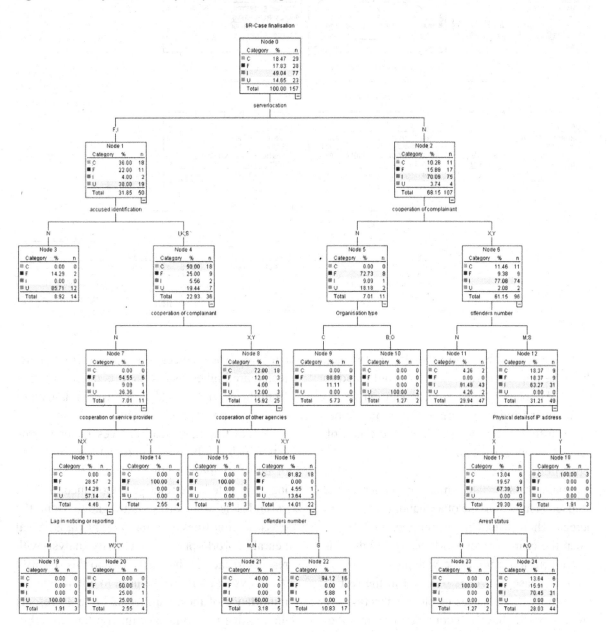

Figure 3. Classification tree for the cybercrimes reported in rest of the country

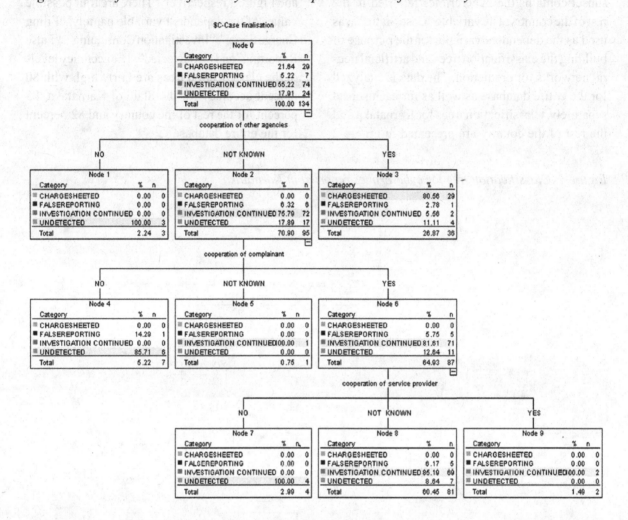

In the case of crimes reported in Karnataka, the most important variables that would lead to filing of a charge sheet are cooperation of the complainant and the tenure of the employee between 6 to 12 months. Similarly, there is a 60 percent chance of charge sheeting when the reputation of the complainant is at stake and the complainant is female while the gender of the accused is male. On the other hand, there is a 78 percent chance that the crime goes undetected when the crime is a network crime and there is no cooperation from the service provider.

In the case of crimes reported in the rest of the country, the chances of charge sheeting are highest when there is cooperation from other agencies. The chances of the crime going undetected are highest when there is no cooperation from the service provider, or the complainant or other agencies. This conclusion is rather obvious.

While the classification trees generate rule sets which can be used to predict the possibility of either charge sheeting or the crime remaining undetected, the relative importance of these variables is very difficult to gauge from the classification trees. On the other hand, artificial neural networks provide sensitivity analysis with respect to each of the variables and this sensitivity analysis in turn can be used to obtain relative importance of these variables. Table 3 presents the relative importance of the top ten variables.

Table 3. Relative importance of the top ten variables

Variable	Relative Importance		
	All India	**Karnataka**	**Rest of India**
Age of accused	0.0776	0.0835	0.0337
Lag in noticing or reporting	0.0389	0.0384	0.0319
Marital status of complainant	0.0388	0.0375	0.0319
Damage amount	0.0387	0.0322	0.0284
Employee tenure	0.0339	0.0365	0.0244
Gender of accused	0.0338	0.0504	0.0293
Offence type	0.0325	N	0.0288
accused identification	0.0332	N	N
cooperation of complainant	0.0322	N	N
Organization type	0.0311	N	N
Information	N	0.0309	N
Offenders number	N	0.0395	N
Age of complainant	N	0.0366	N
Damage to the victim	N	0.0327	N
Occupation of complainant	N	N	0.0329
penal act	N	N	0.0310
Occupation of accused	N	N	0.0262

N: Not in Top ten

These are presented separately for crimes reported in Karnataka, Rest of the country as well as for the entire country.

Seven variables are common across the three models namely, All India, Karnataka and Rest of the country. The age and the gender of the accused are important along with the lag in reporting. The earlier the reporting is done, the higher are the chances of charge sheeting. Similarly the employee tenure and the damage amount are also important factors across all the three models.

These models can be used in conjunction to identify the factors that will be helpful in addressing cybercrime. The classification trees can help in predicting the likelihood of charge sheeting the accused. In case such chances are low for a given case, the tree can help the authorities in focusing on certain aspects of the case. For example, if the FIR is unable to specify the service provider or the server logs and it happens to be network type,

then it is important to the authorities to concentrate on either getting the server logs or zero in on the service provider. Similarly it is imperative that data with respect to the cyber café, various service providers' server logs, type damage that could result to the complainant or the victim from the crime should be collected and analyzed carefully in order to reach the stage for charge sheeting. In most cases, the cooperation of the complainant and other investigating agencies is the most important determinant of the solving the crime. The focus of the investigating agencies should be on continuing cooperation from the complainants.

SUMMARY AND CONCLUSION

The Information Technology Act 2000 enacted by Government of India and the amendments of 2006 address various concerns of cybercrime such as e-commerce frauds, data theft, child pornography, theft of identity documents etc. Even after the enactment of the Information Technology Act 2000 and the amendments, there are a number of uncertainties in the investigation of cybercrime. There is a need to understand and strengthen the existing investigation methods and systems as well as data collection for controlling cybercrime. This study analyzed data with respect to 291 reported cases of cybercrime. The data is divided into two different subsets, the first dealing with the crimes reported in Karnataka and the second dealing with the rest of the country. The study applied the techniques of classification trees and artificial neural networks to analyze the data. Different models were built to identify the important factors that will enable law enforcement agencies to reach the first step in effective prosecution, namely charge-sheeting of cybercrime cases. Through these models it is possible to identify the relative importance of different variables that could lead to charge sheeting of the accused. These models are also capable of predicting the possible outcome of the case. Depending on the prediction, and the chances of reaching the stage of charge sheeting, these models can guide the authorities in focusing their energies on the collection of appropriate information which will increase the chances of charge sheeting. Thus, these models can be used to improve the efficiency of the authorities in solving cybercrimes.

The research reported in this paper contributes to both the stream of the literature that deals with identifying patterns of crime and reportage that can assist with prosecution. Our results clearly show what is important, in the Indian context, to file a charge sheet and prosecute a case. This research shows the possibility and value of using data mining techniques such as classification trees and artificial neural networks. The paper provides concrete evidence of the use and value of such techniques from a practical perspective.

REFERENCES

Anonymous,. (2006). Immunizing the Internet, or: How I learned to stop worrying and love the worm. *Harvard Law Review*, *119*, 2442–2463.

Australian Centre for Policing Research. (2000). *The virtual horizon: Meeting the law enforcement challenges-developing an Australasian law enforcement strategy for dealing with electronic crime*. Retrieved February 10, 2009, from http://www.acpr.gov.au/pdf/ACPR134_1.pdf

Bassett, R., Bass, L., & O'Brien, P. (2006). Computer forensics: An essential ingredient of cyber security. *Journal of Information Science and Technology*, *3*(1), 22–32.

Cangemi, D. (2004). Procedural law provisions of the council of European convention on cybercrime. *International Review of Law Computers & Technology*, *18*(2), 165–171. doi:10.1080/1360086042000223472

Chen, H., Chung, W., Xu, J. J., Qin, G. W. Y., & Chau, M. (2004, April). Crime data mining: A general framework and some examples. *IEEE Computer*, 50-56.

Faraway, J., & Chatfield, C. (1998). Time series forecasting with neural networks: A comparative study using the airline data. *Applied Statistics*, *47*(2), 231–250. doi:10.1111/1467-9876.00109

Hossain, M., & Shahidullah, S. M. (2008). Global-local nexus and the emerging field of criminology and criminal justice in South Asia: Bangladesh case. *Bangladesh e-. Journal of Sociology (Melbourne, Vic.)*, *5*(2), 51–60.

Huey, L., & Rosenberg, R. S. (2004, October). Watching the web: Thoughts on expanding police surveillance opportunities under the cyber-crime convention. *Canadian Journal of Criminology and Criminal Justice*, 597–606.

IISA/UCD. (2006). *Irish cybercrime survey (2006)-the impact of cybercrime on Irish organization.* Retrieved February 10, 2009, from http://www.issaireland.org/ISSA%20UCD%20 Irish%20Cybercrime%20Survey %202006. pdf

Lu, C., Jen, W. Y., Chang, W., & Chou, S. (2006). Cybercrime & cybercriminals: An overview of the Taiwan experience. *Journal of Computers, 1*(6), 1–8. doi:10.4304/jcp.1.6.11-18

McAfee. (2007). *Virtual criminology report - cybercrime: the next wave.* Retrieved February 10, 2009, from http://www.mcafee.com/us/research/ criminology_report/default.html

Nagadevara, V. (2004). *Application of neural prediction models in healthcare.* Paper presented at the Second International Conference on e-Governance, Colombo, Sri Lanka.

Nagadevara, V. (2008). Improving the effectiveness of the hotel loyalty programs through data mining. In Jauhari, V. (Ed.), *Global causes on hospitality industry.* New York: The Haworth Press.

Passas, N., & Vlassis, D. (2004). Background and outline of the 2nd world summit of attorneys general, prosecutors general, chief prosecutors, prosecutors and ministers of justice. *Crime, Law, and Social Change, 47,* 193–200. doi:10.1007/ s10611-007-9074-4

Pocar, F. (2004). New challenges for international rules against cyber-crime. *European Journal on Criminal Policy and Research, 10,* 27–37. doi:10.1023/B:CRIM.0000037565.32355.10

Price Waterhouse Coopers. (2005). *Global economic crime survey.* Retrieved February 10, 2009, from http://www.pwc.com/ro/eng/ins-sol/ survey-rep/PwC_2005_global_crimesurvey.pdf

Richardson, R. (2008). *CSI Computer Crime & Security Survey.* Retrieved February 10, 2009, from http://i.cmpnet.com/v2.gocsi.com/pdf/ CSIsurvey2008.pdf

Ritschard, G., Gabadinho, A., Muller, N. S., & Studer, M. (2008). Mining event histories: A social science perspective. *International Journal of Data Mining. Modelling and Management, 1*(1), 68–90.

TRAI. (2007). *Quarterly performance indicators of Indian telecom services for the quarter ending December 2007.* Retrieved February 10, 2009, from http://www.trai.gov.in/trai/upload/ PressReleases/555/pr10april08no33.pdf

United Nations. (1994). *International review of criminal policy, 43 & 44, 1994.* United Nations manual on the computer and computer related crime.

Wong, B. K., Bodnovich, T. A., & Selvi, Y. (1997). Neural network applications in business: A review and analysis of the literature (1988-1995). *Decision Support Systems, 19,* 301–320. doi:10.1016/ S0167-9236(96)00070-X

This work was previously published in International Journal of Information Systems in the Service Sector, Volume 2, Issue 3, edited by John Wang, pp. 1-12, copyright 2010 by IGI Publishing (an imprint of IGI Global).

Chapter 12
Deploying New Perspectives of Network Organizations for Chronic Diseases' Integrated Management

Isabella Bonacci
Federico II University, Italy

Oscar Tamburis
ICAR – CNR, Italy

ABSTRACT

The social frame of healthcare organizations in Europe (and in particular in the Italian Public Sector), as a combination of relational, formal and informal aspects, is one of their most relevant sources of complexity, which leads to different approaches about decisional, clinical and organizational processes (Cicchetti, 2004). These issues have been enlightened as well by the increasing social incidence of chronic-degenerative pathologies, such as Diabetes Mellitus type 2. In this regard, the Italian national e-government strategy has first pointed out the need for paths of integration and interoperability among information systems to ensure a safe exchange of information (CNIPA, 2008). The activity of "integrated design" of information flows between doctors and patients allows the creation and development of reticular organizational forms in which many non contiguous actors work at the same time on the diagnosis and care process. This paper shows how the adoption of the Social Network Analysis (SNA), as theoretical and methodological perspective that emphasizes the social reality as reticular framework (Moreno, 1987), can provide an innovative approach for the study of the "pathology networks" and the "integrated management" of Diabetes Mellitus type 2, where ICT solutions are (or are about to be) currently involved.

DOI: 10.4018/978-1-4666-0044-7.ch012

Copyright © 2012, IGI Global. Copying or distributing in print or electronic forms without written permission of IGI Global is prohibited.

INTRODUCTION

HealthCare Organizations (HCOs) can be defined as "[...] social entities guided by specific objectives and involved in the processes through which health assistance services are produced and provided to healthy (e.g., prevention) or diseased subjects" (Mapelli, 1999).

Health assistance services spread over a health–disease–health continuum, since the gap between health and disease can be only reduced, so that a disease subject produces another disease subject with different needs (Ruta, 1993). Many levels of assistance complexity and intensity are so covered, comprised within a wider *corpus* of organizational forms that, with its many professional subgroups, complex work processes and power structures, represents a fluid and dynamic context with fewer formalized control mechanisms (Helmreich & Merritt, 1998) and suggests indefinite possible solutions of coordination and work assigning. Issues come from the difficulties to assess the alternative organizational forms proposed for the healthcare sector, in terms of efficacy, efficiency and equity (Grandori, 1999), as well as the different methodological approaches introduced for the study of its complexity: different levels of complexity can be detected in fact, from the agreement degree (among those working in the inside environment) to the uncertainty degree (how the inside environment connects to the outside environment), related in any case to three main different fields: culture and values; technological–formal issues; social legacies (Cicchetti, 2004).

In this dynamic context the emerging organisational form is the network organisation: the development of a reticular organizational structure rises from the need of a higher degree of organizational analysis than what requested for a single company (Martinez, 1997), and from the importance to deal with an interconnected organizations set as a higher ranking actor (Keen, 1990; Rockart & Short, 1991; Bonacci & Tamburis, 2007). The network

appears therefore as the solution to the issues of integration between separated and specialized units (Cicchetti & Mascia, 2007); nonetheless, an accomplished sharing of values, social legacies and formal languages becomes possible in particular only within an "information and communication network", where the knowledge framework that gives origin to the *government of the technological system* (Cosmi, 2003) – meant as pattern of analysis and management of coded information and data flows – takes the name of *Information and Communication Technology*.

THE IMPACT OF ICTS VS. THE LOGICS OF NETWORK

After the First Stage of Discovery of the "Health ICT world" (1989-1999), the Second Stage of Acceptance (1999-2009) began with recognition that nothing was going to happen by osmosis or just because of the enthusiasm of that community alone. The challenges were evident – there was no main stream credibility for health ICT within the technology sector or indeed within healthcare itself; there was no voice for innovation and new ideas; few who were aware or listening to the health telematics community (EHTEL, 2009). Opportunities have been beginning to open up during years. New technologies have been maturing which had relevance to healthcare. The growing pressures of demography, medical advances and patient empowerment were all in sharp contrast with finite resources available to address a growing demand from citizens and patients for more health attention.

The impact of increasing incidence of chronic disease, evidence based medicine, and early glimpses of personalized care, information based management and control, economics of transformation through technology support and development of strategic ideas from worldwide markets have been changing perceptions, priorities and the choice of health business models. In addition, as opportunities emerged, stakeholders began to be more aware of the opportunities and threats associated with ongoing change. There is therefore evidence that, when combined with proper organization, leadership and skills, innovative Information and Communication Technologies (ICTs) can help to address some of the societal challenges to (not only) Europe's healthcare systems, first of all the achievement of the logics of "healthcare network" through which realize a level of technological integration capable of increase synergies between HCOs, and between them and the patients: a network of interconnected HCOs and healthcare operators (General Practitioners, Specialists, …) can lead to access to, deliver and share new forms and channels of relations, apart from consolidating and revitalizing the already existing ones. Nevertheless, researches examining organizational and socio-cultural factors have provided insight into variables which diminish or create barriers to the use of ICTs within HCOs. Recent works have paid attention to the interactive complexity of group works (Goodwin & Goodwin, 1998; Kaplan & Shaw, 2002) demonstrating the need to move outside the traditional individual decision-maker assessment and take account of the context of practice, team integration, and related cognitive as well as socio-cultural issues. Few studies (Santahanam, Guimaraes, & George, 2000; Kaplan, 2001) have traced as well the links between improvements in organizational outcome indicators and a diversity of predictive variables (technical, organizational and socio-cultural factors) within organizations as ICT were implemented. Another body of literature, focused on the diffusion of technological innovation (Rogers, 1995), has identified the processes by which innovation is communicated though certain channels over time among members of a social system: neither here much attention has been paid to the consequences for workers and organizations (and HCOs among these) of adopting technological innovations (Westbrook, Braithwaite, Iedema, & Coiera, 2004).

LITERATURE REVIEW

Our study draws upon two main areas of research in the literature: (i) the network organizations in the healthcare sector, (ii) the *Social Network Analysis* as work methodology. In this section, we provide a brief survey of pertinent studies in each area from the literature.

In a strictly organizational meaning, the network is defined as a set of relations between actors, and ties between subjects and/or systems of coordination and governance, converging upon the same output and/or business process (Grandori, 1999). There are two main branches of research focused on the healthcare networks: the first one aims to analyze the pattern and its strategic and organizational properties from the network *nodes* standpoint, paying attention on their dynamics of aggregation. Many experiences (Cicchetti, 2002; Miolo, Vitali, & Nuti, 2003; among the others) made possible to depict two main categories: the horizontally–integrated networks and the vertically–integrated networks. In the first case, literature widely refers to the so–called "hub & spoke model", where a medical centre of excellence able to provide high specialized performances – often because of higher resources availability – is surrounded by a number of peripheral facilities aimed to less specialized tasks (Cicchetti, 2002; Lega, 2002). In the second case, the network is related to the concept of assistance continuity (Lega, 1998), and the research focuses on the enhancement of the patient assistance path, with particular regard to the prevention performances.

The other main body of literature concerns the kind of flows – meant as exchange of resources – that origin inside the network (*co–ordinate mobilization*: Warren, Stephen, & Bergunder, 1974). Researches focus on the dynamics of integration, coordination and interdependence occurring between two or more organizations (Milner, 1980; Fennell & Warnecke, 1988; Kaluzny & Warnecke, 1996). Such contributes differ from the previous ones because, besides drawing the network organizational framework, highlight the impact on performances level by analyzing management and clinical outcomes: this leads therefore to an evaluation of the efficacy for both the whole network and the single nodes and ties (Provan & Milward, 1995).

The co–ordinate mobilization is a typical form of healthcare services supplying, and is the first stage in a much longer path along which the relational tissue gets steadier thanks to information exchange and agreements settling among the actors involved (e.g., dynamics of patients exchange between HCOs) (Van de Ven, Walker, & Liston, 1979; Van de Ven & Walker, 1984). The networks studies appear as connected to other disciplines, such as sociology, and in particular with the body of literature about the *social network analysis*. Assuming that the relationships occurring between actors are held to actors' roles inside the network (Cross & Parker, 2004; Meneguzzo & Cepiku, 2008), the whole set of nodes/actors (with their peculiar features), and the set of ties (e.g., connections, relations and/or interactions for the exchange of resources) give origin to a *social network* (Powell, 1990), that can be can be articulated on different levels: *interpersonal* (a single person belonging to an organization); *intra–organizational* (a specific people group within an organization); *inter–organizational* (a set of relations existing between organizations). Such levels concern different kind of social ties, from casual contacts, to working relationships, to family bonds (Chiesi, 1999, 2006).

The Social Network Analysis (SNA) is a methodology for the analysis of social relationships, developed from the research of Jacob Levy Moreno (among the others), founder of *sociometry* (a discipline focused on the study of interpersonal relationships), that in 1934 tried for first to visualize the social interactions as reticular objects. The SNA makes a wide use of topics, concepts and instruments coming from the branch of mathematics known as "theory of graphs", focusing especially on the possibility

to analyze, interpret (and somehow foretell) the ties existing between the nodes of a network. In the healthcare sector the organizational actors are strongly interconnected each other, and then influenced by the surrounding social environment, so the SNA appears as the most suitable theoretical and methodological perspective to investigate the spreading of innovations and good practices (clinical, organizational and technological) among healthcare operators, or how multidisciplinary teams for the treatment of chronic–degenerative pathologies work. The above mentioned level of analysis can be featured as follows:

- *Interpersonal*: performance supplying, definition and development of decisional and information processes for practitioners and specialists (Coleman, 1974; Valente, 2002), operations of multifunctional teams (West, Barron, Dowsett, & Newton, 1999);
- *Intra–organizational*: designing of HCOs, where social relations play a key role in the performance analysis of the organizational units (Lomi, 1991; Donatini et al., 2001);
- *Inter–organizational*: designing of assistance networks (Agranoff & McGuire, 2001).

The adoption of the SNA fits with the research objective, because of its capability to feature correctly the organizations involved, by using appropriate sets of indicators and graphic instruments. Within this logic, it becomes possible to investigate any kind of relationships that origin in a healthcare system, comparing therefore the "formal" and the "real" organization frameworks (Cicchetti, 2007); that makes also possible to improve the ability to develop evaluation models that are adaptive and sensitive to the characteristics of wicked problems and provides a strong theoretical basis from which to analyze and interpret findings (Westbrook et al., 2007).

METHODOLOGICAL REMARKS

The present work supports an explorative/descriptive analysis (Yin, 1993; Mari, 1994), featuring as the first step of a wider research path described in its overall in Figure 1. The two main research objectives are:

- Verify if and how the SNA can address the instances of *change* and knowledge management within a territorial context featuring a low use of ICTs and a limited spreading of information flows concerning the chronic patients' care paths;
- Verify if and how the SNA can appear as the "way" to a perspective of *innovation*, whereas the realization of an information framework (*social healthcare network*) for the circulation and the exchange of accurate, individual and complete clinical data, can improve the dynamics of communication and interaction/integration between the subjects involved in the patients' care paths.

The concept of *change* means any kind of modification of the organizational and technological knowledge gained from the outside environment and/or improving the use of resources extant, but not properly exploited (Corti, 2002): this descriptive side of the analysis is enhanced by the increasing body of literature about the network designing in the healthcare sector as well. The explorative analysis refers instead to the concept of *innovation*, meant as any qualitative/quantitative modification of the use of extant technologies, able to lead "somehow" to a very change, perceived as positive (Corti, 2002). The deployment of the analysis of social networks requires a methodology for the evaluation of relational data.

The quantitative–relational approach provided by the SNA features as analysis units the set of relationships that the actors (nodes) involved in the care path (HCOs, GPs, patients) origin inside the network, while the relations' properties (ties) belong to couples of actors, instead of single nodes (Mazzoni, 2007; Marchi, Schifini D'Andrea, Maggino, & Mola, 2007). Strengths of the SNA are the exploitation of the Theory of

Figure 1. The research path

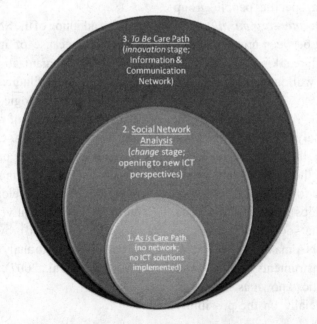

Graphs to handle the relational data (the couple of actors), and the Matrix Algebra to describe the interactions framework (Scott, 2000; Wasserman & Faust, 1996): relational data are first depicted through the use of "n x n" sociometric matrixes, whose rows and columns refer to the nodes, while the cells refer to their connections. The "weight" of each connection depends on the definition of a *suitable evaluation parameter* adopted for drawing the social network.

The graphs (here called "sociograms") are bi–dimensional descriptions of the social relations, wherein the points mean the nodes and the lines mean the ties between couple of nodes. The use of sociograms makes finally possible to highlight many formal network properties (such as density, cohesion, centrality, and connectivity). The analysis of the problematics on a complex environment in which information & communication technologies are increasingly being implemented led to recognize that there aren't suitable evaluation frameworks yet, by which to assess their impact on clinical work and organizational outcomes. The two main challenges the research path should try to address are to conceptualize the design features of an evaluation framework and to specify what data will be gathered and how.

THE EMPIRICAL VERIFICATION

The empirical analysis coming from the research strategy consisted of two main steps:

- The first step focused on the identification of possible areas of implementation of ICT solutions in the Districts of the Local Health Authority "Na 2 Nord" (located in the north of Naples' province, Italy), in relation to the sustainability of programmes of Integrated Management for chronic–degenerative pathologies, in particular Diabetes Mellitus type 2. The quantitative research was founded on a survey administering;

- The second step aimed to elaborate the results achieved using qualitative methods (participant observation, creation of a "Pathology Group"). The implementation of the SNA made possible to draw a network to investigate the relations occurred, according to the logic of disease management.

The sample group consisted of nearly 50 General Practitioners (GPs) and Specialists (in particular diabetologists), working in the Districts of the Local Health Authority Na 2 Nord; chronic–degenerative pathologies, including the Diabetes Mellitus type 2, present similar clinical courses, and their incidence on the population has been increasing mostly because of the raising of life expectancy. In Italy, surveys concerning the Diabetes incidence on national scale are not available, while there are studies performed on local areas (see: Bonora et al., 2004 (Bolzano area); Bruno et al., 2005 (Turin area); Pelella, Tamburis, & Tranfaglia, 2007; Bonacci, Pelella, & Tamburis, 2008 (Benevento area)). In addition, from ISTAT yearbook data (Zaccarin & Rivellini, 2007) emerges that 4,6% of Italians are diabetic, equal to 2,7 millions people (4,9% women and 4,4% men). The standard prevalence increased, during the last years, from 4,2% in 2002 to 4,6% in 2007. The prevalence of Diabetes Mellitus increases with the age, up to the 17,6% in the over 75 age group. In the age group from 35 to 74 years, the prevalence is greater for the men, while in the over 75 age group is greater for the women. The administered 50–item questionnaire for the data collection, mostly structured with fixed questions, was divided in three main areas:

- *Knowledge of the pathology*: the analysis focused on the main topics concerning the handling of the diabetic patient by the GPs, in order to verify their correct behavior as well as the respect of the guidelines for the treatment of the pathology;

- *Approach to the ICT*: the first purpose was to evaluate, among the GPs, their knowledge and experience with information instruments as well as with electronic data delivering and warehousing tools. The second purpose was to analyze their propensity toward the adoption of Electronic Medical Record protocols;
- *Management of communication flows*: the analysis focused on evaluation of the degree of interaction/integration between the subjects involved in the diabetic patient care path.

The answers analysis from the sample group members led to a first "picture" of the three levels of the social network, and to the set of flows occurring among the actors themselves (co–ordinate mobilization). A strong dichotomy appeared between their will to equip with ICT solutions, and the lack of a real sense of their use, as well as their effects on work performances, services efficiency and operators expertise. The emerging scenario showed once one how "the deployment of ICTs, either as change or innovation, is still perceived as an out–of–the–ordinary, avoidable experience: a definitely remarkable chance of improvement for the service performances supplying, but ready to turn out as negative, since cause of modification for actors' behaviors and roles" (Corti, Iasiello, Marino, & Tamburis, 2004).

THE GENERAL CARE PATH (*AS* IS)

Figure 2 describes the General Care Path, as drawn upon the elaboration and the analysis of the questionnaires. The flow chart turned out as the best pattern to highlight the logical sequence of the episodes forming the Care Path in a territorial context, and allocate the performances delivered by the GPs, together with the diabetological team

(composed by diabetologist, diabetic centre, cardiologist, nephrologist, optician, dietician, podiatrist and psychologist) and the territorial hospital(s), for the treatment of a particular kind of patients.

The realization of the General Care Path started with the analysis of the *real* care path adopted by each GP (i.e., the visualization, for the diabetic patients followed, of the actual sequence of the episodes their assistance process is made of). The best assistance path realized by each GP has been named Reference path. The synthesis of the most efficacious (from the clinical standpoint) and most effective (from the organizational standpoint) Reference paths has originated finally the General Care Path (*As Is*). The relational approach overlapped to the previous logical one firstly required, to draw correctly the network, the identification of the best fitting evaluation parameter to assign a weight to the connections found: that was the *therapeutic continuity* settled between every couple of actors of the care path, expressed by a numeric value ranging from 1 to 7, according to the great part of literature. Such step was conducted with the help of the members of the "Pathology Group", comprised by those physicians and administrators belonging to the sample group, that showed higher levels of expertise and collaboration; the output was the sociometric matrix in Figure 4. Finally, dedicated software (UCINET) translated the matrix in a sociogram (see Figure 3). The analysis of the resulting network shows an appearing *structural equivalence* between patient, GP, diabetologist and diabetic centre (e.g., a similitude of their relational framework with the other nodes of the network).

The exploitation of the UCINET software allows pointing out many relevant properties of sociograms, the first of which is the network cohesion, which ranges from 0 to 1. The resulting value is 0.764 (i.e., in the network are present about the 75% of all the possible connections). The density value is confirmed by the standard deviation value (0.4406) that suggests the presence

Figure 2. As Is care path flow chart

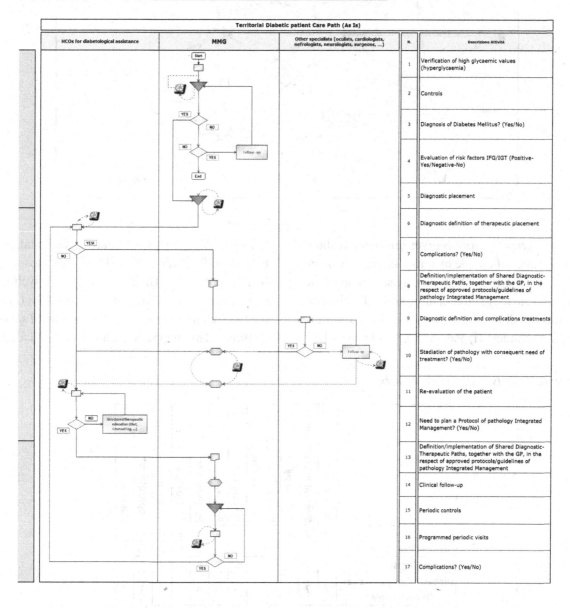

of a significant level of variability in the connections. Such high percentage, rather than being a positive output, highlights instead a non rational (and even mostly redundant) distribution of the connections, centered among the four nodes with the highest *connectivity* values (e.g., the number of nodes that have to be removed in order to disconnect the network on the whole. High values for k(G) mean significant levels of connectivity in the graph/network).

Figure 3. Sociogram of the healthcare network originated from the As Is Care Path

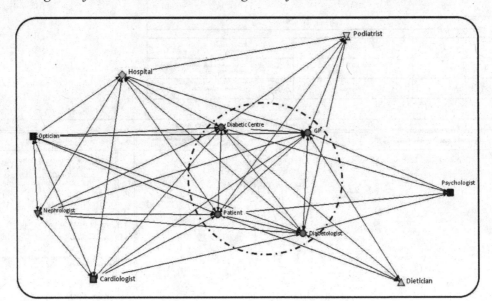

The *cliques analysis* gives information about the number of couple of actors sharing the same group; a clique is a high density subgroup of the network, made of three or more nodes. In this case, it was possible to recognize only four extremely similar cliques: (i) Patient – GP – Diab. – DC/ LHA – Cardiol. – Opt. – Nephrol. – Hospital, (ii) Patient – GP – Diab. – DC/LHA – Pod. – Hospital, (iii) Patient – GP – Diab. – DC/LHA – Psychol., (iv) Patient – GP – Diab. – DC/LHA – Diet (Figure 5). That means the lack of an arranged set of relations. This happens because every diabetic

Figure 4. As Is Sociometric Matrix

	Patient	General Practitioner	Diabetologist	Diabetic Centre / Local Health Authority	Dietician	Podiatrist	Psychologist	Cardiologist	Optician	Nephrologist	Hospital
Patient	7	7	7	7	4	5	4	6	6	6	4
General Practitioner	7	7	7	7	4	6	6	6	6	6	5
Diabetologist	7	7	7	7	6	5	4	4	4	4	4
Diabetic Centre / Local Health Authority	7	7	7	7	5	4	4	4	4	4	4
Dietician	4	4	6	5	7	3	3	3	3	3	3
Podiatrist	5	6	5	4	3	7	3	3	3	3	4
Psychologist	4	6	4	4	3	3	7	3	3	3	3
Cardiologist	6	6	4	4	3	3	3	7	4	4	5
Optician	6	6	4	4	3	3	3	4	7	6	4
Nephrologist	6	6	4	4	3	3	3	4	6	7	4
Hospital	4	5	4	4	3	3	3	5	4	4	7

patient, deprived of a real guide, can actually make different choices along the path, share single parts of the path with other patients, be stuck in a loop with the same episode, or even skip one or more episodes. There is a remarkable heterogeneity among the care paths originally identified by the GPs involved, and in particular there is a gap between those and what recommended in the guidelines for the Integrated Management of Diabetes Mellitus type 2; the SNA provides a "photography" that enlightens the lack of a real *network organization*, although the number of HCOs through which, in the same territorial context, the assistance process of the diabetic patient is supposed to be set and organized: GPs have generally a very low knowledge degree of the care paths followed by their patients; the clinical data are delivered by the patient himself, that moves among the HCOs with his (papery) clinical history.

The deployment of ICT solutions is very limited for all three levels of study (interpersonal, intra– and inter–organizational), since exploited mainly to automate already existing operation processes (Data Resource Technology: Pontiggia,

1997). The final outcome is that the instances of *change* perspective and complexity management (as to culture and values, technological–formal issues and social legacies) have been addressing along an unequal development of those macro–assets (instruments, professional skills, organizational bonds, information) on which ICTs are based on, leading so to an impossibility to come to a rational organization of the assistance supplying processes (Bonacci & Tamburis, 2009).

NETWORK DEVELOPMENTS

By exploiting the SNA to "take snapshots" of the current organization it is possible a longitudinal study of the related network, through which aims to: an efficacious path of patients' empowerment; a more appropriate handling of the disease for the GPs; an improvement of the capabilities of the territorial care supplying facilities. Deploying a sort of "evolution logic", the mentioned instances of change and knowledge management can be interpreted, foretold, and even somehow *driven*: this can be called "innovation". It takes

Figure 5. As Is Cliques Diagram

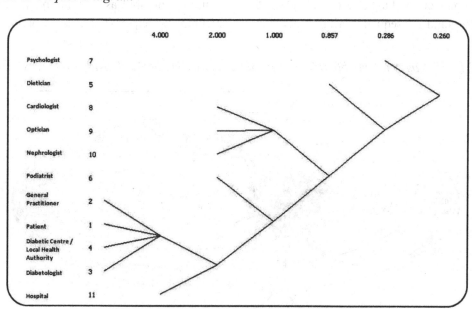

first a passage from a "Data Resource Technology" to a "Communication Technology", and therefore to a "Relation Technology" condition, where ICT should impact pervasively in order to redesign the value chain on the whole. It is supposed to happen through the implementation of an "ERP–like" integrated information framework, supporting an Electronic Health Record system. The realization of an "information connecting tissue" (*middleware*) can become the first step toward the achievement of an interoperating and interconnected environment, where the Care Path itself would get to the status of *social healthcare network*, and GPs would aim to the key role of *process owner* of the integrated management of the pathology, called to:

- Coordinate and control the dynamics of communication and interaction/integration between the subjects involved in the diabetic patient care path;
- Promote the activation of suitable systems for the strategic planning and the performances measurement in a sort of "information virtual ward";

Such network should feature a lower density value (less connections, but better organization of the data flows) and, consequently, a higher number of subgroups, with smaller dimension but a major proximity index (that is the capacity for each node to create ties with the other nodes), thanks to a redefinition of roles and social relationships. In such new view, the strategic subject called to the government and the monitoring of the assistance processes can appear as more "expanded", and feature as a "decision–making composite actor" (Achard, 1999).

CONCLUSIONS AND FUTURE PROSPECTS

The main consequences of the emerging of a new paradigm for the ICT in the healthcare sector, based upon clinical, organizational and administrative information sharing and integration among the operators, is depicted and summarized in Figure 6. The exploitation of social healthcare networks is meant to "compress" the lead line that links the outside environment of the HCOs (inter–organizational perspective) and their inside processes of Healthcare Technology Management and, in particular, deployment of ICT solutions (intra–organizational and interpersonal perspectives), increasing the cohesion of the whole organizational tissue and featuring the SNA as "cultural bond" based upon common principles (Fontana & Lorenzoni, 2004).

Figure 6. The SNA as "cultural bond" between outside environment and inside processes of the HCOs

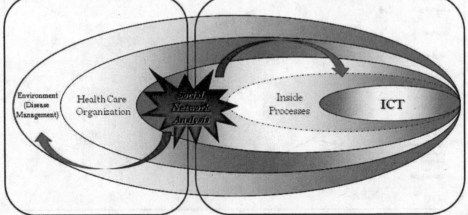

This process could help to redefine the connections between general management and clinical management, allowing a better handling of the main risk concerning the deployment of evolved healthcare technologies, that is an as much intrinsic as unaware dissociation of the medical act between its operative, informative and hierarchical factors.

This is the main reason why the approach suggested in the present work can take a strong competitive advantage from its being focused on a relatively not much explored sector yet, suggesting a large-scale, longitudinal, quali–quantitative research and experimental method analysis of a social network related to the Chronic Diseases' Integrated Management. The next research step will be focused therefore on a deeper investigation of the extant network, already ongoing deep structural changes, to show the advantages that a rational organization of the assistance supplying processes may bring to the treatment of the diabetic pathology and, more in general, to the organization of the healthcare systems.

ACKNOWLEDGMENT

The authors acknowledge the Editor-in-Chief of the journal, Professor John Wang, and the anonymous reviewers for their indispensable input that improved the paper significantly.

REFERENCES

Achard, P. O. (1999). *Economia e organizzazione delle imprese sanitarie*. Milano, Italy: FrancoAngeli.

Agranoff, R., & McGuire, M. (2001). Big questions in public network management research. *Journal of Public Administration: Research and Theory, 11*(3), 295–326.

Bonacci, I., Pelella, E. F., & Tamburis, O. (2008). Fattori di rischio nella gestione delle patologie cronico-degenerative: Analisi dei flussi informativi nel territorio sannita. In *Proceedings of XIII AIES Conference (Associazione Italiana di Economia Sanitaria)*.

Bonacci, I., & Tamburis, O. (2007). Paths of organizational change in the healthcare structures: The role of ICT. In *Proceedings of Mediterranean Conference on Information Systems (MCIS07)* (Vol. 1).

Bonacci, I., & Tamburis, O. (2009). The Social network analysis as key factor for improving interoperability standards on patients care paths. In *Proceedings of VI Conference of the Italian Chapter of AIS (ItAIS)*.

Bonora, E., Kiechl, S., Willeit, J., Oberhollenzer, F., Egger, G., & Meigs, J. B. (2004). Population-based incidence rates and risk factors for type 2 diabetes in white individuals: The Bruneck study. *Diabetes, 53*, 1782–1789. doi:10.2337/diabetes.53.7.1782

Bruno, G., Runzo, C., Cavallo-Perin, P., Merletti, F., Rivetti, M., Pinach, S., Novelli, G., Trovati, M., Cerutti, F., & Pagano, G., & Piedmont Study Group for Diabetes Epidemiology. (2005). Incidence of type 1 and type 2 diabetes in adults aged 30-49 years: Population-based registry in the province of Turin, Italy. *Diabetes Care, 28*, 2613–2619. doi:10.2337/diacare.28.11.2613

Centro nazionale per l'informatica nella Pubblica Amministrazione – CNIPA. (2008). *Piano triennale per l'ICT della pubblica amministrazione centrale per il triennio 2008-2010*.

Chiesi, A. M. (1999). *L'analisi dei reticoli*. Milano, Italy: FrancoAngeli.

Chiesi, A. M. (2006). Perspectives of network analysis applied to social sciences. In *Proceedings of XLIII SIS Conference* (CLEUP), Torino, Italy.

Cicchetti, A. (2002). *L'organizzazione dell'ospedale*. Milano, Italy: Vita e Pensiero Ed.

Cicchetti, A. (2004). *La progettazione organizzativa*. Milano, Italy: FrancoAngeli/Sanità.

Cicchetti, A., & Mascia, D. (2007). Organizzare le reti in sanità: teoria, metodi e strumenti di social network analysis. *Mecosan, 61*, 9–32.

Coleman, J. S. (1974). *Power and the structure of society*. New York: W. W. Norton & Company Inc.

Corti, E. (2002). *Gestione dell'innovazione*. Napoli, Italy: ESI.

Corti, E., Iasiello, F., Marino, A., & Tamburis, O. (2004). Innovazione tecnologica nel contesto sociale e organizzativo. L'impatto delle tecnologie informatiche nell'ospedale di elevata specializzazione: Il caso della Campania. In *Proceedings of XV AiIG Conference (Associazione italiana di Ingegneria Gestionale)*.

Cosmi, L. (2003). Razionalità dei processi di diffusione nei sistemi aziendali di tecnologia sanitaria innovativa. Un modello delle variabili 'non convenzionali'. In *Proceedings of VIII AIES Conference (Associazione Italiana di Economia Sanitaria)*.

Cross, R., & Parker, A. (2004). *The hidden power of social networks: Understanding how work really gets done in organizations*. Boston: Harvard Business School Press.

Donatini, A., Rico, A., D'Ambrosio, M. G., Lo Scalzo, A., Orzella, L., Cicchetti, A., & Profili, S. (2001). Health care system in transition. In *Italy, country profile, European observatory on health care systems*, Copenhagen, Denmark.

European Health Telematics Association – EHTEL. (2009). *Reflections on a decade of eHealth: The second stage in healthcare transformation*. Retrieved October 22, 2009, from http://www.ehtel.org/

Fennell, M. L., & Warnecke, R. B. (1988). *Diffusion of medical innovations: An applied network analysis*. New York: Plenum.

Fontana, F., & Lorenzoni, G. (2004). *Le architetture strategiche nelle aziende sanitarie: una indagine empirica*. Milano, Italy: FrancoAngeli.

Goodwin, C., & Goodwin, M. (1998). Seeing as situated activity: Formulating planes. In Engeström, Y., & Middleton, D. (Eds.), *Cognition and communication at work* (pp. 96–129). Cambridge, MA: CUP.

Grandori, A. (1999). *Organizzazione e comportamento economico*. Bologna, Italy: Il Mulino.

Helmreich, R., & Merritt, A. (1998). *Culture at work in aviation and medicine: National, organizational and professional influences*. Aldershot, UK: Ashgate.

Kaluzny, A. D., & Warnecke, R. B. (1996). *Managing a health care alliance*. San Francisco, CA: Jossey-Bass.

Kaplan, B. (2001). Evaluating informatics applications - some alternative approaches: Theory, social interactionism, and call for methodological pluralism. *International Journal of Medical Informatics, 64*, 39–55. doi:10.1016/S1386-5056(01)00184-8

Kaplan, B., & Shaw, N. (2002). People, organizational and social issues: Evaluation as an exemplar. In Haux, R., & Kulikowski, C. (Eds.), *Yearbook of medical informatics 2002* (pp. 91–99). Stuttgart, Germany: Schattauer.

Keen, P. G. W. (1990). Telecommunications and organizational choice. In Fulk, J., & Steinfield, C. (Eds.), *Organizations and communication technology*. Newbury Park, CA: Sage.

Lega, F. (1998). Scelte strategiche e definizione dei confini dell'ospedale. Dalla struttura focalizzata alla struttura a rete. *Organizzazione sanitaria, 1*, 43-66.

Lega, F. (2002). *Gruppi e reti aziendali in sanità.* Milano, Italy: Egea.

Lomi, A. (1991). *Reti organizzative. Reti, tecniche e applicazioni.* Bologna, Italy: Il Mulino Editore.

Mapelli, V. (1999). Sanità: La rivincita del piano sul mercato. In Bernardi, L. (Ed.), *La finanza pubblica italiana, Rapporto 1999* (pp. 319–341). Bologna, Italy: Il Mulino.

Marchi, M., Schifini D'Andrea, S., Maggino, F., & Mola, T. (2007). *Studio delle reti di supporto: Un'applicazione ai dimessi ospedalieri.* Working paper, University of Florence, Deptartment of Statistics.

Mari, C. (1994). *Metodi qualitativi di ricerca. I casi aziendali.* Torino, Italy: Giappichelli.

Martinez, M. (1997). *Teorie di organizzazione in economia aziendale. Dall'organismo al network.* Milano, Italy: FrancoAngeli.

Mazzoni, E. (2007). La Social network analysis a supporto delle interazioni nelle comunità virtuali per la costruzione di conoscenza. *TD, 35*(2), 54-63.

Meneguzzo, M., & Cepiku, D. (Eds.). (2008). *Network pubblici: Strategia, struttura e governance.* Milano, Italy: McGraw-Hill.

Milner, M. (1980). *Unequal care: A case study of interorganizational relations in health care.* New York: Columbia University Press.

Miolo Vitali, P., & Nuti, S. (2003). *Ospedale in rete e reti di ospedali: Modelli ed esperienze a confronto.* Milano, Italy: FrancoAngeli.

Moreno, J. L. (1987). *Manuale di psicodramma* (*Vol. 2*). Roma, Italy: Astrolabio.

Pelella, E. F., Tamburis, O., & Tranfaglia, R. (2007). Indicatori di qualità nell'attività dei MMG: L'impatto di strumenti economici di efficacia ed efficienza nella gestione delle patologie cronico-degenerative. In *Proceedings of XII AIES Conference (Associazione Italiana di Economia Sanitaria).*

Pontiggia, A. (1997). *Organizzazione dei sistemi informativi. Modelli per l'analisi e per la progettazione.* Milano, Italy: Etaslibri.

Powell, W. W. (1990). Neither market nor hierarchy. *Research in Organizational Behavior, 12,* 295–333.

Provan, K. G., & Milward, H. B. (1995). A preliminary theory of interorganizational network effectiveness: A comparative study of four community mental health systems. *Administrative Science Quarterly, 40,* 1–33. doi:10.2307/2393698

Retrieved September 2, 2008, from www.cnipa. gov.it/site/_files/Piano_triennale_2008_10b.pdf

Rockart, J. F., & Short, J. E. (1991). IT in the 90s: Managing organizational interdependence. *Sloan Management Review,* 7–17.

Rogers, E. (1995). *Diffusion of Innovations.* New York: Free Press.

Ruta, C. (1993). *Sanità & Management.* Milano, Italy: Etaslibri Ed.

Santahanam, R., Guimaraes, T., & George, J. F. (2000). An empirical investigation of ODSS impact on individuals and organizations. *Dec Supp Sys, 30,* 51–72. doi:10.1016/S0167-9236(00)00089-0

Scott, J. (2000). *Social network analysis. A Handbook.* London: Sage.

Valente, A. (Ed.). (2002). *Percorsi e contesti della documentazione e comunicazione scientifica.* Milano, Italy: FrancoAngeli.

Van de Ven, A. H., & Walker, G. (1984). The dynamics of interorganizational coordination. *Administrative Science Quarterly, 29,* 598–621. doi:10.2307/2392941

Van de Ven, A. H., Walker, G., & Liston, J. (1979). Coordination patterns within an interorganizational Network. *Human Relations, 32*(1), 19–36. doi:10.1177/001872677903200102

Warren, R., Stephen, M. R., & Bergunder, A. F. (1974). *The structure of urban reform.* Lexington, MA: Lexington Books.

Wasserman, S., & Faust, K. (1996). *Social network analysis. Method and applications*. Cambridge, MA: Cambridge University Press.

West, E., Barron, D., Dowsett, J., & Newton, J. (1999). Hierarchies and cliques in the social networks of health care professionals: Implications for the design of dissemination strategies. *Social Science & Medicine, 48*, 633–646. doi:10.1016/S0277-9536(98)00361-X

Westbrook, J. I., Braithwaite, J., Georgiou, A., Ampt, A., Creswick, N., Coiera, E. W., & Iedema, R. (2007). Multimethod evaluation of information and communication technologies in health in the context of wicked problems and sociotechnical theory. *Journal of the American Medical Informatics Association, 14*(6), 746–755. doi:10.1197/jamia.M2462

Westbrook, J. I., Braithwaite, J., Iedema, R., & Coiera, E. W. (2004). Evaluating the impact of information communication technologies on complex organizational systems: A multi-disciplinary, multi-method framework. In M. Fieschi et al. (Eds.), *Proceedings of MEDINFO 2004*. Amsterdam: IOS Press.

Yin, R. K. (1993). *Application of case study research*. Newbury Park, CA: Sage.

Zaccarin, S., & Rivellini, G. (2007). *Reti di relazioni e comportamento individuale: L'approccio della social network analysis*. Milano, Italy: ISTAT Office of Milan.

This work was previously published in International Journal of Information Systems in the Service Sector, Volume 2, Issue 3, edited by John Wang, pp. 13-27, copyright 2010 by IGI Publishing (an imprint of IGI Global).

Chapter 13

Marketing and Reputation in the Services Sector:
Higher Education in South Africa and Singapore

Johan De Jager
Tshwane University of Technology, South Africa

Werner Soontiens
Curtin University of Technology, Australia

ABSTRACT

Over the past few decades the tertiary sector has developed from a predominantly inward focussed industry serving public interest to an internationalised and commercially competitive industry. Resulting from this fundamental change is a drive to better understand the most prominent dimensions that impact on internationalisation, more particularly, the expectations and experiences of students. Although some of these can be argued to be country specific, and thus differentiate between markets, others are universal and impact on the overall industry. One of the latter is a pressure to consider and treat students as clients introducing all the dynamics of service delivery and management. The primary objective of this paper is to identify the most important variables related to marketing and reputation issues when selecting a university in South-Africa and compare the same for Singapore students. This study revealed that the most important consideration for the South African sample, regarding marketing and reputation related variables when choosing an institution of higher education, is the academic reputation of the institution, while the marketing activities were regarded as priority by the Singaporean sample.

INTRODUCTION

Various studies emphasize the tendency of universities referring to their students as customers (Eagle & Brennan, 2007; Comm & Mathaisel, 2005; Ho & Hung, 2008) and the increasing im-

portance of comparing educational systems (Wang et al., 2009) and the impact on service providers. Michael (2004) emphasises the vital role of higher education management based on a solid understanding of its fundamental impact on management thoughts and practices currently prevalent in higher education systems. The increased level

DOI: 10.4018/978-1-4666-0044-7.ch013

Copyright © 2012, IGI Global. Copying or distributing in print or electronic forms without written permission of IGI Global is prohibited.

of competition in the education environment has led to institutions of higher education employing managerial techniques to improve the efficiency and quality of their provisions (Eagle & Brennan, 2007; Palihawadana, 1999) and a switch from a passive to a more active market approach (Ivy, 2008). Hemsley-Brown and Oplatka (2006, p. 316) emphasizes that in the context of increasing competition for home-based and overseas students, higher educational institutions now recognize the need to market themselves in a climate of international competitiveness.

If universities are to satisfy student's requirements they should be aware of their own offerings and how these are perceived in the market place. It is important for institutional policy makers to be aware of the influential factors and the associated impact on potential students (Eagle & Brennan, 2007; Moogan & Baron, 2001, p. 197). This impact also refers to the influence of the product offerings on the overall reputation that an institution of higher education builds over a period of time (Gotsi & Wilson, 2001).

In order to maintain students as loyal customers a marketing orientation approach should be followed, implying that various aspects should be taken into consideration. This includes the satisfaction of consumers' needs, the wellbeing of the society and achieving objects over the long term, including profit. This study will mainly investigate the level of importance of some elements of the product offering of two universities, one in South Africa and one in Singapore, to their students. The influence of these elements on the overall reputation of the universities will also be investigated.

MARKETING PRACTICES AND REPUTATION IN THE HIGHER EDUCATION SECTOR

Flavian, Torres, and Guinaliu (2004) argue that large numbers of competitors in a global environ-

ment are constantly attempting to offer something different in their services to distinguish them from competition. Da Silva and Batisda (2007) are of the opinion that relationship building with customers is crucial for commercial survival. This also includes public organisations. The author points out that the building of corporate reputation has become a strategic issue for organisations that requires a series of organisation changes. The building of reputation requires a strong customer-focused orientation, better performance of an organisations day-to-day management and operating activities, more efficient and effective communication with its publics and a greater emphasis on recognition. As a result the author emphasized the importance of increasing an organisations image that is transmitted to consumers. Alsop (2004) explains that the top managements own reputation affects corporate reputation and states that high profile CEO's like Bill Gates still affects the company image and is ultimately accountable for reputation.

Although the paper does not focus on the relationship between marketing and reputation per se, it may be worthwhile clarifying the anticipated relationship of a few related concepts. The image and reputation terminology are sometimes confusing and as a result Gotsi and Wilson (2001) attempt to define the concept of corporate reputation and identify its relationship with corporate image. Gotsi and Wilson (2001) argue that some schools of thoughts view corporate reputation as synonymous with corporate image and further pointed out that the reason for the lack of a single common definition for corporate reputation (and image) mainly derives from the diversity of relevant studies which explore the construct from different disciplinary perspectives. Overall however there is support for a separate but interrelated view. Barich and Kotler (1991) point out that the critical role of institutional image and institutional reputation in customer buying intentions are well known in marketing. Duncan (2005) states that the difference between image and reputation is sometimes confusing because the two are somewhat related. The difference between image and reputation lays in the fact that image can be created and reputation is earned (or maintained). Both these concepts are important and are known as integrity. Raj (1985) points out that institutional image and reputation are important to develop and maintain a loyalty relationship with customers. This is reflected in the trend that students often choose to attend a university based on impressions and experiences by acquaintances. In the university environment image and reputation may also impact on student decisions to enroll or to stay for advanced studies. In other respects institutional image and reputation are considered as two distinct but strongly related social entities (Nguyen & Le Blank, 2001). Rao (1994) as cited in Nguyen and Le Blank (2001) is of the opinion that this relationship is intuitively appealing given the idea that image and reputation may share a certain number of components, while they constitute the global outcome of the process of legitimating or the credentialing mechanism (Tait, de Jager & Soontiens, 2007).

Gotsi and Wilson (2001) came to the conclusion that a corporate reputation is a stakeholders overall evaluation of a company over time. The evaluation is based on the stakeholders' direct experiences with the company and other forms of marketing communications and symbolism that provides information about a company's actions and/or a comparison with the actions of other leading rivals. Ivy (2001) further states that as competition for student's increases and funding decrease, universities need to create and maintain a distinctive image and reputation in the market place. Consequently higher education institutions are becoming increasingly aggressive in their *marketing activities* and need to be clear about their positioning in order to convey a favorable image and reputation to their distinctive interest groups, from students to donors (Russel, 2005; Ivy, 2001; Tait, de Jager, & Soontiens, 2007). The abovementioned clarifies the interrelationship between the creation and maintenance of an

acceptable corporate reputation and an effective corporate marketing activities (marketing communication system) with its publics. The reputation (and image) of universities is thus established and enhanced through interaction with various stakeholders, amongst which students are a prominent group, mostly through various media. Institutional reputation thus engages various media channels (marketing tools) to engage with stakeholders while stakeholders evaluate the institution against the messages. A consistent performance (i.e., service quality) may strengthen the reputation.

Higher Education Institutions should understand their own offerings and how these are perceived in the market place, as these it could have important marketing and management implications. Oldfield and Baron (2000) suggest that there are three underlying factors of higher education service quality that may appeal to stakeholders namely, requisite elements (encounters which are essential to enable students to fulfil their study obligations), acceptable elements (which are desirable but not essential to students) and functional elements (which are of a practical or utilitarian nature). Al these should be communicated with the relevant stakeholders in an acceptable manner. Various factors influence the choice of potential students to study at a specific tertiary institution, including location (Ford, Joseph, & Joseph, 1999; Roberts & Allen, 1997), reputation of academic quality (V88) (Chen & Zimitat, 2006; Landrum, Turrisi, & Harless, 1998; Ivy, 2001), course specifics (V103), (Ford, Joseph, & Joseph, 1999), a safe environment and state of the art facilities and offerings (Comm & Mathaisl, 2005). A recent study (2003) by the Human Sciences Research Council (HSRC) in South Africa has found that the most important influence upon choice of institution is its reputation followed by the geographical location.

Sohail et al. (2003) argues that the introduction of quality control measures has mainly been focussed on non-academic matters. Although the physical environment is overall accepted to impact on the study experience there is little evidence of the actual impact on satisfaction by students. Wakefield and Blodgett (1994) established that the utilitarian nature of facilities such as sporting facilities (V89) and the like does however impact the experience of students who spend a significant amount of time on campus. Oldfield and Baron (2000) found that although modern looking equipment is unimportant, students do find up to date equipment, particularly in information technology, crucial.

The choice of service provider (university) is dominated by the perceived overall academic quality, the quality of academic staff (V91, 92, 93) and the rigour of the program (Soutar & Turner, 2002). From an efficiency perspective, Cloete and Bunting (2000) indicate that institutions with an above average percentage of highly qualified academic staff are generally more efficient universities. A study by Ben Ami (2005) confirmed the importance of highly qualified and skilled academic staff to deliver programs. Research by Tait, Van Eeden & Tait (2002) indicates that presentation of lectures is significantly correlated to the value perception of university studies and the learning process, emphasising the crucial role of lecturing staff for learners. McElwee and Redman (1993) emphasise undergraduate students' lack of knowledge and experience with higher education and therefore have no comparative base or framework of reference from which to make evaluations.

In order to satisfy student requirements, universities must develop an awareness of perceived course offerings. In order to do this effectively institutional policy makers must be aware of the influential factors and the associated impact on potential students, (Moogan, Baron, & Bainbridge, 2001). Emphasizing the importance of identified quality directives in marketing communication (V94) Cheng and Tam (1997) argue in favour of segmenting the market by selecting a target market and positioning.

Institutions operating in the international arena can strengthen their market presence through scholarships and bursaries. The Singaporean Ministry of Education (2007) confirms that Singapore has worked towards its identity of education centre on the back of scholarships (V95) to study in commonwealth countries under the 'education as aid' initiative in the 1970s and 1980s. The United Kingdom and Australia established themselves as major international education providers this way. More recently, the Singaporean government impact the attraction of quality students by providing scholarships and bonds (Ministry of Education, 2000).

Oldfield and Baron (2000) determined that it is also important to note that students perceive a clear distinction between academic and administrative staff roles. In the 'pure service' environment of higher education there is the interactive relationship between students which also impacts on overall expectations and satisfaction of students. Service delivery in this environment is often personalised and dependent on individual technical or customer related skills and personality by for instance career advisors (V112) or other support staff. According to Boulding et al. (1993) a prime issue of poor performance in this environment is not knowing what customers expect and the absence of tangible clues.

Bearing in mind all the above mentioned possible attributes that higher education can contribute to various stakeholders, Balmer and Greyser (2006) state that a key attribute of corporate level-marketing is its concern with multiple exchange relationships with multiple stakeholder groups and networks.

THE SINGAPOREAN TERTIARY EDUCATION ENVIRONMENT

Despite historically having inherited a poorly educated workforce upon independence, the Singapore government acknowledged and committed to the potential and development of human resources as main foundation of the economy. This translated to an investment in education and vocational trading that has consistently been expanded since the 1960s (Sanderson, 2002). Over time the focus has shifted to tertiary education with recognition that an educated and skilled workforce is imperative to meet human resource need, enforce sound moral values and align Singapore in the face of rapid progress and change (Ministry of Information and the Arts, 1998). Traditionally the Singapore government has had a high level of involvement in education driven by the strong conviction that education enhances productivity of the labour force. The Singaporean Ministry of Education (2007) reports that the return on tertiary education is higher compared to non-tertiary education. This provides a further drive to meet the shift of the Singaporean economy to higher value-added and knowledge activities.

Singapore, both by necessity as a small, open economy and by design from an outcomes driven government has emerged as a unique hub of international education which is likely to challenge the traditional western models that have been dominant over the past decades (Sanderson, 2002). The emergence of Singapore as an education hub takes place against the backdrop of being conscious to develop a system that is flexible enough to cater for different students. In view of this, the Singaporean education sector is anticipating the establishment of up to ten specialised institutions by 2010 (Li, 2006).

Overall, in a globalised small and open economy like Singapore, sustainable growth pivots around the growth potential of human capital. A conscious positioning in the knowledge and service based industries further enhances the role of tertiary education and subsequent interest and investment throughout Singapore (Ministry of Education, 2007). In the international education context, Singapore reflects the traditional stages of development. Under the 'education as aid' initiative amongst Commonwealth nations in the 1970s and 1980s Singaporean students received scholarships to study inter alia in Australia and the

United Kingdom. In addition limited local capacity enhanced the outflow of Singaporean students (Sanderson, 2002). Over time, the trend of Singaporeans study abroad has maintained momentum due to low capacity, high entry requirements and government restrictions. Simultaneously Singapore has developed a market for overseas institutions and foreign students to the extent that in 2002 an estimated 11,000 foreign students were enrolled in tertiary education of some sort. The attraction for foreign students is that fees are subsidised by the Singaporean government in a tuition grant that bonds students to stay and work in Singapore for three years after completing their studies (Ministry of Education, 2000).

International education in Singapore is delivered by local universities or foreign universities through either branch campuses or twinning programs with local institutions such as professional bodies. In 2000 there were more than 50 institutions offering tertiary education of which the vast majority was UK and Australian based. Interestingly non-Singaporean universities do not require approval to operate in Singapore or to issue their qualifications. The Singaporean government does however issue licenses to local partner institutions to retain an involvement with foreign universities (Ziguras, 2003). More recently the Singapore government has targeted high end providers such as INSEAD and the Chicago School of Business to establish a local presence. In addition, Curtin University has transformed its presence from an agreement with professional bodies to a full blown presence (Curtin University of Technology, 2008). In reaction to this and in line with Singapore's tradition of allowing market forces to dictate sectors, Singaporean institutions are corporatized and operate autonomously as not-for-profit public companies predominantly owned by the Singapore government (Li, 2006).

Singapore has emerged as the most prominent education provider in Southeast Asia, both as a result of an articulated government direction and its perceived relevance to bridge Asian heritage with Anglo education. To this extent it could be argued that South Africa and Singapore play a similar role in their respective continents and are therefore included in the study.

SOUTH AFRICAN UNIVERSITIES

Universities in South Africa have experienced stagnating and declining budgets and simultaneous pressures to increase enrolments (Samoff, 2001). Since the late nineties South African universities have experienced a gradual decline in student numbers translating in more choice and increased pressures on service delivery by students. Pressures also build up in respect of technological advances and skills with some institutions and staff delivering and using sub-standard computer technology (Miji, 2002; Zaaiman, Van der Flier, & Thijs, 1998).

An assessment of the South African education system indicates that individual universities display unique sets of characteristics with regard to historical origins, faculty and departmental organisation, human resources and student numbers (Cloete & Bunting, 2000). Each of these in turn contributes to the image and reputation of the university. At the same time all universities are governed by common national regulations which imply a level of homogeneity across all players.

South African Universities like other universities in countries such as the United Kingdom and Australia (that have similar educational systems to South Africa) has experienced a dramatic decline in government subsidies and an increase in student fees (Palihawadana, 1999; Soutar & Turner, 2002). This is due to various changes in the respective environments. In South Africa the decline in funding from subsidies is a direct consequence of the trend of falling pass rates (Naidoo, 2003) and subsequently earns less government subsidy. It appears as if tertiary institutions across the globe experiencing increasing market and financial pressures. The result has caused institutions of higher education to engage in more competitive educational practices.

Given the above background, the effects of competition on institutions of higher education, especially in the South African context, can be seen as having far-reaching implications for these institutions. Traditionally, Technikons and Universities have competed indirectly, whereas they now compete directly, ostensibly for the same market. The impact of technology and the demand for a technologically literate workforce has also created a third stream of private educational institutions that not only compete for school-leavers, but also on post-graduate level. Private providers meeting a specialised demand are often highly responsive and provide credentials in areas that the public sector does not (Kruss, 2002). This increased level of competition in the education environment has led to institutions of higher education employing managerial techniques to improve the efficiency and quality of services (Palihawadana, 1999) and switch from a passive to a more active market approach (Naudé & Ivy, 1999). If universities are to satisfy student requirements they must be aware of their own offerings and how these are perceived in the market place. Being aware of the influential factors and the associated impact on potential students is important for institutional policy makers (Moogan et al., 2001).

PROBLEM STATEMENT

Higher education is facing increasingly more challenges on the global arena. As institutions of higher education compete for human and financial capital it is equally important to understand and address the demands of students and industry. This is even more so as universities increasingly develop an international presence and seek to attract international students. Overall the problem is a lack of information to enable institutions of higher education to identify and adhere to students needs in order to attract them from the global market.

OBJECTIVE OF THE STUDY

The primary objective of this study is to identify the most important variables related to marketing and reputation issues when selecting a university in South-Africa and in Singapore as confirmed by students. A secondary objective is to determine whether there are significant differences between South-African and Singaporean students related to marketing and reputation issues when deciding on an educational service provider.

RESEARCH METHODOLOGY

Conceptualising the Purpose of the Investigation

In order to achieve the primary objective of the research, the service quality variables related to marketing and reputation of higher education when choosing an institution of higher education is investigated.

The following secondary objectives were formulated:

- To evaluate the expressed levels of importance of South-African and Singaporean students with regard to these selected higher education challenges;
- To determine the existence of significant differences between the South-African and Singaporean students with regard to their expressed levels of importance with these variables related to higher education.

Research Hypotheses

With regards to the objectives the researchers formulated the following hypotheses:

- **Ho:** There exist no significant differences with regard to the importance of the service variables related to marketing and reputation of higher education between the South-African and the Singaporean samples.
- **Ha:** There exist significant differences with regard to the importance of marketing and reputation of higher education related service variables between the South-African and Singaporean students.

The Sample Framework

A sample of 406 students at the management faculties of a university in South-Africa and a university in Singapore were selected at random after permission was granted to include pre determined classes/courses for the purpose of the survey. All respondents agreed to participate to the survey and were supplied with a self administrative questionnaire after the required process was explained to them. Consequently two hundred and twenty one of the respondents that were issued with a questionnaire were students from a large South-African University while one hundred and eighty five of the respondents were student from a University in Singapore. No questionnaire or part thereof was discarded. The sample comprised of 42% male and 58% female students. The attitudes of the two student samples were tested regarding the importance of pre-identified service quality issues related to marketing and reputation of higher education institutions when selecting a specific institution. The list of variables was based on extensive literature research and the findings of focus groups consisting of students and lecturers.

A summary of the composition of the sample is provided in Table 1.

The Measuring Instrument and Reliability Measures

A structured questionnaire was developed to measure the preferences of students when deciding on a specific institution of higher education. For the purpose of this paper only the variables related to

Table 1. Summary of sample characteristics

	South Africa		Singapore	
	n	%	n	%
University	221	54	185	46
Age				
16-17 years	0	0	0	0
18-19 years	43	19	52	28
20-21 years	43	19	53	29
21-22 years	74	33	80	43
Over 22 years	61	28	0	0
Gender				
Male	77	35	93	50
Female	144	65	92	50
Current Year of Study				
First year	78	36	39	21
Second year	7	3	39	21
Third year	111	51	29	16
Fourth year	24	11	78	42

N = 406

marketing and reputation are included in the study. The questionnaire addressed the following issues.

1.   Section A: Biographical information of the students including their location and methods of awareness of institutions of higher education.
2.   Section B: Service quality variables related to marketing and reputation of higher education institutions were included to determine the level of importance of these aspects.

Section A utilised nominal scales whilst a five-point Likert-type scale was used for Section B to measure the levels of importance with regards to various higher education related services at two institutions of higher education in South-Africa and Singapore. The scales were categorised as 1=very important, 2=important, 3=not important nor unimportant, 4=not important and 5=not important at all. The inputs for section B was gathered through an intensive literature study on

the topic as well as focus group discussions with students enrolled at institutions of higher education. Only marketing and reputation related issues were selected for the purpose of this study.

Data Collection and Analysis

The data was gathered and captured by trained field workers over a period of six months during the second semester of 2006 and the first semester of 2007. The SPSS version 16.0 statistical package was utilised to analyse the data. For this analysis the Kolmogorov-Smirnov Test was employed based on the assumption that if the significant values exceeded 0.5, normality could not be assumed and the researchers had to rely on employing non-parametric analysis techniques. As normality could not be assumed after applying the Kolmogorov-Smirnov Test the researchers employed the Kruskall Wallis test to test the null hypothesis and the alternative hypothesis that there exists no significant difference between the levels of importance between the two groups and there exists significant differences between the groups (South-African & Singaporean students).

An item analysis was carried out to test the validity and the reliability of the questionnaire and an overall Cronbach's alpha of a 0.89 and 0.95 were obtained for the South African sample and Singaporean sample respectively.

FINDINGS OF THE STUDY

Table 2 and Table 3 provide interesting results about sources of information relating to institutions of higher education of the two sample groups. It is clear from the tables that the two sample groups have diverse characteristics in terms of the questions asked. However there are some similarities between the groups.

Both sample groups has indicated that the biggest source of information related to institu-

tions of higher education is their friends. Family members are also an important source of information by the South African sample while the media and press tend to be second most important source of information for the Singaporean sample.

Table 3 indicates that the majority of both sample groups has indicated that a close friend has enrolled at an institution of higher education prior to their enrolment.

According to Table 4 the most important variable in the image and marketing category for South African respondents when choosing an educational institution was the academic reputation of the institution. This variable was rated third by the Singaporean sample. Although no significant differences between the two samples were measured, the South African sample regarded this variable as more important compared to the Singaporean sample and a higher level of consensus was also measured for the latter sample.

Table 2. Methods of awareness of educational institution

How did you become aware of the Educational Institution? (*You may choose more than one option*)	South Africa		Singapore	
	Frequency	%	Frequency	%
Friends	114	51	66	35
Media, press, radio, TV	44	20	41	22
Family member	82	37	25	14
The institution it self	56	25	39	21
Teachers	53	24	21	11
Other	4	2	14	8

Table 3. Persons known that enrolled at an institution of higher education

Indicate who of the following people (familiar to you) has enrolled at a Higher Education Institution. (*You may choose more than one option*)	South Africa		Singapore	
	Frequency	%	Frequency	%
No one	19	9	56	30
Parent / Guardian	59	27	27	15
Brothers or sisters	115	52	39	21
Close friend	128	58	67	36
Other	25	11	6	3

The academic reputation of the faculty was rated as second most important variable by the South African sample and in fifth position by the Singaporean sample. Significant differences were measured between the two sample groups. The South African sample rated it significantly more important compared to their Singaporean counterparts. The reputation of the study program was rated third most important variable in this category by the South African sample. Although the Singaporean sample rated it second most important position, no significant differences were measured between the two sample groups.

The variable that was rated in last position in terms of importance in the image and marketing category is the sport reputation of the institution.

Both samples rated it in ninth position and no significant differences were measured between the two groups.

CONCLUSION AND RECOMMENDATIONS

It is clear from the findings that the two samples have distinctive characteristics that make it obvious that different needs and expectations prevail in terms of service delivery in higher education. Fifty four percent of the respondents were from South Africa and forty six percent from Singapore. While the methods of becoming aware of the educational institution differ significantly, the

Table 4. Level of importance of reputation and marketing when choosing an educational institution

Image and marketing of institution		Singapore		South Africa		
Item	Item wording	Mean	SD	Mean	SD	Results of hypothesis test
V88	Academic reputation of institution	1.763	1.98	1.541	0.92	df = 1 p-value = 0.1280 Conclusions: Ho accepted
V89	Sport reputation of institution	3.209	1.32	2.839	1.26	df = 1 p-value = 0.0188 Conclusions: Ho rejected
V91	Academic reputation of faculty	1.846	1.97	1.632	1.01	df = 1 p-value = 0.0069 Conclusions: Ho accepted
V92	Reputation of lecturers at institution	1.774	1.87	1.744	0.94	df = 1 p-value = 0.9230 Conclusions: Ho accepted
v93	Availability of information about faculty	1.815	1.74	1.775	1.01	df = 1 p-value = 0.1595 Conclusions: Ho accepted
v94	Marketing activities of Institution	1.641	1.84	2.028	1.14	df = 1 p-value = 0.0001 Conclusions: Ho rejected
v95	Scholarships available	2.398	1.15	1.977	1.22	df = 1 p-value = 0.0073 Conclusions: Ho rejected
v103	Reputation of study program	1.752	1.72	1.733	0.91	df = 1 p-value = 0.8227 Conclusions: Ho accepted
v112	Career Advisors (of institution) accessible and informed	2.147	0.82	1.896	1.07	df = 1 p-value = 0.0024 Conclusions: Ho accepted

majority of the respondents in both sample groups became aware of the institution through friends. This confirms that acceptable service provision to existing students is important as word of mouth is an important method of conveying a message about the institution. In terms of familiar persons that have enrolled at an institution of higher education, different results were recorded. Overall however the majority of both sample groups have indicated that a close friend has been enrolled. This confirms the previous statement that word of mouth is a significant method of conveying a positive image of an institution.

It is further clear that the reputation and marketing activities of the two respective institutions are relatively important in the reputation and marketing category with the biggest exceptions being the sport reputation of the institution and scholarships available. The two samples showed remarkable resemblance in the way the importance of the reputation and marketing variables were ranked and can thus be treated more general.

Areas where significant differences were detected in both the ranking of the importance as well as in terms of statistical significance, is the academic reputation of the faculty (which is rated significantly more important by the South African sample – second most important) and the marketing activities of the institution (that was rated significantly more important by the Singaporean sample – rated most important). The relative high level of importance that was attached to both variables (although in different order and not of equal importance by each sample), justifies a followed and response, appropriate contextualized to the specific country. E.g., South Africa's Institutions of higher education should focus on the academic reputation of their respective faculties, while Singaporean institutions would benefit from active and visible general marketing activities or campaigns directed to students. The two most important variables as identified by the two samples will consequently be discussed.

Overall it is important that both institutions should pay special attention to attending to its institutional reputation (including the reputation of the study program) and establish it to an acceptable level. With respect to the various stakeholders of universities this could include involvement in a variety of community service projects and assuring its effectiveness (reputation) in the mind of all interest groups. This may include ensuring that partnerships between the institution and the industry exist. This relationship should include responding to the training needs of the industry and offer courses in line with the needs. Institutional partnerships with the industry are also of importance where joint attempts are attempted to solve problems of mutual interest. Cross department integration should be facilitated in order to contribute to the enhancement of an acceptable reputation of the faculties and consequently of institution in general.

Although the importance of the marketing activities applies mainly to the Singaporean sample, this could also enhance the reputation of the institution. At the marketing communication and service level capabilities should be developed in order to engage in public communication opportunities and to convey messages related to improved satisfaction with regards to services offered. According to Da Silva and Batisda (2007, p. 604) the greatest challenge of a customer relationship management system in order to enhance a company's reputation (through satisfied stakeholders) is the integration of technological resources across all sorts of media and channels of interaction. This should however be preceded by sound and well thought business perspectives that addresses all activities that may have an impact on overall satisfaction.

Faculty related reputation challenges that include the reputation of the lecturers and the reputation of the academic programs offered were also rated relatively important providing an indication that maintaining the overall reputation of the institution should be prioritised and displayed to all the key stakeholders particularly students and end-users of graduates. The overall reputation of the institution is consequently regarded as high priority area to be addressed in the management strategy. This will ensure that the most promising students/employers are attracted. Building and maintaining a good reputation could be done by implementing high quality training of international acceptable standards. International partnerships in training should be high on the agenda and should be emphasised in internal and external communications with employees and alumni. The importance and power of word of mouth communication should not be under estimated as the findings revealed that friends and family were regarded as the biggest source of academic information. Academic institutions' active involvement in research of highly acceptable standard will ensure a good national and international academic standing and hence facilitate these countries developments and competitiveness regionally and beyond.

It is clear that these finding should be followed up by a study investigating the perceived performance of the institutions. The findings of such a study should be incorporated into a strategy to address issues of concern and to take corrective action in order to enhance satisfaction levels of customers (students). It is clear that friends, family and the media have been regarded as main sources of information that that needs to be taken in account when making decisions regarding corporate affairs.

The recreational amenities of the institutions have been rated least important and significant differences exist between the two sample groups with Singaporeans rated it significantly less important compared to the South African sample. Because a significant number of senior students were involved in the survey it may be concluded that at this phase of their academic career, it is agreed upon that academic issues are more important than the extramural activities although a balance should be maintained in life in general.

It is recommended to duplicate the study in other countries in order to confirm similar findings in other regions or to determine whether the findings are country specific.

REFERENCES

Alsop, R. (2004). Corporate reputation: Anything but superficial- the deep but fragile nature of corporate reputation. *The Journal of Business Strategy, 25*(6), 21–29. doi:10.1108/02756660410699900

Balmer, J. M. T., & Greyser, S. A. (2006). Corporate marketing; integrating corporate identity, corporate branding, corporate communications, corporate image and corporate reputation. *European Journal of Marketing, 40*(7-8), 730–741. doi:10.1108/03090560610669964

Barich, H., & Kotler, P. (1991, winter). A framework of marketing image management. *Sloan Management Review*.

Ben-Ami, Z. (2005). *Service quality in tertiary institutions*. Unpublished M.Com dissertation, University of Port Elizabeth, South Africa.

Boulding, W., Kalra, A., Staelin, R., & Zeithaml, V. (1993). A dynamic process of service quality: from expectations to behavioral intentions. *JMR, Journal of Marketing Research, 30*(1), 7–27. doi:10.2307/3172510

Chen, C. H., & Zimitat, C. (2006). Understanding Taiwanese students' decision-making factors regarding Australian international higher education. *International Journal of Educational Management, 20*(2), 91–100. doi:10.1108/09513540610646082

Cheng, Y., & Tam, W. M. (1997). Multi models of quality in Education. *Quality Assurance in Education, 5*(1), 22–31. doi:10.1108/09684889710156558

Cloete, N., & Bunting, I. (2000). *Higher education transformation: Assessing performance in South Africa*. Pretoria, South Africa: Centre for higher education transformation.

Comm, C. L., & Mathaisel, D. F. X. (2005). A case in applying lean sustainability concepts to universities. *International Journal of Sustainability in Higher Education, 6*(2), 134–146. doi:10.1108/14676370510589855

Curtin University of Technology. (2008, August 13). *Curtin appoints pro vice-chancellor for Singapore campus*. Perth, Australia: Curtin University Media Release.

Da Silva, R., & Batisda, L. (2007). Boosting government reputation through CRM. *International Journal of Public Sector Management, 20*(7), 588–607. doi:10.1108/09513550710823506

Duncan, T. (2005). *Advertising and IMC* (2nd ed.). New York: McGraw Hill.

Eagle, L., & Brennan, R. (2007). Are students customers? TQM and marketing perspectives. *Quality Assurance in Education, 15*(1), 44–60. doi:10.1108/09684880710723025

Flavian, C., Torres, E., & Guinaliu, M. (2004). Corporate image measurement. A further problem for the tangibilization of internet banking services. *International Journal of Bank Marketing, 22*(5), 366–384. doi:10.1108/02652320410549665

Ford, J. B., Joseph, M., & Joseph, B. (1999). Importance-performance analysis as a strategic tool for service marketers: The case of service quality perceptions of business students in New Zealand and the USA. *Journal of Services Marketing, 13*(1), 171–186. doi:10.1108/08876049910266068

Gotsi, M., & Wilson, A. M. (2001). Corporate reputation: seeking a definition. *Corporate Communications: An International Journal, 6*(1), 24–30. doi:10.1108/13563280110381189

Hemsley-Brown, J., & Oplatka, I. (2006). Universities in a competitive global marketplace, a systematic review of the literature on higher education marketing. *International Journal of Public Sector Management, 19*(4), 316–338. doi:10.1108/09513550610669176

Ho, H. F., & Hung, C. C. (2008). Marketing mix formulation for higher education. An integrated analysis employing analytic hierarchy process, cluster analysis and correspondence analysis. *International Journal of Educational Management, 22*(4), 328–340. doi:10.1108/09513540810875662

Ivy, J. (2001). Higher education institution image: A correspondence analysis approach. *International Journal of Educational Management, 15*(6), 276–282. doi:10.1108/09513540110401484

Ivy, J. (2008). A new higher education marketing mix: The 7p's for MBA marketing. *International Journal of Educational Management, 22*(4), 288–299. doi:10.1108/09513540810875635

Krone, F., Gilly, M., Zeithaml, V., & Lamb, C. W. (1981). Factors influencing the graduate business school decision. In *Proceedings of the American Marketing Services* (pp. 453-456).

Kruss, G. (2002, April 10). Illuminating private higher education in SA. *Business Day*, 1st ed.

Landrum, R. E., Turrisi, R., & Harless, C. (1998). University Image: The benefits of assessment and modelling. *Journal of Marketing for Higher Education, 9*(1), 53–68. doi:10.1300/J050v09n01_05

Li, X. (2006, January 6). Diversity in Tertiary Education: More opportunities. *The Epoch Times*, 25.

McElwee, G., & Redman, T. (1993). Upward appraisal in practice. *Education + Training, 35*(2), 27–31.

Michael, S. O. (2004). In search of universal principles of higher education management and applicability to Moldavian higher education system. *International Journal of Educational Management, 18*(2), 118–137. doi:10.1108/09513540410522252

Miji, A. (2002). What influences students to university education? Insights from the horse's mouth. *South African Journal of Higher Education, 16*(2), 166–176.

Ministry of Education. (2000). *Higher Education FAQs*. Retrieved from http:www.moe.edu.sg/hed.html

Ministry of Education. (2007, January 19). *Premium on fields of study: The returns to higher education in Singapore* (press release). Retrieved from http:www.mom.gov.sg/mrsd/publication

Ministry of Information and the Arts. (1998). *Singapore 1998*. Singapore: Singapore Government Press.

Moogan, Y. J., & Baron, S. (2001). Timings and trade-offs in the marketing of higher education courses: a conjoint approach. *Marketing Intelligence & Planning, 19*(3), 179–187. doi:10.1108/02634500110391726

Moogan, Y. J., Baron, S., & Bainbridge, S. (2001). Timings and trade-offs in the marketing of higher education courses: a conjoint approach. *Marketing Intelligence & Planning, 19*(3), 179–187. doi:10.1108/02634500110391726

Naidoo, S. (2003, October 15). Asmal calls for controlled student intake. *Business Day*, 1st ed.

Naudé, P., & Ivy, N. (1999). The marketing strategies of universities in the United Kingdom. *International Journal of Educational Management, 13*(3), 126–136. doi:10.1108/09513549910269485

Nguyen, N., & LeBlanc. (2001). Image and reputation of higher education institutions in student's retention decisions. *International Journal of Educational Management, 15*(6), 301–311. doi:10.1108/EUM0000000005909

Oldfield, B., & Baron, S. (2000). Student perceptions of service quality in a UK university business and management faculty. *Quality Assurance in Education, 8*(2), 85–95. doi:10.1108/09684880010325600

Palihawadana, G. H. (1999). Modelling module evolution in marketing education. *Quality Assurance in Education, 7*(1), 41–46. doi:10.1108/09684889910252531

Raj, S. P. (1985). Striking a balance between brand popularity and brand loyalty. *Journal of Marketing, 49*, 53–59. doi:10.2307/1251175

Roberts, D., & Allen, A. (1997). Young applicants perceptions of higher education: *Vol. 2. No. 20.* Leeds, UK: HEIST Publications.

Russel, M. (2005). Marketing education - a review of service quality perceptions amongst international students. *International Journal of Contemporary Hospitality Management, 17*(1), 65–77. doi:10.1108/09596110510577680

Samoff, J. (2001). Education for all in Africa but education systems that serve few well. *Perspectives in Education, 19*(1), 5–28.

Sanderson, G. (2002). International education developments in Singapore. *International Education Journal, 3*(2), 85–103.

Sohail, M. S., Rajdurai, J., & Rahman, N. (2003). Managing quality in higher education: A Malaysian case study. *International Journal of Educational Management, 17*(4-5), 141–147. doi:10.1108/09513540310474365

Soutar, G. N., & Turner, J. P. (2002). Student preferences for university: a conjoint analysis. *International Journal of Educational Management*, *16*(1), 40–45. doi:10.1108/09513540210415523

Tait, M., de Jager, J. W., & Soontiens, W. (2007, September 27-29). *Image and academic expectations of entry-level and senior university students a South African perspective*. Paper presented at the 1ST Biannual International Conference on Strategic Developments in Services Marketing, Chios Island, Greece.

Tait, M., Van Eeden, S., & Tait, A. M. (2002). An exploratory study on the perceptions of previously educationally disadvantaged first year learners of law regarding university education. *South African. The Journal of Higher Education*, *16*(2), 181.

Wakefield, K. L., & Bodgett, J. G. (1994). The importance of servicescapes in leisure service settings. *Journal of Services Marketing*, *8*(3), 66–76. doi:10.1108/08876049410065624

Wang, J., Xia, J., Hollister, K., & Wang, Y. (2009). Comparative analysis of international Education Systems. *International Journal of Information Systems in the Service Sector*, *1*(1), 1–14.

Zaaiman, H., Van der Flier, H., & Thijs, G. D. (1998). Selecting South African higher education students: critical issues and proposed solutions. *South African Journal of Higher Education*, *12*(3), 96–97.

Ziguras, C. (2003). The impact of the GATS on transnational tertiary education: Comparing experiences of New Zealand, Australia, Singapore and Malaysia. *Australian Educational Researcher*, *30*(3), 89–109.

This work was previously published in International Journal of Information Systems in the Service Sector, Volume 2, Issue 3, edited by John Wang, pp. 28-41, copyright 2010 by IGI Publishing (an imprint of IGI Global).

Chapter 14
Data Mining in Nonprofit Organizations, Government Agencies, and Other Institutions

Zhongxian Wang
Montclair State University, USA

Ruiliang Yan
Indiana University Northwest, USA

Qiyang Chen
Montclair State University, USA

Ruben Xing
Montclair State University, USA

ABSTRACT

Data mining involves searching through databases for potentially useful information, such as knowledge rules, patterns, regularities, and other trends hidden in the data. Today, data mining is more widely used than ever before, not only by businesses who seek profits but also by nonprofit organizations, government agencies, private groups and other institutions in the public sector. In this paper, the authors summarize and classify the applications of data mining in the public sector into the following possible categories: improving service or performance; helping customer relations management; analyzing scientific and research information; managing human resources; improving emergency management; detecting fraud, waste, and abuse; detecting criminal activities; and detecting terrorist activities.

INTRODUCTION

Data mining involves searching through databases for potentially useful information such as: knowledge rules, patterns, regularities, and other trends hidden in the data. In order to complete these tasks the contemporary data mining packages offer techniques such as neural networks, inductive learning decision trees, cluster analysis, link analysis, genetic algorithms, visualization etc. (Hand, Mannila, & Smyth, 2001; McPhail, 2008; Ranjan, 2009). In general, data mining is a data analytical technique that assists businesses in learning and understanding their customers so that

DOI: 10.4018/978-1-4666-0044-7.ch014

Copyright © 2012, IGI Global. Copying or distributing in print or electronic forms without written permission of IGI Global is prohibited.

decisions and strategies can be implemented most accurately and effectively to maximize profitability. Data mining is not general data analysis, but a comprehensive technique that requires analytical skills, information construction, and professional knowledge.

Businesses are now facing globalized competition, and are being forced to deal with an enormous amount of data. The vast amounts of data and the increasing technological ability to store it also facilitated data mining. In order to gain a certain level of competitive advantage, data mining is now commonly adopted among businesses. Nowadays, data mining is more widely used than ever before; not only by businesses who seek profits, but also by nonprofit organizations, government agencies, private groups and other institutions in the public sector. Organizations use data mining as a tool to forecast customer behavior, reduce fraud and waste, and assist in medical research.

BACKGROUND

Data mining uses statistical analysis, artificial intelligence, and machine learning technologies to identify patterns that could not be found by manual analysis alone. The primary function of data mining has already amazed many people and is now considered one of the most critical issues towards a business's success. However, data mining was not born all of a sudden. The earliest usage of data mining can be traced back in the World War II years. Data analytical methods such as model prediction, database segmentation, link analysis, and deviation detection, were used for military affairs and demographic purposes by the U.S. government, but data mining had not been seriously promoted until the 1990's (Meletiou & Katsirikou, 2009).

Gramatikov (2006) compared statistical methods to data mining, differentiating them by the ultimate focus of these two tools. Statistical methods use data which is collected with a pre-defined set of questions. Statisticians are looking either for describing parameters of data or making inferences through statistics within intervals. With data mining, knowledge is generated from hidden relations, rules, trends and patterns which emerge as the data are mined.

The reason that data mining has been developed enormously again in the last few years is that huge amount of information was demanded by modern enterprises due to globalization. Important information regarding the markets, customers, competitors, and future opportunities were collected in the form of data to the database and needed data mining to unearth useful information and knowledge. Otherwise, a huge, overloaded, and unstructured database could just make it very difficult for companies to utilize and mislead the database users.

Public administration is, broadly speaking, the study and implementation of policy. The term may apply to government, private sector organizations and groups, and individuals. The adjective 'public' often denotes government at federal, state, and local levels, although it increasingly encompasses nonprofit organizations such as those of civil society or any not specifically acting in self-interest. Then, a long list exists: colleges and universities, health care organizations, charities, as well as postal offices, libraries, prisons, etc.

In the public sector, data mining initially were used as a means to detect fraud and waste, but have since grown into the use for purposes such as measuring and improving program performance. Data mining has been increasingly cited as an important tool for homeland security efforts, crime prevention, medical and educational application to increase efficiency, reduce costs, and enhance research.

BENEFITS OF DATA MINING IN PUBLIC ADMINISTRATION

Data mining techniques offer public sector opportunities to optimize decisions based on general trends extracted from historical data. With the knowledge that can be extracted from the data public organizations can level up its knowledge accumulation strategies and steps. The knowledge that can be derived with the data mining could serve first as a tool for better governance and second as a means for sustaining the organizational knowledge. Data mining technology is applied in different aspects of public administration such as healthcare, immigration, law enforcement and other public sectors to solve specific business or research problems. Examples of application areas follow.

Improving Service or Performance

The purpose of SBA's (Small Business Administration) lender/loan monitoring system is to improve service or performance. The system was developed by Dun & Bradstreet. SBA uses the system to identify, measure, and manage risk in its business loan programs. Its outputs include reports that identify the total amount of loans outstanding for a particular lender and estimate the likelihood of loans becoming delinquent in the future based on predefined patterns (GAO, 2005).

Hospitals are currently using data mining to save money in the long-run by reducing medication errors and the cost of transcribing doctors' dictation. For example, a family practitioner at UW Health's Meadowood clinic, uses the Epic System to order a drug, the computer automatically checks a database of potentially cross-reactions with other medications that the patient is currently taking. This system makes it easier for doctors to do their job very well, and at the same time, this system makes it easier for patients to see their information and interact with doctors. Also, with the growing rate of infection epidemic in hospitals in the United States, some hospitals are adopting data mining techniques to inform doctors on problems they might miss. MedMined of Birmingham is a company that has sold its data analysis services to hospitals to help detect infection in its early stage. Hospitals transmit encrypted data from patient's records to MedMined, which then uses its data mining algorithms to detect unusual patterns and correlations. At first only a few hospitals used this system but now it is becoming a necessity in hospitals (Lok, 2004).

Cahlink (2000) reported that data mining techniques are used by health organizations and hospitals to improve upon work processes. The Center for Disease Control and Prevention National Immunization Program in Atlanta implemented data mining software to allow better tracking of reactions to vaccine. The program has a huge database of adverse reactions to vaccines reported by physicians, clinics, and hospitals, patients and pharmaceutical companies across the nation. Statisticians and federal researchers monitor the data regularly to find problems caused by a single vaccine or vaccine combinations.

Through a cooperative agreement, the FDA's Division of Drug Risk Evaluation in the Office of Drug Safety has been working for almost two years to implement a desktop data-mining software system. This data mining tool will help to evaluate the hundreds of thousands of reports submitted annually to the Adverse Events Reporting System (AERS) - a system that has become more widely available to the public (Anonymous, 2005).

Delavari, Shirazi, and Beikzadeh (2004) showed that higher educational institutes use data mining models to identify which part of their processes can be improved by data mining technology and how they can achieve their goals. Data mining is used in the educational system to allocate resources and staff more efficiently, manage student relations and enhance the performance of the institution and its students and faculty. Databases include information on students and teachers, course schedules, academic performance, test scores, extra-curricular activities, post-graduation activities, etc., all of which can guide an institution on how to improve.

Helping Customer Relations Management (CRM)

Studying consumer behavior is the primary purpose of data mining. Data mining has enabled businesses to provide better customer service through the use of CRM technology. Most federal agencies have different customers such as citizens, businesses, other government agencies and even offices within agencies and each customer interaction provides extensive data which is used to develop new channels of service for customers. CRM is a conglomeration of technologies and management strategies which is used by organizations to control the operational side of their business. CRM is implemented in every department that deals with customers, be it in sales, technical support, customer service or marketing. CRM combines all customer data derived from these departments into one place such that the information can be accessed anywhere. This will enable the company to see the snapshot of a customer's history whenever a customer is contacted.

According to Dean (2001), the government's use of CRM technologies is very different from the private sectors benefits. Businesses use CRM to weed out customers that are costly to serve while the government uses CRM as a tool to help them acquire customers. All the same agencies use CRM to learn about customer habits which is used to create efficiency and cost-savings solutions. The Internal Revenue Service (IRS) uses CRM as a federal tax payment system. IRS uses this system to facilitate the collection of tax payments from corporations. Also, this system is incorporated in the IRS's call center and it help customer service to have access to taxpayer's data to help resolve any issues they may have with their tax payment. This system has been said to help reduce the time it takes taxpayers to phone in payments by more

than 40 percent and the number of taxpayer requests have dropped by 90 percent. The average payment now takes just 2 minutes and 20 seconds, and it happens 100,000 times a day.

CRM has helped governments and businesses to take an inventory of their customers, identify the products and services provided to customers, identify the methods of providing the products and services, and measure the effectiveness of communications with the customers through service channels.

Analyzing Scientific and Research Information

The increasing amount of data accumulated in the healthcare industry creates databases which can serve as basis for data mining. As the healthcare industry continues its work to enhance quality of care, promote services and reduce cost, undiscovered patterns of care will become increasingly transparent, first for physicians, nurses and other clinicians, and ultimately for all consumers of healthcare. Providers are now beginning to recognize the value of data mining as a tool to analyze patient care and clinical outcomes. As providers deploy advanced clinical data systems, more granular, primary data are becoming available for analysis.

In healthcare, increased access to data and information has facilitated the development of new drugs which seem to be produced at ever-increasing speeds, as Boire (2005) claimed. By being able to quickly analyze volumes of data from all kinds of different tests and during different time periods, data mining represents a critical cog within the drug development process. What was once a few years ago almost considered impossible entered the realm of the possible through access to these newfound capabilities due in large part to data mining? According to scientists, this breakthrough discovery of being able to map the DNA genome offers limitless possibilities in the development of new drugs now that specific genes can be isolated.

Data mining gives an opportunity to analyze the actual impact of one variable on another and/or other. The analysis of data mining results enables healthcare industries to discover new approaches in care delivery that consider a multitude of data points. (Business Wire, 2005) reported, a big step forward was achieved in medical research with the help of data mining. Children's Memorial Research Center, a leading U.S. pediatric hospital and research institute, has gained unique insights into tumor classification and treatment strategies with the help of SPSS predictive analysis. The automated extraction of information from biomedical literature promises to play an increasingly important role in text-based knowledge discovery processes.

Managing Human Resources

Consistent with Ashbaugh & Miranda (2002), Human Resource Management System (HRMS) is an integral part of the digital government which streamlines government processes in accounting, payroll and personnel administration. The underlying architecture for digital government is the Internet and integrated administrative systems commonly known as Enterprise Resource Planning (ERP) systems. ERP systems are built on software that integrates information from different applications into a common database. The ERP system and HRM system are the linkage between financial and human resources application through a single database in a software application that is both rigid and flexible. The rigidity comes from the need to standardize processes and deter customers from modifying the underlying software source code. Flexibility refers to the customer's ability to configure the software to collect specific data and other business goals. Business intelligence is a new concept in the public sector, uses advanced analytical tools such as data mining to provide insights into organizations trends and patterns, and helps

organizations to improve their decision-making skills. HRMS and business intelligence can be used to support personnel management decisions, including turnover analysis, recruitment, training analysis, and salary/workforce planning.

US Air Force uses data mining to manage its human resources. U.S. Air Force has signed an $88.5 million, multiyear contract with the Oracle Corp., which includes a closely watched deal to build a new logistics system for the organization. The Air Force's Expeditionary Combat Support System (ECSS) is intended to replace more than 500 legacies IT systems with one integrated, commercial supply chain management system. Oracle was competing against other enterprise resource planning vendors for the ECSS contract. Oracle uses data mining to provide information on promotions, pay grades, clearances, and other information relevant to human resources planning (Cowley, 2005).

Improving Emergency Management

Barnes, Fritz, and Yoo (2007) demonstrated that the σ-tree-based image information mining capability was useful in disaster response planning by detecting blocked access routes and autonomously discovering candidate rescue/recovery staging areas. An image-driven data mining of high-resolution satellite image features in nearshore areas in the aftermath of Hurricane Katrina in Gulfport, MS, were investigated for damage assessments and emergency response planning. Results showed a capability to detect hurricane debris fields and storm-impacted nearshore features and an ability to detect and classify nonimpacted features.

By identifying the core patient treatments provided by the emergency department (ED) and incorporating them into a Discrete Event Simulation model, (Ceglowski, Churilov, & Wasserthiel, 2007) provided insight into the complex relationship between patient urgency, treatment and disposal, and the occurrence of queues for treatment and promoted a generally applicable methodology for identifying bottlenecks in the interface between an ED and a hospital ward.

Along the lines of Hecker and Bruzewicz (2008), since 1998, the US Army Corps of Engineers (USACE) has been responsible for managing activities of the Civil Military Emergency Preparedness (CMEP) program, in Europe and Central Asia. CMEP supports international partner nations' national and regional strategies related to disaster awareness and consequence management for all hazards including the development and exercise of national and regional plans. The use of available technologies including the Internet, remote sensing and Geographic Information Systems (GIS), and reliable civil-military planning processes, are key program components. More than 55 seminars, workshops and Table Top Exercises (TTXs) have occurred since the program's inception. In 2005, USACE developed Emergency Management International (EMI), a program designed to provide CMEP -- and a broader range of USACE expertise -- globally. The authors examined the necessary conditions for effective disaster planning, preparedness and response for large disasters requiring national and international coordination and cooperation and examples of techniques used and outcomes of CMEP activities.

Also, Hesseldahl (2008) discussed Inrix, a company that analyzes data gathered from satellite navigation gear for the real time traffic information it provides, referred to as reality mining. It discussed potential applications for this data, including monitoring contact between employees, urban planning, and emergency management.

Detecting Fraud, Waste, and Abuse

In the government, data mining was initially used to detect financial fraud, waste and abuse. The Department of Agriculture's Risk Management Agency (RMA) uses data mining methods to identify potential abusers, improve program policies and guidance, and improve program performance and data quality. RMA uses information collected from insurance applicants as well as from insurance agents and claims adjusters. The department produces several types of outputs, including lists of names of individuals whose behavior matches patterns of anomalous behavior, which are provided to program investigators and sometimes insurance agencies. In addition it also produces programmatic information, such as how a procedural change in the federal crop insurance program's policy manual would impact the overall effectiveness of the program, and information on data quality and program performance, both of which are used by program managers (GAO, 2005).

Fraud in healthcare is controlled by the use of data mining by federal agencies. The agency can compare costs charged for medical services and find health-care providers overcharging their patients. Data mining is used to compare treatments for different medical conditions to determine if a patient is receiving inadequate or excessive care. Landro (2006) demonstrated that researchers are currently using data mining to review records of infants stored in the database to compare the effectiveness and safety of the narcotics morphine and fentanyl in easing pain. The need to mine existing data is very important in newborn intensive-care units, where different treatments can not always be studied in large scale randomized clinical trials.

Instead of insurance companies continuing to rely on the medical expertise of physicians, as well as other trained clinicians, to manually review insurance claims to detect healthcare fraud and abuse, companies can now use a data mining framework that assesses clinical pathways to construct an adaptable and extensible detection model. As Yang and Hwang noticed (2006) that clinical pathways are driven by physician orders, as well as industry and local standards of clinical care. Pathways provide the medical community with algorithms of the decisions to be made and the care to be provided to a particular patient population. The use of clinical pathways in detecting insurance fraud and abuse by service providers shows a significant promise. A care activity is highly likely to be fraudulent if it orders suspiciously. For example, a typical pattern of physicians is that of ordering noninvasive tests before ordering more invasive ones. Therefore, there is a high probability that the same set of medical activities ordered in a different order is fraudulent or abusive.

Detecting Criminal Activities

Data mining is also used by federal and state agencies to identify criminal activities, fraudulent misuse of governmental credit card, Medicaid and Medicare abuse. The SPSS predictive analytics software is used for crime prevention. This software's ability to detect unusual activity patterns has aided in the detection of credit card and Medicare fraud. In Richmond, Virginia, police use data mining to help them predict where to put patrols for crime prevention. An arm of the U.S. Army's homeland security uses the SPSS software to fight cyber crimes. The Army aims at protecting the databases of utility companies from hackers bent on shutting down these systems from performing (Van, 2005).

IRS uses the system to identify financial crime, including individual and corporate tax fraud. Its outputs include reports containing names, social security numbers, addresses, and other personal information of individuals suspected of financial crime, including individual and corporate tax fraud. Reports are shared with IRS field office personnel, who conduct investigations based on the report's results (GAO, 2005).

Corresponding to Boire (2005), the murder rate of New York City was reduced from 2200 in the late 1970s to between 600-700 murders a year over time. Not undervaluing some other factors like Bill Clinton's bill to increase the number of police officers and zero tolerance policy resulted in the full prosecution of even minor crimes such as the illegal placement of graffiti on public prop-

erty, officials used technology and data mining to analyze data concerning crimes in all sectors of his city. Data mining made it possible to analyze massive amounts of data that allowed uncovering trends and patterns concerning future crime behavior within high risk areas.

An intrusion detection problem is characterized by huge network traffic volumes, difficult to realize decision boundaries between attacks and normal activities and highly imbalanced attack class distribution. Moreover, it demands high accuracy, fast processing times and adaptability to a changing environment. Shafi, Kovacs, Abbass, and Zhu (2009) introduced a better approach for handling the situation when no rules match an input on the test set.

Thammaboosadee and Silparcha (2009) proposed a developed graphical user interface (GUI) prototype, which is supported by the framework of data mining techniques-based criminal judicial reasoning system. The GUI sequences of the prototype are satisfied with criminal judicial procedure in civil law system. As indicated by the authors, initially, the user must build the model by input the existing incident and specifying the detail of objects, elements of crime, charge and judgment. After enough training, the prototype will be ready to determine judgments from new occurred incidents.

Detecting Terrorist Activities

Following the terrorist attacks of September 11, 2001, data mining has been used increasingly as a tool to help detect terrorist threats through the collection and analysis of public and private sector data. Data mining has become one of the key features of many homeland security initiatives and its use has also expanded to other purposes.

In the context of homeland security, data mining can be a potential means to identify terrorist activities, such as money transfers and communications, and to identify and track individual terrorists themselves, such as through travel and immigration records. Some of the homeland security data mining applications represent a significant expansion in the quantity and scope of data to be analyzed. Some efforts that have attracted a higher level of congressional interest include the Terrorism Information Awareness (TIA) project (now-discontinued) and the Computer-Assisted Passenger Prescreening System II (CAPPS II) project (now canceled and replaced by Secure Flight) (Seifert, 2006). Other initiatives that have been the subject of recent congressional interest include the Multi-State Anti-Terrorism Information Exchange (MATRIX), the Able Danger program and data collection and analysis projects being conducted by the National Security Agency (NSA) (News Release, 2006).

Other government data-mining projects include Talon, a program run by the Pentagon's Counterintelligence Field Activity, which collects reports on demonstrators outside U.S. military bases, as maintained by Boyd (2006). Thousands of such reports are stored in a database called Cornerstone and are shared with other intelligence agencies. The Pentagon's Advanced Research and Development Activity based at Fort Meade, Md., runs a research program whose goal is to develop better ways to mine huge databases to help the nation avoid strategic surprises such as those of September 11, 2001.

In proportion to Cao, Zhao, and Zhang (2008), activity data accumulated in real life, such as terrorist activities and governmental customer contacts, present special, structural and semantic complexities. Activity data may lead to or be associated with significant business impacts, and result in important actions and decision making leading to business advantage. For instance, a series of terrorist activities may trigger a disaster to society, and large amounts of fraudulent activities in social security programs may result in huge government customer debt. Uncovering these activities or activity sequences can greatly evidence and/or enhance corresponding actions in business decisions. Cao et al. investigated the

characteristics and challenges of activity data, and the methodologies and tasks of activity mining based on case-study experience in the area of social security.

BARRIERS OF DATA MINING IN PUBLIC ADMINISTRATION

Two precursors are necessary for a successful data mining expedition: a clear formulation of the problem to be solved, and access to relevant data. Complicating the formulations of the problems to be solved and inherent in the public sectors are constraints raised by political opposition, privacy considerations, and concerns arising from the inherent limitations of the technology itself and the competency and hidden agendas of those who would implement the data mining projects and interpret its outputs. The most potent threat to privacy interests created by data mining technology arises from efforts to prevent terrorism in this country and overseas. As a result of anguished inquiries into the failure of the United States military and intelligence branches to detect the risk, and to intercept at least one previously identified terrorist before he boarded the airplane at Newark Airport and participated in the attacks, it became more politically acceptable for politicians and public servants to procure and develop more effective and potentially intrusive data mining techniques in the interest of public safety.

Bagner, Evansburg, Watson, and Welch (2003) observed that building on the USA PATRIOT Act was the Total Information Awareness Project (TIA) developed by the Department of Defense. TIA was designed to collect information on individual's financial transactions, travel records, medical records, and other activities from a wide variety of public and private databases. The data mined from these sources was to be used to prevent terrorism. Unlike the USA PATRIOT Act, which passed through Congress with little opposition, two bills were introduced in Congress to prevent TIA from moving forward. TIA was much broader in scope than the USA PATRIOT Act, and focused on collecting information about ordinary Americans rather than terror suspects. Because TIA was seen as a greater threat to with less return in security, Congress was widely against it. The TIA project has since been scrapped.

FUTURE TRENDS AND RESEARCH DIRECTIONS

The world is fast becoming a global village and with this comes the urgent need for a new generation of computational tools to assist humans in extracting useful information from the rapidly growing volumes of digital data. The future of data mining lies in predictive analysis or *one-click* data mining, accomplished through the simplification and automation of the entire data mining process.

Despite the limitations, data mining will have a tremendous impact on how business is done in the future. As a technology, data mining will become more embedded in a growing number of business applications making it more readily available to a wider market segment. The developers of data mining applications therefore need to develop it into something that most users can work with and that can provide and add value to our everyday lives. Easier interfaces will allow end user analysts with limited technical skills to achieve good results

Predictive Analysis

Augusta (2004) suggested that predictive analysis is one of the major future trends for data mining. Rather than being just about mining large amounts of data, predictive analytics looks to actually understand the data content. They hope to forecast based on the contents of the data. However, this requires complex programming and a great amount of business acumen. They are looking to do more than simply archive data, which is what data min-

ing is currently known for. They want to not just process it, but understand it more clearly which will in turn allow them to make better predictions about future behavior. With predictive analytics you have the program scour the data and try to form, or help form, new hypotheses itself. This shows great promise, and would be a boon for public administration everywhere.

Diversity of Application Domains

Data mining and X" phenomenon, as Tuzhilin (2008) coined, where X constitutes a broad range of fields in which data mining is used for analyzing the data, which has resulted in a process of cross-fertilization of ideas generated within this diverse population of researchers interacting across the traditional boundaries of their disciplines. The next generation of data mining applications covers a large number of different fields from traditional businesses to advance scientific research. Kantardzic and Zurada (2005) observed that with new tools, methodologies, and infrastructure, this trend of diversification will continue each year.

CONCLUSION

Data mining has become an indispensable technology for businesses and researchers in many fields including public administration. Since in public sectors, organizations and decision makers, are dealing with a volume amount of information from the public, a systematic way of collecting data and reading collected data is necessary. This, not only finds the similarities from one case to another, but also identifies unique cases and extreme values. Decision makers, service providers, and researchers are then be able to launch the next action, based on the knowledge discovered from the database and this increases their chances of being right. When the target market is the entire human population in the universe, instead of any other business market, data mining means more than making money for someone's self. Exercising data mining in public administration is to help the public, improve people's lives, and hence benefit the public as a whole.

REFERENCES

Anonymous. (2005, January 28). FDA drug safety reviewers to use data mining tool. *Washington Drug Letter, 37*(5).

Ashbaugh, S., & Miranda, R. (2002). Technology for human resources management: Seven questions and answers. *Public Personnel Management, 31*(1), 7–19.

Augusta, L. (2004, August). The future of data mining - predictive analytics. *DM Review, 14*(8), 16-20, 37.

Bagner, J., Evansburg, A., Watson, V. K., & Welch, J. B. (2003). Senators seek limits on DoD mining of personal data. *Intellectual Property & Technology Law Journal, 15*(5), 19–20.

Barnes, C. F., Fritz, H., & Jeseon, Y. (2007). Hurricane disaster assessments with image driven data mining in high-resolution satellite imagery. *IEEE Transactions on Geoscience and Remote Sensing, 45*(6), 1631–1640. doi:10.1109/TGRS.2007.890808

Boire, R. (2005, October). Future of data mining in marketing (Part 1). *Direct Marketing News.*

Boyd, R. S. (2006, February 2). Data mining tells government and business a lot about you. *Knight Ridder Washington Bureau.*

Business Wire. (2005, March 7). *SPSS predictive analytics accelerating cancer research.* Chicago: Children's Memorial Research Center.

Cahlink, G. (2000, October). Data mining taps trends. *Government Executive, 32*(12), 85–87.

Cao, L., Zhao, Y. C., & Zhang, C. Q. (2008). Activity mining: from activities to actions. *International Journal of Information Technology & Decision Making, 7*(2), 259–273. doi:10.1142/S0219622008002934

Ceglowski, R., Churilov, L., & Wasserthiel, J. (2007). Combining data mining and discrete event simulation for a value-added view of a hospital emergency department. *The Journal of the Operational Research Society, 58*(2), 246–254.

Cowley, S. (2005, October 24). Oracle wins $88.5 million Air Force contract. *IDG News Service.*

Dean, J. (2001). Better business through customers. *Government Executive, 33*(1), 58–60.

Delavari, N., Shirazi, M. R. A., & Beikzadeh, M. R. (2004, May 31-June 2). A new model for using data mining technology in higher educational systems. In *Proceedings 5th International Conference on Information Technology Based Higher Education and Training (ITEHT'04)*, Istanbul, Turkey (pp. 319-324).

GAO. (2005, August). Data mining: Agencies have taken key steps to protect privacy in selected efforts, but significant compliance issues remain (Tech. Rep. No. GAO-05-866, p. 7). Washington, DC: United States Government Accounting Office.

Gramatikov, M. (2006). *Data mining techniques and the decision making process in the Bulgarian Public Administration.* Retrieved December 30, 2009, from http://unpan1.un.org/intradoc/groups/public/documents/nispacee/unpan009209.pdf

Hand, D. J., Mannila, H., & Smyth, P. (2001). *Principles of Data Mining.* Cambridge, MA: MIT Press.

Hecker, E. J., & Bruzewicz, A. J. (2008). Emergency management international: improving national and international disaster preparedness and response. *Int. J. of Emergency Management, 3/4*, 250–260. doi:10.1504/IJEM.2008.025095

Hesseldahl, A. (2008, May 5). A rich vein for reality mining. *BusinessWeek, 4082*, 52-53.

Kantardzic, M. M., & Zurada, J. (Eds.). (2005). *Next generation of data-mining applications*. Washington, DC: IEEE Press.

Landro, L. (2006, January 26). The informed patient: Infant monitors yield new clues; Studies of digital records are used to identify problems with medications. Practices. *Wall Street Journal*, D5.

Lok, C. (2004, October). Fighting infections with data. *Technology Review*, 24.

McPhail, K. (2008). Contributing to sustainable development through multi-stakeholder processes: practical steps to avoid the "resource curse". *Corporate Governance, 8*(4), 471–481. doi:10.1108/14720700810899202

Meletiou, A., & Katsirikou, A. (2009). Methodology of analysis and interrelation of data about quality indexes of library services by using data- and knowledge- mining techniques. *Library Management, 30*(3), 138–147. doi:10.1108/01435120910937311

News Release. (2005). *MATRIX pilot project concludes*. Retrieved December 30, 2009, from http://www.fdle.state.fl.us/press_releases/expired/2005/20050415_matrix_project.html

Ranjan, J. (2009). Data mining in pharma sector: benefits. *International Journal of Health Care Quality Assurance, 22*(1), 82–92. doi:10.1108/09526860910927970

Shafi, K., Kovacs, T., Abbass, H. A., & Zhu, W. (2009). Intrusion detection with evolutionary learning classifier systems. *Natural Computing, 8*(1), 3–27. doi:10.1007/s11047-007-9053-9

Thammaboosadee, S., & Silparcha, U. (2009). A GUI Prototype for the Framework of Criminal Judicial Reasoning System. *Journal of International Commercial Law and Technology, 4*(3), 224–230.

Tuzhilin, A. (2008). Foreword. In J. Wang (Ed.). *Encyclopedia of data warehousing and mining* (4 Volumes, 2nd ed.). Hershey, PA: IGI Global.

Van, J. (2005, October 17). Cybercrime being fought in new ways. *Knight Rider Tribune Business News,* 1.

Vaught, C., Mallett, L., Brnich, M. J., Reinke, D., Kowalski-Trakofler, K. M., & Cole, H. P. (2006). Knowledge management and transfer for mine emergency response. *International Journal of Emergency Management, 3*(2-3), 6.

Yang, W. S., & Hwang, S. Y. (2006). A process-mining framework for the detection of healthcare fraud and abuse. *Expert Systems with Applications, 31*(1), 56–68. doi:10.1016/j.eswa.2005.09.003

This work was previously published in International Journal of Information Systems in the Service Sector, Volume 2, Issue 3, edited by John Wang, pp. 42-52, copyright 2010 by IGI Publishing (an imprint of IGI Global).

Chapter 15
Understanding Expectations, Perceptions and Satisfaction Levels of Customers of Military Engineer Services in India

Anand Parkash Bansal
Indian Institute of Management Bangalore, India

Vishnuprasad Nagadevara
Indian Institute of Management Bangalore, India

ABSTRACT

Customer satisfaction and client orientation concepts are needed in all service providing organisations, including those engaged in construction and infrastructure provision within the public sector where the public perception about their services is at its lowest. This study measures the expectations and percep-tions of various service elements among clients of Military Engineer Services (MES) in India. Customers' survey mode was used to measure the expectations, perception, importance and satisfaction. The perceived quality of services provided by this department was measured with SERVQUAL instrument on selected attributes using the Gap approach for identifying priorities. Additionally, this study also examines the influence of demographic characteristics of clients on expectations and perceptions of the clients. The results can be used by similar organisations for cultural and structural change to increase accountability and performance, in which the results indicate that the three most important dimensions in the order of importance among the clients of MES are tangibles, responsiveness and reliability.

DOI: 10.4018/978-1-4666-0044-7.ch015

Copyright © 2012, IGI Global. Copying or distributing in print or electronic forms without written permission of IGI Global is prohibited.

INTRODUCTION

Execution of public works has been an organized function of the state from the times immemorial in India and elsewhere. But, the inadequate job descriptions, low productivity, indifferent attitude among the employees of public sector organisations are among few of the factors which contribute to inefficiencies in the whole system and poor service delivery to the citizens.

The forces of globalisation and liberalisation and the consequent changes in the economic environment have created new challenges for the government departments the world over. Military Engineer Services (MES) and Central Public works department (CPWD) are among few large departments in Govt. of India that are engaged in the building construction and maintenance industry among other activities. The departments as of now enjoy near monopoly in service provision to clients in their designated jurisdiction under Government of India. The pressure for change is being felt by the users of such organisations from the rapidly changing economic-political environment, increasing demand for better value for money, pressures for greater effectiveness, efficiency and performance, rapid technology changes and increasing awareness; all these factors leading to increasing expectations for citizen participation. The Administrative Reforms Commission (2007) in its recent report titled "Ethics in Governance" recommended for identifying areas within government where existing monopoly of functions could be tempered with competition.

Customer satisfaction and customer orientation concepts are therefore, increasingly being adopted to identify and prioritise the areas for improvement in the quality of services provided by government departments. It is necessary to understand the needs and expectations of the clients and define quality standards according to their expectations. There should also be institutional mechanisms to continuously assess the quality of the service provided and to take appropriate measures to improve the service quality based on the feedback from clients. The focus of the administrators in public sector departments therefore needs change from provision of construction and maintenance services to providing these services with quality above minimum acceptable standards. These departments, however, do not have any arrangements for evaluation of expectations and perceptions of clients and for monitoring client satisfaction.

The obvious approach to gauge the satisfaction level is to ask the clients themselves. Construction and Maintenance of buildings etc. is one of those services that are difficult to measure and monitor, with very little research on service quality in this field. The predominant amount of research on the measurement of service management quality has taken place in the fields of retail industry, health care and financial services. The little amount of research in the construction industry involving empirical surveys has focused on the quality of consultancy services (Hoxley, 1998; Love, Smith, Treloar, & Li, 2000). SERVQUAL based survey using Gap model have also been carried out for service quality in the maintenance of mechanical and engineering services (Wan, Bridge, & Skitmore, 2001).

It was therefore, thought appropriate to have a systematic study and find out the extent of client satisfaction in Public Sector Construction and Maintenance Organisations and to identify the areas for improvement. Military Engineer Services (MES), which is engaged in providing construction and maintenance services for all organs of Ministry of Defence for their infrastructure needs was selected for this study. The focus in this study was on customer satisfaction with particular emphasis on service quality in Public Sector Construction and Maintenance departments so as to provide the necessary inputs and desired impetus to the department to improve and excel in the future. The main objective of the study was to bring out the customer satisfaction gaps and analysis of these gaps. The results of the analysis are used to suggest ways and means to improve the delivery of

Figure 1. Customer-service provider relationship: private sector

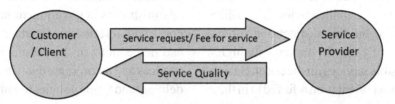

the service and in turn to improve the perception of service quality as experienced by the clients.

LITERATURE REVIEW

Customer / Client Satisfaction

It will be useful to compare the concept of customer in a private sector setting vis-à-vis the clients in the government sector setting. What the customers are to service organisations in private sector, clients are to the government service organisations. A subtle difference may however be drawn between a customer and client. The relation between the customer and the service provider are limited in a sense that the customer purchases the goods or services and pays in return for the services s/he receives. The customer does not have any right or claim on the services provided by the organisation in the absence of a definite agreement/contract. Clients on the other hand receive the professional advice or services from an organisation. In a typical government service organisation with defined geographical jurisdiction, the clients have right or claim over the services it provides. The rights of the clients on these services are however limited to the extent decided by the citizens/taxpayers who are bearers of rights and duties in a framework of community and exercise their control through elected representatives/executive appointed by them for the purpose (Figure 1 and Figure 2).

With the above background the question that arises is "Are all citizens customers, and to what extent should a government treat citizens as its customers?" Customer service advocates argue

that every citizen is a government's customer. But, the government is expected to serve the larger public interest over that of individual citizens. According to Kettl (2000) the citizens as customers have four different perspectives. The citizens could be service recipients, partners, owners and taxpayers. As service recipients, citizens expect high quality services at low or even no cost; as partners, they are to ensure that the services are more effective and are expected to play a strong role different from the passive role as in service recipient role.

Contrary to their role as service recipients, where they might expect virtually unlimited service, as taxpayers they have conflicting priorities in the form of tough management, high efficiency and minimal waste, fraud and abuse from the same government. A balance, however, need to

Figure 2. Customer-service provider relationship: public sector

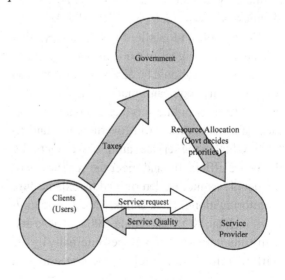

be struck between these two objectives (Dinsdale & Marsden, 1999). The challenge for the public sector is to balance the two distinct and often competing factors of value for money with high quality and accessible services for the client. Basic principle of customer orientation referred to in the context of private service organisations are equally relevant and applicable to government service organisations, which may be termed as citizen/client orientation. The citizen/client orientation as a means for achieving responsive administration requires better understanding of the needs and expectations of citizens on a continuing basis.

Measuring Customer Satisfaction

Public sector organizations have started realizing that not only must they look after their customers but they must also learn from them in terms of customer satisfaction and customer perception of the service. According to Skelcher (1992) this signifies the rejection of the traditional model of uniform services being delivered to passive recipients. "Sometimes organizations make assumptions about what is important to the customer. Once they probe, they may discover that what the customer values is quite different" (Farquhar, 1993). Results of few studies in public sector organizations in the UK indicate that managers frequently overestimate customer expectations (Donnelly, Mike, Wisniewski, Dalrymple, & Curry, 1995).

McDonnell and Gatfield (1998) argued that measures send a signal to an organisation regarding priorities, and it should be obvious that what you don't measure, you can't manage. Traditionally, expenditure on public services is considered as the performance measure in government organizations. Whether the services and assets are actually delivered efficiently and meet the real needs of the people cannot be determined by expenditure monitoring alone (Paul, Balakrishnan, Gopalkumar, Shekhar, & Vivekananda, 2004). These and many other measures developed internally by the staff, therefore, do not reflect the concerns and

priorities of citizens. It is therefore desirable for administrators in government including those in construction sector to understand the expectations and perceptions of the people about the quality services and incorporate them in design of service delivery and frame policies to improve the quality.

Service Quality and Satisfaction

MES like other construction and maintenance agencies is regarded as a service agency. Services have been defined in many ways. Grönroos (1990) defines service as an activity or series of activities of intangible nature that normally takes place between the customer and the service provider. Services are characterised by their intangibility, inseparability of production and consumption, perishability and heterogeneity (Parasuraman, Zeithaml, & Berry, 1981; Parasuraman, Zeithaml, & Berry, 1988). Because of these unique characteristics, measuring service quality poses difficulties for service providers (Bateson, 1995). Service quality therefore is 'whatever a customer says it is' and 'whatever customer perceives it to be' (Buzzel & Gale, 1987). Perceived service quality is therefore viewed as the degree and direction of discrepancy between customers' perceptions and expectations (Zeithaml, Parasuraman, & Berry, 1990).

It is therefore important to understand how the expectations are formed and what their impact is. The expectations are also influenced by the personal values and beliefs. In case of the public services expectations also get influenced by the reputation of the government as a whole. It has also been observed that availability of alternative service providers raises the levels of expectations of adequate service (Zeithaml, Berry, & Parasuraman, 1993). Thus in the end expectations have a central role in impacting the satisfaction.

Service Quality and Its Measurement

The initial research into customer satisfaction measurement involved assessing the determinants of expectations and drivers of satisfaction. Grönroos (1984) identified the two variables of service quality as expected service and perceived service. He observed that the discrepancy between expectations and perceptions is the primary determinant of customers' service quality requirements. Parasuraman, Zeithaml, and Berry (1981) presented the most systematic research programmes in service quality and developed a conceptual model SERVQUAL by using extensive exploratory investigations of quality in variety of service businesses. This model was further refined by Parasuraman, Zeithaml, and Berry (1988) who developed a multiple item scale for measuring consumer perception of service quality with five distinct dimensions i.e., tangibles, reliability, responsiveness, assurance and empathy, after multi stage purification process. This instrument can be suitably modified to adapt to the needs and characteristics of a particular service. It also finds application in categorizing customers into several perceived-quality segments (such as high, medium or low) on the basis of their individual SERVQUAL scores. These segments can be then analysed on the basis of demographic, socio-economic and other profiles, the relative importance of the five dimensions in influencing service quality perceptions and the reasons behind the perceptions reported by them.

Although SERVQUAL is used widely to measure quality, it is not without criticism. Key and Theresia (2001) questioned the assumption of linear relationship between customer satisfaction and service attributes' performance. Paying more attention to a particular service attribute may not always lead to a higher customer satisfaction if there is satiation or if that attribute is taken for granted. Carman (1990) also questioned and criticised the validity of SERVQUAL on the psychometric soundness of the difference between expectations and perceptions, and on the collection of expectations data. Some other researchers (Babakus & Boller, 1992) also endorsed the views and suggested that dimensionality may vary with the type of service under study. Despite these concerns, SERVQUAL questionnaire by far is the most robust instrument and has been applied in many service organisations.

Gap Approach

As per the extended model of Parasuraman et al. (1985) there are seven major gaps in the service quality concept, that are shown in Figure 3. The gaps on the service providers' side include consumer expectations - management perceptions gap; management perceptions - service quality specifications gap; and service delivery - external communication gap among others. The consumer side gap, i.e., the gap 5 between expected service and perceived service is what determines the quality that a consumer perceives. The service quality model essentially states that service quality as perceived by consumers depends on extent and direction of this gap which in turn depends on the nature of gaps on the side of service provider.

Service quality gaps can be used by the managers to identify areas of improvement with larger gaps requiring more attention. If gap scores in some areas turn out to be positive, the managers need to review if that particular service is over provided and to explore the possibility of redeploying the resources. The information derived from the gap analysis can be used by the service providers to evaluate the current service quality, to compare performance across different customer groups and across services, for assessment of the impact of improvement initiatives as well as for understanding internal customer.

Satisfaction - Importance Matrix Approach

Satisfaction-Importance matrix approach (Dutka, 1994) also known as quadrants' approach used in various studies captures the direct comparison of the satisfaction level of the service quality attributes and the importance attached to it as shown in

Figure 3. Model of service quality gaps (source: adapted from Parasuraman, Zeithaml, and Berry (1985); Curry (1999))

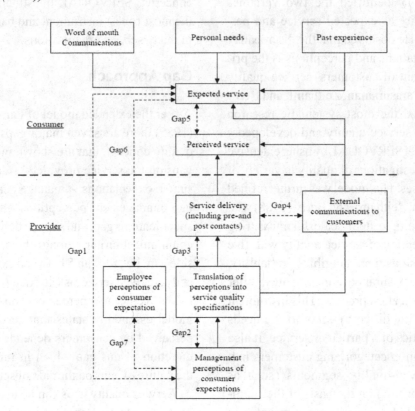

Figure 4. Attributes where the importance is high but satisfaction level is low fall in the "priorities of improvement" quadrant and are the focuses of attention. This approach is somewhat similar to the 'Integrated Model for Measuring Service Quality' (IMMSQ) (Yang, 2003). It involves identification of importance of various attributes and corresponding satisfaction levels. Using similar concept, Yang (2003) plotted degree of importance and satisfaction level of an attributes on the horizontal and vertical dimensions as shown in Figure 5 and named it as 'Importance- Satisfaction' Model.

CMT- Common Measurement Tool

CMT (Common Measurement Tool) is a model developed by The Researchers at the Canadian Centre for Management Development to standardize measurement of customer satisfaction with public services (Schmidt, Faye, Strickland, & Teresa, 1998). The model combines the elements of SERVQUAL and Satisfaction-Importance models to improve the understanding of satisfaction and to highlight priorities for improvement. CMT accordingly measures the expectations of the service factors, perceptions of service experience, level of importance attached to each service element and level of satisfaction with these elements.

The CMT approach is therefore made up of three distinct steps. First, the measures of expectations and perceptions of the service experience (SERVQUAL model) allow the gap analysis approach by comparing expected service quality with experience. In the second step, the users are asked about how important each of the service elements listed are to respondents, followed in the third step by asking about levels of satisfaction with these service elements. This allows the

Figure 4. Satisfaction-importance matrix

		Importance	
		Low	High
Satisfaction (Performance)	High	Unnecessary strengths	Current organization strengths
	Low	Low Priority	Attributes that need attention – **priorities of improvement**

comparison of importance and satisfaction as discussed in quadrants' approach. The Common Measurement Tool was therefore considered to be highly relevant to public sector organisations and has been used in this study with suitable modifications to accommodate the requirements of a public sector construction and maintenance services organisation like MES.

RESEARCH METHODOLOGY

Clients' survey mode has primarily been used in this study to measure the expectations, perceptions and satisfaction of clients about the construction and maintenance services provided by MES. The methodology used in carrying out the research

include identification of important quality attributes, development and pre-testing of appropriate questionnaires, details of sampling plan, data collection and data analysis.

Identification of Attributes and Questionnaire Development

The scale items and framing of questions in SERVQUAL questionnaire to assess the expectations and perceptions were adapted from Parasuraman et al. (1988) with inclusion of few attributes to suit the characteristics of services provided by MES. These attributes for the questionnaire were generated after an exploratory study that involved informal experience survey with key experienced executives and focus group interviews

Figure 5. Importance-satisfaction model (source: adapted from Chang Chow Yang (2003))

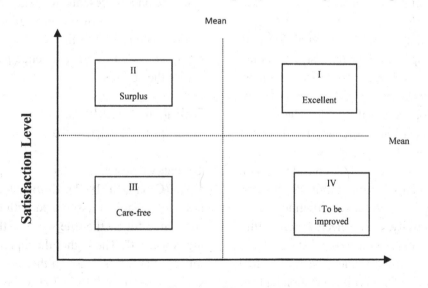

of clients and MES supervisors. In all twenty four attributes (scale items) of the service were identified on five dimensions of service quality (including few questions related to construction quality and specifications provided in buildings). The structure of the set of questionnaires included SERQUAL questionnaire in Part I, A and B, Importance –Satisfaction Survey questionnaire (with 15 identified quality attributes) in Part II, A and B and a separate section at the end to record the socio-demographic details of the respondent. The 7-point Likert scale as recommended by Parasuraman et al. was used as a measure for the expectation and perception attributes with range from 1 (strongly disagree) to 7 (strongly agree). Similarly 5-point Likert scale with levels from 1 (extremely unimportant) to 5 (extremely important) was used for importance-satisfaction survey. Content validity was also ascertained by pre-testing the questionnaire and a review of the questionnaire by academics and practitioners in the field from MES and CPWD. An open ended question was added to capture qualitative remarks and suggestions of respondents.

Sampling Plan

MES provides services to various organs of Ministry of Defense which includes services of construction and maintenance for their administrative, technical, other specialty buildings/structures and housing complexes. There are significant numbers of Defence units located at Bangalore with approx clients' population of 20,000. The sample profile of clients at Bangalore largely represents the configuration of clients in any peace station across the country and can be considered as a representative sample. In all, 31 units/ formations dependent on MES, both for construction and for maintenance activity, were selected from Army and Air Force units located across different parts of Bangalore. Stratified mode of sampling was adopted to have a judicious mix of respondents of various ranks from different units in proportion of

their strength. In each of these units, respondents were randomly selected for the survey. Care was taken to get the feedback from the key officials (in-charge of works matters of their buildings) from each unit in addition to common users. Care was also taken to get the feedback from the troops and air warriors occupying the residential accommodation, which are maintained by MES.

Collection of Data

The respondents were contacted at their workplace or at their place of residence. Personal interaction mode with 'a group of respondents' was resorted to before seeking their individual responses. A series of qualitative questions was also asked in personal interviews with key service provider executives and with commanders from the clients' side to reinforce the quantitative data.

DATA ANALYSIS, INTERPRETATION AND FINDINGS

A total of 300 responses were received, of which 262 turned out to be valid responses. The socio demographic profile of the respondents as observed from the data represents the general distribution of population pattern in a typical defence peace station. The results of this data can therefore be safely extended to other defence peace stations across the country.

Reliability Analysis: Cronbach's Alpha Test

The data was tested for reliability using Cronbach's alpha (Cronbach, 1951). Cronbach's alpha is an index of reliability associated with the variation accounted for by the true score of the "underlying construct". The higher the alpha is, the more reliable the test is. Though there is no generally agreed cut-off, usually 0.7 and above is acceptable (Nunnally, 1978; Streiner & Norman, 1989).

Table 1. Reliability test (Cronbach's Alpha) statistics

Reliability Statistics				
Scale	Coefficient alpha	No of Items	Coefficient alpha	No of Items
SERVQUAL Scale	Expectations (1-7)		Perceptions (1-7)	
Tangibles	0.800	4	0.833	4
Reliability	0.894	8	0.936	8
Responsiveness	0.884	4	0.880	4
Assurance	0.912	5	0.932	5
Empathy	0.841	3	0.855	3
Overall	**0.972**	**24**	**0.976**	**24**
Tangibles	0.573	2	0.827	2
Reliability	0.841	3	0.887	3
Responsiveness	0.800	3	0.843	3
Assurance	0.828	4	0.858	4
Empathy	0.763	3	0.828	3
Overall	**0.943**	**15**	**0.965**	**15**

The range of overall coefficient alpha recorded is 0.943 to 0.976 exceeding the suggested level of 0.70 as recommended by Nunnally (1978). Cronbach's alpha across the five dimensions of service quality also ranged from 0.763 to 0.932 with one exception demonstrating good internal consistency and reliability of scale (Table 1).

Analysis of Expectation-Perception Scores

A test of significance was done on the expectation and perception scores and. The results indicate that there is significant difference in the expectations and perceptions of the clients (Table 2). The mean expectation score is seen to be 5.08 which are on lower side when compared to similar surveys in private sector service organisations. The low expectation scores also reflects on the lack of service alternative from the clients' point of view and to some extent reflects on the reputation of the department among clients.

Gap Analysis

It is important to measure expectations and perceptions of the customers to evaluate the customer satisfaction. Service quality is said to have been achieved when these expectations are met or are exceeded. Service quality fails to be achieved when expectations are not met and a service gap materialises. The gap is the difference between the perceptions and the expectations of a particular service. Larger the gap, greater is the gulf between what the customer expects and what they actually receive. It is normally not possible to exceed the expectations of the customer for variety of reasons. Thus, gaps are usually negative for most of the services, whether it is private or public sector. While scores are most often negative reflecting service shortfalls or gaps, scores less than minus '2' are considered to be strong (McDonnell & Gatfield, 1998). Information on customer expectations can help service providers to understand what customer actually expects from the service.

The SERVQUAL scores were derived from expectation and perception scores by subtracting expectation score from perception score.

Table 2. Perception-expectations gap analysis (all attributes)

S. No	Attributes	N	Means			Std. Dev. Of Means			Std. Errors of Means		
			E	P	PE Gap	E	P	PE Gap	E	P	PE Gap
1	Modern and up to date equipment	262	5.52	3.22	-2.31	1.651	1.671	2.516	0.102	0.103	0.155
2	Good facilities in housing units	262	5.15	3.65	-1.50	1.732	1.693	2.179	0.107	0.105	0.135
3	Good architectural features.	262	5.33	3.69	-1.65	1.704	1.762	2.239	0.105	0.109	0.138
4	Good quality of workmanship in construction and maintenance	260	5.13	3.54	-1.60	1.620	1.756	2.225	0.100	0.109	0.138
5	Quality material for construction and maintenance	262	5.06	3.55	-1.52	1.716	1.630	2.181	0.106	0.101	0.135
6	Pleasing appearance of the service centres	260	5.00	3.56	-1.43	1.617	1.729	2.220	0.100	0.107	0.138
7	Adequate stores/spares for maintenance at service centres	261	5.00	3.31	-1.68	1.718	1.689	2.309	0.106	0.104	0.143
8	Adherence to promise to do something by a certain time	262	4.51	3.28	-1.23	1.885	1.662	2.075	0.116	0.103	0.128
9	Sincere interest in solving user's problem	262	5.11	3.74	-1.37	1.733	1.792	2.282	0.107	0.111	0.141
10	Completion of repair/ maintenance job first time	259	4.90	3.56	-1.32	1.713	1.654	2.199	0.106	0.102	0.137
11	Performs the services at the time they promise to do so	262	4.95	3.55	-1.40	1.756	1.650	2.341	0.109	0.102	0.145
12	Employees normally tell the users exactly when the services will be performed.	262	4.92	3.52	-1.41	1.718	1.699	2.381	0.106	0.105	0.147
13	Employees normally give prompt services to the user.	262	5.06	3.58	-1.48	1.659	1.661	2.133	0.102	0.103	0.132
14	Employees are never too busy to respond to user's request.	261	5.00	3.57	-1.42	1.656	1.692	2.216	0.103	0.105	0.138
15	Employees help instil confidence in users.	262	5.08	3.74	-1.34	1.699	1.711	2.186	0.105	0.106	0.135
16	Users normally feel safe in their transactions	262	5.23	3.87	-1.35	1.558	1.757	2.155	0.096	0.109	0.133
17	Employees are consistently courteous with users.	262	4.98	3.91	-1.08	1.663	1.746	2.132	0.103	0.108	0.132

continues on following page

Table 2. Continued

S. No	Attributes	N	Means			Std. Dev. Of Means			Std. Errors of Means		
			E	P	PE Gap	E	P	PE Gap	E	P	PE Gap
18	Employees have the required knowledge to answer the user's questions.	262	5.10	3.99	-1.11	1.564	1.777	2.262	0.097	0.110	0.140
19	Operating hours are convenient to all users	262	5.16	3.82	-1.33	1.745	1.817	2.252	0.108	0.112	0.139
20	Employees normally understand the specific needs of their users.	262	5.01	3.87	-1.13	1.675	1.769	2.196	0.103	0.109	0.136
21	Availability of required staff (electrician, plumber, mason etc) at the service centres	262	5.19	3.79	-1.41	1.708	1.773	2.240	0.105	0.110	0.138
22	Attention to safety at the work site	261	5.33	3.90	-1.43	1.608	1.809	2.191	0.100	0.112	0.136
23	Coordination of the internal services between different wings of deptt i.e. B/R, E/M, BSO etc.	262	5.21	3.55	-1.66	1.777	1.714	2.358	0.110	0.106	0.146
24	Good specifications in construction & maintenance service	262	5.27	3.84	-1.42	1.676	1.707	2.331	0.104	0.105	0.144

Although, the scale used is strictly ordinal, for statistical analysis purpose it was treated as interval scale. The perceptions, expectations and P-E gap scores for all attributes are shown in Table 2.

For the purpose of gap analysis, the 24 scale items describing various services attribute were classified as per SERQUAL model on 5 dimensions namely tangibles, reliability, responsiveness, assurance and empathy. The gap analysis was then performed on the perception and expectation scores across these dimensions as shown in Table 3. The SERVQUAL scores were also subjected to "Sign test" to see if there is significant difference in the perceptions and expectations of the clients in MES. In the present dataset, the significance level is less than.05 indicating that there is significant difference between the perceptions and expectations of the MES users. The results also show that mostly the SERVQUAL scores are negative, indicating that the service quality falls significantly short of clients' expectations. In the present study, SERVQUAL scores for all dimensions range between (-) 1.26 to (-) 1.72 which are more than (-) 2.0 and can be termed as just about satisfactory.

In most organisations where SERVQUAL surveys have been conducted, reliability has consistently been shown to be the most important determinant of perceptions of service quality followed by responsiveness and empathy (Parasuraman, Zeithaml, & Berry, 1991). Reliability, responsiveness and tangibles in the order of priority were the three most important service quality dimensions in case of CPWD (Joshi, 2006). However in case of MES, as can be inferred from above tables, the tangibles dimension is most significant and contributing to the dissatisfaction to a large extent, understandably so looking at the work culture of MES client organisations. The results further corroborate the findings in some

Table 3. Gap analysis

Dimension	N	Means			Std. Dev. Of Means			Std. Errors of Means		
		E	P	PE	E	P	PE	E	P	PE
Tangibles	262	5.18	3.47	-1.72	1.326	1.400	1.917	0.082	0.086	0.118
Reliability	262	5.04	3.58	-1.45	1.341	1.428	1.757	0.083	0.088	0.109
Responsiveness	262	5.05	3.55	-1.50	1.466	1.450	1.961	0.091	0.090	0.121
Assurance	262	5.15	3.88	-1.26	1.393	1.561	1.885	0.086	0.096	0.116
Empathy	262	5.09	3.81	-1.28	1.475	1.564	1.937	0.091	0.097	0.120

* E= Expectations, P= Perceptions, PE= PE Gap, Std. Dev= standard deviation

studies that tangibles appear to be a more important factor in the facility/equipment-based industries (Lee, Lee, & Yoo, 2000). Within the tangibles the MES clients strongly perceive that the tools and equipments used by MES are outdated. The department seems to be lacking in providing adequate maintenance staff, requisite stores/spares at service centres and in ensuring pleasing appearance of its service centres. Responsiveness and reliability dimensions are next in the order. The department need to improve on delivering the services in time and when promised. Co-ordination among various wings, better facilities in housing units, the customer contact, customer relations and giving more importance to customer interaction are some other areas where improvement is required.

Thus the important dimensions which impact the quality of service provided by MES in general are Tangibles, Responsiveness and Reliability. MES needs to improve on the functioning of their service centres by providing adequate manpower and stores, timely and prompt delivery of services, delivery of services as promised and doing the services right the first time. They also need to pay more attention to the internal co-ordination of different services. The gap analysis was also done separately for Air Force clients and Army clients. The results are tabulated in Table 4.

The expectations of clients, in both Army and Air Force, are not very high and are at almost similar level but the perception differs significantly; Air Force clients carrying better perception about MES service quality. This provides valuable information to further analyse the reasons for better perception and to see if practices in use in Air Force could be adopted in Army.

Table 4. Comparison of expectations and perceptions between air force and army

Dimension	Expectations		Perceptions		PE Gap	
	Army	Air Force	Army	Air Force	Army	Air Force
Tangibles	5.24	5.09	3.29	3.78	-1.94	-1.32
Reliability	5.03	5.04	3.30	4.09	-1.74	-0.95
Responsiveness	5.08	4.99	3.26	4.07	-1.83	-0.92
Assurance	5.09	5.25	3.52	4.53	-1.57	-0.72
Empathy	5.05	5.16	3.45	4.46	-1.60	-0.71
Mean	**5.10**	**5.11**	**3.36**	**4.18**	**-1.74**	**-0.92**

Influence of Demographic Characteristics on Expectations, Perceptions and P-E Gaps

In addition, the customers can be categorized into several perceived-quality segments (such as high, medium or low) on the basis of their individual SERVQUAL scores. The segments so categorised can then be analysed on the basis of demographic, socio-economic and other profiles and the reasons behind the expectations and perceptions reported by them. Total of expectation scores, total perception scores and total of P-E gaps of all respondents were sorted in ascending order and then grouped into quintiles in order to analyse the influence of demographic characteristics on expectations, perceptions and P-E gaps, (Table 5). The top quintile and bottom quintile were then analysed to identify if higher expectations, perceptions or wide P-E gaps are influenced by the demographic characteristics of the clients. The findings of the analysis are given below

Army constitutes a high expectation, low perception group with wide PE gap among the clients. The clients living in Government provided married accommodation as also the clients coming on transfer from field area though do not have very high expectations but can be categorised in the group of low perception with wide PE gap. Middle aged clients also fall into the same group. Similarly Air Force clients can be classified as low expectation, high perception group. The finding has significant policy implication in design of distinct service delivery systems for these groups, one, to manage the expectations by proper information dissemination and two, by improving the services.

Perceived Service Quality (PSQ)

Having analysed gaps, it is important to arrive at some measure for service quality as perceived by MES clients. Parasuraman et al. (1985) defined the construct of service quality as the difference between expected service and perceived service. Perceived service quality is the consumer's judgment about the overall excellence or superiority of a service (Parasuraman, Zeithaml, & Bery, 1988). Researchers have also shown that perceived service quality is an antecedent of the satisfaction (Lee, Lee, & Yoo, 2000). Attempt was therefore made to arrive at the perceived service quality (PSQ) score by taking mean of PE gaps across five dimensions. The PSQ so calculated was 1.44 indicating significant gap between the expectations and perceptions of the clients of MES. This again corroborates the earlier findings in case of gap analysis based on SERVQUAL scores.

Analysis of Importance Scores

Importance survey questionnaire was meant to understand the importance of various attributes to the clients. Importance rankings are derived by computing the mean of importance scores of the attributes (Table 6). The clients have accorded highest importance to 'careful repairs by avoiding damage to the assets'. The next important ranking is given to provision of good facilities in the office units and the technical and procedural knowledge of the staff. The clients have also rated prompt service quite high in order of importance. Quite surprisingly and contrary to the popular understanding among the service providers (as told by key service providers to authors during interviews conducted by them), 'delivery of promise made', 'being kept informed of the status of their complaint' and 'pleasant and neat appearance of the maintenance staff' figure low in importance ratings given by the users as seen from the data analysis.

Analysis of Satisfaction Scores

The satisfaction scores (Table 6) range between 3.26 being the highest for courteous behaviour and easy approachability and 3.22 for helpfulness of MES officers. The satisfaction scores indicate that

Table 5. Variation of P, E and PE Gap Vis-a-Vis Demographics

Category/Group	Overall % distribution within Respondents		Expectations %		Perceptions %		PE Gap %	
	Nos	%	High exp group	Low exp group	High percep group	Low percep group	High PE gap group	Low PE gap group
Defence Organisation								
Army	167	64	79	69	50	94	88	52
Air Force	95	36	21	31	50	6	12	48
Total	262	100	100	100	100	100	100	100
Rank category								
Officer	44	18	10	11	13	10	12	13
JCO	73	30	32	30	28	29	27	33
Other Ranks	114	47	52	57	49	61	61	49
Civilians	13	5	6	2	10	0	0	4
Total	244	100	100	100	100	100	100	100
Gender								
Male	248	95	94	96	96	96	94	94
Female	14	5	6	4	4	4	6	6
Total	262	100	100	100	100	100	100	100
Age Groups								
Young Upto 30 Yrs	28	11	8	14	15	4	4	12
Middle Aged 30-40 Yrs	116	45	44	51	29	63	59	42
Seniors	111	44	48	35	56	33	37	46
Total	255	100	100	100	100	100	100	100
Qualification								
Post Graduate	30	13	9	7	17	4	4	13
Graduate	88	39	28	37	39	19	24	44
10+2	72	32	40	37	29	47	48	33
Matric	38	17	23	19	15	30	24	10
Total	228	100	100	100	100	100	100	100
Background								
Urban	69	30	28	24	32	17	17	20
Rural	161	70	72	76	68	83	83	80
Total	230	100	100	100	100	100	100	100
Last Posting								
Field Area	45	26	26	33	15	42	42	20
Modified Field	20	12	8	17	12	13	8	80
Peace Station	105	62	66	50	73	45	50	-
Total	170	100	100	100	100	100	100	100
Accommodation Living In								
Govt Married Accommodation	167	82	85	83	70	95	90	68

Table 5. Continued

Category/Group	Overall % distribution within Respondents		Expectations %		Perceptions %		PE Gap %	
	Nos	%	High exp group	Low exp group	High percep group	Low percep group	High PE gap group	Low PE gap group
Rented Accommodation	6	3	2	-	2	-	2	3
Singlemen Barracks	31	15	13	17	28	5	7	29
Total	204	100	100	100	100	100	100	100

the clients are generally happy about approachability, courtesy and helping tendency of service providers and are also reasonably satisfied about technical and procedural knowledge of officers and staff of MES. The clients however are not so happy about cleaning up the site after completion of the job, disposal of waste and with the appearance of the maintenance staff. On the lower side 2.82 is the lowest mean score for "cleaning up after completion of job and disposal of waste". The mean score for delivery of promise made and/ or being kept informed of the status of complaint pending arrival of stores is also very low (2.83) indicating that the clients are not very happy on these attributes. There is a need to take concrete steps to improve satisfaction on these attributes. The overall mean satisfaction score across all attributes works out to 3.047 indicating that the clients in general are just satisfied with the services being provided by the service providers.

Table 6. Importance-satisfaction scores

S No	Importance Attribute	I	S
1	Pleasant and neat appearance of the maintenance staff.	3.74	2.87
2	The MES staff should show his identity to users before providing the service.	4.09	3.16
3	Promptness of the service	4.12	3.02
4	Pleasant telephone manners and timeliness of the response to telephonic complaint or messages.	4.14	3.07
5	Delivery of promise made and/or being kept informed of the status of your complaint pending arrival of stores.	4.03	2.83
6	Careful repairs to avoid further damage.	4.21	2.98
7	The follow through to see if you got what you needed.	4.05	2.90
8	Technical and procedural knowledge of the staff.	4.15	3.22
9	Courtesy and guidance provided by the MES officers.	4.09	3.26
10	Hours of service (e.g. maintenance)	4.03	3.09
11	Specifications of the work done	4.05	3.10
12	Facilities provided in the housing units	4.10	3.03
13	Facilities provided in the office units	4.16	3.10
14	Cleaning up after completion of job and disposal of waste.	4.00	2.82
15	The officers are easily approachable, listen to you, assess your need and are helpful.	4.12	3.26
	Overall Mean		**3.047**

I = Mean Expectation Score, S = Mean Satisfaction Score

Importance-Satisfaction Scores: Quadrants' Approach

Quadrants' approach was used to plot the above importance and satisfaction scores as shown in chart (Figure 6). The chart is divided in four quadrants with mean satisfaction and important scores lines splitting the chart into four quadrants.

The two left hand quadrants in the I-S matrix (Figure 7) prepared based on above results contain factors that are considered relatively less important. The top right hand quadrant contains those factors that are considered important and which users are also relatively satisfied with. Endeavour of every service providing organisation should be to have all factors in this quadrant. The bottom right quadrant shows those factors users are less satisfied with but which are also relatively important. These should be seen as the priorities of improvement. The priorities of improvement are "provision of better facilities in the housing units", "promptness of the service" and "Careful repairs by avoiding damage to the assets". It can be seen that these aspects are slightly low in satisfaction scores and with little effort towards improvement can yield higher satisfaction levels. These results, to some extent, corroborate the findings of the GAP analysis to some extent which has brought out that the Tangibles, Responsiveness and Reliability attributes of the department needs strengthening. It can also be seen that the department is relatively strong in the factors like the courtesy, technical knowledge and overall competence of the officers and to some extent in the hours of operations. The area which has little significance on the satisfaction levels is "pleasant and neat appearance of the maintenance staff". "Delivery of promise made", "being kept informed of the status of complaint pending arrival of stores", "follow through to see if client got what s/he needed" and "cleaning up after completion of job and disposal of waste" also fall in the same quadrant, but these aspects are marginally low on importance but substantially low in satisfaction scores and require concerted

efforts for improvement in order to achieve higher satisfaction levels. The areas where MES seems to have deployed more resources are the hours of service i.e., flexibility of service and the specifications of the work done. The quadrant analysis thus clearly brings out the areas or the factors for improvement and MES can chalk out plan of action to improve the satisfaction and quality of the service rendered.

The analysis of data to a large extent corroborates the findings of gap analysis and also provides valuable inputs to formulate priorities for improvement and for optimum deployment of resources available with the organisation.

SUMMARY OF FINDINGS

The findings based on data analyses and their interpretations are listed below. The first observation that could be made is that the marketing concept (i.e., the philosophy that organisational goal attainment depends on understanding the needs and wants of the target market i.e., those of clients, and meeting those needs more efficiently and effectively), as opposed to the production or product concepts, has not been embraced by MES. The clients have rated MES officials very high in their technical and procedural competence, on their approachability as well as on courtesy and manners. The satisfaction levels are also significantly good in the area of specifications/facilities provided by MES in office/OTM (Other than Married) accommodation and also about convenience of working hours of maintenance units of service provider. The strength in these areas does not however reflect in attainment of the underlying organisational goal of user satisfaction. The results of the survey indicate that service delivery is much below the clients' expectations. Successful management of service quality requires regular feedback on what customers expect, and how clients' perceptions of service compare with their expectations. Some of the findings based on data analysis are:

Figure 7. Satisfaction-importance matrix

		Importance	
		Low	High
Satisfaction (Performance)	High	**Unnecessary strengths/ Surplus resources deployment** - Hours of service (e.g. maintenance) - Specifications of the work done	**Current organization strengths** - The MES staff should show his identity to users before providing the service. - Pleasant telephone manners and timeliness of the response to telephonic complaint or messages. - Technical and procedural knowledge of the staff. - Courtesy and guidance provided by the service providers. - Facilities provided in the office units - The officers are easily approachable, listen to you, assess your need and are helpful.
	Low	**Low Priority** -Pleasant and neat appearance of the maintenance staff. -Delivery of promise made and/or being kept informed of the status of your complaint pending arrival of stores. - The follow through to see if you got what you needed. -Cleaning up after completion of job and disposal of waste.	**Attributes that need attention – priorities of improvement** -Facilities provided in the housing units -Promptness of the service - Careful repairs by avoiding damage to the assets.

- The three service quality dimensions identified for improvement in the order of priority are Tangibles, Responsiveness and Reliability.

- The overall mean satisfaction score works out to 3.047 (marginally higher than 3.0 on a scale of 1-5) indicating that the clients in general are just satisfied with the services provided.

- Approximately 56% clients are satisfied with MES services (including 19% in highly satisfied category)

- Mean Expectation score (5.08) is lower when compared to similar surveys for service industry firms in private sector.

- Expectation levels of two clients groups were almost similar but the perception of service quality was significantly higher in one group. About 72% of the Air Force clients are satisfied vis-à-vis only 43% in case of Army.

- Satisfaction level based on P-E gap is significantly higher in young clients as well as among senior clients (those above 40 yrs) compared to the middle aged clients.

- Education level seems to be influencing the satisfaction level with higher satisfaction levels prevailing among graduates and higher qualified clients compared to others.

- Most of the clients coming from a field posting have expressed dissatisfaction with services being provided by service provider, indicating higher expectation levels after serving in field areas.

- 84% of the clients residing in single accommodation are satisfied with the services. The satisfaction level in respect of facilities provided in OTM accommodation is also higher than that with residential accommodation.

- 53% of clients living in residential quarters expressed their dissatisfaction with services. Coupled with the observation that most of the clients have expressed their dissatisfaction with facilities in housing units, it translates into urgent requirement of increased emphasis on improving specifications for married quarters.

- No significant difference was observed between clients of different rank, gender or the background

- The clients are generally happy about technical and procedural knowledge, approachability, courtesy and helping tendency of officers from MES.

- The clients however are not so happy about cleaning up the site after completion of job, disposal of waste and with the appearance of the maintenance staff. Incidentally these aspects have not been given high importance.

- The clients give significantly high importance to prompt service and most of them have expressed dissatisfaction in this regard. The clients also give high importance to careful repairs by tradesmen without damage to the existing assets. Whereas this sounds logical and a very genuine expectation, the satisfaction level is very low in this regard.

CONCLUSION

The analysis of the customer satisfaction data from clients of MES has thrown up very useful information for the service deliverance. The service quality dimensions which prominently run through all the departments for improvements are the Tangibles, Responsiveness and Reliability factors. The service provider was found to be short in these dimensions and therefore needs to put in more efforts and find ways and means for improving them. The improvement of these factors will therefore contribute significantly towards the satisfaction levels of the client. Overall improvement is required on Tangibles, Responsiveness and Reliability.

The units from whom the responses were collected were broadly classified into two major groups for the purpose of data analysis depending on the nature of their duties and the service requirements particular to their organisation. The survey and analysis of the responses from these different groups brought out similar level of expectations but differences in level of perceptions about services. The result demonstrated that no two groups of clients could be treated in the same way when being served for their infrastructure needs. This also gives valuable inputs and insights as to why one group exhibited better perceptions compared to the other. The analysis of data also provides valuable inputs to formulate priorities for improvement and for optimum deployment of resources available with the organisation.

Understanding expectations and perceptions is important as it seems to have a significant impact on the overall satisfaction of the clients. The present survey was conducted during 2008 and is limited to clients belonging to two organisations of defence ministry located at Bangalore. There is scope for working on how services compare across other client groups' and to learn lessons from better performing groups. Further longitudinal research on similar lines could also be used to track change over time, given the differences and changes in the expectations. Expectations indices could be constructed to explore the results. Repeated surveys at reasonable intervals of time can be used to benchmark progress of the services over time.

REFERENCES

Administrative Reforms Commission. (2007). *Ethics in governance*. Retrieved December 14, 2009, from http://darpg.nic.in/arpg-website/4tReport-EthicsinGov.pdf

Babakus, E., & Boller, W. G. (1992). An empirical assessment of the SERVQUAL scale. *Journal of Business Research, 24*(3), 253–268. doi:10.1016/0148-2963(92)90022-4

Bateson, J. E. G. (1995). *Managing services marketing: Text and reading* (3rd ed.). Chicago: The Dryden Press.

Bens, C. K. (1994). Effective citizen involvement: How to make it happen. *National Civic Review*, *83*(1), 32–39. doi:10.1002/ncr.4100830107

Carman, J. M. (1990). Consumer perceptions of service quality: An assessment of the SERVQUAL dimensions. *Journal of Retailing*, *66*(1), 33–55.

Chronbach, L. J. (1951). Coefficient Alpha and the internal structure of tests. *Psychometrika*, *16*(3), 297–334. doi:10.1007/BF02310555

Curry, A. (1999). Innovation in public service management. *Managing Service Quality*, *9*(3), 180–190. doi:10.1108/09604529910267082

Dinsdale, G., & Marsden, B. (1999). *Citizen/client surveys: Dispelling myths and redrawing maps*. Ottawa, Canada: Draft, Canadian Centre for Management Development.

Donnelly, M., Wisniewski, M., Dalrymple, J. F., & Curry, A. C. (1995). Measuring service quality in local government: The SERVQUAL approach. *International Journal of Public Sector Management*, *8*(7), 15–20. doi:10.1108/09513559510103157

Dutka, A. (1994). *AMA handbook for customer satisfaction*. Evanston, Illinois: NTC Business Books.

Farquhar, C. R. (1993). Focusing on the customer. *Canadian Business Review*, *20*(4), 1–14.

Grönroos, C. (1984). A service quality model and its marketing implications. *European Journal of Marketing*, *18*(4), 36–44. doi:10.1108/EUM0000000004784

Grönroos, C. (1990). Relationship approach to marketing in service contexts: The marketing and organizational behaviour interface. *Journal of Business Research*, *20*(1), 3–11. doi:10.1016/0148-2963(90)90037-E

Hoxley, M. (1998). *The impact of competitive fee tendering on construction professional service quality (RICS Research Findings No. 24)*. London: Royal Institute of Chartered Surveyors.

Joshi, A. P. (2006). *Customer satisfaction in Central Public Works Department*. Unpublished post-graduate dissertation, Indian Institute of Management Bangalore, India.

Kettl, D. F. (2002). The transformation of governance: Public administration for twenty-first century [Baltimore, MD: JHU Press.]. *America*, 69–72.

Kotler, P. (2000). *Marketing management: The millennium edition* (6th ed.). Upper Saddle River, NJ: Prentice-Hall.

Lee, H., Lee, Y., & Yoo, D. (2000). The determinants of perceived service quality and its relationship with satisfaction. *Journal of Services Marketing*, *14*(3), 217–231. doi:10.1108/08876040010327220

Likert, R. (1932). A technique for the measurement of attitudes. *Archives de Psychologie*, *22*(140), 1–55.

Love, P., Smith, J., Treloar, G., & Li, H. (2000). Some empirical observations of service quality in construction. *Engineering, Construction, and Architectural Management*, *7*(2), 191–201. doi:10.1108/eb021144

McDonnell, J., & Gatfield, T. (1998). SERVQUAL as a cultural change agent in the Australian public sector. In *Proceedings of the Australian and New Zealand Marketing Academy Conference* (pp. 1528-1539).

Nunnally, J. C. (1978). *Psychometric theory* (2nd ed.). New York: McGraw-Hill.

Parasuraman, A., Zeithaml, V. A., & Berry, L. L. (1985). A conceptual model of service quality and its implications for future research. *Journal of Marketing*, *49*(4), 41–50. doi:10.2307/1251430

Parasuraman, A., Zeithaml, V. A., & Berry, L. L. (1988). SERVQUAL: A multiple item scale for measuring consumer perceptions of service quality. *Journal of Retailing, 64*(1), 12–40.

Parasuraman, A., Zeithaml, V. A., & Berry, L. L. (1991). Refinement and reassessment of the SERVQUAL scale. *Journal of Retailing, 67*(4), 420–450.

Paul, S., Balakrishnan, S., Gopalkumar, K., Shekhar, S., & Vivekananda, M. (2004). State of India's public services: Benchmarks for the states. *Economic and Political Weekly, 39*(9), 920–933.

Review, M. O. R. I. (2002). *Public service reforms: Measuring and understanding customer satisfaction*. London: MORI social Research Institute.

Schmidt, F., & Strickland, T. (1998). *Client satisfaction surveying: Common measurements tool*. Ottawa, Canada: Canadian Centre for Management Development.

Skelcher, C. (1992). Improving the quality of local public services. *Service Industries Journal, 12*(4), 463–477. doi:10.1080/02642069200000059

Streiner, D. L., & Norman, G. R. (1989). *Health measurement scales: A practical guide to their development and use*. New York: Oxford University Press, Inc.

Wan, S. G. K., Bridge, A., & Skitmore, M. (2001). Assessing the service quality of building maintenance providers, mechanical and engineering services. *Construction Management and Economics, 19*(7), 719–726. doi:10.1080/01446190110062104

Yang, C.-C. (2003). Establishment and applications of the integrated model of service quality measurement. *Managing Service Quality, 13*(4), 310–324. doi:10.1108/09604520310484725

Zeithaml, V. A., Berry, L. L., & Parasuraman, A. (1993). The nature and determinants of customer expectations of service. *Journal of the Academy of Marketing Science, 21*(1), 1–12. doi:10.1177/0092070393211001

Zeithaml, V. A., Parasuraman, A., & Berry, L. L. (1990). *Delivering quality service: Balancing customer perceptions and expectations*. New York: The Free Press, McMillan, Inc.

This work was previously published in International Journal of Information Systems in the Service Sector, Volume 2, Issue 3, edited by John Wang, pp. 53-73, copyright 2010 by IGI Publishing (an imprint of IGI Global).

Chapter 16
Service Registry Design:
An Information Service Approach

Luís Ferreira Pires
University of Twente, The Netherlands

Arjen van Oostrum
University of Twente, The Netherlands

Fons Wijnhoven
University of Twente, The Netherlands & Wilhelms University of Muenster, Germany

ABSTRACT

A service registry is a Service-Oriented Architecture (SOA) component that keeps a 'catalogue' of available services. It stores service specifications so that these specifications can be found by potential users. Discussions on the design of service registries currently focus on technical issues, while service registries should take into consideration information needs of business domain users. In this regard, the authors consider service registries as information services and develop a comprehensive framework for designing service registries. This framework introduces aspects that determine a design space for service registries. In this design space, the authors identify views, requirements, processes, and means in the design of a service registry that supports the lifecycle information of a service. A vital part of these requirements is further implemented and demonstrated in a prototype built as a 'proof-of-concept' for the framework. This paper also discusses a case study used to evaluate the prototype. In this case study, a registry prototype has been populated with realistic services of a large insurance company, and 21 experienced IT and business professionals from a consultancy organization evaluated the prototype for its user satisfaction.

DOI: 10.4018/978-1-4666-0044-7.ch016

Copyright © 2012, IGI Global. Copying or distributing in print or electronic forms without written permission of IGI Global is prohibited.

INTRODUCTION

Service-Oriented Architecture (SOA) has been introduced with the promise that by offering functionality as services, business processes supported by these services can be more easily composed and executed (Papazoglou, 2008). However, a successful SOA implementation depends on various factors, like a structured decomposition of processes into services, appropriate management support, and *SOA governance* (Mahajan, 2006). SOA governance offers the measuring and steering capabilities that help organizations reach the objectives of their SOA implementations. A particular aspect of SOA governance involves service offerings, which should comply with organizational policies and norms. An overview of the services available in an organization should be in place, in order to avoid redundant offering of services with similar or identical functionality, or offering of services that are not relevant for any business process. Service lifecycle information is valuable for service developers, owners and providers and should be supported by the registry.

In SOA, a service registry is an architectural component that enables a service provider to publish service descriptions and enables a service consumer to find services based on their descriptions (Alonso, Casati, Kuno, & Vijay, 2004). Consequently, a service registry is like a 'Yellow Pages for services'. Service registry implementations based on standards like UDDI and ebXML mainly store technical information on services by means of a flat data model with limited search capabilities (Luo, Montrose, Kim, Khashnobish, & Kang, 2006). Service registries developed according to these standards are mainly suitable for runtime service users, which are interested in interface definitions and the technologies to reach the service at runtime. However, service specifications are also supposed to be used by enterprise architects, application developers and business process engineers, amongst others (Li et al., 2009). These service registry users often need other sorts of information than runtime users, such as the service goals or business value, which correspond to meta-information about the service (Ran, 2003). Furthermore, this information is meant to be understandable for (non-technical) human users, as opposed to the more technical information supported nowadays (Samavi, Yu, & Topaloglou, 2009).

The work reported in this paper has been motivated by the opportunities offered by service registries with respect to SOA governance once these registries are properly designed, and the need to improve the methods available to design these registries.

This paper provides a framework to design and implement service registries for storing, managing and disclosing service specifications. This requires a design that addresses both the technological and business means necessary to implement service registries that are more suitable to support SOA governance than the service registries available today. We consider a service registry as a special case of an information service, which transfers information goods from suppliers to consumers. We define a design space consisting of aspects (content, use features and revenue) and layers (design problem, business, process, infrastructure, prototyping and exploitation) that are relevant for developing effective information services (Wijnhoven & Kraaijenbrink, 2008).

We consider service registries as information services in order to enhance the satisfaction of the consumers of service specifications. We test the validity of our framework by:

1. Assessing the feasibility of designing useful service registers with this framework. Other approaches could be used for designing service registers, but we believe that by considering service registries as information services we can obtain registries that offer the highest value for their users. This is because the service design theory forces the designer to systematically include the actual

business requirements in the service registry design and to consider the actual value of the information goods (service specifications) that a service registry is expected to deliver to its users.

2. Assessing the relevance of this approach by solving a concrete real life problem with a service registry in a case study. This is achieved by building a service registry prototype as a proof-of-concept that supports part of the aspects covered in our framework.

3. Performing a utility test in which registry users provide feedback by scoring their user satisfaction with the service registry prototype.

These steps correspond to the generate-test cycle of (Hevner, March, & Park, 2004), as shown in Figure 1.

Furthermore, we evaluate our results against design science guidelines of Hevner et al. (2004), such as artifact construction (we define a design methodology and build a concrete service registry), relevance (we address real-life problems) and utility (we test our results). We also contribute to design foundations by providing design constructs for service registries as information services.

This paper presents our design methodology, and illustrates the steps of this methodology, start-

ing from the definition of business requirements and ending at the construction and evaluation of a service registry prototype in a case study. Therefore, the paper is further structured as follows: 'Design Methodology' describes our design methodology, by introducing a design space for service registries. 'Business Requirements' discusses business requirements from the stakeholders of a service registry. 'Process Requirements' discusses process requirements of interest for actors of the service registry processes. 'Infrastructure and Prototype Design' introduces the overall architecture of a service registry, and discusses the choices made in our prototype design and implementation. 'Exploitation and Evaluation' discusses the results of our case study, and 'Conclusion' gives conclusions and suggestions for future work.

DESIGN METHODOLOGY

Design Space

Three aspects should be considered in the design of an information service: the delivery of content to the user and all associated functions (e.g., content acquisition and aggregation), the delivery of use features for a better use and value experience of

Figure 1. Our research approach in terms of design science (Adapted from Hevner et al., 2004)

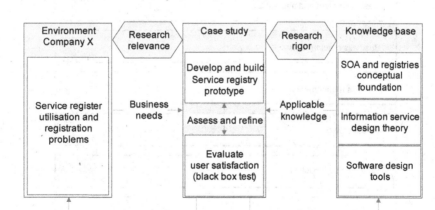

the delivered information good, and the stream of revenues to be realized for the information service to be viable for the content owners and information service providers (Wijnhoven, 2008). In order to support these aspects, we analyze them at different layers. The top layer addresses 'why' the information service should be used ('Design problem and agenda'), the subsequent layers cover 'what' is needed to support the information service ('Business requirements' and 'Process requirements'), and the bottom layer addresses 'how' to design an infrastructure to support it ('Infrastructure'). The infrastructure layer does not only comprise the design of the IT infrastructure such as databases and networking, but also the structuring of employee tasks and tools to support these tasks. However, if we apply only these layers we may obtain a working information service, but for a successful and enduring system we should also consider the construction of a prototype ('Prototype construction') and its exploitation and evaluation for suitability ('Exploitation and evaluation') as explicit design layers.

Figure 2 depicts the resulting design space, which consists of the three aspects, supported by the six layers. Figure 2 shows that eighteen blocks are formed by the crossings of the six rows (layers) and three colored columns (aspects), which indicate the areas that have to be addressed when designing an information service.

Each design, for each type of information service and its instances, is likely to be different from others, due to its particular context. Therefore, it is difficult to prescribe any specific order in which the blocks of Figure 2 should be considered. Top-down, bottom-up and middle-out strategies can be used, as long as the results for each block remain aligned, i.e., they do not contradict each other and the results are mutually supportive.

Content

The content of an information service is some information good, supplemented with some optional information (supportive information or meta-information). In general it is difficult to match these digital goods exactly with the user's demand, since the shear volume of variation options for digital information goods makes it hard to present the user with a limited number of choices. An information service has therefore the task of reducing the amount of possible information good

Figure 2. Design space for information services (Adapted from Wijnhoven, 2008)

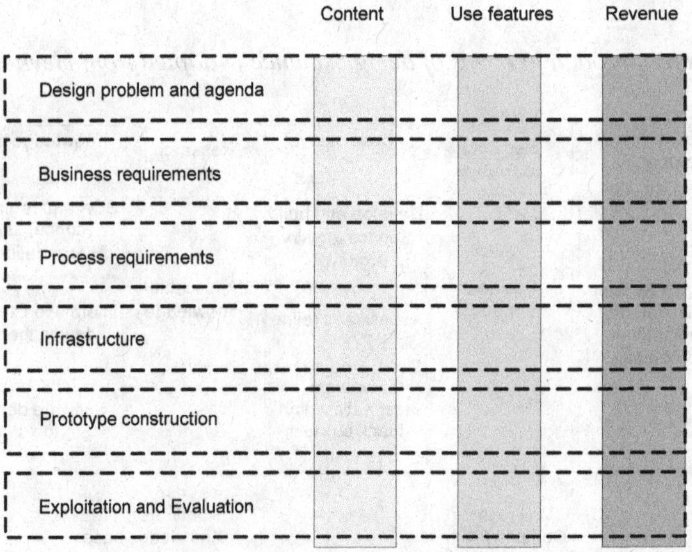

variations to present meaningful and intelligible information to the user.

An information service may transform the information good in order to meet the user's request by delivering just what the user needs. It can do so by altering two dimensions of an information good, namely the Level of Representation (LoR, i.e., the percentage of coverage of all the data that can be delivered) and the Level of Conceptualization (LoC, i.e., the abstraction level of what is delivered, varying from elementary data to theoretical models). By increasing or decreasing either or both levels, the information good can be 'customized' to meet the user's needs.

Since we consider a service registry as an information service, the information good in this case consists of service specifications. The service specification in a service registry can be characterized as process information, in that it can be used to compose business processes. The use of accepted standards can help achieving high quality, and is a prerequisite for exchanging process information (Van der Aalst & Kumar, 2003), which implies that service specifications should be described systematically, preferably by using generally accepted rules or standards. Service specifications should contain both runtime and design-time information, with added supportive information. Not every specification detail is useful for every user, and therefore the LoR can be decreased to present the information that matches the needs of each specific user. For example, some users may only get the interface description as the result of a query. Additionally, the LoC can increase by giving users meta-information in addition to descriptions of how the service specification is used in other situations.

Use Features

Use features can be provided by the information service in order to increase value experience, from which user satisfaction is an important factor. Use features may consist of additional content interaction options, such as advanced search options and extra information about the content. An information service can become more attractive to potential users if it provides use features.

In case of competing service registries that provide the same information good, the support to use features can make a difference for the users to actually use a certain registry. In this paper, for the sake of simplicity we only consider service registries in a single organization or in a network of cooperating organizations. Use features like credibility or quality evaluations of former users can be helpful to decide whether or not to use an information service, but they are not so relevant when the users are obliged to use the service registries of their organization (or organization network), which is the situation considered in this work.

However, since we have aimed to design service registries with a high end-user satisfaction, some use features have been considered in our framework. Examples are help functions to formulate search queries, and the delivery of alternative results, possibly ranked according to their suitability.

Revenue

Although the digital nature of an information good makes distribution inexpensive, costs have to be made in order to create, maintain and provide the information good. In the case of a service registry, the quality of the service specifications has been identified as a key factor, which implies that the maintenance of the service specifications requires extra (human) attention. Revenue streams have to be created to cover the costs of both the service providers and of the organization supporting the service registry. In the case of service registries, information is transparent, in the sense that service specifications should be sampled by service providers, repeatedly used by registry consumers, and their value can be tested once they are acquired. Furthermore, service specifications are meant to generate social benefit in the organization or organization network. According to Womack (2002), since we expect many consumers and relatively few service registries, subsidy and a non-profit organizational unit is required to cope with revenue. However, the consumers still have to pay somehow for their use of the registry in order to create a revenue source to financially support the registry. Possible payment models can be based on subscriptions or on the actual use of the service registry. Payments can be enabled by the actual consumer or sponsor.

BUSINESS REQUIREMENTS

The service registry, as an information service, has several stakeholders. We identified four main stakeholders in an organization with respect to the service registry: *registry consumers*, *service providers*, *organization managers*, and *system and information maintainers*. These stakeholders should have a positive attitude towards the service registry, acknowledge its added-value, and have to be aligned with the goals of the service registry. Assuming these conditions hold, in the sequel we discuss the requirements of the service registry for the business layer for each stakeholder, and we present a value exchange model that considers the contents and revenue aspects of a service registry.

Consumer

Consumers are the end-users of the service registry. These may be people in an organization, or an application or software agent. These users have different demands for information, and therefore we distinguish between them. First, the registry can be used at design-time, where primarily meta-information (e.g., information about the service goals and intended usage) is requested. In this case, our design approach focuses on this (human) end-user. Second, users at runtime have a demand for primarily technical data. To capture

both technical and business aspects of a service from the viewpoint of the different sorts of consumers, we adapt the seven specification levels for business components identified in Fettke and Loos (2003), as shown in Figure 3.

Figure 3 represents the information needs of the design-time service registry end-users, and since the interface level is included, also the needs of the runtime users are covered. These levels are the core information for design-time and runtime reuse of services. The terminology level describes concepts and elements that are used at all levels. The terminology level does not add any specific information to a service specification, but aims at avoiding ambiguity by defining concepts and terms in a structured and consistent way.

Provider

The service provider can be an organization, organizational unit, or any other entity providing some information good. Service registries provide service specifications as information goods, with the purpose of enabling the use of these services by others. Services have a lifecycle as any other IT system, and this lifecycle should be observed

Figure 3. Levels of service specification (Adapted from Fettke & Loos, 2003)

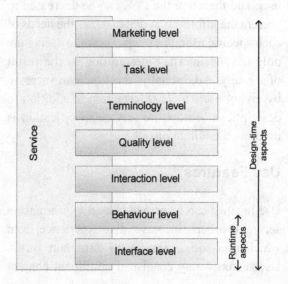

Figure 4. Service lifecycle

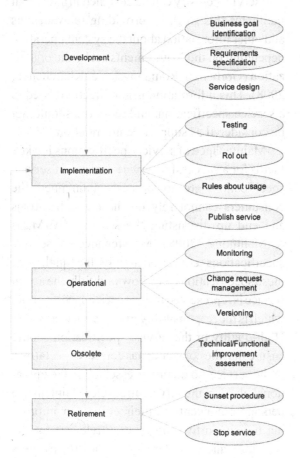

in order to keep the service useful and fit to the overall system architecture. Service providers have the responsibility of maintaining these services according to the service lifecycle.

Figure 4 depicts a service lifecycle in which the service lifecycle descriptions of Afshar (2007) and Larsen and Wilber (2005) are combined. Each lifecycle phase consists of various activities and to perform these activities the service stakeholders need information from earlier activities. For example, the testing activity needs information that has been stored in the service design phase.

A service registry can hold information on the status of the services with respect to their lifecycle. A service specification can be published in the registry already at the beginning of the development phase and can record all relevant informa-

tion for this and the subsequent phases. Lifecycle information at this point should capture the purpose for the development of this service. The stakeholders involved in the service lifecycle can use the service registry to retrieve information, supporting in this way their different information needs. Changes in business needs or technical developments may cause changes in the service (Bose & Suumaran, 2006). During its lifecycle, a service may change quite often, which may improve the value of the service for its users. Before being changed, a service may be evaluated to determine whether the change effort is justifiable. The service registry can support the service lifecycle by providing information not only about the status of a service, but also its change requests or historical change data (Belter, 2008). Service lifecycle management requires supportive information that is directly linked to a specific service, but does not contain any usage information.

Management

The management of an organization is responsible for positioning the service registry in the organization. Management can also take the role of a financial sponsor of the service registry, for example, when the organization elicits and charges all costs through an (internal) cost model. Analogously to application governance in an application portfolio, services can be governed in a service portfolio, allowing managers to measure and steer them. The knowledge on available and popular services in an organization gives the ability to minimize the costs of inefficient services usage, caused by having redundant services and services that are not used at all (Yu, Liu, Bouguettaya, & Medjahed, 2008).

Ideally, all services that are bought or developed should comply with standards, so that their integration in the overall architecture can be facilitated (Bose & Suumaran, 2006). Services should all be published, so that they can be readily found and made available for use. They should be effectively used, so that no unused services are maintained, they should have no redundant functions, so that no extra costs are made to support duplicated functionality, and they should be used under optimal contracts, for example, by offering discounts on the costs per invocation to frequent users. The service registry can be the central place where the information necessary to steer the IT support is stored. This information consists of contracts, service status, service consumers and standards, to name just a few (Li et al., 2009). Along with organizational policies, the readily availability of this information is essential to optimize the service portfolio and minimize costs. The portfolio information related to a service specification is considered to be supportive information (Winkler, Cardoso, & Scheithauer, 2008).

Furthermore, management is normally also interested in information about the use of the service registry itself, especially in case the users of the service registry have to pay for accessing its functionality. This usage information is not directly linked to a certain service specification and is called coordination information. It typically consists of the number of users and the costs related to the use of the service registry.

Maintenance

Maintenance can be divided in maintenance of the service registry as an information system, and maintenance of the service specifications stored in the registry. The technical contents of the service specifications are the responsibility of the service provider, so that here we only consider generic mechanisms for enhancing the quality of these specifications.

Service registry system maintenance concerns processes for functional, application and exploitation management of the service registry software system. The organization in which the service registry is implemented should have proper structures to perform these maintenance tasks.

The service registry can be designed in a way that facilitates this work by providing relevant logs and other information about the system operation depending on the requirements set by the organization (Gorbenko, Romanovsky, & Kharchenko, 2008). This information is not directly related to a service specification, and therefore should not be considered as supportive information.

Maintenance of service specifications is a key factor for a successful service registry. If service specifications are not properly maintained, the consumers cannot rely on these specifications and end up distrusting the services (Al-Masri & Mahmoud, 2008). Maintenance of service specifications concerns mainly the quality of these specifications, i.e., how faithfully the actual service is represented by the service specification, which is the responsibility of the service provider. High-quality of the service specification should ensure that the consumer has correct expectations of the service, so quality is essential in the operational phase in the service lifecycle. Maintenance personnel concentrate their efforts on improving the supportive information relevant for the consumer and provider views. The effectiveness of the service discoveries should be monitored and analyzed in order to improve the matching of service requests to service specifications, and ultimately the services they represent. By assessing the way users search for information, the service specification maintenance can improve the discovery of service specifications.

The terminology level presented in Figure 3 describes terms of the service specification as used at the other levels. These terms can be combined and used to create a domain ontology for service discovery. This ontology can be used for improving search and determining the relevance of a search query result (Verma et al., 2005).

Value Exchange Model

At the business layer we can define the values that are exchanged between stakeholders through the service registry in order to satisfy these stakeholders. The intended interactions with the service registry have been considered to generate requirements for the service registry at this layer. User satisfaction should be enough for the service registry to be used even without obligatory regulations in the organization. A value exchange can refer to the content, use feature, or revenue aspects, and it specifies which values are delivered by a stakeholder in return to other values. The specific realization of these exchanges is ignored at this layer, and is considered at the process layer. Value exchanges between the stakeholders can be modeled, for example, by the e3value technique of Gordijn and Akkermans (2001). In addition to the stakeholders who are directly involved in the exchange of content, the revenue aspect imposes that some form of sponsorship is needed, so that it should also be modeled.

Different alternatives can be chosen when defining value exchanges. For instance, we may have different choices for organizing sponsorship. Figure 5 shows one possible e3value model for the service registry, which consists of a high-level scenario in which the sponsor (possibly the man-

agement of the organization) directly subsidizes the service registry. In a more detailed model, the value exchanges can be further specified, and internal value exchanges can also be modeled.

Figure 5 shows four value exchanges supported by the service registry: (i) the service provider provides a service specification to the service registry, which should pay for the specification in return; (ii) a runtime user can initiate a value exchange in which (some part of) a technical specification is obtained in exchange for a specification fee; (iii) an end-user can pay a specification fee and gets several value objects in return, and (iv) a sponsor can pay for (part of) the specification fee, for instance, in return for feedback and visibility, or to increase the chance that the registry is used by consumers in case these customers are reluctant to use the registry. The service registry offers various use features and search assistance to help the end-user retrieve the (design) service specification. The service registry then delivers a specification, which is the core value of the service registry, i.e., the task of the service registry is to deliver the specification as efficiently as possible. To deliver the specification

Figure 5. High-level e3value model for a service registry

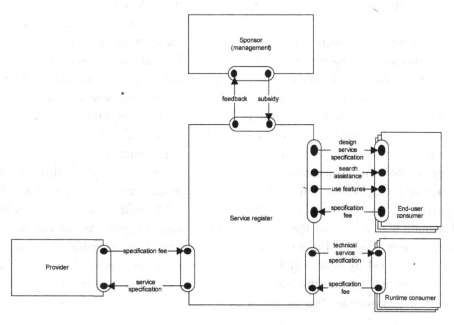

and meet the expectations of its users, the specification should be complete, of high quality and faithfully represent the actual service.

PROCESS REQUIREMENTS

At the process layer, we define the activities for delivering content, facilitating content usage, and handling usage costs and revenues, in contrast with the business layer which ignores all information service internal activities. Requirements for the process layer activities are discussed below by focusing on the interactions with the end-users.

Content Delivery

A service registry delivers service specifications to consumers. In order to perform this task, the service registry aggregates and stores the available service specifications. In order to process a request, the service registry should not perform any interactions with the service provider or other actors. Therefore, the service registry should have stored all the content necessary to answer a request of an end-user before the request is issued. The delivery of results can be customized to meet the request of a human end-user, for instance, by altering the level of representation (LoR). In this case, the service registry does not deliver the entire available service specification, but makes a selection of the available information for the end-user instead. When possible, it can also alter the level of conceptualization (LoC) by delivering fewer details and giving information at a higher abstraction level, like application domain information.

During publication, the information good content (service specification) is delivered by the service provider to the service registry. The end-users demand a high quality of the service specification to achieve a high end-user satisfaction, which is determined by how faithful the service specification represents the actual service. Therefore, before the service specification (or an updated version of this specification) is added to the content base, a series of activities have to be performed on the service specification to ensure that the content meets the quality standards set by the service registry.

Use Facilitation

Along with the content, use features are delivered to positively influence the factors that lead to a high end-user satisfaction. Factors that lead to end-user satisfaction are content, accuracy, format, ease of use and timeliness (Doll & Torkzadeh, 1988). The following requirements can be formulated with respect to these factors:

- Content: the service registry has to deliver the precise information needed by the users. Therefore, the needs of the users have to be determined, e.g., by helping the users formulate their information needs.
- Accuracy: accurate delivery consists of presenting the best matching service specification(s) to the users. The service registry can increase the accuracy by providing alternatives to the users. Using ontologies, the service registry could determine the relevance of the presented results and suggest other specifications which are close enough to the presented ones.
- Format: the presented results should be shown in a clear and useful format. The service registry can assist in this by increasing usability, e.g., by providing different formats so the user can choose the appropriate one. A possibility is to offer the same information in different formats, e.g., in documents using formats like HTML, XML, PDF, MS Excel or MS Word.
- Ease of use: ease of use is increased by providing user-friendly interfaces with help functions and the use of standard information presentation.

- Timeliness: timeliness is influenced by different issues. The technical issue determines the speed at which a request is processed and a response is delivered by the service registry system. The delivery speed is subject to the available processing power, and speed of the computing and networking system. Another issue is the freshness of the service specifications, i.e., whether specifications are still valid or are outdated. While the technical issue can be influenced in the development and deployment of the service registry system, information freshness can be preserved by applying proper maintenance procedures. For example, the service registry system can assign a time-to-live to service specifications, and when the time-to-live of a service specification expires, maintenance personnel can be asked to check whether the specification is still valid or should be updated or removed.

By addressing some of these factors simultaneously when the content is delivered we expect that the experienced value of the content can be enriched.

Handling of Usage Costs and Revenues

The way subsidy is granted, i.e., which revenue model is chosen, determines how the usage costs can be handled. The billing strategies to be used can be a flat-fee subscription or pay-per-unit. Other approaches to cover usage costs (e.g., advertisement, syndication, additional merchandise, pay-per-data-packet) are based upon an open market for content delivery, which is not applicable to most SOA contexts and the setting we consider in this paper. Functional requirements to handle usage costs can be to check the subscription status of the end-users before granting access to the system.

Process Model

Figure 6 shows a process model that incorporates the process requirements described above. It assumes that the maintenance of a service specification is part of the service registry unit.

The actor roles that can be played by the stakeholders and that are relevant in this process have been drawn on the borders of Figure 6. The part of the model that corresponds to each role is indicated with striped lines. Dotted lines indicate a stream of information, while a solid line depicts a process step, possibly containing information elements. More detailed process steps can be drawn by zooming in on process elements. This process model only shows the delivery of content by providers and to consumers. Other processes (involving other stakeholders) could be represented in a similar way.

INFRASTRUCTURE AND PROTOTYPE DESIGN

Figure 2 shows the infrastructure layer immediately below the process requirements layer. The infrastructure layer deals with the mechanisms necessary to support the processes. Since we aim at creating an effective design for a service registry, we consider that a design is effective when it satisfies the end-user in his/her information needs. For this we used the five factors of Doll and Torkzadeh (1988) (content, accuracy, format, ease of use and timeliness) as our main design focus. Below we discuss the means to realize the processes related to the service registry, we introduce our overall architecture, and we present our prototype.

Realization Means

The processes we identified for the service registry (content delivery, use facilitation and handling of usage costs) can be realized using information, technical and organizational means. These means

Figure 6. Process activities chart

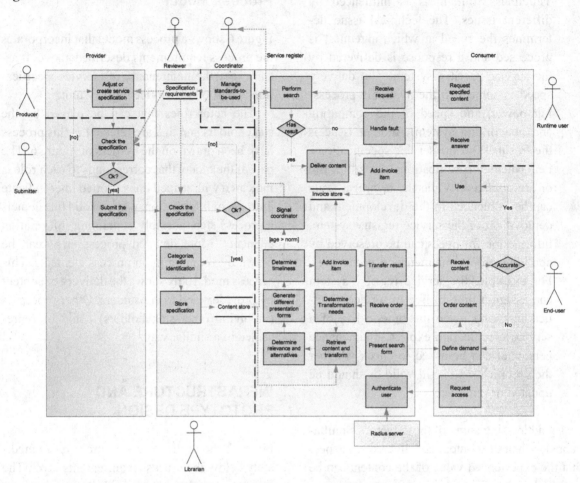

support these processes, and can be identified by systematically investigating what is necessary for each of these processes.

Processes need information to perform tasks for the service registry. Information means consist of the available and accessible data, and mechanisms to allow data to be provided, i.e., the organization of this data and resources, and the management of data freshness (Wijnhoven & Kraaijenbrink, 2008). Technological means are necessary to facilitate the activities of the service registry. Organizational means consist of lists of responsibilities, assignment of tasks and coordination principles. Furthermore, an organization unit can be created to carry the responsibility for the service registry. Table 1 identifies information,

technological and organizational means for each main process, without trying to be comprehensive.

Prototype Construction

In order to evaluate the users' satisfaction with a service registry developed according to our framework; we developed a prototype by focusing on the functional requirements of the end-users, namely the main use case of 'searching for service specifications'. Performance and availability requirements are crucial for a system to be used in production, however, are less relevant when limited functionality is demonstrated in a prototype. The main goal of a service registry is to provide service specifications to human end-users. To be

Table 1. Information, technological and organizational means for the main processes

Process	Information means	Technological means	Organizational means
Content delivery	- List of available service specifications - Requirements for new services - Requirements for standards to use when creating a service specification - Checklists for checking the validity of service specification - Consumers requests - Consumers authentication - List of pending specifications - Information about information consumers needs - Structured data storage and retrieval - Contracts with providers - List of providers - Knowledge about consumer usage - Data models for efficient storage and retrieval	- Tool for syntax checking of service specification - Transformation tool for level of representation - Querying software - Interfaces for receiving content - Communication channel with providers and consumers - Databases to store specifications, requirements and invoices	- Service registry system programmers - Service registry system maintenance people - ICT services management to support client interactions - Providers network - End-user support - Coordinator to create/manage specification requirements - Procedures to add service specifications - Archiving procedures - Librarian - Database administration
Use facilitation	- Data about consumers needs - Supportive information database - Data models for retrieval - Mapping of consumers needs onto available data - Ontology data and relations - Relevance data - Modification date of service specification - Data about preferred user interfaces and possibilities - Links to supportive information (help functions) - Direct links between service specifications and supportive data	- Interfaces - Interactive search determination tool - Search system - Ontology searching mechanism - Data communication network - Presentation/customization tool - Database with feature information - Hard/software platform	- End-user support unit - Librarians to manage supportive information - Librarians to analyze system's usage to improve matching - Provide search and results options to clients - Create and maintain ontological links - Client feedback collection procedure
Costs and revenue management	- Contracts with consumers - Contracts with providers - Data delivery - Data reception - Subscription data	- Billing system - Subscription system - Usage logging system	- Providers ('account management') - Consumers - Sales administration - Contract management

able to provide the specification to the user, the system first needs to know what the user is looking for. From interview sessions with potential service registry users we have learned that the system should be able to search for specifications in different ways, for example, based on the service name or the function provided. The prototype should also assist the user with the formulation of the search question.

We built a prototype that searches available content looking for specifications that match a user query, and presents the results of the search action to the user. The user may further process the results, for example, by exploring the meaning of definitions or by retrieving extra information. The specification levels of a service are therefore presented to the user as additional information. Our prototype has a web interface that can be accessed via an ordinary web browser.

Our prototype was designed by considering the information, technological and organizational means presented in Table 1. Therefore, we defined the data structures for the prototype in a class diagram (information means), the data flows relating data to IT processes in a dataflow diagram (technological means) and the activities of the process for searching service specifications in an activity diagram (organizational means, especially end users support).

Figure 7 shows how the interactions between the consumer and the service registry of Figure 8 for searching service specifications can be refined.

At the beginning the user is expected to enter and submit a query, but can also choose to stop (arrow to the left from Activity 1.0). If the query

Figure 7. Activity diagram for the process of searching for service specifications

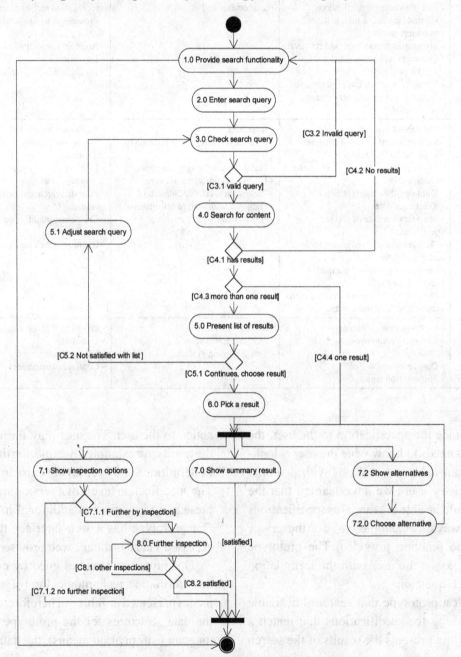

Figure 8. Data Flow Diagram for the 'Search design service specification' process

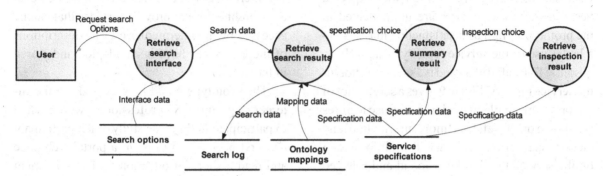

is invalid, the system ignores this query and waits for a new one. The number of returned results determines the next action of the system. If there are multiple results, the user is asked to choose from the list of result options. If there is only one result, the user does not have to choose and the system presents the result summary. If there are no results, the system returns to the initial state and waits for a new query. The search query can be adjusted in case the user is not satisfied with the returned list of results, after which the query is again checked for validity. However, when a result is chosen, the system shows simultaneously the result summary, further inspection options and alternatives. The process stops when the user is satisfied, but the user can also choose an inspection option, after which the result for that inspection is shown. This can be repeated while the alternatives and inspection options remain displayed.

Figure 8 shows a dataflow diagram that represents the data stores used to produce the search results. Some activities do not require any specific data in order to be supported, such as validity checks and user input actions, which may be performed without necessarily using data stores.

When a request for a search action is retrieved by the web server, the user interface for the search form is created. The search options presented to the user are derived from the appropriate data store. By configuring the data store, the service registry can adjust the options that are displayed.

The user submits the search data, and the process uses different data stores to generate the search results. Initially the search data is stored for future analysis. Matching service specifications are derived from the service specifications data store, and ontology mappings are used to determine the relevance of the results and alternatives. When a choice is made from the result list, the summary result for that specification is generated from the service specifications. When the user chooses to inspect the results further (additional information), the relevant specification data is retrieved.

Our prototype implements the process depicted in Figure 7 using the data stores shown in Figure 8. Due to page limitations we omit the class diagram that defines the data structures used in the prototype, which can be found in Van Oostrum (2008).

EXPLOITATION AND EVALUATION

We addressed the 'Exploitation and evaluation' layer of Figure 2 by testing our prototype in a case study. In this case study, we exposed our service registry prototype to experienced IT and business professionals from a consultancy organization, and asked for their opinion on the use of the prototype. We expected that the prototype based on the design as an information service should have a higher user satisfaction than average. An average user satisfaction is defined here as a score of 3 on a five-point scale for measuring user satisfaction.

User satisfaction above average was expected because some use features are implemented in the prototype. High user satisfaction may lead to a better use of the service registry system (Ives, Olson, & Baroudi, 1983), and is a success factor for the service registry. Figure 9 gives a screenshot of our prototype implementation. Some use features are shown on the left bar ('more information' and 'service suggestions'), along with the information on the service that has been found and selected (the Non-life.Endorsement service).

Settings

In the case study we have used descriptions of actual services implemented at the insurance company. This company primarily sells insurances via intermediaries, and has decided to create an SOA architecture to provide services that can be accessed by the intermediaries. The descriptions of these services have been adapted and stored in the prototype.

The prototype could be accessed via the Internet. A group of 89 professionals were invited to participate in this case study. Each participant has first been asked to go to a portal web page and read a short introduction to the assignment before proceeding to the prototype. The participants should perform tasks with the prototype that reflect their actual information needs concerning the search for service information, as they experience in their daily work at the organization. After performing these tasks, each participant has been asked to fill out a short questionnaire to measure

Figure 9. Screenshot of our service registry prototype implementation

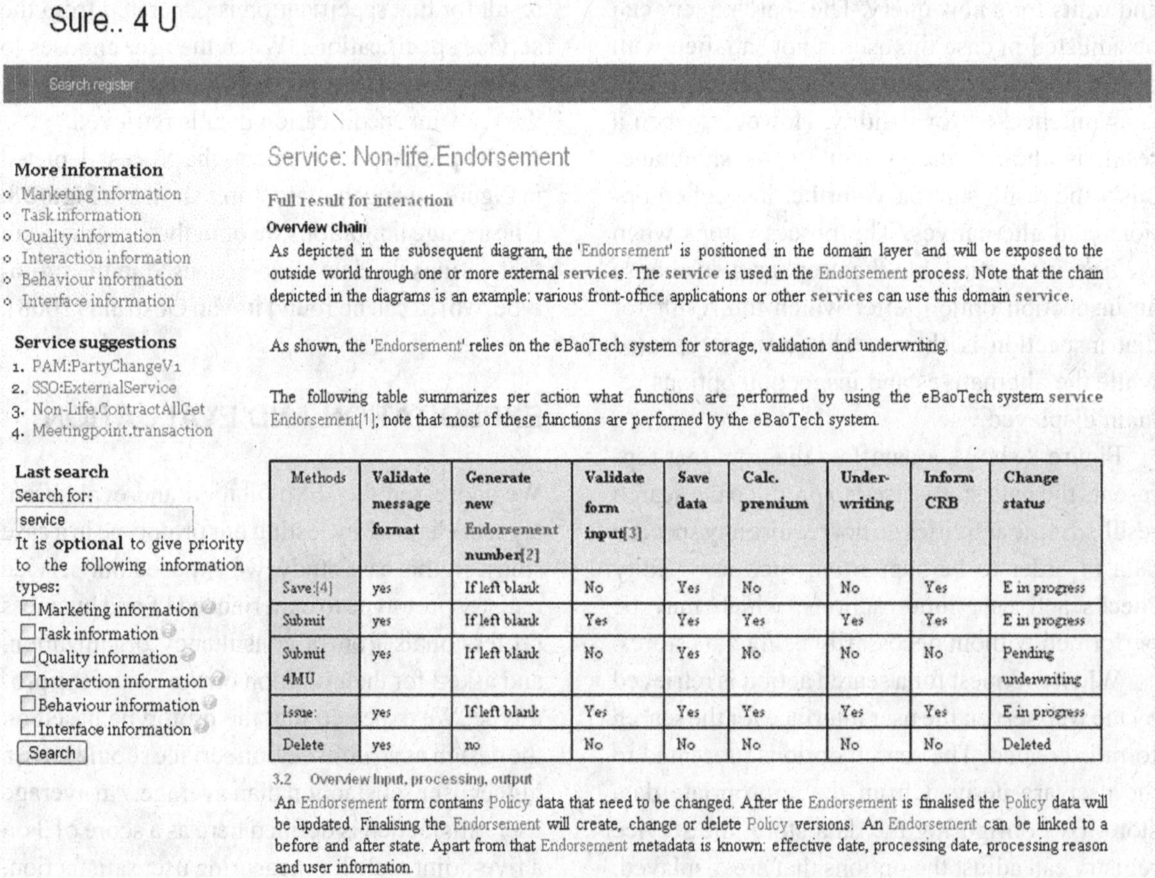

Sure.. 4 U

Search register

More information
○ Marketing information
○ Task information
○ Quality information
○ Interaction information
○ Behaviour information
○ Interface information

Service suggestions
1. PAM:PartyChangeV1
2. SSO:ExternalService
3. Non-Life.ContractAllGet
4. Meetingpoint.transaction

Last search
Search for:
service

It is **optional** to give priority to the following information types:
□ Marketing information
□ Task information
□ Quality information
□ Interaction information
□ Behaviour information
□ Interface information
Search

Service: Non-life.Endorsement

Full result for interaction
Overview chain
As depicted in the subsequent diagram, the 'Endorsement' is positioned in the domain layer and will be exposed to the outside world through one or more external services. The service is used in the Endorsement process. Note that the chain depicted in the diagrams is an example: various front-office applications or other services can use this domain service.

As shown, the 'Endorsement' relies on the eBaoTech system for storage, validation and underwriting.

The following table summarizes per action what functions are performed by using the eBaoTech system service Endorsement[1]; note that most of these functions are performed by the eBaoTech system.

Methods	Validate message format	Generate new Endorsement number[2]	Validate form input[3]	Save data	Calc. premium	Under-writing	Inform CRB	Change status
Save:[4]	yes	If left blank	No	Yes	No	No	Yes	E in progress
Submit	yes	If left blank	Yes	Yes	Yes	Yes	Yes	E in progress
Submit 4MU	yes	If left blank	No	Yes	No	No	No	Pending underwriting
Issue:	yes	If left blank	Yes	Yes	Yes	Yes	Yes	E in progress
Delete	yes	no	No	No	No	No	No	Deleted

3.2 Overview input, processing, output
An Endorsement form contains Policy data that need to be changed. After the Endorsement is finalised the Policy data will be updated. Finalising the Endorsement will create, change or delete Policy versions. An Endorsement can be linked to a before and after state. Apart from that Endorsement metadata is known: effective date, processing date, processing reason and user information.

end-user satisfaction, using questions derived from the model of Doll and Torkzadeh (1988) and a 5-point rating scale.

The insurance company had no service registry before, but kept the service descriptions in separate documents. We used data from these documents to populate the service registry.

Tasks

Each participant was asked to read an introduction and then to perform two simple tasks that reflect the typical information needs of a service registry end-user, and that yield as a result at least one service specification. In this case study we considered a collection of services of an insurance company. The insurance company uses an authentication application that provides validation, authentication and authorization services via an ExternalService. Intermediaries use these and other services to perform various tasks regarding insurance data. These intermediaries sell insurance contracts (with coverage, obligations and rights, which altogether are called a policy) to consumers. The two simple tasks to be performed by the participant consisted of answering two of the following questions:

- Is there a service to 'change a consumer characteristic'?
- What is sent as input to the 'validation' method of the 'ExternalService' service?
- Is 'Cancellation of the entire Policy' one of the supported types of the 'Endorsement' service?
- Can the 'ContractAllGet' service be used to retrieve 'Coverage' details?
- What code is returned by the 'PartyChangeV1' service, in case it completes successfully?

ExternalService, Endorsement, ContractAllGet and PartyChangeV1 are some of the services

that were registered in the service registry prototype for the purpose of our case study.

After the questions were shown, the participant was instructed to follow a link to the prototype, perform the tasks and return to the screen to fill out an evaluation form. The first part of the form contained the questions derived from Doll and Torkzadeh (1988) to measure the end-user satisfaction. These questions were answered on a five point scale, ranging from 1 = 'totally not' to 5 = 'absolutely yes'. Additionally, the participant was inquired about his/her experience with SOA and specifically with service registries, in order to record the skills or expertise level of the participant. Furthermore, the participant was asked to rate his/her overall satisfaction with the prototype on a five point scale, consisting of 1 = 'nonexistent'; 2 = 'poor'; 3 = 'fair'; 4 = 'good' and 5 = 'excellent'. Any additional feedback could be given by the participant on a 'remarks' text field.

Results

From the 89 invitations, 21 persons have actively participated in the research. From these, 17 participants indicated that they had worked with a service registry before. The majority of the participants rated their familiarity with SOA as high (mean of 3.95 on a 5-point scale), and rated their familiarity with the concept of service registry slightly lower (mean of 3.29 on a 5-point scale).

We are aware that the number of participants is too low to draw significant statistical conclusions. Therefore, we carefully use terms like 'suggests' and 'indicates' when discussing the data. Table 2 summarizes the resulting data.

Table 2 shows the average of the accumulated scores and the average of the overall scores indicated by the participants. Scores average denotes the average score of all 12 questions by the 21 participants (so the average of 252 scores). Overall score denotes the average of the score of the 'overall satisfaction' question. The overall score indicated by the participants is close to the scores

Table 2. End user satisfaction scores of service registry users

	Content	Accuracy	Format	Ease of use	Timeliness	Overall score	Scores average
Average	3.52	3.71	3.29	3.36	3.64	3.38	3.50
Standard deviation	0.92	0.59	0.96	0.84	0.81		

average. This suggests that the questions provide a good indication of the user satisfaction. The scores above the 3-point average on a 5-point scale suggest that the participants are more than average satisfied with our prototype.

Table 2 also gives the results for the questions on the factors defined in Doll and Torkzadeh (1988) (contents, accuracy, format, ease of use and timeliness), in terms of the average and standard deviation values. The relatively low standard deviation suggests that the participants rated the content and accuracy generally above 3 points. However, the prototype scores slightly above average for the format and ease of use aspects.

Feedback

Still in the scope of the 'Exploitation and evaluation' layer of Figure 2, we gave the participants an opportunity to give feedback concerning this research. A few participants thought the prototype gave useless details at some service specification levels, while others recognized the usefulness of the division into various information levels (shown in Figure 9 under the 'More information' heading). Some participants would like to know how the prototype would perform in case the search questions were fuzzier.

Although the information in the service specifications was split into the various specification layers, participants still experienced information overload for the full result of a level. This calls for a further reduction of the level of representation of the content, to deliver to the end-user with as few as possible, but yet useful information.

CONCLUSION

The design of a service registry is a complex undertaking due to multiple choices that have to be made about its functionality. By properly scoping the service registry, one can identify the information needs and design requirements of the service registry. We have shown that the design method for information services is useful for developing service registries that fulfill the information needs of its various stakeholders. The design theory forces the designer to approach the service registry by considering its different stakeholders, namely the service providers, management, maintenance personnel and consumers. The design method identifies a design space consisting of layers (design problem, business, process, infrastructure, prototype and exploitation) and aspects (content, use features and revenues) that should be defined for a service registry to fulfill the requirements set by its users. We have also shown how this design theory can be applied, by means of a limited yet representative prototype. Although our case study could give a positive indication of the suitability of our approach, future research could be performed to empirically determine the appropriateness of the design theory for information services that we applied to the design of more realistic service registries, e.g., by evaluating its effectiveness for service registry development projects in product and process dimensions.

The quality of the service specifications (i.e., the content) stored in the registry is quite important in our approach. Previous attempts to create a public service registry have shown that if the information cannot be trusted for its quality, the service registry is marginally used, or not used at all. Therefore, the organization that considers using a service registry should deploy mechanisms to ensure the high quality of the information and to facilitate its usage by end-users (i.e., use features). The service registry is thus more than just a software system, and also requires aligned organizational structures. A separate organizational unit can be created or some roles have to be assigned to employees in order to run and maintain the service registry. Sponsorship could be arranged in order to deal with costs of running and maintain a service registry.

Our design methodology provides a structured design approach for service registries. Service specifications should be available at different levels, both to enable structured storage of service information and to facilitate the addition of use features. These specification levels cover information needs from service registry consumers, allowing end-users to choose their desired level of specification. Both technical and business users should be able to find their desired information.

This paper assumed that the services are already available, and considered the service registry as a means to facilitate service governance. Equally important is to consider the granularity at which services are defined and how this granularity influences the service registry. This is surely an interesting topic to be investigated in the future.

We built a prototype as a 'proof-of-concept' and performed a case study to assess the suitability of our approach. The case study showed a user satisfaction consistently higher than the 3-point average on a 5-point scale. However, due to the small research population size we are aware that these results should be interpreted with care.

In our prototype, the service registry stores meta-information on the service specifications that we found relevant for the case study, but we have not investigated what kind of information is to be stored and what standards are to be used when specifying a service. Further research should be performed to define a domain ontology for service specifications that consists of service specification concepts and their relationships. This ontology could then be used to search for specifications, to reason on the relevance of results, and to suggest other specifications that use different names for the same concept or that use different but strongly related concepts. Furthermore, if consensus can be reached on the service specification concepts, standards can be produced and products can be developed based on these standards. These should facilitate the interoperability between products and ultimately between organizations (Van der Aalst & Kumar, 2003).

ACKNOWLEDGMENT

The authors are thankful to Ordina System Development and Integration B.V. (the Netherlands) for creating the proper environment for performing this work, and to Vikram Sorathia for his contributions to this paper. The authors also acknowledge the Editor-in-Chief of the journal, Professor John Wang, and the anonymous reviewers for their remarks and suggestions to improve this paper.

REFERENCES

Afshar, M. (2007). *SOA governance: Framework and best practices*. Redwood Shores, CA: Oracle Corporation.

Al-Masri, E., & Mahmoud, Q. H. (2008). Toward quality-driven web service discovery. *IT Professional*, *10*(3), 24–28. doi:10.1109/MITP.2008.59

Alonso, G., Casati, F., Kuno, H., & Vijay, M. (2004). *Web services concepts, architectures and applications*. Berlin: Springer.

Belter, R. (2008). Towards a service management system in virtualized infrastructures. In *Proceedings of the IEEE International Conference on Services Computing 2008* (Vol. 2, pp. 47-51). Washington, DC: IEEE Computer Society.

Bose, R., & Suumaran, V. (2006). Challenges for deploying web services-based e-business systems in SMEs. *International Journal of E-Business Research, 2*(1), 1–18.

Doll, W. J., & Torkzadeh, G. (1988). The measurement of end-user computing satisfaction. *Management Information Systems Quarterly, 12*(2), 259–274. doi:10.2307/248851

Fettke, P., & Loos, P. (2003). Specification of business components. In M. Aksit, M. Mezini, & R. Unland (Eds.), *Objects, Components, Architectures, Services, and Applications for a Networked World, International Conference NetObjectDays* (LNCS 2591, pp. 62-75). Berlin: Springer Verlag.

Gorbenko, A., Romanovsky, A., & Kharchenko, V. (2008). How to enhance UDDI with dependability capabilities. In *Proceedings of the 32nd Annual IEEE International Computer Software and Applications Conference* (pp. 1023-1028). Washington, DC: IEEE Computer Society.

Gordijn, J., & Akkermans, H. (2001). Designing and evaluating e-business models. *Intelligent E-Business, 16*(4), 11–17.

Hepworth, M. (2004). A framework for understanding user requirements for an information service: Defining the needs of informal carers. *Journal of the American Society for Information Science and Technology, 55*(8), 695–708. doi:10.1002/asi.20015

Hevner, A. R., March, S. T., & Park, J. (2004). Design science in information systems research. *Management Information Systems Quarterly, 28*(1), 75–105.

Ives, B., Olson, M. H., & Baroudi, J. J. (1983). The measurement of user information satisfaction. *Communications of the ACM, 26*(10), 785–793. doi:10.1145/358413.358430

Lankhorst, M. (2005). *Enterprise architecture at work: Modelling, communication and analysis.* Berlin: Springer.

Larsen, G., & Wilber, J. (2005). *Asset lifecycle management for service-oriented architectures.* Retrieved January 23, 2008, from http://www.ibm.com/developerworks/rational/library/oct05/wilber/

Li, Q., Liu, A., Liu, H., Lin, B., Huang, L., & Gu, N. (2009). Web services provision: Solutions, challenges and opportunities. In *Proceedings of the 3rd International Conference on Ubiquitous Information Management and Communication* (pp. 80-87). New York: ACM.

Luo, J., Montrose, B., Kim, A., Khashnobish, A., & Kang, M. (2006). Adding OWL-S support to the existing UDDI infrastructure. In *Proceedings of the IEEE International Conference on Web Services* (pp. 153-162). Washington, DC: IEEE Computer Society.

Mahajan, R. (2006). SOA and the enterprise: Lessons from the city. In *Proceedings of the IEEE International Conference on Web Services* (pp. 939-944). Washington, DC: IEEE Computer Society.

Papazoglou, M. P. (2008). *Web services: Principles and technologies.* Essex, UK: Pearson Education Limited.

Ran, S. (2003). A model for web services discovery with QoS. *ACM SIGecom Exchanges, 4*(1), 1–10. doi:10.1145/844357.844360

Samavi, R., Yu, E., & Topaloglou, T. (2009). Strategic reasoning about business models: A conceptual modeling approach. *Information Systems and E-Business Management, 7*(2), 171–198. doi:10.1007/s10257-008-0079-z

Van der Aalst, W. M. P., & Kumar, A. (2003). XML-based schema definition for support of interorganizational workflow. *Information Systems Research, 14*(1), 23–46. doi:10.1287/isre.14.1.23.14768

Van Oostrum, A. (2008). *A service register as an information intermediary: towards a structured design approach for service registers*. Unpublished master's thesis, University of Twente, Enschede, the Netherlands.

Verma, K., Sivashanmugam, K., Sheth, A., Patil, A., Oundhakar, S., & Miller, J. (2005). METEOR-S WSDI: A scalable P2P infrastructure of registries for semantic publication and discovery of web services. *Information Technology Management, 6*(1), 17–39. doi:10.1007/s10799-004-7773-4

Wijnhoven, F. (2008). Process design theory for digital information services. In Bernard, A., & Tichkiewith, S. (Eds.), *Methods and tools for effective knowledge life-cycle-management* (pp. 533–546). Berlin: Springer. doi:10.1007/978-3-540-78431-9_31

Wijnhoven, F., & Kraaijenbrink, J. (2008). Product-oriented design theory for digital information services: A literature review. *Internet Research, 18*(1), 93–120. doi:10.1108/10662240810849612

Winkler, M., Cardoso, J., & Scheithauer, G. (2008). Challenges of business service monitoring in the internet of services. In *Proceedings of the 10th International Conference on Information Integration and Web-based Applications & Services* (pp. 613-616). New York: ACM.

Womack, R. (2002). Information intermediaries and optimal information distribution. *Library & Information Science Research, 24*, 129–155. doi:10.1016/S0740-8188(02)00109-3

Yu, Q., Liu, X., Bouguettaya, A., & Medjahed, B. (2008). Deploying and managing web services: Issues, solutions, and directions. *The VLDB Journal, 17*(3), 537–572. doi:10.1007/s00778-006-0020-3

This work was previously published in International Journal of Information Systems in the Service Sector, Volume 2, Issue 4, edited by John Wang, pp. 1-21, copyright 2010 by IGI Publishing (an imprint of IGI Global).

Chapter 17
Operational Performance Analysis of a Public Hospital Laboratory

Kamrul Ahsan
Auckland University of Technology, New Zealand

Abdullahil Azeem
Bangladesh University of Engineering and Technology, Bangladesh

ABSTRACT

Efficient utilization of scarce resources is an issue for any healthcare system. In developing countries, proper tools, techniques, and resources must be widely used in healthcare operational planning. Considering the necessity of effective resource planning, this study focuses on the rural healthcare system of Bangladesh and concentrates on the sub-district government hospital laboratory. The authors' determine possible ways to improve operations of laboratory facilities. To analyze existing system efficiency, sample laboratory data is fed into a simulation model. This paper identifies several possible ways for future expansion and suggests using simulation for better planning and analysis.

INTRODUCTION

The growth of health service systems in many developing countries is hindered due to wasteful planning and operations. Managing health facilities within limited resource and desired service quality is a big challenge for decision makers. Decision-makers need to investigate efficacy and efficiency of existing healthcare systems, and must be able to evaluate the outcomes of any changes they make to these systems (Ahmed & Alkhamis, 2009). In developing countries, proper tools and techniques, and resources for effective planning are important. In this regard, Operations Research (OR) can play an important role. Unfortunately, applications of OR techniques are not widely used by healthcare planners to solve these problems.

DOI: 10.4018/978-1-4666-0044-7.ch017

Copyright © 2012, IGI Global. Copying or distributing in print or electronic forms without written permission of IGI Global is prohibited.

For healthcare programmes, OR study is essential and is a systematic process of identifying and solving programme problems (Fisher, Laing, Stoeckel, & Townsend, 1991). 'The process of OR is designed to increase the efficiency, effectiveness, and quality of services delivered by providers; and the availability, accessibility, and acceptability of services desired by users' (Fisher et al., 1991). Or has been applied in the domain of healthcare for more than 40 years (Brailsford, 2007). Comparing two major developed parts of the world, healthcare OR in the United States has largely been focused on the application of 'hard' OR techniques (Sachdeva, Williams, & Quigley, 2007). In contrast, healthcare OR in Europe, including the UK, are focusing towards 'soft' OR techniques, with growing attempts to combine hard and soft OR methodologies (Lehaney, 1996; Easterby-Smith, Thorpe, & Lowe, 2002). However, OR has had limited success in the implementation of results in practice in the healthcare setting. The outcomes of the research may not be sufficient to motivate a change in practice by physicians, particularly for politically sensitive or controversial decisions (Sachdeva, Williams, & Quigley, 2007; Fone et al., 2003).

In the developing world, application of OR has different meaning. Aggarwal (1994) has pointed out that the concept of OR in developing countries is different from that found in the developed world. The term "OR" may not be used to describe the approach being taken. Decision-makers have different assumptions from those familiar in "traditional" OR methodology. Aggarwal writes: "The primary objective pursued in each case was to make the situation tolerable for as many people as possible." There is considerable interest in the potential for using OR in developing countries. One sign of this is the formation of new societies for OR scientists in countries and regions where no such society had existed. Survey shows that out of 279 OR research studies in West Africa, 33(12%) were conducted on healthcare sector and the sector ranks within top three applications of OR

(Smith, 2008). The formulation of OR models for healthcare decisions in developing countries are important, but at present formulation and solution of healthcare facilities by quantitative models is limited to developed regions only (Parker, 1990). Since 1990, there have been many improvements in using the OR tools and techniques in planning and decision making in developed world. However, the gap still remains between developed and developing world in terms of OR application in healthcare planning. The formulation of 'hard' and 'soft' form of OR models for healthcare decisions in developing countries are important.

In the Ministry of Health and Family Welfare (MOHFW) of Bangladesh, OR processes are not widely used by healthcare planners and service providers. Within the MOHFW there is a tendency for a biased trial and error planning process. The lack of a 'what if?' analysis tool makes existing studies 'barefooted OR' (Rahman, 1998). To improve the current situation, it is important to strengthen and institutionalise the OR process. Recommended strategies to institutionalise OR within the system are to strengthen the capacity of the organisations to conduct and use OR, to improve the methodologies used, and to assist managers to incorporate OR into routine planning and management practice (Population Council, 1998).

One of the priorities of the MOHFW program is to ensure sustainability by improving efficiency through efficient use of human as well as other resources. In recent years there has been increased awareness of the potential impact of OR applications in healthcare planning for Bangladesh. Studies of OR have been carried out by individuals, government organizations, and non-government organizations. One of the pioneers in OR research is the International Center for Diarrhoeal Disease Research, Bangladesh (ICDDR,B). However, most studies (Ahmed, Mozumder, & Barkat-e-khuda, 1999; Barkat-e-khuda, Harbison, & Robinson, 1990; Barkat-e-khuda et al., 1994; Sarker et al., 1999; Stanton & Clemens, 1989;

and other ICDDR,B OR Projects) have been conducted by following empirical research steps and few research (Ahsan & Bartlema, 2004; Ahsan & Bartlema, 2008; Khan, Ali, Ferdousy, & Al-Mamun, 2001; Rahman, 1991; Rahman & Smith, 1999) gives attention to modeling techniques of OR, which are very important in analyzing system performance.

Rahman (1998) classifies OR studies within MOHFW programs into three groups: diagnostic study, field intervention, and evaluation study. These studies are of situational analysis type and lack a simulation analysis tool, which is important for a complete OR study.

Khan et al. (2001) develop a general cost-minimization model of facility location decision for healthcare planning of Bangladesh. Rather than maximizing utilization or minimizing number of deaths, they use a very general social-cost function that combines health outcome measures as well as various cost components. The exercise estimates the number of health centers needed in a region, level of utilization, travel cost and other opportunity costs associated with the utilization of the service by households. The model determines the geographical distance of a health center as the only factor in estimating utilization, but other social and economic factors are not considered explicitly.

Rahman and Smith (2000) review the use of mathematical models of location allocation problems for health service development planning of developing nations. Objective of the location allocation problem is to find the best solution of the problems of locating new facilities for example hospitals, ambulance station. In developing countries, because of poor geographical accessibility, basic healthcare facilities do not reach the majority of the population. Moreover, location allocation decisions of healthcare facilities are normally taken by government officials or locally elected leaders or by both based on pragmatic or political considerations and the results are biased and not give the best solution.

Ahsan and Bartlema (2008) develop a linear programming model to determine the service mix for cost recovery programs in Bangladesh. The research identifies some areas where user fees can be charged and some cost can be recovered from the system for future functional improvement. The research also considers equity and quality of care issues.

In order to have a precise idea about system performance and possible areas of improvement, it is useful to work with some replica of the system. The more realistic the model, the better it will predict the behavior of the real system. Considering the importance and necessity of effective resource planning, this study focuses on rural healthcare systems of Bangladesh and concentrates on simulation study on sub-district level government hospital diagnostic laboratory. The study is performed under the European Union (EU) sponsored Thana Functional Improvement Pilot Project (TFIPP). The objective of TFIPP is to develop an efficient operational system for health services in the country. The aim of the work is to improve the quality of existing health and family welfare services at sub-district level.

The input data for the model has been collected from the daily operations of a Thana Health Complex (THC) laboratory. The main objective of simulation modeling of a laboratory is to obtain a better understanding of operational efficiency. From simulation study, the resources required to provide existing services and necessary resources and methods for capacity expansion have been analyzed. We further look at how to find solutions to eliminate or reduce constraints, a way to improve the process to provide more services, and finally we perform sensitivity analysis of changes in certain decision variables.

In the following section we will give a brief idea about the THC and its laboratory operations. Further, we explain research methodology and the simulation model. We discuss simulation results with sensitivity analysis in the next section. In the last section, we conclude the paper with policy implication and recommendations.

STUDY BACKGROUND

Thana Health Center (THC)

The background of this study is the public health-care system of Bangladesh. The national backbone of primary healthcare is operated by the MOHFW through 398 THCs. Thanas are local government units in sub-district level, which typically have a population in tens to hundreds of thousands. The health delivery system at the thana level consists of a THC organized with comparable medical equipment and personnel, with a facility of 31 beds for indoor patient department (IPD), emergency section, outdoor patient department (OPD), and laboratory or diagnostic laboratory.

In Bangladesh, THCs provide healthcare support at no cost or minimum cost to patient. However, because of scarcity of resources and lack of financial support from the Government, cost-recovery issues are being considered by the Government. In search of better healthcare service quality and efficiency, the Ministry of Health and Family Welfare (MOHFW) of Bangladesh is seeking ways to generate adequate and alternative resources for the public health sector. One of the priorities of the MOHFW is to make the existing system sustainable by improving the quality of service facilities through cost recovery and efficient use of human as well as other resources. Under this plan, the government aims to recover some part of the cost from patients which will contribute towards functional improvement of the system (Ahsan & Bartlema, 2008).

From previous empirical studies (Stanton & Clemens, 1989; Thomas et al., 1998) it has been found that Bangladesh is a potential candidate for the institution of user fees in the healthcare sector. However, major questions arise as to public willingness, whom to charge, service fees, potential services to charge, introduction of cost centers, how to manage funds and lastly who will implement the plan and how it will be implemented. Various studies provide strong evidence that people are willing to pay for different services. Furthermore, it has been found that at present for better service there exist an informal fee business (Killingsworth, 1999; Ruth et al., 2002) among service providers and clients. This money is off the record and taken from the government health service facilities. Even though, it is a moral issue, with the proper policy this money could be used to support the healthcare system.

Typically, THCs are located in suburban areas and through the system the MOHFW provides primary healthcare facilities to 85% of the village population (Ahsan & Bartlema, 2004). There are reasons to believe that the THC in reality does not serve the entire thana, but only the population within a radius of about 10-15km (Ahsan & Bartlema, 2004, p. 470). A typical THC has 50,000 outpatient visits, 2,300 in-patient admissions, and 200 operations a year. In general, a THC has an average of five doctors, six nurses and 31 other staff members. They seem to be quite homogeneous in their basic characteristics, reflecting the fact that they operate according to fixed norms (Rannan-Eliya & Somanathan, 2003). Demand of using THC facilities are increasing with the development of infrastructure facilities and there are pressure to increase the capacity of the facility

Laboratory Operations in THC

THC and the laboratory working hours are from 9:00 to 17:00. According to the source of referral, different types of patients visit the hospital laboratory (Figure 1). Diagnostic tests are conducted on 'first-come-first-serve' and equity basis. Patients requiring tests come from OPD and IPD units. Some come with referral, such as local level doctors or paramedics or private clinics. Though patients come from various sources, they follow more or less the same path within laboratory op-

Figure 1. Types of patient's served by a typical THC laboratory

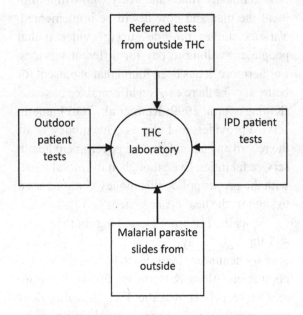

erations. Acute IPD patients for example, do not go to the waiting room. They have test-material taken at bedside and reports are sent to the respective doctor. Usually there are two technicians in the laboratory. The technician registers the test, collects samples, conducts diagnostics tests, and writes and delivers reports to patients.

Generally, the laboratory performs four types of tests. On the basis of category these tests are: blood, stool, urine, and sputum. Details of the tests are shown in Appendix. Patients need a single or a combination of tests. Each test requires different treatment times, and uses different reagents and resources. The fee paid by the patient differs according to the type of test performed. For each test, the time involved to take the sample and to conduct the test is different.

There is no appointment system and patients come to the hospital in their own time. Usually they are from remote places and most patients arrive between 11:00 and 14:00. Rural road infrastructure and weather affect patient arrival. Usually, there are two distinct patient arrival patterns, one

for peak hours (11.00 to 13.00) and the other for usual patient flow.

RESEARCH METHODS

Methods of OR help with managing the important shifts in the balance of healthcare (Royston, 1998). OR methods use in healthcare are brainstorming, Delphi, nominal groups, soft system methods, cognitive mapping, morphological analysis, forecasting, scenario analysis; expert system, neural network; mathematical programming, statistical modelling; simulation, system dynamics; multi-criteria decision making, data envelopment analysis, network analysis; etc. Among the above methods, simulation is one of the most commonly used OR approaches, and is regarded by many as the technique of choice in healthcare (Davies & Davies, 1994).

Simulation Study in Healthcare

Healthcare practitioners need to plan how health system performance can be improved and to consider the effects of introducing certain changes. In order to have a precise idea about these effects and to quantify them, it is useful to work in simulation to make a replica of the system. Models to replicate a hospital system should reflect the issues (Harper, 2002). The more realistic the replica is, the better it will predict the behavior of the real system. With the introduction of graphical interface computing, it is no longer necessary to use sophisticated computer languages in simulation. Rather, models of a system can be made by an expert and used by a practitioner, with little training in how to run the model.

Application of simulation studies are increasing in healthcare system modeling (Sanchez, et al., 2000; Barnes & Quiason, 1997; Baldwin, Eldabi, & Paul, 2004). The technique is popular in health-care because it can handle or incorporate many important features or situations of healthcare sector, such as analysis of uncertainty and variability of different situation, complexity of healthcare organizations, and helping stakeholders with a more realistic picture of the situation (Brailsford, 2007; Banks, 1997).

The application of simulation in healthcare has become popular and numerous studies report success by using simulation with simulation packages. The technique has widely been used in healthcare capacity and operations planning, and assessment for facilities. Historical research shows that simulation studies were conducted to determine patient flow, staff sizing and planning, resource workloads and utilization, operating room efficiency, number of hospital beds, patient occupancy, decision analysis of location allocation of hospitals and layout of hospital facilities. Detail review of simulation studies in healthcare can be obtained in Fon et al. (2003), Jun, Jacobson, and Swisher (1999), Brailsford (2007), and Siassiakos, Ilioudi, and Lazakidou (2008).

The application of simulation modelling in the healthcare sector is not widespread when compared to other sectors such as military, manufacturing and logistics (Eldabi, Paul, & Young, 2007; Baldwin et al., 2004; Sanchez et al., 2000; June et al., 1999). There are also concerns regarding application of simulation methods, simulation methods are less instrumental in addressing the multi-faceted challenges healthcare is facing at present and more importantly in the future (Kuljis, Paul, & Stergioulas, 2007). Literature shows that the application of simulation studies to analyze health facilities and resource planning in a developing country is rare. To our knowledge for Bangladesh there was no such research conducted earlier. Under the TFIPP project, we take the first attempt to conduct simulation application in healthcare planning and decision making for Bangladesh. The motivation behind this study is to analyze the operational performance of a THC laboratory by using a simulation tool.

Simulation Packages and MedModel® Software

The wide use of the object-oriented idea in simulation software design enables analysts to model a system without writing a single line of code. Numerous companies are developing general-purpose software packages incorporating the latest technologies. A detail survey can be obtained from OR/MS Today website (OR/MS Today, 2007). Some software packages are specifically aimed for the healthcare industry, such as ARENA, AgenaRisk, Analytica 4.0, AnyLogic, ExtendSim OR, Lean-Modeler, MedModel Optimization Suite Micro Saint Sharp, SimCad Pro, SIMUL8 and Professional (OR/MS Today, 2007; Caroll, 1996; Keller, 1994). These packages use animation in simulation to present to decision-makers the actual operation of the model and system and, in essence, to sell the insights of the system.

MedModel is owned by ProModel Inc. Beginning with inception in 1993, the software is specially designed to be simple to use and is customized to the needs of healthcare practitioners and planners (Denny, 1997). The software helps to identify new ways to improve patient care, enhance efficiency, optimize staff scheduling, design efficient facility layout, and save money. Details about MedModel can be seen from the software website, (MedModel, 2009)

Data Collection

With the aim of developing a simulation model for the laboratory operations of THC, data have been collected from two THCs located in Bakergonj sub-district of Barisal district and Rajapur sub-district of Jalokati district. These hospitals are within the TFIPP project areas. It is assumed that these hospitals represent the other hospitals of the country, as all THCs are using the same service model and their facilities are very similar regardless of the location of the THC. To collect real life operational data for the model, two monitoring assistants stayed within the THC during the project period of a couple of months. Moreover, the author visited the hospitals to observe first hand the laboratory operational processes and to assist in the data collection process. Collected operational data included arrival pattern, waiting times, types of tests, duration of examinations, analysis, report writing, and handover. Over two month's period, we have collected the data to identify the laboratory patient flow system, laboratory test sample arrival pattern, recorded the number of laboratory tests, processing time at each station. We determine an average arrival pattern and average service time for different types of test. Within the three months period we have collected around 70 sample data. From collected data, we find that patients come for either a single or a combination of tests. We consider each test as an entity. Time distributions from empirical data were used as data input. Arrival pattern distributions are fitted to these data to provide parameters which can be altered in simulation.

MODEL DEVELOPMENT

For laboratory operations of the THC, a simulation model is developed by using MedModel. The laboratory is a single facility location in the model; where test order registration, waiting time, sample collection, sample preparation, analysis, and report collection tasks are conducted routinely. The tasks are consecutive activities which are modeled separately, including time to get from one to another. The ingredients of simulation exercise are time data on entries, exits, activities, time spent on activities, number of patients and movements within the system. Input data is randomly distributed, so consecutive simulation runs will not give the same result.

With the visual interface of MedModel the laboratory operation model is developed. In brief the operational steps of the laboratory modeled in MedModel are shown in Figure 2. Operational

process steps and entity (patient, test and document) movement logic are set according to real work flow. Locations, resources, and entities are elected graphically. Process parameters include single shifts, room capacity, downtimes, and resource and equipment capacity.

It is assumed that at any given moment a maximum of 10 samples can be stored for analysis in the location. The location states are divided into two parts. Some of them are of multiple capacities, and others of single capacity. The waiting room, for example, can be occupied by a maximum of 5 patients, but registration takes place at the desk one-by-one. Other multiple capacity locations are sample collection and report collection. The time spent to move within the laboratory is limited.

RESULTS AND ANALYSIS

Simulation Run

We ran the simulation model for different operating periods and observed the results in terms of location, resource utilization, and by entity (type of test). Simulation results are summarized in tabular form (Table 1 and Table 2). Table 1

Figure 2. Operational steps in a laboratory

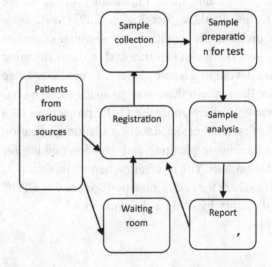

Table 2. Entity (test status) in minutes

Entity name	In system (mins)	In move logic (mins)	Wait for resources (mins)	In operation (mins)
Blood test – routine	101.94	22.22	19.71	60.0
Blood test- special	194.63	25.92	55.27	113.43
Stool	118.86	36.54	40.65	41.57
Sputum	193.35	20.28	65.11	107.85
Urine	155.12	27.21	44.25	83.65
Blood + Urine private	139.00	14.51	27.3	97.1
Urine-private referral	116.00	2.13	43.66	70.2
Blood-private referral	225.65	7.87	71.17	146.6
Malarial parasite	203.40	14.5	92.15	96.73

Table 1. Location status

Location name	Capacity	Total entries mean; (confidence interval)	Full-empty or idle mean; (confidence interval)	% utilization mean; (confidence interval)
Waiting room	5	9.85; (5.6, 14.0)	14.91; (8.0, 21.8)	80.95; (75.2, 86.7)
Registration	1	15.95; (11.3, 20.6)	16.66; (12.25, 21.0)	83.34; (78.9, 87.7)
Sample collection	2	12.65; (8.4, 16.9)	36.15; (8.7, 63.6)	42.52; (17.0, 68.0)
Report preparation	1	9.55; (5.7, 13.3)	90.51; (77.4, 103.6)	9.49; (0, 22.6)
Analysis	10	24.9; (18.9, 30.8)	9.27; (4.4, 14.1)	72.67; (53.5, 91.8)
Report collection	2	15.35; (10.0, 20.6)	64.02; (41.3, 86.8)	27.12; (8.1, 46.0)

gives a summary of location utilization facts for 20 replications. The second column indicates 'capacity' as the maximum number of entity that can be handled for a given number of working hours. In the third column, 'total entries' implies the average and 95% confidence interval of total served tests or results over the day for which the model was run. The fourth column shows average and confidence interval data when a location was wholly idle and there were no tasks. The 'percent utilization' given in the final column means the percentage of the total capacity which was occupied on average during the simulation duration.

On test basis, firstly the simulation model is run for an 8-hour day and found laboratory performs 28 tests per day. The average utilization of laboratory technicians was 85%. Since input patterns are random, obtained results might be for an atypical outcome.

To obtain a better picture of laboratory performance the model is further replicated for a hypothetical month (equivalent to 20 working days). Simulation results were obtained for human resources and resource working status. It was found that in a day, lab technicians were used 68 times for certain services. Each service took approximately 12 minutes. The utilization of resource persons was 84% on average. However, it was at a cost of more waiting time (see column 4 of Table 2), means more queue for the patient and sometimes the system was full and there were no room for new patient. These revels the basic concept of queuing theory that when there are high utilization rate there will be a problem of high queue length.

The output Table 1 for 20 replications, demonstrates that 25 tests were investigated (in analyze section) on average in a month, with 95% confidence interval range of 19 to 31. This implies an average 73% utilization rate, with a standard deviation of 10%. At sample collection point, 13 samples are collected on an average day, with confidence interval of 8.4 to 16.9. Report collection takes place 15 times, and the system was empty 64% of the time.

Further, Table 2 shows that most tests stay within the system for 100 to 225 minutes. The tests are processed an average 54% of the time for some value addition and the rest of the time wait for resources, and move from one place to another. The average amount of time spent for analysis of each test sample is between 20 to 30 minutes per technician. This is based on empirical data and replicates actual performance figures. On a sample basis it can be seen that a special blood test stays in the system for 194 minutes. It is in operation for about 113 minutes (58.28% time), with 55 minutes (28.2% time) of waiting for the resource, and 42 minutes (21.5% time) of movement.

VALIDATION

Validating a model is the process of substantiating the model within the domain of applicability, and testing whether the model is sufficiently accurate for intended application. It is important to determine the degree to which a model corresponds to the real system, or at least accurately represents model specification documents.

During the process of model building the model structure (i.e., the logical relationship between the processes) was kept as close to the real system as possible. Moreover, output from the model was compared to real system data to verify the model. Real system data is obtained from the real patient flow pattern within the subsystems (Table 3). The demands were found from historical data collected by monitoring assistants and the TFIPP. From the model it is found that 25 tests can be performed per day considering the system parameters used. Taking the average over all 55 THC's of the TFIPP project area, 85% of all THC's have daily performance levels below 25 tests (Table 4). Overall, we can conclude that the model replicates actual performance well.

From historical data (Table 3) it was found that on average (in Bakergonj) a laboratory performed 293 tests per month. The data is on a quarterly basis and mean is arithmetic mean. The numbers of OPD visits during Jan-March quarter are almost half of other quarter data. This number does not influence the overall number of test visits. For a 20 working day month the average numbers of tests performed daily are 15, i.e., 54.55% of all THC's have daily performance levels below 15 tests.

Sensitivity Analysis

We find that the system performance is usual in terms of serving the patient and resource utilization. Considering the number of served patient, the system is performing above the average. There are scopes to increase the capacity with additional demand. The laboratory is performing the tests

Table 3. THC performance data for four quarters

	July-Sep	Oct- Dec	Jan-March	April-June	Annual	Monthly (average)
OPD patient visits	10210	10170	5706	13730	39816	3318
IPD	488	587	468	911	2454	205
Laboratory tests	1285	497	675	1061	3518	293

Table 4. Laboratory performance data under TFIPP

Bin range (Number of tests)	Test frequency	Cumulative percentage
3	9	16.36
6	4	23.64
9	7	36.36
12	7	49.09
15	3	54.55
18	7	67.27
21	7	80.00
24	3	85.45
27	5	94.55
30	1	96.36
33	1	98.18
36	0	98.18
More	1	100

it is supposed to, but time is wasted by clients waiting to be served and also there is room for further improvement.

These days' public sector facilities are facing competition from private sector laboratories. If public sector facilities can offer similar or better service at less cost and with better quality, there will be more customers. A separate TFIPP survey found that a good number of patients do to come to the laboratory because of long waiting time and bureaucracy. They are well off and they are going to avail the private facilities and sometimes they pay unofficial fees to bypass the system complicacy.

Considering the market and opportunities, several 'what-if' options are considered to improve efficiency of the system. Several scenarios have been analyzed and compared with the normal condition obtained from 20 replications. The scenarios are such as increasing one key resource (option 1), scratching off administrative tasks from the laboratory technician job (option 2), offering an option for afternoon paying patients (option 3), and a choice for morning paying patients (option 4). The model has been adjusted for the scenarios and discussed the rationales of the options. A brief comparison of the four scenarios with the normal condition can be seen from Table 5.

Option 1: Increasing One More Resource

Adding one laboratory technician, and introduce no further changes in the system, the number of performed tests increases to 34 per day. This is an increase of about one third per month at the cost of one laboratory technician's salary. In terms of income, there is an increase of nearly 512 taka per day, which is considerable, since in our initial scenario, total cost recovered was 348 taka per day. Human resource efficiency remains unaltered, as percentage of utilization stays in the low eighties (82%). Under normal condition it is 84%. This implies that some improvements would be achieved if one laboratory technician were added to increase the team to 3 members.

Table 5. Summary of resource utilization and cost recovery for different scenarios

Variables	Total entries at analysis	Total entries at report collection	% of Manpower utilization	Cost-recovery (Taka)
Normal condition	25	15	84.5	348
Increase one resource	34	22	82.1	512
Job contraction	29	16	83	380
Afternoon paying patients	27	18	83.8	416
Morning paying patients	24	16	90	635

Option 2: Scratching Off Administrative Tasks

The strategy of job-contraction means laboratory technicians concentrate on their specialized professional work and eliminate the tasks of registration and other secretarial jobs. The technicians do not focus on paperwork and these tasks are assumed to be carried out elsewhere by administrative staff. Overall, this strategy increases the number of tests performed from 25 to 29. The income increases from 340 taka to 380 taka per day (s.d.60). Human resource utilization remains constant at 83%. The time gained in removing administrative work from the task description is apparently not used to improve on other performance. It is clear that the improvement achieved by scratching off administrative tasks is negligible. The administrative burden does not appear to be the main bottleneck.

Option 3: Choice for Afternoon Paying Patient

A TFIPP field study identifies that of the total clients, 20% are the wealthiest i.e. the most affluent group. We can assume on the basis of poverty indicators that this population group will be able to pay extra for services provided. We try out the effectiveness of charging fees and offer a special time during the off-peak period which is in the afternoon (2pm to 4pm). We have them contribute an amount which is double the normal price. In this fashion certain exclusivity is guaranteed.

If a separate treatment period for paying patients in the afternoon can be introduced, they will receive a high quality of care, with more time dedicated to each patient. The time involved in taking the sample is unaltered, but there is no wait at registration or before the test starts. Also, report collection is done immediately, and time spent on report taking (explaining results to the patient) increases. This is based on empirical information, which shows that on average the more wealthy patients currently receive better attention. The simulation is thus following actual practice, and not introducing any extraneous change. These patients pay a standard rate twice that of morning rush hour patients. Simulation results show that without any further changes in the system, the total number of tests performed during a normal working day increases from 25 to 27, and report collection from 15 to 18. The number of private tests increases from 2 to 3 per day. Cost recovery increases to 416 taka, from the previous 348 taka per day. Of all costs recovered, 20% are from afternoon paying patients. Human resource utilization is 84%. These are worthwhile improvements without extra costs to the system and are therefore worthy of consideration.

Option 4: Choice for Morning Paying Patient

In order to try out one last scenario, a period for private paying patients in the morning hours (from 9:00 to 11:00) is introduced. Usually, during 9-11 AM there is less patients visit to the laboratory. In this case 24 tests are performed and 16 reports are collected. Utilization percentage remains similar to normal conditions. The generated income goes up to 635 taka per day. The human resource utilization increases to 90% and the number of times resource persons are used for any activity increases to 75. There is some financial gain amongst private tests. This goes against the principle of equity, but provides extra income and better utilizes human resources.

Overall, the existing manpower (two resources) can handle no more than 25 to 30 tests per day. From the analysis, it can be seen that options of afternoon and morning paying patient provisions (options 3 and 4) are more attractive in terms of resource utilization, cost recovery and total number of tests performed. In terms of resource utilization, the option of morning paying patient functions near optimal conditions.

Further, ANOVA analysis is conducted and checked whether model's responses (resource utilization and cost recovery) are not dependent on the others across the options. Our null hypothesis is 'across the options resource utilization does have an effect on cost recovery'. Analysis from Table 5 shows that null hypothesis is not true (test statistics: 51.45> $F_{crictical}$: 5.31), i.e., there are differences among resource utilization and cost recovery across the options, and they are not dependent on each other. Details of ANOVA results can be seen from the Appendix III.

CONCLUSION AND POLICY IMPLICATIONS

The simulation exercise provides a detailed understanding of laboratory operations and helps identify limitations of the current system. The bottleneck in improving performance is identified as incapacity to satisfy demand. This implies that when demand is high, patients have to either go elsewhere or suffer long waiting times, unless they otherwise gain priority.

The simulation has made clear that the laboratory is working well as a unit. Throughput is acceptable, human resources are utilized quite adequately as far as time is concerned, but productivity is low since no more than 2 staff members can treat 25-30 tests per day. The laboratory is simply too small to satisfy demand. Under current practice, the system is covering the demand insufficiently. The laboratory operations need to change the arrival pattern of patients.

There is less room for improvement unless worker productivity can be increased. One possible option of improving worker productivity can be training the laboratory technician. The recommendation is to streamline operations as much as possible, and prioritize according to government health policy criteria. These might be to give the poor or women and children higher priority, or on the contrary create special services for the more privileged. With the development of human resources it is necessary to improve the technical standard of the laboratory with better equipment to speed up services. However, all suggestions are related to budget availability which is a serious constraint of any developing country health system.

This study is an illustration of what is possible with simulation in developing country's healthcare planning. What has been done for the laboratory can of course be repeated for any other THC service? The next step can be to simulate the entire THC, and to draw conclusions on how it is possible to improve the functionalities as a whole.

Potentially, simulation is a useful tool for decision support. The attractive thing about simulation is that it is intuitively easy to understand. It is simple to apply with currently available software, although some basic computer application knowledge is required for data input and model construction. In simulation the model can be repeated many times under different conditions, before real field trials are carried out. Expanding the use of simulation for health system planning in Bangladesh and other developing and emerging economies is recommended. However, implementation depends on government decisions that are often influenced by political considerations.

REFERENCES

Aggarwal, S. C. (1994). Practical applications of OR in an underdeveloped nation. *European Journal of Operational Research*, 77(3), 357–374. doi:10.1016/0377-2217(94)90403-0

Ahmed, K. S., Mozumder, A. K. A., & Barkat-e-khuda. (1999). *Redesigning the operations research project surveillance system* (No. 107). Dhaka, Bangladesh: ICDDRB.

Ahmed, M. A., & Alkhamis, T. M. (2009). Simulation optimization for an emergency department healthcare unit in Kuwait. *European Journal of Operational Research, 198*, 936–942. doi:10.1016/j.ejor.2008.10.025

Ahsan, M. K., & Bartlema, J. (2004). Monitoring healthcare performance by Analytic Hierarchy Process: a developing country perspective. *International Transactions in Operational Research, 11*(4), 465–478. doi:10.1111/j.1475-3995.2004.00470.x

Ahsan, M. K., & Bartlema, J. (2008). Introduction of user fees: a viable means of healthcare financing. *Journal of Health Management, 10*(1), 87–100. doi:10.1177/097206340701000105

Baldwin, L. P., Eldabi, T., & Paul, R. J. (2004). Simulation in healthcare management: a soft approach (MAPIU). *Simulation Modelling Practice and Theory, 12*, 541–557. doi:10.1016/j.simpat.2004.02.003

Banks, J. (1997). The future of simulation software: a panel discussion. In S. Andradottir, K. J. Kealy, D. E. Withers, & B. L. Nelson (Eds), *Proceedings of the 1997 Winter Simulation Conference. Institute of Electrical and Electronics Engineers,* Atlanta (pp. 166-173).

Barkat-e-khuda, Harbison, S. F., & Robinson, W. C. (1990). Is development really the best contraceptive? a 20-year trail in Comilla district. *Population Program Journal, 5*(4), 3–16.

Barkat-e-khuda. Barket, A., Helali, J., Miller, P., & Haaga, J. (1994). *Population policy in Bangladesh: a review of ten priority areas*. Dhaka, Bangladesh: University Research Corporation and the Population Council.

Brailsford, S. C. (2007). Tutorial: Advances and challenges in healthcare simulation modeling. In S. G. Henderson, B. Biller, M. H. Hsieh, J. Shortle, J. D. Tew, & R. R. Barton (Eds.), *Proceedings of the 2007 Winter Simulation Conference* (pp. 1436-1448). Washington, DC: IEEE.

Carroll, D. (1996). MedModel-healthcare simulation software. In J. M. Charnes, D. M. Morrice, D. T. Brunner, & J. J. Swain (Eds.), *Proceedings of the 1996 Winter Simulation Conference,* Coronado, CA (pp. 441-446). Washington, DC: IEEE.

Davies, R., & Davies, H. (1994). Modelling patient flows and resource provisions in health systems. *Omega, 22*, 123–131. doi:10.1016/0305-0483(94)90073-6

Denney, S. H. (1997). MedModel-healthcare simulation software. In S. Andradottir, K. J. Kealy, D. E. Withers, & B. L. Nelson (Eds.), *Proceedings of the 1997 Winter Simulation,* Atlanta (pp. 581-586). Washington, DC: IEEE.

Easterby-Smith, M., Thorpe, R., & Lowe, A. (2002). *Management research: an introduction.* London: Sage.

Eldabi, T., Paul, R. J., & Young, T. (2007). Simulation modelling in healthcare: reviewing legacies and investigating futures. *The Journal of the Operational Research Society, 58*, 262–270.

Fisher, A. A., Laing, J. E., Stoeckel, J. E., & Townsend, J. W. (1991). *Handbook for family planning operation research design.* New York: Population Council.

Fone, D., Hollinghurst, S., Temple, M., Round, A., Lester, N., & Weightman, A. (2003). Systematic review of the use and value of computer simulation modeling in population health and healthcare delivery. *Journal of Public Health Medicine, 25*, 325–335. doi:10.1093/pubmed/fdg075

Jun, J. B., Jacobson, S. H., & Swisher, J. R. (1999). Application of discrete-event simulation in healthcare clinics: a survey. *The Journal of the Operational Research Society, 50*(2), 109–123.

Keller, L. F. (1994). MedModel-specialized software for the healthcare industry. In J. D. Tew, S. Manivannan, D. A. Sadowski, & A. F. Seila (Eds.), *Proceedings of the 1994 Winter Simulation Conference*, Lake Buena Vista, FL (pp. 533-537). Washington, DC: IEEE.

Khan, M. M., Ali, D., Ferdousy, Z., & Al-Mamun, A. (2001). A cost-minimization approach to planning the geographical distribution of health facilities. *Health Policy and Planning, 16*(2), 264–272. doi:10.1093/heapol/16.3.264

Killingsworth, J. R., Hossain, N., Hedrick-Wong, Y., Thomas, S. D., Rahman, A., & Begum, T. (1999). Unofficial fees in Bangladesh: price, equity and institutional issues. *Health Policy and Planning, 14*, 152–163. doi:10.1093/heapol/14.2.152

Klein, R. W., Dittus, R. S., Roberts, S. D., & Wilson, J. R. (1993). Simulation modelling and healthcare decision making. *Medical Decision Making, 13*, 347–354. doi:10.1177/0272989X9301300411

Kuljis, J., Paul, R. J., & Stergioulas, L. K. (2007). Can healthcare benefit from modelling and simulation methods in the same way as business and manufacturing has? In B. Henderson, M.-H. Biller, J. Hsieh, J. D. Shortle, R. Tew, & R. Barton (Eds.), *Proceeding of 39th Winter simulation Conference* (pp. 1449-1453). Washington, DC: IEEE.

MedModel. (2009). *Product summary, MedModel by ProModel*. Retrieved March 25, 2009, from http://www.promodel.com

Parker, B. R. (1990). In quest of useful healthcare decision models for developing countries. *European Journal of Operational Research, 49*(2), 279–288. doi:10.1016/0377-2217(90)90346-D

Population Council. (1998). *Institutionalization of OR*. New York: Population Council.

Rahman, S. (1998). *Barefooted operations research and its extension: locational analysis of public health facilities in rural Bangladesh. Unpublished rep.* Dhaka, Bangladesh: Ministry of Health and Family Welfare.

Rahman, S., & Smith, D. K. (1999). Development of rural health facilities in a developing country. *The Journal of the Operational Research Society, 50*, 892–902.

Rahman, S., & Smith, D. K. (2000). Use of location-allocation models in health service development planning in developing nations. *European Journal of Operational Research, 123*, 437–452. doi:10.1016/S0377-2217(99)00289-1

Rannan-Eliya, R. P., & Somanathan, A. (2003). The Bangladesh health facility efficiency study. In Yazbeck, A. S., & Peters, D. H. (Eds.), *Health policy research in South Asia: Building capacity for reform* (pp. 195–225).

Routh, S., Thwin, A. A., Kane, T. T., & Baqui, A. H. (2000). User-fees for family-planning methods: an analysis of payment behavior among urban contraceptors in Bangladesh. *Journal of Health, Population, and Nutrition, 18*(2), 69–78.

Sachdeva, R., Williams, T., & Quigley, J. (2007). Mixing methodologies to enhance the implementation of healthcare operational research. *The Journal of the Operational Research Society, 58*, 159–167.

Sanchez, S. M., Ogazon, T., Ferrin, D. M., Sepu'lveda, J. A., & Ward, T. J. (2000). Emerging issues in healthcare simulation. In *Proceedings of the 2000 Winter Simulation Conference, Association of Computing Machinery*, New York (pp. 1999-2003).

Sarker, S., Routh, S., & Islam, Z. Barkat-e-khuda, Nasim, S. A., & Khan, Z. A. (1999). *Operations research on ESP delivery and community clinics of Bangladesh* (No. 105). Dhaka, Bangladesh: ICDDR.

Siassiakos, K., Ilioudi, S., & Lazakidou, A. (2008). Simulation and learning environments in healthcare. *International Journal of Healthcare Technology and Management, 9*(2), 155–166. doi:10.1504/IJHTM.2008.017370

Smith, D. K. (2008). A bibliography of applications of operational research in West Africa. *International Transactions in Operational Research, 15*, 121–150. doi:10.1111/j.1475-3995.2008.00625.x

Stanton, B., & Clemens, J. (1989). User fees for healthcare in developing countries: a case study of Bangladesh. *Social Science & Medicine, 29*(10), 1199–1205. doi:10.1016/0277-9536(89)90363-8

Thomas, S., Killingsworth, J., & Acharya, S. (1998). User fees, self-selection and the poor in Bangladesh. *Health Policy and Planning, 13*, 50–58. doi:10.1093/heapol/13.1.50

Today, O. R. M. S. (2007). Simulation software survey. *OR/MS Today*. Retrieved August 19, 2009, from http://www.lionhrtpub.com/orms/surveys/Simulation/ Simulation1.html

APPENDIX

- Laboratory tests performed
- Patient test categories
- ANOVA results

I. Laboratory Tests Carried Out at THC

- Blood tests
  ○ TC, DC, ESR, Hb
  ○ Serum Bilirubin
  ○ ASO Titre
  ○ Widal Test
  ○ Blood Glucose, Blood Grouping(ABO)
  ○ MP
  ○ VDRL
  ○ Hbs Ag
  ○ Serum Cholesterol
- Urine tests - Urine R/E, Urine for PT
- Sputum Tests
- Stool Tests

For practical reason these are grouped into two types, special tests and routine

Special Tests

The special tests are:

1. Urine for PT
2. For Blood
   ○ Serum Bilirubin
   ○ ASO Titre
   ○ Widal Test
   ○ Blood Glucose
   ○ Blood Grouping(ABO)
   ○ VDRL
   ○ Hbs Ag
   ○ Serum Cholesterol

Routine Tests

1. TC, DC, ESR, Hb
2. Urine R/E
3. Stool R/E

4. MP
5. Sputum for AFB

II. Patients Test Categories

1. Client for Blood test
2. Client for Stool test
3. Client for Sputum test
4. Client for Urine test
5. Client for Blood and Stool test
6. Client for Blood and Sputum test
7. Client for Blood and Urine test
8. Client for Stool and Sputum test
9. Client for Stool and Urine test
10. Client for Sputum and Urine test
11. Client for Sputum, Stool and Urine test
12. Client for Sputum, Stool and Blood test
13. Client for Blood, Stool and Urine test
14. Client for Blood, Urine and Sputum test
15. Client for Sputum, Blood, Stool and Urine test

III. ANOVA Result Summary

SUMMARY							
Groups	**Count**	**Sum**	**Average**	**Variance**			
Utilisation	5	423.42	84.684	9.62128			
Cost recovery	5	2291	458.2	13548.2			
ANOVA							
Source of Variation	**SS**	**df**	**MS**	**F**	**P-value**	F_{crit}	
Between Groups	348785.5	1	348785.5	51.45156	9.49E-5	5.317645	
Within Groups	54231.29	8	6778.911				
Total	403016.8	9					

This work was previously published in International Journal of Information Systems in the Service Sector, Volume 2, Issue 4, edited by John Wang, pp. 22-38, copyright 2010 by IGI Publishing (an imprint of IGI Global).

Chapter 18
A Mashup Application to Support Complex Decision Making for Retail Consumers

Steven Walczak
University of Colorado at Denver, USA

Deborah L. Kellogg
University of Colorado at Denver, USA

Dawn G. Gregg
University of Colorado at Denver, USA

ABSTRACT

Purchase processes often require complex decision making and consumers frequently use Web informa-tion sources to support these decisions. However, increasing amounts of information can make finding appropriate information problematic. This information overload, coupled with decision complexity, can increase time required to make a decision and reduce decision quality. This creates a need for tools that support these decision-making processes. Online tools that bring together data and partial solutions are one option to improve decision making in complex, multi-criteria environments. An experiment using a prototype mashup application indicates that these types of applications may significantly decrease time spent and improve overall quality of complex retail decisions.

INTRODUCTION

"Only an inventor knows how to borrow, and every man is or should be an inventor,"
Ralph Waldo Emerson.

DOI: 10.4018/978-1-4666-0044-7.ch018

It has long been recognized that service custom-ers have a dual role, being both consumers and producers (e.g., Chase, 1978; Lovelock & Young, 1979; Mills & Morris, 1986). The production role of the service customer is often referred to as "co-production." Internet-based services are no exception and often require higher levels of

Copyright © 2012, IGI Global. Copying or distributing in print or electronic forms without written permission of IGI Global is prohibited.

co-production than in traditional services (Xue, Harker, & Heim, 2005). While effective IT solutions clearly provide benefits to internal processes, using IT applications in co-production activities has the potential to provide effective and efficient support to both the service customer and the provider. One way to do this is to provide online services that support decision-making needs of consumers.

Many consumer purchases require complex decision making and customers often use online sources for the information needed to select the product or service that best satisfies their needs (Oz, 2007). This information includes product specifications, reviews and ratings, availability, and pricing. Some consumer purchases require the balancing of multiple criteria and require co-ordinating purchases from several vendors (e.g., purchasing an automobile may involve tradeoffs between the cost of vehicle, fuel efficiency, vehicle safety, insurance costs, financing options, non-dealer options, such as GPS or satellite radio add-ons, extended warranties, and maintenance service contracts). The overload of information available from the Web makes finding and using reliable information for multi-criteria decision making problematic (Selamat & Selamat, 2005).

Search engines and other Web search techniques provide consumers with access to large amounts of information; however, the sheer volume of data available can lead to information overload and an inability to apply the information available to the decision-making task. Consumers desire information access during their decision making and such information access produces a more satisfied consumer (Kwon, 2006). However, simply finding appropriate information is not sufficient to enable consumers to adequately evaluate solutions to multi-criteria decision problems (Spira, 2006).

One way the Web is evolving to cope with the increased volume of information is through the development of Web 2.0 applications (e.g., wikis, blogs, social bookmarks and mashups.)

Web 2.0 applications facilitate collaboration and information sharing (O'Reilly, 2005). These new applications are database-driven meaning they are data intensive and the more data they contain the more valuable they become (McFedries, 2006).

Web 2.0 applications provide a more interactive web experience and allow a variety of users, including retailers, manufacturers, consumer rating entities, industry experts, and consumers, to share in the generation, organization, distribution, and utilization of knowledge. These applications have the potential to fundamentally change the way the Internet is used, allowing for new business models based on value-added services. These systems can provide improved information and decision support to enable consumers to make well informed decisions more quickly than with traditional information sources or older standard Web technologies.

This research examines the use of a decision support mashup to facilitate and enhance multi-criteria consumer decision making. The mashup utilizes wiki-based knowledge repositories to improve the information content available for the consumer decision-making process. The primary contribution of our research is the measurement and analysis of actual benefits provided by a mashup. While consumer based mashup applications have increased significantly over the last two years (Fichter & Wisniewski, 2009), these applications are developed to satisfy situated consumer needs and may evaluate perceived benefits. Enterprises considering adopting mashup based decision support applications need to understand the realizable benefits to decision makers, including any reduction in the time required to make a decision and any resulting improvement in the quality of the decision.

An exploratory research experiment is conducted by implementing a prototype mashup application for designing a media room. This purchase decision involves integrating expert information, product specifications, quality ratings, and pricing and availability of the equipment from multiple vendors. In the experiment the media room required a decision involving the following criteria: budget, desired audio quality, desired video quality, room size, anticipated audience, viewing classification, and compatibility of the equipment with physical requirements. The application is evaluated in an experimental setting utilizing a survey. The benefits of mashup decision support application for consumers supported by this empirical evidence are discussed.

BACKGROUND AND RESEARCH HYPOTHESES DEVELOPMENT

Mashup Research

The concept of Web application mashups is relatively new with only a handful of applications available as recently as 2005 (Fichter & Wisniewski, 2009). Borrowing from the radio and video technique of mashing together multiple tracks to produce a new but still familiar song, the concept is applied to the Web when multiple information sources are "mashed" together to enable a much more comprehensive solution to multi-criteria decision-making problems (Oren et al., 2007). Mashups allow end-users to combine information, knowledge, user interface widgets, and APIs from a variety of sources, and integrate them into customized, goal-oriented applications (Albinola, Baresi, Carcano, & Guinea, 2009; Balasubramaniam, Lewis, Simanta, & Smith, 2008).

Due to the emerging popularity of mashup applications a great deal of research is currently being conducted in the development of novel applications and frameworks. For example, there have been a number of articles examining how to integrate heterogeneous data into a common mashup interface (e.g., Murthey et al., 2006; Thor, 2007). This is similar to the research done on data integration addressed in prior IS literature (e.g., Ullman, 1997; Lenzerini, 2002) with a focus on integrating heterogeneous XML and

SOAP resources (Balasubramaniam et al., 2008). Other recent research examines standardized infrastructure frameworks to enable mashup applications to integrate with existing data sources and information flows (Loreto, Mecklin, Opsenica, & Rissanen, 2009; Yu, Kim, Shin, & Jo, 2009).

A second area of research on mashups investigates what data should be combined in a mashup application. Much of this research is focused on the algorithms and technologies that can be used to locate relevant information resources for use in a mashup application. For example, researchers have used artificial intelligence techniques to locate and identify relevant information resources to be used in mashup applications (e.g., Tatemura et al., 2007; Blake & Nowlan, 2008). Another example is the access and data mining of XML databases (Sun & Li, 2009).

Many end-user mashup applications already exist, with over 4300 reported by Programmableweb (2009). Early mashup applications focused primarily in travel and map-related applications (mashworks.net, 2007) and this trend appears to be continuing (Loreto et al., 2009; Yu et al., 2009). However, research evaluating the benefits of mashups as a multi-criteria decision-making tool is nonexistent. This area is the focus of our research study.

Mashup Applications and Multi-Criteria Consumer Decision Problems

Multi-criteria purchase decisions range from very simple to very complex as products and services interact with technology and begin to span different product or service classes and range across different businesses (Froehle & Roth, 2004). Most selection problems require satisfying multiple criteria (Malakooti, 2000). Furthermore, multi-criteria problems are compounded by: time pressure to make the decision, lack of standardized data, presence of non-monetary or intangible attributes, and limited attention and information processing capabilities of decision makers (Ahn, 2003).

As decision making becomes more complex, more functionality is necessitated by decision makers and mashup applications may provide this complex functionality (Obrenović, Gašević, & Eliëns, 2008). Mashup applications have the potential to provide decision support in an integrated manner bringing relevant information into a single location, as opposed to the decentralized architecture of traditional websites. Mashup applications utilize and synthesize a variety of existing and possibly unused information, domain models, and decision support processes. Publicly available services may be incorporated into mashups to extend the current mashup's functionality (Balasubramaniam et al., 2008). Each of these components is integrated into a single online location, typically accessible over the Web or through a company portal.

In order for a mashup application to work it must be able to locate information of interest from relevant information resources and combine or "mash up" that information to provide the information in a more useful format to users. The most common source of information for mashups comes from the Web itself. For example, Amazon.com® makes its catalog available via web services so that its 800,000 marketing affiliates may more easily sell products for Amazon (Manes, 2003). Dollar Rent-A-Car® has exposed its reservation system to provide external partners with information on the availability and price of Dollar cars and to allow them to easily rent Dollar cars (Chen, Jeng, Lee, & Chuang, 2008). As companies make information available on the Web there is an opportunity for other businesses to combine that information in innovative ways to provide value-added services to consumers.

Early research on mashup applications has indicated that mashups will foster business innovation (Dornan, 2007), enable better response to competition, improve customer service (Gaudin, 2007), and increase the scope and utility of existing applications and services (Linthicum,

2007). Mashup applications are demonstrating the efficacy of integrating organizational specific applications with other Web resources such as a mashup application that queries the local power grid to determine when excessive demand is occurring and automatically adjusting various energy consuming features within a building or group of buildings (Sinclair, 2007). The incorporation of business logic and business specific applications into a mashup is the most complex type of mashup (over presentation and data mashups that simply display data in a unified view or perform some combination on the data prior to presentation) (Fichter & Wisniewski, 2009).

Mashups may be combined with wiki technologies to allow information to be incorporated into an integrated knowledge repository that may be easily updated to respond to changes in the information environment. Research on wikis has focused on the use of wikis as a knowledge repository in such domains as encyclopedias (McMullin, 2005) and customer relationship management (Wagner & Majchrzak, 2006). One stream of wiki research has found that wikis are useful for question answering tasks (Jijkoun et al., 2004; Lita, Hunt, & Nyberg, 2004). This suggests that wikis might provide an appropriate knowledge organization for a mashup decision support service to be used by retail consumers.

While the concept of a mashup appears to be a promising innovation, both within the organization and externally for consumers, no prior research has been performed investigating the efficacy and benefits of mashups as a decision-making aide (Venkatesh, Morris, Davis, & Davis, 2003).

Research on the adoption of electronic technologies by consumers (Song, Koo, & Kim, 2007; Tsikriktsis, Lanzolla, & Frohlich, 2004) has largely followed a Technology Acceptance Model (TAM) methodology (Davis, 1989; Venkatesh et al., 2003). TAM proposes that both the perceived ease of use and perceived usefulness drive adoption of technology. In their co-production activities consumers perform this cost (ease of use) /

benefit (usefulness) analysis. Prior research in technology-enabled decision making focuses on the several specific usefulness factors. Gao, Wang, Xu, and Wang (2007), Haubl and Trifts (2000), and Swaminathan (2003) focus on perceived confidence in the decision, knowledge acquisition, and quality of the decision. While not specific to the consumer decision-making task, Seiders, Voss, Godfrey, and Grewal's (2007) SERVCON model provides insight into ease of use factors for service customers.

Research Hypotheses

A mashup application has the potential to provide several direct benefits, including:

- Guiding exploration, discovery, refinement, and articulation of decision-making criteria.
- Facilitating solution of multi-criteria decision problems.
- Enabling knowledge acquisition by users that may improve future decision making and may serve to increase the perceived trust in the developed solution.
- Providing current pricing and product availability information without potential bias.

Ultimately though, the actual and measurable benefits of a mashup multi-criteria decision-making tool are in the reduced time it takes to acquire the knowledge necessary to make the decision and in the resulting improved quality of the decisions made. Both time and decision quality are direct measures of the efficiency and effectiveness of the co-production role of the retail consumer.

H1: Use of the mashup application will decrease the actual time (TIME) spent completing a multi-criteria decision-making problem.
H2: Use of the mashup application will improve the quality (QUAL) of the final decision.

There are, however, perceptual measures of efficiency and effectiveness. That is, the decision-maker may believe that making a decision was easy to make or believe that a very good decision was made. Moreover, these perceptual factors also help lead to adoption and continued usage of technology (Venkatesh et al., 2003) as well as engender customer trust and willingness to transact with a specific service provider or vendor (Gregg & Walczak, 2006). Among the earliest identified benefit to technology-enabled consumer decision making was perceived confidence in the decision (Gao et al., 2007; Haubl & Trifts, 2000; Swaminathan, 2003). Consumers are unlikely to use (or re-use) a technology unless they believe they have made good decisions.

H3: Use of the mashup application will improve the perceived confidence (CONF) in the final decision.

The ease of finding information has a significant impact on user utilization (Diaz-Galiano, Martin-Valdivia, & Ureña-López, 2009) and perceptions on ease of use (Davis, 1989; Venkatesh et al., 2003). Ease of finding information is akin to Seiders et al.'s (2007) convenience constructs, which are related, to re-purchase and positive word of mouth intentions.

H4: Use of the mashup application will improve the perceived ease of finding information (EASE).

Prior research has evaluated similar decision-making technology benefits, but in an isolated manner and only for other non-mashup decision support technologies. The research presented in this article attempts to measure both the actual and perceived benefits to multi-criteria decision making from the innovative mashup technology.

RESEARCH METHODOLOGY

The present research involves the development of a prototype mashup decision support tool tailored to the decision-making task of outfitting a media room. Figure 1 illustrates the multi-criteria decision-making architecture used for this tool. Specific constraints or sets of constraints will drive the information needs and decision-making processes for the mashup application. Following the development of the prototype mashup tool an exploratory experiment is conducted that compares the decision-making behavior, perception, and quality of two subject groups, one using the mashup tool and one using a traditional web-based search.

Mashup Prototype Development

The design of a home media room was selected as the multi-criteria decision-making problem for the prototype because of the numerous decisions and criteria including: video needs (e.g., type, quality, viewing angle and distance, etc.), audio needs (e.g., type, quality, etc.), room utilization (e.g., home theatre, entertainment, mixed usage, etc.), room size and shape, budget, construction possibilities, furniture (e.g., type, arrangement), and ambient lighting and light control, installation, among others. There are also interactions that must be considered such as room size affecting the optimal size television or projection system, creating a complex multi-criteria decision-making problem.

The prototype mashup application used in the experiment considers a smaller subset of the full decision problem to enable subjects to utilize the prototype in a timely manner and to enable a more straightforward evaluation of the results. The media room design mashup prototype included selection of multiple audio and visual components, which included the interaction between these components, subject to budget and room size constraints.

The goal of mash-up applications is to provide a Web-based resource that combines existing content, data or application functionality from multiple sources and allow users adapt those

Figure 1. Multi-criteria decision mashup architecture

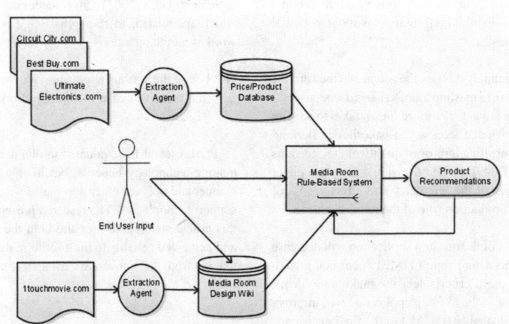

resources to meet their individual information centric and situational application needs (Hoyer & Fisher, 2008). The mashup prototype utilized for this experiment allows users to combine domain specific information from journal articles, commercial websites, third party product review sources (1touchmovie.com, 2007; Consumer Reports, 2007; ITU, 2006; Katzmaier, 2007), and interviews with media room experts with current video and audio component prices and customer ratings extracted from three online stores - Best Buy®, Circuit City®, and Ultimate Electronics® - to facilitate decision making that satisfies a budget constraint. The media room design mashup prototype also combines the application functionality of a wiki, used to organize data from offline sources as well as data extracted from media room information web sites, with a more traditional rule based system, providing users access to decision rules from a variety of expert sources. The ability of the media room mashup to automatically download current inventory and prices from a variety of retailers mimics similar capabilities in e-commerce shopping agents (Gregg & Walczak, 2006) and may also provide a product list that is unbiased since the mashup application is collecting information for uniform presentation from a variety of providers.

An important aspect of mashups is that they allow users to adapt available information and application resources to meet their individual information centric and situational application needs. This was enabled in the media room mashup in a variety of ways. The media room design mashup application does more than simply recommend products. Profiling and preference elicitation is used to enable subjects to discover or refine previously unarticulated decision criteria. The preference elicitation process allows mashup users to select the order of information presentation as well as the types of information that is used as a part of the decision making process. Prior research (Malakooti, 2000) has shown that preference elicitation is beneficial in producing

higher quality decisions in multi-criteria decision problems. As an example of preference modeling in the media room design mashup application, one of the questions asked of a subject is if they feel video or audio quality is more important, which in turn adjusts the recommended budget expenditures for the system components to enable higher quality audio or visual components based on the subject's response and also impacts the types of components recommended. This type of user modeling has been found to be beneficial in prior research (Xiao & Benbasat, 2007), especially when the decision maker is less familiar with product or service attributes.

The media room design mashup utilizes decision tree logic to determine the product characteristics that best meet the subject's needs based on the preference elicitation and recommends products with the appropriate characteristics. The decision tree logic is analogous to the mashup of business processes and business logic discussed in Background section. Subjects may modify their decision profiles and preferences at any time reflecting changes in business logic and the mashup application will automatically adjust its reasoning to satisfy the newly established values for the decision-making constraints. Such modifications may include increasing or decreasing the budget to see a wider or narrower selection of system components that satisfy the current constraints.

Information resources incorporated into the mashup application are used to develop the decision rules and to provide the product options from which subjects may choose. This same information is also exposed to the subjects via the wiki knowledge repository. Similar to the explanation facility in most expert systems (Smedley & Sutton, 2007), background knowledge on audio/visual components and media room design is linked to the preference elicitation portion of the mashup application. In addition to serving as a knowledge acquisition tool for decision makers, the presence of constraint information and reasoning may also serve to increase the trust in any recommended solutions to the multi-criteria decision problem by the user (Pu & Chen, 2007).

After all constraint preference information is collected, the subjects have the opportunity to explore information moderating their decision criteria. The media design mashup application presents lists of specific components to the subject, each of which satisfies all of the specified constraints. The components originally are rank ordered utilizing information on reliability, quality, and customer satisfaction, but may easily be re-ordered by the decision maker using price or other attributes of the individual component (e.g., screen size for televisions). As each component of the overall media room entertainment system is selected, the remaining budget is automatically adjusted to reflect the current decision and re-allocate any additional funds to other components appropriately.

The prototype media room design mashup application is implemented using wiki software written in ASP and a set of HTML/ASP forms to support the preference elicitation and product recommendations. (See Appendix 1 for example screen shots of the prototype mashup tool.) Figure 1 shows the architecture of the prototype mashup. The architecture integrates web-based information resources with a wiki information repository, and a product/pricing information database. These, in turn, provide the information and supporting data for a more traditional rule based system. The actual data specific to media room design is domain specific. The information extraction tools, wiki and other mashup systems are generic and could be populated with data from any decision domain.

Survey Development

The system measured the actual time (TIME) spent participating in the experiment and, for the mashup subjects, the number of information sources visited. The quality of the decision (QUAL) was evaluated by the researchers, who independently judged the decision of each subject. To minimize

bias, this was done in a 'blind' fashion in that the researchers did not know the experimental group of the subjects while performing the evaluation. Factors used to evaluate decision quality included: size and type of television, staying within budget, number of speakers, and receiver and speaker compatibility. Each of these factors had objective standards upon which to assess decision quality. For example, plasma screens are not advised at the altitude in which the subjects reside and experts have clear recommendations of screen size given the size of the room.

A survey was developed to measure the perceptual measures (CONF and EASE) and the research literature was searched for previously used and validated questionnaire items. These were edited only to reflect the context of this experimental study. A candidate list of potential survey questions was identified. An expert panel, including information and web design specialists and decision theorists, evaluated the candidate questions and selected the final survey questions. Table 1 contains the survey questions with citation references. In the actual administration of the survey, the question order was randomized. Questions were presented to the subjects using a 7-point Likert scale, with 1 = Strongly Disagree and 7 = Strongly Agree. Eight demographic questions and an open-ended question, asking simply for additional comments, ended the survey.

The Experiment

The decision making of subjects using the media room design mashup service is compared to subjects solving the same decision task using traditional web search tools. The alternate methodology simulates the common Web-based research methodology of many consumers (75%) who report using the Web to research products prior to purchase (Massey, Khatri, & Montoya-Weiss, 2007).

Since subjects using the mashup are started on the mashup site, subjects using traditional tools

Table 1. Evaluation constructs for mashup decision-making quality and experience

Component	Cronbach alpha	Survey questions/ factors	Sources
Confidence in the decision (CONF)	0.900	• I made a good purchase decision. • I am confident in the choices I made. • I believe that the products I selected were among the best available • I trust the information I got. • I am confident in the choices I made.	Haubl & Trifts (2000) Gao, Wang, Xu, & Wang, 2007 Swaminathan (2003)
Perceived ease of finding information (EASE)	0.866	• It was easy to find the information I needed to make this decision. • I was able to get to information quickly and easily.	Davis (1989) Seiders, Voss, Godfrey & Grewal (2007) Venkatesh, Morris, Davis, & Davis (2003)

are started on a standard Google search page listing consumer electronic stores and media room design sites. Graduate and undergraduate students from information systems, decision sciences, and marketing courses are the subjects. Each student is alternately assigned to one of the two experimental conditions based on the order in which they visited the experiment website, thus producing a random but even distribution of subjects. Those using the mashup service are referred to as 'mashup' subjects. Those using the more common Web-based research, such as a Google search, are referred to as 'traditional' subjects.

The experiment starts by providing each subject with the conditions of the experiment; the subject is to select new audio and video equipment for a media room. A limited number of pre-specified constraints are also provided, including the size and shape of the room (16 by 18 feet), a budget of $4,000, movie watching preference (action/adventure movies over horror or comedy), and room capacity. Relative importance of video quality and audio quality and other criteria are left unspecified for the subjects to use their own preferences. The pre-specified decision constraints and the survey questions are kept visible to the subject throughout the experiment. The subjects are then directed to either the mashup application or the search engine simulator to make their decisions. To evaluate the research hypotheses the survey is administered to both experimental groups.

A total of 56 subjects completed the experiment, 28 in each experimental group. Three additional subjects accessed the experimental website but did not proceed beyond the introduction page. One subject's responses from the mashup experimental group are removed as an outlier. This results in a sample size of 27 users of the mashup tool and 28 users who use a traditional web search. Demographic information may be found in Table 2. Only two subjects, one in each experimental group, reported using the Internet for less than 5 years. Ninety-six percent of subjects reported having made 10 or more online purchases. Only one subject, in the mashing tool experimental group, reported never to have made an online purchase. Five percent reported no prior familiarity with the media room products in this study, 38% had heard of the products but not used them, 31% used the products but felt they didn't know a lot about them, and 25% reported that they both used and knew a lot about the products.

Table 2. Demographic information

	All participants	Mashing-Tool Users	Traditional Web Search
Percent Male	47%	56%	43%
Average Age	24	24	24
Youngest	18	18	18
Oldest	40	40	30

RESULTS AND DISCUSSION

Hypotheses Evaluation

Items for the perceptual measures used in this research, confidence in the decision (CONF) and ease of finding information (EASE), have been previously used in the literature. Both Exploratory and Confirmatory Factor Analysis were performed to verify construct validity using PASW and AMOS. The two-factor model was confirmed which explained 77% of the variance. Confirmatory Factor Analysis also indicated an acceptable fit (GFI = 0.931; CFI = 0.984; RMSEA = 0.047). Scale reliabilities were also acceptable at 0.900 for the CONF construct and 0.866 for the EASE construct (see Table 1).

The means and standard error of the mean are presented in Table 3 for all hypothesized relationships. One-tailed t-tests were performed as follows: The TIME should be less for the mashup subjects than for the traditional subjects, whereas QUAL, CONF, and EASE should be greater for the mashup subjects than for the traditional subjects.

The time (TIME) spent by mashup subjects, as shown in Table 3, is significantly ($p = 0.039$) less than the actual time used by the traditional subjects; thus empirically supporting Hypothesis 1. In fact, the mashup subjects spent on average less than half the time making this complex decision than the traditional group. Additionally, the

mashup subjects showed a much more consistent use of time for performing the decision-making task, with a standard deviation that was less than one fourth of that for the traditional subjects.

Hypothesis 2 addressed the objective assessment of decision quality. Before hypothesis testing, inter-rater agreement was calculated as 0.870, which is significant ($p < 0.000$). Since this value exceeded 0.80, the reliability of the decision quality evaluation was deemed acceptable (Fleiss, 1979). The average objective quality assessment of the mashup group was greater than that of the traditional group ($p = 0.025$) as shown in Table 3, supporting Hypothesis 2.

The survey responses summarized in Table 3 indicate the mashup subjects were not more confident in their decisions nor did they feel that the mashup application made the decision process any easier. Therefore, hypotheses 3 and 4 are not supported.

Our experiment shows definite empirical support for the hypotheses addressing objective measures: Hypothesis 1 (mashup subjects used less time) and Hypothesis 2 (mashup users made better quality decisions.) There was no difference between the groups for the perceptual measures. All participants scored themselves relatively high for confidence in the decision and ease in finding the information. The lack of differences between the mashup and traditional subjects was unexpected compared to previous research with decision

Table 3. Evaluation component means by experimental group and actual time

Component	Mashup Mean (st. error-mean.)	Traditional Search Mean (st. error-mean.)
TIME* (minutes)	21.65 (2.58)	46.39 (10.47)
QUAL** 3-point scale, 3 = high quality decision	2.23 (0.139)	1.81 (0.122)
EASE	5.35 (0.25)	5.41 (0.21)
CONF	5.13 (0.23)	5.29 (0.16)

* Significantly different p = 0.039 – one tailed test Mashup < Traditional

** Significantly different p = 0.025 – one tailed test Mashup > Traditional

support tools and technology (Diehl, Kornish, & Lynch, 2003; Swaminathan, 2003; Venkatesh et al., 2003; Williams, Dennis, Stam, & Aronson, 2007). It could be that the high confidence in the decision for the traditional group came because of the increased expenditure of time. However, it must be remembered that although the group believed they had purchased the best equipment, the actual quality of their decision was lower than that of the mashup group. The use of student subjects participating in a simulated research problem may have impacted the perception of benefit results. Additionally, previous studies utilizing students provided a chance reward of actually receiving the products identified for purchase, giving participants a vested interest in finding high quality solutions. This was not possible for this research study and may not be possible for most high-ticket, complex purchases. Future research may overcome this limitation by examining mashup utilization in real-world settings as opposed to using students in a hypothetical setting.

The experience level of the users also may explain these results. Twenty-five percent rated themselves as having prior experience with the decision domain. Only one respondent had never made an online purchase, most had made over 15. All were experienced Web users. The traditional method of Web browsing may be familiar, and thus not perceived as a particularly cumbersome task. However, imposing the structure of the mashup on the decision process, requiring the subject to articulate preferences, and providing information and/or information links at key decision points, did not degrade the experience for the subjects. The conclusion of formal statistical analysis is that better decisions were achieved in less time using the mashup decision support tool. Both the efficiency and effectiveness of the consumer were positively affected. One can provide decision assistance via a mashup application to consumers resulting in higher quality decision in less time without affecting perceptual factors.

Additional Results

While not part of formal hypothesis testing, some interesting differences were observed between experimental groups. Both groups were to use a $4,000 spending limit and told there was no advantage to under-spending and that the objective was to get the highest quality components to meet the constraints and their own preferences. The traditional subjects spent on average less than the mashup subjects ($3050 versus $3293) and 5 mashup subjects overspent as opposed to 2 traditional subjects. Mashup subjects were given explicit price data throughout the experiment. The system informed them of a relative budget breakdown, a recommended range of how much of their budget to allot to each component. Mashup subjects had updated budgets displayed throughout their decision-making process. They also were explicitly given the option to modify their budgets. Traditional subjects did not have this information and may have viewed the budget as a strict constraint and therefore limited their spending. Given that they made poorer quality decisions, they may have focused on cost to the detriment of other criteria.

From a suppliers' perspective, the fact that the mashup subjects' average spending was closer to the allocated budget may be seen as an advantage, as consumers may invest in higher quality products that would leave them more satisfied with their ultimate purchase decisions. The overspending may also indicate that the mashup users are more willing to explore options outside of their initial set of constraints and this was facilitated by the mashup application. Subjects could see the cost affects of the decisions and trade-offs between decisions. This is summarized nicely by a comment in the open comment section of the survey from one mashup subject: "I found that you need more money to buy what you really want or desire."

The experiment also allowed the information gathering processes of mashup subjects to be assessed. It tracked the pages the subjects accessed and how long they spent reading or interacting with the material on that page. This user interaction data revealed that over 46% of the mashup subjects used the links to access the wiki knowledge base to obtain additional information on media room components and on media room design. These subjects visited an average of 2.33 pages each. This is consistent with prior decision-making research which suggests that users may be unwilling to rely on expert system decisions without an understanding of the information used to make the decision and the decision process (Ye & Johnson, 1995). This is one benefit of using a wiki-based mashup in conjunction with expert or other decision-making aids.

The open-ended question was answered by only a handful of respondents. Subjects from both experimental groups left comments indicating that they enjoyed the experience and that they had not previously thought of making media decisions based on the constraints specified in the experiment. This suggests the utility of a mashup approach to multi-criteria decision making for enabling the ability to explore and review possible constraints impacting the decision-making process and the quality of the corresponding decision.

One final comment from one of the mashup subjects was interesting and holds implications for future mashup research. The comment was: "I liked the site helping me shop. It actually gave me the in-store sales person feeling. And letting me share in the decision and not feel like I was going at this alone was very comforting. I felt like I had a professional A.I. machine keeping me in check." Though not evaluated in the research reported in this article, the above comment indicates that mashups may be able to adequately provide the feel of a mentor or other professional assisting the decision maker.

Implications for Research and Practice

A primary cause of concern is that the subjects of this research did not perceive more confidence nor an ease of finding information in using the mashup

tool even though the study shows that using the mashup application improved both decision time and decision effectiveness. This could be because users in the experiment were only given access to a limited number of information resources as a part of the mashup application. Future studies could use adaptive information extraction agents (e.g., Gregg & Walczak, 2007) to allow users to add their own resources to the mashup tool and determine if that improves user confidence with the decisions made. Future studies should examine whether users would opt to use a mashup tool when it is made available but not required by the experimental design. Research should also examine whether users think they would use a similar tool for future decisions after completing the experiment.

Additional research is also needed to discover why and how users value the information made available by mashups. The fact that nearly half of the mashup users consulted the wiki knowledge repository, even though this was a fictitious, experimental activity, suggests that there is value in providing a mashup that draws from multiple knowledge sources to enhance decision making in complex multi-criteria scenarios. The search for additional information by the experimental subjects could be because it helps them feel more in control over their decision-making activities. Research exploring mashups in more realistic environments, with actual customers, making actual purchases would extend and generalize these results. "Think aloud" research techniques (Van Someren, Barnard, & Sanberg, 1994), where research subjects verbalize their thought processes while working through a cognitive exercise may be useful to broaden understanding of how users interact with mashup technology.

The prototype mashup used in this experiment incorporated only rudimentary decision tree logic, with only several criteria preferences included (some being pre-specified) and as preferences were entered or changed, decision options and/or constraints were updated. Existing research has demonstrated the utility of using more sophisticated techniques for eliciting preferences (Gao et al., 2007; van der Heijden, 2006; Westerman, Tuck, Booth, & Khakzar, 2007) and/or utilizing more complex multi-criteria decision techniques such as the Analytical Hierarchy Process (Chen, 2003; Mustajoki & Hamalainen, 2007; Williams et al., 2007). Further research should explore the utility of incorporating mashup and wiki-based knowledge repositories with additional decision-making techniques. Given that this decision-making aide was shown to improve quality and timeliness, further work should be directed at developing a guided approach for developing the domain-specific parts of the system. This is especially needed for the consumer preference elicitation online survey.

Another limitation of the reported survey results is the small group size of only 56 respondents. Thus the results here should be viewed as exploratory, but the selection of the population should lead to adequate generalization for a well-educated population of users.

Applications of a mashup aided decision tool are ideal in situations where a consumer makes purchase decisions from several different, yet interacting, vendors. Examples include such things as wedding and vacation planning, personal financial management, higher or continuing education, and insurance purchases. Computer-aided decision tools are already used in medical domains to aide patients in making care decisions, e.g., Singh, Cuttler, and Silvers (2004). Information from a source such as WebMD may be combined with decision aides to create treatment or diagnostic mashups, perhaps with a physician and patient sitting side-by-side enabling a truly customized plan of treatment.

The purpose of this research is to evaluate actual and perceived benefits of utilizing a mashup based decision support application. The results show that real benefits occur to mashup users even if the users do not readily perceive these benefits. The development of enterprise mashup applications may be able to overcome this perception deficit by promoting mashup applications and providing motivation for utilization of these applications. As mashup application utility and popularity continues to grow, front-end tools that enable rapid mashup application development are becoming available (Fichter & Wisniewski, 2009). Once service organizations determine which enterprise data is available for consumption by mashup applications and develop a framework for how the mashup applications interact with users, then the basic framework is in place and may be replicated with only the data sources and possibly business rules needing to be changed to provide a wide variety of mashup applications to the organization.

CONCLUSION

Uncertainty in multi-criteria decision problems is produced by lack of information and time pressure to make a decision (Ahn, 2003). The empirical evidence presented shows that the application of mashup decision support overcomes both of these decision-making roadblocks and that furthermore the utilization of a mashup service can greatly improve the quality of consumer decision making in multi-criteria domains.

The design of multi-criteria decision support mashups involves incorporating multiple knowledge resources with decision-making techniques. How to select reliable resources is an open question, but the presented methodology recommends using the presence of individual decision criteria or constraints to assist in identifying needed information resources and decision processes for inclusion in the mashup application.

The profiling and preference gathering methodology of the presented media room design mashup service may serve to help decision makers overcome concerns associated with trying to satisfy multi-criteria, especially for consumers unfamiliar with specific products or service attributes (Malakooti, 2000; Rathnam, 2005; Xiao & Benbasat, 2007).

Future research is needed to further investigate the perceived and actual benefits of mashup service applications, specifically the perceived and actual improvement to the quality of the decisions made and an evaluation of the knowledge sharing capabilities of mashup applications. As implied by the open comment, other capabilities may be achievable through mashup style services including personal shoppers or business mentors to help guide and teach users in effective multi-criteria decision-making processes.

REFERENCES

Ahn, B. S. (2003). Extending Malakooti's model for ranking multicriteria alternatives with preference strength and partial information. *IEEE Transactions on Systems Man and Cybernetics: Part A, 33*(3), 281–287. doi:10.1109/TSMCA.2003.817049

Albinola, M., Baresi, L., Carcano, M., & Guinea, S. (2009). Mashlight: A lightweight mashup framework for everyone. In *Proceedings of WWW2009*. Retrieved October 1, 2009, from http://www.ra.ethz.ch/CDstore/www2009/integror.net/mem2009/papers/paper9.pdf

Balasubramaniam, S., Lewis, G. A., Simanta, S., & Smith, D. B. (2008). Situated software: concepts, motivation, technology, and the future. *IEEE Software, 25*(6), 50–55. doi:10.1109/MS.2008.159

Blake, M. B., & Nowlan, M. F. (2008). Predicting service mashup candidates using enhanced syntactical message management. In *Proceedings of the IEEE International Conference on Services Computing* (pp. 229-236).

Chase, R. (1978). Where does the customer fit in a service operation? *Harvard Business Review, 56*(6), 137–142.

Chen, D. N., Jeng, B., Lee, W. P., & Chuang, C. H. (2008). An agent-based model for consumer-to-business electronic commerce. *Expert Systems with Applications, 34*(1), 469–481. doi:10.1016/j.eswa.2006.09.020

Chen, M. (2003). Factors affecting the adoption and diffusion of XML and Web services standards for E-business systems. *International Journal of Human-Computer Studies, 58*(3), 259–279. doi:10.1016/S1071-5819(02)00140-4

Davis, F. D. (1989). Perceived usefulness, perceived ease of use, and user acceptance of information technology. *Management Information Systems Quarterly, 13*(3), 319–340. doi:10.2307/249008

Diaz-Galiano, M. C., Martin-Valdivia, M. T., & Ureña-López, L. A. (2009). Query expansion with a medical ontology to improve a multimodal information retrieval system. *Computers in Biology and Medicine, 39*(4), 396–403. doi:10.1016/j.compbiomed.2009.01.012

Diehl, K., Kornish, L. J., & Lynch, J. G. (2003). Smart agents: When lower search costs for quality information increase price sensitivity. *The Journal of Consumer Research, 30*(1), 56–71. doi:10.1086/374698

Dornan, A. (2007). Half-baked or mashed: Is mixing enterprise IT and the Internet a recipe for disaster? *Information Week, 10*, 40–48.

Fichter, D., & Wisniewski, J. (2009). They grow up so fast: Mashups in the enterprise. *Online, 33*(3), 54–57.

Fleiss, J. L. (1979). *Statistical methods for rates and proportions* (2nd ed.). New York: Wiley.

Froehle, C. A., & Roth, A. V. (2004). New measurement scales for evaluating perceptions of the technology-mediated customer service experience. *Journal of Operations Management, 22*(1), 1–21. doi:10.1016/j.jom.2003.12.004

Gao, S. J., Wang, H. Q., Xu, D. M., & Wang, Y. F. (2007). An intelligent agent-assisted decision support system for family financial planning. *Decision Support Systems, 44*(1), 60–78. doi:10.1016/j.dss.2007.03.001

Gaudin, S. (2007). IT ditches cost controls to focus on innovation. *Information Week, 128.*

Gregg, D. G., & Walczak, S. (2006). Auction advisor: an agent-based online-auction decision support system. *Decision Support Systems, 41*(2), 449–471. doi:10.1016/j.dss.2004.07.007

Gregg, D. G., & Walczak, S. (2007). Exploiting the information Web. *IEEE Transactions on System. Man and Cybernetics: Part C, 37*(1), 109–125. doi:10.1109/TSMCC.2006.876061

Haubl, G., & Trifts, V. (2000). Consumer decision making in online shopping environments: The effects of interactive decision aids. *Marketing Science, 19*(1), 4–21. doi:10.1287/mksc.19.1.4.15178

Hoyer, V., & Fischer, M. (2008). *Market overview of enterprise mashup tools* (LNCS 5364, pp. 708-721). New York: Springer.

ITU. (2006). *Multichannel stereophonic sound system with and without accompanying picture.* Geneva, Switzerland: International Telecommunication Union.

Jijkoun, V., Mishne, G., Rijke, M. D., Schlobach, S., Ahn, D., & Muller, K. (2004). *Working notes of the CLEF 2004 workshop.* Paper presented at the The University of Amsterdam at QA@CLEF 2004.

Katzmaier, D. (2007). Ultimate HDTV buying guide. *CNet Reviews.* Retrieved December 21, 2007, from http://www.cnet.com/1990-7874_1-5108580-1.html

Kwon, O. B. (2006). Multi-agent system approach to context-aware coordinated web services under general market mechanism. *Decision Support Systems, 41*(2), 380–399. doi:10.1016/j.dss.2004.07.005

Lenzerini, M. (2002). Data integration: A theoretical perspective. In *Proceedings of the Symposium on Principles of Database Systems* (pp. 233-246).

Linthicum, D. (2007). SOA extends its reach: Practical enterprise mash-ups. *InfoWorld, 29*(8), 27–31.

Lita, L. V., Hunt, W. A., & Nyberg, E. (2004). *Resource analysis for question answering.* Paper presented at the Annual Meeting of the Association for Computational Linguistics.

Loreto, S., Mecklin, T., Opsenica, M., & Rissanen, H. (2009). Service broker architecture: Location business case and mashups. *IEEE Communications Magazine, 47*(4), 97–103. doi:10.1109/MCOM.2009.4907414

Lovelock, C. H., & Young, R. F. (1979). Look to consumers to increase productivity. *Harvard Business Review, 57,* 168–178.

Malakooti, B. (2000). Ranking and screening multiple criteria alternatives with partial information and use of ordinal and cardinal strength of preferences. *IEEE Transactions on Systems Man and Cybernetics: Part A, 30*(3), 355–368. doi:10.1109/3468.844359

Manes, A. T. (2003). Web services business models. In *Proceedings of Web services: A manager's guide* (pp. 37–43). Reading, MA: Addison-Wesley.

Mashworks.net. (2007). *Building mash-ups for non-programmers.* Retrieved December 11, 2007, from www.mashworks.net

Massey, A. P., Khatri, V., & Montoya-Weiss, M. M. (2007). Usability of online services: The role of technology readiness and context. *Decision Sciences, 38*(2), 277–308. doi:10.1111/j.1540-5915.2007.00159.x

McFedries, P. (2006). The Web, Take two. *IEEE Spectrum, 43*(6), 68. doi:10.1109/MSPEC.2006.1638049

McMullin, B. (2005). Putting the learning back into learning technology. In G. O'Neill, S.

Mills, P. K., & Morris, J. H. (1986). Clients as "partial" employees of service organizations: Role development in client participation. *Academy of Management Review, 11*(4), 726–735. doi:10.2307/258392

Moore, & B. McMullin (Eds.), *Emerging issues in the practice of university learning and teaching* (pp. 67-76). Dublin: AISHE.

Mustajoki, J., & Hamalainen, R. P. (2007). Smart-Swaps - A decision support system for multicriteria decision analysis with the even swaps method. *Decision Support Systems, 44*(1), 313–325. doi:10.1016/j.dss.2007.04.004

O'Reilly, T. (2005). *What Is Web 2.0: Design patterns and business models for the next generation of software*. Retrieved December 22, 2007, from http://oreillynet.com/pub/a/oreilly/tim/news/2005/09/30/what-is-web-20.html

Obrenović, Z., Gašević, D., & Eliëns, A. (2008). Simulating creativity through opportunistic software development. *IEEE Software, 25*(6), 64–70. doi:10.1109/MS.2008.162

Oren, E., Haller, A., Hauswirth, M., Heitmann, B., Decker, S., & Mesnage, C. (2007). A flexible integration framework for semantic web 2.0 applications. *IEEE Software, 24*(5), 64–71. doi:10.1109/MS.2007.126

Oz, E. (2007). *Foundations of e-Commerce*. Upper Saddle River, NJ: Prentice Hall.

Programmableweb. (2009). *Media room and home theater design and construction*. Retrieved September 23, 2009, from http://www.programmableweb.com

Pu, P., & Chen, L. (2007). Trust-inspiring explanation interfaces for recommender systems. *Knowledge-Based Systems, 20*(6), 542–556. doi:10.1016/j.knosys.2007.04.004

Rathnam, G. (2005). Interaction effects of consumers' product class knowledge and agent search strategy on consumer decision making in electronic commerce. *IEEE Transactions on Systems Man and Cybernetics: Part A, 35*(4), 556–573. doi:10.1109/TSMCA.2005.850606

Reports, C. (2007). HDTV for any budget. *Consumer Reports, 72*, 14.

Seiders, K., Voss, G. B., Godfrey, A. L., & Grewal, D. (2007). SERVCON: Development and validation of a multidimensional service convenience scale. *Journal of the Academy of Marketing Science, 35*(1), 144–156. doi:10.1007/s11747-006-0001-5

Selamat, A., & Selamat, M. H. (2005). Analysis on the performance of mobile agents for query retrieval. *Information Sciences, 172*(3-4), 281–307. doi:10.1016/j.ins.2004.05.005

Sinclair, K. (2007). Building automation: Making money with BAS mash-ups. *Engineered Systems, 24*(8), 25.

Singh, J., Cuttler, L., & Silvers, J. B. (2004). Toward understanding consumers' role in medical decisions for emerging treatments: Issues, framework and hypotheses. *Journal of Business Research, 57*(9), 1054–1065. doi:10.1016/S0148-2963(02)00358-2

Smedley, G., & Sutton, S. G. (2007). The effect of alternative procedural explanation types on procedural knowledge acquisition during knowledge-based systems. *Journal of Information Systems, 21*(1), 27–51. doi:10.2308/jis.2007.21.1.27

Song, J., Koo, C., & Kim, Y. (2007). Investigating antecedents of behavioral intentions in mobile commerce. *Journal of Internet Commerce, 6*(1), 13–34. doi:10.1300/J179v06n01_02

Spira, J. B. (2006). Getting answers to questions. *KM World, 15*(7), 1, 3, 30.

Sun, L., & Li, Y. (2009). Using usage control to access XML databases. *International Journal of Information Systems in the Service Sector, 1*(3), 32–44.

Swaminathan, V. (2003). The impact of recommendation agents on consumer evaluation and choice: The moderating role of category risk, product complexity, and consumer knowledge. *Journal of Consumer Psychology, 13*(1-2), 93–101. doi:10.1207/S15327663JCP13-1&2_08

Tatemura, J., Sawires, A., Po, O., Chen, S., Candan, K., Argrawal, D., & Goveas, M. (2007). Mashup feeds: Continuous queries over Web services. *Internation Conference on Management of Data,* 1128-1120.

Thor, A., Aumueller, D., & Rahm, E. (2007). Data integration support for mashups. In *Proceeding of the International Workshop on Information Integration on the Web,* Vancouver, Canada (pp. 104-109).

1touchmovie.com. (2007). *Media room and home theater design and construction.* Retrieved June 26, 2008, from http://www.1touchmovie.com/theater_design1.html

Tsikriktsis, N., Lanzolla, G., & Frohlich, M. (2004). Adoption of e-processes by service firms: An empirical study of antecedents. *Production and Operations Management, 13*(3), 216–229. doi:10.1111/j.1937-5956.2004.tb00507.x

Ullman, J. D. (1997). *Information integration using logical views* (LNCS 1186, pp. 19-40). New York: Springer.

van der Heijden, H. (2006). Mobile decision support for in-store purchase decisions. *Decision Support Systems, 42*(2), 656–663. doi:10.1016/j.dss.2005.03.006

Van Someren, M., Barnard, Y., & Sanberg, J. (1994). *The think aloud method: A practical guide to modelling cognitive processes.* London: Academic Press.

Venkatesh, V., Morris, M. G., Davis, G. B., & Davis, F. D. (2003). User acceptance of information technology: Toward a unified view. *Management Information Systems Quarterly, 27*(3), 425–478.

Wagner, C., & Majchrzak, A. (2006). Enabling customer-centricity using wikis and the wiki way. *Journal of Management Information Systems, 23*(3), 17–43. doi:10.2753/MIS0742-1222230302

Westerman, S. J., Tuck, G. C., Booth, S. A., & Khakzar, K. (2007). Consumer decision support systems: Internet versus in-store application. *Computers in Human Behavior, 23*(6), 2928–2944. doi:10.1016/j.chb.2006.06.006

Williams, M. L., Dennis, A. R., Stam, A., & Aronson, J. E. (2007). The impact of DSS use and information load on errors and decision quality. *European Journal of Operational Research, 176*(1), 468–481. doi:10.1016/j.ejor.2005.06.064

Xiao, B., & Benbasat, I. (2007). E-commerce product recommendation agents: Use, characteristics, and impact. *Management Information Systems Quarterly, 31*(1), 137–209.

Xue, M., Hein, G. R., & Harker, P. T. (2005). Consumer and co-producer roles in e-service: analysing efficiency and effectiveness of e-service designs. *International Journal of Electronic Business, 3*(2), 174–197. doi:10.1504/IJEB.2005.006909

Ye, L. R., & Johnson, P. E. (1995). The impact of explanation facilities on user acceptance of expert-systems advice. *Management Information Systems Quarterly, 19*(2), 157–172. doi:10.2307/249686

Yu, Y., Kim, J., Shin, K., & Jo, G. S. (2009). Recommendation system using location-based ontology on wireless internet: An example of collective intelligence by using 'mashup' applications. *Expert Systems with Applications, 36*(9), 11675–11681. doi:10.1016/j.eswa.2009.03.017

APPENDIX

Figure 2. Screen shots from the media design mash-up application

Screen shots from the Media Design Mash-up application.

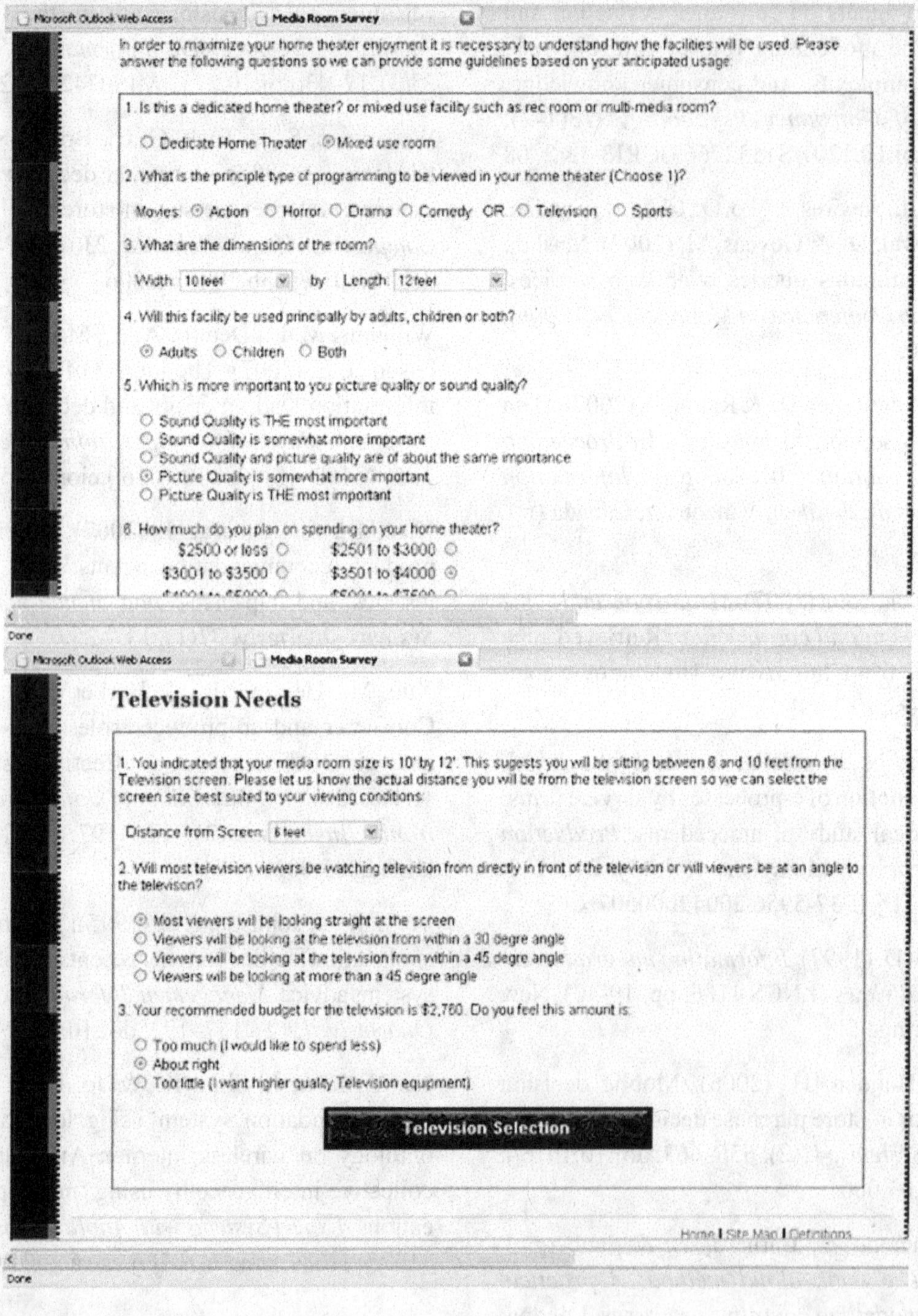

This work was previously published in International Journal of Information Systems in the Service Sector, Volume 2, Issue 4, edited by John Wang, pp. 39-56, copyright 2010 by IGI Publishing (an imprint of IGI Global).

Chapter 19
Using the Critical Incident Technique to Identify Factors of Service Quality in Online Higher Education

María J. Martínez-Argüelles
Open University of Catalonia, Spain

José M. Castán
University of Barcelona, Spain

Angel A. Juan
Open University of Catalonia, Spain

ABSTRACT

Information technologies are changing the way in which higher education is delivered. In this regard, there is a necessity for developing information systems that help university managers measure the quality of online services offered to their students. This paper discusses the importance of considering students' perception of service quality. The authors then identify key factors of service quality, as perceived by students, in online higher education. To this end, the Critical Incident Technique (CIT) is proposed as an effective qualitative methodology. Some benefits of this methodology are highlighted and an exploratory research is carried out in a real environment to illustrate this approach. Results from this research explain which quality dimensions are considered the most valuable to online students. Information provided by this methodology can significantly improve strategic decision-making processes in online universities worldwide.

DOI: 10.4018/978-1-4666-0044-7.ch019

Copyright © 2012, IGI Global. Copying or distributing in print or electronic forms without written permission of IGI Global is prohibited.

INTRODUCTION

Higher education today is undergoing a period of fundamental transformation, triggered particularly by the consequences of the globalization process and by developments in the field of information and communication technologies (ICT). The emergence of an increasingly differentiated demand for education, the need to carry out more commercial activities in order to tap new sources of funding, the new entrants to the high education market –e. g. new online universities that exploit the possibilities offered by ICTs– and the increasing bargaining power of suppliers and customers are only some of the factors that are forcing universities to rethink their traditional roles, to develop new organizational structures and to reposition themselves through strategic direction setting (Moratis & van Baalen, 2002).

These trends and the widespread recognition that the university's invisible product, knowledge, is the most important factor in economic and social growth are the reasons for the increasing competitiveness inside the higher education market all over the world. To survive in this environment, universities should focus on customers' perceptions of service quality –understanding 'service' in the broad sense, including both academic and non academic services– since those perceptions are a key influence on students' decisions when they are choosing or recommending a particular institution.

While there is little disagreement on the importance of service quality issues in higher education, the challenge is to identify and implement the most appropriate measurement tools in order to gain a better understanding of the quality issues that impact on students' service experiences (O'Neill & Palmer, 2004). The problem is that much of the research on this topic has been too highly focused from an academic insider's perspective, presupposing that the inherent knowledge base of those involved in the business of higher education is sufficient for developing student-oriented programs.

Nevertheless, research on service-related business suggests that this 'inside out' decision making is hardly ever successful, because if firms do not know what their own customers' desire is, it is difficult to design programs that match customer expectations of what constitutes a good service. Stated simply, knowing what customers expect is the first and possibly one of the most critical steps in delivering quality (Zeithaml & Bitner, 2003). One of the most important customers of any higher-education offer is the student herself. Even so, her perceptions about the quality of the service being offered are usually omitted in the existing literature about online higher-education.

The purpose of the current article is to investigate how students perceive and evaluate online higher education services. In order to find out the aspects or characteristics that students take into account in their evaluation of the perceived service quality (PSQ) in online higher education environments we have carried out a qualitative analysis using the Critical Incident Technique (CIT). CIT is a procedure in which it is the consumers themselves –in this case the students– who give descriptions of their experience of the service, whether satisfactory or unsatisfactory. After appropriate analysis, these are then grouped to form specific customer requirements or quality dimensions. The results obtained are not only aimed at clarifying the determinants of perceived service quality in online higher education, but also show the advantages of the Critical Incident Technique over other exploratory inductive methods, particularly when research is conducted in online environments, as is the case here.

SERVICE QUALITY IN HIGHER EDUCATION

Following the general pattern set by service industries, the issue of service quality within the higher education sector has received increasing attention in recent years. In particular, there is a clear interest in developing information systems for monitoring students' and groups' activity in online environments, since it can contribute to improve learning processes and, therefore, the quality of the service being offered (Daradoumis et al., 2010; Juan et al., 2009b). Although debate has ranged over various issues, the most dominant theme is the development of valid, reliable and replicable measures of perceived service quality (O'Neill & Palmer, 2004). In the early stages, most models designed to evaluate PSQ focused exclusively on teaching and learning. In the last decade, though, several studies have approached the evaluation of university services from a broad perspective, considering not only the core service (the teaching) but the peripheral or auxiliary administrative and backup services as well (O'Neill & Palmer, 2004; Abdullah, 2005).

This study continues this line of research by applying a holistic conception of service quality in online higher education. Since each and every one of the service interactions between students and the university impact on the overall level of PSQ, knowing the relative importance assigned by students to each of them is vital to be able to pinpoint service quality failures and to direct continuous quality improvement efforts (Aldridge & Rowley, 1998). In this regard, like hospitals or shopping centers, universities constitute a good example of multi-service organization. In organizations of this type, although the central service –the one that defines the organization's mission– is the most important, complementary services also have a decisive impact on PSQ (Gabott & Hogg, 1996; Papa & Avgeri, 2009). In fact, some research shows that while the basic service may be essential to consumer satisfaction, it is not always the only key element in the overall perception of service quality (Bigné et al., 2003; Levy, 2009).

The related literature describes a plethora of measurement tools and techniques for assessing PSQ within the higher education sector. For the most part they are extensions or adaptations of SERVQUAL models (Ford et al., 1993), where service quality is the result of a comparison between expectations and perceptions of performance; SERVPERF (Oldfield & Baron, 2000) which measures service quality considering only consumer perceptions; or IPA (Ford et al., 1999; Joseph et al., 2005), which weights both the perceptions and the importance assigned by consumers to each of the attributes of the service. While those models were initially designed to be applicable across a broad spectrum of service settings, many studies have stressed that the industry-specific characteristics of many services mean that these models should be adapted or supplemented to fit the characteristics of the particular service under analysis (Cox & Dale, 2001; Chen, 2004). Given these considerations, the relatively large number of articles on the subject of evaluating PSQ in higher education is in contrast to the lack of papers regarding higher education in online environments. Recently, however, some authors have considered this is an important research area and, accordingly, some interesting papers have appeared on the subject (Chen et al., 2008; Douglas et al., 2008a; Douglas et al., 2008b; Palmer & Holt, 2009). Following these authors, our work aims to propose and illustrate a methodology for identifying relevant quality dimensions to be considered in educational information systems.

EVALUATION OF SERVICE QUALITY IN ONLINE HIGHER EDUCATION

Probably the two most important long-trends in the business world are the shifting of the economy from goods to services and the rapid extension of the information economy and electronic networks (Jiang & Rosenbloom, 2005). Both trends converge in the concept of online higher education, which provides higher education services over electronic networks, such as the Internet. Learning Management Systems (LMS) are computer-based applications comprising relatively open systems that allow interaction with other students and access to a wide set of electronic teaching resources. However, the feature that defines LMS is the fact that they apply information and communication technologies to general institutional functions such as administration, materials development and distribution, course delivery and monitoring, and complementary advisory and tutorial services (Juan et al., 2009a).

The digital nature the interactions produced in an online environment is a source of some problems for applying the classical PSQ evaluation models. Most of the items used in these scales are linked to the direct interpersonal interaction that characterized 'traditional' services (Makarem et al., 2009). Therefore, even those who advocate the use of these scales in virtual environments acknowledge that, in the absence of these traditional interactions, the scales "would have to be reformulated before they can be meaningfully used in an e-service context" (van Riel et al., 2001, p. 363).

A similar situation occurs with respect to another characteristic of LMS: the absence of physical reference points or indicators of quality of service, such as premises, facilities, and service staff. In the traditional university these tangible elements make up what is known as the 'servicescape' which is a decisive factor in PSQ evaluations (O'Neill & Palmer, 2004). In online learning environments, the student does not have at his/her disposal the conventional physical elements that act as indicators of the quality of service. In their place, the student can only use other variables, such as the aesthetics and ease of use of the online interface, referred to as 'e-scape' (van Riel et al., 2004).

A third element that is distinctive of online learning environments is that students are not just users of university services, but are the universities' 'primary customers'. Consumers are often part of the production and levier processes of services, but in LMS the role of the student is even greater, since it is essential that he/she should be the centre

of the teaching/learning process. Moreover, as the user of a digital interface, the online student will need a certain degree of skill and experience in working with ICTs. Consequently, the students themselves contribute directly to the quality of service delivered and to his/her own (dis)satisfaction.

The aim of this work, the design of an evaluation system for the quality of service, taking into account these and other features of LMS, is –to the best of our knowledge– quite new in the existing literature. Although there are many models for assessing PSQ in online environments are available: the WebQual scale (Loiacono et al., 2000), the SITEQUAL scale (Yoo & Donthu, 2001), the eTAilQ model (Wolfinbarger & Gilly, 2003), the e-SQ model (Zeithaml & Bitner, 2003), or the E-S-QUAL model (Parasuraman et al., 2005), they have been designed exclusively to assess service quality of web sites and, specifically, of online shopping sites. The aforementioned were not designed to evaluate the quality of pure and complex services, such as the educational ones, which do not involve just a single transaction, but multiple interactions that take place over a prolonged time span.

For this reason, we agree with Parasuraman et al. (2005), that an important research priority is to examine the scales in the context of pure service sites to establish how the service quality dimensions change when consumers interact with technology in online environments. Specifically, in the case of online higher education, important questions, both empirical and theoretical, have just begun to be addressed. Most of the published studies focus on specific services –e.g., an online university library (O'Neill, 2003)– or on particular dimensions –as, for instance, teaching resources or development (De Lange et al., 2003; Ellis et al., 2009)–, but to date no holistic evaluation of PSQ, that captures the online student's overall service experience in online learning environments has been carried out. Table 1 shows a summary of the main dimensions of perceived service quality that have been highlighted in previous works in the field of online services. Table 2 shows a similar summary for the field of higher education.

THE CRITICAL INCIDENT TECHNIQUE

Many studies of service quality in higher education have overemphasized the importance of technical –relatively quantifiable– dimensions of service quality. The fact that technical quality is easier to measure has given rise to "a plethora of statistics, indices and league tables covering such issues as student progression rates, the proportion of stu-

dents achieving higher grades and the quality of teaching staff, as measured by their qualifications and research performances" (O'Neill & Palmer, 2004, p. 41). However, less effort has been spent in probing the functional aspects of quality, which are the ones most closely related to students' satisfaction. Functional quality, focused on the more personal aspects of the service encounter, is therefore, by nature, intangible, more difficult to imitate and, as a result, may be used to create a competitive edge.

The identification of the qualitative functional dimensions of service quality was carried out using a qualitative method referred to as the critical

Table 1. Traditional quality dimensions for online services

Author/s	Quality Dimensions
Yoo and Donthu (2001)	Ease of use, aesthetic design, processing speed, security
Loiacono et al. (2002)	Informational fit to task, interactivity, trust, response time, design, intuitiveness, design appeal, innovativeness, flow-emotional appeal, integrated communication, business processes, substitutability
Barnes and Vidgen (2002)	Usability, design, information, trust, empathy
Zeithaml et al. (2002)	Reliability, responsiveness, access, flexibility, ease of navigation, efficiency, assurance/trust, security/privacy, price knowledge, site aesthetics, customization/personalization
Wolfinbarger and Gilly (2003)	Website design, reliability/fulfillment, privacy/security, consumer service
Parasuraman et al. (2005)	Efficiency, fulfillment, reliability, privacy, responsiveness, compensation, contact
Su et al. (2008)	Outcome quality, consumer service, process controllability, ease of use, information quality, website design

Table 2. Traditional quality dimensions for higher education

Author/s	Quality Dimensions
Kwan and Ng (1999)	Course content, concern for student, facilities, assessment, instruction medium, social activities, people
Oldfield and Baron (2000)	Requisite elements, acceptable elements, functional elements
O'Neill and Palmer (2004)	Contact (responsiveness and trust), empathy and logistic (tangibles and reliability)
Lagrosen et al. (2004)	Corporate collaboration, information and responsiveness, courses offered, internal evaluation, computer facilities, collaboration and comparisons, library resources
Sahney et al. (2004)	Competence, attitude, content, delivery, reliability
Marzo-Navarro et al. (2005)	Teaching staff, enrolment and organization
Douglas et al. (2008a)	Teaching, learning and assessment environment (responsiveness, communication, functionality/usefulness) and ancillary services (responsiveness, access, socializing)

incident technique (CIT). CIT was introduced in the social sciences more than fifty years ago by Flanagan (1954) and has been used in a variety of contexts in recent years to explore service research issues. The critical incident technique aims to contribute to improving our understanding of the activity or phenomenon by using an original approach: the reporting of the events that make up a specific experience by the person or persons involved (Schurr, 2007).

The method follows the following steps: Using a survey or a similar procedure, a catalogue of critical incidents is compiled and then analyzed. So the task involves two distinct activities: a) choosing a frame of reference for the incidents recorded, and b) developing –by inductive mechanisms–, a series of categories and subcategories in which the incidents can be classified.

The inductive nature of the CIT makes it particularly appropriate as an exploratory method to deepen our knowledge of a topic or specific phenomenon –such as perceived service quality in online higher education– that has not been widely reported or when used to develop the conceptual structure to be used and tested in subsequent research (Gremler, 2004). The model is flexible and does not have a rigid set of principles to follow, meaning that it can be adapted to the contingencies of a particular subject and makes it especially appropriate in cases in which it is difficult or, as in this study, impossible to determine all the variables a priori (Sweeney & Lapp, 2004).

Furthermore, the fact that it provides information obtained directly from the reports of service recipients helps the researcher to record and understand clearly and holistically the set of cognitive and emotional perceptions that the informant associates with a particular service encounter. This is fundamentally important in the context of service delivery, since the concepts of satisfaction and quality involve a complex psychological process (Zeithaml & Bitner, 2003). In this way, critical incidents highlight this psychological process – without determining a priori what is important and/

or relevant– providing managers and researchers with specific, relevant information that can point to possible areas for improvement (Chell, 1998).

This technique has been widely used to assess the underlying sources of satisfaction and dissatisfaction of consumers of services (Edvardsson & Ross, 2001), but it has hardly ever been applied in the context of e-services (Sweeney & Lapp, 2004; Sur, 2008). In our view, it offers clear advantages in this context over other qualitative techniques and it is a suitable alternative to the discussion group method habitually used in studies of this type (Oldfield & Baron, 2000; O'Neill & Palmer, 2004; Joseph et al., 2005):

- First, since students enrolled on online programs usually combine their studies with their professional activity they do not usually coincide in place and time, so it is difficult to persuade them to participate in synchronous discussion groups or face-to-face interviews.
- In these conditions, furthermore, a bias may appear in the study, as it is probable that students with fewer outside commitments and greater flexibility are likely to participate more, though their preferences may not be representative of the views of the body of students as a whole.

We should also remember that ICTs allow the application of electronic interview procedures that are effective and cheap –for both interviewer and interviewee– and overcome the classic limitations of time and space associated with other procedures. Sending a message to students' personal mailboxes promotes the asynchronous participation of students, as they only have to respond at the time most convenient for them, from wherever they chose, and without the need of having to coincide with the times or places convenient for other students. Moreover, this allows for a reduction of costs for those taking part in the study, not only in terms of avoiding unnecessary travel but, above all, because it cuts the time necessary for participating in the research –in comparison with, for example, what happens in online discussion groups.

Also, this method gives greater flexibility in the design of the research, and in carrying it out, as it encourages the participation of students from different institutions, even if their study and vacation times do not coincide. Similarly, the number of participants taking part in the study can be increased with a reduced marginal cost, as it would only be necessary to forward messages to the corresponding e-mail.

RESEARCH SCENARIO AND RESEARCH METHODOLOGY

The Open University of Catalonia or UOC (http://www.uoc.edu/portal/english) is a fully online university with headquarters in Barcelona, Spain. It was founded in 1995 by the Catalan Government with the mission of "providing people with lifelong learning and education through intensive use of information and communication technologies". According to official data, the UOC offers educational services over the Internet to more than 50,000 students, distributed in several undergraduate and graduate programs. UOC students belong to different parts of the world, but they are mainly located in Spain and South America. About 60% of UOC undergraduate students are adult students (over 30 years old) that typically combine their professional activity and/or family responsibilities with their academic duties. Educational services are delivered by a team composed of more than 2,200 instructors –including UOC faculty and UOC online collaborators, most of these professors from other Spanish universities– and 550 management staff. The UOC uses an asynchronous and student-centered educational model and has already received several international prizes, such as the 2001 ICDE Prize for the best virtual and distance university in the world or the 2004 OEA Prize for educational quality.

In this scenario, the process of data collection of the critical incidents comprises two stages. In the first, the consumers are interviewed and specific information about the service obtained. In the second stage, the data are classified in categories which are intended to represent different dimensions of service quality. In the first stage of our study, an e-mail was sent to a random sample of UOC students. The theory recommends interviewing a minimum between 10 and 20 consumers so that, if one of them provides false or mistaken information, his/her point of view can be compared and contrasted with the data from the other subjects. The selected subjects are usually asked to report between 5 and 10 positive and 5 and 10 negative examples of their experience of the service.

We sent the message to a considerably larger number of students, asking them to record approximately five positive and five negative critical incidents related to the service they receive. We did this because the response rate in online surveys tends to be low –typically between 10% and 30%– and because it was simpler to interview a larger number of subjects than to ask each student to record a higher number of incidents. In this way, we avoid the risk of presenting a complicated and time-consuming survey, which would have an even more negative effect on participation. The main aim of this stage was to obtain a minimum of 200 critical incidents, a number that is considered theoretically adequate. Eventually, a total of 41 (21 men and 20 women) took part, reporting 392 critical incidents, of which twelve were rejected because they had not been correctly formulated. The sample thus comprised 380 valid critical incidents.

The incidents were analyzed in Table 3. First, they were grouped according to type. For each type a sentence was written to describe the incident; both positive and negative incidents were included. Once all the critical incidents were grouped together the above process was repeated, now using the similarity between the sentences

Table 3. Steps in a critical-incident analysis

Step	Description	Key points
1	Generation and collection of critical incidents.	• Messages are sent to students, applying for negative and positive critical incidents. • Collecting critical incidents: specific examples that demonstrate the level of service quality in relation to a specific quality dimension.
2	Classification of critical incidents in groups.	Grouping is based on the similarity of the incidents.
3	Creation of a meaningful definition for each group.	The definitions must be specific and assertive.
4	Classification of the definitions.	• The classification should be based on the similarity of the definitions. • The definitions should describe wishes and/or needs of the customers (each one linked to a quality dimension).
5	Checking the accuracy of the classification process.	• The classification process is carried out by two raters. • The degree of agreement between the two raters is estimated (min. 80%).
6	Checking the relevancy of the included dimensions.	• 10% of the critical incidents are extracted before establishing the dimensions of quality. • Check whether these 10% can be placed in the pre-established dimensions.

describing the incidents as the criterion. We thus obtained a hierarchical relation between critical incidents, their aggregate descriptions and, finally, the dimensions of quality.

The key stage in the process was the creation of the groups. To monitor this process, responsibility for the task was assigned to two different raters: the first established the dimensions of quality following the generalization procedure described above and the second, using the dimensions established, directly assigned each of the critical incidents to one of these dimensions. The accuracy of the distribution process depends on the degree of agreement between the raters, that is, of the percentage of incidents that both place in the same dimension. Total agreement is represented by a score of 1. We obtained a score of 0.91, which should be considered satisfactory, taking into account that the literature considers an index of above 0.8 to be acceptable (Latham et al., 1979).

Finally we checked the accuracy of the dimensions in order to determine whether they were able to define the construct of service quality in its entirety. To do this, we randomly extracted around 10% of the critical incidents (35) and then regrouped and reclassified the remaining incidents in the dimensions. We then re-assigned to these dimensions the 35 critical incidents that we had removed. Since we were able to place all these incidents in the dimensions, we concluded that they presented a reliable reflection of the construct.

EXPERIMENTAL RESULTS

The categorization process highlighted the need to reject incidents which did not contain specific examples or experiences of the service received but reflected more general impressions, such as the advantages of online learning –time saving, availability, ease of access, the opportunity to combine studies and work, etc.– and its drawbacks –the feeling of isolation, the need to adapt to the environment, etc. (Pedró, 2005; Lim et al., 2008; Juan et al., 2008). Among these comments, the opportunity to combine studies and family and professional life was highly valued by a part of the population who otherwise would not be able to study. After this process of refinement we had

350 critical incidents, of which 184 were positive and 166 negative. Once the classification process was completed, and after checking the validity of the process, these critical incidents were finally grouped in 12 dimensions covering 33 definitions. Table 4 shows the most important features of the various dimensions. Figure 1 summarizes this information in a Pareto chart. Notice that all dimensions seem to have a relative importance (i.e., the highest percentage for any dimension is less than 20%). Even so, four dimensions (Learning, Materials, Interface and Responsiveness) account for about 55% of total critical impacts. Examples of positive and negative incidents are shown in Table 5.

The dimension Design and program focus accounted for approximately 5% of all incidents. This dimension covers the study paths offered by the institution and the focus of the program and courses. It represents 5.4% of the positive critical incidents and 4.2% of the negative ones.

The dimension Teaching materials and resources recorded 47 critical incidents (13.4%), 26 positive and 21 negative. The dimension can be divided into three subcategories: contents (e.g., "the materials are up-to-date", "materials are superficial"), format (e.g., "the materials are available in interactive format and on paper", "the materials should be sent on paper") and the library, which the students view as particularly important, since it elicited eight positive and eight negative incidents.

The dimension Learning refers to aspects related to the planning of the learning process, the workload, the usefulness of specific activities, the feedback obtained and the guidance, follow-up and support provided by teachers. This important dimension accounted for almost 20% of all the critical incidents generated (18.5% of the positive incidents and 21.1% of the negative ones).

Assessment of learning accounted for 7.4% of all critical incidents. The students have a high opinion of the 'continuous assessment system' which helps them 'to study and learn' but a negative view of the 'excessive number of tests in some subjects'. Since at half of the institutions analyzed the final assessment is done on brick and mortar campus, the arrangements made for this assessment ("the possibility of choosing the date for the examination among several options" or "the need to go to a particular place to do the examination") was considered as a subcategory.

The dimension Sending of documentation (fulfillment) evaluates the process of delivering documentation to students' homes –either materials and other teaching resources, or administrative documents such as certificates. Though the total percentage of incidents relating to this dimension was low (14), most of them (12) were negative and reported delays.

Two other aspects of service that emerge as fundamental are the Responsiveness, that is, the speed of responses to students' doubts and problems, to do either with the teaching itself or with administrative or technical issues. This dimension accounted for 12.5% of the positive incidents and 7.8% of the negative ones. We also assessed the Accuracy or Appropriate response to incidents and doubts was also assessed. Here there were a greater percentage of negative incidents (9.6%) than positive (5.4%), above all relating to administrative processes. There were also a higher percentage of negative incidents (6.6% vs. 2.7%) in the category Administrative practices (for example, "bureaucratic problems with the secretary's office").

In contrast, one of the dimensions that recorded a higher percentage of positive incidents (9.2% vs. 2.4%) was the student-staff relations, especially the administrative staff (5.4%). The same trend was found (13.6% vs. 3%) in the dimension Relations with other students. The students valued very positively the chance to interact with students "from other places", who are "professionals", and the chance to "make friends" and work together in the learning process, generating a "spirit of solidarity"; they also valued the availability of spaces that promote this interaction.

Table 4. Classification of the dimensions obtained

Dimensions and sub-dimensions	Critical incidents					
	Positive		Negative		Total	
	Number	Percentage	Number	Percentage	Number	Percentage
Design and focus of the program	*10*	*5.43%*	*7*	*4.22%*	*17*	*4.86%*
Focus of the program	6	3.26%	5	3.01%	11	3.14%
Study paths	4	2.17%	2	1.20%	6	1.71%
Teaching materials and resources	*26*	*14.13%*	*21*	*12.65%*	*47*	*13.43%*
Content	14	7.61%	10	6.02%	25	7.14%
Format	4	2.17%	3	1.81%	7	2.00%
Library	8	4.35%	8	4.82%	16	4.57%
Learning	*34*	*18.48%*	*35*	*21.08%*	*69*	*19.71%*
Planning of learning	4	2.17%	3	1.81%	7	2.00%
Workload/level of dedication required	3	1.63%	3	1.81%	6	1.71%
Guidance and follow-up of the learning process	16	8.70%	11	6.63%	27	7.71%
Contribution of the activities to learning	10	5.43%	3	1.81%	13	3.71%
Feedback on the activities	1	0.54%	15	9.04%	16	4.57%
Assessment of learning	*12*	*6.52%*	*14*	*8.43%*	*26*	*7.43%*
Assessment system	10	5.43%	11	6.63%	21	6.00%
Organization of face-to-face final assessment	2	1.09%	3	1.81%	5	1.43%
Responsiveness	*23*	*12.50%*	*13*	*7.83%*	*36*	*10.29%*
Teaching staff	13	7.07%	4	2.41%	17	4.86%
Administrative staff	8	4.35%	8	4.82%	16	4.57%
Computer staff	2	1.09%	1	0.60%	3	0.86%
Accuracy of responses	*10*	*5.43%*	*16*	*9.64%*	*26*	*7.43%*
Teaching staff	5	2.72%	1	0.60%	6	1.71%
Administrative staff	4	2.17%	13	7.83%	17	4.86%
Computer staff	1	0.54%	2	1.20%	3	0.86%
Courtesy	*17*	*9.24%*	*4*	*2.41%*	*21*	*6.00%*
Teaching staff	7	3.80%	2	1.20%	9	2.57%
Administrative staff	10	5.43%	1	0.60%	11	3.14%
Computer staff	0	0.00%	1	0.60%	1	0.29%
Administrative processes	*5*	*2.72%*	*11*	*6.63%*	*16*	*4.57%*
Sending of documentation	*2*	*1.09%*	*12*	*7.23%*	*14*	*4.00%*
Teaching	1	0.54%	5	3.01%	6	1.71%
Administrative	1	0.54%	7	4.22%	8	2.29%
Relations with fellow students	*25*	*13.59%*	*5*	*3.01%*	*30*	*8.57%*
Interaction with other students	13	7.07%	3	1.81%	16	4.57%
Help with learning	4	2.17%	0	0.00%	4	1.14%

continues on following page

Table 4. Continued

Dimensions and sub-dimensions	Critical incidents					
	Positive		Negative		Total	
	Number	Percentage	Number	Percentage	Number	Percentage
Availability of areas of interaction	8	4.35%	2	1.20%	10	2.86%
User's interface	*20*	*10.87%*	*19*	*11.45%*	*39*	*11.14%*
Attractiveness	2	1.09%	1	0.60%	3	0.86%
Easy to connect	3	1.63%	5	3.01%	8	2.29%
Easy to browse	11	5.98%	6	3.61%	17	4.86%
Reliable	3	1.63%	6	3.61%	9	2.57%
Secure	1	0.54%	1	0.60%	2	0.57%
Fees and compensations	*0*	*0.00%*	*9*	*5.42%*	*9*	*2.57%*
Fees	0	0.00%	7	4.22%	7	2.00%
Compensations	0	0.00%	2	1.20%	2	0.57%
TOTAL	*184*	*100.00%*	*166*	*100.00%*	*350*	*100.00%*

Figure 1. Pareto chart for critical incidents by dimension

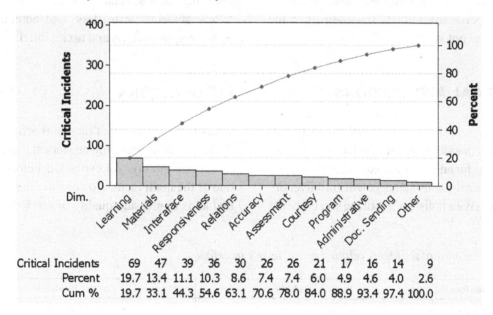

The category User's interface covers the aspects of service relating to the ease of use and the technical functioning of the electronic interface. It includes the physical appearance of the interface, the speed of the connection to the campus at any time (connectivity), the capacity for posting and downloading pages and files reliably (reliability) and security. The highest percentage of positive critical incidents in this dimension is found for ease of browsing, that is, how simple and intuitive the browsing is and the ease of locating informa-

Table 5. Examples of incidents regarding online learning

Learning	Positive incidents	Negative incidents
Planning of learning	"The planning of the entire course is clear from the beginning, there are no last-minute surprises"	"There were changes in the planning of the course and some parts were not offered (...)"
Level of difficulty-dedication	"Requires perseverance and hard work"	"The rhythm is demanding and it's hard to keep up when you're working as well"
Guidance and follow-up	"Excellent guidance from the instructors"	"Some of the instructors just send on the dates of the courses and don't do anything to encourage or guide the students"
Contribution of the activities	"I learnt a lot from the debates"	"Some of the activities require a great deal of work searching the Internet (...); you spend longer looking for information than studying"
Feedback on activities	"Personalized feedback on activities"	"The instructors rarely discuss or comment on the contents of the activities"

tion inside the campus. Some examples of critical incidents for this dimension can be seen in Table 6.

Finally, in the category Fees and compensations only negative incidents are recorded (2.6% of the total of incidents). Some students perceived the courses as "expensive" and stated that they did not receive any refunds if some part of the service does not work.

PRACTICAL APPLICATIONS

This work reveals several important facts that should be considered when developing information systems for online higher-education managers. First of all, total quality management in a university implies to have a holistic view of the service being

offered, which includes not only the learning process section but also other dimensions. Therefore, some relevant quality dimensions that should be included (and measured) in any information system for online higher-education are: learning process, teaching materials and resources, relations with fellow students, instructors' and administrative staff's responsiveness and user's interface.

FUTURE WORK

It has to be noticed that the approach presented in this paper focuses only on students' perception of service quality. As explained before, this is one of the main factors to consider in any model that aims to measure quality of service in online

Table 6. Examples of incidents relating to the user's interface

User's interface	Positive incidents	Negative incidents
Appearance	"Beautiful campus"	"Not very graphic or colorful"
Connectivity	"Access to the campus was problem-free"	"Problems connecting with the campus, at certain times and on certain days"
Browsing	"Browsing the virtual learning environment is very easy "	"Browsing the web is difficult"
Reliability	"(...) everything works well: sending files and downloading materials (...)"	"Errors all the time downloading materials, especially at the start of the course and on Sunday evenings"
Security	"When I lost my access code, the staff asked me a lot of questions to check my identity, quite rightly"	"The antivirus installed makes browsing difficult"

higher education. As discussed through the paper, we have focused in this factor because, despite its relevance, it has been traditionally omitted in most previous works. Nevertheless, in order to develop a more complete model, other relevant factors should also be accounted for, e.g., instructors' perceptions, alumni perceptions, employers' perceptions, etc. Accordingly, the development of a more complete model considering these other factors will guide our future work.

CONCLUSION

The purpose of this paper was to investigate how students perceive online higher education services and which quality dimensions they consider important in their evaluations of the quality of the services they receive. Using the critical incident technique a total of 350 valid critical incidents were reported by 41 respondents selected at random from a database. After a classification process the incidents were grouped into twelve dimensions that account for causes of perceived high and low service quality in the context of online higher education. Results indicated that the learning process is undoubtedly the most important dimension since it plays a major role in the students' quality of service evaluations. Within this area, the most relevant aspect was guidance and follow-up of the learning process by instructors. The second area which featured most was to do with teaching materials and resources and, especially, with their content. These two areas seem to make up the core service of online higher education. The third area is directly related to the fact that the service is offered in an online environment, as it refers to the attributes of the user's interface and, in particular, to how easy it is to surf the virtual campus. The fourth factor, responsiveness, emphasizes the importance, in the framework of e-services, of being able to resolve users' problems and queries quickly, which helps to overcome their sensation of being alone. The rest of the areas, ordered according to their relative importance, are the following: the learning assessment system, the appropriateness of the responses to the questions posed, staff-student relations, the design and focus of the program, the simplicity of the administrative procedures, the efficiency of delivering documentation and, finally, the fees.

The results of the study clarify the determinants of perceptions about e-service quality in online higher education. It seems that online higher education services should be viewed as a composite offer consisting of several dimensions to which students attach different weightings in their evaluations of quality of service. Moreover, by using the critical incident technique, we have confirmed that it is not only possible to capture the full range of customer-service issues and to identify particularly troubling perceptions before they actually become critical, but also we have found it to have a number of advantages over other exploratory measurement techniques in terms of speed, flexibility and cost. These advantages make it especially suitable when evaluating students' perceptions of service quality in online learning scenarios.

ACKNOWLEDGMENT

This work has been partially supported by the HAROSA Knowledge Community of the Internet Interdisciplinary Institute.

REFERENCES

Abdullah, F. (2005). HEdPERF versus SERVPERF: The quest for ideal measuring instrument of service quality in higher education. *Quality Assurance in Education*, *13*(4), 305–327. doi:10.1108/09684880510626584

Aldridge, S., & Rowley, J. (1998). Measuring customer satisfaction in higher education. *Quality Assurance in Education, 6*(4), 197–204. doi:10.1108/09684889810242182

Barnes, S. J., & Vidgen, R. T. (2002). An Integrative Approach to the Assessment of E-commerce quality. *Journal of Electronic Commerce Research, 3*(3), 114–127.

Bigné, E., Sánchez, M. I., & Sánchez, J. (2003). SERVQUAL Reliability and Validity in Travel Agencies. *Annals of Tourism Research, 30*(1), 258–262. doi:10.1016/S0160-7383(01)00090-1

Chell, E. (1998). Critical incident technique. In Symon, G., & Cassell, C. (Eds.), *Qualitative Methods and Analysis in Organisational Research: A practical guide*. London: Sage Publications.

Chen, N., & Lin, K., & Kinshuk. (2008). Analysing users' satisfaction with e-learning using a negative critical incidents approach. *Innovations in Education and Teaching International, 45*(2), 115–126. doi:10.1080/14703290801950286

Chen, Q., Clifford, S. J., & Wells, W. D. (2002). Attitude toward the site II: new information. *Journal of Advertising Research, 42*(2), 33–46.

Cox, J., & Dale, B. G. (2001). Service quality and e-commerce: an exploratory analysis. *Managing Service Quality, 11*(2), 121–131. doi:10.1108/09604520110387257

Daradoumis, A., Faulin, J., Juan, A., Martinez, F., Rodriguez, I., & Xhafa, F. (2010). CRM Applied to Higher Education: Developing an e-Monitoring System to Improve Relationships in e-Learning Environments. *International Journal of Services Technology and Management, 14*(1), 103–125. doi:10.1504/IJSTM.2010.032887

De Lange, P., Suwardy, T., & Mavondo, F. (2003). Integrating a virtual learning environment into an introductory accounting course: determinants of student motivation. *Accounting Education, 12*(1), 1–14. doi:10.1080/0963928032000064567

DeShields, J. Jr, Kara, A., & Kainak, E. (2005). Determinants of business students satisfaction and retention in higher education: Applying Herzberg's two factor theory. *International Journal of Educational Management, 19*(2), 128–135. doi:10.1108/09513540510582426

Douglas, J., McClelland, R., & Davies, J. (2008a). The development of a conceptual model of student satisfaction with their experience in higher education. *Quality Assurance in Education, 16*(1), 19–35. doi:10.1108/09684880810848396

Douglas, J., McClelland, R., Davies, J., & Sudbury, L. (2008b). Using critical incident technique (CIT) to capture the voice of the student. *The TQM Journal, 21*(4), 305–318. doi:10.1108/17542730910965038

Edvardsson, B., & Ross, I. (2001). Critical incident techniques. Towards a framework for analysing the criticality of critical incidents. *International Journal of Service Industry Management, 12*(3), 251–268. doi:10.1108/EUM0000000005520

Ellis, R. A., Ginns, P., & Piggot, L. (2009). E-learning in higher education: some key aspects and their relationship to approaches to study. *Higher Education Research & Development, 28*(3), 303–318. doi:10.1080/07294360902839909

Flanagan, J. C. (1954). The critical incident technique. *Psychological Bulletin, 51*, 327–358. doi:10.1037/h0061470

Ford, J. B., Joseph, M., & Joseph, B. (1993). *Service quality in higher education: a comparison of universities In the United States and New Zealand using SERVQUAL*. Norfolk, VA: Old Dominion University.

Ford, J. B., Joseph, M., & Joseph, B. (1999). Importance-performance analysis as a strategic tool for service marketers: the case of service quality perceptions of business students in New Zealand and the USA. *Journal of Services Marketing, 13*(2), 171–186. doi:10.1108/08876049910266068

Gremler, D. D. (2004). The Critical Incident Technique in Service Research. *Journal of Service Research*, 7(1), 65–89. doi:10.1177/1094670504266138

Hill, Y., Lomas, L., & MacGregor, J. (2003). Students' perceptions of quality in higher education. *Quality Assurance in Education*, 11(1), 15–20. doi:10.1108/09684880310462047

Jiang, P., & Rosenbloom, B. (2005). Customer Intention to Return Online: Price Perception, Attribute-Level Performance, and Satisfaction Unfolding over Time. *European Journal of Marketing*, 39(1), 150–174. doi:10.1108/03090560510572061

Joseph, M., Yakhou, M., & Stone, G. (2005). An educational institution's quest for service quality: customers' perspective. *Quality Assurance in Education*, 13(1), 66–82. doi:10.1108/09684880510578669

Juan, A., Daradoumis, A., Xhafa, F., Caballe, S., & Faulin, J. (Eds.). (2009b). *Monitoring and Assessment in Online Collaborative Environments: Emergent Computational Technologies for E-Learning Support*. Hershey, PA: IGI Global.

Juan, A., Daradoumis, T., Faulin, J., & Xhafa, F. (2009a). A Data Analysis Model based on Control Charts to Monitor Online Learning Processes. *Int. Journal of Business Intelligence and Data Mining*, 4(2), 159–174. doi:10.1504/IJBIDM.2009.026906

Juan, A., Huertas, M., Steegmann, C., Corcoles, C., & Serrat, C. (2008). Mathematical E-Learning: state of the art and experiences at the Open University of Catalonia. *International Journal of Mathematical Education in Science and Technology*, 39(4), 455–471. doi:10.1080/00207390701867497

Kwan, P. Y. K., & Ng, P. W. K. (1999). Quality indicators in higher education – comparing Hong Kong and China's students'. *Managerial Auditing Journal*, 14(1/2), 20–27. doi:10.1108/02686909910245964

Lagrosen, S., Seyyed-Hashemi, R., & Leitner, M. (2004). Examination of the dimensions of quality in higher education. *Quality Assurance in Education*, 12(2), 61–69. doi:10.1108/09684880410536431

LeBlanc, G., & Nguyen, N. (1997). Searching for excellence in business education: an exploratory study of customer impressions of service quality. *International Journal of Educational Management*, 11(2), 72–79. doi:10.1108/09513549710163961

Levy, Y., Murphy, K. E., & Zanakis, S. H. (2009). A Value-Satisfaction Taxonomy of IS Effectiveness (VSTISE): A Case Study of User Satisfaction with IS and User-Perceived Value of IS. *International Journal of Information Systems in the Service Sector*, 1(1), 93–118.

Lim, J., Kim, M., Chen, S. S., & Ryder, C. E. (2008). An Empirical Investigation of Student Achievement and Satisfaction in Different Learning Environments. *Journal of Instructional Psychology*, 35(2), 113–119.

Loiacono, E. T., Watson, R. T., & Goodhue, D. L. (2002). WebQUAL: A Measure of Web Site Quality. *Marketing Theory and Applications, 3*.

Makarem, S. C., Mudambi, S. M., & Podoshem, J. S. (2009). Satisfaction in technology-enabled service encounters. *Journal of Services Marketing*, 23(3), 134–144. doi:10.1108/08876040910955143

Marzo-Navarro, M., Pedraja, M., & Rivera-Torres, M. P. (2005). Measuring Customer Satisfaction in Summer Courses. *Quality Assurance in Education*, 13(1), 53–65. doi:10.1108/09684880510578650

Moratis, L. T., & van Baalen, P. J. (2002). *Management Education in the Network Economy: Its Context, Content and Organization*. Boston: Kluwer Academic Publishers.

O'Neill, M. (2003). The influence of time on student perceptions of service quality. The need for longitudinal measures. *Journal of Educational Administration*, 41(3), 310–324. doi:10.1108/09578230310474449

O'Neill, M., & Palmer, A. (2004). Importance-performance analysis: a useful tool for directing continuous quality improvement in higher education. *Quality Assurance in Education, 12*(1), 39–52. doi:10.1108/09684880410517423

Oldfield, B. M., & Baron, S. (2000). Student perceptions of service quality. *Quality Assurance in Education, 8*(2), 85–95. doi:10.1108/09684880010325600

Palmer, S. R., & Holt, D. M. (2009). Examining student satisfaction with wholly online learning. *Journal of Computer Assisted Learning, 25*(2), 101–113. doi:10.1111/j.1365-2729.2008.00294.x

Papa, M., & Avgeri, M. (2009). Online Services Delivered by NTO Portals: A Cross-Country Examination. *International Journal of Information Systems in the Service Sector, 1*(3), 65–82.

Parasuraman, A., Zeithaml, V. A., & Maholtra, H. (2005). E-S-QUAL: A Multiple-Item Scale for Assessing Electronic Service Quality. *Journal of Service Research, 7*(3), 213–233. doi:10.1177/1094670504271156

Pedró, F. (2005). Comparing Traditional and ICT-Enriched University Teaching Methods: Evidence from Two Empirical Studies. *Higher Education in Europe, 30*(3-4), 399–411. doi:10.1080/03797720600625937

Sahney, S., Banwet, D. K., & Karunes, S. (2004). A SERVQUAL and QFD approach to total quality education: A student perspective'. *International Journal of Productivity and Performance Management, 53*(2), 143–166. doi:10.1108/17410400410515043

Schurr, P. H. (2007). Buyer-Seller relationship development episodes: theories and methods. *Journal of Business and Industrial Marketing, 22*(3), 161–170. doi:10.1108/08858620710741869

Su, Q., Li, Z., & Chen, T. (2008). Conceptualizing consumers' perceptions of e-commerce quality. *International Journal of Retail & Distribution Management, 36*(5), 360–374. doi:10.1108/09590550810870094

Sur, S. (2008). Technology-Based Remote Service Encounters: Understanding Customer Satisfaction and Sustainability. *Journal of Foodservice Business Research, 11*(3), 315–332. doi:10.1080/15378020802317040

Sweeny, J. C., & Lapp, W. (2004). Critical service quality encounters on the Web: an exploratory study. *Journal of Services Marketing, 18*(4), 276–289. doi:10.1108/08876040410542272

van Riel, A. C. R., Lemmink, J., Streukens, S., & Liljander, V. (2004). Boost customer loyalty with online support: the case of mobile telecoms providers. *International Journal of Internet Marketing and Advertising, 1*(1), 4–23. doi:10.1504/IJIMA.2004.003687

van Riel, A. C. R., Liljander, V., & Jurriëns, P. (2001). Exploring consumer evaluations of e-services: a portal site. *International Journal of Service Industry Management, 12*(4), 359–377. doi:10.1108/09564230110405280

Welsh, J. F., & Dey, S. (2002). Quality measurement and quality assurance in higher education. *Quality Assurance in Education, 10*(1), 17–25. doi:10.1108/09684880210416076

Wolfinbarger, M., & Gilly, M. (2003). e-TailQ: Dimensionalizing, Measuring and Predicting e-tail Quality. *Journal of Retailing, 79*(3), 183–198. doi:10.1016/S0022-4359(03)00034-4

Yoo, B., & Donthu, N. (2001). Developing a Scale to Measure the Perceived Quality of an Internet Shopping Site (Sitequal). *Quarterly Journal of Electronic Commerce, 2*(1), 31–46.

Zeithaml, V. A., & Bitner, M. J. (2003). *Services Marketing: Integrating Customer Focus across the Firm*. Boston: Irwin McGraw-Hill.

Zeithaml, V. A., Parasuraman, A., & Maholtra, A. (2002). Service Quality Delivery through Websites: A Critical Review of Extant Knowledge. *Journal of the Academy of Marketing Science, 30*(4), 362–375. doi:10.1177/009207002236911

This work was previously published in International Journal of Information Systems in the Service Sector, Volume 2, Issue 4, edited by John Wang, pp. 57-72, copyright 2010 by IGI Publishing (an imprint of IGI Global).

Compilation of References

1touchmovie.com. (2007). *Media room and home theater design and construction.* Retrieved June 26, 2008, from http://www.1touchmovie.com/theater_design1.html

Abdullah, F. (2005). HEdPERF versus SERVPERF: The quest for ideal measuring instrument of service quality in higher education. *Quality Assurance in Education, 13*(4), 305–327. doi:10.1108/09684880510626584

Abidi, A. (2003). *Customer relationship personalisation on the Internet: a conceptual framework.* Paper presented at the Mass Customisation Conference, Munchen, Germany.

Achard, P. O. (1999). *Economia e organizzazione delle imprese sanitarie.* Milano, Italy: FrancoAngeli.

Adams, B., Berner, E. S., & Wyatt, J. R. (2004). Applying strategies to overcome user resistance in a group of clinical managers to a business software application: A case study. *Journal of Organizational and End User Computing, 16*(4), 55–65.

Administrative Reforms Commission. (2007). *Ethics in governance.* Retrieved December 14, 2009, from http://darpg.nic.in/arpg-website/4tReport-EthicsinGov.pdf

Afshar, M. (2007). *SOA governance: Framework and best practices.* Redwood Shores, CA: Oracle Corporation.

Aggarwal, S. C. (1994). Practical applications of OR in an underdeveloped nation. *European Journal of Operational Research, 77*(3), 357–374. doi:10.1016/0377-2217(94)90403-0

Agranoff, R., & McGuire, M. (2001). Big questions in public network management research. *Journal of Public Administration: Research and Theory, 11*(3), 295–326.

Agrawal, R. (2000). Individual acceptance of information technologies. In Zmud, R. W. (Ed.), *In framing the domains of IT management: Projecting future... through the past* (pp. 85–104). Cincinnati, OH: Pinnaflex Education Resources.

Ahmed, K. S., Mozumder, A. K. A., & Barkat-e-khuda. (1999). *Redesigning the operations research project surveillance system* (No. 107). Dhaka, Bangladesh: ICDDRB.

Ahmed, M. A., & Alkhamis, T. M. (2009). Simulation optimization for an emergency department healthcare unit in Kuwait. *European Journal of Operational Research, 198*, 936–942. doi:10.1016/j.ejor.2008.10.025

Ahn, B. S. (2003). Extending Malakooti's model for ranking multicriteria alternatives with preference strength and partial information. *IEEE Transactions on Systems Man and Cybernetics: Part A, 33*(3), 281–287. doi:10.1109/TSMCA.2003.817049

Ahsan, M. K., & Bartlema, J. (2004). Monitoring healthcare performance by Analytic Hierarchy Process: a developing country perspective. *International Transactions in Operational Research, 11*(4), 465–478. doi:10.1111/j.1475-3995.2004.00470.x

Ahsan, M. K., & Bartlema, J. (2008). Introduction of user fees: a viable means of healthcare financing. *Journal of Health Management, 10*(1), 87–100. doi:10.1177/097206340701000105

Ajzen, I. (1991). The theory of planned behavior. *Organizational Behavior and Human Decision Processes, 50*(2), 179–211. doi:10.1016/0749-5978(91)90020-T

Ajzen, I., & Madden, T. J. (1986). Prediction of goal directed behavior: Attitudes, intentions, and perceived behavioral control. *Journal of Experimental Social Psychology, 22*(5), 453–474. doi:10.1016/0022-1031(86)90045-4

Albinola, M., Baresi, L., Carcano, M., & Guinea, S. (2009). Mashlight: A lightweight mashup framework for everyone. In *Proceedings of WWW 2009*. Retrieved October 1, 2009, from http://www.ra.ethz.ch/CDstore/www2009/integror.net/mem2009/papers/paper9.pdf

Aldridge, S., & Rowley, J. (1998). Measuring customer satisfaction in higher education. *Quality Assurance in Education, 6*(4), 197–204. doi:10.1108/09684889810242182

Ali, J. M. H. (2004). Information technology in the Middle East. *Journal of Global Information Technology Management, 7*(1), 1–4.

Al-Jaghoub, S., & Westrup, C. (2003). Jordan and ict-led development: towards a competition state? *Information Technology & People, 16*(1), 93–110. doi:10.1108/09593840310463032

Al-Masri, E., & Mahmoud, Q. H. (2008). Toward quality-driven web service discovery. *IT Professional, 10*(3), 24–28. doi:10.1109/MITP.2008.59

Alonso, G., Casati, F., Kuno, H., & Vijay, M. (2004). *Web services concepts, architectures and applications*. Berlin: Springer.

Al-Qirim, N. (2007). Championing telemedicine adoption and utilization in healthcare organizations in New Zealand. *International Journal of Medical Informatics, 76*, 42–54. doi:10.1016/j.ijmedinf.2006.02.001

Alsop, R. (2004). Corporate reputation: Anything but superficial- the deep but fragile nature of corporate reputation. *The Journal of Business Strategy, 25*(6), 21–29. doi:10.1108/02756660410699900

Amador, J., & Artalejo, J. R. (2009). The M/G/1 retrial queue: New descriptors of the customer's behavior. *Journal of Computational and Applied Mathematics, 223*(1), 15–26. doi:10.1016/j.cam.2007.12.016

Anders, S. B., & Fischer, C. M. (2004). A hard look at tax software: 2004 survey of New York State practitioners. *The CPA Journal*. Retrieved October 14, 2006, from http://www.nysscpa.org/cpajournal/2004/704/infocus/p18.htm

Andersen, T. J. (2005). The performance effect of computer-mediated communication and decentralized decision making. *Journal of Business Research, 58*(8), 1059–1067. doi:10.1016/j.jbusres.2004.02.004

Anderson, B. (2003, February 25). Fresno County bans diversion of ambulances. *Sacramento Bee*. p. A1.

Anderson, T., Fox, M., & Schwartz, B. N. (2005). History and trends in e-filing: A survey of CPA practitioners. *The CPA Journal*. Retrieved October 14, 2006, from http://www.nysscpa.org/cpajournal/2005/1005/essentials/p66.htm

Anderson, B. D., Manoguerra, A. S., & Haynes, B. E. (1998). Diversion of 911 calls to a poison center. *Prehospital Emergency Care, 2*(3), 176–179. doi:10.1080/10903129808958867

Anite. (2002). *Dynamic packaging: the consumer's choice*. London: Anite Travel Systems.

Anonymous. (2005, January 28). FDA drug safety reviewers to use data mining tool. *Washington Drug Letter, 37*(5).

Anonymous,. (2006). Immunizing the Internet, or: How I learned to stop worrying and love the worm. *Harvard Law Review, 119*, 2442–2463.

Arnold, Y., Leimeister, J. M., & Krcmar, H. (2003). *COPEP: A development process model for a community platform for cancer patients*. Paper presented at the XIth European Conference on Information Systems (ECIS), Naples, Italy.

Artalejo, J. R., & Gómez-Corral, A. (2008). Advances in retrial queues. *European Journal of Operational Research, 189*(3), 1041. doi:10.1016/j.ejor.2007.05.035

Ashbaugh, S., & Miranda, R. (2002). Technology for human resources management: Seven questions and answers. *Public Personnel Management, 31*(1), 7–19.

Aubert, B. A., & Hamel, G. (2001). Adoption of smart cards in the medical sector: The Canadian experience. *Social Science & Medicine, 53*, 879–894. doi:10.1016/S0277-9536(00)00388-9

Auckland, J. S. (2006, April). New Zealand is a nation of dial-up users says statistics NZ. *Computerworld*. Retrieved Oct. 8, 2006, from http://www.computerworld.co.nz/news.nsf/NL/00D725EF22F3F254CC25714200179B6F

Augusta, L. (2004, August). The future of data mining - predictive analytics. *DM Review, 14*(8), 16-20, 37.

Auh, S. (2005). The effects of soft and hard service attributes on loyalty: The mediating role of trust. *Journal of Services Marketing*, *19*(2), 81–92. doi:10.1108/08876040510591394

Australian Centre for Policing Research. (2000). *The virtual horizon: Meeting the law enforcement challenges-developing an Australasian law enforcement strategy for dealing with electronic crime.* Retrieved February 10, 2009, from http://www.acpr.gov.au/pdf/ACPR134_1.pdf

Avital, M., & Te'eni, D. (2006, June 12-14). From generative fit to generative capacity: Exploring an emerging dimension of information systems fit and task performance. In *Proceedings of the 14th European Conference on Information Systems (ECIS)*, Goteburg, Sweden.

Babakus, E., & Boller, W. G. (1992). An empirical assessment of the SERVQUAL scale. *Journal of Business Research*, *24*(3), 253–268. doi:10.1016/0148-2963(92)90022-4

Baba, V. V., & Jamal, M. (1992). Routinization of job context and job content as related to employees' quality of working life: A study of Canadian nurses. *Journal of Organizational Behavior*, *12*(5), 379–386. doi:10.1002/job.4030120503

Baecker, R. M., Grudin, J., Buxton, W. A. S., & Greenberg, S. (1995). Designing to fit human capabilities. In *Human-computer interaction: Towards the year 2000* (pp. 667–680). San Francisco: Morgan Kaufman.

Bae, S. H., Sarkis, J., & Yoo, C. S. (2011). Greening transportation fleets: Insights from a two-stage game theoretic model. *Transportation Research Part E, Logistics and Transportation Review*, *47*(6), 793–807. doi:10.1016/j.tre.2011.05.015

Bagchi, K., Udo, G., & Kirs, P. (2007). Global diffusion of the internet xii: The internet growth in Africa: some empirical results. *Communications of AIS*, *19*, 325–351.

Bagner, J., Evansburg, A., Watson, V. K., & Welch, J. B. (2003). Senators seek limits on DoD mining of personal data. *Intellectual Property & Technology Law Journal*, *15*(5), 19–20.

Balasubramaniam, S., Lewis, G. A., Simanta, S., & Smith, D. B. (2008). Situated software: concepts, motivation, technology, and the future. *IEEE Software*, *25*(6), 50–55. doi:10.1109/MS.2008.159

Baldwin, L. P., Eldabi, T., & Paul, R. J. (2004). Simulation in healthcare management: a soft approach (MAPIU). *Simulation Modelling Practice and Theory*, *12*, 541–557. doi:10.1016/j.simpat.2004.02.003

Ballester, E., & Aleman, L. (2001). Brand trust in the context of consumer loyalty. *European Journal of Marketing*, *35*(11-12), 1238–1258. doi:10.1108/EUM0000000006475

Balmer, J. M. T., & Greyser, S. A. (2006). Corporate marketing; integrating corporate identity, corporate branding, corporate communications, corporate image and corporate reputation. *European Journal of Marketing*, *40*(7-8), 730–741. doi:10.1108/03090560610669964

Bandura, A. (1977). Self-efficacy: Toward a unifying theory of behavioral change. *Psychological Review*, *84*(2), 191–215. doi:10.1037/0033-295X.84.2.191

Bandura, A. (1982). Self-efficacy mechanism in human agency. *The American Psychologist*, *37*(2), 122–147. doi:10.1037/0003-066X.37.2.122

Bandura, A. (1986). *Social foundations of thought and action.* Englewood Cliffs, NJ: Prentice-Hall.

Banks, J. (1997). The future of simulation software: a panel discussion. In S. Andradottir, K. J. Kealy, D. E. Withers, & B. L. Nelson (Eds), *Proceedings of the 1997 Winter Simulation Conference. Institute of Electrical and Electronics Engineers,* Atlanta (pp. 166-173).

Barich, H., & Kotler, P. (1991, winter). A framework of marketing image management. *Sloan Management Review*.

Barkat-e-khuda, Harbison, S. F., & Robinson, W. C. (1990). Is development really the best contraceptive? a 20-year trail in Comilla district. *Population Program Journal*, *5*(4), 3–16.

Barkat-e-khuda. Barket, A., Helali, J., Miller, P., & Haaga, J. (1994). *Population policy in Bangladesh: a review of ten priority areas.* Dhaka, Bangladesh: University Research Corporation and the Population Council.

Barki, H., & Hartwick, J. (1994). Measuring user participation, user involvement, and user attitude. *Management Information Systems Quarterly*, *18*(1), 59–82. doi:10.2307/249610

Barnes, C. F., Fritz, H., & Jeseon, Y. (2007). Hurricane disaster assessments with image driven data mining in high-resolution satellite imagery. *IEEE Transactions on Geoscience and Remote Sensing, 45*(6), 1631–1640. doi:10.1109/TGRS.2007.890808

Barnes, S. J., & Vidgen, R. T. (2002). An Integrative Approach to the Assessment of E-commerce quality. *Journal of Electronic Commerce Research, 3*(3), 114–127.

Baronas, A., & Louis, M. (1988). Restoring a sense of control during implementation: How user involvement leads to system acceptance. *Management Information Systems Quarterly, 12*(1), 111–123. doi:10.2307/248811

Baron, R. B., & Kenny, D. A. (1986). The moderation-mediator variable distinction in social psychological research: Conceptual, strategic, and statistical considerations. *Journal of Personality and Social Psychology, 51*(6), 1173–1182. doi:10.1037/0022-3514.51.6.1173

Baroudi, J., Olson, M., & Ives, B. (1986). An empirical study of the impact of user involvement on system usage and information satisfaction. *Management of Computing, 29*(3), 232–238.

Bartelmus, P. (2010). Use and usefulness of sustainability economics. *Ecological Economics, 69*(11), 2053–2055. doi:10.1016/j.ecolecon.2010.06.019

Barthel, S., Folke, C., & Colding, J. (2010). Social–ecological memory in urban gardens—retaining the capacity for management of ecosystem services. *Global Environmental Change, 20*(2), 255–265. doi:10.1016/j.gloenvcha.2010.01.001

Barton, J. (1994). Choosing to work at night: A moderating influence on individual tolerance to shift work. *The Journal of Applied Psychology, 79*(3), 449–454. doi:10.1037/0021-9010.79.3.449

Barton, J., & Folkard, S. (1991). The response of day and night nurses to their work schedules. *Journal of Occupational Psychology, 64*(3), 207–218.

Bassett, R., Bass, L., & O'Brien, P. (2006). Computer forensics: An essential ingredient of cyber security. *Journal of Information Science and Technology, 3*(1), 22–32.

Bastian, O., Haase, D., & Grunewald, K. (2011). Ecosystem properties, potentials and services – The EPPS conceptual framework and an urban application example. *Ecological Indicators,* In Press, Corrected Proof, Available online Sept. 29, 2011.

Bateson, J. E. G. (1995). *Managing services marketing: Text and reading* (3rd ed.). Chicago: The Dryden Press.

Beck, K. (2000). *Extreme programming explained.* Upper Saddle River, NJ: Addison-Wesley.

Beers, T. M. (2000). Flexible schedules and shift work: Replacing the '9-to-5' workday? *Monthly Labor Review, 123*(6), 33–40.

Beitollahi, H., & Deconinck, G. (2011). A dependable architecture to mitigate distributed denial of service attacks in network-based control systems. *International Journal of Critical Infrastructure Protection,* In Press, Corrected Proof, Available online Sept. 29, 2011.

Beloglazov, A., Abawajy, J., & Buyya, R. (2011). Energy-aware resource allocation heuristics for efficient management of data centers for Cloud computing. *Future Generation Computer Systems,* In Press, Corrected Proof, Available online 4 May 2011.

Belter, R. (2008). Towards a service management system in virtualized infrastructures. In *Proceedings of the IEEE International Conference on Services Computing 2008* (Vol. 2, pp. 47-51). Washington, DC: IEEE Computer Society.

Ben-Ami, Z. (2005). *Service quality in tertiary institutions.* Unpublished M.Com dissertation, University of Port Elizabeth, South Africa.

Benkler, Y. (2000). From consumers to users: Shifting the deeper structures of regulation. *Federal Communications Law Journal, 52*, 561–563.

Bens, C. K. (1994). Effective citizen involvement: How to make it happen. *National Civic Review, 83*(1), 32–39. doi:10.1002/ncr.4100830107

Berger, C., Moslein, K., Piller, F., & Reichwald, R. (2005). Co-designing the customer interface for customer-centric strategies: Learning from exploratory research. *European Management Review, 2*(3), 24–39.

Berghout, B. M., Eminovic, N., Keizer, N. F., & Birnie, E. (2007). Evaluation of general practitioner's time investment during a store-and-forward teledermatology consultation. *International Journal of Medical Informatics, 76*, 384–391. doi:10.1016/j.ijmedinf.2007.04.004

Berners-Lee, T., Hendler, J., & Lassila, O. (2001). The semantic web. *Scientific American, 284*(5), 34–43. doi:10.1038/scientificamerican0501-34

Bernstel, J. (2002). Why Canada wins in online banking. *Banking Marketing, 34*(4), 12–17.

Bhansali, C. (2006a). The question every practicing accountant must ask. *Accounting Technology*, June. Retrieved March 22, 2007, from http://www.webcpa.com/

Bhansali, C. (2006b). A partial solution to a Daunting problem. *Accounting Technology*, September. Retrieved March 22, 2007, from http://www.webcpa.com/

Bible, D. S., & Hsieh, C. H. (1996). Applications of geographic information systems for the analysis of apartment rents. *Journal of Real Estate Research, 12*(1), 79–88.

Biermann, E., Dietrich, W., Rihl, J., & Standl, E. (2002). Are there time and cost savings by using telemanagement for patients on intensified insulin therapy? A randomised, controlled trial. *Computer Methods and Programs in Biomedicine, 69*, 137–146. doi:10.1016/S0169-2607(02)00037-8

Bigné, E., Sánchez, M. I., & Sánchez, J. (2003). SERVQUAL Reliability and Validity in Travel Agencies. *Annals of Tourism Research, 30*(1), 258–262. doi:10.1016/S0160-7383(01)00090-1

Björklund, M. (2011). Influence from the business environment on environmental purchasing — Drivers and hinders of purchasing green transportation services. *Journal of Purchasing and Supply Management, 17*(1), 11–22. doi:10.1016/j.pursup.2010.04.002

Blake, M. B., & Nowlan, M. F. (2008). Predicting service mashup candidates using enhanced syntactical message management. In *Proceedings of the IEEE International Conference on Services Computing* (pp. 229-236).

Blau, G., & Lunz, M. (1999). Testing the impact of shift schedules on organizational variables. *Journal of Organizational Behavior, 20*(6), 933–942. doi:10.1002/(SICI)1099-1379(199911)20:6<933::AID-JOB940>3.0.CO;2-V

Boehm, B. W. (1988). A spiral model of software development and enhancement. *Computer, 21*(5), 61–72. doi:10.1109/2.59

Bøgglid, H., Burr, H., Tüchsen, F., & Jeppesen, J. (2001). Work environment of Danish shift and day workers. *Scandinavian Journal of Work, Environment & Health, 27*(2), 97–105.

Bohle, P., & Tilley, A. J. (1998). Early experience of shiftwork: Influences on attitude. *Journal of Occupational and Organizational Psychology, 71*(1), 61–79.

Boire, R. (2005, October). Future of data mining in marketing (Part 1). *Direct Marketing News*.

Bonacci, I., & Tamburis, O. (2007). Paths of organizational change in the healthcare structures: The role of ICT. In *Proceedings of Mediterranean Conference on Information Systems (MCIS07)* (Vol. 1).

Bonacci, I., & Tamburis, O. (2009). The Social network analysis as key factor for improving interoperability standards on patients care paths. In *Proceedings of VI Conference of the Italian Chapter of AIS (ItAIS)*.

Bonacci, I., Pelella, E. F., & Tamburis, O. (2008). Fattori di rischio nella gestione delle patologie cronico-degenerative: Analisi dei flussi informativi nel territorio sannita. In *Proceedings of XIII AIES Conference (Associazione Italiana di Economia Sanitaria)*.

Bonora, E., Kiechl, S., Willeit, J., Oberhollenzer, F., Egger, G., & Meigs, J. B. (2004). Population-based incidence rates and risk factors for type 2 diabetes in white individuals: The Bruneck study. *Diabetes, 53*, 1782–1789. doi:10.2337/diabetes.53.7.1782

Borg, G. (1998). *Borg's perceived exertion and pain scales*. Champaign, IL: Human Kinetics.

Bosch, L. H. M., & Lange, W. A. M. (1987). Shift work in health care. *Ergonomics, 30*(5), 773–791. doi:10.1080/00140138708969767

Bose, R., & Suumaran, V. (2006). Challenges for deploying web services-based e-business systems in SMEs. *International Journal of E-Business Research, 2*(1), 1–18.

Boulding, W., Kalra, A., Staelin, R., & Zeithaml, V. (1993). A dynamic process of service quality: from expectations to behavioral intentions. *JMR, Journal of Marketing Research, 30*(1), 7–27. doi:10.2307/3172510

Bowen, J., & Chen, S. (2001). The relationship between customer loyalty and customer satisfaction. *International Journal of Contemporary Hospitality Management, 13*(5), 213–217. doi:10.1108/09596110110395893

Boyd, R. S. (2006, February 2). Data mining tells government and business a lot about you. *Knight Ridder Washington Bureau.*

Brailsford, S. C. (2007). Tutorial: Advances and challenges in healthcare simulation modeling. In S. G. Henderson, B. Biller, M. H. Hsieh, J. Shortle, J. D. Tew, & R. R. Barton (Eds.), *Proceedings of the 2007 Winter Simulation Conference* (pp. 1436-1448). Washington, DC: IEEE.

Brink, J. L., Moorman, P. W., Boer, M. F., Pruyn, J. F. A., Verwoerd, C. D. A., & Bemmel, J. H. (2005). Involving the patient: A prospective study on use, appreciation and effectiveness of an information system in head and neck cancer care. *International Journal of Medical Informatics, 74*, 839–849. doi:10.1016/j.ijmedinf.2005.03.021

Brown, D., & Wilson, S. (2009). *The black book of outsourcing: 2009 green outsourcing survey.* John Wiley & Sons Inc.

Brown, M. M., & Brudney, J. L. (2003). Learning organizations in the public sector? A study of police agencies employing information and technology to advance knowledge. *Public Administration Review, 63*(1), 30–43. doi:10.1111/1540-6210.00262

Bruner, G. C., & Kumar, A. (2005). Explaining consumer acceptance of handheld Internet devices. *Journal of Business Research, 58*, 553–558. doi:10.1016/j.jbusres.2003.08.002

Bruno, G., Runzo, C., Cavallo-Perin, P., Merletti, F., Rivetti, M., Pinach, S., Novelli, G., Trovati, M., Cerutti, F., & Pagano, G., & Piedmont Study Group for Diabetes Epidemiology. (2005). Incidence of type 1 and type 2 diabetes in adults aged 30-49 years: Population-based registry in the province of Turin, Italy. *Diabetes Care, 28*, 2613–2619. doi:10.2337/diacare.28.11.2613

Bullinger, H.-J., & Scheer, A.-W. (2003). *Service engineering: Entwicklung und gestaltung innovativer dienstleistungen.* Berlin, Germany: Springer.

Buren, R. M., & Stenzel, W. W. (1984). The impact of police work scheduling on patrol productivity. *Public Productivity Review, 8*(3), 236–252. doi:10.2307/3380465

Bush, C. T. (2000). Accountants are thriving on the Web, says survey. [from http://www.aicpa.org/PUBS/JOFA/joaiss.htm]. *Journal of Accountancy, 190*(5), 20. Retrieved November 23, 2006.

Business Wire. (2005, March 7). *SPSS predictive analytics accelerating cancer research.* Chicago: Children's Memorial Research Center.

Cahlink, G. (2000, October). Data mining taps trends. *Government Executive, 32*(12), 85–87.

Cangemi, D. (2004). Procedural law provisions of the council of European convention on cybercrime. *International Review of Law Computers & Technology, 18*(2), 165–171. doi:10.1080/1360086042000223472

Cao, L., Zhao, Y. C., & Zhang, C. Q. (2008). Activity mining: from activities to actions. *International Journal of Information Technology & Decision Making, 7*(2), 259–273. doi:10.1142/S0219622008002934

Carman, J. M. (1990). Consumer perceptions of service quality: An assessment of the SERVQUAL dimensions. *Journal of Retailing, 66*(1), 33–55.

Carroll, D. (1996). MedModel-healthcare simulation software. In J. M. Charnes, D. M. Morrice, D. T. Brunner, & J. J. Swain (Eds.), *Proceedings of the 1996 Winter Simulation Conference,* Coronado, CA (pp. 441-446). Washington, DC: IEEE.

Cass, H. D., Smith, I., Unthank, C., Starling, C., & Collins, J. E. (2003). Improving compliance with requirements on junior doctors' hours. *British Medical Journal, 327*(2), 270–273. doi:10.1136/bmj.327.7409.270

Ceglowski, R., Churilov, L., & Wasserthiel, J. (2007). Combining data mining and discrete event simulation for a value-added view of a hospital emergency department. *The Journal of the Operational Research Society, 58*(2), 246–254.

Centro nazionale per l'informatica nella Pubblica Amministrazione – CNIPA. (2008). *Piano triennale per l'ICT della pubblica amministrazione centrale per il triennio 2008-2010.*

Chae, Y. M., Lee, J. H., Ho, S. H., Kim, H. J., Jun, K. H., & Won, J. U. (2001). Patient satisfaction with telemedicine in home health services for the elderly. *International Journal of Medical Informatics, 61*, 167–173. doi:10.1016/S1386-5056(01)00139-3

Chang, I. J., Hwang, H. G., Hung, M. C., Lin, M. H., & Yen, D. C. (2007). Factors affecting the adoption of electronic signature: Executives' perspective of hospital information department. *Decision Support Systems*, *44*, 350–359. doi:10.1016/j.dss.2007.04.006

Chase, R. (1978). Where does the customer fit in a service operation? *Harvard Business Review*, *56*(6), 137–142.

Chatzopoulos, K. C., & Economides, A. A. (2009). A holistic evaluation of Greek municipalities' websites. *Electronic Government, an International Journal (EG)*, *6*(2), 193-212.

Chau, P. Y. K., & Hu, P. J. H. (2002). Investigating healthcare professionals' decisions to accept telemedicine technology: An empirical test of competing theories. *Information & Management*, *39*, 297–311. doi:10.1016/S0378-7206(01)00098-2

Chell, E. (1998). Critical incident technique. In Symon, G., & Cassell, C. (Eds.), *Qualitative Methods and Analysis in Organisational Research: A practical guide*. London: Sage Publications.

Chen, H., Chung, W., Xu, J. J., Qin, G. W. Y., & Chau, M. (2004, April). Crime data mining: A general framework and some examples. *IEEE Computer*, 50-56.

Chen, X.D, Lupi, F., An, L., Sheely, R., Viña, A., & Liu, J. (2011). Agent-based modeling of the effects of social norms on enrollment in payments for ecosystem services. *Ecological Modelling*, In Press, Corrected Proof, Available online Sept. 29, 2011.

Chen, C. H., & Zimitat, C. (2006). Understanding Taiwanese students' decision-making factors regarding Australian international higher education. *International Journal of Educational Management*, *20*(2), 91–100. doi:10.1108/09513540610646082

Chen, D. N., Jeng, B., Lee, W. P., & Chuang, C. H. (2008). An agent-based model for consumer-to-business electronic commerce. *Expert Systems with Applications*, *34*(1), 469–481. doi:10.1016/j.eswa.2006.09.020

Cheng, T. C. E., Lam, D. Y. C., & Yeung, A. C. L. (2006). Adoption of internet banking: An empirical study in Hong Kong. *Decision Support Systems*, *42*, 1558–1572. doi:10.1016/j.dss.2006.01.002

Cheng, Y., & Tam, W. M. (1997). Multi models of quality in Education. *Quality Assurance in Education*, *5*(1), 22–31. doi:10.1108/09684889710156558

Chen, I. J., Yang, K. F., Tang, F. I., Huang, C. H., & Yu, S. (2008). Applying the technology acceptance model to explore public health nurses' intentions towards web-based learning: A cross-sectional questionnaire survey. *International Journal of Nursing Studies*, *45*(6), 869–878. doi:10.1016/j.ijnurstu.2006.11.011

Chen, K., & Yen, D. (2004). Improving the quality of online presence through interactivity. *Information & Management*, *42*, 217–226.

Chen, M. (2003). Factors affecting the adoption and diffusion of XML and Web services standards for E-business systems. *International Journal of Human-Computer Studies*, *58*(3), 259–279. doi:10.1016/S1071-5819(02)00140-4

Chen, N., & Lin, K., & Kinshuk. (2008). Analysing users' satisfaction with e-learning using a negative critical incidents approach. *Innovations in Education and Teaching International*, *45*(2), 115–126. doi:10.1080/14703290801950286

Chen, Q., Clifford, S. J., & Wells, W. D. (2002). Attitude toward the site II: new information. *Journal of Advertising Research*, *42*(2), 33–46.

Chiesi, A. M. (2006). Perspectives of network analysis applied to social sciences. In *Proceedings of XLIII SIS Conference* (CLEUP), Torino, Italy.

Chiesi, A. M. (1999). *L'analisi dei reticoli*. Milano, Italy: FrancoAngeli.

Chin, W. W. (1998). Issues and opinions on structural equation modeling. *Management Information Systems Quarterly*, *22*(1), 7–16.

Chin, W. W., Marcolin, B. L., & Newsted, P. R. (2003). A partial least squares latent variable modeling approach for measuring interaction effects: Results from a monte carlo simulation study and an electronic mail adoption study. *Information Systems Research*, *14*(2), 189–217. doi:10.1287/isre.14.2.189.16018

Chiou, J. (2004). The antecedents of consumers' loyalty toward internet service providers. *Information & Management*, *41*, 685–695. doi:10.1016/j.im.2003.08.006

Choo, C. W. (1998). *The knowing organization*. New York: Oxford University Press.

Christou, E., & Kassianidis, P. (2003). Consumers perception and adoption of online buying for travel products. *Journal of Travel & Tourism Marketing, 12*(4), 56–68. doi:10.1300/J073v12n04_06

Chronbach, L. J. (1951). Coefficient Alpha and the internal structure of tests. *Psychometrika, 16*(3), 297–334. doi:10.1007/BF02310555

Cicchetti, A. (2002). *L'organizzazione dell'ospedale*. Milano, Italy: Vita e Pensiero Ed.

Cicchetti, A. (2004). *La progettazione organizzativa*. Milano, Italy: FrancoAngeli/Sanità.

Cicchetti, A., & Mascia, D. (2007). Organizzare le reti in sanità: teoria, metodi e strumenti di social network analysis. *Mecosan, 61*, 9–32.

Clemons, E., Gao, G., & Hitt, L. (2006). When online reviews meet hyperdifferentiation: A study of craft beer industry. In *Proceedings of the 39th Hawaii International Conference on System Sciences*.

Clemons, E., Gu, B., & Spitler, R. (2003). Hyper-differentiation strategies: Delivering value, retaining profits. In *Proceedings of the 36th Hawaii International Conference on System Sciences*.

Cloete, N., & Bunting, I. (2000). *Higher education transformation: Assessing performance in South Africa*. Pretoria, South Africa: Centre for higher education transformation.

Cohort. (2002). *Metropolitan Richmond hospital diversions: A system analysis and change proposal*. Project report, Systems and Information Engineering Executive Master's Program. Charlottesville, VA: University of Virginia.

Coleman, J. S. (1974). *Power and the structure of society*. New York: W. W. Norton & Company Inc.

Colomo-Palacios, R., Gómez-Berbís, J. M., García-Crespo, A., & Puebla-Sánchez, I. (2008). Social global repository: Using semantics and social web in software projects. *International Journal of Knowledge and Learning, 4*(5), 452–464. doi:10.1504/IJKL.2008.022063

Colvin, C. A., & Goh, A. (2005). Validation of the technology acceptance model for police. *Journal of Criminal Justice, 33*(1), 89–95. doi:10.1016/j.jcrimjus.2004.10.009

Comm, C. L., & Mathaisel, D. F. X. (2005). A case in applying lean sustainability concepts to universities. *International Journal of Sustainability in Higher Education, 6*(2), 134–146. doi:10.1108/14676370510589855

Compeau, D. R., & Higgins, C. A. (1995). Computer self-efficacy: Development of a measure and initial test. *Management Information Systems Quarterly, 19*(2), 189–211. doi:10.2307/249688

Compeau, D., & Higgins, C. (1995). Computer self-efficacy: Development of a measure and initial test. *Management Information Systems Quarterly, 19*(2), 189–211. doi:10.2307/249688

Compeau, D., & Higgins, C. (1999). Social cognitive theory and individual reactions to computing technology: A longitudinal study. *Management Information Systems Quarterly, 23*(2), 145–159. doi:10.2307/249749

Corcho, O., Losada, S., & Benjamins, R. (2008). Semantic web-enabled protocol mediation of logistics domain. In García, R. (Ed.), *Semantic web for business: Cases and applications*. Hershey, PA: IGI Global.

Cordner, G. W. (1979). Police patrol work load studies: A review and critique. *Police Studies Intnl Review of Police Development, 2*(2), 50–60.

Corti, E., Iasiello, F., Marino, A., & Tamburis, O. (2004). Innovazione tecnologica nel contesto sociale e organizzativo. L'impatto delle tecnologie informatiche nell'ospedale di elevata specializzazione: Il caso della Campania. In *Proceedings of XV AiIG Conference (Associazione italiana di Ingegneria Gestionale)*.

Corti, E. (2002). *Gestione dell'innovazione*. Napoli, Italy: ESI.

Cosmi, L. (2003). Razionalità dei processi di diffusione nei sistemi aziendali di tecnologia sanitaria innovativa. Un modello delle variabili 'non convenzionali'. In *Proceedings of VIII AIES Conference (Associazione Italiana di Economia Sanitaria)*.

Cowley, S. (2005, October 24). Oracle wins $88.5 million Air Force contract. *IDG News Service*.

Cox, J., & Dale, B. G. (2001). Service quality and e-commerce: an exploratory analysis. *Managing Service Quality, 11*(2), 121–131. doi:10.1108/09604520110387257

Cross, R., & Parker, A. (2004). *The hidden power of social networks: Understanding how work really gets done in organizations.* Boston: Harvard Business School Press.

Crowston, K., Sawyer, S., & Wigand, R. (2001). Investigating the interplay between structure and information and communications technology in the real estate industry. *Information Technology & People, 14*(2), 163–183. doi:10.1108/09593840110695749

Curry, A. (1999). Innovation in public service management. *Managing Service Quality, 9*(3), 180–190. doi:10.1108/09604529910267082

Curtin University of Technology. (2008, August 13). *Curtin appoints pro vice-chancellor for Singapore campus.* Perth, Australia: Curtin University Media Release.

Cushman & Wakefield. (2008). *Marketbeat Q4 2008.* Retrieved August 30, 2009 from http://www.mapic.com/App/homepage.cfm?appname=100543&moduleid=279&campaignid=13036&iUserCampaignID=46044210

Czech Statistical Office. (2002). *Technology used by enterprises.* Retrieved October 11, 2006, from http://www.czso.cz/eng/edicniplan.nsf/o/9602-04-2003-1__technology_used_by_enterprises

Da Silva, R., & Batisda, L. (2007). Boosting government reputation through CRM. *International Journal of Public Sector Management, 20*(7), 588–607. doi:10.1108/09513550710823506

Daenzer, W. F. (1977). *Systems engineering: Leitfaden zur methodischen durchführung umfangreicher planungsvorhaben.* Köln, Zürich: Peter Hanstein.

Dalton, D. R., & Mesch, D. J. (1990). The impact of flexible scheduling on employee attendance and turnover. *Administrative Science Quarterly, 35*(2), 370–387. doi:10.2307/2393395

Daniel, A. (2006, August). Internet usage in Australia. *Kinesis Interactive Design.* Retrieved Oct. 8, 2006, from http://www.kinesis.com.au/article_stats.asp

Daradoumis, A., Faulin, J., Juan, A., Martinez, F., Rodriguez, I., & Xhafa, F. (2010). CRM Applied to Higher Education: Developing an e-Monitoring System to Improve Relationships in e-Learning Environments. *International Journal of Services Technology and Management, 14*(1), 103–125. doi:10.1504/IJSTM.2010.032887

Davies, J., Lytras, M. D., & Sheth, A. P. (2007). Semantic-web-based knowledge management. *IEEE Internet Computing, 11*(5), 14–16. doi:10.1109/MIC.2007.109

Davies, R., & Davies, H. (1994). Modelling patient flows and resource provisions in health systems. *Omega, 22,* 123–131. doi:10.1016/0305-0483(94)90073-6

Davis, F. D. (1989). Perceived usefulness, perceived ease of use, and user acceptance of information technology. *Management Information Systems Quarterly, 13*(3), 319–340. doi:10.2307/249008

Davis, F. D. (1989). Perceived usefulness, perceived ease of use, and user acceptance of information technology. *MIS Quarterly, 13*(3), 319–339. doi:10.2307/249008

Dawes, S. S. (1996). Interagency information sharing: Expected benefits, manageable risks. *Journal of Policy Analysis and Management, 15*(3), 377–394. doi:10.1002/(SICI)1520-6688(199622)15:3<377::AID-PAM3>3.0.CO;2-F

De Lange, P., Suwardy, T., & Mavondo, F. (2003). Integrating a virtual learning environment into an introductory accounting course: determinants of student motivation. *Accounting Education, 12*(1), 1–14. doi:10.1080/0963928032000064567

Dean, A. (2002). Service quality in call centres: Implications for customer loyalty. *Managing Service Quality, 12*(6), 414–423. doi:10.1108/09604520210451894

Dean, J. (2001). Better business through customers. *Government Executive, 33*(1), 58–60.

Delavari, N., Shirazi, M. R. A., & Beikzadeh, M. R. (2004, May 31-June 2). A new model for using data miningtechnology in higher educational systems. In *Proceedings 5th International Conference on Information Technology Based Higher Education and Training (ITEHT'04),* Istanbul, Turkey (pp. 319-324).

Deloitte & Touche. (2005). *Der deutsche pitness- und wellnessmarkt.* Munich, Germany: Deloitte & Touche GmbH.

DeLone, W., & McLean, E. (1992). Information systems success: The quest for the dependent variable. *Information Systems Research, 3*(1), 60–95. doi:10.1287/isre.3.1.60

DeLone, W., & McLean, E. (2003). The DeLone and McLean model of information systems success: A ten-year update. *Journal of Management Information Systems, 19*(4), 9–30.

Demerouti, E., Geurts, S. A. E., Bakker, A. B., & Euwema, M. (2004). The impact of shiftwork on work-home conflict, job attitudes and health. *Ergonomics, 47*(9), 987–1002. doi:10.1080/00140130410001670408

Denney, S. H. (1997). MedModel-healthcare simulation software. In S. Andradottir, K. J. Kealy, D. E. Withers, & B. L. Nelson (Eds.), *Proceedings of the 1997 Winter Simulation,* Atlanta (pp. 581-586). Washington, DC: IEEE.

Dennis, A. R., Wixom, B. H., & Vandenberg, R. J. (2001). Understanding fit and appropriation effects in group support systems via meta-analysis. *Management Information Systems Quarterly, 25*(2), 167–193. doi:10.2307/3250928

Derlet, R. W., Richards, J. R., & Kravitz, R. L. (2001). Frequent overcrowding in U.S. emergency departments. *Academic Emergency Medicine, 8*(2), 151–155. doi:10.1111/j.1553-2712.2001.tb01280.x

DeShields, J. Jr, Kara, A., & Kainak, E. (2005). Determinants of business students satisfaction and retention in higher education: Applying Herzberg's two factor theory. *International Journal of Educational Management, 19*(2), 128–135. doi:10.1108/09513540510582426

Diaz-Galiano, M. C., Martin-Valdivia, M. T., & Ureña-López, L. A. (2009). Query expansion with a medical ontology to improve a multimodal information retrieval system. *Computers in Biology and Medicine, 39*(4), 396–403. doi:10.1016/j.compbiomed.2009.01.012

Dick, A., & Basu, K. (1994). Customer loyalty: towards an integrated framework. *Journal of the Academy of Marketing Science, 22*(2), 99–113. doi:10.1177/0092070394222001

Diehl, K., Kornish, L. J., & Lynch, J. G. (2003). Smart agents: When lower search costs for quality information increase price sensitivity. *The Journal of Consumer Research, 30*(1), 56–71. doi:10.1086/374698

Dinsdale, G., & Marsden, B. (1999). *Citizen/client surveys: Dispelling myths and redrawing maps.* Ottawa, Canada: Draft, Canadian Centre for Management Development.

Dishaw, M. T., & Strong, D. M. (1998). Supporting software maintenance with software engineering tools: A computed task-technology analysis. *Journal of Systems and Software, 44*(2), 107–120. doi:10.1016/S0164-1212(98)10048-1

Dishaw, M. T., & Strong, D. M. (1999). Extending the technology acceptance model with task technology fit constructs. *Information & Management, 36*(1), 9–21. doi:10.1016/S0378-7206(98)00101-3

Doll, W. J., & Torkzadeh, G. (1988). The measurement of end-user computing satisfaction. *Management Information Systems Quarterly, 12*(2), 259–274. doi:10.2307/248851

Doll, W., & Torkzadeh, G. (1998). Developing a multi-dimensional measure of system-use in an organizational context. *Information & Management, 33*(4), 171–185. doi:10.1016/S0378-7206(98)00028-7

Donatini, A., Rico, A., D'Ambrosio, M. G., Lo Scalzo, A., Orzella, L., Cicchetti, A., & Profili, S. (2001). Health care system in transition. In *Italy, country profile, European observatory on health care systems,* Copenhagen, Denmark.

Donnelly, M., Wisniewski, M., Dalrymple, J. F., & Curry, A. C. (1995). Measuring service quality in local government: The SERVQUAL approach. *International Journal of Public Sector Management, 8*(7), 15–20. doi:10.1108/09513559510103157

Dornan, A. (2007). Half-baked or mashed: Is mixing enterprise IT and the Internet a recipe for disaster? *Information Week, 10*, 40–48.

Doty, H., & Glick, W. (1994). Typologies as a unique form of theory building: Towards improvement understanding and modelling. *Academy of Management Review, 19*(2), 230–251. doi:10.2307/258704

Douglas, J., McClelland, R., & Davies, J. (2008a). The development of a conceptual model of student satisfaction with their experience in higher education. *Quality Assurance in Education, 16*(1), 19–35. doi:10.1108/09684880810848396

Douglas, J., McClelland, R., Davies, J., & Sudbury, L. (2008b). Using critical incident technique (CIT) to capture the voice of the student. *The TQM Journal, 21*(4), 305–318. doi:10.1108/17542730910965038

Druckman, A., Chitnis, M., Sorrell, S., & Jackson, T. (2011). Missing carbon reductions? Exploring rebound and backfire effects in UK households. *Energy Policy, 39*(6), 3572–3581. doi:10.1016/j.enpol.2011.03.058

Duffy, D. (2003). Commentary internal and external factors which affect customer loyalty. *Journal of Consumer Marketing, 20*(5), 480–485. doi:10.1108/07363760310489715

Duncan, T. (2005). *Advertising and IMC* (2nd ed.). New York: McGraw Hill.

Dunham, R. (1977). Shift work: A review and theoretical analysis. *Academy of Management Review, 2*(4), 624–634. doi:10.2307/257514

Duray, R. (2000). Approaches to mass customization: Configurations and empirical validation. *Journal of Operations Management, 18*(6), 605–625. doi:10.1016/S0272-6963(00)00043-7

Duray, R. (2002). Mass customization origins: mass or custom manufacturing? *International Journal of Operations & Production Management, 22*(3), 314–330. doi:10.1108/01443570210417614

Duray, R., & Milligan, G. (1999). Improving customer satisfaction through MC. *Quality Progress, 32*(8), 23–41.

Duray, R., Ward, P. T., Milligan, G. W., & Berry, W. L. (2000). Approaches to MC: configurations & empirical validation. *Journal of Operations Management, 18*, 605–625. doi:10.1016/S0272-6963(00)00043-7

Dutka, A. (1994). *AMA handbook for customer satisfaction*. Evanston, Illinois: NTC Business Books.

Eagle, L., & Brennan, R. (2007). Are students customers? TQM and marketing perspectives. *Quality Assurance in Education, 15*(1), 44–60. doi:10.1108/09684880710723025

Easterby-Smith, M., Thorpe, R., & Lowe, A. (2002). *Management research: an introduction*. London: Sage.

Ebbers, W. E., & van Dijk, J. A. G. M. (2007). Resistance and support to electronic government, building a model of innovation. *Government Information Quarterly, 24*(3), 554–575. doi:10.1016/j.giq.2006.09.008

Economides, A. A., & Terzis, V. (2008). Evaluating tax sites: An evaluation framework and its application. *Electronic Government, an International Journal (EG), 5*(3), 321-344.

Edvardsson, B., & Ross, I. (2001). Critical incident techniques. Towards a framework for analysing the criticality of critical incidents. *International Journal of Service Industry Management, 12*(3), 251–268. doi:10.1108/EUM0000000005520

Eldabi, T., Paul, R. J., & Young, T. (2007). Simulation modelling in healthcare: reviewing legacies and investigating futures. *The Journal of the Operational Research Society, 58*, 262–270.

Ellis, R. A., Ginns, P., & Piggot, L. (2009). E-learning in higher education: some key aspects and their relationship to approaches to study. *Higher Education Research & Development, 28*(3), 303–318. doi:10.1080/07294360902839909

Epstein, S. K., & Tian, L. (2006). Development of an emergency department work score to predict ambulance diversion. *Academic Emergency Medicine, 13*(4), 421–426. doi:10.1111/j.1553-2712.2006.tb00320.x

Ernst, G. (2005). Integration von produkt und dienstleistung—hybride wertschöpfung.

European Health Telematics Association - EHTEL. (2009). *Reflections on a decade of eHealth: The second stage in healthcare transformation*. Retrieved October 22, 2009, from http://www.ehtel.org/

Falin, G. A. (1990). Survey of retrial queues. *Queueing Systems, 7*(2), 127–168. doi:10.1007/BF01158472

Famega, C. N. (2005). Variation in officer downtime: A review of the research. *Policing: An International Journal of Police Strategies and Management, 28*(3), 388–414. doi:10.1108/13639510510614528

Fandray, D. (2000). Eight days a week: Meeting the challenge of the 24/7 economy. *Workforce, 79*(9), 35-42.

Faraway, J., & Chatfield, C. (1998). Time series forecasting with neural networks: A comparative study using the airline data. *Applied Statistics, 47*(2), 231–250. doi:10.1111/1467-9876.00109

Farquhar, C. R. (1993). Focusing on the customer. *Canadian Business Review, 20*(4), 1–14.

Fennell, M. L., & Warnecke, R. B. (1988). *Diffusion of medical innovations: An applied network analysis*. New York: Plenum.

Fensel, D. (2002). *Ontologies: A silver bullet for knowledge management and electronic commerce*. Berlin: Springer.

Fensel, D., van Harmelen, F., Horrocks, I., McGuinness, D. L., & Patel-Schneider, P. F. (2001). OIL: An ontology infrastructure for the semantic web. *IEEE Intelligent Systems, 16*(2), 38–45. doi:10.1109/5254.920598

Ferris, C., & Farrell, J. (2003). What are web services? *Communications of the ACM, 46*(6), 31. doi:10.1145/777313.777335

Fettke, P., & Loos, P. (2003). Specification of business components. In M. Aksit, M. Mezini, & R. Unland (Eds.), *Objects, Components, Architectures, Services, and Applications for a Networked World, International Conference NetObjectDays* (LNCS 2591, pp. 62-75). Berlin: Springer Verlag.

Fichter, D., & Wisniewski, J. (2009). They grow up so fast: Mashups in the enterprise. *Online, 33*(3), 54–57.

Fishbein, M., & Ajzen, I. (1975). *Belief, attitude, intention and behavior: An introduction to theory and research*. Reading, UK: Addison-Wesley.

Fishbein, M., & Ajzen, I. (1975). *Belief, attitude, intention and behavior: An introduction to theory and research*. Reading, MA: Addison-Wesley.

Fisher, A. A., Laing, J. E., Stoeckel, J. E., & Townsend, J. W. (1991). *Handbook for family planning operation research design*. New York: Population Council.

Fjermestad, J., & Romano, N. (2003). An integrative implementation framework for electronic customer relationship management: Revisiting the general principles of usability and resistance. In *Proceeding of the Proceedings of the 36th Hawaii International Conference on System Sciences*, Big Island, HI.

Flanagan, J. C. (1954). The critical incident technique. *Psychological Bulletin, 51*, 327–358. doi:10.1037/h0061470

Flavian, C., Torres, E., & Guinaliu, M. (2004). Corporate image measurement. A further problem for the tangibilization of internet banking services. *International Journal of Bank Marketing, 22*(5), 366–384. doi:10.1108/02652320410549665

Fleiss, J. L. (1979). *Statistical methods for rates and proportions* (2nd ed.). New York: Wiley.

Fletcher, K. (1995). *Marketing management and information technology* (2nd ed.). Hertfordshire, UK: Prentice Hall.

Fone, D., Hollinghurst, S., Temple, M., Round, A., Lester, N., & Weightman, A. (2003). Systematic review of the use and value of computer simulation modeling in population health and healthcare delivery. *Journal of Public Health Medicine, 25*, 325–335. doi:10.1093/pubmed/fdg075

Fontana, F., & Lorenzoni, G. (2004). *Le architetture strategiche nelle aziende sanitarie: una indagine empirica*. Milano, Italy: FrancoAngeli.

Fontanella, G. C., & Morabito, R. (2002). Analyzing the trade-off between investing in service channels and satisfying the targeted user service for Brazilian internet service providers. *International Transactions in Operational Research, 9*(3), 247–259. doi:10.1111/1475-3995.00354

Ford, J. B., Joseph, M., & Joseph, B. (1993). *Service quality in higher education: a comparison of universities In the United States and New Zealand using SERVQUAL*. Norfolk, VA: Old Dominion University.

Ford, J. B., Joseph, M., & Joseph, B. (1999). Importance-performance analysis as a strategic tool for service marketers: The case of service quality perceptions of business students in New Zealand and the USA. *Journal of Services Marketing, 13*(1), 171–186. doi:10.1108/08876049910266068

Franke, N., & Piller, F. (2003). Key research issues in user interaction with user toolkits in a mass customization system. *International Journal of Technology Management, 26*(5-6), 578–599. doi:10.1504/IJTM.2003.003424

Franke, N., & Piller, F. (2004). Toolkits for user innovation and design: An exploration of user interaction and value creation. *Journal of Product Innovation Management, 21*(6), 401–415. doi:10.1111/j.0737-6782.2004.00094.x

Frank, I. C. (2001). ED crowding and diversion: Strategies and concerns from across the United States. *Journal of Emergency Nursing: JEN, 27*(6), 559–565. doi:10.1067/men.2001.120244

Froehle, C. A., & Roth, A. V. (2004). New measurement scales for evaluating perceptions of the technology-mediated customer service experience. *Journal of Operations Management, 22*(1), 1–21. doi:10.1016/j.jom.2003.12.004

Fryrear, R., Prill, E., & Worzala, E. M. (2001). The use of geographic information systems by corporate real estate executives. *Journal of Real Estate Research, 22*(1-2), 153–164.

Fung, D., Kung, H., & Barber, C. (1995). The application of GIS to mapping real estate values. *The Appraisal Journal, 16*(11), 446–449.

Furnham, A., & Hughes, K. (1999). Individual difference correlates of nightwork and shift-work rotation. *Personality and Individual Differences, 26*(5), 941–959. doi:10.1016/S0191-8869(98)00199-8

Gagnon, M. P., Godin, G., Gagné, C., Fortin, J. P., Lamothe, L., & Reinharz, D. (2003). An adaptation of the theory of interpersonal behavior to the study of telemedicine adoption by physicians. *International Journal of Medical Informatics, 71*, 103 115. doi:10,1016/S1386-5056(03)00094-7

Gallun, R. A., Heagy, C. D., & Lindsey, H. C. (1993). How CPAs use computers. *Journal of Accountancy, 175*(1), 38–41.

Gao, G., & Hitt, L. (2004). IT and product variety: Evidence from panel data. In *Proceedings of the 25th International Conference on Information Systems (ICIS)*, Washington, DC.

GAO. (2005, August). Data mining: Agencies have taken key steps to protect privacy in selected efforts, but significant compliance issues remain (Tech. Rep. No. GAO-05-866, p. 7). Washington, DC: United States Government Accounting Office.

Gao, S. J., Wang, H. Q., Xu, D. M., & Wang, Y. F. (2007). An intelligent agent-assisted decision support system for family financial planning. *Decision Support Systems, 44*(1), 60–78. doi:10.1016/j.dss.2007.03.001

García Crespo, A., Gómez Berbís, J. M., Colomo Palacios, R., & García Sánchez, F. (2009c). Digital libraries and web 3.0: The CallimachusDL approach. *Computers in human behaviour.*

García Crespo, A., Chamizo, J., Rivera, I., Mencke, M., Colomo Palacios, R., & Gómez Berbís, J. M. (2009a). SPETA: Social pervasive e-tourism advisor. *Telematics and Informatics, 26*(3), 306–315. doi:10.1016/j.tele.2008.11.008

García Crespo, A., Colomo Palacios, R., Gómez Berbís, J. M., & García Sánchez, F. (2009b). *SOLAR: Social link advanced recommendation system*. Future Generation Computer Systems.

Garen, K. (2006). Driving the firm of the future. *Accounting Technology,* June. Retrieved February 9, 2007, from http://www.webcpa.com/

Gaudin, S. (2007). IT ditches cost controls to focus on innovation. *Information Week,* 128.

Gefen, D., & Straub, D. (2005). A practical guide to factorial validity using PLS-graph: Tutorial and annotated example. *Communications of the Association for Information Systems, 16*(5), 91–109.

Geisler, E. (2009). Tacit and explicit knowledge: Empirical investigation in an emergency regime. *International Journal of Technology Management, 47*(4), 273–285. doi:10.1504/IJTM.2009.024430

Giapoulis, A. (1996). *Modelle für effektive konstruktionsprozesse*. Aachen, Germany: Shaker.

Giorgino, T., Azzini, I., Rognonia, C., Quaglinia, S., Stefanelli, M., & Gretter, R. (2005). Automated spoken dialogue system for hypertensive patient home management. *International Journal of Medical Informatics, 74*, 159–167. doi:10.1016/j.ijmedinf.2004.04.026

Glushak, C., Delbridge, T. R., & Garrison, H. G. (1997). Ambulance diversion. Standards and Clinical Practices Committee, National Association of EMS Physicians. *Prehospital Emergency Care, 1*(2), 100–103. doi:10.1080/10903129708958797

Glykas, M., & Chytas, P. (2004). Technological innovations in asthma patient monitoring and care. *Expert Systems with Applications, 27*, 121–131. doi:10.1016/j.eswa.2003.12.007

Gómez-Berbís, J. M., Colomo-Palacios, R., García-Crespo, A., & Ruiz-Mezcua, B. (2008). ProLink: A semantics-based social network for software project. *International Journal of Information Technology and Management*, *7*(4), 392–404. doi:10.1504/IJITM.2008.018656

Goodhue, D. L. (1995). Understanding user evaluations of information systems. *Management Science, 41*, 1827–1844. doi:10.1287/mnsc.41.12.1827

Goodhue, D. L., & Thompson, R. L. (1995). Task-Technology fit and individual performance. *Management Information Systems Quarterly*, *19*(2), 213–237. doi:10.2307/249689

Goodman, B. (1999). Internet telephony and modem delay. *IEEE Network, 13*(3), 8–16. doi:10.1109/65.767132

Goodwin, C., & Goodwin, M. (1998). Seeing as situated activity: Formulating planes. In Engeström, Y., & Middleton, D. (Eds.), *Cognition and communication at work* (pp. 96–129). Cambridge, MA: CUP.

Gorbenko, A., Romanovsky, A., & Kharchenko, V. (2008). How to enhance UDDI with dependability capabilities. In *Proceedings of the 32nd Annual IEEE International Computer Software and Applications Conference* (pp. 1023-1028). Washington, DC: IEEE Computer Society.

Gordijn, J., & Akkermans, H. (2001). Designing and evaluating e-business models. *Intelligent E-Business*, *16*(4), 11–17.

Gotsi, M., & Wilson, A. M. (2001). Corporate reputation: seeking a definition. *Corporate Communications: An International Journal*, *6*(1), 24–30. doi:10.1108/13563280110381189

Gramatikov, M. (2006). *Data mining techniques and the decision making process in the Bulgarian Public Administration*. Retrieved December 30, 2009, from http://unpan1.un.org/intradoc/groups/public/documents/nispacee/unpan009209.pdf

Grandori, A. (1999). *Organizzazione e comportamento economico*. Bologna, Italy: Il Mulino.

Grant, N. (1979). *Time to care*. London: Royal College of Nursing.

Greenberg, B. S., & Wolff, R. W. (1987). An upper bound on the performance of queues with returning customers. *Journal of Applied Probability, 24*, 466–475. doi:10.2307/3214270

Gregg, D. G., & Walczak, S. (2006). Auction advisor: an agent-based online-auction decision support system. *Decision Support Systems, 41*(2), 449–471. doi:10.1016/j.dss.2004.07.007

Gregg, D. G., & Walczak, S. (2007). Exploiting the information Web. *IEEE Transactions on System. Man and Cybernetics: Part C, 37*(1), 109–125. doi:10.1109/TSMCC.2006.876061

Gremler, D. D. (2004). The Critical Incident Technique in Service Research. *Journal of Service Research, 7*(1), 65–89. doi:10.1177/1094670504266138

Gretzel, U., Mitsche, N., Hwang, Y., & Fesenmaier, D. (2004). Tell me who you are and I will tell you where to go: Travel personality testing for DRS. In A. Frew (Ed.), *Proceedings of the ICT in Tourism ENTER 2004*, Vienna, Austria (pp. 205-215). Berlin: Springer Verlag.

Grönroos, C. (1984). A service quality model and its marketing implications. *European Journal of Marketing, 18*(4), 36–44. doi:10.1108/EUM0000000004784

Grönroos, C. (1990). Relationship approach to marketing in service contexts: The marketing and organizational behaviour interface. *Journal of Business Research, 20*(1), 3–11. doi:10.1016/0148-2963(90)90037-E

Gruber, T. R. (1993). A translation approach to portable ontology specifications. *Knowledge Acquisition, 5*(2), 199–220. doi:10.1006/knac.1993.1008

Gruber, T. R. (2008). Collective knowledge systems: Where the social web meets the semantic web. *Web Semantics: Science. Services and Agents on the World Wide Web, 6*(1), 4–13.

Guay, L. (2003). Create your identity, create your product. In *Proceedings of the 2003 World Congress on Mass Customization and Personalization (MCPC 2003)*, Munich, Germany.

Gullkvist, B., & Ylinen, M. (2005). E-accounting systems use in Finnish accounting agencies. In M. Seppä, M. Hannula, A-M. Järvelin, J. Kujala, M. Ruohonen, & T. Tiainen (Eds.) *Frontiers of e-Business Research. Proceedings of the e-Business Research Forum 2005* (pp. 109-117). Tampere, Finland: e-Business Resilience Centre.

Ha, H. (2004). Factors influencing consumer perceptions of brand trust online. *Journal of Product and Brand Management, 13*(5), 329–342. doi:10.1108/10610420410554412

Hand, D. J., Mannila, H., & Smyth, P. (2001). *Principles of Data Mining*. Cambridge, MA: MIT Press.

Hart, C., & Taylor, J. R. (1996). *Value creation through MC: Achieving competitive advantage through mass customization*. Ann Arbor, MI: University of Michigan Business School seminar.

Haubl, G., & Trifts, V. (2000). Consumer decision making in online shopping environments: The effects of interactive decision aids. *Marketing Science, 19*(1), 4–21. doi:10.1287/mksc.19.1.4.15178

Hecker, E. J., & Bruzewicz, A. J. (2008). Emergency management international: improving national and international disaster preparedness and response. *Int. J. of Emergency Management, 3/4*, 250–260. doi:10.1504/IJEM.2008.025095

Hedman, J., & Henningsson, S. (2011). Three strategies for green IT. *IT Professional Magazine, 13*(1), 54–57. doi:10.1109/MITP.2010.141

Helmreich, R., & Merritt, A. (1998). *Culture at work in aviation and medicine: National, organizational and professional influences*. Aldershot, UK: Ashgate.

Hemsley-Brown, J., & Oplatka, I. (2006). Universities in a competitive global marketplace, a systematic review of the literature on higher education marketing. *International Journal of Public Sector Management, 19*(4), 316–338. doi:10.1108/09513550610669176

Hepworth, M. (2004). A framework for understanding user requirements for an information service: Defining the needs of informal carers. *Journal of the American Society for Information Science and Technology, 55*(8), 695–708. doi:10.1002/asi.20015

Hermann, T., Krcmar, H., & Kleinbeck, U. (Eds.). (2005). *Konzepte für das service engineering—modularisierung, prozessgestaltung und produktivitätsmanagement*. Heidelberg, Germany: Physica.

Hess, C., & de Vries, M. (2006). From models to data: A prototype query translator for the cadastral domain. *Computers, Environment and Urban Systems, 30*(5), 529–542. doi:10.1016/j.compenvurbsys.2005.08.008

Hesse, B. W., Sproull, L. S., Kiesler, S. B., & Walsh, J. P. (1993). Returns to science: Computer networks in oceanography. *Communications of the ACM, 36*(8), 90–101. doi:10.1145/163381.163409

Hesseldahl, A. (2008, May 5). A rich vein for reality mining. *BusinessWeek, 4082*, 52-53.

Hevner, A. R., March, S. T., & Park, J. (2004). Design science in information systems research. *Management Information Systems Quarterly, 28*(1), 75–105.

Hill, Y., Lomas, L., & MacGregor, J. (2003). Students' perceptions of quality in higher education. *Quality Assurance in Education, 11*(1), 15–20. doi:10.1108/09684880310462047

Ho, H. F., & Hung, C. C. (2008). Marketing mix formulation for higher education. An integrated analysis employing analytic hierarchy process, cluster analysis and correspondence analysis. *International Journal of Educational Management, 22*(4), 328–340. doi:10.1108/09513540810875662

Holsapple, C. W., Luo, W., & Morton, R. S. (2000). Computer support of shift work: An experiment in a GSS environment. *Journal of Computer Information Systems, 41*(1), 1–6.

Hopkins, C., & Raymond, M. (2004). Consumer responses to perceived telepresence in online advertising: moderating role of involvement. *Marketing Theory, 4*(1-2), 137–162. doi:10.1177/1470593104044090

Hosmer, D., & Lemeshow, S. (2000). *Applied Logistic Regression* (2nd ed.). New York: John Wiley & Sons.

Hossain, M., & Shahidullah, S. M. (2008). Global-local nexus and the emerging field of criminology and criminal justice in South Asia: Bangladesh case. *Bangladesh e-. Journal of Sociology (Melbourne, Vic.), 5*(2), 51–60.

Hoxley, M. (1998). *The impact of competitive fee tendering on construction professional service quality (RICS Research Findings No. 24)*. London: Royal Institute of Chartered Surveyors.

Hoyer, V., & Fischer, M. (2008). *Market overview of enterprise mashup tools* (LNCS 5364, pp. 708-721). New York: Springer.

Hsieh, R. K. C., Hjelm, N. M., Lee, J. C. K., & Aldis, J. W. (2001). Telemedicine in China. *International Journal of Medical Informatics, 61*, 139–146. doi:10.1016/S1386-5056(01)00136-8

Huey, L., & Rosenberg, R. S. (2004, October). Watching the web: Thoughts on expanding police surveillance opportunities under the cyber-crime convention. *Canadian Journal of Criminology and Criminal Justice*, 597–606.

Huffman, C., & Kahn, B. (1998). Variety for sale: Mass customization or mass confusion. *Journal of Retailing, 74*(4), 491–513. doi:10.1016/S0022-4359(99)80105-5

Humby, C., Hunt, T., & Phillips, T. (2003). *Scoring points how tesco is wining customer loyalty*. London: Kogan Page.

Hunton, J., & Beeler, J. (1997). Effects of user participation on systems development: A longitudinal field experiment. *Management Information Systems Quarterly, 21*(4), 359–388. doi:10.2307/249719

Hurrell, J. J. (1987). An overview of organizational stress and health. In L. R. Murphy & T. F. Schoenberg (Eds.), *Stress management in work settings*. Washington, DC: National Institute of Occupational Safety and Health (U.S. Government Printing Office).

IISA/UCD. (2006). *Irish cybercrime survey (2006)-the impact of cybercrime on Irish organization*. Retrieved February 10, 2009, from http://www.issaireland.org/ISSA%20UCD%20Irish%20Cybercrime%20Survey%202006.pdf

ITU. (2006). *Multichannel stereophonic sound system with and without accompanying picture*. Geneva, Switzerland: International Telecommunication Union.

Ives, B., & Olson, H. (1984). User involvement and MIS success: A review of research. *Management Science, 30*(5), 586–603. doi:10.1287/mnsc.30.5.586

Ives, B., Olson, M. H., & Baroudi, J. J. (1983). The measurement of user information satisfaction. *Communications of the ACM, 26*(10), 785–793. doi:10.1145/358413.358430

Ivy, J. (2001). Higher education institution image: A correspondence analysis approach. *International Journal of Educational Management, 15*(6), 276–282. doi:10.1108/09513540110401484

Ivy, J. (2008). A new higher education marketing mix: The 7p's for MBA marketing. *International Journal of Educational Management, 22*(4), 288–299. doi:10.1108/09513540810875635

Jackson, T., & Victor, P. (2011). Productivity and work in the 'green economy': Some theoretical reflections and empirical tests. *Environmental Innovation and Societal Transitions, 1*(1), 101–108. doi:10.1016/j.eist.2011.04.005

Jacobson, I., Booch, G., & Rumbaugh, J. (1999). *The unified software development process*. Glenview, IL: Addison-Wesley Longman.

Jenkin, T., Webster, J., & McShane, L. (2010, Sep). An agenda for "green" information technology systems research. *Information and Organization, 21*(1), 17–40. doi:10.1016/j.infoandorg.2010.09.003

Jiang, J., Waleed, J., Muhanna, A., & Klein, G. (2000). User resistance and strategies for promoting acceptance across system types. *Information & Management, 37*(1), 25–36. doi:10.1016/S0378-7206(99)00032-4

Jiang, P., & Rosenbloom, B. (2005). Customer Intention to Return Online: Price Perception, Attribute-Level Performance, and Satisfaction Unfolding over Time. *European Journal of Marketing, 39*(1), 150–174. doi:10.1108/03090560510572061

Jijkoun, V., Mishne, G., Rijke, M. D., Schlobach, S., Ahn, D., & Muller, K. (2004). *Working notes of the CLEF 2004 workshop*. Paper presented at the The University of Amsterdam at QA@CLEF 2004.

Johnston, R. P. (2005). A tour of tomorrow's technology. [from http://www.aicpa.org/PUBS/JOFA/joaiss.htm]. *Journal of Accountancy, 200*(4), 95–97. Retrieved November 23, 2006.

Jones, M. C., & Young, R. (2006). ERP usage in practice: An empirical investigation. *Information Resources Management Journal, 19*(1), 23–42.

Jones, N. B., & Kochtanek, T. R. (2004). Success factors in the implementation of a collaborative technology and resulting productivity improvements in a small business: An exploratory study. *Journal of Organizational and End User Computing, 16*(1), 1–20.

Joseph, M., Yakhou, M., & Stone, G. (2005). An educational institution's quest for service quality: customers' perspective. *Quality Assurance in Education, 13*(1), 66–82. doi:10.1108/09684880510578669

Joshi, A. P. (2006). *Customer satisfaction in Central Public Works Department.* Unpublished post-graduate dissertation, Indian Institute of Management Bangalore, India.

Juan, A., Daradoumis, A., Xhafa, F., Caballe, S., & Faulin, J. (Eds.). (2009b). *Monitoring and Assessment in Online Collaborative Environments: Emergent Computational Technologies for E-Learning Support.* Hershey, PA: IGI Global.

Juan, A., Daradoumis, T., Faulin, J., & Xhafa, F. (2009a). A Data Analysis Model based on Control Charts to Monitor Online Learning Processes. *Int. Journal of Business Intelligence and Data Mining, 4*(2), 159–174. doi:10.1504/IJBIDM.2009.026906

Juan, A., Huertas, M., Steegmann, C., Corcoles, C., & Serrat, C. (2008). Mathematical E-Learning: state of the art and experiences at the Open University of Catalonia. *International Journal of Mathematical Education in Science and Technology, 39*(4), 455–471. doi:10.1080/00207390701867497

Jun, J. B., Jacobson, S. H., & Swisher, J. R. (1999). Application of discrete-event simulation in healthcare clinics: a survey. *The Journal of the Operational Research Society, 50*(2), 109–123.

Kaluzny, A. D., & Warnecke, R. B. (1996). *Managing a health care alliance.* San Francisco, CA: Jossey-Bass.

Kamali, N., & Loker, S. (2002). Mass customization: On-line consumer involvement in product design. *Journal of Computer-Mediated Communication, 7*(4). Retrieved July 5, 2005 from http://jcmc.indiana.edu/vol7/issue4/loker.html

Kamberovic, R., Meyer, M., & Orth, S. (2005). Eckdaten der deutschen fitnesswirtschaft. 67.

Kandolin, I. (1993). Burnout of female and male nurses in shift work. *Ergonomics, 36*(1-3), 141–147. doi:10.1080/00140139308967865

Kantardzic, M. M., & Zurada, J. (Eds.). (2005). *Next generation of data-mining applications.* Washington, DC: IEEE Press.

Kaplan, B. (2001). Evaluating informatics applications - some alternative approaches: Theory, social interactionism, and call for methodological pluralism. *International Journal of Medical Informatics, 64*, 39–55. doi:10.1016/S1386-5056(01)00184-8

Kaplan, B., & Shaw, N. (2002). People, organizational and social issues: Evaluation as an exemplar. In Haux, R., & Kulikowski, C. (Eds.), *Yearbook of medical informatics 2002* (pp. 91–99). Stuttgart, Germany: Schattauer.

Karahanna, E., Straub, D. W., & Chervany, N. L. (1999). Information technology adoption across time: A cross-sectional comparison of pre-adoption and post-adoption beliefs. *MIS Quarterly, 23*(2), 183–213. doi:10.2307/249751

Kargin, B., Basoglu, N., & Daim, T. (2009). Adoption factors of mobile services. *International Journal of Information Systems in the Service Sector, 1*(1), 15–34.

Katzmaier, D. (2007). Ultimate HDTV buying guide. *CNet Reviews.* Retrieved December 21, 2007, from http://www.cnet.com/1990-7874_1-5108580-1.html

Keen, P. G. W. (1990). Telecommunications and organizational choice. In Fulk, J., & Steinfield, C. (Eds.), *Organizations and communication technology.* Newbury Park, CA: Sage.

Keller, L. F. (1994). MedModel-specialized software for the healthcare industry. In J. D. Tew, S. Manivannan, D. A. Sadowski, & A. F. Seila (Eds.), *Proceedings of the 1994 Winter Simulation Conference,* Lake Buena Vista, FL (pp. 533-537). Washington, DC: IEEE.

Kernane, T. (2008). Conditions for stability and instability of retrial queuing systems with general retrial times. *Statistics & Probability Letters, 78*(18), 3244–3248. doi:10.1016/j.spl.2008.06.019

Kettl, D. F. (2002). The transformation of governance: Public administration for twenty-first century [Baltimore, MD: JHU Press.]. *America,* 69–72.

Khani, P. E., & Zarowin, S. (1994). The technology used by high-tech CPAs. *Journal of Accountancy, 177*(2), 54–58.

Khan, M. M., Ali, D., Ferdousy, Z., & Al-Mamun, A. (2001). A cost-minimization approach to planning the geographical distribution of health facilities. *Health Policy and Planning, 16*(2), 264–272. doi:10.1093/heapol/16.3.264

Khasawneh, A. M., & Stafford, T. F. (2008). Mobile computing in developing nations: the case of use and adoption in Jordan. In *Proceedings of the 2008 Global Information Technology Management Conference,* Atlanta, GA.

Khasawneh, A. M. (2008). Information technology in transitional economies: The mobile internet in Jordan. *Journal of Global Information Technology Management, 11*(3), 4–23.

Killingsworth, J. R., Hossain, N., Hedrick-Wong, Y., Thomas, S. D., Rahman, A., & Begum, T. (1999). Unofficial fees in Bangladesh: price, equity and institutional issues. *Health Policy and Planning, 14,* 152–163. doi:10.1093/heapol/14.2.152

Kim, K. S. (2011). Exploring transportation planning issues during the preparations for EXPO 2012 Yeosu Korea. *Habitat International, 35*(2), 286–294. doi:10.1016/j.habitatint.2010.10.002

Kipp, A., Jiang, T., Fugini, M., & Salomie, I. (2011). Layered Green Performance Indicators. *Future Generation Computer Systems,* In Press, Corrected Proof, Available online Sept. 29, 2011.

Kirmeyer, S. L., & Lin, T.-R. (1987). Social support: Its relationship to observed communication with peers and superiors. *Academy of Management Journal, 30*(1), 138–151. doi:10.2307/255900

Klein, R. W., Dittus, R. S., Roberts, S. D., & Wilson, J. R. (1993). Simulation modelling and health-care decision making. *Medical Decision Making, 13,* 347–354. doi:10.1177/0272989X9301300411

Kleinrock, L. (1996). Nomadicity: Anytime, anywhere in a disconnected world. *Mobile Networks and Applications, 1*(4), 351–357.

Knickman, J. R., Hunt, K. A., Snell, E. K., Marie, L., Alecxih, B., & Kennell, D. L. (2003). Wealth patterns among elderly Americans: Implications for healthcare affordability. *Health Affairs, 22,* 168–174. doi:10.1377/hlthaff.22.3.168

Kogi, K. (1985). Introduction to the problems of shift work. In Folkard, S., & Monk, T. (Eds.), *Hours of work* (pp. 165–182). Chichester, UK: Wiley.

Kotha, S., & Vadlamani, B. (1995). Assessing generic strategies: an empirical investigation of two competing typologies in discrete manufacturing industries. *Strategic Management Journal, 16*(1), 75–83. doi:10.1002/smj.4250160108

Kotler, P. (2000). *Marketing management: The millennium edition* (6th ed.). Upper Saddle River, NJ: Prentice-Hall.

Krol, D., Trawinski, B., & Zawila, W. (2008). Integration of cadastral and financial-accounting systems. *International Journal of Intelligent Information and Database Systems, 2*(3), 370–381. doi:10.1504/IJIIDS.2008.020448

Krone, F., Gilly, M., Zeithaml, V., & Lamb, C. W. (1981). Factors influencing the graduate business school decision. In *Proceedings of the American Marketing Services* (pp. 453-456).

Krueger, M. (2003). Dial-out modem pools. *Buildings, 97*(11), 16.

Kruss, G. (2002, April 10). Illuminating private higher education in SA. *Business Day,* 1st ed.

Kulchitsky, D. R. (2004). Computerization, knowledge, and information technology initiatives in Jordan. *Administration & Society, 36*(1), 3–37. doi:10.1177/0095399703257263

Kuljis, J., Paul, R. J., & Stergioulas, L. K. (2007). Can healthcare benefit from modelling and simulation methods in the same way as business and manufacturing has? In B. Henderson, M.-H. Biller, J. Hsieh, J. D. Shortle, R. Tew, & R. Barton (Eds.), *Proceeding of 39th Winter simulation Conference* (pp. 1449-1453). Washington, DC: IEEE.

Kummerow, M., & Lun, J. C. (2005). Information and communication technology in the real estate industry: Productivity, industry structure and market efficiency. *Telecommunications Policy, 29*(2-3), 173–190. doi:10.1016/j.telpol.2004.12.003

Kwan, P. Y. K., & Ng, P. W. K. (1999). Quality indicators in higher education – comparing Hong Kong and China's students'. *Managerial Auditing Journal, 14*(1/2), 20–27. doi:10.1108/02686909910245964

Kwon, O. B. (2006). Multi-agent system approach to context-aware coordinated web services under general market mechanism. *Decision Support Systems, 41*(2), 380–399. doi:10.1016/j.dss.2004.07.005

Lagoe, R. J., & Jastremski, M. S. (1990). Relieving overcrowded emergency departments through ambulance diversion. *Hospital Topics, 68*(3), 23–27.

Lagoe, R. J., Kohlbrenner, J. C., Hall, L. D., Roizen, M., Nadle, P. A., & Hunt, R. C. (2003). Reducing ambulance diversion: A multihospital approach. *Prehospital Emergency Care, 7*, 99–108. doi:10.1080/10903120390937184

Lagrosen, S., Seyyed-Hashemi, R., & Leitner, M. (2004). Examination of the dimensions of quality in higher education. *Quality Assurance in Education, 12*(2), 61–69. doi:10.1108/09684880410536431

Lai, K.-H., & Wong, C. W. Y. (2012). Green logistics management and performance: Some empirical evidence from Chinese manufacturing exporters. *Omega, 40*(3), 267–282. doi:10.1016/j.omega.2011.07.002

Lake, N., & Hickey, K. (2002). *The customer service workbook*. London: Kogan Page.

Lambert, J., Van Houdt, B., & Blondia, C. (2008). Queues in DOCSIS cable modem networks. *Computers & Operations Research, 35*(8), 2482–2496.

Lamb, J. (2009). *The greening of IT: How companies can make a difference for the Environment*. Pearson. IBM Press.

Lampel, J., & Mintzberg, H. (1996). Customizing MC. *Sloan Management Review, 38*, 21–30.

Landro, L. (2006, January 26). The informed patient: Infant monitors yield new clues; Studies of digital records are used to identify problems with medications. Practices. *Wall Street Journal*, D5.

Landrum, R. E., Turrisi, R., & Harless, C. (1998). University Image: The benefits of assessment and modelling. *Journal of Marketing for Higher Education, 9*(1), 53–68. doi:10.1300/J050v09n01_05

Lane, P. L., Palko, J., & Cronan, T. P. (1994). Key issues in the MIS implementation process: An update using end user computing satisfaction. *Journal of End User Computing, 6*(4), 3–14.

Langegger, A., & Wöß, W. (2007). Product finding on the semantic web: A search agent supporting products with limited availability. *International Journal of Web Information Systems, 3*(1-2), 61–88. doi:10.1108/17440080710829225

Lankhorst, M. (2005). *Enterprise architecture at work: Modelling, communication and analysis*. Berlin: Springer.

Larsen, G., & Wilber, J. (2005). *Asset lifecycle management for service-oriented architectures*. Retrieved January 23, 2008, from http://www.ibm.com/developerworks/rational/library/oct05/wilber/

Lau, F. (1997). A review on the use of action research in information systems studies. In A. S. Lee, J. Liebenau & J. I. DeGross (Eds.), *Information Systems and Qualitative Research: Proceedings of the IFIP TC8 WG 8.2 International Conference on Information Systems and Qualitative Research*, Philadelphia (pp. 31-68). London: Chapman & Hall.

Law, A. M., & Kelton, W. D. (2000). *Simulation modeling and analysis* (3rd ed.). New York: McGraw-Hill.

LeBlanc, G., & Nguyen, N. (1997). Searching for excellence in business education: an exploratory study of customer impressions of service quality. *International Journal of Educational Management, 11*(2), 72–79. doi:10.1108/09513549710163961

Lee, H., Lee, Y., & Yoo, D. (2000). The determinants of perceived service quality and its relationship with satisfaction. *Journal of Services Marketing, 14*(3), 217–231. doi:10.1108/08876040010327220

Lee, R. D., & Tuljapurkar, S. (1994). Stochastic population forecasts for the United States: Beyond high, medium and low. *Journal of the American Statistical Association, 89*, 175–189. doi:10.2307/2290980

Lega, F. (1998). Scelte strategiche e definizione dei confini dell'ospedale. Dalla struttura focalizzata alla struttura a rete. *Organizzazione sanitaria, 1*, 43-66.

Lega, F. (2002). *Gruppi e reti aziendali in sanità*. Milano, Italy: Egea.

Leimeister, J. M., Ebner, W., & Krcmar, H. (2005). Design, implementation and evaluation of trust-supporting components in virtual communities for patients. *Journal of Management Information Systems*, *21*(4), 101–131.

Lenzerini, M. (2002). Data integration: A theoretical perspective. In *Proceedings of the Symposium on Principles of Database Systems* (pp. 233-246).

Levit, K., Smith, C., Cowan, C., Lazeby, H., Sensenig, A., & Catlin, A. (2003). Trends in U.S. healthcare spending 2001. *Health Affairs*, *22*, 154–164. doi:10.1377/hlthaff.22.1.154

Levy, Y., & Green, B. D. (In Press). An empirical study of computer self-efficacy and the technology acceptance model in the military: A case of a U.S. Navy combat information system. *Journal of Organizational and End User Computing*, 1-23.

Levy, Y. (2006). *Assessing the value of e-learning systems*. Hershey, PA: Information Science Publishing.

Levy, Y., Murphy, K. E., & Zanakis, S. H. (2009). A Value-Satisfaction Taxonomy of IS Effectiveness (VS-TISE): A Case Study of User Satisfaction with IS and User-Perceived Value of IS. *International Journal of Information Systems in the Service Sector*, *1*(1), 93–118.

Lewin Group. (2002). *Emergency department overload: A growing crisis*. Chicago: American Hospital Association.

Lexhagen, M. (2009). Customer perceived value of travel and tourism websites. *International Journal of Information Systems in the Service Sector*, *1*(1), 35–53.

Li, Q., Liu, A., Liu, H., Lin, B., Huang, L., & Gu, N. (2009). Web services provision: Solutions, challenges and opportunities. In *Proceedings of the 3rd International Conference on Ubiquitous Information Management and Communication* (pp. 80-87). New York: ACM.

Li, X. (2006, January 6). Diversity in Tertiary Education: More opportunities. *The Epoch Times*, 25.

Liao, C., & Huang, W. (2009). Community adaptability, computer and internet self-efficacy, and intention of blended e-learning. *International Journal of Society Systems Science*, *1*(3), 209–226. doi:10.1504/IJSSS.2009.022816

Liechty, J., Ramaswamy, V., & Cohen, S. H. (2001). Choice menus for mass customization: An experimental approach for analyzing customer demand with an application to a Web-based information service. *JMR, Journal of Marketing Research*, *39*(2), 183–196. doi:10.1509/jmkr.38.2.183.18849

Liederbach, J. (2005). Addressing the "elephant in the living room:" An observational study of the work of suburban police. *Policing: An International Journal of Police Strategies and Management*, *28*(3), 415–434. doi:10.1108/13639510510614537

Likert, R. (1932). A technique for the measurement of attitudes. *Archives de Psychologie*, *22*(140), 1–55.

Lim, J., Kim, M., Chen, S. S., & Ryder, C. E. (2008). An Empirical Investigation of Student Achievement and Satisfaction in Different Learning Environments. *Journal of Instructional Psychology*, *35*(2), 113–119.

Lin, J., Mamykina, L., Lindtner, S., Delajoux, G., & Strub, H. (2006). Fish'n'Steps: Encouraging physical activity with an interactive computer game. In P. Dourish & A. Friday (Eds.), *Proceedings of the International Conference on Ubiquitous Computing*, Orange County, USA (pp. 261-278). Berlin, Germany: Springer.

Linthicum, D. (2007). SOA extends its reach: Practical enterprise mash-ups. *InfoWorld*, *29*(8), 27–31.

Lita, L. V., Hunt, W. A., & Nyberg, E. (2004). *Resource analysis for question answering*. Paper presented at the Annual Meeting of the Association for Computational Linguistics.

Liu, J. E., Pothiban, L., Lu, Z., & Khamphonsiri, T. (2000). Computer knowledge, attitudes, and skills of nurses in People's Hospital of Beijing Medical University. *Computers in Nursing*, *18*(4), 197–206.

Liu, J. G., & Shen, Z. Q. (2011). Low carbon finance: Present situation and future development in China. *Energy Procedia*, *5*, 214–218. doi:10.1016/j.egypro.2011.03.038

Liu, L., & Ma, Q. (2005). The impact of service level on the acceptance of application service oriented medical records. *Information & Management*, *42*, 1121–1135. doi:10.1016/j.im.2004.12.004

Lohr, S. (2009, April 29). Bringing efficiency to the infrastructure. *The New York Times, Energy & Environment*, p. F1.

Lohr, S. (2011, August 23). Why flash is the future of storage in Data centers. *The New York Times,* Technology p.1.

Loiacono, E. T., Watson, R. T., & Goodhue, D. L. (2002). WebQUAL: A Measure of Web Site Quality. *Marketing Theory and Applications, 3*.

Lok, C. (2004, October). Fighting infections with data. *Technology Review*, 24.

Löllgen, H. (2004). Standard der sportmedizin: Das anstrengungsempfinden (RPE, Borg Skala). *Deutsche Zeitschrift fur Sportmedizin, 55*(11), 299–300.

Lomi, A. (1991). *Reti organizzative. Reti, tecniche e applicazioni*. Bologna, Italy: Il Mulino Editore.

Loreto, S., Mecklin, T., Opsenica, M., & Rissanen, H. (2009). Service broker architecture: Location business case and mashups. *IEEE Communications Magazine, 47*(4), 97–103. doi:10.1109/MCOM.2009.4907414

Lorincz, J., Capone, A., & Begušić, D. (2011). Optimized network management for energy savings of wireless access networks. *Computer Networks, 55*(3), 514–540. doi:10.1016/j.comnet.2010.09.013

Lou, H., Luo, W., & Strong, D. (2000). Perceived critical mass effect on groupware acceptance. *European Journal of Information Systems, 9*(2), 91–103.

Lovelock, C. H., & Young, R. F. (1979). Look to consumers to increase productivity. *Harvard Business Review, 57*, 168–178.

Love, P., Smith, J., Treloar, G., & Li, H. (2000). Some empirical observations of service quality in construction. *Engineering, Construction, and Architectural Management, 7*(2), 191–201. doi:10.1108/eb021144

Lu, C., Jen, W. Y., Chang, W., & Chou, S. (2006). Cybercrime & cybercriminals: An overview of the Taiwan experience. *Journal of Computers, 1*(6), 1–8. doi:10.4304/jcp.1.6.11-18

Lucas, H., Walton, E., & Ginzberg, M. (1988). Implementing packaged software. *Management Information Systems Quarterly, 12*(4), 537–549. doi:10.2307/249129

Luen, T. W., & Al-Hawamdeh, S. (2001). Knowledge management in the public sector: Principles and practices in police work. *Journal of Information Science, 27*(5), 311–318. doi:10.1177/016555150102700502

Luo, A., & Olson, J. S. (2006). Informal Communication in Colaboratories. In *Proceedings of the conference on computer-human interaction*. New York: Association for Computing Machinery.

Luo, J., Montrose, B., Kim, A., Khashnobish, A., & Kang, M. (2006). Adding OWL-S support to the existing UDDI infrastructure. In *Proceedings of the IEEE International Conference on Web Services* (pp. 153-162). Washington, DC: IEEE Computer Society.

Lytras, M. D., & García, R. (2008). Semantic web applications: A framework for industry and business exploitation - what is needed for the adoption of the semantic web from the market and industry. *International Journal of Knowledge and Learning, 4*(1), 93–108. doi:10.1504/IJKL.2008.019739

Magrabi, F., Lovell, N. H., & Celle, B. G. (1999). A web-based approach for electrocardiogram monitoring in the home. *International Journal of Medical Informatics, 54*, 145–153. doi:10.1016/S1386-5056(98)00177-4

Mahajan, R. (2006). SOA and the enterprise: Lessons from the city. In *Proceedings of the IEEE International Conference on Web Services* (pp. 939-944). Washington, DC: IEEE Computer Society.

Makarem, S. C., Mudambi, S. M., & Podoshem, J. S. (2009). Satisfaction in technology-enabled service encounters. *Journal of Services Marketing, 23*(3), 134–144. doi:10.1108/08876040910955143

Malakooti, B. (2000). Ranking and screening multiple criteria alternatives with partial information and use of ordinal and cardinal strength of preferences. *IEEE Transactions on Systems Man and Cybernetics: Part A, 30*(3), 355–368. doi:10.1109/3468.844359

Maloney, J. P. (1982). Job stress and the consequences on a group intensive case and non-intensive care nurses. *ANS. Advances in Nursing Science, 4*(2), 31–42.

Maltz, M. D., Gordon, A. C., & Friedman, W. (2000). *Mapping crime in its community setting: Event geography analysis*. New York: Springer Verlag.

Manes, A. T. (2003). Web services business models. In *Proceedings of Web services: A manager's guide* (pp. 37–43). Reading, MA: Addison-Wesley.

Manning, P. K. (1996). Information technology in the police context: The "sailor" phone. *Information Systems Research*, *7*(1), 52–62. doi:10.1287/isre.7.1.52

Mapelli, V. (1999). Sanità: La rivincita del piano sul mercato. In Bernardi, L. (Ed.), *La finanza pubblica italiana, Rapporto 1999* (pp. 319–341). Bologna, Italy: Il Mulino.

Marchi, M., Schifini D'Andrea, S., Maggino, F., & Mola, T. (2007). *Studio delle reti di supporto: Un'applicazione ai dimessi ospedalieri*. Working paper, University of Florence, Deptartment of Statistics.

Marcoulides, G. A., Chin, W. W., & Saunders, C. (2009). A critical look at partial least squares modeling. *Management Information Systems Quarterly*, *33*(1), 171–175.

Marcoulides, G. A., & Saunders, C. (2006). PLS: A silver bullet? *Management Information Systems Quarterly*, *30*(2), iii–ix.

Mari, C. (1994). *Metodi qualitativi di ricerca. I casi aziendali*. Torino, Italy: Giappichelli.

Marsan, M. A., & Meo, M. (2011). Energy efficient wireless Internet access with cooperative cellular networks. *Computer Networks*, *55*(2), 386–398. doi:10.1016/j.comnet.2010.10.017

Martinez, M. (1997). *Teorie di organizzazione in economia aziendale. Dall'organismo al network*. Milano, Italy: FrancoAngeli.

Marzo-Navarro, M., Pedraja, M., & Rivera-Torres, M. P. (2005). Measuring Customer Satisfaction in Summer Courses. *Quality Assurance in Education*, *13*(1), 53–65. doi:10.1108/09684880510578650

Mashworks.net. (2007). *Building mash-ups for non-programmers*. Retrieved December 11, 2007, from www.mashworks.net

Massey, A. P., Khatri, V., & Montoya-Weiss, M. M. (2007). Usability of online services: The role of technology readiness and context. *Decision Sciences*, *38*(2), 277–308. doi:10.1111/j.1540-5915.2007.00159.x

Mathieson, K., Peacock, E., & Chin, W. W. (2001). Extending the technology acceptance model: The influence of perceived user resources. *The Data Base for Advances in Information Systems*, *32*(3), 86–112.

Matsumoto, M. (2010). Development of a simulation model for reuse businesses and case studies in Japan. *Journal of Cleaner Production*, *18*(13), 1284–1299. doi:10.1016/j.jclepro.2010.04.008

Mazzoni, E. (2007). La Social network analysis a supporto delle interazioni nelle comunità virtuali per la costruzione di conoscenza. *TD, 35*(2), 54-63.

McAfee. (2007). *Virtual criminology report - cybercrime: the next wave*. Retrieved February 10, 2009, from http://www.mcafee.com/us/research/criminology_report/default.html

McDonnell, J., & Gatfield, T. (1998). SERVQUAL as a cultural change agent in the Australian public sector. In *Proceedings of the Australian and New Zealand Marketing Academy Conference* (pp. 1528-1539).

McElwee, G., & Redman, T. (1993). Upward appraisal in practice. *Education + Training*, *35*(2), 27–31.

McFedries, P. (2006). The Web, Take two. *IEEE Spectrum*, *43*(6), 68. doi:10.1109/MSPEC.2006.1638049

McMenamin, T. M. (2007). A time to work: Recent trends in shift work and flexible schedules. *Monthly Labor Review*, *139*(12), 3–15.

McMullin, B. (2005). Putting the learning back into learning technology. In G. O'Neill, S.

McPhail, K. (2008). Contributing to sustainable development through multi-stakeholder processes: practical steps to avoid the "resource curse". *Corporate Governance*, *8*(4), 471–481. doi:10.1108/14720700810899202

MedModel. (2009). *Product summary, MedModel by ProModel*. Retrieved March 25, 2009, from http://www.promodel.com

Meletiou, A., & Katsirikou, A. (2009). Methodology of analysis and interrelation of data about quality indexes of library services by using data- and knowledge- mining techniques. *Library Management*, *30*(3), 138–147. doi:10.1108/01435120910937311

Meneguzzo, M., & Cepiku, D. (Eds.). (2008). *Network pubblici: Strategia, struttura e governance*. Milano, Italy: McGraw-Hill.

Mertler, C. A., & Vannatta, R. A. (2001). *Advanced and multivariate statistical methods: Practical application and interpretation*. Los Angeles, CA: Pyrczak Publishing.

Michael, S. O. (2004). In search of universal principles of higher education management and applicability to Moldavian higher education system. *International Journal of Educational Management*, *18*(2), 118–137. doi:10.1108/09513540410522252

Michalowski, M., Ambite, J. L., Thakkar, S., Tuchinda, R., Knoblock, C. A., & Minton, S. (2004). Retrieving and semantically integrating heterogeneous data from the web. *IEEE Intelligent Systems*, *19*(3), 72–79. doi:10.1109/MIS.2004.16

Miji, A. (2002). What influences students to university education? Insights from the horse's mouth. *South African Journal of Higher Education*, *16*(2), 166–176.

Mills, P. K., & Morris, J. H. (1986). Clients as "partial" employees of service organizations: Role development in client participation. *Academy of Management Review*, *11*(4), 726–735. doi:10.2307/258392

Milner, M. (1980). *Unequal care: A case study of interorganizational relations in health care*. New York: Columbia University Press.

Ministry of Education. (2000). *Higher Education FAQs*. Retrieved from http:www.moe.edu.sg/hed.html

Ministry of Education. (2007, January 19). *Premium on fields of study: The returns to higher education in Singapore* (press release). Retrieved from http:www.mom.gov.sg/mrsd/publication

Ministry of Information and the Arts. (1998). *Singapore 1998*. Singapore: Singapore Government Press.

Miniwatts Marketing Group. (2004). *ISOC-ZA trying to lower broadband costs*. Retrieved Oct. 8, 2006, from http://www.internetworldstats.com/af/za.htm

Mintel International Group Ltd. (2005). Retrieved October 14, 2006, from http://www.mintel.com

Miolo Vitali, P., & Nuti, S. (2003). *Ospedale in rete e reti di ospedali: Modelli ed esperienze a confronto*. Milano, Italy: FrancoAngeli.

Mistry, J. J. (2005). A conceptual framework for the role of government in bridging the digital divide. *Journal of Global Information Technology Management*, *8*(3), 28–46.

Moller, C., Chaudhry, S. S., & Jorgensen, B. (2008). Complex service design: A virtual enterprise architecture for logistics service. *Information Systems Frontiers*, *10*(5), 503–518. doi:10.1007/s10796-008-9106-3

Monk, T., & Folkard, S. (1985). Shift work and performance. In Folkard, S., & Monk, T. (Eds.), *Hours of work* (pp. 239–252). Chichester, UK: Wiley.

Moogan, Y. J., Baron, S., & Bainbridge, S. (2001). Timings and trade-offs in the marketing of higher education courses: a conjoint approach. *Marketing Intelligence & Planning*, *19*(3), 179–187. doi:10.1108/02634500110391726

Moon, Y. (2002). Personalization and personality: Some effects of customizing message style based on customer personalities. *Journal of Consumer Psychology*, *12*(4), 313–326. doi:10.1207/15327660260382351

Moore, & B. McMullin (Eds.), *Emerging issues in the practice of university learning and teaching* (pp. 67-76). Dublin: AISHE.

Moore, G. C., & Benbasat, I. (1991). Development of an instrument to measure the perceptions of adopting an information technology innovation. *Information Systems Research*, *2*(3), 192–222. doi:10.1287/isre.2.3.192

Mora, M., Raisinghani, M., O'Connor, R., & Gelman, O. (2009). Toward an integrated conceptualization of the service and service system concepts: A systems approach. *International Journal of Information Systems in the Service Sector*, *1*(2), 36–57.

Moratis, L. T., & van Baalen, P. J. (2002). *Management Education in the Network Economy: Its Context, Content and Organization*. Boston: Kluwer Academic Publishers.

Moreno, J. L. (1987). *Manuale di psicodramma* (*Vol. 2*). Roma, Italy: Astrolabio.

Morshead, D. M. (2002). Stress and shiftwork. *Occupational Health & Safety (Waco, Tex.)*, *71*(4), 36–38.

Mueller, F., & Agamanolis, S. (2005). Sports over a distance. *ACM Computers in Entertainment, 3*(3), 4. doi:10.1145/1077246.1077261

Murugesan, S. (2008). Harnessing green IT: Principles and practices. *IEEE IT Professional, 10*(1), 24–25. doi:10.1109/MITP.2008.10

Mustajoki, J., & Hamalainen, R. P. (2007). Smart-Swaps - A decision support system for multicriteria decision analysis with the even swaps method. *Decision Support Systems, 44*(1), 313–325. doi:10.1016/j.dss.2007.04.004

Myers, M., & Avison, D. (2002). *Qualitative research in information systems*. Thousand Oaks, CA: Sage Publications.

Nagadevara, V. (2004). *Application of neural prediction models in healthcare*. Paper presented at the Second International Conference on e-Governance, Colombo, Sri Lanka.

Nagadevara, V. (2008). Improving the effectiveness of the hotel loyalty programs through data mining. In Jauhari, V. (Ed.), *Global causes on hospitality industry*. New York: The Haworth Press.

Naidoo, S. (2003, October 15). Asmal calls for controlled student intake. *Business Day*, 1st ed.

Naldi, M. (1999). Measurement-based modeling of internet dial-up access connections. *Computer Networks, 31*, 2381–2390. doi:10.1016/S1389-1286(99)00091-2

Naudé, P., & Ivy, N. (1999). The marketing strategies of universities in the United Kingdom. *International Journal of Educational Management, 13*(3), 126–136. doi:10.1108/09513549910269485

Nawar, E. W., Niska, R. W., & Xu, J. (2007). *National hospital ambulatory medical care survey: 2005 Emergency department summary* (Advance data from vital and health statistics No. 386). Hyattsville, MD: National Center for Health Statistics. Retrieved March 30, 2009, from http://www.cdc.gov/nchs/data/ad/ad386.pdf

Neely, K. W., Norton, R. L., & Young, G. P. (1994). The effect of hospital resource unavailability and ambulance diversions on the EMS system. *Prehospital and Disaster Medicine, 9*(3), 172–177.

Neumann, G., & Hottenrott, K. (2002). *Das große buch vom laufen*. Aachen, Germany: Meyer & Meyer.

News Release. (2005). *MATRIX pilot project concludes*. Retrieved December 30, 2009, from http://www.fdle.state.fl.us/press_releases/expired/2005/20050415_matrix_project.html

Nguyen, N., & LeBlanc. (2001). Image and reputation of higher education institutions in student's retention decisions. *International Journal of Educational Management, 15*(6), 301–311. doi:10.1108/EUM0000000005909

Northrop, A., Kraemer, K. L., & King, J. L. (1995). Police use of computers. *Journal of Criminal Justice, 23*(3), 259–275. doi:10.1016/0047-2352(95)00019-M

Novak, D. C., Rowland, D., & DaSilva, L. (2003). Modeling dialup internet access: An examination of user-to-modem ratios, blocking probability, and capacity planning in a modem pool. *Computers & Operations Research, 30*, 1959–1976. doi:10.1016/S0305-0548(02)00119-3

Noy, N. F., & Musen, M. A. (2003). The PROMPT suite: Interactive tools for ontology merging and mapping. *International Journal of Human-Computer Studies, 59*(6), 983–1024. doi:10.1016/j.ijhcs.2003.08.002

Nunnally, J. C. (1978). *Psychometric theory* (2nd ed.). New York: McGraw-Hill.

Nunn, S. (2001). Police information technology: Assessing the effects of computerization on urban police functions. *Public Administration Review, 61*(2), 221–234. doi:10.1111/0033-3352.00024

Nwe, E. S., Adhitya, A., Halim, I., & Srinivasan, R. (2010). Green supply chain design and operation by integrating LCA and Dynamic Simulation. *Computer Aided Chemical Engineering, 28*, 109–114. doi:10.1016/S1570-7946(10)28019-7

O'Neill, M. (2003). The influence of time on student perceptions of service quality. The need for longitudinal measures. *Journal of Educational Administration, 41*(3), 310–324. doi:10.1108/09578230310474449

O'Neill, M., & Palmer, A. (2004). Importance-performance analysis: a useful tool for directing continuous quality improvement in higher education. *Quality Assurance in Education, 12*(1), 39–52. doi:10.1108/09684880410517423

O'Reilly, T. (2005). *What Is Web 2.0: Design patterns and business models for the next generation of software*. Retrieved December 22, 2007, from http://oreillynet.com/pub/a/oreilly/tim/news/2005/09/30/what-is-web-20.html

Obrenović, Z., Gašević, D., & Eliëns, A. (2008). Simulating creativity through opportunistic software development. *IEEE Software*, 25(6), 64–70. doi:10.1109/MS.2008.162

Oexman, R. D., Knotts, T. L., & Koch, J. (2002). Working while the world sleeps: A consideration of sleep and shift work design. *Employee Responsibilities and Rights Journal*, 14(4), 145–157. doi:10.1023/A:1021189305076

Oldfield, B., & Baron, S. (2000). Student perceptions of service quality in a UK university business and management faculty. *Quality Assurance in Education*, 8(2), 85–95. doi:10.1108/09684880010325600

Oon, Y. B., & Khalid, H. M. (2001). Usability of design by customer websites. In Tseng, M. M., & Piller, F. (Eds.), *The Customer Centric Enterprise* (pp. 283–301). New York: Springer.

Oren, E., Haller, A., Hauswirth, M., Heitmann, B., Decker, S., & Mesnage, C. (2007). A flexible integration framework for semantic web 2.0 applications. *IEEE Software*, 24(5), 64–71. doi:10.1109/MS.2007.126

Organisation for Economic Co-operation and Development. (2006). *Innovation and knowledge-intensive activities*. Paris: Author.

Organization for Economic Co-operation and Development. (2002). *The OECD model survey of ICT usage in the business sector*. Retrieved September 8, 2006, from http://www.oecd.org

Oz, E. (2007). *Foundations of e-Commerce*. Upper Saddle River, NJ: Prentice Hall.

Ozen, Ç., & Basoglu, N. (2006, July 9-13). Impact of man-machine interaction factors on enterprise resource planning (ERP) software design. In *Technology Management for the Global Future, 2006 (PICMET 2006)* (Vol. 5, pp. 2335-2341). IEEE.

Pace, R. K., & Gilley, O. W. (1997). Using the spatial configuration of the data to improve estimation. *The Journal of Real Estate Finance and Economics*, 14(3), 333–340. doi:10.1023/A:1007762613901

Pagourtzi, E., Nikolopoulos, K., & Assimakopoulos, V. (2006). Architecture for a real estate analysis information system using GIS techniques integrated with fuzzy theory. *Journal of Property Investment and Finance*, 24(1), 68–78. doi:10.1108/14635780610642971

Palihawadana, G. H. (1999). Modelling module evolution in marketing education. *Quality Assurance in Education*, 7(1), 41–46. doi:10.1108/09684889910252531

Palmer, S. R., & Holt, D. M. (2009). Examining student satisfaction with wholly online learning. *Journal of Computer Assisted Learning*, 25(2), 101–113. doi:10.1111/j.1365-2729.2008.00294.x

Papa, M., & Avgeri, M. (2009). Online Services Delivered by NTO Portals: A Cross-Country Examination. *International Journal of Information Systems in the Service Sector*, 1(3), 65–82.

Papathanassiou, E. (2004). MC: management approaches and internet opportunities in the UK financial sector. *International Journal of Information Management*, 24, 387–399. doi:10.1016/j.ijinfomgt.2004.06.003

Papazoglou, M. P. (2008). *Web services: Principles and technologies*. Essex, UK: Pearson Education Limited.

Parasuraman, A., Zeithaml, V. A., & Berry, L. L. (1985). A conceptual model of service quality and its implications for future research. *Journal of Marketing*, 49(4), 41–50. doi:10.2307/1251430

Parasuraman, A., Zeithaml, V. A., & Berry, L. L. (1988). SERVQUAL: A multiple item scale for measuring consumer perceptions of service quality. *Journal of Retailing*, 64(1), 12–40.

Parasuraman, A., Zeithaml, V. A., & Berry, L. L. (1991). Refinement and reassessment of the SERVQUAL scale. *Journal of Retailing*, 67(4), 420–450.

Parasuraman, A., Zeithaml, V. A., & Maholtra, H. (2005). E-S-QUAL: A Multiple-Item Scale for Assessing Electronic Service Quality. *Journal of Service Research*, 7(3), 213–233. doi:10.1177/1094670504271156

Parker, B. R. (1990). In quest of useful healthcare decision models for developing countries. *European Journal of Operational Research*, 49(2), 279–288. doi:10.1016/0377-2217(90)90346-D

Parker, M. (1996). *Strategic transformation and information technology: Paradigms for performing while transforming*. Englewood Cliffs, NJ: Prentice-Hall.

Passas, N., & Vlassis, D. (2004). Background and outline of the 2nd world summit of attorneys general, prosecutors general, chief prosecutors, prosecutors and ministers of justice. *Crime, Law, and Social Change, 47*, 193–200. doi:10.1007/s10611-007-9074-4

Paul, S., Balakrishnan, S., Gopalkumar, K., Shekhar, S., & Vivekananda, M. (2004). State of India's public services: Benchmarks for the states. *Economic and Political Weekly, 39*(9), 920–933.

Pedró, F. (2005). Comparing Traditional and ICT-Enriched University Teaching Methods: Evidence from Two Empirical Studies. *Higher Education in Europe, 30*(3-4), 399–411. doi:10.1080/03797720600625937

Pelella, E. F., Tamburis, O., & Tranfaglia, R. (2007). Indicatori di qualità nell'attività dei MMG: L'impatto di strumenti economici di efficacia ed efficienza nella gestione delle patologie cronico-degenerative. In *Proceedings of XII AIES Conference (Associazione Italiana di Economia Sanitaria)*.

Peters, L., & Saidin, H. (2000). IT and the mass customisation of services: The challenge of implementation. *International Journal of Information Management, 20*(4), 103–119. doi:10.1016/S0268-4012(99)00059-6

Pham, J. C., Patel, R., Millin, M. G., Kirsch, T. D., & Chanmugam, A. (2006). The effects of ambulance diversion: A comprehensive review. *Academic Emergency Medicine, 13*(11), 1220–1227. doi:10.1111/j.1553-2712.2006.tb01652.x

Piller, F. (2005). *Innovation and Value Co-Creation: Integrating Customers in the Innovation Process*. Cambridge, MA.

Piller, F., Moeslein, K., & Stotko, C. (2004). Does mass customisation pay? An economic approach to evaluate customer integration. *Production & Planning, 15*(4), 435–444. doi:10.1080/0953728042000238773

Piller, F., & Moller, M. (2004). A marketing approach for mass customization. *International Journal of Computer Integrated Manufacturing, 17*(7), 583–593. doi:10.1080/0951192042000273140

Piller, F., Schubert, P., Koch, M., & Möslein, K. (2005). Overcoming mass confusion: Collaborative customer co-design in online communities. *Journal of Computer-Mediated Communication, 10*(4). Retrieved from http://jcmc.indiana.edu/vol10/issue4/piller.html.

Pine, B. J. II. (1993). *Mass customization: The new frontier in business competition*. Boston: Harvard Business School Press.

Pine, B. J. II, Peppers, D., & Rogers, M. (1995). Do you want to keep your customers forever. *Harvard Business Review, 73*(2), 103–114.

Pinhanez, C. (2009). A service science perspective on human-computer interface issues of online service applications. *International Journal of Information Systems in the Service Sector, 1*(2), 17–35.

Pitt, L., Bertham, P., & Watson, R. (1999). Cyberserving: Taming service marketing problems with the world wide web. *Business Horizons, 42*(1), 11. doi:10.1016/S0007-6813(99)80044-5

Pocar, F. (2004). New challenges for international rules against cyber-crime. *European Journal on Criminal Policy and Research, 10*, 27–37. doi:10.1023/B:CRIM.0000037565.32355.10

Pontiggia, A. (1997). *Organizzazione dei sistemi informativi. Modelli per l'analisi e per la progettazione*. Milano, Italy: Etaslibri.

Population Council. (1998). *Institutionalization of OR*. New York: Population Council.

Powell, W. W. (1990). Neither market nor hierarchy. *Research in Organizational Behavior, 12*, 295–333.

Prawitt, D., Romney, M., & Zarowin, S. (1997). A journal survey: The software CPAs use. [from http://www.aicpa.org/PUBS/JOFA/joaiss.htm]. *Journal of Accountancy, 183*(2), 52–66. Retrieved November 23, 2006.

Pretorius, A. J. (2005). Visual analysis for ontology engineering. *Journal of Visual Languages and Computing, 16*(4), 359–381. doi:10.1016/j.jvlc.2004.11.006

Price Waterhouse Coopers. (2005). *Global economic crime survey*. Retrieved February 10, 2009, from http://www.pwc.com/ro/eng/ins-sol/survey-rep/PwC_2005_global_crimesurvey.pdf

Programmableweb. (2009). *Media room and home theater design and construction.* Retrieved September 23, 2009, from http://www.programmableweb.com

Provan, K. G., & Milward, H. B. (1995). A preliminary theory of interorganizational network effectiveness: A comparative study of four community mental health systems. *Administrative Science Quarterly, 40,* 1–33. doi:10.2307/2393698

Prud'hommeaux, E., & Seaborne, A. (2008). *SPARQL query language for RDF.* Retrieved August 30, 2009 from http://www.w3.org/TR/rdf-sparql-query

Punkett, J. L., & Lundman, R. J. (2003). Factors affecting homicide clearances: Multivariate analysis of a more complete conceptual framework. *Journal of Research in Crime and Delinquency, 40*(2), 171–193. doi:10.1177/0022427803251125

Pu, P., & Chen, L. (2007). Trust-inspiring explanation interfaces for recommender systems. *Knowledge-Based Systems, 20*(6), 542–556. doi:10.1016/j.knosys.2007.04.004

Rahman, S. (1998). *Barefooted operations research and its extension: locational analysis of public health facilities in rural Bangladesh. Unpublished rep.* Dhaka, Bangladesh: Ministry of Health and Family Welfare.

Rahman, S., & Smith, D. K. (1999). Development of rural health facilities in a developing country. *The Journal of the Operational Research Society, 50,* 892–902.

Rahman, S., & Smith, D. K. (2000). Use of location-allocation models in health service development planning in developing nations. *European Journal of Operational Research, 123,* 437–452. doi:10.1016/S0377-2217(99)00289-1

Raj, S. P. (1985). Striking a balance between brand popularity and brand loyalty. *Journal of Marketing, 49,* 53–59. doi:10.2307/1251175

Ranjan, J. (2009). Data mining in pharma sector: benefits. *International Journal of Health Care Quality Assurance, 22*(1), 82–92. doi:10.1108/09526860910927970

Rannan-Eliya, R. P., & Somanathan, A. (2003). The Bangladesh health facility efficiency study. In Yazbeck, A. S., & Peters, D. H. (Eds.), *Health policy research in South Asia: Building capacity for reform* (pp. 195–225).

Ran, S. (2003). A model for web services discovery with QoS. *ACM SIGecom Exchanges, 4*(1), 1–10. doi:10.1145/844357.844360

Rapoport, R. N. (1970). Three dilemmas in action research. *Human Relations, 23*(4), 499–513. doi:10.1177/001872677002300601

Rathnam, G. (2005). Interaction effects of consumers' product class knowledge and agent search strategy on consumer decision making in electronic commerce. *IEEE Transactions on Systems Man and Cybernetics: Part A, 35*(4), 556–573. doi:10.1109/TSMCA.2005.850606

Reddy, M., & Dourish, P. (2002). A finger on the pulse: Temporal rhythms and information seeking in medical work. In *Proceedings of the conference on computer supported collaborative work.* New York: Association for Computing Machinery.

Redelmeier, D. A., Blair, P. J., & Collins, W. E. (1994). No place to unload: A preliminary analysis of the prevalence, risk factors, and consequences of ambulance diversion. *Annals of Emergency Medicine, 23*(1), 43–47. doi:10.1016/S0196-0644(94)70006-0

Reinhardt, U. E. (2000). Healthcare for the aging baby boom: Lessons from abroad. *The Journal of Economic Perspectives, 14,* 71–83.

Reports, C. (2007). HDTV for any budget. *Consumer Reports, 72,* 14.

Retrieved September 2, 2008, from www.cnipa.gov.it/site/_files/Piano_triennale_2008_10b.pdf

Review, M. O. R. I. (2002). *Public service reforms: Measuring and understanding customer satisfaction.* London: MORI social Research Institute.

Rialle, V., Lamy, J. B., Noury, N., & Bajolle, L. (2003). Telemonitoring of patients at home: A software agent approach. *Computer Methods and Programs in Biomedicine, 72,* 257–268. doi:10.1016/S0169-2607(02)00161-X

Richards, J. R., Navarro, M. L., & Derlet, R. W. (2000). Survey of directors of emergency departments in California on overcrowding. *The Western Journal of Medicine, 172*(6), 385–388. doi:10.1136/ewjm.172.6.385

Richardson, R. (2008). *CSI Computer Crime & Security Survey*. Retrieved February 10, 2009, from http://i.cmpnet.com/v2.gocsi.com/pdf/CSIsurvey2008.pdf

Richardson, L. D., Asplin, B. R., & Lowe, R. A. (2002). Emergency department crowding as a health policy issue: Past development, future directions. *Annals of Emergency Medicine, 40*(4), 388–393. doi:10.1067/mem.2002.128012

Ringle, C. M., Wende, S., & Will, A. (2005). *SmartPLS 2.0 (beta)*. Retrieved March 11, 2009 from http://www.smartpls.de/

Ritschard, G., Gabadinho, A., Muller, N. S., & Studer, M. (2008). Mining event histories: A social science perspective. *International Journal of Data Mining. Modelling and Management, 1*(1), 68–90.

Roberts, D., & Allen, A. (1997). Young applicants perceptions of higher education: *Vol. 2. No. 20*. Leeds, UK: HEIST Publications.

Rocheleau, B. (1993). Evaluating public sector information systems. *Evaluation and Program Planning, 16*, 119–129. doi:10.1016/0149-7189(93)90023-2

Rockart, J. F., & Short, J. E. (1991). IT in the 90s: Managing organizational interdependence. *Sloan Management Review*, 7–17.

Rodriguez, M., Sirmans, C. F., & Marks, A. P. (1995). Using geographic information systems to improve real estate analysis. *Journal of Real Estate Research, 10*(2), 163–174.

Rogers, E. (1995). *Diffusion of Innovations*. New York: Free Press.

Routh, S., Thwin, A. A., Kane, T. T., & Baqui, A. H. (2000). User-fees for family-planning methods: an analysis of payment behavior among urban contraceptors in Bangladesh. *Journal of Health, Population, and Nutrition, 18*(2), 69–78.

Rowley, J. (2005). The four cs of customer loyalty. *Marketing Intelligence & Planning, 23*(6), 574–581. doi:10.1108/02634500510624138

Roxas, M. L., Peek, L., Peek, G., & Hagemann, T. (2000). A preliminary evaluation of professional accounting services: Direct marketing on the Internet. *Journal of Services Marketing, 14*(7), 595–605. doi:10.1108/08876040010352763

Russel, M. (2005). Marketing education - a review of service quality perceptions amongst international students. *International Journal of Contemporary Hospitality Management, 17*(1), 65–77. doi:10.1108/09596110510577680

Ruta, C. (1993). *Sanità & Management*. Milano, Italy: Etaslibri Ed.

Saari, T. (2002). Designing mind-based media and communications technologies. In *Proceedings of Presence 2002 Conference*, Porto, Portugal.

Saari, T., & Turpeinen, M. (2003). *Psychological customisation of information: Basic concepts, system architecture and applications*. Paper presented at the Mass customisation Conference, Munchen, Germany.

Sachdeva, R., Williams, T., & Quigley, J. (2007). Mixing methodologies to enhance the implementation of healthcare operational research. *The Journal of the Operational Research Society, 58*, 159–167.

Sagie, A., & Krausz, M. (2003). What aspects of the job have most effect on nurses? *Human Resource Management Journal, 13*(1), 46–62. doi:10.1111/j.1748-8583.2003.tb00083.x

Sahney, S., Banwet, D. K., & Karunes, S. (2004). A SERVQUAL and QFD approach to total quality education: A student perspective'. *International Journal of Productivity and Performance Management, 53*(2), 143–166. doi:10.1108/17410400410515043

Samavi, R., Yu, E., & Topaloglou, T. (2009). Strategic reasoning about business models: A conceptual modeling approach. *Information Systems and E-Business Management, 7*(2), 171–198. doi:10.1007/s10257-008-0079-z

Samoff, J. (2001). Education for all in Africa but education systems that serve few well. *Perspectives in Education, 19*(1), 5–28.

Sanchez, S. M., Ogazon, T., Ferrin, D. M., Sepu'lveda, J. A., & Ward, T. J. (2000). Emerging issues in healthcare simulation. In *Proceedings of the 2000 Winter Simulation Conference, Association of Computing Machinery*, New York (pp. 1999-2003).

Sanderson, G. (2002). International education developments in Singapore. *International Education Journal, 3*(2), 85–103.

Santahanam, R., Guimaraes, T., & George, J. F. (2000). An empirical investigation of ODSS impact on individuals and organizations. *Dec Supp Sys, 30,* 51–72. doi:10.1016/S0167-9236(00)00089-0

Sarker, S., Routh, S., & Islam, Z. Barkat-e-khuda, Nasim, S. A., & Khan, Z. A. (1999). *Operations research on ESP delivery and community clinics of Bangladesh* (No. 105). Dhaka, Bangladesh: ICDDR.

Schaper, L. K., & Pervan, G. P. (2003). ICT and OTs: A model of information and communication technology acceptance and utilization by occupational therapists. *International Journal of Medical Informatics, 71,* 103–115. doi:10.1016/S1386-5056(03)00094-7

Scheer, A.-W., & Spath, D. (2004). *Computer aided service engineering.* Berlin, Germany: Springer.

Schikora, P. F., & Godfrey, M. R. (2003). Efficacy of end-user neural network and data mining software for predicting complex system performance. *International Journal of Production Economics, 84,* 231–253.

Schikora, P. F., & Godfrey, M. R. (2006). Connect time limits and customer service levels in dial-up modem pools. *Journal of Network and Systems Management, 14*(2), 181–188. doi:10.1007/s10922-006-9031-z

Schmidt, F., & Strickland, T. (1998). *Client satisfaction surveying: Common measurements tool.* Ottawa, Canada: Canadian Centre for Management Development.

Schull, M. J., Lazier, K., Vermeulan, N., Mauhenney, S., & Morrison, L. J. (2003). Emergency department contributors to ambulance diversion: A quantitative analysis. *Annals of Emergency Medicine, 41*(4), 467–476. doi:10.1067/mem.2003.23

Schull, M. J., Mamdani, M. M., & Fang, J. (2004). Community influenza outbreaks and emergency department ambulance diversion. *Annals of Emergency Medicine, 44*(1), 61–67. doi:10.1016/j.annemergmed.2003.12.008

Schultze, U., & Orlikowski, W. J. (2004). A practice perspective on technology-mediated network relations: The use of internet-based self-serve technologies. *Information Systems Research, 15*(1), 87–106. doi:10.1287/isre.1030.0016

Schurr, P. H. (2007). Buyer-Seller relationship development episodes: theories and methods. *Journal of Business and Industrial Marketing, 22*(3), 161–170. doi:10.1108/08858620710741869

Schwabe, G., & Krcmar, H. (2000a). *Digital material in a political work context—The case of Cuparla.* Paper presented at the 8th European Conference on Information Systems (ECIS 2000), Vienna, Austria.

Schwabe, G., & Krcmar, H. (2000b). *Piloting a socio-technical innovation.* Paper presented at the 8th European Conference on Information Systems (ECIS 2000), Vienna, Austria.

Schwarzer, R. (2004). *Psychologie des gesundheitsverhaltens. Einführung in die gesundheitspsychologie* (3rd ed.). Göttingen, Germany: Hogrefe.

Schwarz, N., Bauer, A., & Haase, D. (2011). Assessing climate impacts of planning policies—An estimation for the urban region of Leipzig (Germany). *Environmental Impact Assessment Review, 31*(2), 97–111. doi:10.1016/j.eiar.2010.02.002

Scott, J. (2000). *Social network analysis. A Handbook.* London: Sage.

Scriba, P. C., & Schwartz, F. W. (2004). Bewegung. Prävention und gesundheitsförderung—wege zur innovation im gesundheitswesen? *Internist, 45*(2), 157–165. doi:10.1007/s00108-003-1131-1

Seiders, K., Voss, G. B., Godfrey, A. L., & Grewal, D. (2007). SERVCON: Development and validation of a multidimensional service convenience scale. *Journal of the Academy of Marketing Science, 35*(1), 144–156. doi:10.1007/s11747-006-0001-5

Selamat, A., & Selamat, M. H. (2005). Analysis on the performance of mobile agents for query retrieval. *Information Sciences, 172*(3-4), 281–307. doi:10.1016/j.ins.2004.05.005

Shadbolt, N., Hall, W., & Berners-Lee, T. (2006). The semantic web revisited. *IEEE Intelligent Systems, 21*(3), 96–101. doi:10.1109/MIS.2006.62

Shafi, K., Kovacs, T., Abbass, H. A., & Zhu, W. (2009). Intrusion detection with evolutionary learning classifier systems. *Natural Computing, 8*(1), 3–27. doi:10.1007/s11047-007-9053-9

Sheehan, J. (2006). Understanding service sector and innovation. *Communications of the ACM, 49*(7), 43–48. doi:10.1145/1139922.1139946

Siassiakos, K., Ilioudi, S., & Lazakidou, A. (2008). Simulation and learning environments in healthcare. *International Journal of Healthcare Technology and Management, 9*(2), 155–166. doi:10.1504/IJHTM.2008.017370

Sigala, M., & Christou, E. (2005, July 27-31). MC in the travel trade: Reality check in the Greek travel-tour operator sector. In *Proceedings of the Annual I-CHRIE Convention*, Las Vegas, NV.

Sigala, M. (2002). The evolution of Internet pedagogy: Benefits for tourism and hospitality education. *Journal of Hospitality, Leisure. Sports and Tourism Education, 1*(2), 29–45.

Sigala, M. (2005). Integrating customer relationship management in hotel operations: Managerial and operational implications. *International Journal of Hospitality Management, 24*(3), 391–413. doi:10.1016/j.ijhm.2004.08.008

Sigala, M. (2006). Mass customisation implementation models and customer value in mobile phones services: Preliminary findings from Greece. *Managing Service Quality, 16*(4), 395–420. doi:10.1108/09604520610675720

Silver, J. (2004). *Attributional coding in essential guide to qualitative methods in organizational research*. Thousand Oaks, CA: SAGE Publications.

Simon, J. S., Rundall, T. G., & Shortell, S. M. (2007). Adoption of order entry with decision support for chronic care by physician organizations. *Journal of the American Medical Informatics Association, 14*, 432–439. doi:10.1197/jamia.M2271

Sinclair, K. (2007). Building automation: Making money with BAS mash-ups. *Engineered Systems, 24*(8), 25.

Singh, J., Cuttler, L., & Silvers, J. B. (2004). Toward understanding consumers' role in medical decisions for emerging treatments: Issues, framework and hypotheses. *Journal of Business Research, 57*(9), 1054–1065. doi:10.1016/S0148-2963(02)00358-2

Sivadas, E., & Baker-Prewitt, J. (2002). An examination of the relationship between service quality, customer satisfaction, and store loyalty. *International Journal of Retail & Distribution Management, 28*(2), 73–82. doi:10.1108/09590550010315223

Skelcher, C. (1992). Improving the quality of local public services. *Service Industries Journal, 12*(4), 463–477. doi:10.1080/02642069200000059

Smedley, G., & Sutton, S. G. (2007). The effect of alternative procedural explanation types on procedural knowledge acquisition during knowledge-based systems. *Journal of Information Systems, 21*(1), 27–51. doi:10.2308/jis.2007.21.1.27

Smith, D. K. (2008). A bibliography of applications of operational research in West Africa. *International Transactions in Operational Research, 15*, 121–150. doi:10.1111/j.1475-3995.2008.00625.x

Sohail, M. S., Rajdurai, J., & Rahman, N. (2003). Managing quality in higher education: A Malaysian case study. *International Journal of Educational Management, 17*(4-5), 141–147. doi:10.1108/09513540310474365

Song, J., Koo, C., & Kim, Y. (2007). Investigating antecedents of behavioral intentions in mobile commerce. *Journal of Internet Commerce, 6*(1), 13–34. doi:10.1300/J179v06n01_02

Soutar, G. N., & Turner, J. P. (2002). Student preferences for university: a conjoint analysis. *International Journal of Educational Management, 16*(1), 40–45. doi:10.1108/09513540210415523

Spath, D., & Demuß, L. (Eds.). (2006). *Entwicklung hybrider produkte—gestaltung materieller und immaterieller leistungsbündel* (2nd ed.). Berlin, Germany: Springer.

Spira, J. B. (2006). Getting answers to questions. *KM World, 15*(7), 1, 3, 30.

Spira, J. (1996). Mass customization through training at Lutron Electronics. *Computers in Industry, 30*(3), 171–174.

Spohrer, J., & Kwan, S. K. (2009). Service science, management, engineering, and design (SSMED): An emerging discipline - outline & references. *International Journal of Information Systems in the Service Sector, 1*(3), 1–31.

Sproull, L., & Kiesler, S. (1986). Reducing social context cues: electronic mail in organizational communication. *Management Science, 32*(11), 1492–1512. doi:10.1287/mnsc.32.11.1492

Sprugeon, A., & Cooper, C. L. (2000). Working time, health, and performance. In Cooper, C. L., & Robertson, I. T. (Eds.), *International review of industrial and organizational psychology* (*Vol. 15*). Chichester, UK: Wiley.

Staab, S., Studer, R., Schnurr, H. P., & Sure, Y. (2001). Knowledge processes and ontologies. *IEEE Intelligent Systems, 16*(1), 26–34. doi:10.1109/5254.912382

Stafford, T. F., Turan, A. H., & Khasawneh, A. M. (2006). Middle East.com: diffusion of the internet and online shopping in Jordan and Turkey. *Journal of Global Information Technology Management, 9*(3), 43–61.

Stanton, B., & Clemens, J. (1989). User fees for healthcare in developing countries: a case study of Bangladesh. *Social Science & Medicine, 29*(10), 1199–1205. doi:10.1016/0277-9536(89)90363-8

Stephens, C., & Long, N. (2000). Communication with police supervisors and peers as a buffer of work-related traumatic stress. *Journal of Organizational Behavior, 21*, 407–424. doi:10.1002/(SICI)1099-1379(200006)21:4<407::AID-JOB17>3.0.CO;2-N

Sterne, J. (2000). *Customer service on the internet: building relationships, increasing loyalty, and staying competitive* (2nd ed.). New York: Wiley.

Stevens, G., Wulf, V., Rohde, M., & Zimmermann, A. (2006). *Ubiquitous fitness support starts in everyday's context.* Paper presented at the 6th World Conference on the Engineering of Sport, Munich, Germany.

Streiner, D. L., & Norman, G. R. (1989). *Health measurement scales: A practical guide to their development and use.* New York: Oxford University Press, Inc.

Stubkjær, E. (2000, August 13-29). Information communities - A case study in the ontology of real estate. In B. Brogaard (Ed.), Rationality and Irrationality, *Proceedings of the 23rd International Wittgenstein Symposium*, Kirchberg am Wechsel, Austria (Vol. 8, No. 2, pp. 159-166).

Studer, R., Benjamins, V. R., & Fensel, D. (1998). Knowledge engineering: Principles and methods. *Data & Knowledge Engineering, 25*(1-2), 161–197. doi:10.1016/S0169-023X(97)00056-6

Sun, L., & Li, Y. (2009). Using usage control to access XML databases. *International Journal of Information Systems in the Service Sector, 1*(3), 32–44.

Su, Q., Li, Z., & Chen, T. (2008). Conceptualizing consumers' perceptions of e-commerce quality. *International Journal of Retail & Distribution Management, 36*(5), 360–374. doi:10.1108/09590550810870094

Sur, S. (2008). Technology-Based Remote Service Encounters: Understanding Customer Satisfaction and Sustainability. *Journal of Foodservice Business Research, 11*(3), 315–332. doi:10.1080/15378020802317040

Swaminathan, V. (2003). The impact of recommendation agents on consumer evaluation and choice: The moderating role of category risk, product complexity, and consumer knowledge. *Journal of Consumer Psychology, 13*(1-2), 93–101. doi:10.1207/S15327663JCP13-1&2_08

Sweeny, J. C., & Lapp, W. (2004). Critical service quality encounters on the Web: an exploratory study. *Journal of Services Marketing, 18*(4), 276–289. doi:10.1108/08876040410542272

Szyperski, N. (1971). Zur wissensprogrammatischen und forschungsstrategischen orientierung der betriebswirtschaft. *Zeitschrift für Betriebswirtschaft, 23*, 261–282.

Tait, M., de Jager, J. W., & Soontiens, W. (2007, September 27-29). *Image and academic expectations of entry-level and senior university students a South African perspective.* Paper presented at the 1ST Biannual International Conference on Strategic Developments in Services Marketing, Chios Island, Greece.

Tait, M., Van Eeden, S., & Tait, A. M. (2002). An exploratory study on the perceptions of previously educationally disadvantaged first year learners of law regarding university education. *South African. The Journal of Higher Education, 16*(2), 181.

Targowski, A. (2009). The architecture of service systems as the framework for the definition of service science scope. *International Journal of Information Systems in the Service Sector, 1*(1), 54–77.

Tatemura, J., Sawires, A., Po, O., Chen, S., Candan, K., Argrawal, D., & Goveas, M. (2007). Mashup feeds: Continuous queries over Web services. *Internation Conference on Management of Data*, 1128-1120.

Taylor, S., & Todd, P. (1995). Assessing IT usage: The role of prior experience. *MIS Quarterly, 19*(4), 561–570. doi:10.2307/249633

Tayyebi, A., Pijanowski, B. C., & Tayyebi, A. H. (2011). An urban growth boundary model using neural networks, GIS and radial parameterization: An application to Tehran, Iran. *Landscape and Urban Planning, 100*(1-2), 35–44. doi:10.1016/j.landurbplan.2010.10.007

Te'eni, D. (2005). Designs that fit: An overview of fit conceptualizations in Human Computer Interaction. In Zhang, P., & Galletta, D. (Eds.), *Human-Computer Interaction and Management Information Systems – Foundations. Advances in Management Information Systems, 4.* Armonk, NY: M. E. Sharpe.

Tebbutt, D., Atherton, M., & Lock, T. (2008). *Green IT for Dummies*. John Wiley & Sons.

Terpsiadou, M. H., & Economides, A. A. (2009). (in press). The use of information systems in the Greek public financial services: The case of TAXIS. *Government Information Quarterly*.

Thammaboosadee, S., & Silparcha, U. (2009). A GUI Prototype for the Framework of Criminal Judicial Reasoning System. *Journal of International Commercial Law and Technology, 4*(3), 224–230.

The slow death of dial-up. (2007). *The Economist, 382*(8519), 13-14.

The use of economic valuation to create public support for green infrastructure investments in urban areas. *Landscape and Urban Planning*, In Press, Corrected Proof, Available online 20 August 2011.

The White House. (2004). *Policy for a common identification standard for federal employees and contractors*. Retrieved March 16, 2008 from http://www.whitehouse.gov/news/releases/2004/08/20040827-8.html

Thomas, S., Killingsworth, J., & Acharya, S. (1998). User fees, self-selection and the poor in Bangladesh. *Health Policy and Planning, 13*, 50–58. doi:10.1093/heapol/13.1.50

Thompson, R. L., Higgins, C. A., & Howell, J. M. (1991). Personal computing: Toward a conceptual model of utilization. *MIS Quarterly, 15*(1), 124–143. doi:10.2307/249443

Thor, A., Aumueller, D., & Rahm, E. (2007). Data integration support for mashups. In *Proceeding of the International Workshop on Information Integration on the Web*, Vancouver, Canada (pp. 104-109).

Titus, J. (2007). Dial-up modems still ring a bell. *Electronic Component News, 51*(12), 21.

Today, O. R. M. S. (2007). Simulation software survey. *OR/MS Today*. Retrieved August 19, 2009, from http://www.lionhrtpub.com/orms/surveys/Simulation/Simulation1.html

Topacan, U., Basoglu, A. N., & Daim, T. U. (2008, July 27-31). Exploring the success factors of health information service adoption. In *Portland International Conference on Management of Engineering & Technology, 2008 (PICMET 2008)* (pp. 2453-2461). IEEE.

TRAI. (2007). *Quarterly performance indicators of Indian telecom services for the quarter ending December 2007*. Retrieved February 10, 2009, from http://www.trai.gov.in/trai/upload/PressReleases/555/pr10april08no33.pdf

Trappey, A. J. C., Trappey, C. V., & Wu, C.-R. (2010). Genetic algorithm dynamic performance evaluation for RFID reverse logistic management. *Expert Systems with Applications, 37*(11), 7329–7335. doi:10.1016/j.eswa.2010.04.026

Tsikriktsis, N., Lanzolla, G., & Frohlich, M. (2004). Adoption of e-processes by service firms: An empirical study of antecedents. *Production and Operations Management, 13*(3), 216–229. doi:10.1111/j.1937-5956.2004.tb00507.x

Tucker, A. L., Edmondson, A. C., & Spears, S. (2002). When problem solving prevents organizational learning. *Journal of Organizational Change Management, 15*(2), 122–137. doi:10.1108/09534810210423008

Tung, F. C., Chang, S. C., & Chou, C. M. (2008). An extension of trust and TAM model with IDT in the adoption of the electronic logistics information system in HIS in the medical industry. *International Journal of Medical Informatics, 77*, 324–335. doi:10.1016/j.ijmedinf.2007.06.006

Turban, E. (2004). *Electronic commerce 2004: a managerial perspective* (International ed.). Upper Saddle River, NJ: Prentice Hall.

Turban, E., Lee, J. K., King, D., & Chung, H. M. (2003). *Electronic commerce - a managerial perspective*. Upper Saddle River, NJ: Prentice Hall.

Tuzhilin, A. (2008). Foreword. In J. Wang (Ed.). *Encyclopedia of data warehousing and mining* (4 Volumes, 2nd ed.). Hershey, PA: IGI Global.

U.S. General Accounting Office. (2003). *Hospital emergency departments: Crowded conditions vary among hospitals and communities* (GAO-03–460). Washington, DC: Author. Retrieved March 30, 2009, from http://www.gao.gov/new.items/d03460.pdf

U.S. House of Representatives. (2001). *National Preparedness: Ambulance Diversions Impede Access to Emergency Rooms*. Washington, DC: Special Investigative Division, Minority Staff for Representative Henry A. Waxman, Committee on Government Reform, U.S. House of Representatives.

Ullman, J. D. (1997). *Information integration using logical views* (LNCS 1186, pp. 19-40). New York: Springer.

Ulrich, H. (1981). Die betriebswirtschaftslehre als anwendungsorientierte sozialwissenschaft. In M. N. Geist & R. Köhler (Eds.), *Die führung des betriebes. Festschrift für curt sandig* (pp. 1-26), Stuttgart, Germany: Poeschel Verlag. Heidelberg,Springer, S. Verein Deutscher Ingenieure. (2004). *VDI richtlinie 2223—methodisches entwerfen technischer produkte*. Berlin, Germany: Beuth.

United Nations. (1994). *International review of criminal policy, 43 & 44, 1994*. United Nations manual on the computer and computer related crime.

Valente, A. (Ed.). (2002). *Percorsi e contesti della documentazione e comunicazione scientifica*. Milano, Italy: FrancoAngeli.

Van de Ven, A. H., & Walker, G. (1984). The dynamics of interorganizational coordination. *Administrative Science Quarterly, 29*, 598–621. doi:10.2307/2392941

Van de Ven, A. H., Walker, G., & Liston, J. (1979). Coordination patterns within an interorganizational Network. *Human Relations, 32*(1), 19–36. doi:10.1177/001872677903200102

Van der Aalst, W. M. P., & Kumar, A. (2003). XML-based schema definition for support of interorganizational workflow. *Information Systems Research, 14*(1), 23–46. doi:10.1287/isre.14.1.23.14768

van der Heijden, H. (2006). Mobile decision support for in-store purchase decisions. *Decision Support Systems, 42*(2), 656–663. doi:10.1016/j.dss.2005.03.006

Van Oostrum, A. (2008). *A service register as an information intermediary: towards a structured design approach for service registers*. Unpublished master's thesis, University of Twente, Enschede, the Netherlands.

van Riel, A. C. R., Lemmink, J., Streukens, S., & Liljander, V. (2004). Boost customer loyalty with online support: the case of mobile telecoms providers. *International Journal of Internet Marketing and Advertising, 1*(1), 4–23. doi:10.1504/IJIMA.2004.003687

van Riel, A. C. R., Liljander, V., & Jurriëns, P. (2001). Exploring consumer evaluations of e-services: a portal site. *International Journal of Service Industry Management, 12*(4), 359–377. doi:10.1108/09564230110405280

Van Someren, M., Barnard, Y., & Sanberg, J. (1994). *The think aloud method: A practical guide to modelling cognitive processes*. London: Academic Press.

Van, J. (2005, October 17). Cybercrime being fought in new ways. *Knight Rider Tribune Business News*, 1.

Vandermeulen, V., Verspecht, A., Vermeire, B., Van Huylenbroeck, G., & Gellynck, X. (2011).

Vatariasusombut, B. (2004). How to retain online customers. *Communications of the ACM, 47*(6), 65–69.

Vaught, C., Mallett, L., Brnich, M. J., Reinke, D., Kowalski-Trakofler, K. M., & Cole, H. P. (2006). Knowledge management and transfer for mine emergency response. *International Journal of Emergency Management, 3*(2-3), 6.

Velte, T., Velte, A., & Elsenpeter, R. (2008). *Green IT:Reduce your information system's environmental impact while adding to the bottom line*. McGraw-Hill.

Venkatesh, V., & Bala, H. (2008). Technology acceptance model 3 and a research agenda on Interventions. *Decision Sciences, 39*(2), 273–315. doi:10.1111/j.1540-5915.2008.00192.x

Venkatesh, V., & Davis, F. D. (1996). A model of the antecedents of perceived ease of use: Development and test. *Decision Sciences, 27*(3), 451–481. doi:10.1111/j.1540-5915.1996.tb01822.x

Venkatesh, V., & Davis, F. D. (2000). A theoretical extension of the technology acceptance model: Four longitudinal field studies. *Management Science, 45*(2), 186–204. doi:10.1287/mnsc.46.2.186.11926

Venkatesh, V., Morris, M. G., Davis, G. B., & Davis, F. D. (2003). User acceptance of information technology: Toward a unified view. *MIS Quarterly, 27*(3), 425–478.

Verma, K., Sivashanmugam, K., Sheth, A., Patil, A., Oundhakar, S., & Miller, J. (2005). METEOR-S WSDI: A scalable P2P infrastructure of registries for semantic publication and discovery of web services. *Information Technology Management, 6*(1), 17–39. doi:10.1007/s10799-004-7773-4

Vessey, I., & Galletta, D. (1991). Cognitive fit: An empirical study of information acquisition. *Information Systems Research, 2*(1), 63–84. doi:10.1287/isre.2.1.63

Vilke, G. M., Simmons, C., Brown, L., Skogland, P., & Guss, D. A. (2001). Approach to decreasing emergency department ambulance diversion hours. *Academic Emergency Medicine, 8*(5), 526.

Voiculescu, A. (2000). *Strategic implications of electronic commerce for UK businesses.* Retrieved October 14, 2006, from http://www.aurelvoiculescu.com/

von Lengerke, T., & John, J. (2005). Gesundheitsökonomische aspekte der adipositas—bisherige ergebnisse der kooperativen gesundheitsforschung (KORA). *Cardio News, 8*(3), 46.

W3C. (2004). *Web services architecture.* Retrieved August 30, 2009 from http://www.w3.org/TR/2004/NOTE-ws-arch-20040211

Wagner, C., & Majchrzak, A. (2006). Enabling customer-centricity using wikis and the wiki way. *Journal of Management Information Systems, 23*(3), 17–43. doi:10.2753/MIS0742-1222230302

Wahl, T., & Sindre, G. (2009). A survey of development methods for semantic web service systems. *International Journal of Information Systems in the Service Sector, 1*(2), 1–16.

Wakefield, K. L., & Bodgett, J. G. (1994). The importance of servicescapes in leisure service settings. *Journal of Services Marketing, 8*(3), 66–76. doi:10.1108/08876049410065624

Walczak, S. & Parthasarathy, M. (2006). Modeling online service discontinuation with nonparametric agents. *Information Systems and e-business Management, 4*(1), 49-70.

Wang, J., Xia, J., Hollister, K., & Wang, Y. (2009). Comparative analysis of international Education Systems. *International Journal of Information Systems in the Service Sector, 1*(1), 1–14.

Wan, S. G. K., Bridge, A., & Skitmore, M. (2001). Assessing the service quality of building maintenance providers, mechanical and engineering services. *Construction Management and Economics, 19*(7), 719–726. doi:10.1080/01446190110062104

Warren, P. (2006). Knowledge management and the semantic web: From scenario to technology. *IEEE Intelligent Systems, 21*(1), 53–59. doi:10.1109/MIS.2006.12

Warren, R., Stephen, M. R., & Bergunder, A. F. (1974). *The structure of urban reform.* Lexington, MA: Lexington Books.

Wasserman, S., & Faust, K. (1996). *Social network analysis. Method and applications.* Cambridge, MA: Cambridge University Press.

Weber, B. R. (1990). Application of geographic information systems to real estate market analysis and appraisal. *The Appraisal Journal, 58*(1), 127–132.

Weber, T. C., & Allen, W. L. (2010). Beyond on-site mitigation: An integrated, multi-scale approach to environmental mitigation and stewardship for transportation projects. *Landscape and Urban Planning, Volume, 96*(4), 240–256. doi:10.1016/j.landurbplan.2010.04.003

Website Optimization, L. L. C. (2006). *Home connectivity in the US.* Retrieved Oct. 8, 2006, from http://www.websiteoptimization.com/bw/0603/

Welsh, J. F., & Dey, S. (2002). Quality measurement and quality assurance in higher education. *Quality Assurance in Education, 10*(1), 17–25. doi:10.1108/09684880210416076

Westbrook, J. I., Braithwaite, J., Iedema, R., & Coiera, E. W. (2004). Evaluating the impact of information communication technologies on complex organizational systems: A multi-disciplinary, multi-method framework. In M. Fieschi et al. (Eds.), *Proceedings of MEDINFO 2004*. Amsterdam: IOS Press.

Westbrook, J. I., Braithwaite, J., Georgiou, A., Ampt, A., Creswick, N., Coiera, E. W., & Iedema, R. (2007). Multimethod evaluation of information and communication technologies in health in the context of wicked problems and sociotechnical theory. *Journal of the American Medical Informatics Association, 14*(6), 746–755. doi:10.1197/jamia.M2462

West, E., Barron, D., Dowsett, J., & Newton, J. (1999). Hierarchies and cliques in the social networks of health care professionals: Implications for the design of dissemination strategies. *Social Science & Medicine, 48*, 633–646. doi:10.1016/S0277-9536(98)00361-X

Westerman, S. J., Tuck, G. C., Booth, S. A., & Khakzar, K. (2007). Consumer decision support systems: Internet versus in-store application. *Computers in Human Behavior, 23*(6), 2928–2944. doi:10.1016/j.chb.2006.06.006

Wetzels, M., Odekerken-Schröder, G., & Van-Oppen, C. (2009). Using PLS path modeling for assessing hierarchical construct models: Guidelines and empirical illustration. *Management Information Systems Quarterly, 33*(1), 177–195.

Wigand, R., Picot, A., & Reichwald, R. (1998). Information, organization and management: Expanding corporate boundaries. Chichester, UK: Wiley.

Wijnhoven, F. (2008). Process design theory for digital information services. In Bernard, A., & Tichkiewith, S. (Eds.), *Methods and tools for effective knowledge life-cycle-management* (pp. 533–546). Berlin: Springer. doi:10.1007/978-3-540-78431-9_31

Wijnhoven, F., & Kraaijenbrink, J. (2008). Product-oriented design theory for digital information services: A literature review. *Internet Research, 18*(1), 93–120. doi:10.1108/10662240810849612

Williams, M. L., Dennis, A. R., Stam, A., & Aronson, J. E. (2007). The impact of DSS use and information load on errors and decision quality. *European Journal of Operational Research, 176*(1), 468–481. doi:10.1016/j.ejor.2005.06.064

Wilson, C. (2009). Putting the green in green. *Telephony, 250*(5), 36–37.

Wilson, E. V., & Lankton, N. K. (2004). Modeling patients' acceptance of provider-delivered e-health. *Journal of the American Medical Informatics Association, 11*(4), 241–248. doi:10.1197/jamia.M1475

Wilson, M. (2009). Survey: Green IT now essential. *Chain Store Age, 85*(7), 52–52.

Winkler, M., Cardoso, J., & Scheithauer, G. (2008). Challenges of business service monitoring in the internet of services. In *Proceedings of the 10th International Conference on Information Integration and Web-based Applications & Services* (pp. 613-616). New York: ACM.

Witte, E. (1997). Feldexperimente als innovationstest—die pilotprojekte zu neuen vedien. *Zeitschrift für betriebswirtschaftliche* [zfbf]. *Forschung, 49*(5), 419–436.

Wolff, R. W. (1989). *Stochastic modeling and the theory of queues*. Englewood Cliffs, NJ: Prentice Hall.

Wolfinbarger, M., & Gilly, M. (2003). e-TailQ: Dimensionalizing, Measuring and Predicting e-tail Quality. *Journal of Retailing, 79*(3), 183–198. doi:10.1016/S0022-4359(03)00034-4

Womack, R. (2002). Information intermediaries and optimal information distribution. *Library & Information Science Research, 24*, 129–155. doi:10.1016/S0740-8188(02)00109-3

Wong, A., & Sohal, A. (2003). Service quality and customer loyalty perspectives on two levels of retail relationships. *Journal of Services Marketing, 17*(5), 495–513. doi:10.1108/08876040310486285

Wong, B. K., Bodnovich, T. A., & Selvi, Y. (1997). Neural network applications in business: A review and analysis of the literature (1988-1995). *Decision Support Systems, 19*, 301–320. doi:10.1016/S0167-9236(96)00070-X

Wulf, V., Moritz, E., Henneke, C., Al-Zubaidi, K., & Stevens, G. (2004). Computer supported collaborative sports: Creating social spaces filled with sports activities. In *Proceedings of the Third International Conference on Entertainment Computing (ICEC 2004)* (pp. 80-89). Springer.

Xiao, B., & Benbasat, I. (2007). E-commerce product recommendation agents: Use, characteristics, and impact. *Management Information Systems Quarterly*, *31*(1), 137–209.

Xue, M., Hein, G. R., & Harker, P. T. (2005). Consumer and co-producer roles in e-service: analysing efficiency and effectiveness of e-service designs. *International Journal of Electronic Business*, *3*(2), 174–197. doi:10.1504/IJEB.2005.006909

Yager, R. R. (1988). On ordered weighted averaging aggregation operators in multicriteria decisionmaking. *IEEE Transactions on Systems, Man, and Cybernetics*, *18*(1), 183–190. doi:10.1109/21.87068

Yang, B. H., & Rhee, S. (2000). Development of the ring sensor for healthcare automation. *Robotics and Autonomous Systems*, *30*, 273–281. doi:10.1016/S0921-8890(99)00092-5

Yang, C.-C. (2003). Establishment and applications of the integrated model of service quality measurement. *Managing Service Quality*, *13*(4), 310–324. doi:10.1108/09604520310484725

Yang, T., & Templeton, J. G. C. (1987). A survey of retrial queues. *Queueing Systems*, *2*(3), 201–233. doi:10.1007/BF01158899

Yang, W. S., & Hwang, S. Y. (2006). A process-mining framework for the detection of healthcare fraud and abuse. *Expert Systems with Applications*, *31*(1), 56–68. doi:10.1016/j.eswa.2005.09.003

Ye, L. R., & Johnson, P. E. (1995). The impact of explanation facilities on user acceptance of expert-systems advice. *Management Information Systems Quarterly*, *19*(2), 157–172. doi:10.2307/249686

Yin, R. K. (1993). *Application of case study research*. Newbury Park, CA: Sage.

Yoo, B., & Donthu, N. (2001). Developing a Scale to Measure the Perceived Quality of an Internet Shopping Site (Sitequal). *Quarterly Journal of Electronic Commerce*, *2*(1), 31–46.

Young, R. F. (2010). Managing municipal green space for ecosystem services. *Urban Forestry & Urban Greening*, *9*(4), 313–321. doi:10.1016/j.ufug.2010.06.007

Yu, Q., Liu, X., Bouguettaya, A., & Medjahed, B. (2008). Deploying and managing web services: Issues, solutions, and directions. *The VLDB Journal*, *17*(3), 537–572. doi:10.1007/s00778-006-0020-3

Yusof, M. M., Kuljis, J., Papazafeiropoulou, A., & Stergioulas, L. K. (2008). An evaluation framework for health information systems: Human, organization and technology-fit factors (HOT-fit). *International Journal of Medical Informatics*, *77*, 386–398. doi:10.1016/j.ijmedinf.2007.08.011

Yu, Y., Kim, J., Shin, K., & Jo, G. S. (2009). Recommendation system using location-based ontology on wireless internet: An example of collective intelligence by using 'mashup' applications. *Expert Systems with Applications*, *36*(9), 11675–11681. doi:10.1016/j.eswa.2009.03.017

Zaaiman, H., Van der Flier, H., & Thijs, G. D. (1998). Selecting South African higher education students: critical issues and proposed solutions. *South African Journal of Higher Education*, *12*(3), 96–97.

Zaccarin, S., & Rivellini, G. (2007). *Reti di relazioni e comportamento individuale: L'approccio della social network analysis*. Milano, Italy: ISTAT Office of Milan.

Zarowin, S. (2003). Hot stuff: What you need and what you don't your technology setup may be sufficient for your needs. [from http://www.aicpa.org/PUBS/JOFA/joaiss.htm]. *Journal of Accountancy*, *195*(4), 28. Retrieved November 23, 2006.

Zarowin, S. (2004). Top tools for CPAs: Technology products that make your work go faster and smoother. [from http://www.aicpa.org/PUBS/JOFA/joaiss.htm]. *Journal of Accountancy*, *194*(5), 26. Retrieved November 23, 2006.

Zarowin, S. (2006). Rate yourself in the paperless race: Have you overcome your resistance to the new technology? [from http://www.aicpa.org/PUBS/JOFA/joaiss.htm]. *Journal of Accountancy*, *201*(5), 50–54. Retrieved February 17, 2007.

Zedeck, S., Jackson, S. E., & Marca, E. S. (1983). Shift work schedules and their relationship to health, adaptation, satisfaction, and turnover intention. *Academy of Management Journal*, *26*(2), 297–310. doi:10.2307/255977

Zeithaml, V. A., Berry, L. L., & Parasuraman, A. (1993). The nature and determinants of customer expectations of service. *Journal of the Academy of Marketing Science*, *21*(1), 1–12. doi:10.1177/0092070393211001

Zeithaml, V. A., & Bitner, M. J. (2003). *Services Marketing: Integrating Customer Focus across the Firm*. Boston: Irwin McGraw-Hill.

Zeithaml, V. A., Parasuraman, A., & Berry, L. L. (1990). *Delivering quality service: Balancing customer perceptions and expectations*. New York: The Free Press, McMillan, Inc.

Zeithaml, V. A., Parasuraman, A., & Maholtra, A. (2002). Service Quality Delivery through Websites: A Critical Review of Extant Knowledge. *Journal of the Academy of Marketing Science*, *30*(4), 362–375. doi:10.1177/009207002236911

Zeng, T. Q., & Zhou, Z. (2001). Optimal spatial decision making using GIS: A prototype of a real estate geographical information system. *International Journal of Geographical Information Science*, *15*(4), 307–321. doi:10.1080/136588101300304034

Zhang, D., Chen, M., & Zhou, L. (2005). Dynamic and personalized web services composition in e-business. *Information Systems Management*, *22*(3), 50–65. doi:10.1201/1078/45317.22.3.20050601/88745.7

Zhang, H., Liu, L., & Li, T. (2011). Designing IT systems according to environmental settings: A strategic analysis framework. *The Journal of Strategic Information Systems*, *20*(1), 80–95. doi:10.1016/j.jsis.2011.01.001

Zhang, P., & Na, L. (2004). An assessment of human-computer interaction research in management information systems: Topics and methods. *Computers in Human Behavior*, *20*(2), 125–147. doi:10.1016/j.chb.2003.10.011

Ziguras, C. (2003). The impact of the GATS on transnational tertiary education: Comparing experiences of New Zealand, Australia, Singapore and Malaysia. *Australian Educational Researcher*, *30*(3), 89–109.

Zmud, R. (1979). Individual differences and MIS success: A review of the empirical literature. *Management Science*, *25*(10), 966–979. doi:10.1287/mnsc.25.10.966

About the Contributors

John Wang is a full professor at Montclair State University. Having received a scholarship award, he came to the USA and completed his PhD in operations research from Temple University. He has published more than 100 refereed papers and six books. He has also developed several computer software programs based on his research findings. He is the Editor of the *Encyclopedia of Data Warehousing and Mining, 1st and 2nd Edition*. Also, he is the Editor-in-Chief of *International Journal of Applied Management Science, International Journal of Information Systems and Supply Chain Management, International Journal of Data Analysis Techniques and Strategies*. He has served as a guest editor and referee for many other highly prestigious journals. His long-term research goal is on the synergy of operations research, data mining and cybernetics.

* * *

A.S.N. Murthy is an Electronics and Communication engineer from Andhra University. He studied Management (PGDBM) from XLRI, Jamshedpur and also from Indian Institute of Management (IIM), Bangalore, and Law from Kuvempu University. He has done a two-year dissertation titled Predictive models for Cyber Crime: Law enforcement perspective. He worked in MMTC (The Minerals and Metals Trading Corporation of India), an international trading company for about seven years (1985-1992) in several managerial positions. He joined the prestigious Indian Police Service, a Civil Service under the Government of India, in 1993, and was allotted to work in Karnataka state. For his meritorious work, he was awarded Police medal by the President of India on the occasion of Independence Day 2008. He held posts of Superintendent of Police of Chitradurga, Dharwad and Koppal districts. He is presently holding the charge of Deputy Inspector General of Police responsible for financial management of the 90,000 strong police department of Karnataka.

Abdullahil Azeem is an Associate Professor in the Department of Industrial and Production Engineering in Bangladesh University of Technology, Bangladesh. He obtained his PhD degree from the University of Western Ontario, Canada. His publications have appeared in many peer reviewed journals such as International Journal of Production Economics, International Journal of Advanced Manufacturing Technology, International Journal of Machine Tools and Manufacture, International Journal of Quality and Innovation. His research interests include supply chain management, health care management, production management, and manufacturing system.

Abey Kuruvilla is an assistant professor in operations management at the University of Wisconsin-Parkside. He has a BTech degree in mechanical engineering from University of Kerala, India, and MS and PhD degrees in industrial engineering from the University of Louisville, KY. Dr. Kuruvilla's research interests are ambulance diversion in emergency medical systems, healthcare management and operations management in the service sectors. He has also developed a research interest in the online language learning industry.

Ahmad Al-Khasawneh (*) is a Director eLearning Centre and vice president assistant of Hashemite University in Jordan. Dr. Khasawneh holds the *Ph.D.* and M.S. of Information Systems Technology, and Computer Engineering both from Newcastle University, Australia and B.S in Computer and Automatic Control Engineering, Jordan. Dr. Khasawneh has a 13-years experience in ICT field and in ICT applications. He has been managing Galileo and Royal Jordanian Airlines R&D project since 1994, ranging from instrumentation development, to network deployment to IT applications. Dr. Khasawneh acts as technical advisor to the Royal Jordanian Galileo (NDC Jordan) director on issues related to the development of travel industry and ICT strategy, and the establishment of strategic partnerships with other airlines and international ICT vendors.

Anand Parkash Bansal, an Electrical Engineer is working as Joint Director (Planning and Services) with Military Engineer Services at Pune, India. After graduation, he obtained specialization in Electrical and Mechanical Engineering from College of Military Engineering, Pune, India. He has also specialized in "Public Policy and Management" from Indian Institute of Management Bangalore and from Maxwell School of Citizenship and Public Affairs, Syracuse University, USA. Presently a professional in the service sector, he has held various prestigious appointments in his department and has many awards to his credit including Prestigious "VB Tawadey Memorial Medal". He has special interest in the field of CRM, project management, Public Private Partnership and Automation. His case studies and research papers have been presented and published in various international and national level conferences and seminars.

Anastasios A. Economides received the Dipl.Eng. degree in electrical engineering from the Aristotle University of Thessaloniki, in 1984. Holding a Fulbright and a Greek State Fellowship, he received the MSc and the PhD degrees in computer engineering from the University of Southern California, Los Angeles, in 1987 and 1990, respectively. At graduation, he received the Outstanding Academic Achievement Award from the University of Southern California. Currently, he is an associate professor and chairman of the Information Systems Department at the University of Macedonia, Thessaloniki, Greece. He is the director of CONTA (COmputer Networks and Telematics Applications) Laboratory. His research interests include techno-economics of networks and e-services. He has published over one hundred fifty peer-reviewed papers. He has been the plenary speaker in two international conferences. He has served on the editorial board of several international journals, on the program committee of many international conferences, and as a reviewer for many international journals and conferences.

Angel A. Juan is an Associate Professor of Simulation and Data Analysis in the Computer Science Department at the Open University of Catalonia (Barcelona, Spain). He also collaborates, as a Lecturer of Applied Statistics, with the Department of Applied Mathematics I at the Technical University of Catalonia. He holds a Ph.D. in Applied Computational Mathematics (UNED), an M.S. in Information Technology (Open University of Catalonia), and an M.S. in Applied Mathematics (University of Valencia). His research interests include computer simulation, educational data analysis and mathematical e-learning.

Ángel García-Crespo is the Head of the SofLab Group at the Computer Science Department in the Universidad Carlos III de Madrid and the Head of the Institute for promotion of Innovation Pedro Juan de Lastanosa. He holds a PhD in Industrial Engineering from the Universidad Politécnica de Madrid (Award from the Instituto J.A. Artigas to the best thesis) and received an Executive MBA from the Instituto de Empresa. Professor García-Crespo has led and actively contributed to large European Projects of the FP V and VI, and also in many business cooperations. He is the author of more than a hundred publications in conferences, journals and books, both Spanish and international.

Arjen van Oostrum obtained his master's degree in Business Information Technology (BIT) from the School of Management and Governance of the University of Twente, Enschede, the Netherlands, in 2008. His master's final project has been performed in the scope of an internship at Ordina System Development and Integration B.V., the Netherlands. His main interest is the application of technological solutions to business challenges. He currently works as a trainee for a semi-governmental organization responsible for the storage and processing of information of all Dutch health-care organizations. He also runs a private company that develops advanced web applications.

Brian D. Neureuther is an associate professor of operations/supply chain management at the State University of New York at Plattsburgh. He received his PhD in production and operations management from Texas Tech University in 1999. His research interests include simulation, quality control, supply chain management, service operations management, and mathematical modeling. He is a member of the Production and Operations Management Society, the Institute for Operations Research and Management Science, and APICS. His work has appeared in journals such as the *International Journal of Production Economics, IEEE Transactions on Semiconductor Manufacturing, Production Planning and Control, the Journal of Marketing Channels, the International Journal of Information Systems and Supply Chain Management, and the Quality Management Journal*.

Efstratios C. Emmanouilidis graduated from the Hellenic Officers Military Academy, in 1996. In 2002, he graduated from the School of Computer Programmers of the Hellenic Army. Holding a Hellenic Army Fellowship, he received the MSc degree in information systems from the University of Macedonia, Thessaloniki, Greece, in 2005. In 2006, he graduated from The School of Research and Informatics Officers of the Hellenic Army. Currently, he is a military Officer at the rank of Captain and serves in Research and Informatics Corps of Hellenic Army. His research interests include statistics analysis and programming.

Fernando Paniagua Martín has been a Faculty Member of the Computer Science Department at the Carlos III Technical University of Madrid since 2005. Currently, he is completing his PhD in Computer Science in the Universidad Carlos III de Madrid. He also holds a Master in Computer Science and Technology. He has been working as software engineer and project manager in several companies. His research interests include Software Engineering, Audio-visual accessibility on the Web, Web 2.0 and Computer Supported Cooperative Work.

Fons Wijnhoven is Associate Professor of Knowledge Management & Information Systems at the University of Twente since 2002, and received a PhD in MIS in 1995. He researches the development and exploitation of information services in companies, between companies, and in networks of expertise. Last decade over 50 of his articles appeared in academic journals, and he (co-)authored several books. He teaches in the programs of Business Information Technology, Industrial Engineering & Management, Business Administration, and Public Administration of the University of Twente. He is an associate of the national research school on operations management, BETA, and member of the Center of Telematics and Information Technology of the University of Twente. He has been affiliated to the Helsinki School of Economics (1994), Nijenrode Business School (1998), the Finnish InfWest program (2003-2005), and has been a guest professor in information management at the Wilhelms-University of Muenster (Germany) in 2009.

Helmut Krcmar is a full professor of information systems and holds the chair for information systems at the Department of Informatics, Technische Universitaet Muenchen (TUM), Germany since 2002. He worked as post doctoral fellow at the IBM Los Angeles Scientific Center, as assistant professor of information systems at the Leonard Stern School of Business, NYU, and at Baruch College, CUNY. From 1987 to 2002 he was chair for information systems, Hohenheim University, Stuttgart. His research interests include information and knowledge management, IT-enabled value Webs, service management, computer supported cooperative work, and information systems in health care and eGovernment.

Ibrahim Obeidat is the Chair of Computer Information System Department of Hashemite University in Jordan. He has received his Bsc in electrical engineering from Jordan, his master from the New York Institute of Technology, and his PhD from George Washington University, United States of America. His research interests lays in Computer Science and Networking. He has experience in networking reliability. Prior to joining the Hashemite University of Jordan, Dr. Obeidat held several key positions with major international ICT and IS consultancy and solutions firms.

Isabella Bonacci is Research Professor of Corporate Organization at the Federico II University, Naples, and at the Second University of Naples (SUN), Italy. She obtained her Ph.D in Business Economics and the degree in Economics both from Federico II University of Naples. She was visiting scholar at the CMER, INSEAD Institute, Fontainebleau, France. Her research interests include economics of information systems, corporate relationships and new organizational forms, strategic use of ICTs to improve public corporate performances, with particular concern for the healthcare sector. She presented her research at several national and international conferences, including the Italian Chapter of AIS (ItAIS), the Mediterranean Conference of Information Systems (MCIS), and the International Conference of Society for Global Business & Economic Development (SGBED). Her articles and works appeared in Politiche Sanitarie and for the Italian Society of Health Technology Assessment (SIHTA). She also published several book chapters.

Iyad Al Azzam is a lecturer and a faculty member at faculty of Information Technology. He has received his Bsc in Computer Science from Jordan University of Science and Technology, Jordan, his Master from Metropolitan University, UK. He has presented numerous articles in national and international conferences. His research interests lays in management information systems and electronic business.

Jan Marco Leimeister is a full professor of information systems and holds the Chair for Information Systems at Kassel University since 2008, He is furthermore a research group manager at the Computer Science Department at Technische Universität München, Munich, Germany. He runs research groups on virtual communities, eHealth,ubiquitous/mobile computing and manages several publicly funded research projects. His teaching and research areas include eHealth, online communities, IT innovation management, service science, ubiquitous and mobile computing, computer supported cooperative work, and information management.

Johan De Jager holds a PhD degree and is Research and Innovation Professor of the Department Marketing, Logistics and Sport management at the Tshwane University of Technology in Pretoria, South Africa. His major areas of interest are marketing of non profit organisations and services like health care and higher education. His major responsibilities are the supervising of post graduate students and conducting other marketing related research projects. He represents the Faculty of Management Sciences in a number of committees. Johan regularly acts as external examiner, locally and in various African countries. He also serves on the executive board of three international academic conferences and acts as referee for various scientific academic outputs.

José M. Castán is a Professor of Business Organization at the University of Barcelona (Spain). He had been also an Associate Professor for more than a decade in the Business Organization Department at the Technical University of Catalonia (Spain). He holds a Ph.D. in Economics and Business Administration (University of Barcelona). His research interests include logistics, quality, business organization and strategic management. He has published several books, papers and proceedings regarding these fields.

Juan Miguel Gómez-Berbís is an Associate Professor at the Computer Science Department of the Universidad Carlos III de Madrid. He holds a PhD in Computer Science from the Digital Enterprise Research Institute (DERI) at the National University of Ireland, Galway and received his MSc in Telecommunications Engineering from the Universidad Politécnica de Madrid (UPM). He was involved in several EU FP V and VI research projects and was a member of the Semantic Web Services Initiative (SWSI). His research interests include semantic web, semantic web services, business process modelling, b2b integration and, recently, bioinformatics.

Kamrul Ahsan is a senior lecturer of management in the Faculty of Business, Auckland University of Technology, New Zealand. He holds a Ph.D. degree in industrial engineering and management from Tokyo Institute of Technology, Japan. His current research interests include health care management, sustainable supply chain, project performance analysis, and project contract modeling. His publications have appeared in peer-reviewed journals such as International Journal of Project Management, International Transactions in Operational Research, Asia Pacific Journal of Operational Research (APJOR), Journal of Health Management, and International Journal of Industrial Engineering. He has taken part in a number of international conferences and worked as reviewer for many international journals.

Luís Ferreira Pires is an Associate Professor at the Faculty of Electrical Engineering, Mathematics and Computer Science of the University of Twente, Enschede, the Netherlands since 1994. He obtained his PhD degree in 1994 from the University of Twente and his Master's degree in 1989 from the 'Escola Politécnica da Universidade de São Paulo', São Paulo, Brazil. His research interests include design methodologies for distributed systems, architecture of distributed systems, modeling and specification techniques, middleware platforms and distributed applications. Lately he has been working on the application of model-driven architecture and semantic web technologies to the design of context-aware applications and services. He published around 100 papers in international workshops, conferences and journals. He is currently responsible for the courses 'Programming 1 / 2', 'Java Middleware Technologies' and 'Service-oriented architecture with Web services' at the University of Twente.

María J. Martínez-Argüelles is an Associate Professor of Economics and Business Administration at the Open University of Catalonia (Barcelona, Spain). She holds a Ph.D. in Economics and Business Administration (University of Barcelona), and a M.S. in Economics (Pompeu Fabra University). Her research interests include organization management, quality and e-learning. She has published several papers, book chapters and proceedings regarding these fields.

Marianna Sigala is Assistant Professor at the Democritus University, Greece. Before joining Democritus University, she had been lecturing at the Universities of the Aegean (Greece) and the universities of Strathclyde and Westminster in the UK. Her interests include productivity and service quality management, Information and Communication Technologies (ICT) applications in tourism and hospitality, and e-learning. She has professional experience from the Greek hospitality industry and contributed to several international research projects. Her work has been published in several academic journals and international conferences. She is the co-chair of the Euro-CHRIE Special Interest Group (SIG) in ICT in Hospitality and she currently serves at the Board of Directors of I-CHRIE, IFITT and HeAIS.

Michael R. Godfrey joined the Supply Chain & Operations Management faculty at the University of Wisconsin Oshkosh in 2001. He teaches manufacturing planning & control, analytical methods, and supply chain management at the undergraduate level and operations & process management in the MBA program. He has published in the *Journal of Business Logistics*, the *International Journal of Production Economics*, *Six Sigma Forum Magazine*, and the *Journal of Network and Systems Management*.

Mohammad Bsoul (PhD) is a assistant professor at Prince Al-Hussein bin Abdullah II Faculty of Information Technology. He has received his Bsc in Computer Science from Jordan University of Science and Technology, Jordan, his Master from University of Western Sydney, Australia and his PhD from Loughborough University, United Kingdom. He has presented numerous articles in national and international conferences. His research interests lays in Networking and Performance Management.

Nuri Basoglu is an associate professor in Department of Management Information Systems, Bogazici University, Istanbul, Turkey. His research interests are socio-technical aspects of IS, customer-focused product development, information technology adaptation and wireless service design, intelligent adaptive human computer interfaces, information systems strategies. He has published articles in journals such as *Technology Forecasting and Social Change, Journal of High Technology Management* and *Technology in Society, International Journal of Services Sciences*. Dr. Basoglu received his BS in industrial engineering, Bogazici University in Turkey, MS and PhD in business administration, Istanbul University.

Oscar Tamburis (*) is a Researcher at CNR (Italian Research National Council), Institute of High Performances Networks, Naples, and Dept. of Technology Innovation, Rome, Italy. He obtained his Ph.D degree in Management of Healthcare Organizations and the degree in Management and Industrial Engineering both from Federico II University of Naples. His research interests include the role of ICTs in the organisational change of public services, with particular concern for the healthcare sector. He presented his research at several national and international conferences, including the Italian Association for Healthcare Economics (AIES), the Italian Chapter of AIS (ItAIS), the Mediterranean Conference of Information Systems (MCIS), and the International Conference of Society for Global Business & Economic Development (SGBED). His articles appeared in the International Journal of Electronic Healthcare and International Journal of Healthcare Technology and Management and Hospital IT Europe.

Paul F. Schikora is associate professor of operations management in the College of Business at Indiana State University. He earned his PhD in operations management from Indiana University's Kelley School of Business in 1999. He earned his MS degree in logistics management from the U. S. Air Force Institute of Technology, and his BS degree in management from the Illinois Institute of Technology. He has 11 years experience as a United States Air Force officer in logistics and transportation management, and currently holds a commission in the U.S. Air Force reserve. His work has been published in the *Quality Management Journal, International Journal of Production Economics, Journal of Network* and *Systems Management and IEEE Transactions on Semiconductor Manufacturing.* His research interests include process simulation, quality management and improvement, manufacturing scheduling, and information systems management. Dr. Schikora is a member of the Decision Sciences Institute, American Society for Quality, Production and Operations Management Society, and APICS.

Qiyang Chen is a Professor of MIS in School of Business, Montclair State University. He earned his Ph.D. in information systems from the University of Maryland, Baltimore. His research interests are in the areas of human-computer interaction, database development, soft computing and information resource management. His recent publications are in the International Journal of Human-Computer Interactions, Human System Management, Journal of Neural Network Computing and Applications, etc. Dr. Chen has consulted with industry on various issues in information systems and regularly serves in program committees for national and international conferences.

Rahul De' is the Hewlett-Packard Chair Professor in ICT for Sustainable Economic Development at IIM Bangalore. He has a B.Tech. from the Indian Institute of Technology, Delhi, an MBA University of Delhi, and a Ph.D. from the Katz Graduate School of Business, University of Pittsburgh, U.S.A. Since 1990, he has taught Information Systems and Management Science courses in various universities in the United States, India, France, Spain and Sweden. His research interests are in E-Governance and applications of ICT for development; and impacts of Free and Open Source software and its role in government. He has interests in data mining, analytics and applied Artificial Intelligence. He has published over 40 articles in international journals, refereed conference proceedings and as chapters in books. In 2009, Dr De' was awarded the Outstanding Paper Award for Most Interdisciplinary and Innovative Research at the 8th International Conference on Electronic Government held in Linz, Austria.

Ricardo Colomo-Palacios is an Associate Professor at the Computer Science Department of the Universidad Carlos III de Madrid. His research interests include applied research in People in IT, Software Process Improvement, Software Project Management and Business Information Systems. He received his PhD in Computer Science from the Universidad Politécnica of Madrid (2005). He also holds a MBA from the Instituto de Empresa (2002). He has been working as software engineer, project manager and software engineering consultant in several companies including Spanish IT leader INDRA.

Roslin V. Hauck is an Assistant Professor of Business Information Systems at Illinois State University. She received her Ph.D. from the Management Information Systems Department at the University of Arizona. Her research interests include organizational change, technology adoption, and the use of technology for communication and knowledge management. She has published in a number of journals including *Journal of Information Systems Education*, *Decision Support Systems*, *Journal of International Management Studies*, and *Journal of the American Society for Information Science and Technology*. She teaches courses in business systems analysis and information systems in organizations and has received numerous teaching awards at the college and university levels.

Ruben Xing received his PhD, Master of Science (M.S), and Master of Arts (M.A) in from Columbia University, New York. Having worked for more than 15 years, Dr. Xing has held senior IT management positions at several large financial conglomerates like Merrill Lynch, Citigroup, First-Boston/Credit Suisse in metropolitan New York. His current research interests include Broadband and Wireless Communications, the Internet transformations and security, Disaster Recover/Business Continuity Planning, and Supply Chain Management.

Ruiliang Yan is an assistant professor of marketing at Indiana University Northwest. He received his PhD in marketing from the University of Wisconsin, Milwaukee. He has published one book and a number of articles in the different refereed journals. He also is serving as referee for many highly prestigious journals. He specializes in marketing modeling, retailing and supply chain management.

Sherry M.B. Thatcher is an Associate Professor of Management at the University of Louisville. She received her Ph.D. from the Management Department at the Wharton School of the University of Pennsylvania. Her research revolves around teams and includes creativity, diversity faultlines, identity recognition, the social effects of computer communication technologies, and team conflict. She has published in a number of journals including The Academy of Management Journal, The Academy of Management Review, Organizational Science, Journal of Management, and The International Journal of Networking and Virtual Organizations.

Suraj Alexander is a professor in the Department of Industrial Engineering at the University of Louisville. He has a BS degree in mechanical engineering from I.I.T, Madras, and MS and PhD degrees in industrial engineering and operations research, from the Virginia Polytechnic Institute and State University. Before entering academia, he worked as an equipment design engineer for Corning, Inc. His current research interests are in the areas of quality assurance, process monitoring, diagnosis and control, decision support systems, and logistics. Dr. Alexander is a fellow of the Institute of Industrial Engineers and the American Society for Quality. He is a registered professional engineer in Kentucky, and a certified quality engineer.

Suzanne Weisband is an Associate Professor in Management Information Systems at the University of Arizona. She received her Ph.D. in Social and Decision Sciences and Policy Analysis from Carnegie Mellon University. Her research examines the socio-technical aspects of large scale distributed collaboration, leadership, telemedicine services over time, work practices of system administrators, and how interruptions affect work performance. She has published her work in leading management and information systems journals. Her most recent book, <u>Leadership at a Distance</u>, was published by Psychology Press in 2008. Her research has been funded by NSF and the Army Research Institute for the Social and Behavioral Sciences.

Theon L. Danet resides in Newport News, Virginia. She received her BS from the University of Maryland, her MBA from the Florida Institute of Technology, and her Ph.D. from Nova Southeastern University. She has been employed with NASA Langley Research Center for the past eight years as an Information Technology Specialist in charge of various projects. Before that, she was an Information Technology instructor and Webmaster at the Military Traffic Management Command on Fort Eustis in Newport News, Virginia. Dr. Danet served in the Army for six years as a Cryptographic Communication Specialist. She lived in Germany for two years and then had an opportunity to work for General Colin Powell's communication team in the Pentagon for three years.

Tugrul Daim is an associate professor of engineering and technology management at Portland State University. He is published in many journals including *Technology in Society*, *Technology Forecasting and Social Change*, *Int'l J of Innovation and Technology Management*, *Technology Analysis and Strategic Management*, and *Technovation*. Dr.Daim received his BS in mechanical engineering from Bogazici University in Turkey, MS in mechanical engineering from Lehigh University in Pennsylvania, another MS in engineering management from Portland State University and a PhD in systems science-engineering management from Portland State University.

Umit Topacan is a MA student in the Department of Management Information Systems at Bogazici University, Istanbul, Turkey. He received his BS in computer education and educational technologies from the same university. His research interests include technology management, information technology adoption, health information services and service development. He has work experiences both of academia as a teaching and research assistantship; and private sector as IT consultant.

Uta Knebel is a full-time researcher at the chair for information systems, Technische Universitaet Muenchen, Germany, since 2005. She works on projects related to IT-supported product-service bundles for the sports industry and RFID. Her research interests include IT-supported health interventions, ubiquitious computing, mobile commerce, IT innovation management, and adaption/diffusion of innovations.

Vishnuprasad Nagadevara is a Professor in the Quantitative Methods and Information Systems Area at the Indian Institute of Management Bangalore. His current interests are Data Mining techniques and applications, Application of Operations Research Techniques, Project Management, Project Evaluation and Information Technology Applications. A graduate from Agriculture College, Bapatla, he did his Post Graduation at GB Pant University of Agriculture and Technology and obtained his Doctorate from Iowa State University, USA in Economics and Operations Research. He also worked at Iowa State University. Dr. Nagadevara has published a number of articles in India and abroad on Data Mining, Application of

Statistical Methods and Operations Research Techniques. He also participated and presented papers in national and international conferences. He was the Volume Editor for the book "Operations Research Methods for Agricultural Decisions", published by Iowa State University Press. He was also the Dean of IIM Bangalore from 1997 to 2000.

Werner Soontiens is currently employed as Professor and Dean International of the Curtin Business School overseeing the strategic intent and operational implementation of courses in commerce in various international locations. Before this he was Head: School of Management, Curtin Business School and Program Director: International Business. On the lecturing front he acts as unit controller for International Management and Global Business Environment which is offered in 8 different locations throughout Southeast Asia. In addition, he teaches International Business related content in graduate and postgraduate courses both in Australia, Asia and China. He represents the faculty of business on a number of university committees and was appointed as member and chair of various sub-committees. Furthermore, Werner plays an active role in the recruitment of on-campus international students.

Yair Levy is an Associate Professor of Information Systems (IS) at the Graduate School of Computer and Information Sciences at Nova Southeastern University. He is the director of the Center for e-Learning Security Research (http://CeLSR.nova.edu/). During the mid to late 1990s, Dr. Levy helped NASA develop e-learning platforms and manage Web infrastructures. He earned his Bachelor's degree in Aerospace Engineering from the Technion, Israel Institute of Technology. He received his MBA with MIS concentration and Ph.D. in Management Information Systems from Florida International University. His current research interests include e-learning security and users perceptions of IS. He has authored a book and numerous research publications that appear in IS journals, conference proceedings, invited book chapters, and encyclopedias. Dr. Levy is the editor-in-chief for the International Journal of Doctoral Studies (IJDS) and serves on editorial board of other recognized scholarly journals. To find out more about Dr. Levy, please visit his site: http://scis.nova.edu/~levyy/.

Zhongxian Wang is a professor at Montclair State University, New Jersey, USA. Professor Wang teaches Operations Analysis, Production/Operations Management, Decision Support & Expert Systems, Business Statistics, Operations Research, and Management Sciences. He is a member of Institute for Operations Research and the Management Sciences (INFORMS), Information Resources Management Association (IRMA), The Decision Sciences Institute (DSI), The Production and Operations Management Society (POMS).

Index

911 call data 1, 3, 7
911 calls 1-8
911 patients 2

A

accounting office 1-2, 10, 46-49, 54, 56, 60-61, 63-64, 217
ADSL - See Asymmetric Digital Subscriber Line.
Adverse Events Reporting System (AERS) 210
AI - See artificial intelligence.
ambulance diversion 1-4, 9-10
American Institute of Certified Public Accountants (AICPA) 47, 64
Analytical Periodic Statement (APS) 46, 58
artificial intelligence (AI) 122, 125, 191, 209, 279
artificial neural networks (ANN) 155, 171-174, 176
Asymmetric Digital Subscriber Line (ADSL) 55, 63

B

bandwidth throttling 43
Borg scale 17, 20, 24

C

cable network 30
Central Bureau of Investigation (CBI) 167-168
centralized identification systems (CIS) 105-106, 108, 110, 113, 115
Central Public works department (CPWD) 220, 226, 229, 237
Certified Public Accountants (CPA) 47, 64
charge-sheeting 166-167, 176
Chronic Diseases' Integrated Management 178, 189
CIS - See centralized identification systems.
CIT - See Critical Incident Technique.
Civil Military Emergency Preparedness (CMEP) 213
classification trees 166, 171, 173-176

client orientation 219, 222
cliques analysis 186
CMT - See Common Measurement Tool.
collaborative sports 12, 24
commercially competitive industry 193
Common Measurement Tool (CMT) 224-225
Community Platform Engineering Process (CoPEP) 14, 22
computerized centralized user identification 105
Computer Security Institute (CSI) 169, 177
computer self-efficacy (CSE) 95, 101, 105-111, 113-116, 118
computer use 46, 74, 91, 94-96
control systems 68, 151
CoPEP - See Community Platform Engineering Process.
CPA - See Certified Public Accountants.
CPWD - See Central Public works department.
criminal activities 208, 214
Critical Incident Technique (CIT) 295-296, 299-300, 307-309
CRM - See Customer Relationship Management.
Cronbach's Alpha 105, 110-111, 201, 226-227
CSE - See computer self-efficacy.
CSI - See Computer Security Institute.
customer productivity 25, 36, 39-43
Customer Relationship Management (CRM) 58-59, 63, 116, 120, 157, 203, 205, 211, 280, 308
customer satisfaction 155, 163-165, 219-220, 222-224, 227, 236-238, 284, 308-310
customer service 25, 27-29, 31-33, 37, 41, 43-44, 48, 160-161, 165, 211, 221, 280, 290
customer value 135-138, 140-144, 151, 153, 157
cybercrime 166-170, 172-177, 218
cyber-stalking 168
cyber-terrorism 168

D

data backup systems 50
dataflow diagram 252-253
data mining 30, 44, 166, 170, 176-177, 208-218,
    279, 309
Data Over Cable Service Interface Specification
    (DOCSIS) 30, 44
decision support 69, 78, 80, 177, 271, 277-282,
    286-287, 289, 291-293
decision-support systems 295
dependent variable 109, 113, 115, 173
design science 239, 241, 258
developed countries 12, 167
dial-up modem pool (DMP) 25-33, 41, 43
diversion statistics 2
diversion status 2-3
DMP - See dial-up modem pool.
DOCSIS - See Data Over Cable Service Interface
    Specification.

E

e3value technique 247
e-accounting 46, 48, 64
e-commerce 145, 158, 162, 168, 176, 283, 292-293,
    308, 310
ED - See Emergency Department.
ED directors 2
ED diversion status 2
ED saturation 1
ED staff 1
ED visits 1
efficient utilization 260
e-finance 46
e-government 46-49, 63, 114, 167, 178
electronic services (e-services) 46, 48, 57, 61, 63-
    64, 66, 135, 151-154, 300, 307, 310
emergency care 1-2, 8-9
Emergency Department (ED) 1-4, 9-10, 23, 44,
    100, 132, 134, 155, 164-165, 177, 190-191,
    205-206, 212-213, 217-218, 237, 272, 290
emergency management 1, 208, 212-213, 217-218
Emergency Medical Systems (EMS) 1-3, 6, 9
EMS - See Emergency Medical Systems.
EMS agencies 2-3, 6
Enterprise Resource Planning (ERP) 58-59, 79,
    116, 188, 212
e-services - See electronic services.
European Union (EU) 48, 114, 262

F

faceted search 129-130
face-to-face support 15
first come, first served (FCFS) 28

G

GDP - See gross domestic product.
Geographic Information Systems (GIS) 120, 132-
    134, 213
government agencies 105-107, 114-115, 169, 208-
    209, 211
Graphical User Interfaces (GUI) 123-124, 126, 214,
    218
gross domestic product (GDP) 67

H

HCO - See HealthCare Organizations.
healthcare industry 66, 211, 265, 273
healthcare operational planning 260
HealthCare Organizations (HCO) 78, 107, 178-179,
    265
healthcare system 68, 180-181, 189, 260, 262-264
health expenditures 67
higher education 193-196, 198-207, 217, 295-300,
    307-310
HRMS - See Human Resource Management Sys-
    tem.
human-computer interface 47, 65, 133, 149
Human Resource Management System (HRMS)
    212
hybrid products 11-12

I

ICDDR,B - See International Center for Diarrhoeal
    Disease Research, Bangladesh.
ICT - See information and communication technol-
    ogy.
ICT infrastructure 46, 48-49, 63
IMMSQ - See Integrated Model for Measuring
    Service Quality
implementation success 105-110, 113-114
indoor patient department (IPD) 263-264
industry accountants 47
information and communication technology (ICT)
    46-49, 52-56, 63-65, 80, 88, 133, 135-136, 138,
    142-145, 150-151, 153, 155, 162, 166-167,
    178-180, 183-184, 187-189, 296

information services 66, 72, 137-138, 141, 143-145, 151, 153, 239-242, 256, 259
information systems (IS) 1-7, 10-14, 17, 19, 21-34, 36-37, 39-50, 52, 54, 56-61, 63, 65-70, 72-77, 79-84, 86-145, 149-189, 192-199, 201-204, 207-224, 226-227, 229-231, 233-236, 238-272, 276-290, 292-303, 305-307, 309-311
Information Technology (IT) 1-5, 11-14, 16-17, 19-22, 24, 27, 29-34, 37, 39-43, 46-50, 52, 54-55, 57-58, 60, 63, 66, 68, 71, 73-75, 78-81, 83, 87-93, 95-100, 102-103, 106-108, 110, 113-115, 118, 121, 123-126, 128-129, 131-132, 137-139, 141-143, 145, 149-156, 158-170, 175-176, 181, 186-188, 191, 194-196, 198, 201-204, 209-217, 220-224, 227, 229, 231, 234-237, 239, 242-244, 246-249, 252-253, 255, 257, 259, 261-271, 277-278, 280-281, 287-288, 290-291, 293, 296-298, 300-301, 303, 305-307
Inland Revenue Services (IRS) 211, 214
integrated management 178, 183, 187-189
Integrated Model for Measuring Service Quality (IMMSQ) 224
Integrated Services Digital Network (ISDN) 55, 63
intelligent monitoring 68
International Center for Diarrhoeal Disease Research, Bangladesh (ICDDR,B) 261-262
Internet banking 78, 158, 162, 205
Internet use 49, 54, 56
IPD - See indoor patient department (IPD).
IRS - See Inland Revenue Services.
IS - See information systems.
ISDN - See Integrated Services Digital Network.
IS success model 108
ISU - See IS usage.
IS usage (ISU) 105, 108-113, 119
IT - See Information Technology.
iterative development 11, 14
IT management 66, 100

J

J2EE - See Java to Enterprise Edition.
Java software 126
Java to Enterprise Edition (J2EE) 19, 126-127

K

knowledge acquisition 126, 133, 281, 283, 292
knowledge management 88, 103, 122, 132, 134, 182, 187, 218
knowledge management systems 88
knowledge rules 208

L

LAN - See Local Area Networks.
Learning Management Systems (LMS) 297-298
Level of Conceptualization (LoC) 243, 248
Level of Representation (LoR) 243, 248, 256
LMS - See Learning Management Systems.
LoC - See Level of Conceptualization.
Local Area Networks (LAN) 47, 49-51, 63
logistic model 3-4, 6
logistic regression 1, 3, 5, 9, 112
LoR - See Level of Representation.

M

mashup application 277-290
mass customization (MC) 135-145, 149-157
MAST - See Metropolitan Ambulance Services Trust.
MAUT - See Multi Attribute Utility Theory.
MC - See mass customization.
media rooms 277
MES - See Military Engineer Services.
Metropolitan Ambulance Services Trust (MAST) 1, 3, 8
Military Engineer Services (MES) 219-220, 222, 225-226, 229-231, 233-236
Ministry of Health and Family Welfare (MOHFW) 261-263, 273
mobile information systems 13
Mobile Sports Companion (MSC) 11, 13-15, 17, 19-22
modem-equipped computer 26
modem pool 25-26, 28, 31, 44
modem-to-modem connection 26
MOHFW - See Ministry of Health and Family Welfare.
MSC - See Mobile Sports Companion.
Multi Attribute Utility Theory (MAUT) 125
multi-criteria decision making 264, 277-278, 281, 288

N

Natural Language Processing (NLP) 125, 131
network organizations 178, 180
neural nets 166
NLP - See Natural Language Processing.
nonprofit organizations 208-209

O

OECD - See Organization for Economic Co-operation and Development.
OLR - See ordinal logistic regression.
online environments 296-298, 307
online higher education 295-298, 300, 306-307
online learning 298, 302, 306-307, 309-310
online travel services 135, 144, 151
OPD - See outdoor patient department.
operational planning 260
Operations Research (OR) 1, 3-4, 7, 11-17, 19-22, 24-33, 36, 44, 47, 49-50, 52, 54-59, 66, 68-72, 74-75, 81-83, 88-94, 98-100, 106-107, 109-110, 112-114, 118, 121-131, 136, 138, 140-145, 149-152, 155, 159-163, 166, 168-172, 174-176, 178-182, 184, 186-187, 195-197, 199, 203-204, 208-216, 221-223, 226-227, 231, 233-234, 236, 240, 242-245, 247-249, 251, 255-257, 260-271, 273-274, 277-285, 287-290, 296-298, 300-303
orbit queue 27-28, 31-32, 34
Ordered Weighted Averaging (OWA) 125, 134
ordinal logistic regression (OLR) 112-113
organizational environment 66
organizational forms 87-88, 99-100, 178-179
organizational variables 88, 101
Organization for Economic Co-operation and Development (OECD) 48, 65
outdoor patient department (OPD) 263, 268
OWA - See Ordered Weighted Averaging.
OWL - See Web Ontology Language.

P

P2P - See Peer-to-Peer.
Partial Least Square (PLS) 105, 111-113, 116-117
pathology networks 178
PCA - See Principal Component Analysis.
Peer-to-Peer (P2P) 50, 259
Perceived Service Quality (PSQ) 222, 231, 237, 295-298, 300
personalised tourism 136
personalised travel services 136
personal training 12-13
physiological outcomes 88
PLS - See Partial Least Square.
police organization 87, 89, 94
political barriers 92
predictive model 30, 113, 166
Principal Component Analysis (PCA) 105, 110-111
private groups 208-209

private sector 169, 209, 214, 221, 227, 235, 269
product development 11-12, 136
product-service bundle 11, 13, 17
product-service packages 11-12
prototype mashup 277-278, 282, 284, 288
prototype mashup application 277-278, 282
PSQ - See Perceived Service Quality.
PSTN - See Public Switched Telephone Network.
public administration 101, 103, 189, 209-210, 215-217, 237
public health operations 260
public sector 101, 103-104, 178, 198, 205, 208-210, 212, 219-222, 225, 227, 237, 269
Public Switched Telephone Network (PSTN) 55

Q

qualitative methodology 295

R

RDF - See Resource Description Framework.
remote medical procedures 68
research information 208, 211
Resource Description Framework (RDF) 124-127, 130, 133
resource utilization 100, 260, 266, 268-271
Retail Real Estate Agencies (RREA) 120-121, 127, 131
retrial queue 25, 27-28, 30, 33, 43-45
Risk Management Agency (RMA) 213
routinization 89-90, 94, 99, 101
RREA - See Retail Real Estate Agencies.

S

SBA - See Small Business Administration.
SEM - See structured equation modeling.
semantic annotation 123, 126-127, 131
semantic web 120-123, 126, 131-134, 292
SERREA 120-121, 123-125, 127-131
service discovery 239, 246, 257
service operations 30, 260
Service-Oriented Architecture (SOA) 239-240, 249, 254-255, 257-258, 291
service provider 20, 27, 31, 172, 174-175, 196, 199, 219, 221-223, 226, 234-236, 240, 244, 246-248, 281
Service Quality (SERVQUAL) 66, 106, 157, 163-165, 195, 199-200, 204-206, 219-227, 229-231, 234-238, 260, 263, 295-302, 306-311
service registry 239-241, 243-257

service sector 10, 23-24, 45-46, 65, 86, 100, 103-104, 106, 114, 119, 121, 133-134, 137, 155-157, 165, 177, 192, 207, 218, 238, 259, 276, 293-294, 309-311
SERVQUAL - See Service Quality.
shift work 87-91, 97-104
Small Business Administration (SBA) 210
smart homes 68
SNA - See Social Network Analysis.
SOA - See Service-Oriented Architecture.
SOA governance 239-240, 257
social environment 66, 181
social healthcare network 182, 188
Social Network Analysis (SNA) 178, 180-183, 187-192
social variables 88
software engineering 12, 102
structured equation modeling (SEM) 111

T

TAM - See Technology Acceptance Model.
task-technology fit (TTF) 78, 87, 89-92, 99, 102, 155
Technology Acceptance Model (TAM) 68, 75-76, 78-80, 87, 91, 98-99, 101-102, 104, 116, 140, 196, 204, 280
technology characteristics 66
technology fears 158
telecommunication systems 68
temporal boundaries 88
terrorist activities 208, 214-215
tertiary education 196-197, 205, 207
tertiary sector 193
Thana Functional Improvement Pilot Project (TFIPP) 262, 265, 268-270
Thana Health Complex (THC) 262-266, 268, 271, 275
Theory of Planned Behavior (TPB) 68, 78, 91
Theory of Reasoned Action (TRA) 67-68, 76, 91

therapeutic continuity 184
Three-Tier-Model 12
TIA - See Total Information Awareness Project.
time limits 25, 27, 31-34, 36-44
Total Information Awareness Project (TIA) 215-216
TPB - See Theory of Planned Behavior.
TRA - See Theory of Reasoned Action.
training habits 17
TTF - See task-technology fit.

U

UI - See user involvement.
unidimensional IS usage 108
URES - See user's resistance.
user behavior 22, 66, 77
user characteristics 66-67, 74-75, 77, 145, 149, 154
user involvement (UI) 105-111, 113-116, 118, 152
user satisfaction 65, 69, 87, 94, 103, 106, 150, 156, 234, 239, 241, 243, 247, 253-254, 256-257, 309
user's resistance (URES) 105, 108-111, 113, 118

V

Value Aided Tax (VAT) 46, 57, 61, 63-64
Varimax rotation 105, 110
VAT - See Value Aided Tax.
Verein Deutscher Ingenieure (VDI) 12, 24
Voice over Internet Protocol (VoIP) 30, 54, 63

W

WAN - See Wide Area Networks.
Web 2.0 131, 153-154, 278, 292
Web 2.0 applications 278, 292
Web interface 15-16, 126, 251
Web Ontology Language (OWL) 125-127
weight classification 17
Wide Area Networks (WAN) 49, 220, 238
workscore 3